RHETORICAL CRITICISM

Fourth Edition

RHETORICAL CRITICISM

Exploration and Practice

Fourth Edition

Sonja K. Foss
University of Colorado at Denver

WAVELAND
PRESS, INC.
Long Grove, Illinois

For information about this book, contact:
Waveland Press, Inc.
4180 IL Route 83, Suite 101
Long Grove, IL 60047-9580
(847) 634-0081
info@waveland.com
www.waveland.com

10-digit ISBN 1-57766-586-4
13-digit ISBN 978-1-57766-586-1

Printed in the United States of America

7 6 5 4

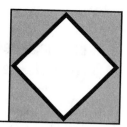

Contents

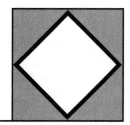

Preface

Rhetorical criticism is not a process confined to a few assignments in a rhetorical or media criticism course. It is an everyday activity we can use to understand our responses to symbols of all kinds and to create symbols of our own that generate the kinds of responses we intend. I hope this book not only provides guidelines for understanding and practicing critical analysis but also conveys the excitement and fun that characterize the process.

I am grateful to a number of people who have assisted me throughout my work on this project. Ernest G. Bormann, Cindy L. Griffin, D. Lynn O'Brien Hallstein, Kellie Hay, and Debian L. Marty read portions of the manuscript and provided invaluable suggestions that significantly improved the work. William Waters's ideas were instrumental in creating the steps of generative criticism in chapter 11. Karen A. Foss, Robert Trapp, and Richard L. Johannesen read the entire manuscript of the first edition, which formed the basis for this version, and Karen A. Foss read many of the chapters for this edition. Their gifts of time, energy, and support are particularly appreciated. I also value the comments of a number of professional colleagues that improved this edition in significant ways: Bernard J. Armada, Richard Enos, Sara E. Hayden, Xing Lu, and Clarke Rountree.

Many others contributed in other significant ways to the book. Diana Brown Sheridan, Xing Lu, Laura K. Hahn, and Michelle A. Holling provided research support and assistance with bibliographies with competence, care, and efficiency. My thanks to Karen A. Foss, Bernard J. Armada, and Robert Trapp for providing me with excellent samples of their students' work. I also appreciate the scholars whose work I have included for their willingness to share their critical essays; their excellent models of criticism both enrich and clarify the approaches they illustrate. Thanks to Kimberly C. Elliott, who pursued permissions for copyrighted material with perseverance, technological wizardry, and creativity, and ευχάριστώ πολύ to Gordana Lazić for locating photographs for inclusion in this edition with efficiency and good humor. Finally, this book is also a product of the questions, insights, and essays of criticism of the students in my rhetorical criticism courses at the University of Denver, the University of Oregon, Ohio State University, and the University of Colorado Denver.

Three people deserve special thanks. My publishers, Carol Rowe and Neil Rowe, provided their usual enthusiastic support, amazing freedom, and just the right amount of prodding to produce this revision. My husband, Anthony J. Radich, himself a superb rhetorical critic, contributed to this project constant good humor, support, and love.

PART 1

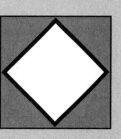

Introduction

The Nature of Rhetorical Criticism

We live our lives enveloped in symbols. How we perceive, what we know, what we experience, and how we act are the results of the symbols we create and the symbols we encounter in the world. We watch movies and television, listen to speeches by political candidates, notice ads on billboards and buses, choose furniture and works of art for our apartments and houses, and talk with friends and family. As we do, we engage in a process of thinking about symbols, discovering how they work, and trying to figure out why they affect us. We choose to communicate in particular ways based on what we have discovered. This process is called *rhetorical criticism*, and this book provides an opportunity for you to develop skills in the process and to explore the theory behind it.

Rhetoric

A useful place to start in the study of rhetorical criticism is with an understanding of what rhetoric is. Many of the common uses of the word *rhetoric* have negative connotations. The term commonly is used to mean empty, bombastic language that has no substance. Political candidates and governmental officials often call for "action not rhetoric" from their opponents or from the leaders of other nations. In other instances, *rhetoric* is used to mean flowery, ornamental speech laden with metaphors and other figures of speech. Neither of these conceptions is how rhetoric is used in rhetorical criticism, and neither is how the term has been defined throughout its long history as a discipline dating back to the fifth century BC. In these contexts, rhetoric is defined as the human use of symbols to communicate. This definition includes three primary dimensions: (1) humans as the creators of rhetoric; (2) symbols as the medium for rhetoric; and (3) communication as the purpose for rhetoric.

3

Humans as the Creators of Rhetoric

Rhetoric involves symbols created and used by humans. Some people debate whether or not symbol use is a characteristic that distinguishes humans from all other species of animals, pointing to research with chimpanzees and gorillas in which these animals have been taught to communicate using signs. As far as we know, humans are the only animals who create a substantial part of their reality through the use of symbols. Every symbolic choice we make results in seeing the world one way rather than another. When we change the symbols we use to frame an event, our experience of the event is altered. In contrast to the experience of animals, human experience changes as symbols change. Thus, *rhetoric* is limited to human rhetors as the originators or creators of messages.

Symbols as the Medium for Rhetoric

A second primary concept in the definition of rhetoric is that rhetoric involves symbols rather than signs. A symbol is something that stands for or represents something else by virtue of relationship, association, or convention. Symbols are distinguished from signs by the degree of direct connection to the object represented. Smoke is a sign that fire is present, which means that there is a direct relationship between the fire and the smoke. Similarly, the changing color of the leaves in autumn is a sign that winter is coming; the color is a direct indicator of a drop in temperature. A symbol, by contrast, is a human construction connected only indirectly to its referent. The word *cup*, for example, has no natural relationship to an open container for beverages. It is a symbol invented by someone who wanted to refer to this kind of object; it could have been labeled a *fish*, for example. The selection of the word *cup* to refer to a particular kind of container is arbitrary.

The following example illustrates the distinction between a symbol and a sign. Imagine someone who does not exercise regularly agreeing to play tennis for the first time in many years. Following the match, he tells his partner that he is out of shape and doesn't have much stamina. The man is using symbols to explain to his partner how he is feeling, to suggest the source of his discomfort, and perhaps to rationalize his poor performance. The man also experiences an increased heart rate, a red face, and shortness of breath, but these changes in his bodily condition are not conscious choices. They communicate to his partner, just as his words do, but they are signs directly connected to his physical condition. They thus are not rhetorical. Only his conscious use of symbols to communicate a particular condition is rhetorical.

The intertwining of signs and symbols is typical of human communication. For instance, a tree standing in a forest is not a symbol. It does not stand for something else; it simply is a tree. The tree could become a symbol, however, if someone chooses it to communicate an idea. It could be used in environmental advocacy efforts as a symbol of the destruction of redwood forests, for example, or as a symbol of Jesus's birth when it is used as a Christmas tree. Humans use all sorts of nonrhetorical objects in rhetorical ways, turning them into symbols in the process.

Although rhetoric often involves the deliberate and conscious choice of symbols to communicate with others, actions not deliberately constructed by rhetors also can be interpreted symbolically. Humans often choose to interpret something rhetorically that the rhetor did not intend to be symbolic. Someone can choose to give an action or an object symbolic value, even though it was not intended as part of the message. Often, in such cases, the meaning received is quite different from what the creator of the message intends. When the United States deliberately deploys an aircraft carrier off the coast of North Korea, it has performed a rhetorical action to warn Pyongyang not to continue with its program to develop nuclear weapons. Both sides read the message symbolically, and there is no doubt about the meaning. If a U.S. reconnaissance plane accidentally strays over North Korea without the purpose of communicating anything to North Korea, however, the pilot is not engaged in rhetorical action. In this case, however, the North Koreans can choose to interpret the event symbolically and take retaliatory action against the United States. Any action, whether intended to communicate or not, can be interpreted rhetorically by those who experience or encounter it.

The variety of forms that symbols can assume is broad. Rhetoric is not limited to written and spoken discourse; in fact, speaking and writing make up only a small part of our rhetorical environment. Rhetoric, then, includes nondiscursive or nonverbal symbols as well as discursive or verbal ones. Speeches, essays, conversations, poetry, novels, stories, comic books, Web sites, television programs, films, art, architecture, plays, music, dance, advertisements, furniture, automobiles, and dress are all forms of rhetoric.

Communication as the Purpose of Rhetoric

A third component of the definition of rhetoric is that its purpose is communication. Symbols are used for communicating with others or oneself. For many people, the term *rhetoric* is synonymous with *communication*. The choice of whether to use the term *rhetoric* or the term *communication* to describe the process of exchanging meaning is largely a personal one, often stemming from the tradition of inquiry in which a scholar is grounded. Individuals trained in social scientific perspectives on symbol use often prefer the term *communication*, while those who study symbol use from more humanistic perspectives tend to select the term *rhetoric*.

Rhetoric functions in a variety of ways to allow humans to communicate with one another. In some cases, we use rhetoric in an effort to persuade others—to encourage others to change in some way. In other instances, rhetoric is an invitation to understanding—we offer our perspectives and invite others to enter our worlds so they can understand us and our perspectives better. Sometimes, we use rhetoric simply as a means of self-discovery or to come to self-knowledge. We may articulate thoughts or feelings out loud to ourselves or in a journal and, in doing so, come to know ourselves better and perhaps make different choices in our lives.

Another communicative function that rhetoric performs is that it tells us what reality is. Reality is not fixed but changes according to the symbols we use to talk about it. What we count as real or as knowledge about the world depends on how we choose to label and talk about things. This does not mean that things do not really exist—that this book, for example, is simply a figment of your imagination. Rather, the symbols through which our realities are filtered affect our view of the book and how we are motivated to act toward it. The frameworks and labels we choose to apply to what we encounter influence our perceptions of what we experience and thus the kinds of worlds in which we live. Is someone an *alcoholic* or *morally depraved?* Is a child *misbehaved* or *suffering from ADD?* Is an unexpected situation a *struggle* or an *adventure?* Is a coworker's behavior *irritating* or *eccentric?* The choices we make in terms of how to approach these situations are critical in determining the nature and outcome of the experiences we have regarding them.

Rhetorical Criticism

The process you will be using for engaging in the study of rhetoric is rhetorical criticism. It is a qualitative research method that is designed for the systematic investigation and explanation of symbolic acts and artifacts for the purpose of understanding rhetorical processes. This definition includes three primary dimensions: (1) systematic analysis as the act of criticism; (2) acts and artifacts as the objects of analysis in criticism; and (3) understanding rhetorical processes as the purpose of criticism.

Systematic Analysis as the Act of Criticism

We are responding to symbols continually, and as we encounter symbols, we try to figure out how they are working and why they affect us as they do. We tend to respond to these symbols by saying "I like it" or "I don't like it." The process of rhetorical criticism involves engaging in this natural process in a more conscious, systematic, and focused way. Through the study and practice of rhetorical criticism, we can understand and explain why we like or don't like something by investigating the symbols themselves—we can begin to make statements about messages rather than statements about our feelings. Rhetorical criticism, then, enables us to become more sophisticated and discriminating in explaining, investigating, and understanding symbols and our responses to them.

Acts and Artifacts as the Objects of Criticism

The objects of study in rhetorical criticism are symbolic acts and artifacts. An act is executed in the presence of a rhetor's intended audience—a speech or a musical performance presented to a live audience, for example. Because an act tends to be fleeting and ephemeral, making its analysis difficult, many rhetorical critics prefer to study the artifact of an act—the text, trace, or tangible evidence of the act. When a rhetorical act is transcribed and printed, posted on a Web site, recorded on film, or preserved on canvas, it becomes a rhetorical artifact that then is accessible to a wider audience than the one that witnessed the rhetorical act. Both acts and artifacts are objects of rhetorical criticism. But because most critics use the tangible product as the basis for criticism—a speech text, a building, a sculpture, a recorded song, for example—the term *artifact* will be used in this book to refer to the object of study. The use of the term is not meant to exclude acts from your investigation but to provide a consistent and convenient way to talk about the object of criticism.[1]

Understanding Rhetorical Processes as the Purpose of Criticism

The process of rhetorical criticism often begins with an interest in understanding particular symbols and how they operate. A critic may be interested in a particular kind of symbol use or a particular rhetorical artifact—the Holocaust Museum in Washington DC or Amy Winehouse's music, for example—and engages in criticism to deepen appreciation and understanding of that artifact. Critics of popular culture such as restaurant, television, theatre, film, and music critics are these kinds of critics—they tend to be most interested in understanding the particular experience of the restaurant or CD they are reviewing. But criticism undertaken primarily to comment on a particular artifact tends not to be "enduring; its importance and its functions are immediate and ephemeral."[2] Once the historical situation has been forgotten or the rhetor—the creator of the artifact—is no longer the center of the public's attention, such criticism no longer serves a useful purpose if it has been devoted exclusively to an understanding of a particular artifact.

In contrast to critics of popular culture, rhetorical critics don't study an artifact for its qualities and features alone. Rhetorical critics are interested in discovering what an artifact teaches about the nature of rhetoric—in other words, critics engage in rhetorical criticism to make a contribution to rhetorical theory.[3] *Theory* is a tentative answer to a question we pose as we seek to understand the world. It is a set of general clues, generalizations, or principles that explains a process or phenomenon and thus helps to answer the question we asked. We are all theorists in our everyday lives, developing explanations for what is happening in our worlds based on our experiences and observations. If a friend never returns your phone calls, e-mails, or text messages, for example, you might come to the conclusion—or develop the theory—that the friendship is over. You have asked yourself a question about the state of the friendship, collected some evidence (made phone calls and sent e-mail and text messages and observed that they were not returned), and reached a tentative conclusion or claim (that the other person no longer wishes to be your friend).

In rhetorical criticism, the theorizing that critics do deals with explanations about how rhetoric works. A critic asks a question about a rhetorical process or phenomenon and how it works and provides a tentative answer to the question. This answer does not have to be fancy, formal, or complicated. It simply involves identifying some of the basic concepts involved in a rhetorical phenomenon or process and explaining how they work. Admittedly, the theory that results is based on limited evidence—in many cases, one artifact. But even the study of one artifact allows you to step back from the details of a particular artifact to take a broader view of it and to draw some conclusions about what it suggests concerning some process of rhetoric.

The process of rhetorical criticism does not end with a contribution to theory. Theories about rhetorical criticism enable us to develop a cumulative body of research and thus to improve our practice of communication. The final outcome of rhetorical criticism is a contribution to the improvement of our abilities as communicators. As a rhetorical critic, you implicitly suggest how more effective symbol use may be accomplished. In suggesting some theoretical principles about how rhetoric operates, you provide principles or guidelines for those of us who want to communicate in more self-reflective ways and to construct messages that best accomplish our goals.[4] As a result of our study of these principles, we should be more skilled, discriminating, and sophisticated in our efforts to communicate in talk with our friends and families, in the decoration of our homes and offices, in the choices we make about our dress, and in our efforts to present our ideas at school or at work.

Knowledge of the operation of rhetoric also can help make us more sophisticated audience members for messages. When we understand the various options available to rhetors in the construction of messages and how they function together to create the effects they produce, we are able to question the choices others make in the construction of acts and artifacts. We are less inclined to accept existing rhetorical practices and to respond uncritically to the messages we encounter. As a result, we become more engaged and active participants in shaping the nature of the worlds in which we live.

Notes

[1] This distinction is suggested by Kathleen G. Campbell, "Enactment as a Rhetorical Strategy/ Form in Rhetorical Acts and Artifacts," Diss. University of Denver 1988, pp. 25–29.

[2] Karlyn Kohrs Campbell, "Criticism: Ephemeral and Enduring," *Speech Teacher*, 23 (January 1974), p. 11.

[3] More elaborate discussions of rhetorical criticism as theory building can be found in: Roderick P. Hart, "Forum: Theory-Building and Rhetorical Criticism: An Informal Statement of Opinion," *Central States Speech Journal*, 27 (Spring 1976), 70–77; Richard B. Gregg, "The Criticism of Symbolic Inducement: A Critical-Theoretical Connection," in *Speech Communication in the 20th Century*, ed. Thomas W. Benson (Carbondale: Southern Illinois University Press, 1985), pp. 42–43; and Campbell, "Criticism," pp. 11–14.

[4] Discussions of rhetorical criticism to increase the effectiveness of communication can be found in: Robert Cathcart, *Post Communication: Criticism and Evaluation* (Indianapolis: Bobbs-Merrill, 1966), pp. 3, 6–7, 12; and Edwin Black, *Rhetorical Criticism: A Study in Method* (Madison: University of Wisconsin Press, 1978), p. 9.

Doing Rhetorical Criticism

The definitions of *rhetoric* and *rhetorical criticism* in chapter 1 have provided a starting place for understanding rhetorical criticism. Knowledge about what rhetorical criticism *is* does not automatically translate into the ability to *do* criticism, however. This chapter is designed to provide an overview of the actual process of producing an essay of criticism. At the end of the chapter is a discussion of the standards used to evaluate essays of criticism.

Because this textbook is a first experience with rhetorical criticism for many of you, you probably will feel more comfortable initially practicing rhetorical criticism using specific methods. Using these methods enables you to begin to develop your critical skills and to learn the language and basic procedures of criticism. This chapter, then, provides you with information about how to do criticism when your starting point is a formal method of criticism. A variety of these methods are presented in chapters 3 through 10. In chapter 11, a different way of approaching criticism is presented—generative criticism—an approach you probably will want to try as your skills as a critic grow. Using this approach, you will create a method or framework for analyzing an artifact from the data of the artifact itself.

Your starting place, then, is with a method of criticism—either one you have chosen or one selected for you by your professor. When you begin with a particular method, the process of rhetorical criticism involves four steps: (1) selecting an artifact; (2) analyzing the artifact; (3) formulating a research question; and (4) writing the essay.

Selecting an Artifact

Your first step is to find an artifact to analyze that is appropriate for the method you will be applying. The artifact is the data for the study—the rhetorical act, event, or product you are going to analyze. It may be any instance of symbol use that is of interest to you and seems capable of generating insights about rhetorical processes—a song, a poem, a speech, a work of art, or a building, for example.

An artifact is appropriate for a method in two ways. It first must contain the kinds of data that are the focus of the units of analysis of the method. Units of analysis focus attention on certain dimensions of an artifact and not others. A critic cannot possibly examine all of the features of an artifact, so units of analysis serve as a vehicle or lens for you to use to examine the artifact. They are scanning devices for picking up particular kinds of information about an artifact, directing and narrowing the analysis in particular ways, revealing some things and concealing others. Units of analysis are things like strategies, types of evidence, values, word choice, and metaphors. If you are using the narrative method, for example, you will need an artifact that is a narrative or story or that includes a story within it. If you are using metaphor criticism, you will need an artifact that contains some obvious metaphors.

The artifact you choose also should be something you really like or really dislike, something that puzzles or baffles you, or something that you cannot explain. We have such responses to the artifacts around us all the time—we love a particular song, we cannot understand why a singer has the appeal that she does, we marvel at the artistry involved in a quilt, or we cannot figure out what the message of a building is supposed to be. Let your interest in your daily encounters with artifacts guide you in your selection of an artifact. Your interest in, passion for, and curiosity about an artifact are important initial ingredients for writing an essay of criticism.

Analyzing the Artifact

The second step in the process of criticism is to code or analyze your artifact using the procedures of the method. Each method of criticism has its own procedures for analyzing an artifact, and at this step you apply the units of analysis provided by the method. If you are applying metaphor analysis, for example, you will be involved in coding your artifact for metaphors. If you are applying the cluster method, you will be identifying key terms in the artifact and finding the terms that cluster around them. This is the step, then, at which you engage in a close and systematic analysis of the artifact and become thoroughly familiar with the dimensions highlighted by your method.

An easy way to do the coding of your artifact is to write or type your notes about the artifact in a list, leaving some space between each "code" or observation that you make. Physically cut the observations you have made apart so that each idea or observation is on a separate strip of paper. Then group the strips that are about the same thing and put them in one pile. Group the strips that are about something else and put them in another pile. What is in these piles will depend on the method of criticism you are using—perhaps different fantasy themes, different metaphors, or different elements of narratives, for example. Play around with different ways to organize your piles. The strips of paper allow you to group and regroup your codings into different categories and encourage you to experiment with multiple ways of conceptualizing the data of your artifact.

Formulating a Research Question

The research question is what you want to find out about rhetoric by studying an artifact. It suggests what your study contributes to our understanding of how rhetorical processes work—your contribution, in other words, to rhetorical theory. Although you may choose to state your research question as a thesis statement instead of an actual question in your essay, you want to be able to articulate what your research question is in your mind because it encourages you to be very clear about your objective in your analysis. Research questions are questions such as: "How does an ambiguous artifact persuade?" "What strategies can help people regain credibility after they have been humiliated?" "What strategies do marginalized groups use to challenge a dominant perspective?" or "How does a political leader construct a nation as an enemy?"

To create a research question, use the principle behind *Jeopardy* and create a question for which the analysis you have just completed is the answer. Use your findings to discover what is most significant, useful, or insightful about your artifact and make that focus into a research question. If your analysis reveals, for example, that an artifact is making a highly controversial topic seem normal, your research question might be something like, "What rhetorical strategies facilitate the normalization of a controversial perspective?"

Research questions tend to be about four basic components of the communication process—the rhetor, the audience, the situation, and the message. If you are having trouble developing a research question, identifying the arena in which your study belongs might help you formulate your question.

1. *Rhetor.* Some research questions deal with the relationship between rhetors and their rhetoric. Questions that focus on the rhetor might be concerned with the motive of the rhetor, the worldview of the rhetor, or how the rhetoric functions for the rhetor. "How do cowboy references function in the rhetoric of politicians?" is a research question that has the rhetor as a focus.

2. *Audience.* Some research questions are concerned with the relationship between an artifact and an audience. Although rhetorical criticism does not allow you to answer questions about the actual effects of rhetoric on an audience, you can ask questions about the kind of audience an artifact constructs as its preferred audience or how an artifact functions to facilitate the development of certain values or beliefs in an audience. A research question centered on audience is: "What is the ideal audience constructed by and for reality TV shows?"

3. *Situation.* Other research questions deal with the relationship between an artifact and the situation or context in which the artifact is embedded. Such questions might deal with the impact of a situation on an

artifact, the rhetor's definition of a situation in an artifact, or whether the artifact adequately addresses an exigence in a particular situation. Research questions in which situation is central are: "How do political leaders define exigencies following a national crisis?" "What is the impact of those definitions on perceptions of the crisis?"

4. *Message.* Most research questions in rhetorical criticism deal with the message. The focus is on the specific features of the artifact that enable it to function in particular ways. Such questions might deal with the kinds of arguments constructed, the types of metaphors used, the key terms used, or a combination of rhetorical strategies and characteristics that create a particular kind of artifact. Research questions that focus on method are questions such as: "What are the features of effective apologies?" or "How does rhetoric generate support for propositions that are contrary to cultural norms?"

When you formulate your research question, try to avoid three mistakes that beginning critics sometimes make as they create research questions. One is to make the question too broad and generic. A question such as "How does political rhetoric about war function?" is too broad and unfocused to answer through the rhetorical analysis of one or even several artifacts. Try to narrow the scope of the question by paying attention to the specific features of the artifact that are most interesting to you. You then might narrow the question to one such as "What rhetorical strategies do political leaders use to justify unpopular wars?"

A second problem that can occur with research questions is that the wording of the questions does not allow the exploration and explanation of anything interesting. Yes-or-no questions, which typically begin with *do,* are one example: "Do political leaders justify unpopular wars?" Not only do these kinds of questions require simple yes-or-no answers, but the answers to them are usually obvious—of course political leaders try to justify unpopular wars. An easy way to make sure your research question is one that takes advantage of the interesting and useful insights your analysis has produced is to begin your question with words and phrases such as *How? In what way? What are the rhetorical processes used in?* or *What are the rhetorical strategies used to?*

There is one more thing to avoid as you develop your research question. Do not include your specific artifact or data in your research question. Although there are exceptions with some methods of criticism (such as the ideological approach), the question usually should be larger than the artifact you are analyzing. You should be able to use any number of artifacts to answer the question rather than being limited to the one you chose to study. Turn the question that fits the analysis of your artifact into a more general one by making the elements of the question more abstract. Instead of a question such as, "How did George W. Bush reassure citizens after the terrorist attacks of September 11?," your question could be, "What rhetorical strategies do political leaders use to reassure citizens after catastrophic events?" Instead of a question such as, "How does the National Rifle Association make its ideology palatable to resistant audiences?," your question could be, "How do organizations with strong ideologies construct messages that appeal to normally resistant audiences?"

Writing the Essay

After you have analyzed your artifact, you are ready to write your essay of criticism. Think of doing the analysis and writing the essay as two separate processes. All of the thinking you have done and the steps you have gone through to conduct your analysis are not included in your essay. What you want to put on paper is the end result of your analysis so that you produce a coherent, well-argued essay that reports your insights. An essay of criticism includes five major components: (1) an introduction, in which you discuss the research question, its contribution to rhetorical theory, and its significance; (2) a description of your artifact and its context; (3) a description of your method of analysis; (4) a report of the findings of the analysis; and (5) a discussion of the contribution your analysis makes to rhetorical theory. These components do not need to be discussed in separate sections or identified with headings, but you want to include these topics in your essay in some way.

Introduction

Your task in the introduction to the essay is the task of the introduction of any paper. You want to orient the reader to the topic and present a clear statement of purpose that organizes the essay. In the introduction, identify the research question the analysis answers, although you do not have to state the question as an actual question in your essay. It usually is stated as the purpose or thesis statement in your essay, using words such as "I will argue," "I will suggest," or "I will explore." If the research question you have formulated, for example, is "What are the functions of reality-television shows for audiences?," you may want to state it in your essay in this way: "In this essay, I will explore the functions of reality-television shows for their audiences to try to discover the appeal of such programs."

A major purpose of the introduction is to generate interest so that your readers will want to read your essay, even if they have no initial curiosity about your artifact. One way to invite them into the essay is by suggesting that they will learn something important or significant to them. If possible, think of some real-life examples of rhetorical processes with which your readers have had experience that relate to your analysis. If you are analyzing a speech by an NRA member to gun-control supporters, for example, you might provide examples of individuals who have attempted to persuade those who hold views that are hostile to theirs. If you are analyzing a speech in which a rhetor attempts to synthesize two polarized positions, you might argue that this artifact is a model of how rhetors can create identification between opposing positions. Knowledge about how to do this, you can suggest, is important for managing conflict effectively between other opposing factions.

Another way to generate interest is by providing information about other studies that have been done on the artifact you are analyzing that are incomplete, inadequate, or do not provide a satisfactory explanation for it. You also can suggest that your study is important because it extends, elaborates on, builds on, or in some way adds to knowledge that already exists concerning a particular rhetorical process. When you discuss why the knowledge about the rhetorical process to which you are contributing is important, you are addressing the "so what?" question in research. This question asks you to consider why the reader should care about the topic and continue to read the essay.

Description of the Artifact

If the readers of your essay are to understand your analysis of an artifact, they must be somewhat familiar with the artifact itself. To acquaint readers with the artifact, provide a brief overview or summary of the artifact near the beginning of the essay. Give readers whatever information they need to understand the artifact and to be able to follow your analysis. If you are analyzing a film, for example, tell when the film was released and who directed it and provide an overview of the film's plot, major characters, and significant technical features. If you are analyzing a speech, include in the description of the artifact the major arguments presented by the rhetor and any significant features of the rhetor's delivery, the occasion, and the response of the audience. You also want to provide the context for the artifact, locating it within the social, political, and economic arrangements of which it is a part. If, for example, you are analyzing a Harry Potter book or movie, give a brief explanation of the Harry Potter phenomenon—tell who the author of the books is, the number of books in the series, the number of books sold, the amount of money generated at the box office by the films, and the controversies the phenomenon has generated among some religious groups.

Your description of the artifact is, to some extent, an interpretation of the artifact. You cannot tell the reader everything about the artifact, so you must make decisions about what to feature in the description. In this process, you want to describe and thus to highlight aspects of the artifact that are most important for and relevant to the analysis that will follow. Do not describe the artifact in too much detail here. You will reveal a great deal about what the artifact is like as you present the findings of your analysis, so details that will emerge later in your analysis do not need to be included in your introduction. This is the place to provide a broad overview of the artifact, knowing that readers will become much more familiar with your artifact later.

In the description of the artifact, also provide a justification for why that artifact is a particularly appropriate or useful one to analyze in order to answer the research question. Many different artifacts can be used for answering the same research question, so provide an explanation as to why analyzing your artifact is a good choice for explaining the specific rhetorical process your research question addresses. Many kinds of reasons can be used to justify your artifact. You might explain why the artifact is important in historical context. Perhaps the artifact represents a larger set of similar texts that are culturally significant. Perhaps the artifact you are analyzing has won many prestigious awards or has been highly successful in generating money. Perhaps the artifact has reached large numbers of people or created an unusual response. Perhaps the rhetorical techniques used in the artifact warrant exploration.

Description of the Method

You need to cover one more topic to complete readers' understanding of what will happen in the essay—a description of the method used to analyze the artifact. Identify the method you are using, explain who created the method (if one person is identifiable with the method), define its key concepts, and briefly lay out its basic tenets or procedures. If you are using the fantasy-theme method of criticism, for example, your description might include mention of its creator, Ernest Bormann; a definition of its basic terms, *fantasy theme* and *rhetorical vision*; and a brief explanation of the method's assumptions.

Report of the Findings of the Analysis

The report of the findings of your analysis constitutes the bulk of the essay. In this section, lay out for readers the results of your analysis of the artifact. Tell what you discovered from an application of the method of criticism to the artifact and provide support for your discoveries from the data of the artifact. If you used pentadic analysis as your method, for example, you would identify the terms of act, purpose, agent, agency, and scene for your artifact. If you analyzed the artifact using the fantasy-theme method, this section would be organized around the fantasy themes of settings, characters, and actions evident in your artifact and the rhetorical vision they create.

Bring in relevant literature as you explain your findings to elaborate on or extend your ideas. Be sure that you feature your ideas in your analysis section, making the thesis statements of your paragraphs about *your* ideas and not echoes of the ideas of others. Any theories or concepts you believe are relevant to your analysis should be used to support, elaborate on, and extend your ideas rather than letting the ideas of others subsume yours.

If you used the technique of cutting apart your observations on individual strips of paper in the coding step, you have available to you a very easy way to write up your analysis. Organize the piles in the order in which you want to talk about the components of your findings. When you are ready to write a section of your analysis, take the pile relevant to the topic of the section and sort the strips of paper within it, laying out the pieces in the order in which you want to discuss ideas and examples and eliminating those you do not want to include in your essay. As you write, connect the topics of the strips with transitions, previews, summaries, and interpretations.

This approach facilities writing your essay. You have the freedom to write the sections of the analysis in any order—you do not have to begin with the first component of the schema. Each pile contains all of your ideas relevant to a section; you do not need to see what happens in one section to be able to write the next. Another advantage of this system is that you cannot lose track of where you are because the ideas of your schema are clearly organized, and all the content you want to discuss is identified and waiting in the piles.

Contribution to Rhetorical Theory

Your essay ends with a discussion of the contribution your analysis makes to rhetorical theory. This contribution is your answer to your research question. At this point in the essay, move away from your specific artifact or data and answer your research question more generally and abstractly. Transcend the specific data of your artifact to focus on the rhetorical processes with which you are concerned. Suggest to your readers how your analysis of your artifact provides an answer to the larger issue with which your essay is concerned, discussing the implications or significance of the contribution you mentioned in the introduction. Perhaps you also can suggest how the new knowledge you have generated can make human communication better in some way.

Your contribution to rhetorical theory is likely to be made in one of two ways: identifying new *concepts* or identifying new *relationships* among concepts. Concepts and relationships are the two basic elements of theories. Concepts are the components, elements, or variables the theory is about. The concepts tell what you are looking at and what you consider important. Statements of relationship are explanations about how the concepts are related to one another. They identify patterns in the relationships among variables or concepts, and they tell how concepts are connected. One rhetorical theory concerning the process of credibility, for example, suggests that, to be credible, a rhetor must demonstrate intelligence, moral character, and good will toward the audience. The concepts of the theory are intelligence, moral character, and good will, and the theory posits that all three of these concepts, interacting together and displayed in an artifact itself, contribute to an audience's perception that the rhetor is credible; this is a statement of relationship. Your analysis can contribute to rhetorical theory, then, by identifying important concepts in a rhetorical process, by suggesting how concepts relate to one another, or by doing both.

Although you cannot generalize your findings to other artifacts like yours or to artifacts characterized by similar rhetorical processes to make a contribution to rhetorical theory, you can make a contribution without moving beyond the particular artifact you have studied. David Zarefsky calls this kind of contribution a "theory of the particular case" and suggests that your analysis of your artifact—the particular case—allows you to suggest a theory that "more fully encompasses the case than do the alternatives." You are able to provide an initial general understanding of some aspect of rhetoric on the basis of the necessarily limited evidence available in the artifact.[1]

The idea that you can and should make a contribution to rhetorical theory in an essay of criticism makes many beginning rhetorical critics uncomfortable. You may feel as though you are not expert enough to develop a theory or to contribute to our understanding of how rhetoric works, or you may feel that you have not yet earned the right to make such contributions.

You are an expert, however, in your way of seeing—in the application of your perspective on the world. This is a perspective that belongs to no one else. You will see things in an artifact that no one else sees, and making a contribution to rhetorical theory is the way in which you can share your unique perspective and offer a new understanding of an artifact. Also remember that the perspective you share with others is not coming out of thin air—you will have the backing of the careful and systematic analysis you have completed as the basis on which to make your contribution to rhetorical theory.

Standards of Evaluation for Critical Essays

What makes one essay of criticism better than another? By what standards is an essay of criticism judged? Rhetorical criticism is a different kind of research from quantitative research, so it is not judged by the standards that are used for such research. In quantitative research, the basic standards of evaluation are validity—whether researchers are measuring what they claim they are measuring—and reliability—replicability of results if the same set of objects is measured repeatedly with the same or comparable measuring instruments. In contrast, the standards of evaluation in rhetorical criticism are justification, reasonable inference, and coherence.

The standards used in rhetorical criticism to judge analyses of artifacts are rooted in two primary assumptions. One assumption is that objective reality does not exist. As discussed in chapter 1, those of us who study rhetoric believe that reality is constituted through the rhetoric we use to talk about it; it is a symbolic creation. Thus, the artifact you are analyzing does not constitute a reality that can be known and proved. You cannot know what the artifact "really" means because there are as many realities about the artifact as there are vocabularies from which to conduct inquiry about it.

A second assumption on which the standards of rhetorical criticism are built is very much related to the first: A critic can know an artifact only through a personal interpretation of it. You cannot be objective, impartial, and removed from the data because you bring to the critical task particular values and experiences that are reflected in how you see and write about an artifact. As a result of these assumptions, your task as a critic is to offer one perspective on an artifact—one possible way of viewing it. You are not concerned with finding the true, correct, or right interpretation of an artifact. Consequently, two critics may analyze the same artifact, ask the same research question, and come up with different conclusions, and the essays they write both can be excellent essays of criticism.

Justification

The primary standard used in judging an essay of criticism is justification—the argument made by a critic.[2] You must be able to justify what you say or offer reasons in support of the claims you make in your report of your findings. All of the ways in which we judge arguments, then, apply to judgments about the quality of a critical essay. You must have a claim—the conclusion of the argument you are seeking to justify. The claim is the answer to the question, "Where are we going?" You must provide evidence to support the claim you are making and have sufficient evidence from the artifact to back up your claim. This evidence constitutes the grounds of your argument—the data from the artifact on which the argument is based. Grounds provide the answer to the question, "What do we have to go on?"

The easiest way for an audience to see that the artifact is as you claim it to be is to use ample quotations from a discursive artifact and ample descriptions of the dimensions of a visual one. You also must quote the evidence accurately, and the evidence you cite should be representative of the artifact as a whole. This standard of adequate, accurate documentation requires that what you say exists in an artifact is, in fact, there.

Reasonable Inference

A second standard by which arguments are judged and that also applies to essays of criticism is reasonable inference. What this means is that you must show how you moved from the data of the artifact to the claims you are making. As you write your essay, you must show the reader how the claims you make reasonably can be inferred from your data. If, for example, you suggest that the straight lines on a building suggest rigidity, you would want to explain how you inferred rigidity from straight lines—perhaps because of their "straight-and-narrow" nature or their visual lack of variation and deviation.

What you are doing here is explicating the warrants of your claim. The warrant authorizes movement from the grounds to the claim and answers the question, "How do we justify the move from these grounds to that claim?"[3] Although your readers must be able to follow you from the data to your claims, they do not have to agree with those claims. They do not have to come up with the same claims that you did to judge your essay to be rigorous or excellent. Each critic brings a unique framework and biases to the process, so complete agreement on the interpretation of an artifact is not likely. Your readers, however, should be able to see and appreciate how you arrived at your claims.

Coherence

A third criterion by which essays of rhetorical criticism are judged is coherence. You must order, arrange, and present your findings so they are congruent and consistent. Congruence means that your findings do not contradict one another and are internally consistent. It also means that all of the major dimensions of the artifact are included in the schema or theory you present of your findings—nothing major is left hanging, unable to be explained. Parallel constructs and labels for your findings create coherence as well—the labels should be parallel in terms of level of abstraction and language.

If your findings include three major strategies, those strategies should be equally concrete or abstract, equally specific or general, and their wording should match one another in length, tone, and type of vocabulary. For example, labels for the three strategies of *using rhetoric to make oneself suffer, pleading,* and *a rhetor's development of a new plan to convince a teenage audience* are at different levels of abstraction and use different voice and language forms. More parallel labels for these strategies might be *suffering, pleading,* and *innovating.*

Coherence also requires that a critic do sufficient analysis of the findings to present them in an insightful and useful way. If you are doing a metaphor analysis, for example, you could report your findings as a list of the metaphors used by the rhetor in the artifact. To satisfy the criterion of coherence, however, you would engage in an additional act of analysis. You would want to organize the metaphors into categories and provide an interpretation of those categories in a coherent framework. The act of presenting your findings in a coherent way usually provides many more insights into your data.

The criteria for evaluating an essay of criticism point to the essence of rhetorical criticism as an art, not a science. In rhetorical criticism, artifacts are dealt with more as the artist deals with experience than as the scientist does. As a rhetorical critic, you are required to bring a variety of creative abilities to bear throughout the process of rhetorical criticism—writing in a way that is not dull, helping the reader envision and experience an artifact as you do, conveying your interest in and perhaps passion for an artifact, persuading readers to view the artifact's contribution to rhetorical theory as you do, and offering a compelling invitation to readers to experience some aspect of the world in a new way.[4]

What Comes Next

The chapters that follow are designed to provide additional guidelines for you as a rhetorical critic. They provide formal methods of rhetorical criticism that will give you practice developing your skills in the art of rhetorical criticism. To help you become comfortable with the critical process and to learn to produce excellent criticism, the chapters include four components, each offering a different opportunity for exploring the method and the kinds of insights it can produce for an artifact.

Each chapter begins with a theoretical overview of the critical method, including a discussion of its origins, assumptions, and units of analysis. The second part of the chapter details the procedures or steps for applying the method to an artifact. This is followed by sample essays in which the method has been used. Some of the sample essays were written by students who were just learning about criticism, as you are, and some were written by seasoned rhetorical critics. If you are a beginning critic with no experience in rhetorical criticism, you probably will find the essays by the students shorter, simpler, and more accessible, but all of the essays were selected because they model the application of a method with particular clarity. Each chapter ends with a list of additional samples of essays in which the method that is the subject of the chapter has been used. These lists of samples are not exhaustive; they are designed simply to serve as places to start if you wish to locate other samples of the method.

Seven of the chapters are organized alphabetically: cluster, fantasy-theme, generic, ideological, metaphor, narrative, and pentadic criticism. The steps in the process of rhetorical criticism discussed in this chapter are repeated in each of these seven chapters to provide a basic framework for criticism that remains constant regardless of your method, artifact, or research question. The chapters on neo-Aristotelian criticism and generative criticism are not in alphabetical order. Neo-Aristotelian criticism is presented first because it was the first method of criticism developed in the communication field and served as an exigence to which the other formal methods responded. It differs from the others in that it dictates a particular end for criticism, and it is rarely used by rhetorical critics today. The chapter on generative criticism concludes the book because it involves a different process for doing criticism than the process presented in the other chapters. In the generative approach, a critic generates a method or an explanatory schema from the data of the artifact itself. Generative criticism is an advanced approach to criticism that you will be ready to try after you have gained practice in criticism by using some of the formal methods of criticism.

You are about to embark on an exciting adventure that will engage and stimulate your critical thinking skills and challenge you to develop more sophisticated writing skills. If you are like most rhetorical critics, you will find yourself engaged, intrigued, inspired, and sometimes frustrated and baffled as you work through critical methods and develop analyses of artifacts. The process of rhetorical criticism is demanding and difficult, but it is also fun. It is a skill that will enable you to analyze the worlds others have created and to choose more deliberately the symbolic worlds that you yourself inhabit.

Notes

[1] David Zarefsky, "The State of the Art in Public Address," in *Texts in Context: Critical Dialogues on Significant Episodes in American Political Rhetoric*, ed. Michael C. Leff and Fred J. Kauffeld (Davis, CA: Hermagoras, 1989), pp. 22–23.

[2] A good discussion of the role of argument in rhetorical criticism is provided by Wayne Brockriede, "Rhetorical Criticism as Argument," *Quarterly Journal of Speech*, 60 (April 1974), 165–74. Barbara A. Larson suggests that Stephen Toulmin's model of argument can be used to connect data and claims in rhetorical criticism in "Method in Rhetorical Criticism: A Pedagogical Approach and Proposal," *Central States Speech Journal*, 27 (Winter 1976), 297–301.

[3] Claims, grounds, and warrants are components of the layout of an argument suggested by Stephen Toulmin. For more detail on his model of argument, see: Stephen Toulmin, *The Uses of Argument* (Cambridge, UK: Cambridge University Press, 1958); Stephen Toulmin, Richard Rieke, and Alan Janik, *An Introduction to Reasoning* (New York: Macmillan, 1984); and Sonja K. Foss, Karen A. Foss, and Robert Trapp, *Contemporary Perspectives on Rhetoric*, 3rd ed. (Long Grove, IL: Waveland, 2002), ch. 5.

[4] For more detailed discussions of standards for judging rhetorical criticism, see: Sonja K. Foss, "Criteria for Adequacy in Rhetorical Criticism," *Southern Speech Communication Journal*, 48 (Spring 1983), 283–95; and Philip Wander and Steven Jenkins, "Rhetoric, Society, and the Critical Response," *Quarterly Journal of Speech*, 58 (December 1972), 441–50.

Neo-Aristotelian Criticism
Genesis of Rhetorical Criticism

The first formal method of rhetorical criticism developed in the communication field is called the *neo-classical, neo-Aristotelian,* or *traditional* method of criticism. In 1925, Herbert A. Wichelns detailed the central features of the neo-Aristotelian method in "The Literary Criticism of Oratory."[1] Until Wichelns's essay, critics did not use specific guidelines for criticism, and there was no clear understanding of what rhetorical criticism was. Because Wichelns's essay provided "substance and structure to a study which heretofore had been formless and ephemeral . . . it literally *created* the modern discipline of rhetorical criticism."[2] Donald C. Bryant explained the significant impact Wichelns's essay had on the practice of rhetorical criticism:

> [It] set the pattern and determined the direction of rhetorical criticism for more than a quarter of a century and has had a greater and more continuous influence upon the development of the scholarship of rhetoric and public address than any other single work published in this century.[3]

In his essay, Wichelns began by distinguishing literary criticism from rhetorical criticism, asserting that rhetorical criticism "is not concerned with permanence, nor yet with beauty," as is literary criticism. Rather, it "is concerned with effect. It regards a speech as a communication to a specific audience, and holds its business to be the analysis and appreciation of the orator's method of imparting his ideas to his hearers."[4] Wichelns's distinction reflects the origins of the communication discipline in departments of English. Early theorists in communication wanted to develop their field as a separate and legitimate discipline.

Wichelns's major contribution to the development of neo-Aristotelianism was that he listed the topics that should be covered in the study of a speech. A critic, he suggested, should deal with these elements: the speaker's personality, the public character of the speaker or the public's perception of the speaker, the audience, the major ideas presented in the speech, the motives to which the speaker appealed, the nature of the speaker's proofs, the speaker's judgment of human nature in the audience, the arrangement of the speech, the speaker's mode of expression, the speaker's method of speech preparation, the manner of delivery, and the effect of the discourse on the immediate audience and its long-term effects.[5]

Many of these topics were discussed by Aristotle in the *Rhetoric* and by other classical rhetoricians such as Cicero and Quintilian. Because Wichelns did not discuss how a critic should analyze these topics, critics turned to classical sources for elaboration of Wichelns's guidelines. They began to use the classical canons of rhetoric—invention, organization, style, memory, and delivery—as units of analysis and named the approach *neo-Aristotelianism*. The ancient rhetorical theorists provided the framework for criticism, the topics covered, and the perspectives taken on them.

Numerous critical studies that followed solidified Wichelns's suggested approach to rhetorical criticism. The widespread use of neo-Aristotelianism was particularly evident in the two-volume *A History and Criticism of American Public Address*, edited by William Norwood Brigance and published in 1943.[6] In the studies included in this work, authors guided their critical efforts with the Aristotelian pattern alone or in combination with those of other classical rhetoricians. Wichelns's method became more firmly fixed in 1948 with the publication of *Speech Criticism*, in which Lester Thonssen and A. Craig Baird presented an elaborate system for the practice of rhetorical criticism based on the topics suggested by Wichelns and the writings of classical rhetoricians.[7]

As a consequence of the adoption of neo-Aristotelianism as virtually the only method of rhetorical criticism in the early years of the communication field, the practice of rhetorical criticism was limited in subject matter and purpose. Rhetorical criticism became the study of speeches because the approach required that a critic determine the effect of rhetoric on the immediate audience. Neo-Aristotelianism thus was not used to study written discourse or nondiscursive rhetoric. Neo-Aristotelianism also led to the study of single speakers because the sheer number of topics to cover relating to the rhetor and the speech made dealing with more than a single speaker virtually impossible. Thus, various speeches by different rhetors related by form or topic were not included in the scope of rhetorical criticism.[8]

The single speakers who were the focus of study were limited further in that they tended to be individuals of the past—generally elite men—who had made significant contributions in the realm of public affairs. A critic was required to determine a number of details about the speaker's life, public character, and the audience for the speech at the time. Such data were only available for famous people because their speeches were the ones that were saved and archived.

Neo-Aristotelian criticism was virtually unchallenged as the method to use in rhetorical criticism until the 1960s, when the orthodoxy that had developed in rhetorical criticism began to be criticized on a number of grounds. One criticism was that the work on which neo-Aristotelianism was based, Aristotle's *Rhetoric*, was not intended as a guide for critics. The *Rhetoric* and other classical works that were being used to guide the critic were designed to teach others how to speak well. Nothing in them suggested they were to be used to appraise discourse.[9]

The concern with effects that derived, in part, from an emphasis on teaching effective speech led to another problem with neo-Aristotelianism. Critics of neo-Aristotelianism argued that an exclusive concern with effects does not always produce significant criticism. "Did the speech evoke the intended response from the immediate audience?" and "Did the rhetor use the available means of persuasion to achieve the desired response?" are not always the most appropriate questions to ask about a rhetorical artifact. These questions also do not always produce significant insights into an artifact. As Otis M. Walter pointed out, a critic who is studying Jesus's Sermon on the Mount using the neo-Aristotelian approach asks whether Jesus used the means of persuasion available to him. But this question may not produce a significant answer. More interesting might be questions such as, "Were Jesus's means of persuasion consistent with his ethical doctrines?" or "What changes in Old Testament morality did Jesus present?"[10] But neo-Aristotelian criticism does not allow a critic to explore these questions. As Karlyn Kohrs Campbell explained, neo-Aristotelianism excludes "all *evaluations* other than the speech's potential for evoking intended response from an immediate, specified audience."[11]

Still others objected to neo-Aristotelianism on the grounds that the works on which it was based—Aristotle's *Rhetoric* and other classical writings—were written at a time and in the context of cultures that were different in values, orientation, and knowledge from ours. Yet, critics using the neo-Aristotelian mode of criticism assumed that what were believed to be ideal rhetorical principles in ancient Greek and Roman cultures are the same today. In other words, critics of neo-Aristotelianism suggested, rhetorical principles have undergone change since their formulation in classical Greek and Roman times, and later cultures have modified or extended those principles.[12] To use only classical tenets of rhetoric as units of analysis in criticism was to ignore a large body of new scholarship about rhetorical principles.

Yet another criticism of neo-Aristotelianism concerned its rational bias. As Campbell explained, a basic assumption of the approach was that our unique attribute is the capacity to be rational, and humans are able to engage in persuasion and be subject to it only because they are rational beings. Thus, rhetoric was seen as the art of reasoned discourse or argumentation. Emotional and psychological appeals exist and affect persuasion, neo-Aristotelianism suggests, but they are secondary to judgments resulting from rational means of persuasion. One consequence, explained Campbell, was that "'true' or 'genuine' rhetoric" became "the art by which men are induced to act in obedience to reason in contrast to 'false' or 'sophistic' rhetoric which uses any and all means to produce acquiescence."[13] Critics and theorists operating out of this approach either had to denigrate or ignore nonrational appeals and attempt, generally fruitlessly, to distinguish between rational and nonrational appeals.

Another criticism of neo-Aristotelianism as the presiding method of criticism was that it encouraged the mechanical application of categories to rhetoric, with the result that the work that critics did sometimes was unimaginative and self-fulfilling. Critics set out to find the particular rhetorical techniques suggested by classical rhetoricians in the artifacts they were studying—techniques such as logical argument and emotional appeals—and, indeed, did find them being used in the speeches they were analyzing. But rather than helping a critic understand and illuminate the speeches using these units of analysis, neo-Aristotelianism sometimes became "a mechanical accounting or summing up of how well" a speech fit "an *a priori* mold."[14]

Today, critics who use the neo-Aristotelian approach to analyze rhetoric are few, and essays that feature the method rarely find their way into the journals and convention programs of the communication field. Criticisms of how the neo-Aristotelian framework limited the potential of criticism led, in the 1960s, to pluralism in critical approaches. As evident in the remaining chapters of this book, a wide variety of approaches now characterize rhetorical criticism. Discussions and defenses of neo-Aristotelianism ended largely in the early 1970s.[15]

As the first critical approach developed in the communication field, neo-Aristotelianism served to differentiate the discipline from literature and literary criticism and helped to legitimize it by focusing on its classical roots. While you may not choose to use this approach in critical essays, understanding its basic components will facilitate your understanding of the approaches discussed in the remainder of the book, for they were developed largely in response to both the strengths and limitations of neo-Aristotelian criticism.

Procedures

Using the neo-Aristotelian method of criticism, a critic analyzes an artifact in a four-step process: (1) selecting an artifact; (2) analyzing the artifact; (3) formulating a research question; and (4) writing the essay.

Selecting an Artifact

The neo-Aristotelian method of criticism was developed to analyze speeches, so speeches are particularly good artifacts to select for this method of criticism. If you are not interested in analyzing a speech, selecting a discursive text rather than an entirely visual one will maximize the insights your criticism produces because most of the units of analysis of neo-Aristotelianism deal with linguistic dimensions of rhetoric. Because the method includes an investigation of the rhetor, you also want to select an artifact produced by a rhetor about which some biographical information is available.

Analyzing the Artifact

Neo-Aristotelian criticism involves three basic steps: (1) reconstructing the context in which the artifact occurred; (2) application of the five canons to the artifact; and (3) assessing the impact of the artifact on the audience.[16]

Reconstructing the Context

Connecting the rhetorical artifact with its context helps a critic discover how various components of the context affected the rhetoric that was formulated. A critic investigates three major components of the context—the rhetor, the occasion, and the audience.

A critic begins by discovering information about the rhetor. The aim of this inquiry is not to develop a typical biography of the individual's life. Rather, the purpose is to study the individual as a rhetor and to discover links between rhetorical efforts and the rhetor's history, experience, and character. For example, you may want to seek information about early environmental influences on the rhetor's attitudes, motivation, and communication skills. Other areas to investigate include whether the rhetor had formal training in the rhetorical medium selected for expression, the rhetor's previous experience with the subject and the medium, the rhetor's rhetorical philosophy or principles, and methods of rhetorical preparation. Finally, try to discover the motivating forces of the rhetor—why the rhetor chose to produce this rhetoric on this particular occasion and what the rhetor sought to accomplish.

After investigating the background of the rhetor to discover its effects on the rhetorical artifact, a critic turns to an examination of the occasion on which the rhetoric was presented. The rhetorical act is affected by factors in the occasion, so your task here is to determine the elements in the occasion that influenced the rhetor in choice of subject and approach or the peculiar demands of the time and place when the rhetoric occurred. Pay attention to the historical antecedents of the rhetoric, the specific events that gave rise to and followed it, and the social and cultural attitudes toward the topic of the rhetoric.

A critic completes the examination of the context by looking at the audience for the rhetoric. The rhetor constructs rhetoric to accomplish a particular goal for a specific individual or group. Knowing about the audience, then, helps you understand why the rhetor selected particular strategies. The same forces that helped to shape the occasion for the rhetor also affect the audience, so you probably already know something about the audience through investigating the occasion. Additional lines of inquiry to pursue are the composition of the audience, the rhetor's reputation with this audience, and the listeners' knowledge about and attitudes toward the rhetor's subject.

Applying the Canons

The second component of neo-Aristotelian criticism is the analysis of the artifact itself using the five canons of classical rhetoric. In classical Greek and Roman times, when the study of rhetoric began, rhetoric was divided into five parts. These five parts of or canons of rhetoric are the steps that go into the process of public speaking.[17] They are: (1) invention, the location and creation of ideas and materials for the speech; (2) organization, the structure or arrangement of the speech; (3) style, the language of the speech; (4) memory, mastery of the subject matter, which may include the actual memorizing of the speech; and (5) delivery, management of the voice and gestures in the presentation of the speech.

Invention.   A critic's concern in applying the canon of invention is with the speaker's major ideas, lines of argument, or content. Invention is based on two major forms of proof. External or inartistic proofs are those the rhetor uses from other sources but does not create, including the testimony of witnesses and documents such as contracts and letters. Internal or artistic proofs, those that the rhetor creates, fall into three categories: (1) *logos* or logical argument; (2) *ethos* or the appeal of the rhetor's character; and (3) *pathos* or emotional appeal.

Logos deals with the logical or rational elements of the rhetoric and with the effect of these elements on the audience. In discovering the rhetor's use of logical appeals, a critic identifies the argument or thesis the rhetor is presenting and determines how that thesis is developed and supported. The evidence presented to enforce or support the point is evaluated in terms of the beliefs of the audience and the context of the rhetoric. Whether the evidence is the quoting of experts, statistical summaries, personal experience, or some other form, a critic examines it to see whether it is relevant to the thesis being developed, whether the evidence is consistent, and whether sufficient evidence has been supplied to make the point.

A rhetor cannot simply present evidence to the audience; something must be done with the evidence to encourage the audience to come to some conclusion based on it. This is the process of reasoning, which assumes two major forms—inductive and deductive. In inductive reasoning, a series of specific examples is used to draw a general conclusion. Six cases in which individuals who talked on cell phones while driving were involved in serious accidents could be used by a rhetor, for example, to make the point that people should not simultaneously drive and talk on cell phones. Deductive reasoning, in contrast, begins with a generalization that is acceptable to the audience, and the rhetor then applies the generalization to a specific case. A rhetor who begins with the generalization that smoking and lung cancer are linked may conclude, using deductive reasoning, that those in the audience who smoke are in danger of developing the disease. A critic, then, assesses both the evidence and the reasoning used by the rhetor to develop the thesis.

The second form of artistic proof, *ethos*, is what we today call *credibility*. It deals with the effect or appeal of the speaker's character on the audience. Your concern in analyzing *ethos* is with how the rhetor's character, as known to the audience prior to the speech and as presented to the audience during the speech, facilitates the acceptance of belief on the part of the audience. Credibility is demonstrated by a rhetor largely through the display of three qualities in the rhetorical act: (1) moral character or integrity, achieved by linking the message and rhetor with what the audience considers virtuous; (2) intelligence, evident in a display of common sense, good taste, and familiarity with current topics and interests; and (3) good will, the establishment of rapport with the audience through means such as identifying with the audience members or praising them.

The third form of artistic proof, *pathos*, concerns appeals designed to generate emotions in the audience. Here, a critic identifies the emotions generated by the speech—perhaps fear, shame, or pity—and explains how those emotions put the listeners in a particular frame of mind to react favorably to the rhetor's purpose.

Organization.   The second major area of the rhetorical artifact a critic analyzes using the neo-Aristotelian method is its arrangement or structure. Your task here is to determine the general pattern of arrangement adopted for the rhetoric—for example, a chronological order, where material is divided into time units, or a problem-solution order, where a discussion of a problem is followed by suggested solutions to it. Determine which aspects of the content are given emphasis in the rhetoric through the structure and the various functions the parts of the artifact perform. Emphasis can be determined by discovering which parts of the rhetoric are given greater weight through their placement at the beginning or end, the topic on which the rhetor spends the most time, and the ideas the rhetor repeats. Your task is also to assess the results of the arrangement of the discourse in its entirety to discover if the organization of the speech is consistent with the subject and purpose of the discourse and is appropriate for the audience.

Style.   The canon of style deals with the language used by the rhetor. A critic assesses how particular kinds of words or other symbols are used by the rhetor to create varying effects and how the symbols are arranged to form larger units such as sentences, figures of speech, images, and so on. Analysis of style involves determining the general effect that results—common and ordinary, forceful and robust, or stately and ornate, for example. In general, a critic's concern in examining style is with whether the language style contributes to the accomplishment of the rhetor's goal and helps to create the intended response.

Delivery.   The canon of delivery is concerned with the speaker's manner of presentation. In the application of this canon, a critic investigates the influence of delivery on the success of the rhetorical artifact. In a public speech, delivery involves the rhetor's mode of presentation—whether the speech is delivered impromptu, from memory, extemporaneously, or by reading from a manuscript. The bodily action of the rhetor while delivering the rhetoric—posture, movement, gestures, and eye contact—and how the appearance and physical characteristics of the rhetor affected the audience are also part of your examination of delivery. Assessment of the vocal skill of the rhetor, including how articulation, pronunciation, rate of speech, and pitch contributed to the audience's acceptance of the message—if that information is available—completes your analysis of delivery.

Memory.   Although memory also is among the five classical canons of rhetoric, it was not dealt with systematically by Aristotle. Partly for this reason and also because many speeches are not memorized (and memory is irrelevant to most nondiscursive forms of rhetoric), this canon often is not applied by the neo-Aristotelian critic. When it is, it deals with the rhetor's control of the materials of the speech and the relation of memory to the mode of presentation selected.

The neo-Aristotelian method, with its application of the five canons to an artifact, asks much of the critic. To cover all of the canons thoroughly in a short artifact is often difficult, and the critic cannot do justice either to the artifact or the analysis. Thus, you sometimes will see neo-Aristotelian critics focus on only one or two of the canons in their analyses. Such a focus allows them to dissect an artifact more deeply and to pay most attention to those features of it that make the most difference in that artifact's persuasiveness. You may want to exercise this same option if you choose to use neo-Aristotelian criticism as a critical method.

Assessing the Effects

At the conclusion of criticism using neo-Aristotelianism, a critic judges the effects of the rhetoric. Because the rhetoric was designed to accomplish some goal—the rhetor sought a response of some kind—your task is to determine whether or not this goal was met or what happened as a result of the rhetoric. There is no single measure of effectiveness, and how you choose to assess the effects depends on the characteristics of the rhetorical artifact itself, the rhetor's intention, the audience to which the rhetoric is addressed, and the context in which the rhetoric is presented. The effectiveness of a speech frequently is judged by the immediate and/or long-term response of the audience—either those changes immediately visible in the audience or those that emerge at a later time.

Formulating a Research Question

The research question asked about artifacts in neo-Aristotelian criticism is: "Did the rhetor use the available means of persuasion to evoke the intended response from the audience?"

Writing the Essay

After completing the analysis, you are ready to write your essay, which includes five major components: (1) an introduction, in which you discuss the research question, its contribution to rhetorical theory, and its significance; (2) a description of the artifact and its context; (3) a description of the method of criticism—in this case, neo-Aristotelian criticism; (4) a report of the findings of the analysis, in which you explicate the rhetor's choices through application of the five canons to your artifact; and (5) a discussion of the contribution the analysis makes to rhetorical theory.

Sample Essays

The two essays that follow demonstrate the neo-Aristotelian approach to criticism. Forbes Hill's essay on a speech by Richard Nixon not only provides an illustration of neo-Aristotelian criticism but also an assessment of the value of this critical approach. Gary W. Brown uses neo-Aristotelian criticism to analyze the rhetoric of Saddam Hussein during the Persian Gulf War in 1991. The research question guiding both analyses is: "Did the rhetor select the best rhetorical options available to him to evoke the intended response from the audience?"

Notes

[1] Herbert A. Wichelns, "The Literary Criticism of Oratory," in *Studies in Rhetoric and Public Speaking in Honor of James A. Winans*, ed. A. M. Drummond (New York: Century, 1925), pp. 181–216. A more accessible source for the essay is Herbert A. Wichelns, "The Literary Criticism of Oratory," in *Methods of Rhetorical Criticism: A Twentieth-Century Perspective*, ed. Bernard L. Brock and Robert L. Scott, 2nd ed. (Detroit: Wayne State University Press, 1980), pp. 40–73.

[2] Mark S. Klyn, "Toward a Pluralistic Rhetorical Criticism," in *Essays on Rhetorical Criticism*, ed. Thomas R. Nilsen (New York: Random House, 1968), p. 154.

[3] Donald C. Bryant, ed., *The Rhetorical Idiom: Essays in Rhetoric, Oratory, Language, and Drama* (Ithaca: Cornell University Press, 1958), p. 5.

[4] Wichelns, in Brock and Scott, p. 67.

[5] Wichelns, in Brock and Scott, pp. 69–70.

[6] William Norwood Brigance, ed., *A History and Criticism of American Public Address*, 2 vols. (New York: McGraw-Hill, 1943). A third volume was published in 1955: Marie Kathryn Hochmuth, ed., *A History and Criticism of American Public Address, III* (New York: Longmans, Green, 1955).

[7] Lester Thonssen and A. Craig Baird, *Speech Criticism* (New York: Ronald, 1948). In the second edition of the book, a third author was added: Lester Thonssen, A. Craig Baird, and Waldo W. Braden, *Speech Criticism*, 2nd ed. (New York: Ronald, 1970).

[8] G. P. Mohrmann and Michael C. Leff point out that neo-Aristotelianism itself does not preclude the study of discourse larger than a single speech; in fact, Aristotle discusses oratorical genres—deliberative or political speaking, forensic or legal speaking, and epideictic or ceremonial speaking. The notion of genres was not incorporated into the neo-Aristotelian approach because of Wichelns's determination that the purpose of rhetorical criticism was to uncover effects on the specific audience. See G. P. Mohrmann and Michael C. Leff, "Lincoln at Cooper Union: A Rationale for Neo-Classical Criticism," *Quarterly Journal of Speech*, 60 (December 1974), 463.

[9] Edwin Black, *Rhetorical Criticism: A Study in Method* (Madison: University of Wisconsin Press, 1978), p. 33; and Otis M. Walter, "On the Varieties of Rhetorical Criticism," in *Essays in Rhetorical Criticism*, ed. Thomas R. Nilsen (New York: Random, 1968), p. 162.

[10] Walter, pp. 162–65.

[11] Karlyn Kohrs Campbell, "The Forum: 'Conventional Wisdom—Traditional Form': A Rejoinder," *Quarterly Journal of Speech*, 58 (December 1972), 454.

[12] Black, p. 124.

[13] Karlyn Kohrs Campbell, "The Ontological Foundations of Rhetorical Theory," *Philosophy and Rhetoric*, 3 (Spring 1970), 98.

[14] Douglas Ehninger, "Rhetoric and the Critic," *Western Speech*, 29 (Fall 1965), 230.

[15] See, for example: J. A. Hendrix, "In Defense of Neo-Aristotelian Rhetorical Criticism," *Western Speech*, 32 (Fall 1968), 216–52; Forbes I. Hill, "Conventional Wisdom—Traditional Form: The President's Message of November 3, 1969," *Quarterly Journal of Speech*, 58 (December 1972), 373–86; Campbell, "The Forum," pp. 451–54; Forbes I. Hill, "The Forum: Reply to Professor Campbell," *Quarterly Journal of Speech*, 58 (December 1972), 454–60; and Mohrmann and Leff, pp. 459–67.

[16] The summary of these procedures is brief. Much more detail about them is available in Thonssen, Baird, and Braden.

[17] Although these canons were formulated to apply to public speaking and neo-Aristotelian criticism originally was applied to speeches, the canons can be applied to rhetorical acts and artifacts of various kinds. Admittedly, in such an application, the canons and neo-Aristotelian criticism must be stretched. For an example of this kind of expansion of the canons, see Nancy Harper, *Human Communication Theory: The History of a Paradigm* (Rochelle Park, NJ: Hayden, 1979), pp. 181–261.

Conventional Wisdom—
Traditional Form—
The President's Message of November 3, 1969

Forbes Hill

More than one critique of President Nixon's address to the nation on November 3, 1969, has appeared,[1] which is not remarkable, since it was the most obvious feature of the public relations machine that appears to have dammed back the flood of sentiment for quick withdrawal of American forces from Southeast Asia. To be sure, the dike built by this machine hardly endured forever, but some time was gained—an important achievement. It seems natural, then, that we should want to examine this obvious feature from more than one angle.

Preceding critiques have looked at Nixon's message from notably nontraditional perspectives. Stelzner magnified it in the lens of archetypal criticism, which reveals a non-literary version of the quest story archetype, but he concluded that the President's is an incomplete telling of the story that does not adequately interact with the listeners' subjective experiences. Newman condemned the message as "shoddy rhetoric" because its tough stance and false dilemmas are directed to white, urban, uptight voters. Campbell condemned it on the basis of intrinsic criticism because though its stated purposes are to tell the truth, increase credibility, promote unity, and affirm moral responsibility, its rhetoric conceals truth, decreases credibility, promotes division, and dodges moral responsibility. Then, stepping outside the intrinsic framework, she makes her most significant criticism: the message perpetuates myths about American values instead of scrutinizing the real values of America.

I propose to juxtapose these examinations with a strict neo-Aristotelian analysis. If it differs slightly from analyses that follow Wichelns[2] and Hochmuth-Nichols,[3] that is because it attempts a critique that reinterprets neo-Aristotelianism slightly—a critique guided by the spirit and usually the letter of the Aristotelian text as I understand it. What the neo-Aristotelian method can and should do will be demonstrated, I hope, by this juxtaposition.

Neo-Aristotelian criticism compares the means of persuasion used by a speaker with a comprehensive inventory given in Aristotle's *Rhetoric*. Its end is to discover whether the speaker makes the best choices from the inventory to get a favorable decision from a specified group of auditors in a specific situation. It does not, of course, aim to discover whether or not the speaker actually gets his favorable decision; decisions in practice are often upset by chance factors.[4] First the neo-Aristotelian critic must outline the situation, then specify the group of auditors and define the kind of decision they are to make. Finally he must reveal the choice and disposition of three intertwined persuasive factors—logical, psychological, and characterological—and evaluate this choice and disposition against the standard of the *Rhetoric*.

From *Quarterly Journal of Speech*, 58 (December 1972), 373–86. Used by permission of the Speech Communication Association [National Communication Association] and the author.

The Situation

The state of affairs for the Nixon Administration in the fall of 1969 is well known. The United States had been fighting a stalemated war for several years. The cost in lives and money was immense. The goal of the war was not clear; presumably the United States wanted South Viet Nam as a stable non-Communist buffer state between Communist areas and the rest of Southeast Asia. To the extent that this goal was understood, it seemed as far from being realized in 1969 as it had been in 1964. In the meantime, a large and vocal movement had grown up, particularly among the young, of people who held that there should have been no intervention in Viet Nam in the first place and that it would never be possible to realize any conceivable goal of intervention. The movement was especially dangerous to the Administration because it numbered among its supporters many of the elements of the population who were most interested in foreign policy and best informed about it. There were variations of position within the peace movement, but on one point all its members were agreed: the United States should commit itself immediately to withdraw its forces from Viet Nam.

The policy of the Nixon Administration, like that of the Johnson Administration before it, was limited war to gain a position of strength from which to negotiate. By fall 1969 the Administration was willing to make any concessions that did not jeopardize a fifty-fifty chance of achieving the goal, but it was not willing to make concessions that amounted to sure abandonment of the goal. A premature withdrawal amounted to public abandonment and was to be avoided at all costs. When the major organizations of the peace movement announced the first Moratorium Day for October 15 and organized school and work stoppages, demonstrations, and a great "March on Washington" to dramatize the demand for immediate withdrawal from Viet Nam, the Administration launched a counterattack. The President announced that he would make a major address on Viet Nam November 3. This announcement seems to have moderated the force of the October moratorium, but plans were soon laid for a second moratorium on November 15. Nixon's counterattack aimed at rallying the mass of the people to disregard the vocal minority and oppose immediate withdrawal; it aimed to get support for a modified version of the old strategy: limited war followed by negotiated peace. The address was broadcast the evening of November 3 over the national radio and television networks.

The Auditors and the Kind of Decision

An American President having a monopoly of the media at prime time potentially reaches an audience of upwards of a hundred million adults of heterogeneous backgrounds and opinions. Obviously it is impossible to design a message to move every segment of this audience, let alone the international audience. The speaker must choose his targets. An examination of the texts shows us which groups were eliminated as targets, which were made secondary targets, and which were primary. The speaker did not address himself to certain fanatical opponents of the war: the ones who hoped that the Viet Cong would gain a signal victory over the Americans and their South Vietnamese allies, or those who denied that Communist advances were threats to non-Communist countries, or those against any war for any reason. These were the groups the President sought to isolate and stigmatize. On the other hand, there was a large group of Americans who would be willing to give their all to fight any kind of Communist expansion anywhere at any time. These people also were not a target group: their support could be counted on in any case.

The speaker did show himself aware that the Viet Cong and other Communist decision-makers were listening in. He represented himself to them as willing and anxious to negotiate and warned them that escalation of the war would be followed by effective retaliation. The Communists constituted a secondary target audience, but the analysis that follows will make plain that the message was not primarily intended for them.

The primary target was those Americans not driven by a clearly defined ideological commitment to oppose or support the war at any cost. Resentment of the sacrifice in money and lives, bewilderment at the stalemate, longing for some movement in a clearly marked direction—these were the principal aspects of their state of mind assumed by Nixon. He solicited them saying "tonight—to you, the great silent majority of my fellow Americans—I ask for your support."[5]

His address asks the target group of auditors to make a decision to support a policy to be continued in the future. In traditional terms, then, it is primarily a deliberative speech. Those who receive the message are decision-makers, and they are concerned with the past only as it serves as analogy to future decisions. The subjects treated are usual ones for deliberation: war and peace.[6]

Disposition and Synopsis

The address begins with an enthymeme that attacks the credibility gap.[7] Those who decide on war and peace must know the truth about these policies, and the conclusion is implied that the President is going to tell the truth. The rest of the *proem* is taken up by a series of questions constructing a formal partition of the subjects to be covered. The partition stops short of revealing the nature of the modification in policy that constitutes the Nixon plan. The message fits almost perfectly into the Aristotelian pattern of *proem*, narrative, proofs both constructive and refutative, and epilogue. Just as *proem* has served as a general heading for a synoptic statement of what was done in the first few sentences, so the other four parts will serve us as analytical headings for a synopsis of the rest.

The narrative commences with Nixon's statement of the situation as he saw it on taking office. He could have ordered immediate withdrawal of American forces, but he decided to fulfill "a greater obligation . . . to think of the effect" of his decision "on the next generation, and on the future of peace and freedom in America, and in the world." Applicable here is the precept: the better the moral end that the speaker can in his narrative be seen consciously choosing, the better the *ethos* he reveals.[8] An end can hardly be better than "the future of peace and freedom in America, and in the world." The narrative goes on to explain why and how the United States became involved in Viet Nam in the first place. This explanation masquerades as a simple chronological statement—"Fifteen years ago . . ." but thinly disguised in the chronology lie two propositions: first, that the leaders of America were right in intervening on behalf of the government of South Viet Nam; second, that the great mistake in their conduct of the war was over-reliance on American combat forces. Some doubt has been cast on the wisdom of Nixon's choice among the means of persuasion here. The history, writes one critic, "is a surprising candidate for priority in any discussion today. . . . The President's chief foreign policy advisors, his allies on Capitol Hill, and the memorandum he got from the Cabinet bureaucracy all urged him to skip discussions of the causes and manner of our involvement. Yet history comes out with top billing."[9] This criticism fails to conceive the rhetorical function of the narrative: in the two propositions the whole content of the proofs that follow is foreshadowed, and foreshadowed in the guise of a non-controversial statement about the historical facts. Among traditional orators this use of the narrative to foreshadow proofs is common, but it has seldom been handled with more artistry than here.

Constructive proofs are not opened with an analytical partition but with a general question: what is the best way to end the war? The answer is structured as a long argument from logical division: there are four plans to end American involvement; three should be rejected so that the listener is left with no alternative within the structure but to accept the fourth.[10] The four plans are: immediate withdrawal, the consequences of which are shown at some length to be bad; negotiated settlement, shown to be impossible in the near future because the enemy will not negotiate in earnest; shifting the burden of the war to the Vietnamese with American withdrawal on a fixed timetable, also argued to have bad consequences; and shifting the burden of the war to the Vietnamese with American withdrawal on a flexible schedule, said to have good consequences, since it will eventually bring "the complete withdrawal of all United States *combat ground* forces," whether earnest negotiations become possible or not. Constructive proofs close with one last evil consequence of immediate withdrawal: that it would lead eventually to Americans' loss of confidence in themselves and divisive recrimination that "would scar our spirit as a people."

As refutative proof is introduced, opponents of the Administration are characterized by a demonstrator carrying a sign, "Lose in Viet Nam"; they are an irrational minority who want to decide policy in the streets, as opposed to the elected officials—Congress and the President—who will decide policy by Constitutional and orderly means. This attack on his presumed opponents leads to a passage which reassures the majority of young people that the President really wants peace as much as they do. Reassuring ends with the statement of Nixon's personal belief that his plan will succeed; this statement may be taken as transitional to the epilogue.

The epilogue reiterates the bad consequences of immediate withdrawal—loss of confidence and loss of other nations to totalitarianism—it exhorts the silent majority to support the plan, predicting its success; it evokes the memory of Woodrow Wilson; then it closes with the President's pledge to meet his responsibilities to lead the nation with strength and wisdom. Recapitulation, building of *ethos*, and reinforcing the right climate of feeling—these are what a traditional rhetorician would advise that the epilogue do,[11] and these are what Nixon's epilogue does.

Indeed, this was our jumping-off place for the synopsis of the message: it falls into the traditional paradigm; each frame of the paradigm contains the lines of argument conventional for that frame. The two unconventional elements in the paradigm—the unusual placement of the last evil consequence of immediate withdrawal and the use of the frame by logical division for the constructive proofs—are there for good rhetorical reasons. That last consequence, loss of confidence and divisive recrimination, serves to lead into the refutation which opens with the demonstrator and his sign. It is as if the demonstrator were being made an example in advance of just this evil consequence. The auditor is brought into precisely the right set for a refutation section that does not so much argue with opponents as it pushes them into an isolated, unpopular position.

Because of the residues-like structure, the message creates the illusion of proving that Vietnamization and flexible withdrawal constitute the best policy. By process of elimination it is the only policy available, and even a somewhat skeptical listener is less likely to question the only policy available. Approaching the proposal with skepticism dulled, he perhaps does not so much miss a development of the plan. In particular, he might not ask the crucial question: does the plan actually provide for complete American withdrawal? The answer to this question is contained in the single phrase, "complete withdrawal of all United States *combat ground* forces." It is fairly clear, in retrospect, that this phrase concealed the intention to keep in Viet Nam for several years a large contingent of air and support forces. Nixon treats the difference between plan three, Vietnamization and withdrawal on a fixed schedule, and plan four, Vietnamization and withdrawal on a flexible schedule, as a matter of whether or not the schedule is announced in advance. But the crucial difference is really that plan three was understood by its advocates as a plan for quick, complete withdrawal; plan four was a plan for partial withdrawal. The strategic reason for not announcing a fixed schedule was that the announcement would give away this fact. The residues structure concealed the lack of development of the plan; the lack of development of the plan suppressed the critical fact that Nixon did not propose complete withdrawal. Although Nixon's message shows traditionally conventional structure, these variations from the traditional show a remarkable ability at designing the best adaptations to the specific rhetorical situation.

Logical and Psychological Persuasive Factors

Central to an Aristotelian assessment of the means of persuasion is an account of two interdependent factors: (1) the choice of major premises on which enthymemes[12] that form "the body of the proof" are based, and (2) the means whereby auditors are brought into states of feeling favorable to accepting these premises and the conclusions following from them. Premises important here are of two kinds: predictions and values. Both kinds as they relate to good and evil consequences of the four plans to end American involvement, will be assessed. The first enthymeme involving prediction is that immediate withdrawal followed by a Communist takeover would lead to murder and imprisonment of innocent civilians. This conclusion follows from the general predictive rule: the future will resemble the past.[13] Since the Communists murdered and imprisoned opponents on taking over North Viet Nam in 1954 and murdered opponents in the city of Hue in 1968, they will do the same when they take over South Viet Nam. Implied also is an enthymeme based on the value premise that security of life and freedom from bondage are primary goods for men;[14] a Communist takeover would destroy life and freedom and therefore destroy primary goods for men.

Presumably no one would try to refute this complex of enthymemes by saying that life and freedom are not primary goods, though he might argue from more and less;[15] more life is lost by continuing the war than would be lost by a Communist takeover, or American-South Vietnamese political structures allow for even less political freedom than the Communist alternatives. Nixon buries these questions far enough beneath the surface of the message that probably auditors in the target group are not encouraged to raise them. One could also attack the predictive premise: after all, the future is not always the past writ over again. But this kind of refutation is merely irritating; we know that the premise is not universally true, yet everyone finds it necessary to operate in ordinary life as if it were. People on the left of the target group, of course, reject the evidence—North Viet Nam and Hue.

A related prediction is that immediate withdrawal would result in a collapse of confidence in American leadership. It rests on the premise that allies only have confidence in those who both have power and will act in their support.[16] If the United States shows it lacks power and will in Viet Nam, there will be a collapse of confidence, which entails further consequences: it would "promote recklessness" on the part of enemies everywhere else the country has commitments, i.e., as a general premise, when one party to a power struggle loses the confidence of its allies, its enemies grow bolder.[17] The conclusion is bolstered by citations from former presidents Eisenhower, Johnson, and Kennedy: the statement of the "liberal saint," Kennedy, is featured.

It is difficult to attack the related premises of these tandem arguments. They rest on what experience from the sandbox up shows to be probable. The target group consists of people with the usual American upbringing and experience. Someone will question the premises only if he questions the worldview out of which they develop. That view structures the world into Communist powers—actual or potential enemies—and non-Communist powers—allies. America is the leader of the allies, referred to elsewhere as the forces of "peace and freedom" opposed by "the forces of totalitarianism." Because of its association with freedom, American leadership is indisputably good, and whatever weakens confidence in it helps the enemies. Only a few people on the far left would categorically reject this structure.

The foregoing premises and the worldview fundamental to them are even more likely to be accepted if the auditors are in a state of fear. Fear may be defined as distress caused by a vision of impending evil of the destructive or painful kind.[18] This message promotes a state of fear by the nature of the evil consequences developed—murder and imprisonment of innocents, collapse of leadership in the free world, and reckless aggressiveness of implacable enemies. America is the prototype of a nation that is fearful; her enemies are watching their opportunities all over the globe, from Berlin to the Middle East, yes even in the Western Hemisphere itself. The enemies are cruel and opposed to American ideals. They are strong on the battlefield and intransigent in negotiations. Conditions are such that America's allies may lose confidence in her and leave her to fight these enemies alone. But these circumstances are not too much amplified: only enough to create a state of feeling favorable to rejecting immediate withdrawal, not so much as to create the disposition for escalation.

Nixon claims to have tried hard to make a negotiated settlement, but he could not make one because the Communists refused to compromise. The evidence that they would not compromise is developed at length: public initiatives through the peace conference in Paris are cited, terms for participation of the Communist forces in internationally supervised elections offered, and promises made to negotiate on any of these terms. Then there were private initiatives through the Soviet Union and directly by letter to the leaders of North Viet Nam, as well as private efforts by the United States ambassador to the Paris talks. These efforts brought only demands for the equivalent of unconditional surrender. The citation of evidence is impressive and destroys the credibility of the position that negotiations can bring a quick end to the war.

Nixon does not explicitly predict that the plan for negotiated settlement will not work ever; on the contrary, he says that he will keep trying. But if the auditor believes the evidence, he finds it difficult to avoid making his own enthymeme with the conclusion that negotiated settlement will never work; the major premise is the same old rule, the future will be like the past. Nixon gives another reason, too: it will not work while the opposite side "is convinced that all it has to do is to wait for our next concession, and our next concession after that one, until it gets everything it wants." The major premise—no power convinced that victory is probable by forcing repeated concessions will ever compromise—constitutes a commonplace of bargaining for virtually everyone.

Peace is seen in these arguments as almost an unqualified good. Although compromise through bargaining is the fastest way to peace, the other side must make concessions to assure compromise. Reasons for continuing the war, such as an ideological commitment, are evil. There is no glory in war and prolonging it is not justified by political gains made but only by a commitment to higher values like saving lives and preserving freedom. Prolonging the war is also justified as avoiding future wars by not losing Southeast Asia altogether and not promoting the spirit of recklessness in the enemies. "I want," states Nixon, "to end it [the war] in a way which will increase the chance that their [the soldiers'] younger brothers and their sons will not have to fight in some future Vietnam. . . ."

A listener is prone to reject the likelihood of a negotiated peace if he is angry with his opponents. Anger is a painful desire for revenge and arises from an evident, unjustified slight to a person or his friends.[19] People visualizing revenge ordinarily refuse compromise except as a temporary tactic. Nixon presents the American people as having been slighted: they value peace, and their leaders have with humility taken every peace initiative possible: public, private, and secret. The Communist powers wish to gain politically from the war; they have rebuffed with spite all initiatives and frustrated our good intentions by demanding the equivalent of unconditional surrender. Frustration is, of course, a necessary condition of anger.[20] Again, Nixon does not go too far—not far enough to create a psychological climate out of which a demand for escalation would grow.

Nixon announces that his plan for Vietnamization and American withdrawal on a flexible timetable is in effect already. Its consequences: American men coming home, South Vietnamese forces gaining in strength, enemy infiltration measurably reduced, and United States' casualties also reduced. He predicts: policies that have had such consequences in the past will have them in the future, i.e., the future will be like the past. Again, the undisputed value that saving lives is good is assumed. But in this case the argument, while resting on an acceptable premise, was, at the time of this speech, somewhat more doubtful of acceptance by the target group. The evidence constitutes the problem: obviously the sample of the past since the policy of Vietnamization commenced was so short that no one could really judge the alleged consequences to be correlated with the change in policy, let alone caused by it. There is, then, little reason why that audience should have believed the minor premise—that the consequences of Vietnamization were good.

A temporizing and moderate policy is best presented to auditors who while temporarily fearful are basically confident. Nothing saps the will to accept such a proposal as does the opposite state, basically fearful and only temporarily confident. Confidence is the other side of the coin from fear: it is pleasure because destructive and painful evils seem far away and sources of aid near at hand.[21] The sources of aid here are the forces of the Republic of South Viet Nam. They have continued to gain in strength and as a result have been able to take over combat responsibilities from American forces. In contrast, danger from the enemy is receding—"enemy infiltration . . . over the last three months is less than 20 per cent of what it was over the same period last year." Nixon assures his auditors that he has confidence the plan will succeed. America is the "strongest and richest nation in the world"; it can afford the level of aid that needs to be continued in Viet Nam. It will show the moral stamina to meet the challenge of free world leadership.

For some time rumors about gradual American withdrawal from Viet Nam had been discounted by the peace movement. The only acceptable proof of American intentions would be a timetable showing withdrawal to be accomplished soon. Thus the third plan: withdrawal on a fixed timetable. Nixon predicts that announcing of a timetable would remove the incentive to negotiate and reduce flexibility of response. The general premise behind the first is a commonplace of bargaining: negotiations never take place without a *quid pro quo*; a promise to remove American forces by a certain date gives away the *quid pro quo*. For most Americans, who are used to getting things by bargaining, this premise is unquestionable. Only those few who think that the country can gain no vestige of the objective of the war are willing to throw away the incentive. The premises behind the notion of flexibility—that any workable plan is adaptable to changes in the situation—is a commonplace of legislation and not likely to be questioned by anyone. Nixon adds to this generally acceptable premise a specific incentive. Since withdrawal will occur more rapidly if enemy military activity decreases and the South Vietnamese forces become stronger, there is a possibility that forces can be withdrawn even sooner than would be predicted by a timetable. This specific incentive is illusory, since it is obvious that one can always withdraw sooner than the timetable says, even if he has one; it is hard to see how a timetable actually reduces flexibility. Everyone makes timetables, of course, and having to re-make them when conditions change is a familiar experience. But the average man who works from nine to five probably thinks that the government should be different: when it announces a timetable it must stick to it; otherwise nothing is secure. This argument may seem weak to the critic, but it is probably well directed to the target group. The real reason for not announcing a timetable has already been noted.[22]

One final prediction is founded on the preceding predictions—whenever a policy leads to such evil consequences as movement of Southeast Asia into alliance with the enemy and a new recklessness on the part of enemies everywhere, it will eventually result in remorse and divisive recrimination which will, in turn, result in a loss of self-confidence. Guiltlessness and internal unity, the opposites of remorse and recrimination, are here assumed as secondary goods leading to self-confidence, a primary good. The enthymeme predicting loss of self-confidence consequent on immediate withdrawal is summary in position: it seems to tie together all previous arguments. It comes right after a particularly effective effort at *ethos* building—the series of statements developed in parallel construction about not having chosen the easy way (immediate withdrawal) but the right way. However, it rests on the assumption that the long term mood of confidence in the country depends on the future of Southeast Asia and the recklessness of our enemies. Since these two factors are only an aspect of a larger picture in which many other events play their parts, it is surely not true that they alone will produce a loss of confidence. The enthymeme based on this assumption, placed where it is, however, does not invite questioning by the target group. Doubtful though it may look under searching scrutiny, it has an important function for the structure of psychological proof in this message. It reinforces the vague image of the danger of facing a stronger enemy in a weakened condition: America itself would be less united, less confident, and less able to fight in the future if this consequence of immediate withdrawal were realized.

Other things being equal, the more commonplace and universally accepted the premises of prediction in a deliberative speech, the more effective the speech. This is especially true if they are set in a frame that prepares the auditor psychologically for their acceptance. There is almost no doubt that given the policy of the Nixon Administration—Vietnamization and partial withdrawal on a flexible schedule not announced in advance—the message shows a potentially effective choice of premises. In some cases it is almost the only possible choice. Likewise the value structure of the message is wisely chosen from materials familiar to any observer of the American scene: it could be duplicated in hundreds of other messages from recent American history.

Several additional value assumptions are equally commonplace. Betraying allies and letting down friends is assumed to be an evil, and its opposite, loyalty to friends and allies the virtue of a great nation. This premise equates personal loyalty, like that a man feels for his friend, with what the people of the whole nation should feel for an allied nation. Many people think this way about international relations, and the good citizens of the target group can be presumed to be among them.

Policies endorsed by the people they are supposed to help are said to be better policies than those not endorsed by them. This statement undoubtedly makes a good political rule if one expects participation in the execution of policy of those to be helped. Policies that result from the operation of representative government are good, whereas those made on the streets are bad. This value is, of course, an essential of republican government: only the most radical, even of those outside the target group, would question it. Finally, Nixon assumes that the right thing is usually the opposite of the easy thing, and, of course, *he* chooses to do the right thing. Such a value premise does not occur in rhetorics by Aristotle or even George Campbell; it is probably a peculiar product of Protestant-American-on-the-frontier thinking. Its drawing power for twentieth-century urban youngsters is negligible, but the bulk of the target group probably is made up of suburbanites in the 30–50 category who still have some affinity for this kind of thinking.

Some shift from the traditional values of American culture can be seen in the tone of Nixon's dealing with the war: the lack of indication that it is glorious, the muted appeal to patriotism (only one brief reference to the first defeat in America's history), the lack of complete victory as a goal. But nowhere else does the culture of the post-atomic age show through; by and large the speech would have been applauded if delivered in the nineteenth century. That there has been a radical revolution of values among the young does not affect the message, and one might predict that Nixon is right in deciding that the revolution in values has not yet significantly infected the target group.

Characterological and Stylistic Factors

Nixon's choice of value premises is, of course, closely related to his *ethos* as conveyed by the speech. He promises to tell the truth before he asks the American people to support a policy which involves the overriding issues of war and peace—phraseology that echoes previous Nixonian messages. He refrains from harsh criticism of the previous administration; he is more interested in the future America than in political gains; such an avowal of disinterestedness is the commonest topic for self-character building.

Nixon is against political murders and imprisonments and active pushing initiatives for peace. He is flexible and compromising, unlike the negotiators for the enemy. He chooses the right way and not the easy way. He is the champion of policy made by constitutional processes; his opponents conduct unruly demonstrations in the streets. But he has healthy respect for the idealism and commitment of the young; he pledges himself in the tradition of Woodrow Wilson to win a peace that will avoid future wars. He has the courage to make a tasteful appeal to patriotism even when it's unpopular. Such is the character portrait drawn for us by Richard Nixon: restrained not hawkish, hard-working and active, flexible, yet firm where he needs to be. He seems an American style democrat, a moral but also a practical and sensitive man. The message is crowded with these overt clues from which we infer the good *ethos* of political figures in situations like this. Any more intensive development of the means of persuasion derived from the character of the speaker would surely have been counter-productive.

The language of Nixon's message helps to reinforce his *ethos*. His tone is unbrokenly serious. The first two-thirds of the message is in a self-consciously plain style—the effort is clearly made to give the impression of bluntness and forthrightness. This bluntness of tone correlates with the style of deliberative argumentation:[23] few epideictic elements are present in the first part of the speech. Everything seems to be adjusted to making the structure of residues exceedingly clear.

About two-thirds of the way through, the message shifts to a more impassioned tone. The alternative plans are collapsed into two, thus polarizing the situation: either immediate withdrawal or Nixon's plan for Vietnamization and unscheduled withdrawal. From here on parallel repetitions are persistent, and they serve no obvious logical function, but rather function to deepen the serious tone. There is, in short, an attempt to rise to a peroration of real eloquence. The qualities aimed at in the last third of the message seem to be gravity and impressiveness more than clarity and forthrightness. The effort seems to tax the speechwriter's literary skill to the limit, and the only new phrases he comes up with are the "silent majority" and the description of the energies of the young as "too often directed to bitter hatred against those they think are responsible for the war." All else is a moderately skillful pastiche of familiar phrases.

General Assessment

A summary answer can now be given to the question, how well did Nixon and his advisors choose among the available means of persuasion for this situation? The message was designed for those not ideologically overcommitted either to victory over Communism or to peace in any case while frustrated by the prolonged war. It operates from the most universally accepted premises of value and prediction; it buries deep in its texture most premises not likely to be immediately accepted. Enough of the means for bringing auditors into states of fear, anger, and confidence are used to create a psychological climate unfavorable to immediate withdrawal and favorable to Vietnamization. The goals—life, political freedom, peace, and self-confidence—are those shared by nearly all Americans, and connections of policies to them are tactfully handled for the target group. The structure is largely according to tradition: it can best be seen as falling into the four parts, and the right elements are contained in each of the parts. Two minor variations from the traditional are artfully designed to realize evident psychological ends. Conventional wisdom and conventional value judgments come dressed in conventional structure. The style of the narrative and proofs reflects adequately Nixon's reliance on clearly developed arguments from accepted premises; the style of the latter part of the message shows a moderately successful attempt at grandeur. In choice and arrangement of the means of persuasion for this situation this message is by and large a considerable success.

Neo-Aristotelian criticism tells a great deal about Nixon's message. It reveals the speechwriter as a superior technician. It permits us to predict that given this target group the message should be successful in leading to a decision to support the Administration's policies. It brings into sharp focus the speechwriter's greatest technical successes: the choice of the right premises to make a version of the domino theory plausible for these auditors and the creation of a controlled atmosphere of fear in which the theory is more likely to be accepted. Likewise, the choice of the right means of making success for peace negotiations seems impossible and the building of a controlled state of anger in which a pessimistic estimate of the chances for success seems plausible. Also the finely crafted structure that conceals exactly what needs to be concealed while revealing the favored plan in a context most favorable to its being chosen.

What neo-Aristotelianism does not attempt to account for are some basic and long-run questions. For instance, it does not assess the wisdom of the speaker's choice of target audience as does Newman, who wanted the President to alleviate the fears of the doves. All critics observe that Nixon excludes the radical opponent of the war from his audience. Not only is this opponent excluded by his choice of policy but even by the choice of premises from which he argues: premises such as that the Government of South Viet Nam is freer than that of North Viet Nam, or that the right course is the opposite of the easy one. Radical opponents of the war were mostly young—often college students. The obvious cliché, "they are the political leadership of tomorrow," should have applied. Was it in the long run a wise choice to exclude them from the target? An important question, but a neo-Aristotelian approach does not warrant us to ask it. There is a gain, though, from this limitation. If the critic questions the President's choice of policy and premises, he is forced to examine systematically all the political factors involved in this choice. Neither Newman nor Campbell do this in the objective and systematic fashion required by the magnitude of the subject. Indeed, would they not be better off with a kind of criticism that does not require them to do it?

Nor does the neo-Aristotelian approach predict whether a policy will remain rhetorically viable. If the critic assumes as given the Nixon Administration's choice of policy from among the options available, he will no doubt judge this choice of value and predictive premises likely to effect the decision wanted. To put it another way, Nixon's policy was *then* most defensible by arguing from the kinds of premises Nixon used. It seems less defensible at this writing, and in time may come to seem indefensible even to people like those in the target group. Why the same arguments for the same policy should be predictably less effective to people so little removed in time is a special case of the question, why do some policies remain rhetorically viable for decades while others do not. This question might in part be answered by pointing, as was done before, to the maturing of the students into political leadership. But however the question might be answered, neo-Aristotelianism does not encourage us to ask it. As Black truly said, the neo-Aristotelian comprehends "the rhetorical discourse as tactically designed to achieve certain results with a specific audience on a specific occasion,"[24] in this case that audience Nixon aimed at on the night of November 3, 1969.

Finally, neo-Aristotelian criticism does not warrant us to estimate the truth of Nixon's statements or the reality of the values he assumes as aspects of American life. When Nixon finds the origin of the war in a North Vietnamese "campaign to impose a Communist government on South Vietnam by instigating and supporting a revolution," Campbell takes him to task for not telling the truth. This criticism raises a serious question: are we sure that Nixon is not telling the truth? We know, of course, that Nixon oversimplifies a complex series of events—any speaker in his situation necessarily does that. But will the scholar of tomorrow with the perspective of history judge his account totally false? Campbell endorses the view that basically this is a civil war resulting from the failure of the Diem government backed by the United States to hold elections under the Geneva Agreements of 1954. But her view and Nixon's are not mutually exclusive: it seems evident to me that both the United States and the Communist powers involved themselves from the first to the extent they thought necessary to force an outcome in their favor in Viet Nam. If a scientific historian of the future had to pick one view of the conflict or the other, he would probably pick Nixon's because it more clearly recognizes the power politics behind the struggle. But I am not really intending to press the point that Campbell commits herself to a wrong view, or even a superficially partial one. The point is that she espouses here a theory of criticism that requires her to commit herself at all. If anyone writing in a scholarly journal seeks to assess the truth of Nixon's statements, he must be willing to assume the burden of proving them evidently false. This cannot be done by appealing to the wisdom of the liberal intellectuals of today.[25] If the essential task were accomplished, would the result be called a *rhetorical* critique? By Aristotle's standards it would not, and for my part I think we will write more significant criticism if we follow Aristotle in this case. To generalize, I submit that the limitations of neo-Aristotelian criticism are like the metrical conventions of the poet—limitations that make true significance possible.

Notes

[1] Robert P. Newman, "Under the Veneer: Nixon's Vietnam Speech of November 3, 1969," *Quarterly Journal of Speech*, 56 (Apr. 1970), 168–178; Hermann G. Stelzner, "The Quest Story and Nixon's November 3, 1969 Address," *Quarterly Journal of Speech*, 57 (Apr. 1971), 163–172; Karlyn Kohrs Campbell, "An Exercise in the Rhetoric of Mythical America," in *Critiques of Contemporary Rhetoric* (Belmont, CA: Wadsworth, 1972), pp. 50–58.

[2] Herbert A. Wichelns, "The Literary Criticism of Oratory," in Donald C. Bryant, ed., *The Rhetorical Idiom: Essays in Rhetoric, Oratory, Language, and Drama* (1925; rpt. Ithaca: Cornell Univ. Press, 1958), pp. 5–42.

[3] Marie Hochmuth [Nichols], "The Criticism of Rhetoric," in *A History and Criticism of American Public Address* (New York: Longmans, Green, 1955) III, 1–23.

[4] Aristotle, *Rhetoric* I. 1. 1355b 10–14. "To persuade is not the function of rhetoric but to investigate the persuasive factors inherent in the particular case. It is just the same as in all other arts; for example, it is not the function of medicine to bring health, rather to bring the patient as near to health as is possible in his case. Indeed, there are some patients who cannot be changed to healthfulness; nevertheless, they can be given the right therapy." (Translation mine.) I understand the medical analogy to mean that even if auditors chance to be proof against any of the means of persuasion, the persuader has functioned adequately as a rhetorician if he has investigated these means so that he has in effect "given the right therapy."

[5] Text as printed in *Vital Speeches*, 36 (15 Nov. 1969), 69.

[6] Aristotle *Rhetoric* I. 4. 1359b 33–1360a 5.

[7] Aristotle *Rhetoric* III. 14. 1415a 29–33. Here Nixon functions like a defendant in a forensic speech. "When defending he will first deal with any prejudicial insinuation against him . . . it is necessary that the defendant when he steps forward first reduce the obstacles, so he must immediately dissolve prejudice."

[8] See Aristotle *Rhetoric* III. 16. 1417a 16–36.

[9] Newman, p. 173.

[10] See Aristotle *Rhetoric* II. 23. 1398a 30–31. This basic structure is called method of residues in most modern argumentation textbooks.

[11] Aristotle *Rhetoric* III. 19. 1419b 10–1420a 8.

[12] For the purpose of this paper the term enthymeme is taken to mean any deductive argument. Aristotle gives a more technical definition of enthymeme that fits into the total design of his organon; in my opinion it is not useful for neo-Aristotelian criticism.

[13] Remarkably enough Aristotle does not state this general rule, though it clearly underlies his treatment of the historical example, *Rhetoric* II. 20.

[14] See Aristotle *Rhetoric* I. 6. 1362b 26–27 for life as a good; I. 8. 1366a for freedom as the object of choice for the citizens of a democracy.

[15] The subject of *Rhetoric* I. 7. Chaim Perelman and L. Olbrechts-Tyteca, commenting on this chapter, indicate that there is usually a consensus on such statements as 'life is good'; the dispute is over whether life is a greater good than honor in this particular situation. See *The New Rhetoric: A Treatise on Argumentation*, trans. John Wilkinson and Purcell Weaver (Notre Dame: Univ. of Notre Dame Press, 1969), pp. 81–82.

[16] See Aristotle *Rhetoric* II. 19. 1393a 1–3.

[17] This principle follows from *Rhetoric* II. 5. 1383a 24–25.

[18] Aristotle *Rhetoric* II. 5. 1382a 21–22. Aristotle treated the *pathe* as states of feeling that a man enters into because he draws certain inferences from the situation around him: he sees, for example, that he is the type of man who experiences pity when faced with this type of victim in these circumstances. The means of getting a man to draw inferences are themselves logical proofs; hence *pathos* does not work apart from the logical proofs in a message but through them. See Aristotle *Rhetoric* II. 1. 1378a 19–28 and my explication in James J. Murphy, ed. *A Synoptic History of Classical Rhetoric* (New York: Random House, 1972).

[19] Aristotle *Rhetoric* II. 2. 1378a 30–32.

[20] Aristotle *Rhetoric* II. 2. 1379a 10–18.

[21] Aristotle *Rhetoric* II. 5. 1383a 16–19.

[22] Since he gave this speech Nixon has made a general timetable for American withdrawal, thus, presumably, showing that he was not utterly convinced by his own argument. But he has never quite fixed a date for complete withdrawal of all American support forces from Viet Nam; he has been consistent in maintaining that withdrawal as a bargaining point for negotiation with the Viet Cong and North Vietnamese.

[23] See Aristotle *Rhetoric* III. 12. 1414a 8–19.

[24] Edwin B. Black, *Rhetorical Criticism: A Study in Method* (New York: Macmillan, 1965), p. 33.

[25] Richard H. Kendall, writing a reply to Newman, "The Forum," *Quarterly Journal of Speech*, 56 (Dec. 1970), 432, makes this same point, particularly in connection with Newman's implication that ex-President Johnson was a fraud. "If so, let us have some evidence of his fraudulent actions. If there is no evidence, or if there is evidence, but an essay on the rhetoric of President Nixon does not provide proper scope for a presentation of such evidence, then it seems to me inclusion of such a charge (or judgment) may fall into the category of gratuitous." Newman in rejoinder asks, "Should such summary judgments be left out of an article in a scholarly journal because space prohibits extensively supporting them? Omission might contribute to a sterile academic purity, but it would improve neither cogency nor understanding." I would certainly answer Newman's rhetorical question, yes, and I would go on to judge that view of criticism which encourages such summary judgments not to be a useful one.

Vietnamization Speech

Richard Nixon
November 3, 1969

Good evening, my fellow Americans: Tonight I want to talk to you on a subject of deep concern to all Americans and to many people in all parts of the world—the war in Vietnam.

I believe that one of the reasons for the deep division about Vietnam is that many Americans have lost confidence in what their Government has told them about our policy. The American people cannot and should not be asked to support a policy which involves the overriding issues of war and peace unless they know the truth about that policy.

Tonight, therefore, I would like to answer some of the questions that I know are on the minds of many of you listening to me.

How and why did America get involved in Vietnam in the first place?

How has this administration changed the policy of the previous administration?

What has really happened in the negotiations in Paris and on the battlefront in Vietnam?

What choices do we have if we are to end the war?

What are the prospects for peace?

Now, let me begin by describing the situation I found when I was inaugurated on January 20.

- The war had been going on for 4 years.
- 31,000 Americans had been killed in action.
- The training program for the South Vietnamese was behind schedule.
- 540,000 Americans were in Vietnam with no plans to reduce the number.
- No progress had been made at the negotiations in Paris and the United States had not put forth a comprehensive peace proposal.
- The war was causing deep division at home and criticism from many of our friends as well as our enemies abroad.

In view of these circumstances there were some who urged that I end the war at once by ordering the immediate withdrawal of all American forces.

From a political standpoint this would have been a popular and easy course to follow. After all, we became involved in the war while my predecessor was in office.

I could blame the defeat which would be the result of my action on him and come out as the peacemaker. Some put it to me quite bluntly: This was the only way to avoid allowing Johnson's war to become Nixon's war.

But I had a greater obligation than to think only of the years of my administration and of the next election. I had to think of the effect of my decision on the next generation and on the future of peace and freedom in America and in the world.

Let us all understand that the question before us is not whether some Americans are for peace and some Americans are against peace. The question at issue is not whether Johnson's war becomes Nixon's war.

The great question is: How can we win America's peace?

Well, let us turn now to the fundamental issue. Why and how did the United States become involved in Vietnam in the first place?

Fifteen years ago North Vietnam, with the logistical support of Communist China and the Soviet Union, launched a campaign to impose a Communist government on South Vietnam by instigating and supporting a revolution.

In response to the request of the Government of South Vietnam, President Eisenhower sent economic aid and military equipment to assist the people of South Vietnam in their efforts to prevent a Communist takeover. Seven years ago, President Kennedy sent 16,000 military personnel to Vietnam as combat advisers.

Four years ago, President Johnson sent American combat forces to South Vietnam.

Now, many believe that President Johnson's decision to send American combat forces to South Vietnam was wrong. And many others—I among them—have been strongly critical of the way the war has been conducted.

But the question facing us today is: Now that we are in the war, what is the best way to end it?

In January I could only conclude that the precipitate withdrawal of American forces from Vietnam would be a disaster not only for South Vietnam but for the United States and for the cause of peace.

For the South Vietnamese, our precipitate withdrawal would inevitably allow the Communists to repeat the massacres which followed their takeover in the North 15 years before.

- They then murdered more than 50,000 people and hundreds of thousands more died in slave labor camps.
- We saw a prelude of what would happen in South Vietnam when the Communists entered the city of Hue last year. During their brief rule there, there was a

bloody reign of terror in which 3,000 civilians were clubbed, shot to death, and buried in mass graves.

- With the sudden collapse of our support, these atrocities of Hue would become the nightmare of the entire nation—and particularly for the million and a half Catholic refugees who fled to South Vietnam when the Communists took over in the North.

For the United States, this first defeat in our Nation's history would result in a collapse of confidence in American leadership, not only in Asia but throughout the world.

Three American Presidents have recognized the great stakes involved in Vietnam and understood what had to be done.

In 1963, President Kennedy, with his characteristic eloquence and clarity, said: "we want to see a stable government there, carrying on a struggle to maintain its national independence."

"We believe strongly in that. We are not going to withdraw from that effort. In my opinion, for us to withdraw from that effort would mean a collapse not only of South Vietnam, but Southeast Asia. So we are going to stay there."

President Eisenhower and President Johnson expressed the same conclusion during their terms of office.

For the future of peace, precipitate withdrawal would thus be a disaster of immense magnitude.

- A nation cannot remain great if it betrays its allies and lets down its friends.

- Our defeat and humiliation in South Vietnam without question would promote recklessness in the councils of those great powers who have not yet abandoned their goals of world conquest.

- This would spark violence wherever our commitments help maintain the peace— in the Middle East, in Berlin, eventually even in the Western Hemisphere.

Ultimately, this would cost more lives.

It would not bring peace; it would bring more war.

For these reasons, I rejected the recommendation that I should end the war by immediately withdrawing all of our forces. I chose instead to change American policy on both the negotiating front and battlefront.

In order to end a war fought on many fronts, I initiated a pursuit for peace on many fronts.

In a television speech on May 14, in a speech before the United Nations, and on a number of other occasions I set forth our peace proposals in great detail.

- We have offered the complete withdrawal of all outside forces within 1 year.

- We have proposed a cease-fire under international supervision.

- We have offered free elections under international supervision with the Communists participating in the organization and conduct of the elections as an organized political force. And the Saigon Government has pledged to accept the result of the elections.

We have not put forth our proposals on a take-it-or-leave-it basis. We have indicated that we are willing to discuss the proposals that have been put forth by the other side. We have declared that anything is negotiable except the right of the people of South Vietnam to determine their own future. At the Paris peace conference, Ambassador Lodge has demonstrated our flexibility and good faith in 40 public meetings.

Hanoi has refused even to discuss our proposals. They demand our unconditional acceptance of their terms, which are that we withdraw all American forces immediately and unconditionally and that we overthrow the Government of South Vietnam as we leave.

We have not limited our peace initiatives to public forums and public statements. I recognized, in January, that a long and bitter war like this usually cannot be settled in a public forum. That is why in addition to the public statements and negotiations I have explored every possible private avenue that might lead to a settlement.

Tonight I am taking the unprecedented step of disclosing to you some of our other initiatives for peace—initiatives we undertook privately and secretly because we thought we thereby might open a door which publicly would be closed. I did not wait for my inauguration to begin my quest for peace.

- Soon after my election, through an individual who is directly in contact on a personal basis with the leaders of North Vietnam, I made two private offers for a rapid, comprehensive settlement. Hanoi's replies called in effect for our surrender before negotiations.

- Since the Soviet Union furnishes most of the military equipment for North Vietnam, Secretary of State Rogers, my Assistant for National Security Affairs, Dr. Kissinger, Ambassador Lodge, and I, personally, have met on a number of occasions with representatives of the Soviet Government to enlist their assistance in getting meaningful negotiations started. In addition, we have had extended discussions directed toward that same end with representatives of other governments which have diplomatic relations with North Vietnam. None of these initiatives have to date produced results.

- In mid-July, I became convinced that it was necessary to make a major move to break the deadlock in the Paris talks. I spoke directly in this office, where I am now sitting, with an individual who had known Ho Chi Minh [President, Democratic Republic of Vietnam] on a personal basis for 25 years. Through him I sent a letter to Ho Chi Minh.

I did this outside of the usual diplomatic channels with the hope that with the necessity of making statements for propaganda removed, there might be constructive progress toward bringing the war to an end. Let me read from that letter to you now.

> Dear Mr. President
>
> I realize that it is difficult to communicate meaningfully across the gulf of four years of war. But precisely because of this gulf, I wanted to take this opportunity to reaffirm in all solemnity my desire to work for a just peace. I deeply believe that the war in Vietnam has gone on too long and delay in bringing it to an end can benefit no one—least of all the people of Vietnam. . . .
>
> The time has come to move forward at the conference table toward an early resolution of this tragic war. You will find us forthcoming and open-minded in a common effort to bring the blessings of peace to the brave people of Vietnam. Let history record that at this critical juncture, both sides turned their face toward peace rather than toward conflict and war.

I received Ho Chi Minh's reply on August 30, 3 days before his death. It simply reiterated the public position North Vietnam had taken at Paris and flatly rejected my initiative. The full text of both letters is being released to the press.

- In addition to the public meetings that I have referred to, Ambassador Lodge has met with Vietnam's chief negotiator in Paris in 11 private sessions.
- We have taken other significant initiatives which must remain secret to keep open some channels of communication which may still prove to be productive.

But the effect of all the public, private, and secret negotiations which have been undertaken since the bombing halt a year ago and since this administration came into office on January 20, can be summed up in one sentence: No progress whatever has been made except agreement on the shape of the bargaining table.

Well now, who is at fault?

It has become clear that the obstacle in negotiating an end to the war is not the President of the United States. It is not the South Vietnamese Government.

The obstacle is the other side's absolute refusal to show the least willingness to join us in seeking a just peace. And it will not do so while it is convinced that all it has to do is to wait for our next concession, and our next concession after that one, until it gets everything it wants.

There can now be no longer any question that progress in negotiation depends only on Hanoi's deciding to negotiate, to negotiate seriously.

I realize that this report on our efforts on the diplomatic front is discouraging to the American people, but the American people are entitled to know the truth—the bad news as well as the good news—where the lives of our young men are involved.

Now let me turn, however, to a more encouraging report on another front.

At the time we launched our search for peace I recognized we might not succeed in bringing an end to the war through negotiation. I, therefore, put into effect another plan to bring peace—a plan which will bring the war to an end regardless of what happens on the negotiating front.

It is in line with a major shift in U.S. foreign policy which I described in my press conference at Guam on July 25. Let me briefly explain what has been described as the Nixon Doctrine—a policy which not only will help end the war in Vietnam, but which is an essential element of our program to prevent future Vietnams.

We Americans are a do-it-yourself people. We are an impatient people. Instead of teaching someone else to do a job, we like to do it ourselves. And this trait has been carried over into our foreign policy.

In Korea and again in Vietnam, the United States furnished most of the money, most of the arms, and most of the men to help the people of those countries defend their freedom against Communist aggression.

Before any American troops were committed to Vietnam, a leader of another Asian country expressed this opinion to me when I was traveling in Asia as a private citizen. He said: "When you are trying to assist another nation defend its freedom, U.S. policy should be to help them fight the war but not to fight the war for them."

Well, in accordance with this wise counsel, I laid down in Guam three principles as guidelines for future American policy toward Asia:

- First, the United States will keep all of its treaty commitments.
- Second, we shall provide a shield if a nuclear power threatens the freedom of a nation allied with us or of a nation whose survival we consider vital to our security.
- Third, in cases involving other types of aggression, we shall furnish military and economic assistance when requested in accordance with our treaty com-

mitments. But we shall look to the nation directly threatened to assume the primary responsibility of providing the manpower for its defense.

After I announced this policy, I found that the leaders of the Philippines, Thailand, Vietnam, South Korea, and other nations which might be threatened by Communist aggression, welcomed this new direction in American foreign policy.

The defense of freedom is everybody's business not just America's business.

And it is particularly the responsibility of the people whose freedom is threatened.

In the previous administration, we Americanized the war in Vietnam. In this administration, we are Vietnamizing the search for peace.

The policy of the previous administration not only resulted in our assuming the primary responsibility for fighting the war, but even more significantly did not adequately stress the goal of strengthening the South Vietnamese so that they could defend themselves when we left.

The Vietnamization plan was launched following Secretary Laird's visit to Vietnam in March. Under the plan, I ordered first a substantial increase in the training and equipment of South Vietnamese forces.

In July, on my visit to Vietnam, I changed General Abrams' orders so that they were consistent with the objectives of our new policies. Under the new orders, the primary mission of our troops is to enable the South Vietnamese forces to assume the full responsibility for the security of South Vietnam.

Our air operations have been reduced by over 20 percent.

And now we have begun to see the results of this long overdue change in American policy in Vietnam.

- After 5 years of Americans going into Vietnam, we are finally bringing American men home. By December 15, over 60,000 men will have been withdrawn from South Vietnam—including 20 percent of all of our combat forces.

- The South Vietnamese have continued to gain in strength. As a result they have been able to take over combat responsibilities from our American troops.

Two other significant developments have occurred since this administration took office.

- Enemy infiltration, infiltration which is essential if they are to launch a major attack, over the last 3 months is less than 20 percent of what it was over the same period last year.

- Most important—United States casualties have declined during the last 2 months to the lowest point in 3 years.

Let me now turn to our program for the future.

We have adopted a plan which we have worked out in cooperation with the South Vietnamese for the complete withdrawal of all U.S. combat ground forces, and their replacement by South Vietnamese forces on an orderly scheduled timetable. This withdrawal will be made from strength and not from weakness. As South Vietnamese forces become stronger, the rate of American withdrawal can become greater.

I have not and do not intend to announce the timetable for our program. And there are obvious reasons for this decision which I am sure you will understand. As I have indicated on several occasions, the rate of withdrawal will depend on developments on three fronts.

One of these is the progress which can be or might be made in the Paris talks. An announcement of a fixed timetable for our withdrawal would completely remove any incentive for the enemy to negotiate an agreement. They would simply wait until our forces had withdrawn and then move in.

The other two factors on which we will base our withdrawal decisions are the level of enemy activity and the progress of the training programs of the South Vietnamese forces. And I am glad to be able to report tonight progress on both of these fronts has been greater than we anticipated when we started the program in June for withdrawal. As a result, our timetable for withdrawal is more optimistic now than when we made our first estimates in June. Now, this clearly demonstrates why it is not wise to be frozen in on a fixed timetable.

We must retain the flexibility to base each withdrawal decision on the situation as it is at that time rather than on estimates that are no longer valid. Along with this optimistic estimate, I must—in all candor—leave one note of caution.

If the level of enemy activity significantly increases we might have to adjust our timetable accordingly.

However, I want the record to be completely clear on one point. At the time of the bombing halt just a year ago, there was some confusion as to whether there was an understanding on the part of the enemy that if we stopped the bombing of North Vietnam they would stop the shelling of cities in South Vietnam. I want to be sure that there is no misunderstanding on the part of the enemy with regard to our withdrawal program.

We have noted the reduced level of infiltration, the reduction of our casualties, and are basing our withdrawal decisions partially on those factors.

If the level of infiltration or our casualties increase while we are trying to scale down the fighting, it will be the result of a conscious decision by the enemy.

Hanoi could make no greater mistake than to assume that an increase in violence will be to its advantage. If I conclude that increased enemy action jeopardizes our remaining forces in Vietnam, I shall not hesitate to take strong and effective measures to deal with that situation.

This is not a threat. This is a statement of policy, which as Commander in Chief of our Armed Forces, I am making in meeting my responsibility for the protection of American fighting men wherever they may be.

My fellow Americans, I am sure you can recognize from what I have said that we really only have two choices open to us if we want to end this war.

- I can order an immediate, precipitate withdrawal of all Americans from Vietnam without regard to the effects of that action.

- Or we can persist in our search for a just peace through a negotiated settlement if possible, or through continued implementation of our plan for Vietnamization if necessary—a plan in which we will withdraw all of our forces from Vietnam on a schedule in accordance with our program, as the South Vietnamese become strong enough to defend their own freedom.

I have chosen this second course.

It is not the easy way.

It is the right way.

It is a plan which will end the war and serve the cause of peace—not just in Vietnam but in the Pacific and in the world.

In speaking of the consequences of a precipitate withdrawal, I mentioned that our allies would lose confidence in America.

Far more dangerous, we would lose confidence in ourselves. Oh, the immediate reaction would be a sense of relief that our men were coming home. But as we saw the consequences of what we had done, inevitable remorse and divisive recrimination would scar our spirit as a people.

We have faced other crises in our history and have become stronger by rejecting the easy way out and taking the right way in meeting our challenges. Our greatness as a nation has been our capacity to do what had to be done when we knew our course was right.

I recognize that some of my fellow citizens disagree with the plan for peace I have chosen. Honest and patriotic Americans have reached different conclusions as to how peace should be achieved.

In San Francisco a few weeks ago, I saw demonstrators carrying signs reading: "Lose in Vietnam, bring the boys home."

Well, one of the strengths of our free society is that any American has a right to reach that conclusion and to advocate that point of view. But as President of the United States, I would be untrue to my oath of office if I allowed the policy of this Nation to be dictated by the minority who hold that point of view and who try to impose it on the Nation by mounting demonstrations in the street.

For almost 200 years, the policy of this Nation has been made under our Constitution by those leaders in the Congress and the White House elected by all of the people. If a vocal minority, however fervent its cause, prevails over reason and the will of the majority, this Nation has no future as a free society.

And now I would like to address a word, if I may, to the young people of this Nation who are particularly concerned, and I understand why they are concerned, about this war.

I respect your idealism.

I share your concern for peace.

I want peace as much as you do.

There are powerful personal reasons I want to end this war. This week I will have to sign 83 letters to mothers, fathers, wives, and loved ones of men who have given their lives for America in Vietnam. It is very little satisfaction to me that this is only one-third as many letters as I signed the first week in office. There is nothing I want more than to see the day come when I do not have to write any of those letters.

- I want to end the war to save the lives of those brave young men in Vietnam.

- But I want to end it in a way which will increase the chance that their younger brothers and their sons will not have to fight in some future Vietnam someplace in the world.

- And I want to end the war for another reason. I want to end it so that the energy and dedication of you, our young people, now too often directed into bitter hatred against those responsible for the war, can be turned to the great challenges of peace, a better life for all Americans, a better life for all people on this earth.

I have chosen a plan for peace. I believe it will succeed.

If it does succeed, what the critics say now won't matter. If it does not succeed, anything I say then won't matter.

I know it may not be fashionable to speak of patriotism or national destiny these days. But I feel it is appropriate to do so on this occasion.

Two hundred years ago this Nation was weak and poor. But even then, America was the hope of millions in the world. Today we have become the strongest and richest nation in the world. And the wheel of destiny has turned so that any hope the world has for the survival of peace and freedom will be determined by whether the American people have the moral stamina and the courage to meet the challenge of free world leadership.

Let historians not record that when America was the most powerful nation in the world we passed on the other side of the road and allowed the last hopes for peace and freedom of millions of people to be suffocated by the forces of totalitarianism.

And so tonight—to you, the great silent majority of my fellow Americans—I ask for your support.

I pledged in my campaign for the Presidency to end the war in a way that we could win the peace. I have initiated a plan of action which will enable me to keep that pledge.

The more support I can have from the American people, the sooner that pledge can be redeemed, for the more divided we are at home, the less likely the enemy is to negotiate at Paris.

Let us be united for peace. Let us also be united against defeat. Because let us understand: North Vietnam cannot defeat or humiliate the United States. Only Americans can do that.

Fifty years ago, in this room and at this very desk, President Woodrow Wilson spoke words which caught the imagination of a war-weary world. He said: "This is the war to end war." His dream for peace after World War I was shattered on the hard realities of great power politics and Woodrow Wilson died a broken man. Tonight I do not tell you that the war in Vietnam is the war to end wars. But I do say this: I have initiated a plan which will end this war in a way that will bring us closer to that great goal to which Woodrow Wilson and every American President in our history has been dedicated—the goal of a just and lasting peace.

As President I hold the responsibility for choosing the best path to that goal and then leading the Nation along it.

I pledge to you tonight that I shall meet this responsibility with all of the strength and wisdom I can command in accordance with your hopes, mindful of your concerns, sustained by your prayers.

Thank you and goodnight.

The Power of Saddam Hussein's War Rhetoric

Gary W. Brown

In January, 1991, the United States and its allies, Great Britain, France, and Saudi Arabia, initiated a war with Iraq in response to Iraq's invasion of Kuwait in August of 1990. Although the United States and its allies won the war quickly, another less destructive—yet equally important—war was being fought while the air and ground campaigns occurred. This was a war of words that involved campaigns by the two sides to instill public support for the war and their respective causes. In sharp contrast to the clear victory that the United States and its allies obtained as a result of the air and ground campaign, the outcome of the war of the rhetoric that occurred during the conflict proved to be less decisive.

From a Western perspective, Saddam Hussein was a ruthless tyrant who would stop at nothing to conquer the world and to eliminate any opposition to him. His rhetoric during the war, usually disseminated through radio addresses, often was discredited by the Western listener. Yet, how was Hussein's rhetoric viewed from the perspective of his own people or of the people of Iraq's neighboring nations? That is the question I wish to address in this essay.

Using neo-Aristotelian criticism, I will examine how influential Saddam Hussein's war rhetoric was for those in his own country and neighboring countries using as my artifact five daily radio addresses Hussein presented during February, 1991. The tapes of the short-wave radio addresses used for my analysis were obtained by a classmate whose boyfriend was stationed in Saudi Arabia during the war. These tapes contained Hussein's speeches in Arabic, which I translated into English. I lived in Kuwait and had taken two years of intensive Arabic language classes as a requirement for graduating from the American School of Kuwait, the high school I attended. I will proceed, in my analysis, by examining the context in which the speeches were presented, analyzing the speeches by applying the five canons of rhetoric, and assessing the success of Hussein's rhetoric for its intended audience.

Context

I will examine three areas that will help provide the context for the artifact: Hussein as a rhetor, the occasions on which the rhetoric was presented, and the audience to whom the rhetoric was addressed.

Information about Hussein's background helps to explain the motives for and nature of his war rhetoric. First, Hussein is Muslim, and his rhetoric was directed at a Muslim audience, which means his rhetoric was not typical of rhetorics that embody Western ideologies. Rather, his speeches deal with philosophies and background experiences that are completely foreign to us. In most of his speeches, he devoted a great deal of time to praising Allah, for example. Thus, in order to criticize the war rhetoric of Hussein effectively, my examination of the artifact must take place, as far as is possible, through the eyes of a Muslim rather than those of a Westerner.

At the time he gave the speeches, Hussein was the political as well as the military leader of Iraq. This position had an impact on the way he addressed his people as well

This essay was written while Gary W. Brown was a student in Karen A. Foss's rhetorical criticism class at Humboldt State University in 1991. Used by permission of the author.

as on the flavor and tone of his rhetoric. Hussein was interested in maintaining his power and prestige, and his rhetoric reflected a desire for dominance and authority.

Although Hussein was the military leader of Iraq as well as its political leader, curiously, he never served in the military. Not until he became the leader of Iraq did he have any extensive training in military strategy and tactics. This factor may have affected audiences' assessment of his war rhetoric. Military leaders from both his and other countries may not have responded favorably to his war rhetoric simply because of his lack of a military background. This lack of military experience, however, may have been of less importance to the average listener with little or no military background. Thus, Hussein's rhetoric probably was targeted to the untrained military public rather than to the trained military.

In terms of the occasion for the radio addresses, an all-out confrontation between the United States and its allied forces and Iraq was underway. Baghdad, Iraqi military targets, and Iraqi troops constantly were being bombed by the allies. Because of this heavy air assault, I assume that morale in Iraq was low. In an attempt to increase morale and public support for Iraq, Hussein made irregularly timed addresses over short-wave radio to inform his people of war-worthy news such as allied "defeats." These radio addresses came at a time when the leader of Iraq was under severe criticism by both his own people and many other nations around the world.

The intended audiences for these radio broadcasts consisted primarily of the people of Iraq and the neighboring "friendly" nations that border Iraq. Evidence for these as his intended audience comes first from the fact that the addresses were spoken in the Arabic language. In addition, the common, ordinary words and phrases he used seemed to be directed at the average Arab citizen. Very little effort was made to discuss sophisticated and technical specifications about war strategies or the like. In fact, very little, if any, time was spent by Hussein in dealing with such topics. Rather, he chose to read scriptures from the Koran and to denounce the evil Western societies, strategies that seemed designed to motivate and strengthen general Arab public opinion in support of Hussein.

The Arabic audiences to which Hussein's speeches were addressed were, like Hussein, Muslim. They shared the same background philosophies and ideologies as Hussein, and they all possessed a certain amount of national and racial pride about their heritage. There also existed a high degree of tension and animosity toward Western societies, especially the United States, which probably heightened the Arab audiences' national pride.

Another hidden audience that could have been a target audience that Hussein was trying to reach was the Western societies themselves. Such descriptions as "the allies will drown in their own pools of blood" or "the holy mother war to end all wars and bring the downfall of Western societies" were presented with a possible intent to scare Western audiences and encourage the allied forces to move back due to a lack of Western public support.

Analysis of Hussein's Rhetoric

I now will examine Hussein's rhetoric itself by applying the five canons of rhetoric to the radio addresses. I will examine how Hussein used (1) invention; (2) organization; (3) style; (4) memory; and (5) delivery in order to create a rhetoric that was effective for his audience.

Invention

In terms of invention, the major sources on which Hussein depended for logical proof was the Koran, the holy book of Muslims; traditional Arab tribal laws; and

Arab unity against evil Western societies. In his speeches, every movement he made, such as the initial attack on Kuwait, was justified by the Koran and Allah. In Arab society and culture, if an individual is able to perform an action with little or no opposition, then, in God's eyes, that person is assumed to be correct and that individual's action is justified by Allah. Because Hussein's military was successful in conquering Kuwait in a matter of days with very little resistance, Arab logic dictated that Hussein must have been right in Allah's eyes.

Using this logic, Hussein was able to justify his action to the Arab people. In all five radio broadcasts I analyzed, Hussein justified his right to take over Kuwait. In his first public radio announcement shortly after the air raids began, for example, he stated, "God has given us the strength and power to rid Kuwait of its corrupt and sinful leaders." Thus, Hussein used the logic that Allah had given him the power to conquer Kuwait to set it straight; he removed the responsibility for the action from himself and attributed it to God. In this way, Hussein tried to establish his *ethos* among the people of his nation and those of other neighboring Arab countries.

In addition, Kuwait always has been considered part of Iraq by the Iraqis. This idea can be traced back to tribal conflicts, when the Bedouins migrated around the Middle East during the different seasons. Part of the land now found in Kuwait, as far as the Iraqis are concerned, belongs to members of tribes whose descendants currently inhabit Iraq. Thus, in their minds, Kuwait actually belongs to Iraq, a belief that aided Hussein in justifying his conquering of Kuwait.

Hussein's third major argument, which remained consistent throughout the radio addresses, was the appeal to other Arabic nations to help Iraq fight off the "evil" Western societies that interfered with Arab business. He developed this argument in two ways: (1) He sought to instill or reinforce a sense of racial prejudice; and (2) He sought to draw attention away from the Kuwait issue by trying to involve Israel in the conflict.

In several radio addresses before and during the air and ground campaign, Hussein called upon other "Arab brothers" to help Iraq "conquer and humiliate" the United States and its allies. Hussein developed this argument by employing *logos, ethos,* and *pathos.* He relied on the logic that Arab "brothers must stick together to fight off evil Bush and his minions." The logic assumed that all Arab brothers would converge together regardless of past conflicts that may have occurred: "You are all, in the eyes of Allah, Arab brothers. We all need to come together to rid ourselves of the evil menace that infects our lands."

Hussein also was trying to establish his *ethos* in the speeches. He accomplished this by indicating repeatedly that all the Arab people were "brothers" as well as Muslims who must fight together for a common cause. By referencing his identity as a Muslim as well as an Arab and showing that the majority of the inhabitants of the allied nations were neither, he provided a reason to support his war efforts. This argument also showed signs of *pathos* for similar reasons. Because Hussein and the residents of Iraq were both Muslim and Arab, he hoped to stir up emotions to sway other Muslims and Arabs to help Iraq fight.

Hussein also developed his appeal to fight evil Western societies by taking the focus off of the Kuwait conflict and placing it on the Palestinian issue. He tried to pull other Arab nations into the conflict by addressing an issue that was a political "hot potato" in the Arab culture's eyes. Perhaps Hussein realized the reservations that other nations possessed about entering into his "holy war." Bringing up Iraq's commitment to help the Palestinians regain the land from Israel that was "rightfully theirs" was a means Hussein used to encourage other Arab nations to fight on the side of Iraq in the war. As a consequence of this argument, Hussein could be seen as a leader who was attempting to settle the Palestinian dispute, thus contributing to his *ethos*. He could be perceived as a leader who was fighting for the good of all Arab people because he was addressing an issue close to the hearts of all Arabs.

Organization

An examination of the organization of Hussein's radio addresses reveals a consistent pattern. Each speech began with a quote or paraphrase from the Koran, the holy book of the Muslim faith. This was followed by praise for the strength and courage of the Iraqi citizens who were enduring constant air raids by allied forces. He also reassured his people that Iraq would prevail and would be victorious in the war. Hussein concluded the speeches by criticizing the Western allied nations. He used such descriptive terms as "evil corrupt society" or "evil President Bush" to help instill emotional hatred of the allies. Finally, he again appealed to other Arabs to join the fight that Iraq entered in order to help the Palestinian cause.

Style

The style of speech Hussein used during his addresses also played a critical role in their effectiveness. Hussein used the classical Arabic dialect rather than any other dialect of Arabic, a style that helped give him authority. Classical Arabic is used as both the diplomatic and religious languages of Iraq. Thus, simply using classical Arabic promotes an image of prestige and grace. To use an example of how effective this style of Arabic is, let me use an example of how this dialect might apply to Western languages. The President of the United States, when addressing the nation, would not use slang terms. Rather, he or she purposely would use a somewhat formal style because it would be appropriate for a leadership role. The same argument can be made for the use of classical Arabic. In the minds of Arabs, a leader who uses this dialect of the language is both eloquent and appropriate.

By using classical Arabic, Hussein also was assured that every Arab citizen was able to understand his speech. Many different dialects exist in the Arab language, and I know from my own experience in Kuwait that if I attempted to speak a different dialect of Arabic to an individual unfamiliar with it, that person would have no idea what I was saying. Because classical Arabic is the dialect taught in the schools of Arab nations, however, all Arabs would have been able to understand the words of Hussein regardless of their local dialects.

Because the classical Arabic style is used as the written language of the Koran, Hussein's use of this form also contributed to his credibility as a religious authority. Hussein had declared this war a holy war, and by using the holy language, Hussein reinforced this image. In essence, Hussein used the classical Arabic to establish himself as a religious leader protected by Allah.

Delivery

The delivery of Hussein's addresses also helped to promote a sense of authority and control for his listeners. Hussein's style of delivery was dynamic and energetic, particularly when he read from the Koran. His delivery style, in fact, helped to create the impression that he was passionate about the cause.

I believe that Hussein's speeches were prepared much earlier than the dates on which they were delivered. Most of the wording in the speech was carefully chosen so as not to insult any potential allies of Iraq. Also, the vividness of the descriptive language used to condemn the United States (such as "let them lie drowning in their own pools of blood for their persistence" or "Allah sheds the dust upon the evil machines [the war machines used by the allies] to protect the true followers of Muhammad") suggests that much preparation went into the speeches before they were delivered.

Memory

The last canon I will use to analyze the effectiveness of Hussein's radio addresses is memory. As I have suggested, I believe the speeches were prepared prior to their delivery. I also believe the speeches were written in manuscript form and read over the radio. On occasion, Hussein seemed to stumble on certain words, after which he quickly corrected himself. I suspect this was due to misreading his script.

Assessment of Effects

The creation of memorable speeches constituted only part of the purpose of Hussein's rhetoric. The other part is how effective the rhetoric was in meeting its objectives. In spite of the outcome of the military campaign, I argue that his rhetoric was successful. Although many Arab nations did not go to the aid of Iraq, Hussein was successful in obtaining some sympathy from Muslim nations as well as other nations around the world. The most memorable example of such a case occurred when the United States bombed a "public residence." When Hussein sharply accused the United States of intentionally killing innocent citizens, many Arab nations announced their agreement with his position and suggested their disgust with the United States' action. Hussein's attempts to address the Palestinian issue as well as Iraq's attempt to sign a peace treaty with Russia also contributed to the speeches' effectiveness. All these attempts by Iraq to address political problems and peaceful solutions to issues concerning the Arab community helped create a feeling of sympathy for Iraq.

Hussein's speeches did help to promote Arab pride. As reports from CNN and other network news stations illustrated, many Arabs felt that the Iraqi leader's attempt to address the Palestinian issue, as well as to fight the allies for the good "of the Arab people," was a valiant attempt on Hussein's part. They argued that the Palestinian issue had become public once again and had helped to establish a sense of Arab "brotherhood" and unity. If the military campaign had not been so one-sided in favor of the allies, I believe that stronger Arab unity eventually would have created problems for the allied forces.

Finally, Hussein was successful in reaching his intended audience, evidenced in the fact that many Arabs from nations other than Iraq were willing to join the Iraqi army and fight for Hussein. Once again, the concept of Arab "brotherhood" was a strong political theme that Hussein used to his advantage.

The allied nations may have won the military campaign, but I am less sure that they achieved such a decisive victory from a rhetorical standpoint. If the Iraqi forces had been more successful in fighting off the allies, I believe that, given time, Hussein would have proved to be a deadly rhetorical weapon by influencing other Arab nations to fight for his cause. In fact, Hussein was successful in achieving many of the goals he set out to accomplish through the use of his rhetoric. In addition, after the victory by the allied nations, Hussein remained in power. Potentially, Hussein could have suffered defeat and been forced to resign as the Iraqis' leader, but this did not occur. This may not have been the case had he not used rhetoric effectively to bring Arabs together in a spirit of unity and pride.

Withdrawal from Kuwait

Saddam Hussein
February 26, 1991

In the name of God, the merciful, the compassionate. O great people, O stalwart men in the forces of jihad and faith, glorious men of the Mother of Battles, O zealous, faithful, and sincere people in our glorious nations, and among all Muslims and all virtuous people in the world, O glorious Iraqi women, in such circumstances and times, it is difficult to talk about all that should be talked about, and it is difficult to recall all that has to be recalled. Despite this, we have to recall what has to be recalled, and say part—a principal part—of what should be said.

We start by saying that on this day, our valiant armed forces will complete their withdrawal from Kuwait. And on this day, our fight against aggression and the ranks of infidelity, joined in an ugly coalition comprising 30 countries, which officially entered war against us under the leadership of the United States of America—our fight against them would have lasted from the first month of this year, starting with the night of 16–17 January, until this moment in the current month, February. It was an epic duel which lasted for two months, which came to confirm clearly a lesson that God has wanted as a prelude of faith, impregnability, and capability for the faithful, and a prelude to an abyss, weakness, and humiliation which God almighty has wanted for the infidels, the criminals, the traitors, the corrupt and the deviators.

To be added to this is the military and nonmilitary duel, including the military and the economic blockade, which was imposed on Iraq and which lasted throughout 1990 until today, and until the time God almighty wishes it to last. Before that, the duel lasted in other forms for years before this time. It was an epic struggle between right and wrong; we have talked about this in detail on previous occasions.

It gave depth to the age of the showdown for the year 1990, and the already elapsed part of the year 1991. Hence, we do not forget because we will not forget this great struggling spirit, by which men of great faith stormed the fortifications and the weapons of deception and the Croesus' [Kuwaiti rulers] treachery on the honorable day of the call. They did what they did within the context of legitimate deterrence and great principled action.

All that we have gone through or decided within its circumstances, obeying God's will and choosing a position of faith and chivalry is a record of honor, the significance of which will not be missed by the people and nation and the values of Islam and humanity. Their days will continue to be glorious, and their past and future will continue to relate the story of a faithful, jealous, and patient people who believed in the will of God and in the values and stands accepted by the Almighty for the Arab nation in its leading role and for the Islamic nation in the essentials of its true faith and how they should be. These values—which had their effect in all those situations, offered the sacrifices they had offered in the struggle, and symbolized the depth of the faithful character in Iraq—will continue to leave their effects on souls. They will continue to reap their harvest, not only in terms of direct targets represented in the slogans of their age—whether in the conflict between the oppressed poor and the unjust and opportunist rich, or between faith and blasphemy, or between injustice, deception, and treachery on the one hand and fairness, justice, honesty, and loyalty on the other—but also the indirect targets as well. This will shake the opposite ranks and cause them to collapse after everything has become clear. This will also add faith to the faithful, now that the minds and eyes have been opened and the hearts are longing for what the principles, values, and stances should long for and belong to.

The stage that preceded the great day of the call on 2 August 1990 had its own standards, including dealing with what is familiar and inherited during the bad times, whether on the level of relations between the ruler and the ruled, or between the leader and the people he leads. The relations between the foreigners among the ranks of infidelity and oppression and among the region's states and the world had their own standards, effects, and privileges that were created by the Arab homeland's circumstances, and which were facilitated by propaganda, which no one could expose more than it has now been exposed. The conflict was exacerbated by the vacuum that was created by the weakness of one of the two poles that used to represent the two opposite lines in the world. After 2 August 1990, however, new concepts and standards were created. This was preceded by a new outlook in all walks of life, in relations among peoples, relations among states, the relations between the ruler and the ruled, and by standards of faith and positions; patriotism, pan-Arabism, and humanitarianism; jihad, faith, Islam, fear and non-fear; restlessness and tranquility; manhood and its opposite; struggle, jihad, and sacrifice; and readiness to do good things and their opposite.

When new measures spring forth and the familiar, failed, traitorous, subservient, corrupt [people] and tyrants are rejected, then the opportunity for the cultivation of the pure soil will increase in its scope, and the seeds of this plant will take root deep in the good land, primarily the land of the Arabs, and the land of revelation and the messages, and the land of prophets. God says: "Like a goodly tree, whose root is firmly fixed, and its branches reach to the heavens. It brings forth its fruit at all times, by the leave of its Lord" [Koranic verse].

Then, everything will become possible on the road of goodness and happiness that is not defiled by the feet of the invaders or by their evil will or the corruption of the corrupt among those who have been corrupted and who spread corruption in the land of the Arabs. Moreover, the forces of plotting and treachery will be defeated for good. Good people and those who are distinguished by their faith and by their faithful, honorable stands of jihad will become the real leaders of the gathering of the faithful everywhere on earth, and the gathering of the corruption, falsehood, hypocrisy, and infidelity will be defeated and meet the vilest fate. The earth will be inherited, at God's order, by His righteous slaves. "For the earth is God's to give as a heritage to such of His servants as He pleaseth; and the end is best for the righteous" [Koranic verse].

When this happens, the near objectives will not only be within reach, available and possible, but also the doors will be open without any hindrance which might prevent the achievement of all the greater, remoter, and more comprehensive objectives to the Arabs, Muslims, and humanity at large.

Then, also, it will be clear that the harvest does not precede the seeding and that the threshing floor and the yield are the outcome of a successful seeding and a successful harvest.

The harvest in the Mother of Battles has succeeded. After we have harvested what we have harvested, the greater harvest and its yield will be in the time to come, and it will be much greater than what we have at present, in spite of what we have at present in terms of the victory, dignity, and glory that was based on the sacrifices of a deep faith which is generous without any hesitation or fear. It is by virtue of this faith that God has bestowed dignity upon the Iraqi mujahidin and upon all the depth of this course of jihad at the level of the Arab homeland and at the level of all those men whom God has chosen to be given the honor of allegiance, guidance, and honorable position, until He declares that the conflict has stopped or amends its directions and course and the positions in a manner which would please the faithful and increase their dignity.

O valiant Iraqi men, O glorious Iraqi women, Kuwait is part of your country and was carved from it in the past. Circumstances today have willed that it remain in the state in which it will remain after the withdrawal of our struggling forces from it. It hurts you that this should happen.

We rejoiced on the day of the call when it was decided that Kuwait should be one of the main gates for deterring the plot and for defending all Iraq from the plotters. We say that we will remember Kuwait on the great day of the call, on the days that followed it, and in documents and events, some of which date back 70 years.

The Iraqis will remember and will not forget that on 8 August 1990 Kuwait became part of Iraq legally, constitutionally, and actually. They remember and will not forget that it remained throughout this period from 8 August 1990 until last night, when withdrawal began, and today we will complete withdrawal of our forces, God willing. Today, certain circumstances made the Iraqi Army withdraw as a result of the ramifications which we mentioned, including the combined aggression by 30 countries. Their repugnant siege had been led in evil and aggression by the machine and the criminal entity of America and its major allies.

These malicious ranks took the depth and effectiveness of their aggressiveness not only from the aggressive premeditated intentions against Iraq, the Arab nation, and Islam, but also from the position of those who were deceived by the claim of international legitimacy. Everyone will remember that the gates of Constantinople were not opened before the Muslims in the first struggling attempt, and that the international community consigned dear Palestine's freedom and independence to oblivion.

Whatever the suspect parties try, by virtue of the sacrifices and struggle of the Palestinians and Iraqis, Palestine has returned anew to knock at the doors closed on evil.

Palestine returned to knock on those doors to force the tyrants and the traitors to a solution that would place it at the forefront of the issues that have to be resolved—a solution that would bring dignity to its people and provide better chances for better progress.

The issues of poverty and richness, fairness and unfairness, faith and infidelity, treachery and honesty and sincerity have become titles corresponding to rare events and well-known people and trends that give priority to what is positive over what is negative, to what is sincere over what is treacherous and filthy, and to what is pure and honorable over what is corrupt, base, and lowly. The confidence of the nationalists and the faithful mujahidin and the Muslims has grown bigger than before, and hope grew more and more. Slogans have come out of their stores to occupy strongly the facades of the pan-Arab and human jihad and struggle. Therefore, victory is great, now and in the future, God willing.

Shout for victory, O brothers, shout for your victory and the victory of all honorable people, O Iraqis. You have fought 30 countries, and all the evil and the largest machine of war and destruction in the world that surrounds them. If only one of these countries threatens anyone, this threat will have a swift and direct effect on the dignity, freedom, or life of this or that country, people, and nation.

The soldiers of faith have triumphed over the soldiers of wrong. O stalwart men, your God is the one who granted your victory. You triumphed when you rejected, in the name of faith, the will of evil which the evildoers wanted to impose on you to kill the fire of faith in your hearts. You have chosen the path you have chosen, including acceptance of the Soviet initiative, but those evildoers persisted in their path and methods, thinking that they can impose their will on Iraq, as they imagined and hoped. This hope of theirs may remain in their heads, even after we withdraw from Kuwait. Therefore, we must be cautious, and preparedness to fight must remain at the highest level.

O you valiant men, you have fought the armies of 30 states and the capabilities of an even greater number of states which supplied them with the means of aggression and support. Faith, belief, hope, and determination continue to fill your chests, souls, and hearts. They have even become deeper, stronger, brighter, and more deeply rooted. God is great, God is great, may the lowly be defeated. Victory is sweet with the help of God.

Note: This speech by Saddam Hussein was given during the time of the speeches analyzed by Gary W. Brown, but it is not necessarily one of the speeches he analyzed.

Additional Samples of Neo-Aristotelian Criticism

Anderson, Jeanette. "Man of the Hour or Man of the Ages? The Honorable Stephen A. Douglas." *Quarterly Journal of Speech*, 25 (February 1939), 75–93.

Bauer, Marvin G. "Persuasive Methods in the Lincoln-Douglas Debates." *Quarterly Journal of Speech*, 13 (February 1927), 29–39.

Brigance, William Norwood, ed. *A History and Criticism of American Public Address*. Vol. I. New York: McGraw-Hill, 1943, numerous essays, pp. 213–500.

Brigance, William Norwood, ed. *A History and Criticism of American Public Address*. Vol. II. New York: McGraw-Hill, 1943, numerous essays, pp. 501–992.

Casmir, Fred L. "An Analysis of Hitler's January 30, 1941 Speech." *Western Speech*, 30 (Spring 1966), 96–106.

Dell, George W. "The Republican Nominee: Barry M. Goldwater." *Quarterly Journal of Speech*, 50 (December 1964), 399–404.

Hochmuth, Marie Kathryn, ed. *A History and Criticism of American Public Address*. Vol. III. New York: Longmans, 1955, numerous essays, pp. 24–530.

McCall, Roy C. "Harry Emerson Fosdick: Paragon and Paradox." *Quarterly Journal of Speech*, 39 (October 1953), 283–90.

Miller, Joseph W. "Winston Churchill, Spokesman for Democracy." *Quarterly Journal of Speech*, 28 (April 1942), 131–38.

Mohrmann, G. P., and Michael C. Leff. "Lincoln at Cooper Union: A Rationale for Neo-Classical Criticism." *Quarterly Journal of Speech*, 60 (December 1974), 459–67.

Peterson, Owen. "Keir Hardie: The Absolutely Independent M. P." *Quarterly Journal of Speech*, 55 (April 1969), 142–50.

Reid, Ronald F. "Edward Everett: Rhetorician of Nationalism, 1824–1855." *Quarterly Journal of Speech*, 42 (October 1956), 273–82.

Stelzner, Hermann G. "The British Orators, VII: John Morley's Speechmaking." *Quarterly Journal of Speech*, 45 (April 1959), 171–81.

Thomas, Gordon L. "Aaron Burr's Farewell Address." *Quarterly Journal of Speech*, 39 (October 1953), 273–82.

Thomas, Gordon L. "Benjamin F. Butler, Prosecutor." *Quarterly Journal of Speech*, 45 (October 1959), 288–98.

Wills, John W. "Benjamin's Ethical Strategy in the New Almaden Case." *Quarterly Journal of Speech*, 50 (October 1964), 259–65.

Wilson, John F. "Harding's Rhetoric of Normalcy, 1920–1923." *Quarterly Journal of Speech*, 48 (December 1962), 406–11.

PART 2

Critical Approaches

Cluster Criticism

The rhetorical theorist and critic who probably has had the greatest impact on rhetorical criticism as it is practiced today is Kenneth Burke, a "specialist in symbol-systems and symbolic action."[1] Burke's interdisciplinary work crosses the disciplines of philosophy, literature, linguistics, rhetoric, sociology, and economics. Burke spent his life exploring language and its nature, functions, and consequences in books such as *Permanence and Change, Counter-Statement, Attitudes Toward History, The Philosophy of Literary Form, A Grammar of Motives*, and *A Rhetoric of Motives*.[2]

Burke defines rhetoric as "the use of words by human agents to form attitudes or to induce actions in other human agents."[3] The inducement that characterizes rhetoric takes place, Burke suggests, through the process of identification. Individuals form selves or identities through various properties or substances, which include such things as physical objects, occupations, friends, activities, beliefs, and values. As they ally themselves with various properties or substances, they share substance with whatever or whomever they associate and simultaneously separate themselves from others with whom they choose not to identify. Burke uses the term *consubstantial* to describe this association. As two entities are united in substance through common ideas, attitudes, material possessions, or other properties, they are consubstantial.[4] Two artists are consubstantial, for example, in that they share an interest in art. Roommates are consubstantial in that they share living space and a lease agreement.

Burke uses the term *identification* synonymously with *consubstantiality*. Shared substance constitutes an identification between an individual and some property or person: "To identify A with B is to make A 'consubstantial' with B."[5] Burke also equates *persuasion* with *consubstantiality*, seeing persuasion as the result of identification: "You persuade a man only insofar as

63

you can talk his language by speech, gesture, tonality, order, image, attitude, idea, *identifying* your ways with his."[6]

Identification cannot be understood apart from division, which Burke sometimes calls *alienation* or *dissociation*. Human beings are inevitably isolated and divided from one another as a result of their separate physical bodies. The *"individual centrality of the nervous system"* requires that what "the body eats and drinks becomes its special private property; the body's pleasures and pains are exclusively its own pleasures and pains."[7] Although, in the process of identification, "A is 'substantially one' with a person other than himself . . . he remains unique, an individual locus of motives. Thus he is both joined and separate, at once a distinct substance and consubstantial with another."[8]

In division lies a basic motive for rhetoric: People communicate in an attempt to eliminate division. Burke asserts that if individuals were "not apart from one another, there would be no need for the rhetorician to proclaim their unity."[9] Only because of their separation or division do individuals communicate with one another and try to resolve their differences. Paradoxically, then, identification is rooted in division.[10]

One of the ways in which rhetors attempt to create identification is by naming or defining situations for audiences. A speech or a poem, for example, is "a *strategy for encompassing a situation.*"[11] A rhetor sizes up a situation and names its structure and outstanding ingredients. The Constitution of the United States, for example, names a situation concerned with political governance. Calling a person a *friend* or naming the admission standards to a school *rigorous* tells the qualities of the situation that the rhetor deems important.

Rhetoric does not simply provide a name for a situation, however. It also represents a creative strategy for dealing with that situation or for solving the problems inherent in it. Rhetoric offers commands or instructions of some kind, helping individuals maneuver through life and helping them feel more at home in the world. Because rhetoric is a rhetor's solution to perceived problems, it constitutes "equipment for living"[12]—a chart, formula, manual, or map that an audience may consult in trying to decide on various courses of action.

A rhetorical act or artifact provides assistance to its audience in a number of ways. It may provide a vocabulary of thoughts, actions, emotions, and attitudes for codifying and thus interpreting a situation. It may encourage the acceptance of a situation that cannot be changed, or it may serve as a guide for how to correct a situation. In other instances, it may help rhetors justify their conduct, turning actions that seem to be unethical or absurd into ones considered virtuous or accurate. Rhetoric, then, provides an orientation in some way to a situation and provides assistance in adjusting to it.[13]

At the same time that artifacts are functioning to provide equipment for living for audiences, they are revealing the worldview or what Burke calls the *terministic screen*s of the rhetors who created them. The terms we select to describe the world constitute a kind of screen that directs attention to particular aspects of reality rather than others. Our particular vocabularies constitute a reflection, selection, and deflection of reality.[14] Many of our observations, then, *"are but implications of the particular terminology in terms of which the observations are made. In brief, much that we take as observations* about 'reality' may be but the spinning out of possibilities implicit in our particular choice of terms."[15] There are as many different terministic screens as there are people. As Burke suggests, "We can safely take it for granted that no one's 'personal equations' are quite identical with anyone else's" because they are the product of the "peculiar combination of insights associated" with their idiosyncratic combinations of experiences.[16] From the infinite terms available to rhetors, they put together components of rhetoric in a way that reflects who they are, the subjects about which they are engrossed, and the meanings they have for those subjects.

Rhetorical critics can gain insights into rhetors by analyzing the terministic screens evidenced in their rhetoric. Critics can *"track down the kinds of observation implicit in the terminology"* a rhetor has chosen, whether the *"choice of terms was deliberate or spontaneous."*[17] Burke explains the basic approach: "If a writer speaks of life on a mountain, for instance, we start with the impertinent question, 'What is he talking about?' We automatically assume that he is not talking about life on a mountain (not talking *only* about that). Or if he gives us a long chapter on the sewers of Paris, we ask: 'Why that?'—and no matter how realistic his account of the locale may be, we must devote our time to a non-realistic interpretation of his chapter."[18] Cues to rhetors' worldviews and meaning are available by charting the important ingredients of their terministic screens and "noting what follows what."[19]

Burke offers many critical approaches to help a critic discover rhetors' worldviews through an investigation of the rhetoric that constitutes their terministic screens. His notions of identification,[20] representative anecdote,[21] perspective by incongruity,[22] motivational orders,[23] form,[24] and redemption[25] have been used as critical methods for this purpose. Two samples of Burkean methods are included in this book to illustrate the kinds of insights Burkean criticism produces. Cluster criticism is the focus of this chapter, and pentadic criticism is the subject of chapter 10.

In cluster criticism, the meanings that key symbols have for a rhetor are discovered by charting the symbols that cluster around those key symbols in an artifact. Burke explains the central idea of cluster analysis: "Now, the work of every writer [rhetor] contains a set of implicit equations. He uses 'associational clusters.' And you may, by examining his work, find 'what goes with what' in these clusters—what kinds of acts and images and personalities and situations go with his notions of heroism, villainy, consolation, despair, etc."[26] In other words, the task of a critic using this method is to note "what subjects cluster about other subjects (what images *b, c, d* the poet [rhetor] introduces whenever he talks with engrossment of subject *a*)."[27] Burke provides a simple example of how terms that cluster around key terms can illuminate the meanings the rhetor has for those key terms. Speaking about a man with a tic who spasmodically blinks his eyes when certain subjects are mentioned, Burke suggests that if "you kept a list of these subjects, noting what was said each time he spasmodically blinked his eyes, you would find what the tic was 'symbolic' of."[28]

The equations or clusters that a critic discovers in a rhetor's artifact generally are not conscious to the rhetor. As Burke explains, although a rhetor is "perfectly conscious of the act of writing, conscious of selecting a certain kind of imagery to reinforce a certain kind of mood, etc., he cannot possibly be conscious of the interrelationships among all these equations."[29] As a result, the clusters manifest in someone's rhetoric can "reveal, beneath an author's 'official front,' the level at which a lie is impossible. If a man's virtuous characters are dull, and his wicked characters are done vigorously, his art has voted for the wicked ones, regardless of his 'official front.' If a man talks dully of *glory*, but brilliantly employs the imagery of *desolation*, his *true subject* is desolation."[30] A cluster analysis, then, provides "a survey of the hills and valleys" of the rhetor's mind,[31] resulting in insights into the meanings of key terms and thus a worldview that may not be known to the rhetor.

Procedures

Using the cluster method of criticism, a critic analyzes an artifact in a four-step process: (1) selecting an artifact; (2) analyzing the artifact; (3) formulating a research question; and (4) writing the essay.

Selecting an Artifact

Both discursive and nondiscursive artifacts are appropriate for application of the cluster method of criticism. Because the method requires you to identify key terms and the terms that cluster around them, select an artifact that is long enough and complex enough to contain several terms that cluster around the key terms in the artifact. An advertisement with only a few lines of text or a short poem, for example, may not provide enough data for a cluster analysis.

Analyzing the Artifact

Cluster analysis involves three basic steps: (1) identifying key terms in the artifact; (2) charting the terms that cluster around the key terms; and (3) discovering an explanation for the artifact.

Identifying Key Terms

The first step in cluster criticism is to select the key terms in the artifact. Generally, try to select no more than five or six terms that appear to be the most significant for the rhetor. The task of analysis becomes more complex with each term you add.

Significance of terms is determined on the basis of frequency or intensity. A term that is used over and over again by a rhetor is likely to be a key term in that person's thought and rhetoric, so if one term frequently appears in the artifact, that term probably should be selected as one of the rhetor's key terms. In Martin Luther King, Jr.'s speech, "I Have a Dream," for example, *dream* is such a term. A second criterion to use in selecting the rhetor's key terms is intensity. A term may not appear very often in a rhetor's work, but it may be critical because it is central to the argument being made, represents an ultimate commitment, or conveys great depth of feeling. It is a term whose removal would change the nature of the text significantly. In many of George W. Bush's speeches dealing with the aftermath of the terrorist attacks of September 11, *evil* was a key term because it was used as the starting point for many of his arguments and was the focus of the conclusion of many of his speeches. Its intensity suggests that *evil* was a key term in those speeches.

Often, the terms that are key for rhetors function as god and devil terms. God terms are ultimate terms that represent the ideal for a rhetor, while devil terms represent the ultimate negative or evil for a rhetor.[32] In the speeches of many politicians, for example, *terrorism* and *security* are key terms, with *terrorism* a devil term and *security* a god term.

If the artifact you are analyzing is nondiscursive, such as a work of art, the key terms are not words but visual elements. Colors, shapes, or images can serve as key terms. The key terms of the Vietnam Veterans Memorial in Washington DC, for example, are its black color, its V shape, and its listing of the names of those who died in Vietnam by date of death.

Charting the Clusters

After you have identified the key terms in the artifact, chart the clusters around those key terms. This process involves a close examination of the artifact to identify each occurrence of each key term and identification of the terms that cluster around each key term. Terms may cluster around the key terms in various ways. They simply may appear in close proximity to the term, or a conjunction such as *and* may connect a term to a key term. A rhetor also may develop a cause-and-effect relationship between the key term and another term, suggesting that one depends on the other or that one is the cause of the other.

A paragraph from Supreme Court Justice Clarence Thomas's speech to the National Bar Association in 1998 illustrates the process of identifying the terms that cluster around a key term—in this case, the term of *criticism*:

> Of course there is much **criticism** of the court by this group or that, depending on the court's decisions in various highly publicized cases. Some of the **criticism** is profoundly uninformed and unhelpful. And all too often, uncivil second-guessing is not encumbered by the constraints of facts, logic or reasoned analysis. On the other hand, the constructive and often scholarly **criticism** is almost always helpful in thinking about or rethinking decisions. It is my view that constructive **criticism** goes with the turf, especially when the stakes are so high and the cases arouse passions and emotions, and, in a free society, the precious freedom of speech and the strength of ideas. We at the court could not possibly claim exemption from such **criticism**. Moreover, we are not infallible, just final.[33]

In this speech, *criticism* is a key term. Terms that cluster around the key term of criticism in this paragraph are: *court, group, decisions, uninformed, unhelpful, constructive, helpful, turf, scholarly, constructive, cases, (no) exemption,* and *not infallible.*

Discovering an Explanation for the Artifact

At this step of the process, a critic attempts to find patterns in the associations or linkages discovered in the charting of the clusters as a way of making visible the worldview constructed by the rhetor. If a rhetor often or always associates a particular word or image with a key term, that linkage suggests that the key term's meaning for the rhetor is modified or influenced by that associated term. If the terms *surveillance* and *violation of privacy*, for example, usually appear with *freedom* in a rhetor's speeches, you may speculate that the rhetor's view of freedom is constrained by these terms associated with security. Security is necessary to ensure freedom, this rhetor appears to believe, and, as a result, freedom is not a feeling of being unbound and unrestrained. Although you would want to chart all of the clustering terms around *criticism* before you looked for patterns in the clusters of Clarence Thomas's speech, the analysis of the one paragraph begins to suggest that, for Thomas, criticism is a group activity (it involves the court, scholars, and groups), and it is about standards of judgment, whether those standards are about who is subject to criticism or what types of criticism are appropriate.

At this point, an agon analysis may help you discover patterns in the clusters you have identified. Agon analysis is the examination of opposing terms and involves looking for terms that oppose or contradict other terms in the rhetoric. Note whether key terms emerge in opposition to other key terms. Such a pattern may suggest a conflict or tension in the rhetor's worldview or may make explicit the allies and enemies or the god and devil terms in the rhetor's world. In the contexts surrounding the key terms, look for opposing terms that cluster around a key term—perhaps suggesting some confusion or ambiguity on the part of the rhetor about that term. If *freedom* and *surveillance* are both terms that cluster around *patriotism*, for example, you might surmise that, for this rhetor, a conflict exists between freedom and restriction in the meaning of patriotism.

As a result of your charting of the terms that cluster around the key terms, you have a kind of dictionary for the rhetor's key terms. This dictionary suggests the meanings of the key terms for the rhetor and lays out any relationships that emerged among key terms or clustering terms. Your task now is to identify which of the clusters are most interesting and significant and have the most explanatory value for your artifact. You probably chose to analyze your artifact because there is some aspect of the artifact that doesn't fit or that you can't explain. Perhaps you like the artifact and cannot explain its appeal for you. Perhaps it disturbs you, but you don't know why. Perhaps it seems unusual in some way. The clusters you have identified around key terms can provide an explanation for your initial reactions.

Once again, use the principles of frequency and intensity to discover what is significant about the artifact and provides an explanation for it. If you discover that many similar terms cluster around all or most of the rhetor's key terms, frequency—a pattern you observe in which the same feature recurs—suggests an important insight into the rhetor's worldview. A major revelation also might emerge from just one of the key terms and its clusters—an insight based on intensity—and you might choose this as your focus in explaining the artifact.

Formulating a Research Question

Knowing the meanings of key terms for a rhetor can be the basis for understanding many different rhetorical processes, so the research questions asked by critics using the cluster method of criticism vary widely. The explanations you develop for your artifact from charting its clusters can suggest questions about, for example, the strategies that are used to accomplish particular objectives, the kinds of meaning that are being communicated, or the implications of particular constructions of meaning for rhetorical processes or public controversies.

Writing the Essay

After completing the analysis, you are ready to write your essay, which includes five major components: (1) an introduction, in which you discuss the research question, its contribution to rhetorical theory, and its significance; (2) a description of the artifact and its context; (3) a description of the method of criticism—in this case, cluster criticism; (4) a report of the findings of the analysis, in which you explain the key terms, the terms that cluster around them, and the meanings for the key terms suggested by the clustered terms; and (5) a discussion of the contribution the analysis makes to rhetorical theory.

Sample Essays

In the sample essays that follow, the cluster method of criticism is used to answer various research questions. Kathaleen Reid analyzes a nondiscursive text, a painting by Hieronymus Bosch, as a way to answer the question: "How do viewers establish the meanings of ambiguous messages?" In "A Cluster Analysis of Enron's Code of Ethics," Kimberly C. Elliott analyzes the ethics manual for the failed Enron corporation to answer the question: "How do organizations use new meanings to persuade their members to adhere to prescribed organizational values?" Erin E. Bassity analyzes P!NK's song "Dear Mr. President," asking the question, "What strategies can a rhetor use to generate or restore hope?"

Notes

[1] William H. Rueckert, *Kenneth Burke and the Drama of Human Relations*, 2nd ed. (Berkeley: University of California Press, 1982), p. 227.

[2] For an overview of Burke's rhetorical theory, see Sonja K. Foss, Karen A. Foss, and Robert Trapp, *Contemporary Perspectives on Rhetoric*, 3rd ed. (Long Grove, IL: Waveland, 2002), pp. 187–232.

[3] Kenneth Burke, *A Rhetoric of Motives* (1950; rpt. Berkeley: University of California Press, 1969), p. 41.

[4] Substance is discussed in: Burke, *A Rhetoric of Motives*, pp. 20–24; and Kenneth Burke, *A Grammar of Motives* (1945; rpt. Berkeley: University of California Press, 1969), pp. 21–23, 57.

[5] Burke, *A Rhetoric of Motives*, p. 21.

[6] Burke, *A Rhetoric of Motives*, p. 55.

[7] Burke, *A Rhetoric of Motives*, p. 130.

[8] Burke, *A Rhetoric of Motives*, p. 21.

[9] Burke, *A Rhetoric of Motives*, p. 22.

[10] For additional discussions of division, see Burke, *A Rhetoric of Motives*, p. 150; and Kenneth Burke, *The Philosophy of Literary Form: Studies in Symbolic Action* (1941; rpt. Berkeley: University of California Press, 1973), p. 306.

[11] Burke, *The Philosophy of Literary Form*, p. 109.

[12] Burke, *The Philosophy of Literary Form*, pp. 293–304.

[13] Burke discusses the ways in which rhetoric functions to provide assistance in orientation and adjustment in Kenneth Burke, *Counter-Statement* (1931; rpt. Berkeley: University of California Press, 1968), pp. 154–56; and Burke, *The Philosophy of Literary Form*, pp. 64, 294, 298–99.

[14] Kenneth Burke, *Language as Symbolic Action: Essays on Life, Literature, and Method* (Berkeley: University of California Press, 1966), p. 45.

[15] Burke, *Language as Symbolic Action*, p. 46.

[16] Burke, *Language as Symbolic Action*, p. 52.

[17] Burke, *Language as Symbolic Action*, p. 47.

[18] Kenneth Burke, *Attitudes Toward History* (1937; rpt. Berkeley: University of California Press, 1984), p. 191.

[19] Burke, *Attitudes Toward History*, p. 191.

[20] See, for example, Chester Gibson, "Eugene Talmadge's Use of Identification During the 1934 Gubernatorial Campaign in Georgia," *Southern Speech Journal*, 35 (Summer 1970), 342–49.

[21] Barry Brummett explores this notion as a critical tool in "Burke's Representative Anecdote as a Method in Media Criticism," *Critical Studies in Mass Communication*, 1 (June 1984), 161–76.

[22] An example is James L. Hoban, Jr., "Solzhenitsyn on Detente: A Study of Perspective by Incongruity," *Southern Speech Communication Journal*, 42 (Winter 1977), 163–77.

[23] See, for example, Karen A. Foss, "Singing the Rhythm Blues: An Argumentative Analysis of the Birth-Control Debate in the Catholic Church," *Western Journal of Speech Communication*, 47 (Winter 1983), 29–44.

[24] An example is Jane Blankenship and Barbara Sweeney, "The 'Energy' of Form," *Central States Speech Journal*, 31 (Fall 1980), 172–83.

[25] For an example, see Barry Brummett, "Burkean Scapegoating, Mortification, and Transcendence in Presidential Campaign Rhetoric," *Central States Speech Journal*, 32 (Winter 1981), 254–64.

[26] Burke, *The Philosophy of Literary Form*, p. 20.

[27] Burke, *Attitudes Toward History*, p. 232.

[28] Burke, *The Philosophy of Literary Form*, p. 20.

[29] Burke, *The Philosophy of Literary Form*, p. 20.

[30] Burke, *Attitudes Toward History*, p. 233.

[31] Burke, *Attitudes Toward History*, pp. 232–33.

[32] Burke, *A Grammar of Motives*, p. 74; Burke, *A Rhetoric of Motives*, pp. 298–301; and Richard M. Weaver, *The Ethics of Rhetoric* (South Bend, IN: Regnery/Gateway, 1953); pp. 211–32.

[33] Clarence Thomas, "I am a Man, a Black Man, an American," speech to the National Bar Association, Memphis, Tennessee, July 29, 1998. Available at http://douglass.speech.nwu.edu/thom_b30.htm.

The Hay-Wain
Cluster Analysis in Visual Communication
Kathaleen Reid

The popularity of the fifteenth-century painter Hieronymus Bosch has fluctuated dramatically over the last five centuries. This fluctuation is due, in part, to his surrealistic style; his paintings are executed in brilliant colors and with bold presentation, which was a major deviation from the style typical of the fifteenth century. Also contributing to his on-again, off-again popularity were his apparently mystical statements about humanity's plight here on earth. The paintings depict torment, suffering, and unearthly terrors.

Art historians have debated the meaning behind Bosch's visions, but few of their methods have unraveled successfully the cloud of mystery that still envelops his work. What is of concern in this paper is how a rhetorical methodology can be used to understand forms of visual communication such as the painting of Bosch. Also of concern are further issues that apply both to traditional visual media (such as painting) and to modern technological media (such as photography and video): the fixed versus fleeting nature of visual communication (e.g., photographs versus film) and the transition of meaning (including shifts of meaning that occur within a culture as a result of time) through visual images.

The Hay-Wain by Bosch is an example of medieval visual communication designed specifically for use by the public, functioning in ways similar to contemporary mass communication. Originally a triptych, a three-part altar piece, this painting depicts the medieval story of the creation, the fall, and the potential redemption or destruction of humankind. Placed in a cathedral where the populace would have congregated on a regular basis, the triptych would have been viewed simultaneously by all individuals attending worship services. The audience would have been composed of rich and poor, noble and simple, scholars and tradesmen, clergy and laymen. In this way, the painting would function as a form of public visual communication for a diverse audience; therefore, such a painting as this might be considered a predecessor of contemporary mass communication.[1]

The Hay-Wain and other such paintings designed specifically for public audiences provide contemporary public communication scholars with an opportunity to examine early forms of visual communication in which the author of the work presents a narrative through full control over the manipulation of the materials, the ideas, and the representations of objects found within the work. Thus, these early paintings like contemporary narrative film can present stories that may have highly subjective simultaneous representations of natural, supernatural, and ideological worlds.

This juxtaposition of the natural and supernatural may result in potentially more ambiguous, difficult messages in both film and traditional media. A rhetorical methodology such as Burke's cluster analysis may aid viewers in establishing the meanings of ambiguous messages. Applying the methodology to a piece of visual communication such as *The Hay-Wain* simplifies the task of attributing meaning, since the static nature of the painting eliminates the dimensions of movement and time that add complexities to study of film and video.

From *Journal of Communication Inquiry*, 14 (Summer 1990), 40–54. Used by permission of the Iowa Center for Communication Study and the author.

The Hay-Wain by Hieronymus Bosch, 1485–1490. (Image also included in color photo gallery.)

In this paper, the visual communication of Bosch's painting—*The Hay-Wain*—has been analyzed in order to: (1) test the applicability of a rhetorical methodology to visual communication and (2) demonstrate how such a methodology can help the audience derive meaning from a highly subjective visual communication such as *The Hay-Wain*, which is often assessed as being so idiosyncratic that its meaning must remain a mystery.

Background

Hieronymus Bosch Van Aeken was born around 1450 in southern Holland. His family originally may have been from Aachen, but Bosch was born in a quiet town in the central lowlands called 's Hertogenbosch, which was less than two days' journey from the Dutch artistic capitals of Haarlem and Delft. Bosch was a member of a highly puritanical, nonclerical organization called the Brotherhood of Our Lady, whose staunch religious *Weltanschauung* may have influenced Bosch's artistic visions. He married into a wealthy family, and he had no children. Little else is known of his personal life, except that he died in 1516.

Several attempts have been made to understand Bosch's work, efforts made particularly difficult because of the lack of information about Bosch. Charles de Tolnay (1965) has made the most complete catalog of Bosch's work, dividing it into three major periods (early, middle, and late). Bosch became more esoteric throughout his career, de Tolnay asserts, moving from traditional approaches to Biblical topics to a more introspective view of creation, redemption, and damnation.

Another of Bosch's chroniclers, Max Friedlander (1969), has sought to find explanations of the artist's unique style and themes in his personal characteristics. He attempts to link what was known about Bosch as a person with the subject matter and themes of his work and suggests that Bosch's idiosyncratic personality explains his divergence from the mainstream of art during the fifteenth century. Friedlander never explains fully, however, what impact Bosch's personality might have had on his individual works.

Still other theories exist to explain why Bosch painted as he did. Cuttler (1968) and Combe (1946) have suggested that belief in alchemy and superstition could have influenced the artistry of someone like Bosch. Bax (1979) suggests that popular folklore and contemporary prose seem an integral part of Bosch's work.

A Rhetorical Perspective

As the above scholarship indicates, Bosch's paintings have been interpreted most often from one of two perspectives: (1) as a product of his personality, or (2) as a product of his environment. Since neither of these deductive methods seems to explain satisfactorily his motive and uniqueness, another approach that may be more adequate is the analysis of a single work without allowing either his personality or history to overshadow its content. Thus, the critic could move from the painting to the man rather than moving from the man to the communication.

One potentially useful perspective for analyzing the meaning behind a form of visual communication, especially work as complex as that of Bosch, is derived from rhetoric. In the past, rhetoric was limited to the study of discursive communication, but, recently, a broader definition has expanded the arena for rhetorical criticism to include non-discursive communication. These non-discursive forms of communication function in a way that is similar to discourse in that they transmit information and evoke some response from the audience. Here the non-discursive form being examined is visual communication, defined as communication through visual forms such as painting, photography, videography, and film.

That such human activity is within the purview of rhetorical criticism was suggested by the Committee on the Advancement and Refinement of Rhetorical Criticism (Sharf, 1979), which reported that the rhetorical critic "studies his subject in terms of its suasory potential or persuasive effect. So identified, rhetorical criticism may be applied to any human act, process, product or artifact" (Sharf, 1979, p. 21). Karlyn Kohrs Campbell echoed this sentiment by asserting that "if criticism is to fulfill its function, the rhetorical critic must proclaim: Nothing that is human symbolization is alien to me" (1974, p. 14).

Foss and Radich suggest that art is a form of visual communication that is within the scope of rhetoric because it is a "conscious production to evoke a response" (1980, p. 47). Burke lends further credence to the view that a painting is a visual communicative act when he states:

> For when an art object engages our attention, by the sheer nature of the case we are involved in at least as much of a communicative relationship as prevails between a pitchman and a prospective customer. (1964, p. 106)

Thus, visual communication such as painting can be defined in a way that is similar to verbal communication based on its ability to engage our attention to evoke responses.

This basic parallel between visual and verbal rhetoric—that both convey information and evoke some response from an audience—can be found in the aesthetics studies of art history. Egbert notes that the artist "is intent on expressing something which he feels can best be said through the medium of his art . . ." (1944, p. 99). Gombrich stresses the importance of good articulation in the rhetorical process. When commenting on the works of artists like Constable, he says, "All human communication is through symbols, through the medium of a language [he includes the visual arts in his notion of language] and the more articulate that language the greater the chance for the message to get through" (1960, p. 385).

Just as others use words to describe things, "the artist uses his categories of shapes and color to capture something universally significant in the particular" (Arnheim, 1971, p. vi). Kleinbauer states that "an artist may deliberately or even unconsciously conceal or transfigure his intention, thoughts and experience in his work" (1971, p. 68). These and other theorists indicate that the artist uses his or her techniques as a medium of rhetoric for expressing ideas and experiences just as verbal rhetoric functions to express the experiences of the speaker.

Schools such as the Prague Structuralists reinforce the phenomenological position that both verbal and visual rhetoric function as social artifacts in the communication process. They study how the relationships between creator of the artifact and the interpreter function in forming our society. Their work, especially that of Lotman and Mukarovsky, presents both verbal and visual communication as part of the communication process that constitutes our entire social system (Lotman, 1976; Mukarovsky, 1977; Morawsky, 1974; Lucid, 1977; Bailey, Matejka, & Steiner, 1980).

Methodology for the Analysis of Bosch's Works

Perhaps one key to unraveling the mystery of Bosch lies in his use of symbolic counterpoint—the juxtaposition of various elements within a single setting.

> Simultaneously attracted by the joys of the flesh and seduced by the promises of asceticism, too much a believer to fall into heresy, but too clear-sighted not to see through the short-comings of the clergy and the evils of the world, dazzled by the beauty and wonders of nature and unwilling to recognize their divine or human value, contenting himself with the *docta ignorantia*, Bosch lays bare the contradictions of his age and makes them the subject of his artistic production. (De Tolnay, 1965, p. 49)

If the juxtaposition of elements is viewed as basic to the structure of his works, then a method to describe this structure may be of value in understanding Bosch.

Burke contends that a communicator consciously or unconsciously juxtaposes ideas within a communication act, showing how he or she sees the meaning of terms. This process of clustering of ideas gives evidence of the communicator's motive for the rhetorical act or work. Burke asserts that the motive and the form of a rhetorical act are inseparable.

In *A Grammar of Motives*, Burke states, "There must . . . be some respect in which the act is a *causa sui*, a motive of itself" (1945, p. 66) and that when one is searching for motives of the communicator, "the thinker will in effect locate the motive under the head of the Act itself" (1945, p. 69). So each act has within it some measure of motive directing the communicator. Duncan clarifies Burke's position: ". . . as we think about human motives, it becomes increasingly obvious that they depend on the forms of communication available to us . . ." (1954, p. xvii).

In order to reveal this motive, Burke develops, in *Attitudes Toward History*, a methodology for discovering what elements are associated with what other elements in the mind of the communicator (1937, p. 233). This methodology is called "cluster analysis," which he clarifies in later essays (Burke, 1954, 1957). Cluster analysis asks "what follows what?" and is concerned with the examination of elements that are linked together by the communicator.

The methodology consists of three steps. The first is the selection of key terms, or the important elements used in the rhetoric. The key terms are selected because of their high frequency and/or high intensity of use (Rueckert, 1963, p. 84). Frequency refers to how often the term is repeated, and intensity refers to how significant the term appears to be in the work. Wong (1972) discusses principles of design and notes that the main elements of design in a painting consist of color, line, form, value, texture, rhythm, balance, repetition, similarity, and other design elements. These are used as key terms in this analysis.

The second step is to identify what clusters around each key term each time it appears in painting. This is a description of what elements are adjacent to or in close radius to each key term.

The third step is interpretation of the clusters. In this step, each cluster is analyzed to reveal what potential messages are being presented by the communicator. The interpretations revealed then are examined as a whole to determine an overall interpretation of the painting and a possible explanation of the communicator's motive for creating the work.

While cluster analysis generally has been applied to written discourse, such as Berthold's (1976) analysis of Kennedy's Presidential speeches, it also should provide valuable insights into visual communication.

The Hay-Wain

One aspect of Burke's method of cluster analysis is that each communication act is in itself a microcosm of an individual's motives. Thus, to assess these motives, the critic can survey, in detail, a single communicative act to derive understanding of motive. Because Bosch's paintings universally contain contradictory elements I have narrowed the scope of this investigation to a single work—*The Hay-Wain*. Not only is it one of Bosch's most recognizable works, but many art historians have selected it as highly representative of his paintings in general. The work is a triptych—composed of three panels—and is attributed to the start of Bosch's middle period, painted sometime around 1485–1490.

The central panel of the painting shows a hay wagon overflowing with hay and drawn by a team of minotaur-like creatures. The wagon is surrounded by peasants clamoring to grab pieces of hay, while other peasants are crushed beneath the wheels. Common interpretation suggests that this scene was taken from a Flemish proverb that says that the world is a haystack from which each person plucks what he or she can. Behind the wagon is a procession headed by clerical figures who look down upon the melee from horseback with stoic aloofness. On top of the hay are lovers, flanked by an angel and a demon. This central, frantic scene is counterpointed by the depiction of everyday activities—such as a woman changing a baby's diaper, another cooking food, and a patient being tended by a medieval physician in the foreground. Above hovers a large cloud containing the Christ figure, with His hands raised in a blessing.

The left panel is a traditional visualization of the story of creation and follows Adam and Eve from their "birth" to their expulsion from the Garden. Executed mainly in tranquil blues and greens, this panel portrays a peaceful environment except for three elements: rebellious angels being cast from the heavens, the serpent tempting the couple inside the Garden, and the archangel with drawn sword guarding the entrance to the Garden.

In stark contrast to the left panel, the right panel is a scene of unearthly horrors, with demons attacking naked humans in front of a tower. The whole panel is crowned with violent reds and oranges, representing fire and smoke. Colors are flat and bold. The figures seem to bathe in the light, turning them shades of pink and orange, totally different from the jaundiced skin of those in the center panel and from the skin tones provided by the blues and greens of the left panel.

Key Elements

The figures in this painting appear small and somewhat weightless as they engage in numerous activities. Still dominant is Bosch's concern with color. The golden mass of hay on the wagon is the central focus and part of the first and most striking key term—gold color. In *The Hay-Wain*, the use of the bright golden color dominating the central panel is a significant design element. By its dominance—via size and intensity or brightness—it attracts the eye more rapidly than other important, yet less significant design elements. By its eminence and brightness, the gold color shows high intensity; therefore, it is considered a major key term.

While the golden color was the most dominant and intense design element, repetition and similarity were the major criteria for choosing the other key terms. These were the arch shape, ladders, clerics, couples, fish, and the boar. Similarity was a strong criterion for choosing the two arches as key elements. They are of the same elongated form and both serve the same function as portals or entry ways. The same is true of the ladders. Two ladders are parallel in structure, length, and usage.

The other key terms—clerics, couples, fish, and boars—were chosen because of frequency; they each occur in the painting three or more times. Clerics are presented in three places. Four couples—as prototypes of the original Adam and Eve—appear. The fish or variations of the fish appear three times and the same is true for the boar. Because the image of the boar is connected to that of the fish in two places, the boar and the fish are treated as one unit.

Clusters around Key Elements

Gold Color. The golden-yellow color that pervades the painting is one of its most striking elements. The two golden clouds that float in the blue sky contain the figure of God as judge and the figure of Christ. The God-judge figure is surrounded by the rebellious angels who are being cast from heaven. Their blue and light-red tones contrast with the bright yellow of the cloud in which they are placed. The golden cloud is matched by a similar one in the upper portion of the center panel. Within this cloud, Christ is isolated from others. His hands, with their bleeding wounds, are raised as if in blessing, and the light-red drapery surrounding His pierced body is similar in color to the clothing of the God-judge figure.

Most of the gold color is found in the central panel. Creating a large golden triangle, the large patch of color includes the majority of the center ground and has as its central focus the hay wagon. Within this golden triangle are many scenarios: people fighting, others scrambling to grab a piece of hay, a woman tending an injured man, peasants being crushed by the wagon, a boar's head and a fish roasting over a fire, and anthropomorphic creatures such as the boar-like demonic figure pulling the wagon toward hell. At the apex of the triangle is a soberly clad pilgrim. Standing with his staff, he carries a small child on his shoulders and is accompanied by an adolescent. The small trio seems separated from the crowd; yet, they are a part of life on earth as they stand adjacent to women involved in everyday activities.

Ladders. Bosch has incorporated two similar ladders in *The Hay-Wain*. These are parallel in design and structure, one resting against the wagon in the center panel and the other leaning against the tower in the right panel. The ladder of the center panel is held by a member of the crowd, apparently attempting to climb toward the couple on top. The ladder of the right panel holds a demon who is climbing it in order to work on building the tower. Members of the clergy and nobility are next to the center ladder. At the base of the ladder in the right panel, a group of demons in animalistic form leads a naked human toward the tower.

Arches. Two arches are significant elements. These two key terms are similar not only in size and shape but also similar in function and location within the painting. The similar function is that they are both entry ways, one in the left panel and one in the right. The left-panel arch is the entrance into the pastoral Garden of Eden, which is barred by the archangel who threatens the now-guilty Adam and Eve. The other arch symmetrically positioned in the right panel is filled with blackness. Before it cowers a figure reminiscent of Adam, who is being pushed toward the portal by a demon with a staff.

Couples. Bosch has included several couples in *The Hay-Wain*, all of whom have either a good or evil supernatural figure near them. Adam and Eve are shown in a number of vignettes: in one, depicting the creation, God as creator is standing with them; the fall of humankind is depicted in the vignette containing the couple and the serpent. The most prominent pair are being thrown out of the Garden by the archangel, and their flight leads the viewer directly into the center panel with all of its banality and travail. The second prominent couple sits on top of the hay wagon, flanked by an angel and a demon. This pair enjoys the music of a lute player, and they are oblivious to the turmoil just below their feet. They do not display the anguish of those who struggle to attain the heights of the wagon, but they are equally unaware that the wagon is being dragged toward damnation.

Fish and Boar. A fish appears on the spit by the fire in the center panel, waiting to serve as nourishment for the humans around it. The immediate environment suggests the humdrum of everyday life, with the fish being just one more artifact of human existence. In the same panel, however, the fish symbol begins to change. It becomes a demonic half-fish, half-human creature that is helping pull the wagon into hell. In the right panel, the fish symbol is perverted even more, so that now the fish feeds upon the human rather than the opposite. This scene also is surrounded by activities, but these are the activities of hell, such as an emaciated black-hooded demonic priest carrying a human on a spit, animals attacking men, and other grotesque torture of humans.

Because of the similarity of their treatment, the boar is placed in the same cluster as the fish. The boar's head, along with the fish, is being roasted over the open fire. It, too, will serve as part of a meal for the women around the fire. Boar-headed creatures also are found pulling the wagon toward hell. Unlike the fish, the boar is not as clearly found in the right panel—though some demonic faces are reminiscent of a boar.

Clerics. Church figures appear in opposite corners of the center panel. In the upper left, prelates mounted on horses observe the anguish of the peasants as they fight around the wagon. In the lower right corner, nuns carry hay to a priest who calmly sits oblivious to what is happening around him. These people are outside the flow of action but have potentially significant positions. In the right panel, directly across from the black-hooded priest located in the central panel, is a black-hooded demonic priest who carries a human thrust upon a spit-like staff. This demonic cleric is a mocking replica of the priest sitting amongst the nuns in the center panel.

Interpretation of Clusters

Examination of the clusters in *The Hay-Wain* reveals a common theme—that of transition. Whether the symbols in each cluster reveal a physical transition such as the moving hay wagon or a more esoteric transition such as the moral transition of Adam and Eve, this theme is suggested in each cluster.

Gold Color. While the golden-color cluster is the most dominant key term and gives an underlying commonality to the diverse elements contained within the cluster, it is also the most confusing. Contained within this large cluster are terms of both good and evil. Because it represents warmth, prosperity, and power in most cultures, it lends a positive atmosphere to the cluster. This positiveness is offset somewhat by such negative elements as greed and conflict as people struggle for handfuls of hay.

The God-judge figure in the gold cluster immediately and visually transmits the concept of transition as the rebellious angels are forced to leave the heavens. The second element, Christ with hands raised, does not indicate transition visually; yet, traditionally in the Christian religion, Christ represents the greatest of all transitions. He descends from heaven to earth and ascends back to heaven. He was God who became human and the One who moved from life to death, from immortal to mortal and from temporal to eternal. Via Him, humans also may attain these characteristics, thereby moving the individual past human limitations.

With the hay wagon in the gold-color cluster, Bosch presents the viewer with both a physical transition—the journey along the earthly trail—and an esoteric transition—the journey of greed that takes a person from life on earth to life in hell. The pilgrim shares this same duality, both a physical and an esoteric transition. Physically, the pilgrim is on a journey through the plane containing the mob surrounding the hay wagon. Also, by definition, a pilgrim refers to a wayfarer on a spiritual journey as he or she seeks to make the transition from a mundane plateau to a more holy place.

Ladders. The first prominent ladder in this painting speaks of an important transition, for the individual may follow the ladder in the central panel to the false plateau atop the hay wagon, or he or she may continue in an upward direction toward Christ. The parallel ladder in the right panel allows the person ascending to reach the top of the tower, while the viewer's eye again allows for a transition from the bottom of the ladder to the ladder's ultimate direction—into the depths of hell where the fire burns the brightest.

Arches. The two major arches function as portals, openings leading from one setting to another. The concept of transition is found in the left panel, as the arch is the doorway from earthly life to paradise. The interior side of the portal is smooth and straight, seemingly indicating an easy movement from paradise to outside, while movement in the opposite direction is much more difficult because of the archangel guarding the rough-hewn facade on the outer side of the portal. Although some light flows through the archway, the rocky exterior, irregular and rugged, seems to denote this as a portal from God's grace into the travails of humanity. In contrast, the corresponding archway in the right panel is smooth and sleek. This architecturally precise portal makes entrance into the black interior easy, while the demon holding a wooden beam seems to block anything trying to exit the interior of the tower. The darkness of the interior of a building that has no roof speaks of a transition into an unnatural, black void.

Couples. Major transitional aspects can be noted among the couples. In the left panel, Adam and Eve make both moral and immortal-mortal transitions as they succumb to the temptation presented by the serpent in the garden. The transition from one life to another is presented in the couple's removal from a perfect garden, which required no work, to a life of toil outside the gates of paradise. Both physical and spiritual journeys are presented in the couple on the wagon in the center panel. Physically, they are being transported, while spiritually they are continuing in a destructive, even if entertaining, direction. Thus, when the couples are followed through the narrative via the composition leading from one vignette to the next, we can note the idea of transition on both physical and metaphoric levels.

Fish and Boar. Both the fish and boar representations suggest a transition of power. Both are presented in a traditional fashion such as food being prepared for a household. The next appearance of a fish and boar is in anthropomorphic form, human legs with either a boar or fish head, and they are part of the power that pulls the loaded wagon toward hell. The right panel, while not clearly presenting the boar, does present the fish in its final form—a red-eyed monster that has human legs instead of fins. But more grotesque than its form is its action: it is swallowing a human being. This is the ultimate transition in power. Instead of the fish functioning as nourishment for the humans who control the animals, the fish now feasts upon the humans whom they now control.

Clerics. Even if it has not actually occurred yet, the prelates astride their horses seem to present the transition of the church from an organization that is deeply involved in the concerns of the people to an organization of clerics who merely observe, not prevent, the people moving in the direction of damnation. The group of nuns is located at the entrance of hell, and although they are not as compositionally active in carrying the eye from the center panel to the right as are the half-humans pulling the wagon, they are still part of the visual transition into hell. That they are part of the transition seems incongruous with their role as representatives of religion. Perhaps more fascinating is Bosch's placement of the black-hooded demon immediately adjacent to the black-hooded priest. Though located in separate panels, their physical proximity causes the viewer to recognize immediately the similarity between the two figures. This presents the illusion of a transition from an easy-going priest to a sadistic ogre.

In summary, the two major themes derived from this interpretation center around transition. The first theme deals with the transition of life from that which is good and innocent to that which eventually may be and most often is destructive. Only two of the transitions are positive: the Christ figure, who offers salvation through a transition from mortal to immortal life, and the pilgrim, who seeks to attain a higher spiritual being. Except for the pilgrim, no other human on earth seems exempt from a destructive transition, and even the success of the pilgrim is questioned since the path appears difficult to follow. The second theme is the transition of power from the humans to outside forces, whether they are supernatural animals that become masters of human beings or the Christ figure as master when the individual chooses the difficult route along with the pilgrim.

In numerous ways the transitions suggest the loss of the "autonomous" individual. In each vignette of couples, supernatural figures such as imps and angels can be found, and power over the individual shifts to those beings. The center panel demonstrates the loss of power as individuals strive to control each other as they fight one another for the hay. The major and final transition of power to others outside of the self is shown in the right panel. While the center panel shows that humans have delusions of power in their attempts to control each other and the animals (roasting the fish and boar, prelates riding on horses), the right panel illustrates the final, most tragic transition of power: the animals mutilate and torture the humans, who had controlled them in the center panel.

Bosch seems to be motivated in *The Hay-Wain* by an over-riding pessimism that indicates that all the world is doomed for destruction. He does provide a limited amount of optimism by placing the Christ figure and the pilgrim within the gold cluster suggesting warmth, prosperity, power, and security. That touch of optimism, however, seems largely overshadowed by the sweeping movement of the entire painting toward hell. Thus, Bosch seems motivated to shove people out of their complacent acceptance of life viewed only from a single perspective, although he seems to doubt his ability to produce change in the perspectives and direction of most individuals.

Also revealed in the analysis were four important presuppositions. These reinforce Bosch's motive for persuading individuals to consider the transitions of their lives. As the painting indicates, he is predominantly concerned with the spiritual and moral transitions, not the physical.

The Ambiguity of Human Existence. Ambiguity, uncertainty of a symbol's meaning, is one of the first presuppositions generally noted about the paintings of Bosch. In one place, a symbol has one meaning and in another place, its counterpart has an opposite meaning. This is demonstrated, for example, by his use of the arch shape, where one arch leads into a beautiful garden and the other into a tower of punishment for humans. Duality also is seen in the ladder symbol, where one ladder leads to Christ and salvation, and the other points toward blackness, fire, and eternal torture.

Such contradictions with their resulting ambiguity suggest that Bosch understood the reflexive nature of symbols. The reflexivity that he demonstrated using the arch, ladder, and fish illustrates his consciousness of the complexity of the many facets of life. As a result, Bosch perceived life as being ambiguous, with the artifacts of life drawing meaning from their surroundings; their meanings are not fixed. These artifacts can fall on the side of good or evil, and Bosch's placement of elements seems to state his recognition of right and wrong. He seems to believe that anything can be an instrument of salvation or perdition.

Demonstration of the Reality of the Supernatural. The supernatural elements are not treated as dreams or figments of the imaginations of the individuals within the painting; rather, they are treated the same way as the human, earthly figures. This can be seen with clusters surrounding the couples and, in particular, with the archangel guarding the entrance to the garden. The archangel with drawn sword is truly there, as he refuses to allow Adam and Eve to reenter the garden. The couples in the garden also are in a pastoral setting that is treated as natural and real. One couple is seated above the hay wagon happily singing with the angel and demon perched near their shoulders being as clearly and naturally depicted as the couple.

Further evidence of this treatment of the supernatural as the natural can be seen in the gold-color cluster. The Christ figure's physical portrayal is as accurate as the painting of the pilgrim at the apex of the golden triangle. Also within the golden cluster are the anthropomorphic figures that are pulling the wagon. In particular, the boar-headed creatures are as real as the boar's head roasting over the fire near the everyday activities of the women in the foreground. This portrayal of anthropomorphic creatures as being as real as the people in the crowd makes this painting gruesome. The strife and death shown in the golden triangle are mere forerunners of that which follows in the right panel, where humans suffer eternal torture.

Bosch shows the viewer a hideousness that is a tangible, real entity. His view of hell is as real in his mind and in this painting as is the common daily life portrayed in the center panel. This is indeed no dream, but rather a *wakeful reality* in which humans must overcome depravity just as surely as they must overcome the trials of earthly existence.

Choice in Life. Bosch made clear that one must select a path of salvation or destruction and that one must seek guidance in order to complete the journey successfully. He depicts the people with decisions to be made; decisions that have direct impact upon their current lives. They choose to fight or not fight for the hay, for example, and for their eternal destiny. These are illustrated by the clusters around the gold color. Only the pilgrim seems to have the strength to make the difficult choice. At the apex of the triangle, he must choose one of two paths. One of those paths is difficult; it goes against the cultural customs and norms such as grabbing pieces of the hay. The pilgrim must traverse through the crowd and climb higher than those around him. He must not stop on the false plateau atop the hay wagon, where the couple sits. Rather, he must continue toward the next golden cloud of color—toward Christ, who acts as intercessor for the pilgrim on the long, difficult journey.

Questioning the Role of the Church. In this painting, the clergy are not acting in their traditional role of "priests for confession"; instead, Church officials are following the wagon of destruction. The other members of the Church are now nuns, whose interaction with people outside the Church is limited to the one playing cat's cradle. This lack of interaction seems to indicate more concern with internal problems than with caring for those around them in dire need of help. Bosch does not want to exclude the Church from the life drama of salvation, but he has difficulty justifying the excesses of the clergy that infected the Church of the fifteenth century. He could not bring himself to give the clergy a key role, but neither could he bring himself to exclude them, depicting them as he viewed their lack of effectiveness in aiding humanity.

On the basis of these four indicators, the basic motive of *The Hay-Wain* is reinforced. It seems to be that Bosch had a high level of concern for his fellow human beings who cannot act alone and who must eventually face the reality of perdition if they continue in their current direction.

This motive is enhanced further by noting the relationships of the indicators to each other. The high levels of ambiguity in the painting generally confuse viewers and lead them to conclude that Bosch is either inconsistent or a mystic who follows his own rules of logic. However, if we take that ambiguity as simply an indicator of his recognition that things are not always as they first appear, and that there are two sides to a coin, then internal consistency demands that Bosch note both sides and that he question whether or not something is always as good as it first seems.

The second indicator, demonstration of the supernatural as real, takes this ambiguity into a level that incorporates the earthly and the supernatural. It explains why so many seemingly harmless things on earth can have a flip side that is detrimental for people. For example, a common wagon becomes an instrument of destruction for the people snatching at the hay. It suggests the potential of a greed that can destroy totally and the supernatural forces that affect the individual's decisions.

If Bosch held these presuppositions, as *The Hay-Wain* indicates, then he would be highly concerned about the plight of those around him. He deals with these presuppositions by illustrating the difficulty of choosing the right path. This is accomplished by placing the pilgrim at a distance from the Christ-figure, who can provide salvation. Yet he gives hope by placing Christ in a bright golden cloud that the pilgrim can keep in sight as he traverses the tumultuous path on earth.

Another way in which Bosch acts upon these presuppositions is to question the role of the Church. This questioning is natural since traditionally the Church's major responsibility is for the spiritual and physical lives of the people. Therefore, Bosch would seek to evaluate how well the Church's representatives were performing, since failure on their part could have severe consequences for individuals.

The basic motivation of concern for others, which I have derived, may seem too simple and too obvious. However, Bosch's complexity of design and his mixing of cues (i.e., a nun playing cat's cradle instead of binding the wounds of the injured) confuses the casual observer who then questions what his true stance and motive might have been. This cluster analysis, which began by examining clusters of elements around key symbols of the painting, shows that Bosch indeed did hold and express a consistent perspective regarding human life on earth.

Conclusion

The purposes of this paper were to: (1) discover whether highly subjective visual communication such as the work of Bosch can be deciphered; and (2) to test whether a rhetorical methodology such as Burke's cluster analysis can be applied to visual communication. Although, by its nature, cluster analysis permits the discovery and analysis of the structure of a form of visual communication first and foremost, it also suggests dimensions of the communicator's character. This methodology has revealed enough insights to affirm that Bosch was not so idiosyncratic that he cannot be understood.

The cluster analysis reveals repeated patterns of elements within the painting that had high levels of consistency. While the consistency found may be the result of the critic's biases, I propose that enough clarity exists to suggest that Bosch, though intricate and complex, is not as bewildering as many observers assume. The consistencies found through cluster analysis support the idea that this work is not simply a private language of a communicator who cannot be understood except by his contemporaries. For through an analysis such as this, the critic can examine the underlying framework of the paintings, "what goes with what," and determine what synonyms and metaphors Bosch has expressed in his communication.

The cluster analysis reveals one of the major conflicts in Bosch's work that accounts for much of the confusion surrounding his work regarding intended meaning. The conflict is defined as the point at which traditional cultural images such as the figure of Christ meet and clash with incongruities. Such conflict is found in the distant figure of Christ, seemingly isolated from others, in *The Hay-Wain*. Bosch takes the traditional and places it in a context that at first is confusing: Why is the figure of Christ so distant? Why is Christ not interacting with those in the groups around Him? Perhaps, Bosch is asking the viewer, as well as himself, to contemplate the role of traditional Christian spirituality in the midst of the fluctuating Western world of the fifteenth and early sixteenth centuries.

Whether this questioning reflects Bosch's own private skepticism and doubt or whether it is a rhetorical tool to push viewers to face issues regarding their psychological and physical destiny cannot be determined by this study. Whichever is the case, this painting by Bosch has continued through the years as a rhetorical device that challenges the observer to question his or her own understanding of the issues portrayed in the process of trying to understand Bosch.

The primary purpose of the paper, to test whether a rhetorical methodology can be applied to visual communication, however, raises a number of issues that should be considered. Cluster analysis is based on the assumption that the connotative meaning of a term can be known by examining the context of that element. Questions arise as to how those connotative meanings are derived and interpreted when cluster analysis is applied to visual communication.

One area of concern is with the data—the paintings by Bosch. The nature of this form of communication is fixed rather than fleeting. An important distinction between visual communication such as painting and photography and other types of communication is that the forms within painting and photography are "fixed."[2] The advantage is that there is no need to halt a process as when "freezing" a frame in film or when using recordings. While cluster analysis could be applied to fleeting communication (incorporating paralinguistics and other aspects of the spoken word) perhaps it is most easily applied to fixed data where the structure and context of elements can be more easily examined, collected, and interpreted.

Another issue is to what extent we should treat the visual communication as a language. If, in using cluster analysis, we do indeed treat visual images as language, we ignore differences between the images and full language systems. In other words, we need to examine to what extent Burke's methodological procedures are grounded in his understanding of language systems and are at least partially ruled by those presuppositions.

Like other forms of nonverbal communication that are not full language systems, some basic questions may need to be asked: (1) Is there a given rule structure governing how visual symbols should be put together, just as there is a full rule structure for use of verbal language? (2) Based on Burke's ideas of the distinction between verbal and nonverbal communication, can visual communication reference the negative (communicate absence of joy, absence of pain)? (3) Can the visual communications be self-reflective—talk about themselves as in verbal language, when Mary says that Joe says that Bill says that Janie says? (4) We know that visual communication is not time bound in the sense that it can depict events of yesterday and today as well as project scenes into the future. But does visual communication have full ability to indicate past, present, and future tense? Can it depict present perfect, past perfect, or future perfect tense? What about the subjunctive mood?[3] Perhaps these four areas are not crucial for the use of cluster analysis and interpretation; however, these are ways in which visual communication may differ from verbal communication that could present potential problems if we treat the two in the same manner.

Still another issue revealed in this application of cluster analysis to visual communication concerns methodology. A major drawback to examining a painting or photograph rather than discourse is that the critic is presented with a more limited number of symbols. A comparison to clarify my point would be to look at the difference between a short poem by e. e. cummings as compared to a lengthy address by President J. F. Kennedy. Social artifacts such as paintings, photographs, and poems that contain fewer elements may create problems in generating sufficient material to study when using the methodology of cluster analysis.

A final issue in this kind of application involves interpretation. A major problem here concerns the high level of reflexivity found in visual communication. While written and spoken language is reflexive, it expresses as much by what is between words as by the words themselves; there is even more reflexivity in visual communication, since elements such as those found in paintings are not always as specific as words for describing the communicator's intentions. This high level of reflexivity allows for more multiple realities than do words. The extent to which the visual communicator and viewer have similar interpretations is based on the extent of their shared knowledge and understanding of the elements (Merleau-Ponty, 1964, 1968).

Despite these issues that arise from the application of cluster analysis, the rhetorical perspective helps open the door for more research regarding visual communication. However, further research needs to be done in order to establish more clearly the boundaries of cluster analysis and how it might relate to contemporary media such as film and video that have a fleeting rather than fixed nature. I hope this application of cluster analysis can challenge and encourage others within the field of communication to apply this method to "fleeting" communication and to explore further the issues raised.

Notes

[1] The distinction that often is made between fine arts, mass mediated, and applied arts is subject to much debate. Dondis (1973), for instance, suggests that the dichotomy between fine and applied arts is false. He notes the varying historical perspectives, emphasizing that groups such as the Bauhaus made no distinctions. Painting, architecture, photography, all were assumed to have similar communicative functions. Dondis further emphasizes his point by noting that "the idea of a 'work of art' [fine art] is a modern one, reinforced by the concept of the museum as the ultimate repository of the beautiful. . . . This attitude removes art from the mainstream, gives it an aura of being special and petty, reserves it for an elite, and so negates the true fact of how it is struck through our lives and our world. If we accept this point of view, we abdicate a valuable part of our human potential. We not only become consumers with not very sharp criteria, but we deny the essential importance of visual communication both historically and in our own lives" (1973, p. 6). Contemporary critics who view Bosch's *Hay-Wain* in the art museum must remember that the current setting was not its original. It was not designed with the purpose of being simply a work of fine art; rather, its form and function was one of public communication.

[2] This characteristic is based on Ricoeur's (1971, p. 529) notion of fleeting versus fixed communication. He notes that spoken language is fleeting, and the written text is fixed. The major distinction between them is their temporal aspects. Fleeting communication is the "instance of discourse," while fixed communication exists and continues over time in the form originally intended by the communicator.

[3] For further elaboration of these concepts see Burgoon and Saine (1978, pp. 18–20). In addition to these four questions by Burgoon and Saine, other works that question similarities and differences among visual art and other forms of rhetoric include Barthes (1977, pp. 32–51) and Eco (1976, pp. 190–216).

References

Arnheim, R. (1971). *Art and Visual Perception*. Berkeley: University of California.

Bailey, R. W., Matejka, L., and Steiner, P. ([1978] 1980). *The Sign: Semiotics around the World*. Reprint. Ann Arbor, MI: Slavic Publications.

Barthes, R. (1977). *Image Music Text*. New York: Hill and Wang.

Bax, D. (1979). *Hieronymus Bosch: His Picture-Writing Deciphered*. Montclair, NJ: Abner Schram.

Berthold, C. A. (1976). "Kenneth Burke's Cluster-Agon Method: Its Development and an Application." *Central States Speech Journal*, 27, 302–09.

Burgoon, J. K. and Saine, T. (1978). *The Unspoken Dialogue*. Boston: Houghton Mifflin.

Burke, K. (1945). *A Grammar of Motives*. New York: Prentice-Hall.

Burke, K. (1954). "Fact, Inference, and Proof in the Analysis of Literary Symbolism," in Bryson, L. (ed.), *Symbols and Values: An Initial Study* (pp. 283–306). New York: Harper and Brothers.

Burke, K. (1957). *Philosophy of Literary Form*. Rev. ed. New York: Vintage.

Burke, K. ([1937] 1961). *Attitudes Toward History*. Reprint. Boston: Beacon Press.

Burke, K. (1964). On Form. *Hudson Review*, 17, 106.

Campbell, K. K. (1974). Criticism: Ephemeral and Enduring. *Speech Teacher*, 23, 14.

Combe, J. (1946). *Jheronimus Bosch*. Paris, France: Pierre Tisne.

Cuttler, C. D. (1968). *Northern Painting from Puccelle to Bruegel/Fourteenth, Fifteenth, and Sixteenth Centuries*. New York: Holt, Rinehart and Winston.

De Tolnay, C. (1965). *Hieronymus Bosch*. New York: Reynal.

Dondis, D. A. (1973). *A Primer of Visual Literacy*. Cambridge: Massachusetts Institute of Technology.

Duncan, H. D. (1954). Introduction to *Performance and Change*, by K. Burke. Indianapolis: Bobbs-Merrill.

Eco, U. (1976). *A Theory of Semiotics*. Bloomington: Indiana University Press.

Egbert, D. D. (1944). "Foreign Influences in American Art," in Bowers, D. F. (ed.), *Foreign Influences in American Life: Essays and Critical Bibliographies* (pp. 99–126). Princeton: Princeton University Press.

Foss, S. K. and Radich, A. J. (1980). The Aesthetic Response to Nonrepresentational Art: A Suggested Model. *Review of Research in Visual Arts Education*, 12(4), 40–49.

Friedlander, M. J. ([1937] 1969). *Early Netherlandish Painting*. Vol. 5, *Geertgen tot Sint Jans and Jerome Bosch*. Reprint, with translation by H. Norden. New York: Frederick Praeger.

Gombrich, E. H. (1960). *Art and Illusion: A Study in the Psychology of Pictorial Representation*. New York: Pantheon Books.

Guillaud, J. and M. (in collaboration with Isabel Matco Gomez) (1989). *Hieronymus Bosch: The Garden of Earthly Delights*. Ian Robson, Translator. New York: Clarkson N. Potter.

Kleinbauer, W. E. (1971). *Modern Perspectives in Western Art History*. New York: Holt, Rinehart and Winston.

Lotman, Y. (1976). *Analysis of the Poetic Text*. Ed. D. B. Johnson. Ann Arbor: Ardis.

Lucid, D. P., ed. (1977). *Soviet Semiotics*. Baltimore: Johns Hopkins University Press.

Merleau-Ponty, M. (1964). *Signs*. Evanston: Northwestern University Press.

Merleau-Ponty, M. (1968). *The Visible and the Invisible*. Ed. C. Lefort. Evanston: Northwestern University Press.

Morawsky, S. (1974). *Inquiries into the Fundamentals of Aesthetics*. Cambridge: Massachusetts Institute of Technology.

Mukarovsky, J. (1977). *The Word and Verbal Art*. Ed. J. Burbank and P. Steiner. New Haven: Yale University Press.

Reid-Nash, K. (1984). *Rhetorical Analysis of the Paintings of Hieronymus Bosch*. University of Denver.

Ricoeur, P. (1971). The Model of the Text: Meaningful Action Considered as a Text. *Social Research*, 38, 529–62.

Rueckert, W. H. (1963). *Kenneth Burke and the Drama of Human Relations*. Minneapolis: University of Minnesota Press.

Sharf, B. F. (1979). Rhetorical Analysis of Nonpublic Discourse. *Communication Quarterly*, 21(3), 21–30.

Wong, W. (1972). *Principles of Two-dimensional Design*. New York: Van Nostrand Reinold.

A Cluster Analysis of Enron's Code of Ethics

Kimberly C. Elliott

Enron is a name known worldwide for American corporate corruption, ethical fail-ure, executive misconduct, and financial collapse. Most anyone told of Enron's *Code of Ethics* responds with surprise that the company even had one. The published *Code,* once distributed to all Enron employees, became such a curiosity after the company's failure that the Smithsonian Institution acquired a copy of the document for display. Indeed, a common understanding of the meaning of *ethics* coupled with even a cursory understand-ing of how Enron operated suggests that ethics had little bearing upon Enron's operations.

In his book *The Words We Live By,* Brian Burrell explains, "A code [of ethics] must address questions involving moral choice—what people ought to do, as opposed to what they are required to do. Any set of rules that is made mandatory, therefore, can-not be about ethics." A code of ethics, then, "cannot properly be about ethics unless it restricts its scope to ideals, suggestions, goals, and general principles. What is ethical is clearly and easily distinguishable from what is merely required." [1]

If Enron's ethics are listed in their entirety within its *Code of Ethics,* then Burrell's description of ethics validates a common perception: Enron had virtually no ethics. Cluster analysis of the *Code* reveals Enron's consistent equation of legal requirements and ethics. Far from distinguishing between what is *merely required* and what is ethical, the company implies that they are one and the same. By doing so, the company assigns what Kenneth Burke calls a "new meaning" to the word *ethics.* With new meanings, Burke explains, we are asked to "alter our orientations." [2]

Enron's new meaning of *ethics* suggests some explanation for its now-legendary organizational ethical failure wherein many individual employees seemed to have lost or suspended any basic understanding of what is right or wrong. With this cluster analysis, I will seek some insight into how an organization might use *new meanings* to persuade its members to set aside their own values and judgments in favor of adhering to prescribed organizational values and rules.

Background

On December 2, 2001, Enron Corp. filed for Chapter 11 bankruptcy protection following a failed merger attempt, massive financial losses, a swift and precipitous fall in its market value, the launch of a Securities and Exchange Commission investigation into some of its activities, and amid emerging reports of staggering executive miscon-duct that included personal enrichment. Not only was Enron's bankruptcy filing the largest in U.S. history, but the failure of Enron launched a severe crisis of confidence in corporate America's ethics. Three months later, a company publication dated July 2000, entitled the *Enron Code of Ethics,* was a top-selling item in eBay's online auctions, commanding up to $225 per copy. One former employee offered a copy in perfect con-dition, stating that it had "never been read." Observers might have concluded that Enron's ethical void grew from employee indifference to the *Code of Ethics.* My analysis of the document suggests otherwise. Close adherence to the *Enron Code of Ethics* would not have yielded ethical employee behavior because the document is not about ethics.

This essay was written while Kimberly C. Elliott was a student in Sonja K. Foss's rhetorical criticism class at the University of Colorado Denver in 2003. Used by permission of the author.

At Enron, ethics were defined by and limited to laws. Cluster analysis of the company's *Code of Ethics* suggests that Enron's leadership either mistook legal compliance and protection of company assets for ethical conduct or simply applied the *Code of Ethics* title to its legal compliance manual after writing it. The result is either an unlikely title for the document's content or unlikely content for the document's title.

Previously published analyses of the document have assumed the *Code of Ethics* was about ethics. In other words, reliance was placed upon the title rather than its incongruous contents. Ethical theorists and business journalists have discussed various reasons that simply having a code of ethics does not ensure ethical behavior, neglecting to discuss what having a code of ethics that does not address ethics might cause. Evaluations consistently have concluded that the company's "ethical lapses" resulted from disregard for its own *Code of Ethics*. Few writers have made any reference at all to the contents of the document. Comments appear to have been guided instead by writers' own notions of what a code of ethics is rather than what Enron's *Code of Ethics* was. They ascribed their own meaning to *ethics* rather than Enron's *new meaning*.

Those writers who did reference the *Code's* contents tended to focus on five particular pages, which differ significantly from the document's other 59 pages. Page 2 presents a letter from Kenneth L. Lay, Chairman and Chief Executive Officer, to the document's intended audience, "officers and employees of Enron Corp." Page 3, entitled "How to Use this Booklet," explains that employees must sign a "Certificate of Compliance," assuring the company they will "comply with the policies stated herein." Pages 4, 5, and 6 comprise a multi-purpose section entitled "Principles of Human Rights." Writers have noted repeatedly the irony of Lay's stated interest in the company's reputation given that he was subsequently faulted for leading the company into extreme disrepute. Some writers have commented on the four "values" stated in the "Principles of Human Rights" section. I have not yet found an existing reference to the *Enron Code of Ethics* that acknowledges the final 59 pages of the document, which outline various laws and internal policies that regulate employee behavior and the consequences for failure to abide by them.

Method

Cluster analysis was developed by Kenneth Burke as a method for gaining insight into a rhetor's worldview. The critic selects the target artifact's key terms and observes those terms that cluster around them for the purpose of learning more about how the rhetor associates particular concepts. In this analysis, I have selected the key terms *ethics, laws, the Company,* and *employees* to analyze Enron's *Code of Ethics*.

Some question may arise regarding the identity of the rhetor in this artifact. The Enron *Code of Ethics* is unattributed, as is customary of such corporate documents. Any discussion of its authorship is therefore speculative. Although I have no company-provided information regarding its authorship, the *Code of Ethics* appears to have been written by more than one person. Its tone and language use vary dramatically among sections, significantly undermining the consistency of the document. For example, the "Principles of Human Rights" section repeatedly uses the term *we* to refer to employees, managers, and directors. The section concerned with insider trading labels employees *personnel, employees,* and *you,* forsaking the term *we*. The "Use of Communication and Services Equipment" section labels employees *users* of services and equipment.

If the *Code of Ethics* were written by more than one author, any attempt to gain insight into the author's worldview might be fruitless as any number of worldviews may be represented. Within this analysis, I will attribute any emerging worldview to the company rather than to the individual or individuals who wrote the document. Although such personification of a corporation may be problematic, I think one can treat a widely distributed document issued under a company's name and the signature of its CEO as a representation of the company's position.

Analysis

In the Enron *Code of Ethics*'s foreword, CEO Kenneth L. Lay does not even mention ethics or the title of the document. Instead, he describes the contents of "this booklet" as "certain policies" approved by the Board of Directors and intended to "keep [the company's] reputation high." The instructions for "How to Use this Booklet" describe it as "a set of written policies dealing with rules of conduct" rather than a code of ethics. The only section of the document that even aspires to anything resembling ethics is the three-page section subtitled "Principles of Human Rights." Even Enron's discussion of human rights outlines laws, crimes, and punishments. The section contains the company's *vision*, a term often used synonymously elsewhere with *mission statement* and *values*. "Principles of Human Rights" apparently was considered an appropriate heading under which to publish the company's *vision* and *values* because "Enron's Vision and Values are the platform upon which our human rights principles are built." This statement suggests that "Principles of Human Rights" is Enron's name for "conduct that will help us achieve our mission in accordance with our values." This is hardly a common application suggested by the term "Principles of Human Rights." It is more likely a *new meaning*.

The "Principles of Human Rights" section includes Enron's *vision*; four *values*; a rephrased version of the Golden Rule ("at Enron, we treat others as we expect to be treated ourselves"); a toothless "belief" in non-discrimination that offers no expansion of federal non-discrimination laws; an assertion of dedication to obey "all applicable laws and regulations including, but not limited to, the U.S. Foreign Corrupt Practices Act"; a commitment to safety through compliance with various laws; a belief in "playing an active role in every community in which we operate"; a belief in "fair compensation" for employees; and an assertion that all of the aforementioned comprise "principles." Those "principles" are then distilled into "policies and procedures," which are equated with "written guidelines" that mandate "compliance with the law" under threat of "disciplinary action, which may include termination." By the conclusion of the "Principles of Human Rights" section on page 6 of the document, the company has issued its first threat of severance to employees and dramatically challenged any preconceived notion readers may have of "Human Rights."

The four stated *values* are the only items in the document that may be construed to be ethics. They are *respect, integrity, communication*, and *excellence*. *Respect* is a second reiteration of the Golden Rule. *Integrity* is described as honest behavior pertaining specifically to "customers and prospects." The *communication* value states that "we have an obligation to communicate." The value of *excellence* at Enron means "the very best in everything we do." Individuals familiar with a wider range of values will note the frugality of Enron's collection. Some also might find *new meanings* in Enron's version of those definitions. Readers may observe that the remainder of the stated "Principles of Human Rights" does not necessarily have any obvious connection to the four *values*, despite the company's assertion that the values are the *platform* upon which the *principles* are built. Six pages into this document, one senses that its authors built upon a hill of sand rather than a platform of any sort. The remaining 90% of the text, however, shores up the structure by attaching it to rigid laws, rules, regulations, and policies.

Key Term: *Ethics*

Lay's foreword describes employee responsibility to conduct "the affairs of the companies in accordance with all applicable laws and in a moral and honest manner." This is the sole appearance of the word *moral* in the document. Because many rhetors use the words *moral* and *ethical* interchangeably, this cluster analysis notes that the terms *applicable laws* and *honest* cluster around the sole appearance of the word *moral* in this document. One may gain some insight into Lay's notion of ethics from both his usage of the word *moral* and his reference to the company's *Code of Ethics* as "certain policies" and "this booklet" rather than by its title.

Accordingly, the *Enron Code of Ethics* makes little mention of ethics. The word *ethics* and its adjective form *ethical* appear only seven times in the 64-page document. This contrasts with the word *laws (or law),* which appears more than 100 times. Nevertheless, this document was presented by virtue of its title as a *Code of Ethics* rather than a *Legal Compliance Manual,* so the document's treatment of the word *ethics* is central to this analysis.

The words *ethics* and *ethical* are surrounded by legal and compliance matters in all but one instance. One mention of *ethical* concerns the company's reputation rather than any legal compulsion for ethical conduct. The terms clustering around *ethics* and *ethical* include *laws and regulations, policies, guidelines, standards, violations, disciplinary action, legal obligations,* and *legal uses.* The *Code* references ethics in conjunction with such terms as *the law and ethical standards, principles and business ethics,* and *ethical and legal uses.*

Primary assertions often pertain to laws, with mentions of ethics serving as afterthoughts. The *Code* states, for example, "we are dedicated to conducting business according to all applicable local and international laws and regulations, including, but not limited to, the U.S. Foreign Corrupt Practices Act, and with the highest professional and ethical standards." The terms clustered around *ethics* strongly suggest that the company equates legal compliance with ethical conduct. This view of ethics finds value in what employees must do under the law and threat of punishment rather than what they ought to do because it is the right thing to do.

Key Term: *Laws*

The document names 11 federal laws and several types of unnamed laws and the punishments the company and its employees may face for noncompliance. The terms *moral, honest, ethical,* and *values* cluster around the words *law* and *laws* to suggest strongly the equation of laws with ethics. Other terms, including *compliance, in accordance, commitment, faithfully,* and *obey* signal unconditional acceptance of the authority of law. For example, the *Code* asserts, "laws, regulations, and standards are designed to safeguard the environment, human health, wildlife, and natural resources. Our commitment to observe them faithfully is an integral part of our business and of our values." In one succinct statement, the *Code* claims, "laws and regulations affecting the Company will be obeyed." Lay's foreword tells officers and employees, "we are responsible for conducting the business affairs of the companies in accordance with all applicable laws and in a moral and honest manner."

Other terms clustered around the key term *law* recognize the consequences of failure to comply with laws, including *violations, abuses, consequences,* and *penalties.* The words *company* and *employee* also cluster around the words *law* and *laws,* indicating both who must obey the laws and who suffers from disobedience. At Enron, "compliance with the law and ethical standards are conditions of employment, and violations will result in disciplinary action, which may include termination."

Key Term: *The Company*

The words clustering around the term *the Company,* which is always thus capitalized, and *Enron Corp.* often demonstrate esteem for *the Company* through words like *honest, proud, respected, important, integrity, excellence,* and *quality.* Far more prevalent, however, are terms indicating a desire to protect the company from harm imposed by employees and their potential failures to comply with various laws and internal policies. Such words clustered around *the Company* include *trade secrets, proprietary information, interests, confidentiality, unique assets, valuable, property,* and *reputation,* all things the company seeks to protect.

An example of such clustering is "employees will maintain the confidentiality of the Company's sensitive or proprietary information." Another part of Enron's *Code of Ethics* explains that all products of employees' work are "the sole and exclusive property of the Company." Further, "the Company's confidential and proprietary information could be very helpful to suppliers and the Company's competitors, to the detriment of the Company." One might surmise that protecting company information is the highest priority by noting that 22 of the 64 pages of the *Code of Ethics* mandate specific employee behaviors surrounding company information. The plan for implementing that protection shows up in other terms clustering around *the Company,* including *policies, rules of conduct, applicable laws, standards, laws, regulations, regulatory requirements,* and *rights.*

Key Term: *Employees*

The *Code of Ethics* lists and describes dozens of ways that employees can harm both themselves and the company. This document, which proclaims such extensive company vulnerability to employee misdeeds, is heavily populated with terms clustered around references to employees that describe employee misbehavior in terms of criminal conduct. Employees are referenced as *you, we, personnel, employees,* and *users* within the *Code of Ethics.* The terms of criminal conduct that cluster around those labels include *violate, illegal behavior, not authorized, infringe, unauthorized disclosure, misappropriation, counterfeit, failure to comply, abusing, criminal offense, criminal conduct, wrongdoers, harassment,* and *intimidation.* Clusters indicate that the company approves of employee efforts to *avoid actions, abide by the letter and spirit of laws, maintain confidentiality, refrain, honor obligations, laws, rules, regulations, standards, compliance,* and *duty.*

The word *employee* is also often surrounded by terms describing consequences for failure to behave as prescribed. These terms include *sanction, corrective action, losing privileges, disciplinary action, suspend, dismiss, termination, prosecuted to the full extent of the law, criminal penalties, civil penalty, criminal fine, jail term, prosecution, will not tolerate,* and *liable.* In one mention, for example, "any breach of this policy may subject employees to criminal penalties." One statement in the code proclaims in an enlarged, all-caps font, "FAILURE TO ABIDE BY THESE RESTRICTIONS MAY SUBJECT EMPLOYEES TO CIVIL AND/OR CRIMINAL PROSECUTION."

The last sentence of the document is a final, exponentially redundant threat issued to employees: "An employee who violates any of these policies is subject to disciplinary action including but not limited to suspension or termination of employment, and such other action, including legal action, as the Company believes to be appropriate under the circumstances." Cluster analysis reveals that the company considers employees to pose grave danger to both themselves and the company. Further, the company's attempt to mitigate that perceived danger is revealed as the invocation of threats to employees' continued employment, personal freedom, and financial security. In short, the company attempts to scare employees into the legal compliance that it equates with ethical conduct.

Conclusion

Kenneth Burke explains that, "if we change our ways of acting to bring them more into accord with the new meanings (rejecting old means and selecting new means as a better solution for the problem as now rephrased), we shall bring ourselves and our group nearer to the good life."[3] If Enron were to preface its *Code of Ethics* by paraphrasing Burke to suit its application, it might have said, "if you change your ways to behave according to *The Company's Code of Ethics*, both you and *The Company* will achieve more success." The original problem of ethics is to answer the question, "What is the right thing to do?" The rephrased problem at Enron was, "What will the law permit us to do?"

Cluster analysis reveals a *new meaning* assigned to the word *ethics* at Enron. By publishing a 64-page *Code of Ethics* that contains only a trace of codified ethics, Enron effectively announced that it had no ethics to anyone rejecting the *new meaning* offered within the document. Rejection of the *new meaning* was unlikely, however, among the *Code of Ethics's* intended audience members—the company's employees—because their success in the organization required them to subjugate their own values and judgment to *The Company's* ethics. The prescribed behavior masqueraded as the right thing to do by wearing the title *Code of Ethics*. The document therefore carried a moral imperative for employees in addition to requiring compliance in order to avoid being fired, fined, or imprisoned.

Enron frames individual employees as inherently dangerous, unruly, and unimportant entities capable of becoming and being safe, ethical, and validated through compliant membership in the inherently good, valuable, and ethical organization. Presenting this formula for success as an Enron employee under the title *Code of Ethics* suggests that success comes through ethical behavior at Enron. Acceptance of the *new meaning* of *ethics* is framed as the key to employee redemption within the organization.

With its *Code of Ethics*, Enron demonstrates a bold attempt to assign a *new meaning* to *ethics*. This analysis revealed a variety of methods used to gain acceptance of the *new meaning*: (1) the lures of success and continued membership in the organization; (2) a moral imperative and the implied threat of being judged unethical; and (3) the overt threats of sanction, severance from the organization, criminal penalties, and civil penalties. Cluster analysis of the document offers some insight into how one organization used *new meanings* to persuade its members to accept a prescribed definition of *ethics* over their own preexisting definitions.

Notes

[1] Brian Burrell, *The Words We Live By: The Creeds, Mottoes, and Pledges That Have Shaped America* (New York: Free, 1997), p. 98.

[2] Kenneth Burke, *Permanence and Change: An Anatomy of Purpose*, 3rd ed. (Berkeley: University of California Press, 1984), p. 81.

[3] Burke, p. 81.

Rhetorical Strategies for Generating Hope:
A Cluster Analysis of P!NK's "Dear Mr. President"
Erin E. Bassity

There are many times when rhetors want to generate a sense of hope in an audience. One such situation occurs when a desired objective has not been achieved, as when a group fails to win a contract or a competition. At other times, a rhetor may want to generate hope to motivate a group to continue engaging in some activity, even when attainment of the objective for doing the activity seems nowhere in sight—continuing efforts to rebuild New Orleans following Hurricane Katrina, for example. Rhetors also might seek to instill hope in audience members when they are in the midst of negative conditions and see no way out. Because hope—and, conversely, a lack of hope—can have major consequences for how people work together, their level of motivation to perform, and their tenacity, understanding how it may be generated or restored is important to understand. In this essay, I explore rhetorical strategies that rhetors can use to generate or restore hope in an audience.

The artifact I will analyze to explore the generation of hope is P!NK's song, "Dear Mr. President," sung with the Indigo Girls. This song appears on the album *I'm Not Dead*, released in 2006, and it became a top-five hit in several countries, including Germany and Australia. P!NK is Alicia Beth Moore, an American singer-songwriter who released her first record, *Can't Take Me Home*, in 2000. It went double platinum in the U.S., sold four million copies worldwide, and produced two U.S. top-ten singles— "There You Go" and "Most Girls." P!NK has won Grammy awards for best pop collaboration with vocals and has acted in films such as *Ski to the Max* and *Catacombs*. She was prompted to write "Dear Mr. President" to deal with the negative feelings she had toward the Bush administration and the Iraq War. In the song, P!NK asks Bush to talk with her and raises questions about how he deals with unsolved issues such as homelessness, education, gay and lesbian rights, and war. Although her song appears to be addressed to President George W. Bush, I suggest it is directed at the larger audience of those who listen to the album and the song. One of the primary functions the song performs, I will argue, is to generate hope in this larger audience.

I will analyze "Dear Mr. President" using cluster analysis, a method of criticism developed by Kenneth Burke. It is designed to discover the clusters or equations in an artifact that may not be conscious to the rhetor. The method involves identifying the key terms in an artifact through frequency of appearance or intensity, charting the terms that cluster around those key terms, and using the clustering terms to discover the rhetor's worldview and an explanation for it.

Analysis of "Dear Mr. President"

Three key terms characterize "Dear Mr. President": *Mr. President, father,* and *hard work*. The first term is a constellation of terms that all point to the person of the president of the United States, so it includes *Mr. President* and *you*. I treated both of these as the same key term and sought to discover the terms that clustered around the two terms as one.

This essay was written while Erin E. Bassity was a student in Sonja K. Foss's rhetorical criticism class at the University of Colorado Denver in 2006. Used by permission of the author.

Mr. President. The terms that cluster around the key term of *Mr. President* are *pretend, questions, honestly, feel, see, pray, sleep, mirror, dream, walk, head, eye, why, lonely boy, left behind, cells,* and *hell.* These terms group into two categories—an altered, abnormal state and a state of awareness. The clustering terms that create a sense of an altered state are: *pretend, dream, sleep, hell, pray, lonely boy, left behind,* and *cells. Pretend* is a fantasy state in which actions are not real, *dream* and *sleep* represent an altered state in which an individual is in a different reality from a waking reality, *hell* is believed by some to be a state in which some people reside after death, and *pray* suggests a strategy that is different from the strategies many individuals use for achieving goals. The term *lonely boy* suggests an altered state in two ways: *Boy* suggests a state of innocence and unawareness that is different from the normal adult state, while *lonely* suggests an abnormal, childhood state, a period of time expected to be characterized by fun and friends rather than isolation. *Left behind* suggests a condition that is not where most others are—again, an atypical, abnormal state, while the *cells* of prisons also suggest a physical location in which most people do not reside.

The clustering terms around *Mr. President* that group into the category of awareness are: *look, eye, feel, walk, head, why, questions, honestly,* and *why.* Most of these terms—*look, eye, feel, walk,* and *head*—deal with the senses and the ways in which individuals gather information. The remaining clustering terms—*questions, honestly,* and *why*—suggest a stance of seeking information that is accurate, honest, and critical.

The key term of *father* generates a meaning of dysfunctional family through the terms that cluster around it. Clustering around the term of *father* are: *daughter's rights, taking away, hate, gay, first lady, whiskey,* and *cocaine.* In this cluster, deviation from the norm is evident, suggesting a dysfunctional family. The terms of *daughter's rights, taking away, gay,* and *hate* suggest issues that gay and lesbian children often face within families if they are gay and their parents are not supportive of that identity. Instead of the compassion, love, and support families are expected to demonstrate toward one another, these families hate their children and take away their rights. *Whisky* and *cocaine* add to the dysfunction of the family—a problem with alcoholism and drugs for a family member. The father is seen as the head of a dysfunctional family, and although he could do much to remedy the ills of the family, the fact that he is part of the problem makes it difficult for him to do so.

The third key term in the song is *hard work.* The terms that cluster around this key term are: *minimum wage, baby, rebuilding, house, bombs, bed,* and *cardboard box.* The terms *house, bed, baby,* and *minimum wage* suggest integral concepts to working families or concepts over which working families often struggle. These create a meaning for *hard work* of a commitment to do what is necessary to provide a home for the family. The terms *rebuilding, cardboard box,* and *bombs* suggest that catastrophe or trauma has occurred, resulting in homelessness. These terms suggest that such events can interrupt hard work and the effects it is designed to produce.

The picture that emerges from the clustering terms around the three key terms of *Mr. President, father,* and *hard work* is one of terrible things that have happened. Efforts to make a good life are disrupted by events such as bombs that produce terrible consequences such as living in cardboard boxes. The person who could do something about such things—the literal head of the family or the metaphoric head of the nation—is dysfunctional and unable to act in the ways that he should to address these problems. The audience is left disappointed and discouraged at such a state of affairs.

There is an acknowledgment on P!NK's part, then, of the awful conditions that need to be changed in the terms that cluster around *hard work*—conditions and situations that result in all sorts of negative things for many people. The terms that cluster around *Mr. President* concerning the seeking of information also reinforce the notion that things are not as they should be and need to be changed. Without acknowledgment of current negative conditions, P!NK's audience might think she was being idealistic or denying reality, and her audience would be less inclined to follow her rhetorically.

P!NK's effort to generate hope is the result of the majority of the terms she clusters around the key term of *Mr. President*. She attributes his lack of productive action to the fact that he has been in an altered state, where his awareness is low or nonexistent. While this may appear to be a condition that might cause disappointment in an audience, I suggest that it can be a source of hope because this is not a static condition; rather, it is a condition from which someone can emerge, awaken, and move into a new state.

The terms that cluster around *father* are negative—just like those that cluster around *hard work*. But they, too, are things that can be changed, often in relatively simple ways—by changing one's mind, as in the case of hate, for example. The clustering terms are so negative that most people would not want to live in a family under the conditions the terms reference. The intensity of the negative conditions suggest, then, that those conditions themselves might prompt change. There is another reason for hope suggested by the clustering terms around *father*. *Whisky* and *cocaine* represent problems the audience knows the president had at one time in his life but that are no longer problems for him—his former addictions are now under control. They provide evidence that, in fact, he can change. The two key terms related to the president are ones that suggest he is not immovable or immutable—he can change so that he can address problematic conditions.

A cluster analysis of P!NK's "Dear Mr. President" suggests a number of rhetorical strategies that are available for rhetors who want to generate or restore hope in an audience. One part of the strategy is to include in the rhetorical appeal recognition of what has gone wrong so that the audience believes the rhetor accurately understands the current situation. This strategy shows that the rhetor has appropriate knowledge to be engaging in a rhetoric of hope and also has empathy for the current situation of the audience.

A focus on current conditions, however, must be combined with a discussion of some vehicle or means by which a transformation can take place. One of the easiest ways to do this is to suggest that someone who has the capacity to contribute in major ways to creating the desired changes is not stuck in a place of nonresponsiveness or dysfunction but has the capacity to change. Even more effective is to show that this individual has changed in the past in difficult situations and was successful at maintaining those changes. Hope can be generated, then, through the use of rhetorical strategies that combine recognition of a current negative situation with depiction of an obstacle to change as having the capacity to and showing evidence of change.

Dear Mr. President

P!NK

Dear Mr. President,
Come take a walk with me.
Let's pretend we're just two people and
You're not better than me.
I'd like to ask you some questions if we can speak honestly.

What do you feel when you see all the homeless on the street?
Who do you pray for at night before you go to sleep?
What do you feel when you look in the mirror?
Are you proud?

How do you sleep while the rest of us cry?
How do you dream when a mother has no chance to say goodbye?
How do you walk with your head held high?
Can you even look me in the eye
And tell me why?

Dear Mr. President,
Were you a lonely boy?
Are you a lonely boy?
Are you a lonely boy?
How can you say
No child is left behind?
We're not dumb and we're not blind.
They're all sitting in your cells
While you pave the road to hell.

What kind of father would take his own daughter's rights away?
And what kind of father might hate his own daughter if she were gay?
I can only imagine what the first lady has to say
You've come a long way from whiskey and cocaine.

How do you sleep while the rest of us cry?
How do you dream when a mother has no chance to say goodbye?
How do you walk with your head held high?
Can you even look me in the eye?

Let me tell you 'bout hard work
Minimum wage with a baby on the way
Let me tell you 'bout hard work
Rebuilding your house after the bombs took them away
Let me tell you 'bout hard work
Building a bed out of a cardboard box
Let me tell you 'bout hard work
Hard work
Hard work

You don't know nothing 'bout hard work
Hard work
Hard work
Oh

How do you sleep at night?
How do you walk with your head held high?
Dear Mr. President,
You'd never take a walk with me.
Would you?

Lyrics downloaded February 8, 2008 from
http://www.azlyrics.com/lyrics/pink/dearmrpresident.html

Additional Samples of Cluster Criticism

Berthold, Carol A. "Kenneth Burke's Cluster-Agon Method: Its Development and an Application." *Central States Speech Journal*, 27 (Winter 1976), 302–09.

Cooks, Leda, and David Descutner. "Different Paths from Powerlessness to Empowerment: A Dramatistic Analysis of Two Eating Disorder Therapies." *Western Journal of Communication*, 57 (Fall 1993), 494–514.

Corcoran, Farrel. "The Bear in the Back Yard: Myth, Ideology, and Victimage Ritual in Soviet Funerals." *Communication Monographs*, 50 (December 1983), 305–20.

Courtright, Jeffrey L. "'I Am a Scientologist': The Image Management of Identity." In *Public Relations Inquiry as Rhetorical Criticism: Case Studies of Corporate Discourse and Social Influence*. Ed. William N. Elwood. Westport, CT: Praeger, 1995, pp. 69–84.

Crowell, Laura. "Three Sheers for Kenneth Burke." *Quarterly Journal of Speech*, 63 (April 1977), 152–67.

Foss, Sonja K. "Women Priests in the Episcopal Church: A Cluster Analysis of Establishment Rhetoric." *Religious Communication Today*, 7 (September 1984), 1–11.

Heinz, Bettina, and Ronald Lee. "Getting Down to the Meat: The Symbolic Construction of Meat Consumption." *Communication Studies*, 49 (Spring 1998), 87–99.

Lee, Sang-Chul, and Karlyn Kohrs Campbell. "Korean President Roh Tae-Woo's 1988 Inaugural Address: Campaigning for Investiture." *Quarterly Journal of Speech*, 80 (February 1994), 37–52.

Marston, Peter J., and Bambi Rockwell. "Charlotte Perkins Gilman's `The Yellow Wallpaper': Rhetorical Subversion in Feminist Literature." *Women's Studies in Communication*, 14 (Fall 1991), 58–72.

Mechling, Elizabeth Walker, and Jay Mechling. "Sweet Talk: The Moral Rhetoric Against Sugar." *Central States Speech Journal*, 34 (Spring 1983), 19–32.

Pullum, Stephen J. "Common Sense Religion for America: The Rhetoric of the Jewish Televangelist Jan Bresky." *Journal of Communication and Religion*, 15 (March 1992), 43–54.

Fantasy-Theme Criticism

The fantasy-theme method of rhetorical criticism, created by Ernest G. Bormann, is designed to provide insights into the shared worldview of groups.[1] Impetus for the method came from the work of Robert Bales and his associates in their study of communication in small groups. Bales discovered the process of group fantasizing or dramatizing as a type of communication that occurs in groups.[2] He characterized fantasizing communication in this way: "The tempo of the conversation would pick up. People would grow excited, interrupt one another, blush, laugh, forget their self-consciousness. The tone of the meeting, often quiet and tense immediately prior to the dramatizing, would become lively, animated, and boisterous, the chaining process, involving both verbal and nonverbal communication, indicating participation in the drama."[3]

Bormann extended the notion of fantasizing discovered by Bales into a theory (symbolic convergence theory) and a method (fantasy-theme criticism) that can be applied not only to the study of small groups but also to all kinds of rhetoric in which themes function dramatically to connect audiences with messages. In contexts larger than small groups, fantasizing or dramatizing occurs when individuals find some aspect of a "message that catches and focuses their attention until they imaginatively participate in images and actions stimulated by the message."[4]

Symbolic convergence theory is based on two major assumptions. One is that communication creates reality. As chapter 1 describes, reality is not fixed but changes as our symbols for talking about it change. A second assumption on which symbolic convergence theory is based is that symbols not only create reality for individuals but that individuals' meanings for symbols can converge to create a shared reality or community consciousness. Convergence, in the theory, refers "to the way two or more private symbolic worlds incline toward each other, come more closely together, or even overlap during certain processes of communication."

Convergence also means consensus or general agreement on subjective meanings, as Bormann explains: "If several or many people develop portions of their private symbolic worlds that overlap as a result of symbolic convergence, they share a common consciousness and have the basis for communicating with one another to create community, to discuss their common experiences, and to achieve mutual understanding."[5] Meanings are not all that are shared in symbolic convergence. Participants "have jointly experienced the same emotions; they have developed the same attitudes and emotional responses to the personae of the drama; and they have interpreted some aspect of their experience in the same way."[6]

Evidence of symbolic convergence can be discerned through frequent mention of a theme, a narrative, or an analogy in a variety of messages in different contexts. The war on drugs discussed by many politicians exemplifies such a theme. Widespread appeal of an advertising theme also may indicate a convergence. The "Got milk?" advertising campaign by the National Dairy Council, for example, caught the imagination of the American public and has chained out in various ways. In the Denver International Airport, for example, travelers leaving the security area encounter a sign, "Got laptop?" A Kinko's copy shop has a sign on its recycling bin that asks "Got trees?" A catalog advertises a doormat featuring an image of a cat and the words "Got mouse?," and a book of cookie recipes is titled *Got Milk?* All of these are evidence that the slogan has chained out because it is easily recognized and resonates with many people in a number of different contexts.

Evidence of the sharing of fantasies includes cryptic allusions to symbolic common ground. When people have shared a fantasy theme, they have charged that theme with meanings and emotions that can be set off by an agreed-upon cryptic symbolic cue, whether a code word, phrase, slogan, or nonverbal sign or gesture. These serve as allusions to a previously shared fantasy and arouse the emotions associated with that fantasy. Among a group of college students who lived together in a dorm, for example, *sweet red grape* might serve as a symbolic cue that evokes fond memories of dorm parties where they drank cheap red wine.

The basic unit of analysis of symbolic convergence theory and fantasy-theme criticism is the fantasy theme. *Fantasy*, in the context of symbolic convergence theory, is not used in its popular sense—as something imaginary and not grounded in reality. Instead, *fantasy* is "the creative and imaginative interpretation of events,"[7] and a *fantasy theme* is the means through which the interpretation is accomplished in communication. A fantasy theme is a word, phrase, or statement that interprets events in the past, envisions events in the future, or depicts current events that are removed in time and/or space from the actual activities of a group. The term *fantasy* is designed to capture the constructed nature of the theme. Fantasy themes tell a story about a group's experience that constitutes a constructed reality for the participants.

A fantasy theme depicts characters, actions, and settings that are removed from an actual current group situation in time and place. Bormann distinguishes between a dramatic situation that takes place in the immediate context of a group and a dramatized communication shared by a group:

If, in the middle of a group discussion, several members come into conflict, the situation would be dramatic, but because the action is unfolding in the immediate experience of a group it would not qualify as a basis for the sharing of a group fantasy. If, however, a group's members begin talking about a conflict some of them had in the past or if they envision a future conflict, these comments would be dramatizing messages.[8]

In addition to their dramatic nature, fantasies are characterized by their artistic and organized quality. While experience itself is often chaotic and confusing, fantasy themes are organized and artistic. They are designed to create a credible interpretation of experience—a way of making sense out of experience. Thus, fantasy themes are always ordered in particular ways to provide compelling explanations for experiences. All fantasy themes involve the creative interpretation of events, but the artistry with which the fantasies are presented varies. Some groups construct fantasies "in which cardboard characters enact stereotyped melodramas," while others participate in "a social reality of complexity peopled with characters of stature enacting high tragedies."[9]

A close relationship exists between fantasies and argumentation in that shared fantasies provide the ground for arguments or establish the assumptive system that is the basis for arguments. Argumentation requires a common set of assumptions about the proper way to provide good reasons for arguments, and fantasy themes provide these assumptions. Bormann provides an example of the connection between fantasy themes and arguments:

> For instance, the Puritan vision gave highest place to evidence not of the senses but to revelations, from God. The assumptive system undergirding the Puritan arguments was a grand fantasy type in which a god persona revealed the ultimate truth by inspiring humans to write a sacred text. Supplementing this core drama was the fantasy type in which the god persona inspired ministers to speak the truth when preaching and teaching. These fantasy types provided the ultimate legitimization for the Bible as a source of revealed knowledge and for the ministers as the proper teachers of biblical truths.[10]

Other shared fantasies provide different kinds of assumptions for argumentation than did the Puritan vision. Scientists, for example, assume that argument is based on the careful observation of facts, while lawyers use precedent or past experience as the basis for argument. These groups share different fantasy themes as the basis for their construction of arguments.

The fantasy themes that describe the world from a group's perspective are of three types, corresponding to the elements necessary to create a drama: setting themes, character themes, and action themes. Statements that depict where the action is taking place are setting themes. They not only name the scene of the action but also describe the characteristics of that scene. Character themes describe the agents or actors in the drama, ascribe characteristics and qualities to them, and assign motives to them. Often, some characters are portrayed as heroes, while others are villains; some are major characters, while others are supporting players. Action themes, which also can be called *plotlines*, deal with the actions in which the characters in the drama engage.

When similar scenarios involving particular setting, character, and action themes are shared by members of a community, they form a fantasy type. A fantasy type is a stock scenario that encompasses several related fantasy themes. Once a fantasy type has developed, rhetors do not need to provide an audience with details about the specific fantasy themes it covers. They simply state the general story line of the fantasy type or refer to one of the fantasy themes in the scenario, and the audience is able to call up the specific details of the entire scenario. If a fantasy type has formed, a student in a university community can say, for example, "Students are fed up with professors who are so busy with their own research that they don't have time for students," and an entire scenario is called up among audience members. The success of the type shows that audience members have shared specific fantasies about teachers who are unprepared for class, who do not hold office hours, and who return exams and papers late or not at all.

Fantasy types encourage groups to fit new events or experiences into familiar patterns. If a new experience can be portrayed as an instance of a familiar fantasy type, the new experience is brought into line with a group's values and emotions and becomes part of its shared reality. If the members of a university community, for example, share a fantasy type that the State Board of Higher Education does not support a university, the forced retirement of the university's president by the board may be interpreted as a continued lack of support for the school, and the incident is incorporated into the group's reality.

The second primary unit of analysis in fantasy-theme criticism is the rhetorical vision. A rhetorical vision is a "unified putting together of the various shared fantasies"[11] or a swirling together of fantasy themes to provide a particular interpretation of reality. It contains fantasy themes relating to settings, characters, and actions that together form a symbolic drama or a coherent interpretation of reality. A rhetorical vision shared by college students at many state institutions, for example, might include hostile legislators as character themes, the legislature as a setting theme, and cutting funds to the university as an action theme.

The presence of a rhetorical vision suggests that a rhetorical community has been formed that consists of participants in the vision or members who have shared the fantasy themes.[12] The people who participate in a rhetorical vision, then, constitute a rhetorical community. They share common symbolic ground and respond to messages in ways that are in tune with the rhetorical vision:

> They will cheer references to the heroic persona in their rhetorical vision. They will respond with antipathy to allusions to the villains. They will have agreed-upon procedures for problem-solving communication. They will share the same vision of what counts as evidence, how to build a case, and how to refute an argument.[13]

The motives for action for a rhetorical community reside in its rhetorical vision. Each rhetorical vision contains as part of its substance the motive that impels the participants. As Bormann explains: "Motives do not exist to be expressed in communication but rather arise in the expression itself and come to be embedded in the drama of the fantasy themes that generated and serve to sustain them."[14] Bormann provides some examples of how participation in a rhetorical vision motivates individuals to particular action:

> The born-again Christian is baptized and adopts a life-style and behavior modeled after the heroes of the dramas that sustain that vision. . . . Likewise the convert to one of the countercultures in the 1960s would let his hair and beard grow, change his style of dress, and his method of work, and so forth.[15]

Actions that make little sense to someone outside of a rhetorical vision make perfect sense when viewed in the context of that vision because the vision provides the motive for action. The willingness of terrorists to die in support of a cause, for example, may seem absurd to most of us. Once we discover the rhetorical vision in which these terrorists participate, however, we have a much better idea of why they are motivated to sacrifice their lives for that cause.

Procedures

Using the fantasy-theme method of criticism, a critic analyzes an artifact in a four-step process: (1) selecting an artifact; (2) analyzing the artifact; (3) formulating a research question; and (4) writing the essay.

Selecting an Artifact

The artifact you select for a fantasy-theme analysis should be one where you have some evidence that symbolic convergence has taken place—that people have shared fantasy themes and a rhetorical vision. Any artifact that is popular—an advertisement, a song, a book, or a film, for example—is likely to show evidence of such symbolic convergence. An artifact produced by a major public figure, such as a U.S. president's speech or a commencement address by a talk-show host, also typically constitutes evidence of symbolic convergence because it incorporates themes the rhetor knows will resonate with the audience. Both discursive and nondiscursive artifacts can be used with the fantasy-theme method of criticism.

Analyzing the Artifact

Analysis of an artifact using fantasy-theme analysis involves two steps: (1) coding the artifact for setting, character, and action themes; and (2) constructing the rhetorical vision(s) from the fantasy themes.

Coding for Fantasy Themes

The first step in the fantasy-theme method of criticism is to code the artifact for fantasy themes. This involves a careful examination of the artifact, sentence by sentence in a verbal text or image by image in a visual artifact. Pick out each reference to settings, characters, and actions. This coding process can be illustrated in the first two stanzas from P!NK's song, "Dear Mr. President":

Dear Mr. President,
Come take a walk with me.
Let's pretend we're just two people and
You're not better than me.
I'd like to ask you some questions if we can speak honestly.

What do you feel when you see all the homeless on the street?
Who do you pray for at night before you go to sleep?
What do you feel when you look in the mirror?
Are you proud?[16]

The setting themes you would code in these stanzas are: *street* and *night*. Setting themes suggest where the action takes place or characteristics of the places in which the action occurs. This excerpt is relatively unusual in that it contains few setting themes. There is nothing wrong with your artifact or your coding if you find fewer themes in one category than in another. That is important information about how the rhetor has set up the world.

Character themes to code in the song are: *Mr. President, me, we, two people, I,* and *homeless.* Here, *Mr. President* and *you* are referring to the same character, *I* and *me* refer to the same character, and *two people* and *we* refer to the same set of characters, so your coding would reveal four characters—the president, the narrator, the two of them together, and the homeless. To keep *two people* as a character separate from the president and the narrator might seem odd, but the two of them together seem to be functioning differently from how the two characters function individually. Further coding and your later analysis would let you know whether you have four characters here or just three—the president, the narrator, and the homeless.

In some texts, you might find some nonhuman entities engaging in human-like action. If so, they should be coded as characters—perhaps something like *the earth* or *music*—although there are no such characters in this passage. If the artifact contains descriptions of characters, code those as character themes. *Not better than me,* for example, also would be coded as a character theme because it describes and fills out the picture of the character of the *two people.* If more than one setting is presented, note which characters appear in which settings.

Then code the actions in which the characters are shown engaging as action themes, noting the character to whom the action is linked: *take a walk* (president and narrator), *pretend* (president and narrator), *ask questions* (narrator), *speak honestly* (president and narrator), *feel* (president), *see* (president), *pray* (president), *sleep* (president), and *look in mirror* (president). Note that you do not code anything in the text that is not a setting, character, or action theme, so *Are you proud?* is not coded in this method.

At this preliminary stage of the coding, you may not always be sure if a theme belongs in one category or another—settings, characters, or actions. A word such as *America,* for example, may function both as a setting and a character. If the appropriate category is unclear, code it in both categories initially. Decisions you make in the next step of looking for patterns as you construct the rhetorical vision will determine in which category the word or phrase best belongs.

Constructing the Rhetorical Vision

Your second step in a fantasy-theme analysis is to look for patterns in the fantasy themes and to construct the rhetorical vision from the patterns. Begin by determining which of the fantasy themes appear to be major themes and which are minor themes. Those that appear most frequently are major themes that become the subject of the analysis, and those that appear only once or infrequently are discarded as not important parts of the rhetorical vision. In "Dear Mr. President," for example, the character of the homeless may appear only once, while the president appears several times. The president would be considered a major character in the vision, but the homeless would not. The fact that the character of homeless people appears implicitly in a later stanza with the line "Building a bed out of a cardboard box," however, may keep the homeless in your analysis as a major character.

Your next task is to construct the rhetorical vision from the patterns of fantasy themes you discovered. This involves looking at the major setting themes you identified and linking them with the characters depicted in those settings and the actions those characters are performing. There may be more than one rhetorical vision in your artifact. Some rhetorical communities participate in numerous dramas, with each one developed around a different topic. By linking setting themes with the appropriate characters and actions, you can discover if more than one rhetorical vision exists. If two setting themes appear in the artifact—America and Iraq, for example—the characters of good citizens engaged in the art of working to support their families would be combined with the setting of America to create one rhetorical vision. The characters of terrorists seeking to harm American soldiers would be placed in the setting of Iraq to form another vision.

Formulating a Research Question

Knowing the rhetorical vision of an artifact can be the basis for understanding many different rhetorical processes, so the research questions asked by critics using fantasy-theme analysis vary widely. You can ask questions, for example, about strategies used to accomplish specific objectives, the kinds of messages that are being communicated through particular rhetorical visions, the functions of particular rhetorical visions, or the implications of certain rhetorical visions for rhetorical processes or social controversies.

Writing the Essay

After completing the analysis, you are ready to write your essay, which includes five major components: (1) an introduction, in which you discuss the research question, its contribution to rhetorical theory, and its significance; (2) a description of the artifact and its context; (3) a description of the method of criticism—in this case, fantasy-theme analysis; (4) a report of the findings of the analysis, in which you reveal the fantasy themes and rhetorical vision(s) identified in your analysis; and (5) a discussion of the contribution the analysis makes to rhetorical theory.

Sample Essays

The sample essays that follow illustrate applications of fantasy-theme analysis to various kinds of artifacts. The research question that guides Eleanor M. Novek's analysis of a prison newspaper is, "How do prisoners resist imprisonment to endure and transcend the prison experience?" In Kelly Mendoza's analysis of the song "One Tree Hill" by U2, fantasy-theme criticism is used to explore the question, "What strategies does a rhetor use to cope emotionally with the loss of sudden death?" Kimberly A. McCormick and David Weiss analyze a mural in the parking lot of a Planned Parenthood clinic in Albuquerque, New Mexico, to explore the question, "How can a subversive art form articulate socially acceptable views of controversial issues?"

Notes

[1] Overviews of fantasy-theme criticism are provided by Bormann in: Ernest G. Bormann, "Fantasy and Rhetorical Vision: The Rhetorical Criticism of Social Reality," *Quarterly Journal of Speech*, 58 (December 1972), 396–407; Ernest G. Bormann, "Symbolic Convergence Theory: A Communication Formulation," *Journal of Communication*, 35 (Autumn 1985), 128–38; and Ernest G. Bormann, John F. Cragan, and Donald C. Shields, "In Defense of Symbolic Convergence Theory: A Look at the Theory and Its Criticisms After Two Decades," *Communication Theory*, 4 (November 1994), 259–94. For other information on and samples of the fantasy-theme approach, see John F. Cragan and Donald C. Shields, *Applied Communication Research: A Dramatistic Approach* (Long Grove, IL: Waveland, 1981). For a critique of and a defense of the usefulness of fantasy-theme criticism, see: G. P. Mohrmann, "An Essay on Fantasy Theme Criticism," *Quarterly Journal of Speech*, 68 (May 1982), 109–32; Ernest G. Bormann, "Fantasy and Rhetorical Vision: Ten Years Later," *Quarterly Journal of Speech*, 68 (August 1982), 288–305; and G. P. Mohrmann, "Fantasy Theme Criticism: A Peroration," *Quarterly Journal of Speech*, 68 (August 1982), 306–13. Additional critiques of fantasy-theme analysis include: Stephen E. Lucas, rev. of *The Force of Fantasy: Restoring the American Dream*, by Ernest G. Bormann, *Rhetoric Society Quarterly*, 16 (Summer 1986), 199–205; and Charles E. Williams, "Fantasy Theme Analysis: Theory vs. Practice," *Rhetoric Society Quarterly*, 17 (Winter 1987), 11–20.

[2] Robert Freed Bales, *Personality and Interpersonal Behavior* (New York: Holt, Rinehart and Winston, 1970), pp. 136–55.

[3] Bormann, "Fantasy and Rhetorical Vision," p. 397.

[4] Ernest G. Bormann, Roxann L. Knutson, and Karen Musolf, "Why Do People Share Fantasies? An Empirical Investigation of a Basic Tenet of the Symbolic Convergence Communication Theory," *Communication Studies*, 48 (Fall 1997), 255.

[5] Ernest G. Bormann, "Symbolic Convergence: Organizational Communication and Culture," in *Communication and Organizations: An Interpretive Approach*, ed. Linda L. Putnam and Michael E. Pacanowsky (Beverly Hills: Sage, 1983), p. 102.

[6] Bormann, "Symbolic Convergence Theory," p. 104.

[7] Ernest G. Bormann, "How to Make a Fantasy Theme Analysis," unpublished essay, p. 4.

[8] Ernest G. Bormann, *The Force of Fantasy: Restoring the American Dream* (Carbondale: Southern Illinois University Press, 1985), pp. 4–5.

[9] Bormann, *The Force of Fantasy*, p. 10.

[10] Bormann, *The Force of Fantasy*, pp. 16–17.

[11] Bormann, "Symbolic Convergence Theory," p. 114.

[12] Bormann, *The Force of Fantasy*, p. 8.

[13] Bormann, "Symbolic Convergence Theory," p. 115.

[14] Bormann, "Fantasy and Rhetorical Vision," p. 406.

[15] Bormann, "Fantasy and Rhetorical Vision," pp. 406–07.

[16] Downloaded February 8, 2008, from
http://www.azlyrics.com/lyrics/pink/dearmrpresident.html.

"Heaven, Hell, and Here"
Understanding the Impact of Incarceration through a Prison Newspaper

Eleanor M. Novek

I wonder, how many has this bed slept . . .
I wonder, how many has this bed wept . . .
I wonder, how many has this bed kept . . .
I wonder how many souls this bed has met . . .
I wonder, if memories keep . . . will I at last weep
For me?

("This Bed," *Insight*—the newspaper which is the focus of this article)

Introduction

Historically, some societies have regarded prisons as reformatories for wrongdoers, while others have considered them a means of punishment for lawbreakers. In recent decades, public policy in the United States has unreservedly embraced the latter view. Since the 1970s, Franklin suggests, citizens have supported

> the unrestrained growth of the prison system, harsh mandatory sentences, a "lock 'em up and throw away the key" media campaign, "three strikes and you're out" laws, a stampede toward capital punishment, the creation of "supermax" penitentiaries, and abandonment of all pretense that prison should be designed for rehabilitation. (Franklin, 1998, p. 15)

Consequently, the nation's incarceration rates have more than tripled in the last 20 years (Maguire & Pastore, 2002), and the U.S. now incarcerates more of its own citizens than any other country in the world (The Sentencing Project, 2003). Today, one in every 143 adults in the United States is incarcerated in a state or federal prison or a local jail, the majority convicted of non-violent offenses (Harrison & Beck, 2003). More than 2.1 million men and women are imprisoned, while another 4.7 million are on probation or parole (U.S. Department of Justice, 2003). In addition, the criminal justice system's racially discriminatory rates of arrest, conviction, and sentencing (Harrison & Beck, 2003), its brutal handling of incarcerated women (Human Rights Watch, 1996), and the neglect of pandemics of tuberculosis, AIDS, and hepatitis among inmates (Farmer, 2002) are earning the condemnation of human rights groups around the world.

Prison newspapers reflect the everyday realities of this situation. In these publications, incarcerated people describe their own subjection and the determining power of the criminal justice system; the experiences of their bodies and minds behind bars and barbed wire; their interactions with fellow prisoners, guards, administrators, and the courts; the turning points that led them to prison and that will shape their futures when they return to society. The stories in prison newspapers capture the quotidian atmosphere of the penitentiary as it is lived and understood by the people confined there. The public forum they construct is precious to their writers and audiences, and important also to scholars of communication and media.

This article illuminates the world of a state prison for women through interpretive textual analysis of a prison newspaper. The newspaper was established in 2001 at a state prison for women in the northeastern U.S. The publication comes out of a journalism class taught by the author and a colleague, and is produced entirely by inmates of the prison. After situating the prison newspaper as a tool of ideological struggle, I use symbolic convergence theory to provide a fantasy theme analysis of the texts and illuminate the rhetorical vision they create for their authors and audiences. Constructing a rhetorical vision of "Heaven, hell, and here," the newspapers tell a tale of intense suffering, but also express inmates' struggle to overcome the degradations of confinement with spirituality, compassion, pragmatism, and even humor.

Prison Newspapers and Ideological Struggle

Fiske (1989) argues that dominant institutions and actors in a society have the ability to construct the common sense of that social order in a way that supports their own interests. "Their power is the power to have their meaning of self and of social relations accepted or consented to by the people" (p. 9). When subjugated people attempt to challenge the dominant definitions with meanings of their own, they are committing acts of defiance, for any alternative expression of meanings that establishes social differences "maintains and legitimates those meanings and those differences" (Fiske, 1993, p. 9).

Oppositional expressions of meaning sometimes take the form of "outsider journalism," a form of alternative media created by groups that are not only overlooked by the mainstream media, but also marginalized and despised by society. Historically, outsider journalism has emerged from populations with a dramatic sense of alienation, a sense of themselves as pariahs or outlaws. Scholarship on outsider journalism has focused on publications produced, among others, by prisoners (Gaucher, 2002; Morris, 2002; Novek, 2005), militant gays and lesbians (Streitmatter, 1995), dissident GIs in the Vietnam War (Lewes, 2001), gay men with AIDS (Long, 2000), and homeless people (Howley, 2003; Torck, 2001).

Outsider journalism creates alternative public spheres for publication of the views, opinions, and perspectives of marginalized constituencies (Howley, 2003). Operating outside the norms and standards of mainstream media, such publications build community among their audiences out of the common experiences of adversity and outlaw status. Outsider journalism can be characterized by a tenacious insistence on its own value despite the recognition of the outcast position of its authors. It privileges the lived experience and authentic expression of its authors' voices over other forms of expression. These periodicals offer their writers identity, a sense of agency in the face of oppression, and connection to a similarly situated audience.

Prison newspapers are a form of outsider journalism that involves the creation of alternative meanings by people who are not only dominated, but also disenfranchised and suppressed—as Gaucher (2002) calls them, the "silenced majority." Prisoners are fully encompassed by the institutions in which they live. Foucault (1979) observed that prisons seek to manage and monitor human behavior absolutely; they assume absolute authority over incarcerated people, controlling their bodies, restricting every aspect of their conduct and work, and dictating their mental, moral, and spiritual attitudes, in some cases for their entire lives. The rule and value systems that manage prisoners do not acknowledge their humanity or value; rather, they are motivated by society's desire to isolate and categorize deviant behavior in order to control and punish it.

In the face of such domination, prison newspapers function as notable, if modest, demonstrations of inmate agency. According to historian James McGrath Morris (2002), the first known prison newspaper in the United States appeared in 1800; a New York attorney used the aptly named *Forlorn Hope* to crusade against debtors' prisons while he was locked up in one. Over time, prison newspapers have struggled to be instruments of prison reform and prisoners' rights, particularly the right to be heard (Morris, 2002). For example, the *Prison News Service,* which operated from 1980 to 1996 in Toronto, focused on the practices and politics of imprisonment and prisoners' accounts of their repression (Gaucher, 2002). The *Prison Legal News,* published by civilian volunteers but edited by inmates of the Washington State Reformatory, informed inmates of their rights under the law and helped them in their legal battles while incarcerated (Morris, 2002). *The Angolite,* published at the infamous Louisiana State Penitentiary at Angola, won a George Polk Award for its frank and graphic exposé of rape and sexual violence in prison.

Gaucher (1999, 2002) observes that the penal press was widely appreciated in the United States and around the world after World War II. High-profile dissidents like Alexander Solzhenitsyn of Russia and Brendan Behan of Ireland were celebrated for prison memoirs of political resistance, while Jean Genet of France and Chester Himes of the United States became well-known for novels portraying common criminals in the penal system (Gaucher, 2002). The beginnings of an international network of penal editors and writers contributed to increased public interest in prison writings. In the 1960s and 1970s, however, as the writings of American prisoners began to take a more political and critical tone, U.S. prison officials and judges cracked down on what they saw as a threat to the social order. They moved to censor and suppress inmate writers, barring prisoners from contact with the news media and banning or curtailing prison publications (Gaucher, 1999).

In 1979, after David Berkowitz, the "Son of Sam" killer, appeared poised to earn high fees for a book deal related to his crimes, public outcry led the New York legislature to pass a law redirecting any profits from the book to victims' families (Timmons, 1995). Similar remedies, called "Son of Sam" laws, sprang up around the country in an effort to stop prisoners from making money from their prison writings, although Timmons (1995) notes that most have been found unconstitutional. Ongoing efforts by state legislatures continue to stifle prison writers, even after probation, and even when their writings are not based on the crimes they committed (Timmons, 1995). A recent example of this was the lawsuit brought by the state of Connecticut against eight inmates whose writings were published in 2003 in an edited collection by Wally Lamb; the suit was settled with the inmates agreeing to (re)pay the state part of its costs for imprisoning them (Singer, 2004).

Hamilton (1993) contends that alternative newspapers form "a cultural site at which various institutions, social formations, and ideologies are dynamically, contentiously, and always tentatively negotiated" (p. 255). Prison newspapers, although they face great constraints, are sites where the competing ideologies surrounding the meaning of prison in U.S. society struggle with each other. They also contain the discursive and self-reflexive resistance of an oppressed population "sharing a unique history and destiny" (Steiner, 1983, p. 4) and struggling for a sense of solidarity and support. However, while the phenomenon of contemporary prison writing per se continues to be well examined by scholars of literature, criminal justice, and sociology (see Davies, 1990; Dowd, 1996; Franklin, 1998; Lamb & Women of York Correctional Institution, 2003; Scheffler, 2002; and numerous others), the surviving internal publications of prisoners—newspapers, magazines, newsletters—are largely overlooked.[1]

The Limits of Journalistic Freedom in Custody

Erving Goffman (1961), in analyzing asylums and prisons as total institutions, found prison newspapers to be somewhat toothless, because they require the good will of penal authorities to survive. Sneed and Stonecipher (1986) note that a prisoner's opportunity to take part in the creation of an institutional publication is mainly "a privilege extended by prison authorities for good behavior" (p. 54). Corrections officials who tolerate such publications may view them as a way of keeping inmates busy, co-opting criticism, and making their institutions appear progressive to outsiders (Novek, 2005). It is true that relatively few prison newspapers are openly oppositional; to the contrary, as Morris (2002) observes, prison journalists must decide "whether to be the inmates' advocate, an independent chronicler, or the administration's mouthpiece" (p. 14), and the self-interest that informs that decision often muzzles them.

Sneed and Stonecipher (1986) see inmate newspapers as "a forum for limited freedom of expression within a walled-off society where authoritarian rule presides" (p. 53). As such, inmate newspapers face a level of restraint unheard of in commercial newspapers. The viewpoints expressed in some publications merely echo those of their institutions' administrations, Goffman remarked (1961); in exchange, the authors receive modest recognition for their language skills and the right to voice some complaints. In other publications, prisoners have spoken out bluntly and paid a price for their honesty.

During their sentences, most inmates prefer to keep their heads down and stay invisible, prison author Victor Hassine noted in an interview:

> The minute you stand out for something, whether it's good or bad, you're going to get people on one side of you or the other, and you can't handle that in prison because the guy that's on the other side of you today may be insignificant, tomorrow it may be the warden and you're in trouble. (Gaucher, 1999, p. 110)

When inmates express themselves in writing, they stand out. Repressive wardens and administrators have cracked down on critical writers and editors with solitary confinement and other harsh penalties (Morris, 2002). Prison guards may join in the punishment; McMaster (1999) notes that prison journalists face a constant threat of retribution from custodial officers: "Chronic cell searches, harassment, censorship and long-term segregation are all on the agenda" (p. 48). It is also common for prison newspapers to be shut down suddenly and arbitrarily.

During the last quarter of the 20th century, a number of cases involving inmates' constitutional rights to a free press, freedom of association, and freedom of expression passed through the courts (Morris, 2002), but the Supreme Court has never definitively ruled against the censorship of prison newspapers. According to Sneed and Stonecipher (1986), the federal courts have questioned the states' "unbridled authority" to regulate the content of prison publications (p. 53), but they generally find the speech rights of prisoners less compelling than "the state's objectives of security, order and rehabilitation" (p. 50). To all intents and purposes, Morris (2002) argues, this means that the courts tolerate censorship or suppression whenever a prison administration wants to impose it. Observing broader legislative restrictions on inmate correspondence and authorship of all types for the last two decades, Gaucher (1999) points to an ongoing trend toward "censorship as part of the court sentence, and the definition of the writing, past or future, as part of the offense" (p. 23) for increasing numbers of prisoners.

In addition to the threat of institutional censorship, prison journalists may also gag themselves in fear of their readers. Disgruntled fellow inmates often view journalists as snitches: "Not surprisingly, inmates are often sensitive about having a reporter, especially one of their own, prowling about and writing things they would prefer remain out of print" (Morris, 2002, p. 14). Prison writers routinely face physical and psychological threats from inmates who want to stifle them out of the belief "that it is taboo to openly discuss any aspect of our hidden society" (McMaster, 1999, p. 51). In a 1980 interview in *Time,* award-winning Louisiana prison journalist Wilbert Rideau acknowledged the intimidation he faced from fellow inmates in writing his investigative stories: "You're in a world where everybody plays for keeps" (Morris, 2002, p. 166).

The growth of the incarcerated population is also silencing prisoners by making it harder to sustain publication of inmate newspapers. Gloomily referring to prison journalism as "an artifact of penal history" (p. 187), Morris (2002) observes that the cost of housing an ever-increasing inmate population in recent decades is contributing to the demise of prison newspapers around the country. Overcrowding and violence have put many of the nation's prisons into "virtually a perpetual lockdown, preventing any inmate journalists from doing their work" (p. 188). As their corrections budgets are stretched to breaking point, some states are even considering reducing inmates' daily rations; in such circumstances, the modest funds necessary to print an inmate newspaper may be seen as frivolous. Though Morris recorded the existence of almost 200 prison publications over time, he was only able to establish that eight were still being published when his *Jailhouse Journalism* was published in 2002.

Making Sense of the Prison Experience Together

Whether called newspapers, newsletters, magazines, or 'zines, outsider journalism does not resemble commercial news publications. Outsider journalists often reject conventions of mainstream journalism such as the use of "official sources" and the stance of professional objectivity. For example, the authors of street newspapers analyzed by Howley (2003) did not seek expertise from elected officials, business leaders, or academics: "Rather, expert knowledge is constructed through and draws upon the everyday lived experience of the working poor, the homeless and those who work on their behalf. . . . Reporters recount incidents and conversations on street corners, in social service offices, at soup kitchens and food banks" (pp. 284–285).

In the early gay and lesbian press analyzed by Streitmatter (1995), essays about personal experience, short stories, and poetry dominated the editorial content. "Other elements in the editorial mix included detailed descriptions of research projects on homosexuality, as well as book reviews, lists of recent books and articles of interest to gay readers, and a letters to the editor section" (p. 439). When news briefs began to appear, they were often accompanied by subjective comments from the editors, who encouraged readers to express their opinions as well.

Such personal expressions have been a common feature of outsider journalism. In the 19th century, Steiner (1992) observed, women established independent media to express and dramatize their interests, "to nourish and defend an identity that imbues their lives with meaning" (p. 121). These publications offered solidarity and practical advice for social change. "They taught suffragists how to argue and defend themselves, why to sacrifice, when to renounce. They explained and exhorted. They celebrated both the togetherness of this community and its apartness from larger society" (Steiner, 1983, p. 4).

Like other forms of outsider journalism, prison newspapers allow their creators and audiences to share small acts of defiance within the larger context of their subjugation. These acts of resistance offer the possibility of growth and new ways of seeing. Freire (1980) notes that many oppressed people "have adapted to the structure of domination in which they are immersed, and have become resigned to it" (p. 32). Conditioned to fear freedom, he argues, oppressed people must learn new ways of envisioning themselves in relation to others. Even within the most threatening structures of domination, Conquergood (1995) argues, "people in myriad and creative ways carve out space for resisting, contesting, subverting authority, and refurbishing their own identity and dignity" (p. 85). Once imagined, Fiske (1989) observes, the "interior resistance of fantasy" (p. 10) does more than just allow people to evade the dominant constructions that oppress them—it also provides them with a basis for social action and external resistance to dehumanizing treatment.

The dawning of this resistance may be understood through Bormann's (1982) symbolic convergence theory, where convergence refers to the way that certain processes of communication allow "two or more private symbolic worlds [to] incline towards each other, come more closely together, or even overlap" (p. 51). Drama-based messages known as "fantasy themes" tap into a group's common experiences or sets of interpretations, and are repeated and imparted in ways that feel important and exhilarating to participants (Stone, 2002). Such symbolic sharing, Bormann (1982) argues, structures a shared social reality for the participants that enables social action.

Inmate journalists do much more than describe the bleak realities of prison. Through discourse, they construct multiple meanings of prison life for themselves and their audiences. Stories and articles written by inmates highlight common themes and repeat dramatizing messages about familiar contextual truths. Over time, they create a rhetorical vision, which Bormann (1982) defines as "a unified putting-together of various shared scripts which provides a broader view of a culture's social reality" (p. 52). By allowing incarcerated people to imagine and construct meanings of self and social relations that they appreciate and benefit from, prison journalism may provide a tool for transformation.

This article provides a fantasy theme analysis of a prison newspaper and explores the symbolic convergence of its messages. It describes how the rhetorical vision created by one newspaper, produced at a state prison for women, allows inmates to create or sustain survivor identities and build community with one another under the most oppressive conditions. When these prisoners share their rhetorical vision of "Heaven, hell, and here," they become what Bormann (1982) calls a "rhetorical community." That is, the recognition of their shared fate binds them together in understanding and solidarity. This article describes how a prison newspaper gives voice to incarcerated women and bears witness to the effects of imprisonment on their lives. It also illuminates some of the ways in which the newspaper empowers its creators and audiences to endure and transcend the prison experience.

Methodology: Producing and Analyzing a Prison Newspaper

Communication scholars are increasingly aware of the need to draw public attention to prisons while also engaging with the plight of inmates inside them. A growing number (including Conquergood, 2002; Hartnett, 1998; Valentine, 1998; and others) have worked in prisons as volunteer educators and civil rights advocates. In September of 2001, in partnership with a fellow communication professor, I began teaching a journalism class at a minimum- to maximum-security facility in the northeastern United States. The institution, called Clara Barton State Prison for Women here, is home to approximately 1,100 women. It is located in rolling countryside, about an hour's drive from a large city and just off a heavily trafficked interstate highway. The facility has a minimum-security wing, a maximum-security wing, and a treatment wing for mentally ill and drug-addicted inmates.

A prison term does little to equip a woman with economic survival skills for use when she leaves the institution; rather, it is likely to damage whatever social capital and emotional reserves she may possess. Incarceration suddenly and traumatically separates many women from their children and families, and exiles them from their own communities. At the same time, prison routines appear structured to undermine any sense of trust or cooperation that may develop among inmates. Elsewhere, I have theorized that the social routines of news making may be used by at-risk youth to cultivate a sense of community and make a difference in their lives (Novek, 1995). Similarly, I anticipated that the prison journalism class would offer participants an instrument for self-expression, an enhanced sense of self-efficacy, social support, and a chance to build proficiencies in writing, research, editing, and desktop publishing that might some day enhance their employment options.

The prison had sponsored an inmate newspaper intermittently in the past, but the most recent publication, essentially a one-woman operation, had died out when its editor got into trouble a few years back; this new initiative would eventually expose more than 100 women to the technical skills of journalism. The twice-monthly classes covered news judgment, developing story ideas, writing in news style, interviewing, opinion writing, editing, grammar, spelling and punctuation, page design, and the use of word processing and layout software. Students were encouraged to write news articles that focused on the facts of their daily lives and experiences. Occasionally, passionate debates would take place on current events or controversial stories from the mainstream press.

More than 80 women inmates took part in the classes during the project's first two and a half years. They were free to join or drop out as they wished; some only came to class once or twice, and some remained actively engaged during the entire period described here. After an initial development stage, the classes began producing a regular monthly newspaper. Called here *Insight*, it contained news and feature articles, opinion columns, personal narratives, poetry, recipes, puzzles, and cartoons. (A detailed description is found below.) Between September 2001 and January 2004, the journalism classes produced 16 issues of the newspaper.

The focus of this article is the body of texts published in *Insight* during the first 30 months of the prison journalism project. In February 2004, I obtained a census of the 16 issues produced to that date, consisting of 610 articles, and subjected them to a preliminary content analysis.[2] I identified the categories of subject matter covered by the authors, the frequency with which these topics appeared in the newspaper, and the rate of authorship among the most prolific contributors. Ernest Bormann's symbolic convergence theory was used as an analytical framework for in-depth qualitative interpretive analysis of the broad fantasy themes that recur in the published articles. These themes provided evidence of the rhetorical vision created by the newspaper and the meaning of the texts for their authors.

As discussed above, issues of confidentiality are paramount in prison settings. To protect the privacy of the participants, I have concealed the name and location of the institution, the title of the publication, and the identities of the inmates whose writings are quoted in this study. All names in the article are pseudonyms. At the time of this writing, the newspaper continues to operate, and a number of inmates from the class continue to take part in it.

Format and Content of a Prison Publication

Insight is a publication produced by and for women serving time at the Clara Barton prison, and is not intended for the eyes of civilians (though guards and civilian employees read it too). Each issue of the 24- to 47-page publication is typed and edited on a computer at Clara Barton. Stapled at one edge and decorated with clip-art and fancy fonts, *Insight* resembles the home-made newsletters and fan magazines of earlier decades. Occasional bursts of color ink highlight the cover, which the women often choose to adorn with large clip-art illustrations with seasonal meaning, like an eagle in July or a flower in May. Although the women wanted the publication to be produced commercially on newsprint, to look like a real newspaper, the professors were never able to arrange either permission or funding for this. Instead, *Insight* was printed at a men's prison on 8 1/2 by 11-inch office paper provided by the state.

Inside, the papers displayed one to three items per page. Although the newspaper staff sometimes had a hard time keeping track of all submissions and occasionally lost articles, virtually every piece of writing submitted was printed. About one-third of the articles in the sample followed at least some journalistic norms; they were fact-based stories built on written reports, interviews, or the author's eyewitness observation of events. Another third were opinion columns, giving voice to the authors' personal beliefs or attitudes. The remainder of the articles were unstructured personal narratives, poetry, microwave recipes, and word puzzles. Photos were rare because cameras are forbidden at the prison, but occasionally a civilian employee had permission to take photos at special programs or visitor speeches, and these were made available to the newspaper. Inmates occasionally produced drawings or cartoons and these, along with creative fonts and more clip-art, decorated the newspaper's inside pages.

Many articles in *Insight* were contributed by the general population of the prison, but members of the journalism class made up the foundation of the newspaper staff. It was they who performed the editing and composition of the publication each month. They were also its most prolific contributors. Looking at the frequency of publication for authors hints at the newspaper's importance in the lives of some inmates. Of the more than 80 women who took part in the journalism classes over two and a half years, 14 women produced 353 of the 610 articles, or 58% of the total. The most productive writer was responsible for 9.3% of all the articles published in the newspaper in its first two and a half years.

Another factor that contributed to the paper's content was its leadership. As various women cycled through the position of editor (sometimes appointed by prison staff, sometimes volunteering for the job), their personalities lent the paper distinctive tones.

When a risk-taking inmate would take on the role of editor, her influence would be seen in assertive editorializing and a preference for controversial topics, such as prison health care, domestic violence, or flaws in the nation's criminal justice system. At other times, a more cautious woman would edit the publication, and its flavor would grow less critical, even ingratiating. Maintaining a stable editorial presence proved an almost impossible task; prison routines constantly disrupted inmates' jobs, living conditions, and custodial status (Novek, 2005). In addition, inmates with volatile tempers and bruised egos squabbled over how they thought the newspaper should look and read, and no editor was able to maintain a coherent editorial voice for very long.

The editor's job was not an easy one. Many of the articles submitted for publication were filled with misspellings and errors in grammar and punctuation.[3] Yet the writers resisted suggestions that any part of their articles should be edited or revised; when a new issue of the prison newspaper came out, they would carefully scrutinize its pages, looking for any changes to their work, which they found insulting. They were not likely to accept these suggestions from the professors, either. When editing was taught in the classes, some women would say that only the original author knew what she meant and, therefore, no one else should suggest improvements to her work. These writers fiercely protected their written pieces as extensions of themselves. Editors or other members of the newspaper staff who took it upon themselves to correct errors in grammar and spelling risked an angry confrontation.

Where journalistic norms appear in the paper at all, they may have been due in part to the presence of the author and her colleague. We encouraged the women to write about anything that interested them, but stressed the importance of factual sources and solid reporting. We brought in newspaper articles, journalism textbooks, reference works, and other information resources for them to use. However, most of the women were more comfortable writing in their own voices than citing sources; they valued their own experiences more than the opinions of other people, especially people deemed authorities, and felt that their heartfelt expressions were the best way to reach out to their readers.

Without question, the most powerful influence on the newspaper's content was the superintendent's censoring eye. When out of the hearing range of prison staff or corrections officers, many inmates were highly derogatory about Clara Barton prison's policies and conditions. They complained about the stifling heat and lack of ventilation in summer, the mailroom's confiscation of letters and family photos, life-threatening medical misdiagnosis and neglect, incompetent dental care, unclean and contaminated food, crowded and unsanitary bathrooms, and other hardships. But the journalists had to balance their desire to criticize in a public forum with their fear of offending the superintendent and bringing punishment down upon themselves. They knew the superintendent would read each issue of the newspaper before it went to the printer and reject any materials deemed unacceptable. Such complaints made for rowdy class discussions but rarely appeared as news articles; and when they did, they were often pulled out of the newspaper by prison officials.

After a few issues, this censorship seemed to develop a predictable pattern: critical news stories about broad topics, including the nation's criminal justice system, drug abuse, and domestic violence, were allowed to run unexpurgated. Articles that criticized the prison administration or conditions at this specific institution were likely to be censored. Several items were removed from each issue, including critical articles and cartoons or images considered disrespectful (once, a clip-art of a flying duck). Authors whose writings made the superintendent angry were sometimes yelled at but, to my knowledge, none were punished to the degree reported in men's prisons with newspapers (Morris, 2002). However, as the superintendent began to delegate responsibility for censoring the newspaper to staff members, censorship became more erratic, with the focus shifting from spelling or grammatical errors to topical material to certain forms of religious expression.

Informed by three years of participant observation, teaching at the prison, and working closely with a number of the women on their writings, I identified 16 distinct categories of subject matter in the articles published in the prison newspaper. Following are brief descriptions of these individual topic areas, in descending order of their prevalence:

1. Spiritual: Articles that focus on religion or a higher power. Most of the writings analyzed here refer to Christianity or Islam, with a few references to Judaism, yoga, or other beliefs.

2. General interest: Recipes, book reviews, and other neutral topics of the sort that might be found in the back pages of a local commercial newspaper.

3. Programming: Fact-based coverage of events, classes, and educational or cultural programs that occurred at the prison.

4. Prison life: Descriptions of life experiences and general conditions behind bars.

5. Self-help: Offers of emotional comfort, support, or advice, in an inspirational tone where religion is not the primary emphasis.

6. Critique of society: Judgments of social ills, such as the prison system, drugs, violence, politics, and other topics that affect society as a whole.

7. Medical: Reports or personal narratives about prison health care, whether focused on inmate medical treatment in the U.S. in general or conditions at this prison.

8. Family: Articles about families, children, and parenting, with advice about parenting from prison or being separated from family members.

9. Confession: Accounts of the author's experiences, background, crimes, or life before incarceration.

10. Meta-coverage: Articles that pertain explicitly to the inmate newspaper itself, such as discussions of its staff and procedures, calls for articles, and so on.

11. Legal issues: Laws and policies of special interest to inmates, such as mandatory sentencing guidelines, custody rights, loss of voting rights, and so on.

12. Domestic violence: Reports about violence, abuse, or mistreatment by a family member or romantic partner.

13. Staff profile: Interview-based articles about prison staff members. These were likely to be seen as threats to security and removed by the superintendent.

14. Critique of the facility: Articles critical of specific policies or practices at this prison. Only a few of these avoided expurgation.

15. Entertainment: Articles or puzzles with no news focus, meant only to amuse.

16. Inmate profile: Interview with an inmate. Very few of these were produced.

This initial discussion of the prison newspaper has described the appearance and format of the publication and represented the variety of its themes and coverage; the following qualitative interpretive analysis of its fantasy themes offers a deeper exploration of the texts.

Heaven, Hell, and Here: Constructing the Prison in the Mind

According to Ernest Bormann (1982), a fantasy theme is a dramatizing message in which characters engage symbolically in acts and settings somewhere other than the "here-and-now" of the people involved in the communication (p. 52). Fantasy themes offer people a way to make their common experiences visible and shape them into social knowledge. When fantasy themes are successful, the rhetorical vision they generate allows people "to create community, to discuss their common experiences, and to achieve mutual understanding" (p. 51).

As prisoners make meaning of the prison experience and express it in their news-paper, the shared social knowledge they create builds a sense of community. Using excerpts from representative newspaper articles to support my claims, I will argue that inmate journalists create a rhetorical vision of "Heaven, hell, and here," constructing the prison as a place of both torment and transcendence. The articles in the inmate newspaper delineate the intense sufferings of incarcerated women while also high-lighting their determination to overcome adversity with spirituality, optimism, and resolve. The newspapers articulate the spirit of resistance, pragmatic creativity, and even humor that enable some women to survive the prison experience. The three fan-tasy themes identified here are not simply present in some of the authors' work; rather, they represent dominant premises that emerge repeatedly in the newspaper content.

For some of the women writing articles for the prison newspaper, the prison seems to represent a site of salvation. In the first recurrent fantasy theme, which I des-ignate "heaven," prison is portrayed as a place of transformation and transcendence. The penitentiary is seen as a kind of hard-knocks boot camp experience of tough love that rescues a woman from her weaker self and sets her on the path to righteousness and hope. Articles referring to this theme suggest that being locked up actually offers a troubled woman opportunities for personal development, temporary respite from her vulnerability on the street, an ideal of female solidarity, and the possibility of religious or spiritual enlightenment.

A writer using these narratives typically identifies herself as a lost soul, wandering through her life in a daze of drugs or violence (or both) until some crisis precipitates her arrest and conviction. Once incarcerated, the woman begins to examine her past behaviors and the underlying emotional pain that caused them. She rejects these and vows to reform herself, often embracing religion as a tool for this purpose. One woman writes:

> Was I arrested or rescued? Being on the streets, hanging out in places where danger constantly lurked, using drugs and doing things that were not good for me, was leading me to an early grave. Prison has given me a new understanding of what freedom means. I was rescued from self-destruction.[4]

The endless conflict of inmate life and the arbitrariness of prison rules are seen by some authors as catalysts that strengthen them and prepare them for greater chal-lenges in life:

> Prison for me is one of the best places to make a positive change in one's life. If you can make it here, you can make it anywhere in the world. I say that because I have been forced to deal with people from all walks of life. Every day is filled with the unexpected, from the time I awake until bedtime. What is a rule today may change tomorrow. People I laughed with in the morning may end up cussing me out by night.

The authors of many such articles state that imprisonment allowed them to be con-templative for the first time in their lives, initiating growth and transformation. Some encourage their fellow inmates to educate themselves intellectually and spiritually while incarcerated, so that they can be more worthy members of their communities upon their release:

> Being in prison can be used as a time of reflection on the changes you want to make for yourself and give you an opportunity to implement them before you get out. Time here can be used to develop skills that will help you be able to keep a job, or learn how to apply for a job. There may not be a whole bunch of opportunities in prison, but there are more opportunities here than others have.

For many women, imprisonment involves painful separation from their loved ones. Some whose writing reflects the fantasy theme of prison as "heaven" describe discovering a sense of empathy and connection to other women inmates, a recogni-tion of their shared plight and social support that eases the loneliness of incarceration. They describe the relief of coming to see what they hold in common with fellow pris-oners and reaching out to them for emotional encouragement and advice. One writer describes a road trip with four other women taken to a public hospital because they needed chemotherapy or tests that the prison hospital could not provide. Despite their serious health conditions, the women are strip-searched before and after the trip and chained and shackled while riding in the prison van. Even so, the writer is able to feel uplifted by the experience:

> We all hobble to the van, talking, laughing, finally on our way. We are talking, sharing stories, and laughing, but we are all listening to each other. Stroke, tumors, diabetes, cancer, it doesn't matter to these fearless five what our illness is. We will do the legwork and survive, even in here. . . . I feel the hope in these women and pray that it will continue to grow and become contagious.

This pattern resonates with a fantasy theme identified by Bormann (1977) as "fetching good out of evil" (p. 181). In this fantasy theme, used by colonial preachers in the 18th century, certain people are chosen by God but fail to live up to their cove-nant. The people experience a time of troubles as the result of this sin, but the troubles are seen as the working of God to bring his people back into the fold (Bormann, 1977). In the prison newspaper *Insight,* the heroines of "heaven" narratives tend to be the authors themselves. They may have broken laws and hurt others in the past, but the prison's harsh mercies have forced them to look inside themselves and repent. As their writings testify, out of the evil of prison comes the good of repentance and the productive return to society.

If some writers are able to look past their sufferings to view the prison experience in an optimistic light, others see it as a dreadful place with no redeeming potential. The fantasy theme identified here as "hell" speaks to the women's sense of loss of identity, lack of emotional contact and support, feelings of guilt and worthlessness, physical distress, and the merciless passage of time. For many women, the most pain-ful aspect of prison is their separation from families and loved ones. While inmates experience physical pain and discomfort, their loss of connection to other people causes the deepest damage. Newspaper articles articulate how the true "hell" of the prison experience lies in its heartlessness and isolation. "Prison life is a very lonely life," one woman writes. "You're taken from comfort and consistency and tossed into loneliness and pain. First comes shock, eventually acceptance, and finally utter loneliness. Nothing is familiar, everyone is a stranger. You're apart from your family, and you have no friends."

Ritchie (2002) estimates that 75% of women in prison are mothers, and two-thirds have children under the age of 18. Often, the forced separation of inmate mothers and their children has been sudden and unexpected, and prisoners' longing for their children is acute. "Whether the judge realized it or not, by far the greatest punishment he inflicted on me was separating me from my children," one inmate wrote. In a wrenching first-person account, another young woman describes giving birth to her son while serving a sentence and then having to relinquish the child to the authorities after three days.

> I only had three days to bond with (my son), but it was the best three days in my life. . . . It's the third day and we are ready to be released, except to different destinations. I gave him all the kisses I could before leaving; it felt like my heart wanted to stop. They finally took my son back to the nursery while they shackled me to come back to prison.

Inmates face many difficulties in trying to maintain family contact. The prison is a long journey from many of the women's home towns, and visitors are crowded into dirty transportation vans, screened through metal detectors, checked by drug-sniffing dogs, and herded into crowded visitation areas where there is no privacy or touching. Prisoners anticipating visitors get pat-searched before visits and strip-searched afterwards. While this experience is "very humiliating and degrading," one woman writes, for most inmates, "the hardest thing is watching your family leave when you can't go with them." Others write about the prohibitively high cost of collect phone calls from the prison and difficulties in sending or receiving mail—liberties taken for granted by outsiders, but vitally important to incarcerated women.

Conversely, other writers have suffered because of family contact; as they serve their time, memories of betrayals and cruelty from years ago surface, and the women seek to purge these thoughts with the pen. Girshick (1999) notes that more than 40% of incarcerated women report a history of physical or sexual abuse. Some authors write poems to an abusive lover or describe beatings and other violence at the hands of a parent. One writer describes how she had been molested by her grandfather as a child, and now suspects that he had abused her cousins while she was locked up.

> I have spent the last five years in prison. Why? Because my caretaker chose to abuse me. . . . I will never give up trying to get my life together. I do wish, however, that I had spoken out all those years ago. If I did, I would not be in prison and my abuser would not be walking around jeopardizing other children's lives as we speak.

Despite their emotional suffering, prisoners are encouraged to hold their feelings inside, even when grieving over a death. When a parent or sibling dies, an inmate who can pay for transportation may be granted a fleeting visit to the funeral home, isolated from other family members for a 15-minute viewing of the body, her hands still in cuffs and her feet shackled. If the loved one is not an immediate family member (e.g., only an aunt or grandparent), a grief visit will be denied. Many inmates learn of the deaths of loved ones weeks after they occur, through the mail. In the aftermath, they must hide their pain; one woman was warned by a social worker not to express her sorrow vocally, lest she be isolated from the general population and placed on suicide watch:

> Meaning, you can cry in your room, but if you cry and are too emotional any-where else, you would be put in "lock" or back to maximum security. They are basically saying that you cannot be upset, because everyone will think that something is wrong with you.

Both the "heaven" and "hell" fantasy themes are passionate visions, but a more down-to-earth view appears in the prison newspaper as well. This fantasy theme, which I designate as "here," constructs the prison as a place of extremity where resilient women, finding themselves sorely tested, rise to the challenge of dealing with the present and preparing for the future resourcefully. These narratives offer determined examples of strategic, creative, and sometimes even humorous efforts to resist the prison's mechanisms of emotional and social obliteration. No doubt some of the writers are too emotionally or educationally disadvantaged to act on their own advice, but the fantasy theme of "here" allows the women to envision themselves as competent agents capable of independent thought and action nonetheless.

A number of authors using "here" narratives focus on trying to maintain one's health in the prison setting, where diseases like HIV and hepatitis C are rampant and medical care is hard to get. Although incarcerated women have few resources for dealing with life-threatening infectious diseases or medical conditions, such as diabetes and breast cancer, numerous articles offer basic facts on these ailments and urge readers to stay well-informed. One writer tells inmates what to do when they believe prison authorities are intentionally ignoring their requests for medical care—according to Farmer (2002), this common concern in correctional facilities is well-grounded in evidence:

> Utilize any "administrative remedies" available to you, and keep copies of any letter or complaint that you have written to the medical department, the superintendent, ombudsman, etc. Keep copies of any replies, or note any failure to reply to your complaint. Try to retain more than one set of records, and try to keep one set of records with someone on the outside, for safekeeping, in case yours is "lost."

Another author urges women with HIV to "start a journal and write down your thoughts and questions you may have for your physician or counselor, and take all prescribed medications."

Other writers focus on mental health issues. One woman encourages her fellow inmates to "develop a humor habit" and laugh as often as possible: "Although I can't change my life, I can change my attitude. Laughter, real laughter, is my trick." Another writer urges her fellow inmates to overcome their fears of rejection and keep reaching out to their distant children, even when all they receive by return mail is silence.

> You may have no way of knowing whether or not your child is receiving your correspondence, but if there is any chance that your child is receiving your letters, you must continue to write on a regular basis, even if they never respond. Our children need to know that our devotion to them is unwavering and that our love for them is unconditional.

Prison imposes economic hardship on female inmates and their families. Many inmates were the heads of single-parent households before they were imprisoned and have no other means of support. Yet while incarcerated, they need cash for necessities like personal hygiene products and postage stamps. Some also try to supplement the bland, starchy prison diet with a modest list of food and snack items stocked by the prison commissary. The women must also pay any fines they are liable for, and some try to send money home to their families as well. Therefore, they may work long hours in the prison kitchen, the commissary, or the sewing factory, while others earn small amounts as janitors, office assistants, or health care aides for mentally ill inmates. These jobs pay very little, from about 58 cents an hour to $6 a day; yet some writers see even these minuscule earnings as building blocks that can lead them toward an independent life:

> The money that we receive in this place should be spent very wisely because one day we are leaving this place and who wants to leave here broke? If you can only save $5 a month, that is $60 more dollars (a year) that you can take with you home.

There are not enough jobs to go around, and not all inmates desire to work; some occupy their time by taking classes whenever a rare vacancy opens up. The prison offers classes in high school equivalency subjects, office skills, communication, accounting, and vocational subjects like horticulture, upholstery, and hair styling. Another writer of the "here" theme encourages her peers to

> use the time that we are sentenced to find something you can do to improve yourself. If you can remember the words to your favorite rap, then you can remember to stimulate your brain through education. In return, it will help you to a marketable skill that will help you to prosper in life outside prison.

But waiting lists for the formal classes are long, and state funding only pays for spaces for women under the age of 26. Many women are restless and bored. For some, the newspaper itself offers a diversion, a sense of solidarity with other women, and a place to exercise the intellect. They enjoy the discussions of current events, books, and politics that journalism classes often involve. One woman writes:

> This will really catch your attention because it is an enjoyable skill. It helps us to expand in various areas of life. It is about enlightening other women, helping them to motivate themselves, and giving them a push in a positive direction.

Another thanks the prison superintendent for allowing the women the privilege of publishing a newspaper:

> This paper gives each and every one of us who has a voice a chance to participate. The articles are informative, entertaining and enlightening. Most of the stories come from the heart. We would like to say Thank You for allowing us to do this paper.

Some authors may write comments like these to curry favor with prison officials, but others sincerely appreciate the role of the newspaper in their lives. Their articles encourage others to get benefit from involvement as well.

Finally, a number of articles in the "here" fantasy theme express a cynical or playful attitude that brings humor to a somber place. When a big-city paper sends a reporter to interview some of the women at the Clara Barton prison, an inmate writer sarcastically critiques the melodramatic coverage. She observes that the professional reporter has focused on the depression and despair of the women interviewed, to the exclusion of all else. "The title gives the impression that all women at this facility sit in their living areas and cry, 'Poor me,' 'Why me?' and 'Not me,'" she complains. "What about more attention given to healing, insight, overcoming obstacles, growth, self-discovery, (and) learning?" Another author uses poetry to take ironic aim at a practice that is anything but funny:

Hold your arms in front, handcuffs lock them in.
Spin toward the wall. Does this chain make me look thin?
Hold your right foot up as it's shackled above your boot.
Now hold out the left. Aren't these chains and padlocks cute?
We all fall in line, they're between us with a gun
We're chained, cuffed, shackled—do they really think we'll run?

Whenever incarcerated women write, Scheffler (2002) contends, they affirm their own self-worth and condemn the institution that "attempts to destroy their humanity in the name of justice" (p. xvii). Writing for *Insight* offers inmates a way to create alternative meanings from the experience of prison and to generate a sense of empowerment. The arguments made by these articles affirm the authors' value as human beings.

The fantasy themes identified here are central premises of the prison newspaper. The "heaven" theme portrays the prison as a true penitentiary, an experience that claims good out of evil by transforming the prisoner into a better person. In this view, prison offers troubled women a chance to forsake the behaviors that led to incarceration and claim new ways of being. The fantasy theme of "hell" describes the prison as a place of punishment where the women's social isolation produces acute suffering. This bleak perspective puts special emphasis on the pain of incarcerated women deprived of loving personal relationships and social support. The "here" fantasy theme reveals the prison as a liminal space of extremity where women faced with extraordinary challenges can rise to cope with them. Even if, in reality, the inmates cannot carry out the solutions discussed in these narratives, this viewpoint allows them to see themselves as capable agents in a social setting, ready to act on their own behalf whenever conditions permit.

Conclusion: The Inside Value of Outsider Journalism

As a form of outsider journalism, prison newspapers are a type of alternative medium created by people who are marginalized and despised by society. These publications involve the creation of texts and meaning under conditions of explicit subjugation. As such, they offer a valuable record of prison life as lived and interpreted by those closest to the experience, but also provide important sites of ideological struggle over the meaning and consequence of prison in society. Inmate newspapers construct a public forum that allows incarcerated people to challenge society's definitions of them with oppositional meanings rich in lived experience, self-expression, and group vision.

While prison newspapers enhance our understanding of prison life from the point of view of inmates, their limited accessibility puts them, unfortunately, out of the reach of most outside readers. Not only are these periodicals subject to threats and constraints of every description, but also, in recent years, more existing papers have shut down than new papers have emerged. Even where they survive, prison newspapers are a truly ephemeral form of alternative media. They are not advertised, reviewed, or celebrated; and, with a handful of exceptions, they are not catalogued, preserved, or archived like other texts.

However, the valuable public space created by prison newspapers is treasured by its authors and audiences, and should also be important to scholars of communication and media. Through the outsider journalism of an inmate-created newspaper, incarcerated women construct a rhetorical vision of the institution that shapes their lives. They build community through shared narratives of personal transformation and suffering and share small acts of resistance within a larger context of oppression. The newspapers articulate the spirit of resistance and pragmatic creativity that may enable some women to survive the prison experience with their sense of self more or less intact. By allowing incarcerated people to imagine and construct their own meanings of self and social relations, prison journalism provides a worthy tool of transcendence and transformation.

Notes

[1] In part this may be due to the simple difficulty of obtaining such texts. Contemporary prison publications are not readily available to outside audiences, or catalogued, preserved, or archived like other newspapers or magazines, and surviving historical collections are scattered and incomplete.

[2] Any single textual item submitted for publication by an inmate has been counted here as an "article." This includes texts in conventional narrative or journalistic form as well as other formats such as poetry, recipes, puzzles, cartoons with writing on them, or briefs. Illustrations without textual messages are considered graphics and are too few to analyze; most of the published illustrations were clip-art.

[3] According to the U.S. Department of Justice (2001), approximately 70% of prison inmates perform at the two lowest measurable literacy levels; 11% percent of this group have learning disabilities. Education programs in prisons, especially in women's prisons, are quite limited, often focusing on high school equivalency certification and vocational training. The women working on the inmate newspaper displayed a broad array of literacy abilities, ranging from very elementary levels to college-level fluencies.

[4] The inmate publication uses bylines and identifies the writers by name, but in order to protect the privacy of the women, this article does not use their names. I also omit article headlines, page numbers, dates, or other specific details that might facilitate the identification of a specific writer. The institution and the publication are referred to by pseudonyms.

Acknowledgments

The author gratefully acknowledges that this article was produced with the aid of a Community Action Grant from the American Association of University Women. She thanks her research partner, Dr. Rebecca Sanford of Monmouth University. An earlier version of this paper was presented at the Association for Education in Journalism and Mass Communication conference in Toronto in August 2004.

References

Bormann, E. G. (1977). Fetching good out of evil: A rhetorical use of calamity. *Quarterly Journal of Speech, 65,* 130–139.

Bormann, E. G. (1982). The symbolic convergence theory of communication: Applications and implications for teachers and consultants. *Journal of Applied Communication Research, 10,* 50–61.

Conquergood, D. (1995). Between rigor and relevance: Rethinking applied communication. In K. Cissna (Ed.), *Applied communication in the 21st century* (pp. 79–96). Mahwah, NJ: Erlbaum.

Conquergood, D. (2002). Lethal theatre: Performance, punishment, and the death penalty. *Theatre Journal, 54,* 339–367.

Davies, I. (1990). *Writers in prison.* Toronto: Between the Lines.

Dowd, S. (1996). *This prison where I live: The PEN anthology of imprisoned writers.* London: Cassell.

Farmer, P. (2002). The house of the dead: Tuberculosis and incarceration. In M. Mauer & M. Chesney-Lind (Eds.), *Invisible punishment: The collateral consequences of mass imprisonment* (pp. 239–257). New York: The New Press.

Fiske, J. (1989). *Reading the popular.* Cambridge, MA: Unwin Hyman, Inc.

Fiske, J. (1993). *Power plays, power works.* London: Verso.

Foucault, M. (1979). *Discipline and punish: The birth of the prison* (A. Sheridan, Trans.). New York: Vintage Books.

Franklin, H. B. (1998). Introduction. In H. B. Franklin (Ed.), *Prison writing in 20th century America* (pp. 1–18). New York: Penguin Books.

Freire, P. (1980). *The pedagogy of the oppressed.* New York: Continuum Publishing.

Gaucher, B. (1999). Inside looking out: Writers in prison. *The Journal of Prisoners on Prisons, 10,* 14–31.

Gaucher, B. (2002). *The Journal of Prisoners on Prisons:* An ethnography of the prison industrial complex in the 1990s. In B. Gaucher (Ed.), *Writing as resistance:* The Journal of Prisoners on Prisons *Anthology (1988–2002)* (pp. 5–30). Toronto: Canadian Scholars' Press, Inc.

Girshick, L. B. (1999). *No safe haven: Stories of women in prison.* Boston, MA: Northeastern University Press.

Goffman, E. (1961). *Asylums: Essays on the social situation of mental patients and other inmates.* Chicago: Aldine Publishing Co.

Hamilton, J. (1993). Educating patriots, recruiting radicals: The migrant camp newspaper at Arvin, California. *Communication, 13,* 255–275.

Hamilton, J. (1997). Migrant space, migrant community: Williams, Bakhtin, and cultural analysis. *Communication Review, 2,* 381–418.

Harrison, P., & Beck, A. (2003, July). Prisoners in 2002. *Bureau of Justice Statistics Bulletin.* U.S. Department of Justice, Office of Justice Programs. Retrieved February 12, 2004, from http://www.ojp.usdoj.gov/bjs/pub/pdf/p02.pdf

Hartnett S. (1998). Lincoln and Douglas meet the abolitionist David Walker as prisoners debate slavery: Empowering education, applied communication, and social justice. *Journal of Applied Communication Research, 26*(2), 232–253.

Howley, K. (2003). A poverty of voices: Street papers as communicative democracy. *Journalism, 4,* 273–292.

Human Rights Watch. (1996, December). *All too familiar: Sexual abuse of women in U.S. state prisons.* New York: Human Rights Watch. Retrieved June 6, 2002, from http://www.hrw.org/summaries/s.us96d.html

Lamb, W., & the Women of York Correctional Institution (2003). *Couldn't keep it to myself: Testimonies from our imprisoned sisters.* New York: HarperCollins.

Lewes, J. (2001). Envisioning resistance: The GI underground press during the Vietnam War. *Media History, 7,* 137–150.

Long, T. L. (2000). Plague of pariahs: AIDS 'zines and the rhetoric of transgression. *Journal of Communication Inquiry, 24,* 401–411.

Maguire, K., & Pastore, A. (Eds.). (2002). *Sourcebook of criminal justice statistics* [Online]. Retrieved February 12, 2004, from http://www.albany.edu/sourcebook/

McMaster, G. (1999). Maximum ink. *Journal of Prisoners on Prisons, 10,* 46–52.

Morris, J. M. (2002). *Jailhouse journalism. The Fourth Estate behind bars.* New Brunswick, NJ: Transaction Publishers.

Novek, E. (1995). Buried treasure: The community newspaper as an empowerment strategy for African American high school students. *Howard Journal of Communications, 6,* 69–88.

Novek, E. (2005). "The devil's bargain": Censorship, identity and the promise of empowerment in a prison newspaper. *Journalism, 6,* 5–23.

Ritchie, B. (2002). The social impact of mass incarceration on women. In M. Mauer & M. Chesney-Lind (Eds.), *Invisible punishment: The collateral consequences of mass imprisonment* (pp. 136–149). New York: The New Press.

Scheffler, J. A. (2002). Preface. In J. A. Scheffler (Ed.), *Wall tappings: An international anthology of women's prison writings, 2000 A.D. to the present* (pp. xxi–xliv). New York: The Feminist Press at the City University of New York.

Sentencing Project, The. (2003). *U.S. prison populations: Trends and implications.* Retrieved February 12, 2004, from http://www.sentencingproject.org/pdfs/1044.pdf

Singer, S. (2004). Eight inmates in Connecticut prison agree to pay state portion of book royalties. *Associated Press State and Local Wire.* April 19, 2004, BC cycle. Available online from Lexis-Nexis Academic Universe.

Sneed, D., & Stonecipher, H. (1986). More freedom for the prison press: An emerging First Amendment issue. *The Journalism Quarterly, 63,* 48–54.

Steiner, L. (1983). Finding community in nineteenth century suffrage periodicals. *American Journalism, 1,* 1–15.

Steiner, L. (1992). The history and structure of women's alternative media. In L. Rakow (Ed.), *Women making meaning: New feminist directions in communication* (pp. 121–143). New York: Routledge.

Stone, J. (2002). Using symbolic convergence theory to discern and segment motives for enrolling in professional master's degree programs. *Communication Quarterly, 50,* 227–240.

Streitmatter, R. (1995). Creating a venue for the "love that dare not speak its name": Origins of the gay and lesbian press. *Journalism and Mass Communication Quarterly, 72,* 436–447.

Timmons, K. M. (1995, Summer). Natural born writers: The law's continued annoyance with criminal authors. *29 Georgia Law Review* 1121, pp. 1121–1169. Available online from Lexis-Nexis Academic Universe.

Torck, D. (2001). Voices of homeless people in street newspapers: A cross-cultural exploration. *Discourse and Society, 12,* 371–392.

U.S. Department of Justice (2003). Summary findings. *Bureau of Justice Statistics.* Retrieved February 12, 2004, from http://www.ojp.usdoj.gov/bjs/correct.htm

U.S. Department of Justice (2001). Summary findings. *Bureau of Justice Statistics.* Retrieved June 6, 2002, from http://www.ojp.usdoj.gov/bjs/correct.htm

Valentine, K. (1998, Fall). "If the guards only knew": Communication education for women in prison. *Women's Studies in Communication, 21*(2), 238–243.

Coping with Loss
U2's "One Tree Hill"

Kelly Mendoza

On July 3, 1986, a drunk driver killed Greg Carroll, roadie and assistant to U2, in an accident in Dublin, Ireland. Bono, the singer of U2, was devastated by Carroll's sudden death. On July 10, he spoke and sang at Carroll's funeral in Wanganui, New Zealand, and two days later wrote lyrics to "One Tree Hill" in honor of his friend Carroll. The song, a response to the extremely painful experience of grieving and loss, suggests strategies that individuals may use to cope with the mysterious and difficult subject of death. In this essay, I analyze "One Tree Hill" to explore the strategies a rhetor uses to cope emotionally with the loss of sudden death.

"One Tree Hill" is on U2's *The Joshua Tree* album, released in 1987. The lyrics to the song appear to be written for a funeral because noted under the lyrics on the album insert are the words, "Greg Carroll's Funeral, Wanganui, New Zealand, 10th July 1986" (although the lyrics actually were written *after* Carroll's funeral). On the last page of the album insert is the text, "To the Memory of Greg Carroll 1960–1986." The song "One Tree Hill" refers to the highest of the volcanic hills that overlook Aukland, New Zealand, and Bono apparently knew this place was very special to Carroll. The song itself is neither extremely slow nor sad; in fact, it has an upbeat melody (unlike many songs that deal with death and dying). Bono sings the song in a loud and strong voice.

The critical method I use to explore "One Tree Hill" is fantasy-theme criticism, developed by Ernest G. Bormann to investigate a shared worldview among a group of individuals. There are two units of analysis in fantasy-theme criticism. The first is the fantasy theme, an interpretation through communication that is organized and artistic and assumes the form of settings, characters, and actions. The second unit of fantasy-theme criticism is the rhetorical vision, the grouping together of several shared fantasy themes to create a worldview.

Rhetorical Vision

Identification of the character, action, and setting themes of "One Tree Hill" reveals two primary categories of fantasy themes in the song. One set involves violence and the other nonviolence. Below are the individual fantasy themes in each of these categories:

Violence

The fantasy themes connected to violence are as follows:

Characters	Actions	Settings
day	begs	
(your) sun	leaves no shadows	
scars	carved into stone	face of earth
(our) world		firezone, heart of darkness
poets	speak their hearts	
poets	bleed for (speaking)	

This essay was written while Kelly Mendoza was a student in Sonja K. Foss's rhetorical criticism class at the University of Colorado Denver in 2000. Used by permission of the author.

Characters	Actions	Settings
Jara	sang his song	hands of love
(Jara's) blood	still cries	ground
bullets	rape the night	
stars	fall	

In the category of fantasy themes concerned with violence, non-human characters (*day, sun, scars, world, blood, bullets,* and *stars*) perform somewhat violent actions, such as *begs for mercy, leaves no shadows, carved, cries, rape,* and *fall.* The *bullets* perform the most extreme and sudden violence—the act of *rape.* These actions reveal a nature that is unpredictable and unforgiving. In contrast, whenever human characters (*poets* and *Jara*) speak or sing, they get hurt—both of them *bleed.*

Raging heat exists in the war zone of nature. For example, the *sun* is so *bright* that it seems to scorch the earth, the *sun leaves no shadows,* and the *day begs the night for mercy.* The *firezone* setting describes a fiery war zone because when poets speak here, their *hearts bleed.* After *Jara sang his song* (his *weapon*), his *blood cried* from the *ground.* This category illustrates a hot and dry desert of nature's violent and war-like elements and bloodshed that exists only on earth. Humans, however, have no violent influence here.

Nonviolence

The fantasy themes connected to nonviolence are as follows:

Characters	Actions	Settings
we	turn away to face	cold, enduring chill
moon	is up and over	One Tree Hill
we	see the sun go down	your eyes
you	ran like a river	sea
you	know	
it	runs like a river	sea
	(runs) like a river	sea
I	don't believe	red
moon	has turned red	One Tree Hill
we	run like a river	sea
	(run) like a river	sea

The category of nonviolence is submissive and calm. The human characters (*I, we,* and *you*) do not perform violent actions or even try to fight against the violence of nature but *run, turn away,* or *see* the violence nature performs. The moon character acts with the same passivity as the human characters because it goes *up and over* and *has turned.* Because the *moon* looks over earth and is separate from earth, it is not a part of earth's violent nature. The *moon,* like human characters, observes the violence going on and, unlike the *sun,* it cannot *carve scars* onto the *face of earth.*

In contrast to the heat and war featured in the category of violence, the prevailing image of the category of nonviolence is coolness and calmness. The actions that the humans and the moon perform in this category are passive. To add to the calmness of the actions, the water of the *river* and the *sea* are a part of this category. In these waters exist a coolness and a flowing that are in extreme contrast to the dry heat of nature's *firezone.* The coolness *runs like a river* to the wide body of calmness—the *sea.*

The setting of one tree on a hill represents the only part of the violent earth that is passive, barren, neutral, and safe. The *moon* performs its actions only around One

Tree Hill, suggesting that this place is calm and cool. Perhaps the one tree is a metaphor for a person (possibly Carroll) on the hill, and this is the only place on earth that is not violent where a person can stand (but must stand alone in death).

The two different patterns created by the fantasy themes in the song—violence and nonviolence—create an overall rhetorical vision. Bono's rhetorical vision or worldview is that humans ultimately find some sort of balance, comfort, understanding, and commonality (*we run like a river to the sea*) in the face of a violent, unfair, and unpredictable nature that kills. This vision also suggests that humans should not try to fight against the extreme forces of nature but accept them with passivity.

Because of the circumstances of Carroll's accident—he was hit by a drunk driver—one might expect Bono's rhetorical vision to blame drunk drivers and the careless actions of human beings. Instead, Bono associates death with the harshness and unpredictability of nature. The rhetorical vision of the song is antithetical to a stereotypical blaming of humans for causing tragic events. The rhetor surrenders to and accepts the force of nature's laws as an explanation for his friend's death.

A fantasy-theme analysis of Bono's lyrics in "One Tree Hill" suggests rhetorical strategies that are available to any individual who seeks to cope with the death of a loved one. The construction of a world in which elements of nature (over which humans have no control) are given agency for death removes the blame and guilt many humans feel regarding a loved one's death. By removing the agency from human actions, mourners may find comfort in the fact that they cannot prevent death. The violent picture created in this song suggests a relentless war, with death seeming to provide a relief from the heat, fire, and violence. These dramatic images encourage mourners to let go of a loved one in an act of relief. Another strategy for coping with the loss of death is the depiction of the human actions in the song. Humans are shown as passive and accepting, viewing death as a natural process that requires no opposing action. Typical responses to death of resistance and rage are not presented as useful options because they serve only to perpetuate the violence that death involves. Bono recommends instead a peaceful acquiescence to a very normal event.

One Tree Hill

Bono and U2

We turn away to face the cold, enduring chill
As the day begs the night for mercy
Your sun so bright it leaves no shadows, only scars
Carved into stone on the face of earth
The moon is up and over One Tree Hill
We see the sun go down in your eyes
You ran like a river to the sea
Like a river to the sea
And in our world a heart of darkness, a firezone
Where poets speak their hearts, then bleed for it
Jara sang his song a weapon, in the hands of love
You know his blood still cries from the ground
It runs like a river to the sea
Like a river to the sea
I don't believe in painted roses or bleeding hearts
While bullets rape the night of the merciful
I'll see you again when the stars fall from the sky
And the moon has turned red over One Tree Hill
We run like a river to the sea
Like a river to the sea

Lyrics downloaded November 25, 2003, from
http://www.atu2.com/lyrics/songinfo.src?SID=297

The Sociopolitical Messages of Graffiti Art

Kimberly A. McCormick and David Weiss

Public art, graffiti included, is a raw yet emotional demonstration of worldviews. Although graffiti artists frequently are viewed as anti-establishment, their art, paradoxically, can represent established or mainstream views. Often, as McCormick (2002) noted, graffiti artists express dominant values, such as life-affirming or religious ideals, through icons that offer a multitude of interpretations. Frequently, however, these expressions are not analyzed for their implicit messages; the illegal form or placement of the art becomes the focus for many viewers rather than the societally compatible content of its message. As a result, graffiti tends to be assessed primarily as a rebellious, vandalistic, selfish expression of territoriality (e.g., Gomez, 1993; Grant, 1996); an expression of frustration or resistance (e.g., Boland & Hoffman, 1983; Bruner & Kelso, 1980); or the expression of negative components of identity (e.g., Bowen, 1999; Grant, 1996).

Our goal in this essay is to investigate the means by which a subversive art form can articulate socially acceptable views of controversial issues. We believe that graffiti can serve positive societal functions, such as constructing ideal visions of society, affirming the identities of viewers, offering perspectives on social issues, and facilitating pride in viewers. We seek to discover the rhetorical means by which graffiti can be interpreted positively in such ways by viewers.

To discover how a subversive art form can articulate socially acceptable views of controversial issues, we explicate the rhetorical vision of a subversive culture by uncovering the characteristics of a work of art: an outdoor graffiti-style mural. The mural is spray painted on a 100-foot-long, five-foot-high privacy wall of cinder block that forms the western perimeter of the parking lot of a Planned Parenthood clinic in a lower income commercial area of Albuquerque, New Mexico. The clinic serves as the northern boundary of the lot and the far right end of the mural. The wall, parking lot, and clinic are located directly off busy, gritty San Mateo Boulevard, clearly visible to passing cars and pedestrians. Visitors to the clinic have no choice but to see the wall. While not technically "graffiti" in that Planned Parenthood commissioned the art, the person who painted the mural, "Sug," is a local Albuquerque artist best known for his illegal graffiti art. The mural contains a number of standard elements of the graffiti genre: the use of spray paint, the primacy and style of the artist's signature, bold outlining of words and letters, the contrasting size of words within set phrases, the anthropomorphizing of animal figures, and the splitting of quotations into separate word strings.

Because the wall is so much longer than it is high, there is an inescapable horizontality to the mural. An observer's eye moves from left to right across the wall rather than up and down. Further, because the Planned Parenthood clinic is adjacent to the right end of the wall (at the mural's "conclusion" rather than at its "beginning"), an observer—particularly a client of Planned Parenthood—may experience the mural as a comment on the clinic, a preparation for a visit, or a post-visit endorsement of the clinic's functions and philosophies.

This essay was written while Kimberly A. McCormick and David Weiss were students in Karen A. Foss's rhetorical criticism class at the University of New Mexico in 2002. Used by permission of the authors.

We describe the elements of the artifact from left to right. The mural's first element is a piece (the graffiti term for *masterpiece*), a stylized signature, in which the artist has rendered his alias, *SUG*, in bold sky-blue illegible letters. A stone-gray background shaped like a hill that spans the height of the wall is visible behind the piece. A ribbon of royal blue water extends to the right from the hill across the length of the mural, serving as a literal link visually connecting the mural's disparate foreground elements.

To the right of the hill is a small symbol painted in black. The symbol, shaped like a mirror image of the letters *OK,* is the Chinese character *hé,* which means peace. To its right, a saguaro cactus extends from the base of the wall to its top. Sitting in the "elbow" of the saguaro's left "arm" is a small gray bird with an open beak. The river flows to the right across the earth, past the cactus and a buzzard wearing a brown short-sleeved garment with beige stripes. Extending from its arms and from behind its head are feathers in the style of a Native American headdress.

The river flows behind the buzzard into a gray mountain strewn with watermelons. A second river runs below it, coursing into the next visual element, the word *FIRST,* rendered in bold capitals. Beneath it is the word *AMENDMENT* in plain black uppercase letters. From the right of *FIRST,* the river flows into a second cactus hosting a bird. This cactus resembles a prickly-pear bush, and the bird is large and brown with powerful-looking wings. Three more watermelons sit on the mountainside to the right of the cactus and bird.

Leaning against the side of the mountain is the next figure. Unlike the birds and cacti, which are painted in bold colors and convey three dimensionality, this next figure is flat and black, like a cut-out paper doll. It is Kokopelli, the legendary Hopi character who appears in petroglyphs throughout the Southwest. As is the case with most renditions of Kokopelli, this one is holding a flute to his mouth. Unlike most, however, this one has the word *TOLERANCE* flowing on a pennant from the flute.

To the right of *TOLERANCE* is the sloping edge of the next mountain. Superimposed over this mountain's face is another creature: a gray-green dragon. It is mostly torso and head, the latter little more than a long snout open to reveal sharp white teeth. Its pointy, blood-red tongue protrudes menacingly from its mouth. A flame shoots out from the creature's right ear, while other flames descend from the open snout and flicker around the dragon's head. A red apple sits on the mountain to the right of the dragon's claw. It is partially obscured by another blue-and-gray *FIRST* below a plain black *AMENDMENT.* The upper river flows behind *FIRST,* then re-emerges near a group of apples and from there into the next figure: a dark-brown-skinned woman wearing a red, yellow, green, and black turban.

In an angle formed by the edge of the river and the slope of the mountain is another section of text: *ONE'S PHILOSOPHY, ONE'S EXPERIENCES, ONE'S EXPOSURE TO THE RAW EDGES OF HUMAN EXISTENCE.* . . . . An arrow at the end of the text points to a large stylized sun drawn in the manner of the Zia symbol, in yellow with black outlines. This Zia is a circle from which four "wings"—curved like the blades of a fan—radiate. The river flows under the Zia, then re-emerges as three separate, parallel tributaries. Between the upper and middle branches is a continuation of the earlier text: *ONE'S RELIGIOUS TRAINING, ONE'S ATTITUDE TOWARD LIFE AND FAMILY AND THEIR VALUES, AND THE.* Beneath the middle branch, the text continues: *MORAL STANDARDS ONE ESTABLISHES AND SEEKS TO.* Finally, below the lower branch, the text concludes with *OBSERVE ARE LIKELY TO COLOR ONE'S THINKING AND CONCLUSIONS.* . . . *—JUSTICE BLACKMUN.*

Fantasy Themes

To illuminate the rhetorical vision characterized by the mural, we use the fantasy-theme method of criticism. Fantasy-theme analysis, derived from Bormann's (1972) symbolic convergence theory, applies the central metaphor of drama to examine an artifact in terms of its settings, characters, and actions. Although characters are the most evident thematic components of the mural, we first describe its settings to provide the context for the characters and the actions they perform.

Settings

While the actions presented in the mural take place in a literal (that is, geographical) setting—New Mexico—the settings that more effectively establish the rhetorical vision are temporal: past, present, and future. The mural, however, is not a triptych; there are not clear visual divisions of past, present, and future. Further, visual movement from left to right does not necessarily correlate with the passage of time. Rather, elements of the three temporal settings are strewn throughout the work, suggesting a blurring of time boundaries or perhaps a spatio-temporal location that simultaneously comprises components of different eras.

Helping the viewer sort out this pastiche is the river. Its blue horizontal bands move continuously rightward, touching or approaching nearly every discrete element of the mural and providing a visual link across time. As it moves from left to right, it variously connects with or nears "past" components (Kokopelli, the words *FIRST AMENDMENT*, the traditionally dressed buzzard, the dragon, the dark-skinned woman); "present" or timeless components (mountains, cacti, watermelons, apples, the gray and brown birds, the Zia sun); and "future" components (the dragon, which represents past as well as future, and the word *TOLERANCE*). The elements connected by the river, however, are not arranged linearly from left to right to suggest an orderly chronology from past to present.

Characters

As described above, the mural contains a multiplicity of visual and lexical characters. We see these components not as an army of characters but as traits of two primary character themes—New Mexico and the Director.

A variety of traits, which can be classified as geographical, botanical, zoological, spiritual, and cultural, represent the character of New Mexico. The geographical elements are the mountains, river, and desert-region earth tones. The presence of watermelons and apples on the mountains locate them specifically in the Albuquerque region because *watermelon* in Spanish is *sandia* and *apple* is *manzano*; the Sandias and the Manzanos are the two mountain ranges forming Albuquerque's eastern boundary. The Manzano Mountains were named for the apple orchards located in their foothills, while the Sandia range was named for the mountains' watermelon-like color at sunset. Because the mountains note the location as Albuquerque, the river running through the mural is the Rio Grande. Light brown, the dominant New Mexican earth tone, represents the region's desert landscape. Botanical elements of New Mexico include cacti and the apples, and indigenous birds—a buzzard, a roadrunner, and a hawk—reference the zoological traits of New Mexico.

There are two spiritual aspects of New Mexico in the mural. The first is the Zia sun, an ancient symbol of universal harmony that was originated by New Mexico's indigenous Zia Pueblo Indians; it is now the sole visual element of the state flag. The second spiritual figure is Kokopelli, an early Hopi symbol of fertility, harmony, and peace.

Finally, the cultural elements of the mural represent New Mexico's diversity, both historical and idealized. The artist's signature piece, *SUG*, alludes to his urban, graffiti-art subculture. The Chinese character *hé* represents not only peace and harmony but also New Mexico's Asian peoples. The buzzard's blanket and decorative feathers symbolize the Mexican and Native American cultures central to New Mexico's history. The dark-skinned woman and her red, yellow, green, and black turban reference New Mexico's early African heritage.

The second character theme is the Director of the drama, giving instructions to New Mexico. Viewers do not actually see the Director. Rather, they infer his or her "off-stage" presence from the visual manifestation of four elements, one visual and three lexical. The presence of the dragon makes visible the Director's warning to New Mexico about the ever-present danger to the state posed by nuclear war. The reference here is to the scientists who worked on the Manhattan Project in Los Alamos in the 1940s, who referred to the process of armoring the first atomic bomb as "tickling the dragon's tail." But the presence of atomic energy in New Mexico can be found even closer to the mural's site than Los Alamos; sizable portions of America's nuclear stockpile were stored beneath the Manzano Mountains from 1952 to 1992. The "music" emanating from Kokopelli's flute literally illustrates the Director's demand for tolerance. The prominence and repetition of the words *FIRST AMENDMENT* evidence the value the Director places on American freedoms. Finally, the Director imposes his or her philosophy on New Mexico through the excerpt from Justice Harry Blackmun's *Roe v. Wade* opinion.

Actions

New Mexico's action themes are primarily narrative. As if painting a visual autobiography, New Mexico discloses its history and describes its present. The disclosure of history is accomplished through the symbolic portrayal of the various cultures that have contributed to the region. Mexico is recalled by the buzzard's clothing. The Zia sun, the fluting Kokopelli, and the buzzard's decorative feathers represent indigenous Native nations. The black woman's presence affirms the part Africans and African Americans played in the state's very early history. New Mexico hails its present primarily through its presentation of the natural world. Mountains, cacti, birds, and the river, while obviously also part of the state's past, are still very much a part of its present.

Although perhaps redundant, the Director's role is precisely that: to direct the other character in the drama. To a limited degree, the Director points out to New Mexico the glories and tragedies of its past and sets standards of behavior for its present. But this character's more important action is forecasting and guiding, creating or modeling a vision of the future for New Mexico. The Director cautions New Mexico about the evil lurking within its own borders, the danger of nuclear proliferation. This brings to the forefront of New Mexico's consciousness the destruction wrought in its own past as well as an ongoing threat. The menacing dragon gives visual form to the voice of contemporary anti-nuclear discourse and also predicts what the future might tragically hold should nothing be done to change the current course of events.

The Director orchestrates Kokopelli's "music," the piping of the word *TOLER-ANCE*. This is a condition not yet achieved (and therefore neither a past nor present reality) but potentially achievable in the future. Finally, the Director provides a guiding philosophy for New Mexico through the recitation of the excerpt from Blackmun's *Roe v. Wade* opinion. This action has ramifications for past, present, and future. The decision was written in the 1970s; is still part of present U.S. law, albeit tenuously; and, ideally, represents a standard that can be upheld in the future.

Rhetorical Vision

The fantasy themes in the mural establish a rhetorical vision of a sociopolitical utopia. The utopian worldview is motivated by a need to eradicate ignorance, which is manifested by intolerance, the flouting of First Amendment principles, a lack of appreciation for history, complacency in the face of ever-present nuclear danger, and a lack of respect for basic human rights. In the rhetorical vision, the setting themes and action themes support the dominant, although not overwhelming, character themes. Within the temporal setting, past and present serve as an important prologue to the future, the temporal "location" of the utopian vision's realization. Within the character and action themes, New Mexico establishes history and context, while the Director articulates prescriptions for the future.

The artist of the mural illustrates New Mexico's past and present through the repeated inclusion of established features of the state: its landscape, flora and fauna, indigenous cultures, and spiritual symbols. By using these familiar elements, the rhetor allows the participants in the rhetorical vision to situate themselves in a current place and time upon first approaching the artifact. These temporal and geographic benchmarks serve as a necessary foundation for the yet-to-be established sociopolitical utopia. The visual references to *sandias* (watermelons) and *manzanos* (apples) even can be seen as an inside joke by those New Mexicans and other Spanish speakers who recognize the visual pun as an allusion to the names of the local mountain ranges. The images of Kokopelli and Zia, long-revered Native American symbols, similarly call out to present-day members of local Native cultures as well as to members of those cultures who have arrived more recently in New Mexico. Even New Mexican population groups as numerically underrepresented as African Americans and Asian Americans are included in the rhetorical vision, thanks to the presence of the turbaned woman and the Chinese *hé* symbol. The blue stream gives life and movement to all aspects of the mural, just as the Rio Grande has given life and movement to all of New Mexico's cultures and, should it be allowed to survive, would be a critical element of a New Mexican utopian future.

The rhetor locates the Director peripherally in the past and present and centrally in the future. With the dragon, the Director addresses controversial aspects of New Mexico's nuclear past—specifically the Manhattan Project—as well as current concerns about the state's reliance on the nuclear energy industry, as epitomized by Los Alamos and Sandia National Laboratories. The dragon is clearly a threatening manifestation. In addition to breathing fire, it has a deformed, grotesque body, sharp teeth, and a protruding red tongue. While "tickling the dragon" may have been a tongue-in-cheek allusion to tampering with nuclear weapons in the 1940s, the dragon's present and future roles in the rhetorical vision articulated by the Director are anything but humorous.

For the most part, however, the Director's contributions to the present and future aspects of the rhetorical vision are positive. Through the Director, the mural telegraphs the rhetorical vision's valuation of core American freedoms with the words *FIRST AMENDMENT.* With only two boldly painted words, the rhetor reminds view-

Mural by Sug at Planned Parenthood clinic, Albuquerque, New Mexico, 2002. Photograph by David Weiss.

ers of their rights in a multiplicity of domains: religion, speech, the press, peaceable assembly, and protest. The words *FIRST AMENDMENT,* however, are not a mere reminder of the role these rights have played in the collective past. They are also a call to action, an announcement of the need to foreground First Amendment rights in the present and—perhaps even more important—to establish the future sociopolitical utopia upon the principles embodied by the Amendment.

With *TOLERANCE,* the Director links all three of the temporal settings of the rhetorical worldview. Tolerance is another foundational element of the utopian future; surely, the rhetor is not claiming that tolerance has been practiced in the past or is an actual lived ideal of the present. Yet, by having the word *TOLERANCE* emanate from the flute of Kokopelli, perhaps the most omnipresent symbol of this region's ancient past, the Director is able to suggest that tolerance is or should be a timeless New Mexican value.

The excerpt from Justice Blackmun's *Roe v. Wade* opinion also links the three temporal settings but does so in a way that subtly spells out tensions between present reality and the vision of a utopian future. The section of the Blackmun text included in the mural concerning one's philosophy and experiences ends with an ellipsis. The actual Blackmun quotation, however, ends with the words *about abortion,* which are omitted from the mural's text. The incomplete Blackmun sentence on the mural wall and the Planned Parenthood abortion clinic located immediately adjacent to the wall serve as an enthymeme: members of the rhetorical community must mentally fill in the blanks, supplying the words that are only hinted at by the ellipsis.

By including almost all of a key passage from the *Roe v. Wade* decision and purposely omitting the two words that encapsulate the nature of that decision—it was about abortion, after all—the Director and rhetor underscore the critical difference between the temporal settings of present and future articulated in the rhetorical vision.

In the present, the word *abortion* and the phrase *right to abortion* are highly politicized and inevitably polarizing. They are often omitted from contemporary discourse, euphemized or obliquely referred to as *choice, reproductive freedom,* or *control over one's fertility.* Consequently, the ellipsis at the end of the Blackmun quotation signals the present setting of the mural's rhetorical vision, a time during which certain bold truths cannot be safely uttered. In the rhetorical vision's future, however, to rely on enthymeme will not be necessary. In the sociopolitical utopia of the rhetorical worldview, a time and place in which tolerance and respect for First Amendment rights are foundational, there will be safety to make such bold statements directly and completely.

Conclusion

The graffiti artist's worldview, often inaccurately characterized by society as subversive, actually may converge with the values and motives of the dominant culture. The revulsion much of society claims to have for graffiti art may stem from the inability to recognize that the art can reflect rather than contradict society's own worldviews. Hence, graffiti art can articulate socially acceptable views of sociopolitically controversial issues, such as tolerance for diversity, demand for universal freedoms, recognition of past and possible future mistakes, diligence in protecting lands and peoples, and a command for the freedom and respect to make choices about our lives in much the same way as expressions offered by any other artist or thoughtful individual: by describing and prescribing what the world would look like if we could grasp and enact all of these ideals.

Different elements motivate characters to perform actions within a drama. Beauty, religion, family, money, love, hatred, and myriad other ideas and emotions motivate people. However, the prospect of a perfect place, ideal in its social, political, and moral aspects—a utopia—can motivate even the most skeptical, subjugated, cynical, disconfirmed individuals. The ideologies of those who normally do not have a voice or whose voices are not often recognized—voices included in the mural—may be the voices necessary to create such a utopia.

References

Bales, R. (1970). *Personality and interpersonal behavior.* New York: Rinehart and Winston.

Boland, R., & Hoffman, R. (1983). Humor in a machine shop: An interpretation of symbolic action. In L. Pondy, P. Frost, G. Morgan, & T. Dandridge (Eds.), *Organizational symbolism* (pp. 187–198). Greenwich, CT: JAI.

Bormann, E. (1972). Fantasy and rhetorical vision: The rhetorical criticism of social reality. *Quarterly Journal of Speech, 58,* 396–407.

Bowen, T. E. (1999). Graffiti art: A contemporary study of Toronto artists. *Studies in Art Education, 41,* 22–40.

Bruner, E., & Kelso, J. (1980). Gender differences in graffiti: A semiotic perspective. *Women's Studies International Quarterly, 3,* 239–252.

Gomez, M. (1993). The writing on our walls: Finding solutions through distinguishing graffiti art from graffiti vandalism. *University of Michigan Journal of Law Reform, 26,* 633–707.

Grant, C. (1996). Graffiti: Taking a closer look. *FBI Law Enforcement Bulletin, 65,* 11–15.

McCormick, K. (2002, June). *A content analysis of graffiti in Albuquerque.* Paper presented at the annual meeting of the Hawaii International Conference on Social Sciences, Honolulu, HI.

Rodriguez, A., & Clair, R. (1999). Graffiti as communication: Exploring the discursive tensions of anonymous texts. *Southern Communication Journal, 65,* 1–15.

Additional Samples of Fantasy-Theme Criticism

Benoit, William L., Andrew A. Klyukovski, John P. McHale, and David Airne. "A Fantasy Theme Analysis of Political Cartoons on the Clinton-Lewinsky-Starr Affair." *Critical Studies in Media Communication*, 18 (December 2001), 377–94.

Bishop, Ronald. "The World's Nicest Grown-Up: A Fantasy Theme Analysis of News Media Coverage of Fred Rogers." *Journal of Communication*, 53 (March 2003), 16–31.

Bormann, Ernest G. "A Fantasy Theme Analysis of the Television Coverage of the Hostage Release and the Reagan Inaugural." *Quarterly Journal of Speech*, 68 (May 1982), 133–45.

Bormann, Ernest G. "Fetching Good Out of Evil: A Rhetorical Use of Calamity." *Quarterly Journal of Speech*, 63 (April 1977), 130–39.

Bormann, Ernest G. "The Eagleton Affair: A Fantasy Theme Analysis." *Quarterly Journal of Speech*, 59 (April 1973), 143–59.

Bormann, Ernest G. *The Force of Fantasy: Restoring the American Dream*. Carbondale: Southern Illinois University Press, 1985.

Brown, William R. "The Prime-Time Television Environment and Emerging Rhetorical Visions." *Quarterly Journal of Speech*, 62 (December 1976), 389–99.

Cragan, John F. "Rhetorical Strategy: A Dramatistic Interpretation and Application." *Central States Speech Journal*, 26 (Spring 1975), 4–11.

Cragan, John F., and Donald C. Shields. *Applied Communication Research: A Dramatistic Approach*. Long Grove, IL: Waveland, 1981, several essays.

Doyle, Marsha Vanderford. "The Rhetoric of Romance: A Fantasy Theme Analysis of Barbara Cartland Novels." *Southern Speech Communication Journal*, 51 (Fall 1985), 24–48.

Duffy, Margaret. "High Stakes: A Fantasy Theme Analysis of the Selling of Riverboat Gambling in Iowa." *Southern Communication Journal*, 62 (Winter 1997), 117–32.

Edwards, Janis L., and Huey-Rong, Chen. "The First Lady/First Wife in Editorial Cartoons: Rhetorical Visions Through Gendered Lenses." *Women's Studies in Communication*, 23 (Fall 2000), 367–91.

Endres, Thomas G. "Rhetorical Visions of Unmarried Mothers." *Communication Quarterly*, 37 (Spring 1989), 134–50.

Ford, Leigh Arden. "Fetching Good Out of Evil in AA: A Bormannean Fantasy Theme Analysis of *The Big Book* of Alcoholics Anonymous." *Communication Quarterly*, 37 (Winter 1989), 1–15.

Foss, Karen A., and Stephen W. Littlejohn. "*The Day After*: Rhetorical Vision in an Ironic Frame." *Critical Studies in Mass Communication*, 3 (September 1986), 317–36.

Foss, Sonja K. "Equal Rights Amendment Controversy: Two Worlds in Conflict." *Quarterly Journal of Speech*, 65 (October 1979), 275–88.

Garner, Ana, Helen M. Sterk, and Shawn Adams. "Narrative Analysis of Sexual Etiquette in Teenage Magazines." *Journal of Communication*, 48 (Autumn 1998), 59–78.

Glaser, Susan R., and David A. Frank. "Rhetorical Criticism of Interpersonal Discourse: An Exploratory Study." *Communication Quarterly*, 30 (Fall 1982), 353–58.

Haskins, William A. "Rhetorical Vision of Equality: Analysis of the Rhetoric of the Southern Black Press During Reconstruction." *Communication Quarterly*, 29 (Spring 1981), 116–22.

Hensley, Carl Wayne. "Rhetorical Vision and the Persuasion of a Historical Movement: The Disciples of Christ in Nineteenth Century American Culture." *Quarterly Journal of Speech*, 61 (October 1975), 250–64.

Hubbard, Rita C. "Relationship Styles in Popular Romance Novels, 1950 to 1983." *Communication Quarterly*, 33 (Spring 1985), 113–25.

Huxman, Susan Schultz. "Perfecting the Rhetorical Vision of Woman's Rights: Elizabeth Cady Stanton, Anna Howard Shaw, and Carrie Chapman Catt." *Women's Studies in Communication*, 23 (Fall 2000), 307–36.

Ilkka, Richard J. "Rhetorical Dramatization in the Development of American Communism." *Quarterly Journal of Speech*, 63 (December 1977), 413–27.

Kidd, Virginia. "Happily Ever After and Other Relationship Styles: Advice on Interpersonal Relations in Popular Magazines, 1951–1973." *Quarterly Journal of Speech*, 61 (February 1975), 31–39.

King, Andrew A. "Booker T. Washington and the Myth of Heroic Materialism." *Quarterly Journal of Speech*, 60 (October 1974), 323–27.

Koester, Jolene. "The Machiavellian Princess: Rhetorical Dramas for Women Managers." *Communication Quarterly*, 30 (Summer 1982), 165–72.

Kroll, Becky Swanson. "From Small Group to Public View: Mainstreaming the Women's Movement." *Communication Quarterly*, 31 (Spring 1983), 139–47.

Nimmo, Dan, and James E. Combs. "Fantasies and Melodramas in Television Network News: The Case of Three Mile Island." *Western Journal of Speech Communication*, 46 (Winter 1982), 45–55.

Porter, Laurinda W. "The White House Transcripts: Group Fantasy Events Concerning the Mass Media." *Central States Speech Journal*, 27 (Winter 1976), 272–79.

Putnam, Linda L., Shirley A. Van Hoeven, and Connie A. Bullis. "The Role of Rituals and Fantasy Themes in Teachers' Bargaining." *Western Journal of Speech Communication*, 55 (Winter 1991), 85–103.

Swartz, Omar. *The View from* On the Road: *The Rhetorical Vision of Jack Kerouac.* Carbondale: Southern Illinois University Press, 1999.

West, Mark, and Chris Carey. "(Re)Enacting Frontier Justice: The Bush Administration's Tactical Narration of the Old West Fantasy after September 11." *Quarterly Journal of Speech*, 92 (November 2006), 379–412.

Zagacki, Kenneth S., and Dan Grano. "Radio Sports Talk and the Fantasies of Sport." *Critical Studies in Media Communication*, 22 (March 2005), 45–63.

Generic Criticism

Generic criticism is rooted in the assumption that certain types of situations provoke similar needs and expectations in audiences and thus call for particular kinds of rhetoric. Rather than seeking to discover how one situation affects one particular rhetorical act, the generic critic seeks to discover commonalities in rhetorical patterns across recurring situations. The purpose of generic criticism is to understand rhetorical practices in different time periods and in different places by discerning the similarities in rhetorical situations and the rhetoric constructed in response to them—to discover "how people create individual instances of meaning and value within structured discursive fields."[1] As rhetors develop messages, genres influence them to shape their materials to create particular emphases, to generate particular ideas, and to adopt particular personae. Similarly, audience members' recognition of a particular artifact as belonging to a specific genre influences their strategies of comprehension and response.[2]

The French word *genre* is the term used to refer to a distinct group, type, class, or category of artifacts that share important characteristics that differentiate it from other groups. A rhetorical genre is a constellation, fusion, or clustering of three different kinds of elements so that a unique kind of artifact is created. One element is *situational* requirements or the perception of conditions in a situation that call forth particular kinds of rhetorical responses. A genre also contains *substantive* and *stylistic* characteristics of the rhetoric—features of the rhetoric chosen by the rhetor to respond to the perceived requirements of particular situations. Substantive characteristics are those that constitute the content of the rhetoric, while stylistic characteristics constitute its form.[3] The third element of a rhetorical genre, the *organizing principle*, is the root term or notion that serves as an umbrella label for the various characteristic features of the rhetoric. It is the label for the internal dynamic of the constellation that is formed by the substantive, stylistic, and situational features of the genre.[4]

If there is a genre of eulogistic discourse, for example, then speeches of eulogy for Eleanor Roosevelt, John Lennon, Ronald Reagan, and soldiers killed in the Iraq War should be similar in significant aspects. They should share situational, stylistic, and substantive strategies as well as an organizing principle that binds them together. While strategic responses and stylistic choices, in isolation, may appear in other rhetorical forms, what is distinctive about a genre of rhetoric is the recurrence of the forms together, unified by the same organizing principle. A genre, then, is not simply a set of features that characterizes various rhetorical acts but a set of interdependent features.

The roots of the notion of genre and thus of generic criticism can be traced to the writings of Aristotle and other classical rhetoricians. Much of classical rhetorical theory is based on the assumption that situations fall into general types, depending on the objective of the rhetoric. Classical rhetoricians divided rhetoric into three types of discourse—deliberative or political, forensic or legal, and epideictic or ceremonial. Each of these types has distinctive aims—expedience for deliberative speaking, justice for forensic speaking, and honor for epideictic speaking. They have distinctive strategies as well—exhortation and dissuasion for deliberative speaking, accusation and defense for forensic speaking, and praise and blame for epideictic speaking.[5] Thus, classification of discourse on the basis of similar characteristics and situations has been part of the tradition of the communication field since its inception.

The first person to use the term *generic criticism* in the communication discipline was Edwin Black in his critique of neo-Aristotelianism in 1965. He proposed as an alternative to the traditional method of criticism a generic frame that included these tenets: (1) "there is a limited number of situations in which a rhetor can find himself"; (2) "there is a limited number of ways in which a rhetor can and will respond rhetorically to any given situational type"; and (3) "the recurrence of a given situational type through history will provide a critic with information on the rhetorical responses available in that situation."[6] Black suggested, then, that distinctive, recurrent situations exist in which discourse occurs and encouraged critics to analyze historical texts to describe their common features.

Lloyd F. Bitzer's notion of the rhetorical situation, presented in 1968, also contributed to the development of generic criticism. Bitzer's focus on recurring situations was particularly significant for generic criticism: "From day to day, year to year, comparable situations occur, prompting comparable responses; hence rhetorical forms are born and a special vocabulary, grammar, and style are established."[7] Although his conceptualization of the rhetorical situation has generated controversy,[8] it further developed the theoretical base for generic criticism.

Yet another contribution to the development of generic criticism was a conference held in 1976 called "'Significant Form' in Rhetorical Criticism." Sponsored by the Speech Communication Association (now the National Communication Association) and the University of Kansas, the conference was organized around the idea of significant form, which referred to recurring patterns in discourse or action. These patterns include the "repeated use of images, metaphors, arguments, structural arrangements, configurations of language or a combination of such elements into what critics have termed 'genres' or 'rhetorics.'"[9] The result of the conference was a book, *Form and Genre: Shaping Rhetorical Action,* edited by Karlyn Kohrs Campbell and Kathleen Hall Jamieson, which provided theoretical discussions of the concept of genre and included samples of generic criticism.

Anthony Paré and Graham Smart expanded the study of genre by focusing specifically on rhetorical genres in organizational settings. They define genre as a distinctive profile of regularities across four dimensions: (1) textual features such as styles of texts and modes of argument; (2) regularities in the composing process such as information gathering and analysis of information; (3) regularities in reading practices such as where, when, and why a document is read; and (4) the social roles performed by writers and readers so that no matter who acts as social worker, judge, or project manager, the genre is enacted in much the same way. Paré and Smart believe this view of genres in organizations explains how the effective production of discourse and knowledge occurs within organizations.[10]

The work of Mikhail Bakhtin also has been influential in the development of genre studies. Bakhtin asserts that we

> speak only in definite speech genres, that is, all our utterances have definite and relatively stable typical *forms of construction of the whole.* Our repertoire of oral (and written) speech genres is rich. We use them confidently and skillfully *in practice,* and it is quite possible for us not even to suspect their existence *in theory.*

Bakhtin suggests that even "in the most free, the most unconstrained conversation, we cast our speech in definite generic forms, sometimes rigid and trite ones, sometimes more flexible, plastic, and creative ones." Among the speech genres that are widespread in everyday life are the various genres of greetings, farewells, congratulations, information about health, and the like. These genres have official, respectful forms as well as intimate, familiar ones.[11]

The Sydney School of genre studies, named after its primary institutional base in the University of Sydney's Department of Linguistics, offers another contribution to genre studies—the study of genres to effect social change. Michael Halliday, who once headed the department, sought to bring linguists and educators together to create a literacy pedagogy appropriate for a multicultural society.[12] The result was the use of generic analysis to probe systems of belief, ideologies, and values. The work of the members of this school encourages critics to ask questions about genres such as: How do some genres come to be valorized? In whose interest is such valorization? What kinds of social organization are put in place or kept in place by such valorization? What does participation in a genre do to and for an individual or a group? What opportunities do the relationships reflected in and structured by a genre afford for humane creative action or, alternatively, for the domination of others? Do genres empower some people while silencing others? What representations of the world are entailed in genres? These questions suggest as an agenda for the next phase of generic studies a critical examination of issues such as the nature of the sanctioned representations in genres and their implications for people's lives, the degree of accessibility of a genre to potential users, and genre maintenance as power maintenance. More generally, the Australian genre researchers contribute to generic criticism an explicit acknowledgment of the political dimensions of genres.[13]

Other efforts to link genres to issues of power and ideology include those of critical discourse analysis (CDA) scholars. CDA is primarily concerned with demonstrating issues of power and dominance in private and public discourse, and critics who work in this tradition go beyond identifying the components of genres and seek to expose the values and beliefs of the society that shape the construction of particular genres. Their efforts, then, are devoted to discovering the role that power and ideology play in the construction and interpretation of genres.[14]

Procedures

Using generic criticism, a critic analyzes an artifact in a four-step process: (1) selecting an artifact; (2) analyzing the artifact; (3) formulating a research question; and (4) writing the essay.

Selecting an Artifact

Your choice of an artifact or artifacts for generic criticism depends on the kind of analysis you are doing. As explicated below, generic criticism involves three options—generic description, generic participation, and generic application. If you are interested in generic description, your artifacts should be a variety of texts that appear, on the surface, to share some rhetorical similarities. These artifacts can come from different time periods and be of various forms—speeches, essays, songs, works of art, and advertisements, for example—if they all seem similar in nature and function. If your goal is generic participation, choose an artifact that seems like it should belong to or has been assigned to a particular genre but does not seem to fit. If you are doing generic application, your artifact should be one that you want to assess in terms of how well it conforms to the genre of which it is a part. This should be an artifact that, for some reason, leads you to question how it is functioning in the context of its genre.

Analyzing the Artifact

Generic criticism involves three different options for a critic, with each leading to a different contribution to the understanding of genres—generic description, generic participation, and generic application.[15] The first option is generic description, where you examine several artifacts to determine if a genre exists. This is an inductive operation, in which you begin with a consideration of specific features of artifacts and move to a generalization about them in the naming of a genre. The second option, generic participation, is a deductive procedure in which you move from consideration of a general class of rhetoric to consideration of a specific artifact. Here, you test a specific artifact against a genre to discover if it participates in that genre. The third option is generic application—also a deductive procedure—that involves application of a generic model to particular artifacts in order to assess them.

Generic Description

In the attempt to describe a genre, a critic examines various artifacts to see if a genre exists. Your purpose in generic description is to define a genre and formulate theoretical constructs about its characteristics. Generic description involves four steps: (1) observing similarities in rhetorical responses to particular situations; (2) collecting artifacts that occur in similar situations; (3) analyzing the artifacts to discover if they share characteristics; and (4) formulating the organizing principle of the genre.

The first step of generic description is your observation that similar situations, removed from each other in time and place, seem to generate similar rhetorical responses. In other words, you speculate that a genre of rhetoric exists. Your suspicion of the presence of a genre is not to be confused with a preconceived framework that predicts or limits the defining characteristics of the genre. Rather, your hunch simply serves as a prod to begin an investigation to see if a genre exists and, if so, what elements characterize it. If your starting place is the idea that the messages produced in situations when someone announces the intention to run for public office seem to share characteristics, that idea does not dictate that you will discover certain characteristics. All you know at this point is that the situations seem similar, and the rhetoric in these situations also may share commonalities.

The second step is the collection of a varied sample of artifacts that may represent the genre. Identify rhetorical acts in which the perceived rhetorical situation appears similar or search out contexts that seem to be characterized by similar constraints of situation. If you suspect a genre of rhetoric may exist in which individuals announce their candidacy for office, for example, you would want to collect instances where individuals have announced their intention to run for office. A study by James S. Measell began in a similar fashion. He noticed that similar rhetorical situations were faced by Abraham Lincoln and William Pitt, the prime minister of England during the French Revolution. Both Lincoln and Pitt needed to justify "their administrative policy to withhold the privileges of habeas corpus,"[16] so the rhetoric of Lincoln and Pitt on the topic became the data for his study.

The third step in the process is close analysis of the artifacts collected to discover if there are substantive or stylistic features shared in the various artifacts you have collected. Here, you seek commonalities in how the rhetors dealt with the perceived problem in the situation. In the process of discovering similarities and differences among the rhetorical acts under study, you are not confined to looking for particular kinds of strategies or to using one critical method. Ideally, you allow the artifacts being studied to suggest the important similarities and differences, focusing on those elements that stand out as critical. These might be metaphors, images, sentence structure, failure to enact arguments, or an infinite variety of other elements. You may discover, for example, substantive strategies—those that deal primarily with content—such as use of metaphors dealing with family or the expression of self-sacrifice. Stylistic strategies—those that deal largely with form—may include elements such as adoption of a belligerent tone or use of ambiguous terminology. You may choose to focus on units of analysis suggested in other critical methods such as neo-Aristotelianism or fantasy-theme analysis. Neo-Aristotelian criticism could be used at this stage of generic description to discover similarities among the various artifacts in the use of emotional appeals, for example. Using fantasy-theme criticism, you could choose to search for commonalities in depictions of characters, settings, and actions.

In the process of textual analysis to discover rhetorical strategies, you may want to perform subsample comparisons of the artifacts you are investigating to identify subclasses of a genre. You may seek to determine, for example, if a genre of resignation rhetoric exists and, in the process, discover variants of resignation rhetoric, each characterized by a somewhat different set of rhetorical strategies. You may need to distinguish, then, among various characteristics, seeing some as paradigm cases of a genre, some as borderline cases, and some as characteristics of a subgenre.[17] B. L. Ware and Wil A. Linkugel's essay on speeches of apology is an example of the delineation of subgenres; they identify four different subgenres of apologetic discourse: absolutive, vindicative, explanative, and justificative.[18]

If sufficient similarities are noted to continue the search for a genre, the fourth step for a critic in the process of generic description is to formulate the organizing principle that captures the essence of the strategies common to the sample collected. In her analysis of *Seinfeld, Beavis and Butt-head*, and *The Howard Stern Show* as examples of a possible genre of humorous incivility, for example, Laura K. Hahn names closure to new perspectives as the organizing principle. What brings the shows' substantive and stylistic characteristics together, she suggests, is an active resistance to diverse perspectives.[19] This act of labeling the organizing principle actually may occur simultaneously with the delineation of substantive and stylistic strategies because the elements identified may come to your attention grouped around an obvious core or principle. Regardless of the order in which the steps occur, at the end of this process, you have formulated a list of rhetorical characteristics that appear to define a genre and an organizing principle that unites them.

You may have difficulty deciding whether or not a particular characteristic is a distinguishing feature of a genre. In such instances, the following questions may help you determine if it is one that contributes to a distinct genre:

- Can rules be named with which other critics or observers can concur in identifying characteristics of rhetorical practice when they are confronted with the same examples? Not only must the distinguishing features of a genre be namable but also the rules that are serving as guides for you in making distinctions among characteristics in different artifacts. These rules, of course, do not specify precisely how the rhetorical act is to be performed. A genre is not formulaic because there is always another strategy that a rhetor can use to meet the requirements of the situation. But a genre establishes bounded options for rhetors in situations, and naming the rules that define those options can help clarify whether a characteristic is part of a genre or not.[20]

- Are the similarities in substantive and stylistic strategies clearly rooted in the situations in which they were generated? In other words, does the way in which the situation is defined require the inclusion of an element like this in the artifact? Simply the appearance of one characteristic in several artifacts does not mean it was devised to deal with the same perceived situational constraints. Refer frequently to the description of the perceived situation to establish that the similarities are not simply coincidental but are grounded in some aspect of that situation. [21]

- Would the absence of the characteristic in question alter the nature of the artifact? A genre is created from a fusion of characteristics, and all are critical in the dynamic of that fusion. Simply saying that a certain element appears in all of the artifacts under study is not enough. A genre exists only if each element is fused to the other elements so its absence would alter the organizing principle. A genre is given its character by a fusion of forms and not by its individual elements.[22]

- Does the characteristic contribute to insight about a type of rhetoric or simply lead to the development of a classification scheme? The test of a genre is the degree of understanding it provides of the artifacts. Insight—and not neatness of a classification scheme—is your goal in generic description. If the discovery of similarities among artifacts classifies but does not clarify, it may not be particularly useful.[23]

Description of a genre, then, in which various artifacts are examined to see if a genre exists, is one option for the generic critic. This procedure involves examining a variety of artifacts that seem to be generated in similar situations to discover if they have in common substantive and stylistic strategies and an organizing principle that fuses those strategies. If, in fact, they do, you have developed a theory of the existence of a genre.

Generic Participation

A critic who engages in generic participation determines which artifacts participate in which genres. This involves a deductive process in which you test an instance of rhetoric against the characteristics of a genre. Generic participation involves three steps: (1) describing the perceived situational requirements, substantive and stylistic strategies, and organizing principle of a genre; (2) describing the perceived situational requirements, substantive and stylistic strategies, and organizing principle of an artifact; and (3) comparing the characteristics of the artifact with those of the genre to discover if the artifact belongs in that genre. You then use these findings to confirm the characteristics of the genre or to suggest modifications in it.

As an example of this process, let's assume you are interested in discovering if the rhetoric used by the director of the UFO museum in Roswell, New Mexico, constitutes conspiracy rhetoric. For a study of generic participation, you first would turn to earlier studies in which the characteristics of conspiracy rhetoric are delineated and then would see what elements characterize the speeches of the director. Comparison of the two sets of features would enable you to discover if those speeches participate in a genre of conspiratorial discourse.

Generic Application

A third option is open to a critic who is interested in studying genres—generic application. Rather than simply determining if a particular artifact belongs in a particular genre, you use the description of the genre to evaluate particular instances of rhetoric. Your task here is to apply the situational, stylistic, and substantive elements that characterize a genre to a specific artifact that has been defined as participating in that genre in order to assess it. On the basis of the application of the generic characteristics to the specific model, you are able to determine if the artifact is a good or poor example of the genre.

Four basic steps are involved in generic application (the first three are the same as the steps for generic participation): (1) describing the perceived situational requirements, substantive and stylistic strategies, and organizing principle of a genre; (2) describing the perceived situational requirements, substantive and stylistic strategies, and organizing principle of an artifact that is representative of that genre; (3) comparing the characteristics of the artifact with those of the genre; and (4) evaluating the artifact according to its success in fulfilling the required characteristics of the genre.

In using generic features to evaluate an artifact, a critic draws critical insights about the effectiveness of a particular artifact in fulfilling perceived situational demands. When a generic form is used by a rhetor, it creates expectations in the audience members, who perceive and evaluate rhetoric in terms of generic classifications and expect a particular style and certain types of content from particular types of rhetoric. If the rhetoric does not fulfill these expectations, the audience is likely to be confused and to react negatively. Body art, for example, a form of visual and performance art, tends to violate the genre of visual art. Visitors to galleries expect to see art framed and hanging on walls—the generic form of visual art. Instead, they encounter works such as *Transfixed*, in which body artist Chris Burden had himself nailed to the roof of a Volkswagen bug and had the engine run at full speed for two minutes. While viewers may come to realize that the breaking of the generic frame is done intentionally by the artist/rhetor to encourage viewers to question the definition of art, the violation of generic expectations may create confusion, frustration, and rejection of the artwork by viewers—at least initially.[24]

A critic also may discover that generic violations increase an artifact's effectiveness, as is the case with Sergio Leone's film *Once Upon a Time in the West*. Viewers expect a film in the genre of the Western tradition but find many violations of the genre—in unusual costumes worn by the cowboys, comic characters, the slow unfolding of scenes, and difficulty telling the heroes from the villains. These violations, however, create an experience for the viewer that is positive rather than negative. Evaluation of artifacts, whether positive or negative, is made on the basis of the suasory impact of the artifacts that results from their fulfillment or violation of generic expectations.

Formulating a Research Question

Your research questions in generic criticism will vary according to whether you are engaged in generic description, participation, or application. In generic description, your research questions are: "Does a genre exist among a set of artifacts? If so, what are the characteristics of the genre?" In generic participation, your research question is: "Does this artifact participate in a particular genre?" In generic application, the question with which you are concerned is: "Is this artifact successful in fulfilling the required characteristics of its genre?"

Writing the Essay

After completing the analysis, you are ready to write your essay, which includes five major components: (1) an introduction, in which you discuss the research question, its contribution to rhetorical theory, and its significance; (2) a description of the artifact(s) and their contexts; (3) a description of the method of criticism—in this case, generic analysis and the specific type in which you are engaged—generic description, generic participation, or generic application; (4) a report of the findings of the analysis, in which you reveal the connections you have discovered between your artifact(s) and a genre; and (5) a discussion of the contribution the analysis makes to rhetorical theory.

Sample Essays

The five sample essays that follow illustrate some of the options open to a critic who engages in generic criticism. Joshua Gunn's essay is an example of generic description. He seeks to establish a genre of exorcism and to discover how it functions as it is applied in presidential rhetoric. Sharon M. Varallo is interested in discovering if a genre of family photographs exists and is guided by the research question, "What rhetorical means do families use to construct themselves as a unit?" The next two essays are samples of generic participation. Danielle Montoya engages in an analysis of generic participation to discover if Ansel Adams's photograph "Discussion on Art" reflects attributes of Adams's artistic genre and, if so, how it participates in communicating the artist's perspective. In her essay, Lacey Stein asks whether a video by Common fits into the genre of rap music videos. "The Rhetoric of Huey P. Newton" by Davi Johnson is a sample of both generic participation and generic application. She establishes that the rhetoric of Black Panther Huey P. Newton fits the characteristics of the genre of the jeremiad and, in particular, of the Afro-American jeremiad and then evaluates his use of that generic form. Her primary research question is, "Can a conventional rhetorical genre be used to foster radical social change?"

Notes

1 Charles Bazerman, "Systems of Genres and the Enactment of Social Intentions," in *Genre and the New Rhetoric*, ed. Aviva Freedman and Peter Medway (London: Taylor & Francis, 1994), p. 79.

2 Richard M. Coe, "'An Arousing and Fulfillment of Desires': The Rhetoric of Genre in the Process Era—and Beyond," in *Genre and the New Rhetoric*, ed. Aviva Freedman and Peter Medway (London: Taylor & Francis, 1994), p. 182.

3 For a useful description of substance and form as they relate to genre, see Carolyn R. Miller, "Genre as Social Action," *Quarterly Journal of Speech*, 70 (May 1984), 159.

4 For a discussion of strategies and organizing principle, see: Karlyn Kohrs Campbell and Kathleen Hall Jamieson, "Form and Genre in Rhetorical Criticism: An Introduction," in *Form and Genre: Shaping Rhetorical Action*, ed. Karlyn Kohrs Campbell and Kathleen Hall Jamieson (Falls Church, VA: Speech Communication Association, [1978]), pp. 18, 21, 25; Karlyn Kohrs Campbell and Kathleen Hall Jamieson, "Rhetorical Hybrids: Fusion of Generic Elements," *Quarterly Journal of Speech*, 68 (May 1982), 146; Jackson Harrell and Wil A. Linkugel, "On Rhetorical Genre: An Organizing Perspective," *Philosophy and Rhetoric*, 11 (Fall 1978), 263–64; and Robert L. Ivie, "Images of Savagery in American Justifications for War," *Communication Monographs*, 47 (November 1980), 282.

5 Aristotle, *Rhetoric*, 1.5–10. For a more elaborate discussion of genre in the *Rhetoric*, see G. P. Mohrmann and Michael C. Leff, "Lincoln at Cooper Union: A Rationale for Neo-Classical Criticism," *Quarterly Journal of Speech*, 60 (December 1974), 463. For a discussion of differences between contemporary notions and Aristotle's notion of genre, see Thomas M. Conley, "Ancient Rhetoric and Modern Genre Criticism," *Communication Quarterly*, 27 (Fall 1979), 47–48.

6 Edwin Black, *Rhetorical Criticism: A Study in Method* (Madison: University of Wisconsin Press, 1978), p. 133.

7 Lloyd F. Bitzer, "The Rhetorical Situation," *Philosophy and Rhetoric*, 1 (Winter 1968), 13.

8 Among the essays that deal with Bitzer's notion of the rhetorical situation are: Lloyd F. Bitzer, "The Rhetorical Situation," *Philosophy and Rhetoric*, 1 (Winter 1968), 1–14; Richard L. Larson, "Lloyd Bitzer's 'Rhetorical Situation' and the Classification of Discourse: Problems and Implications," *Philosophy and Rhetoric*, 3 (Summer 1970), 165–68; Arthur B. Miller, "Rhetorical Exigence," *Philosophy and Rhetoric*, 5 (Spring 1972), 111–18; Richard E. Vatz, "The Myth of the Rhetorical Situation," *Philosophy and Rhetoric*, 6 (Summer 1973), 154–61; Scott Consigny, "Rhetoric and Its Situations," *Philosophy and Rhetoric*, 7 (Summer 1974), 175–86; Barry Brummett, "Some Implications of 'Process' or 'Intersubjectivity': Postmodern Rhetoric," *Philosophy and Rhetoric*, 9 (Winter 1976), 21–51; David M. Hunsaker and Craig R. Smith, "The Nature of Issues: A Constructive Approach to Situational Rhetoric," *Western Speech Communication*, 40 (Summer 1976), 144–56; Lloyd F. Bitzer, "Functional Communication: A Situational Perspective," in *Rhetoric in Transition: Studies in the Nature and Uses of Rhetoric*, ed. Eugene E. White (University Park: Pennsylvania State University Press, 1980), pp. 21–38; and Richard A. Cherwitz and James W. Hikins, *Communication and Knowledge: An Investigation in Rhetorical Epistemology* (Columbia: University of South Carolina Press, 1986).

9 Karlyn Kohrs Campbell and Kathleen Hall Jamieson, "Acknowledgements," in *Form and Genre: Shaping Rhetorical Action*, ed. Karlyn Kohrs Campbell and Kathleen Hall Jamieson (Falls Church, VA: Speech Communication Association, [1978]), p. 3.

10 Anthony Paré and Graham Smart, "Observing Genres in Action: Towards a Research Methodology," in *Genres and the New Rhetoric*, ed. Aviva Freedman and Peter Medway (London: Taylor & Francis, 1994), pp. 146–54.

11 M. M. Bakhtin, *Speech Genres and Other Late Essays*, trans. Vern W. McGee, ed. Caryl Emerson and Michael Holquist (Austin: University of Texas Press, 1986), pp. 78–79.

12 Michael A. K. Halliday, *An Introduction to Functional Grammar* (London: Edward Arnold, 1985). For a history of the Sydney School, see Bill Cope, Mary Kalantzis, Gunther Kress, and Jim Martin, "Bibliographic Essay: Developing the Theory and Practice of Genre-Based Literacy," comp. Lorraine Murphy, in *The Powers of Literacy: A Genre Approach to Teaching Writing*, ed. Bill Cope and Mary Kalantzis (Pittsburgh: University of Pittsburgh Press, 1993), pp. 231–47.

13 Many scholars continue to raise questions about and refine generic criticism. See, for example, Herbert W. Simons and Aram A. Aghazarian, *Form, Genre, and the Study of Political Dis-

course (Columbia: University of South Carolina Press, 1986); Thomas Conley's essay in Simons and Aghazarian's volume: "The Linnaean Blues: Thoughts on the Genre Approach," pp. 59–78; and William L. Benoit, "Beyond Genre Theory: The Genesis of Rhetorical Action," *Communication Monographs*, 67 (June 2000), 178–92.

[14] Mohammed Nahar Al-Ali, "Religious Affiliations and Masculine Power in Jordanian Wedding Invitation Genre," *Discourse & Society*, 17 (November 2006), 696–97.

[15] These three options were suggested by Harrell and Linkugel, pp. 274–77.

[16] James S. Measell, "A Comparative Study of Prime Minister William Pitt and President Abraham Lincoln on Suspension of Habeas Corpus," in *Form and Genre: Shaping Rhetorical Action*, ed. Karlyn Kohrs Campbell and Kathleen Hall Jamieson (Falls Church, VA: Speech Communication Association, [1978]), p. 87.

[17] For more discussion of this process, see Herbert W. Simons, "'Genre-alizing' About Rhetoric: A Scientific Approach," in *Form and Genre: Shaping Rhetorical Action*, ed. Karlyn Kohrs Campbell and Kathleen Hall Jamieson (Falls Church, VA: Speech Communication Association, [1978]), p. 41.

[18] B. L. Ware and Wil A. Linkugel, "They Spoke in Defense of Themselves: On the Genre Criticism of Apologia," *Quarterly Journal of Speech*, 59 (October 1973), 282–83. They define the subgenres in this way: In the absolutive subgenre, the speaker seeks acquittal; in the vindictive subgenre, preservation of the accused's reputation and recognition of the rhetor's worth as a human being relative to that of the accusers; in the explanative subgenre, understanding by the audience of the rhetor's motives, actions, or beliefs so it will be unable to condemn; and in the justificative subgenre, understanding and approval.

[19] Laura K. Hahn, "A Generic Analysis of the Rhetoric of Humorous Incivility in Popular Culture," Diss. Ohio State University 1999.

[20] For more on the notion of rules, see: Campbell and Jamieson, "Introduction," pp. 295–96; and Simons, p. 37.

[21] This notion receives some treatment in: Stephen E. Lucas, "Genre Criticism and Historical Context: The Case of George Washington's First Inaugural Address," *Southern Speech Communication Journal*, 51 (Summer 1986), 356–57; and Campbell and Jamieson, "Form and Genre in Rhetorical Criticism," p. 22.

[22] Campbell and Jamieson, "Form and Genre in Rhetorical Criticism," pp. 23–24.

[23] This notion was suggested by: Campbell and Jamieson, "Form and Genre in Rhetorical Criticism," p. 18; Walter R. Fisher, "Genre: Concepts and Applications in Rhetorical Criticism," *Western Journal of Speech Communication*, 44 (Fall 1980), 291; and Roderick P. Hart, "Contemporary Scholarship in Public Address: A Research Editorial," *Western Journal of Speech Communication*, 50 (Summer 1986), 292.

[24] For a discussion of body art and its function for an audience, see Sonja K. Foss, "Body Art: Insanity as Communication," *Central States Speech Journal*, 38 (Summer 1987), 122–31. For more discussion and examples of the impact of genres on audience expectations, see Kathleen M. Hall Jamieson, "Generic Constraints and the Rhetorical Situation," *Philosophy and Rhetoric*, 6 (Summer 1973), 166–67.

The Rhetoric of Exorcism
George W. Bush and the Return of Political Demonology
Joshua Gunn

Ever since the commercial airline missiles destroyed New York City's World Trade Center on 9/11/01, images of violence and catastrophe have seared the collective mind. A popular image shot by freelance photographer Mark Phillips seemed to capture the face of a demon in a large plume of smoke emanating from one of the twin towers [see snopes.com/rumors/wtcface.asp for images]. Soon after the Associated Press secured one-time printing rights to the so-called "smoke demon" image, it became available to Internet users who quickly disseminated it with foreboding commentary about the Christian apocalypse. For many evangelical Protestants in particular, the smoke demon provided evidence that the "current seat of Satan's power" resides in American financial institutions, and that the demise of the World Trade Center is a sign from God (or the Devil) that the end-time is near (Mikkelson & Mikkelson). The goal of this essay is to show how speech writers used a similar, demonic anthropomorphism to craft a righteous presidential rhetoric that helped overcome the widespread experience of anomie and speechlessness caused by the violence of 9/11.

To this end the essay proceeds in four parts. Part one provides a context for the study by describing the recent increase of demonic rhetoric in popular culture. Part two locates the demonic in relation to the religious genres of exorcism and conversion, two iterations of the larger cultural form of religious transformation. In part three, I examine the parallels between exorcism and the political purging of figurative bodies, specifically those that appear in the speeches of George W. Bush in the aftermath of 9/11. Finally, the essay concludes with a discussion of the implications of such a reading for rhetorical theory and practice, focusing particularly on the continued relevance of genre to the study of political discourse.

Demons and Possession in Popular Culture

The Demonic Default

Similar to the childhood game of seeing animals in clouds or finding "the face of Mother Theresa in a cinnamon bun," the attribution of form, particularly a human-like form, to an otherwise vague and diffuse stimulus is a perceptual illusion termed "pareidolia" (Carroll, 2002). According to the anthropologist Stewart Guthrie, pareidolic anthropomorphisms, such as the smoke demon, frequently concern religious figures, for the attribution of form to the ineffable in general is the psychological basis of religion (also see Cassirer).[1] Guthrie also claims that religious anthropomorphisms tend to attribute a given deity or supernatural figure with *the power of speech* (198). Gods and demons speak, and they often have the power to mute speech. From an evangelical perspective, for example, one could claim that Satan's destructive power on 9/11 momentarily robbed the U.S. citizenry of its voice, its power to name, and thereby its ability to comprehend and cope; with destruction and death, Satan silences.

Joshua Gunn, *The Rhetoric of Exorcism: George W. Bush and the Return of Political Demonology.* Reprinted by permission of Routledge.

The ineffability of 9/11 has created numerous rhetorical acts designed to restore the voice and security of the polity, including a litany of rituals, speeches, and performances mourning the loss of the dead, commemorating rescue efforts, and celebrating communal bonds. Speakers who sought to assuage audiences by amplifying the virtues of the American people repeatedly used the words courage, honor, freedom, trust, and faith. In other words, the Western terminological repertoire for expressing goodness, secular and divine, is large. Those who sought to characterize the "terrorists" or their deeds, however, were limited in their expression. They described the terrorists' intent and motives as "evil," reducing human action to inhuman motion and thereby dehumanizing the racial/religious Other as monsters controlled by a malevolent force.

The rhetorical invention of evil is difficult because Westerners have a limited repertoire of language for characterizing it. Historically, of course, the demonic personifications of religious discourse have provided the bulk of Western representations of evil (see Russell *The Devil;* Delbanco).[2] Jeffrey Burton Russell, an expert on the study of the problem of evil, suggests that the paucity of terms for characterizing evil is related to the ineffability of evil itself, defined as "the abuse of a sentient [or pain conscious] being" (Russell, *Devil* 17). Russell argues that evil "is never abstract" because an identifiable victim always exists. In most cultures, argues Russell, "evil is felt as a purposeful force . . . [and is] personified" (Russell, *The Devil* 17; also see Russell, *Satan;* Russell, *Lucifer;* and Russell, *Mephistopheles).* The ineffability of evil, the speechlessness caused by human suffering, demands an identifiable purpose or cause (also see O'Leary 3–19; 34–44). In light of Guthrie's anthropomorphic thesis, it makes sense that demons and monsters represent, literally and figuratively, the purpose or forces behind needless suffering in the popular imagination; demons are ready-made cultural signifiers, handy *topoi* for restoring speech.

Edward J. Ingebretsen claims that demons and monsters are handy signifiers because their creation and destruction is a "soul-deep" narrative form in U.S. popular culture. Monster-making is a uniquely American "pedagogy of fear" that justifies otherwise unacceptable violence by de-humanizing and demonizing the Other (19–41). Declaring something or someone as evil or possessed by evil (a monster) is part of an American political fantasy that establishes or prioritizes certain beliefs, attitudes, and values in relation to some governing norm and through the destruction of the "abnormal" (Ingebretsen 3).[3] The Salem Witch Trials and the Red Scare, hate crimes and riots, murder mysteries and slasher horror films, are examples. Ingebretsen suggests that the success and persistence of the demonic and monstrous relate to the pleasures of repetition, the erotics of frustration and satiation, as the stories of the creation and destruction of a monster or demon surface repeatedly in different guises. Of course, the rhetorical concept for Ingebretsen's "narrative formula," for the recognition and pleasure of a repetitious narrative form, is that of genre (see Burke, *Counter-statement,* 29–44). In the following sections I suggest that exorcism, understood as a violent, ritual cleansing of a body, has reemerged as a significant generic form of demon-making in three interrelated domains: the mass media; the ritual practice of Catholics and Protestants; and presidential speech craft.

Millennialism and Demonic Possession

Sociologist Michael W. Cuneo argues that the greatest popular interest in exorcism to date emerged in the latter half of the twentieth century as a consequence of its representation by the entertainment industry. "Exorcism became a raging concern in the United States," says Cuneo, "only when the popular entertainment industry jacked up the heat. Only with the release of [the film] *The Exorcist* and the publication of [the book] *Hostage to the Devil* . . . did fears of demonization become widespread" (272). The recent, popular interest in exorcism also suggests a millennial stimulus in the form of Satanic thrillers, such as *End of Days* and Polanski's *The Ninth Gate,* and possession thrillers, such as MGM's *Stigmata,* Warner Brother's re-release of *The Exorcist,* Paramount's *Bless the Child,* and New Line Studio's *Lost Souls.* Showtime produced a widely watched film, *Possessed,* based on the "real life" story that inspired *The Exorcist.* Numerous books about demonic possession have also recently appeared, from Cuneo's paperback reprint *American Exorcism,* to less secular how-to's such as Bob Larson's *In the Name of Satan: How the Forces of Evil Work and What You Can Do to Defeat Them,* and Doris M. Wagner's *How to Cast Out Demons: A Guide to the Basics.* Just prior to the attacks on 9/11, these films and books defused demonic images and themes into popular news articles and television programs.

Although the public's preoccupation with the rhetoric of evil in popular discourse indicates a continued fascination with the demonic,[4] critics have given little attention to ritual exorcism as a generic form or as a rhetorical means for *naming the ineffable* in order to cope with social realities.[5] If *The Exorcist* film represents disturbances in "American consciousness" as Thomas Frentz and Thomas Farrell suggest (40–47), then recent media interest in the demonic marks the resurgence of a latent theological form deserving more attention. I suspect that scholars do not discuss exorcism as a rhetorical form because the rite is less obvious than forms such as the American monomyth (e.g., the singular plot of a selfless hero fighting evil; see Brookey and Westerfelhaus). More important, I think that the scholarly blindness to supernatural cultural forms is related to a tacit agnosticism in political and rhetorical scholarship. David S. Gutterman argues that many contemporary political scholars ignore the theological and regard less moderate religious groups—particularly the "Bible-believing" Christians—as a "problem public" with extreme beliefs and social activities. Further, although a number of rhetorical scholars identify the interrelationship between religion and politics, this work usually focuses on the historical past (see Darsey 175–198 for one notable exception). Scholars of political rhetoric sometimes ignore the profound interconnections among religion, spirituality, and *contemporary* political discourse. "Scholars of politics in the United States—and political theorists in particular," argues Gutterman, "can continue to ignore Bible-believing Christians and the pervasive relation between religion and politics at their own risk" (par. 2). The religious themes of conversion and transformation in Bush's campaign manifesto, *A Charge to Keep,* make a strong case for not taking the risk.

Toward a Generic Revivalism

Genre as the Verbal Character of Unconscious Forms

The unfashionability of generic criticism may also be a reason for the lack of attention given to religious forms in recent years. The poststructuralist turn, in particular, has encouraged moving away from genres and similar "modern" conceits in favor of genealogical and cartographic modes of criticism (Callinicos 1–8; Hebdige 62–66). In rhetorical, literary, film, and cultural studies, some critics dismiss generic criticism as "formulaic." For example, Fredric Jameson noted that "genre criticism [has been] thoroughly discredited by modern literary theory and practice" (105).

Other scholars attack generic criticism as pointless exercises in taxonomy (Conley; also see Benoit).

These dismissals of generic criticism lead to a misunderstanding of genre as an essence or invariant structure that inheres in a given text. *Genres are not "in" texts* but, rather, exist in the popular imagination—ultimately in the minds of audiences, rhetors, and critics (Campbell & Jamieson, "Introduction" 294). The charge of "formulaic" representation is an essentialist misunderstanding of genre. Genres do not predetermine texts in a strong sense; they bind what is rhetorically possible in terms of precedent and memory. Genres can be deterministic only if (a) they exist objectively in texts; and (b) texts are discrete unities that lack intertextual reference.

Rather than existing *in texts,* genres are concrete labels for shared patterns or social forms that inhere in the popular imagination. These forms emerge in different ways and permutations and depend on the context in which they appear. Genres reside in the collective, mental space of a community or audience, and assume a *content* within a given context. Once an audience identifies the repetition of an underlying social form within a rhetorical act, it becomes a "genre." Social forms are diffuse organizing structures that hold some predictive value, and genres are retroactive, critical descriptions that identify a pattern among a set of texts (Rosemarin 3–22). Hence, genres are expressions of social forms that are more akin to myth and archetype than textual template. In other words, the generic field is the social field, the collective mental life of a given audience. Hence many of the critics of genre fail to recognize the mental *topography* within which social forms operate.

By focusing on the shared consciousness of a community, and in particular, those elements of communal consciousness that are often repressed or only available as *traces* in texts, a critic can better capture the goal of generic criticism and explain the dynamic features of genres. Characterizing genres in this manner emphasizes their *psychological status* over their textual manifestations. Once we recognize social forms function largely unconsciously, then genres become their conscious, linguistic representations. Genres are thus best understood as a kind of "symbolic-" or "social action" in the collective psyche or popular imagination (see Miller), and generic criticism should be recast as an attempt to *restore social forms to their verbal character.*[6]

Religious Transformation and the Genre of Exorcism

Exorcism is a generic pattern that participates in the larger theological form of *religious transformation.* In a religious context, exorcism is the dialectical counterpart to religious conversion. Both exorcism and conversion share two elements of transformation: (1) an individual experiences a state of crisis; and (2) by turning to God or some other transcendent power, the crisis is resolved or managed. The most familiar genre of transformation is religious conversion, and it relates to the narrative pattern in Christian discourse that features a "sinner" or imperfect individual in crisis who willingly turns to God for help (Gutterman par. 8). More broadly, William James characterized conversion as "the process, gradual or sudden, by which a self hitherto divided becomes unified and consciously right [,] superior [,] and happy, in consequence of its firmer hold upon religious realities" (171). Exorcism is closely related to conversion because it also involves a divided self, but exorcism is distinct in two important ways. First, whereas conversion seems to focus on the mind/soul (*nous*), the genre of exorcism emphasizes corporeal metaphors, frequently locating the body as a terrain for symbolic warfare. Second, whereas the transformation of conversion is freely willed, exorcism is a forced transformation from without, as the source of the "divided self" or possession is an evil, controlling entity.

Unlike a number of conversion genres particular to the West (e.g., being "born again"), exorcism is a religious transformation of *global* significance. Exorcisms are practiced by Hindu priests in Northern India, by Javanese leaders in Indonesia, and by faith healers in Sri Lanka (Dwyer; Headley; Kapferer). Closer to home, possession by good spirits (ancestors) as well as the exorcism of evil spirits comprise important rituals in the Vodou religion of Haiti, as well as its many iterations in North America (Brown, 1991). Hence, as a form of religious transformation, the purging of polluting spirits from a public body may resonate across cultures.

The Catholic exorcism performed in the widely known film, *The Exorcist* (1973), closely resembles the official rite described in *The Roman Ritual,* including the proper garments to be worn and ritual items to be used. In general, the Catholic ritual highlights the importance of speech and incantation. Dialoguing with the demon is important in order to prove that the "bad voice," in fact, belongs to a foreign, supernatural entity and not the diseased mind of the presumed victim. The ritual proceeds in four basic steps: First, the exorcist immobilizes the possessed (by restraints or with the help of aids) and demands the demon to appear; second, the demon is forced to name him/her or themselves (in *The Exorcist* the possessing entity is the biblical multitude known as "Legion") and an interrogation of its supernaturalness ensues; third, after the demon is identified, the exorcist forcefully demands the demon to depart and to restore the control of the human soul to his or her body; and forth, the demon departs the host body and the ritual is ended (Ellis 32–35).

It should be stressed that the ending of *The Exorcist,* which depicts a successful expulsion of a demon from a young woman, does not reflect the accounts of literal exorcisms past and present. Exorcisms in the sixteenth and seventeenth centuries, for example, document repeat failures. One historian remarked that the repeat performances of exorcisms reveal a "slightly comic determination of the [possessing] devils to regain entry into the bodies from which they have been evicted" (Connor 158). In this sense, exorcisms resemble many forms of psychological therapy; both require repeat treatments to identify and manage a problem (see Cuneo 270–281).

The Catholic rite of exorcism illustrated in *The Exorcist* differs significantly from a competing brand of exorcism currently on the rise in the United States. Most of the how-to books available on the topics of exorcism and spiritual warfare are not Catholic, but rather reflect the beliefs of a growing number of evangelical Protestants who practice "deliverance." Deliverance is part of a religious movement that believes demons create personal and social ills.[7] The demons cause everything from alcoholism to homosexuality. The demon's "point of entry" into a human host is opened by (1) personal sin; (2) involvement in the occult (including reading a *Harry Potter* novel or one's daily horoscope in the newspaper); and/or (3) ancestral sin, which is passed on in cursed family lines (Wise 62–66).

Bob Larson is the most dominant and vocal Deliverance leader in the United States. His recent Christian radio program and many books on Satanism and the occult built a large, media-based ministry headquartered in Denver, Colorado. Every year Larson travels around the country conducting workshops and "Freedom Forums" that culminate in mass exorcisms. Larson's exorcisms resemble the Catholic ritual by following the familiar pattern of (1) calling the demon forth; (2) naming the demon; (3) battling the demon; and (4) expelling it. The ritual differs from the Catholic rite because it is less dialogical and is part of a complex, confrontational spectacle.

First, for deliverance a team of aids restrains the possessed person while Larson literally screams at the demon to depart ("Let her go!" Larson yells). Larson's exorcisms are very physical. The possessed struggles against his or her restraints, sometimes passing out. Larson frequently touches the possessed person by pressing his hand or a Bible on his or her forehead. Larson's tone is angry and his resolve unyielding, insisting the possessed let the invading entity name itself. Second, Larson's exorcism style locates the "seat of the demon" or the point of demonic entry in *personal neuroses and anxieties,* which he repeatedly tells his audiences to access and experience in order to uncover a hidden evil force. Most people do not realize they have demons, claims Larson, and the best way to discover them is to relive a profound, painful experience or to reencounter a profoundly negative emotion that he terms the "point of pain." In fact, shortly before the exorcisms begin Larson commands audience members to "go to your deepest fears, your deepest source of pain." Third, Larson's rituals resemble the democratic element of Protestant tradition insofar as the aim of exorcism is "not to give a voice to the devil," but rather to give or restore the good voice of the victim during dispossession in order to empower him or her (Connor 158).

Understanding the difference between Catholic and evangelical Protestant styles of exorcism figure in the discussion of political discourse below because the more recognizably subdued, ritualized, and dialogic character of the Catholic rite makes it more difficult to recognize evangelical Protestant exorcism at work. Below, I suggest that the more confrontational, less dialogic brand of exorcism informs the kind of demonization found in Cold War rhetoric, as well as the recent war rhetoric of George W. Bush.

Examples of the Political Purging of Bodies

When audiences are subjected to (1) the construction of a rhetorical body; (2) demonology as an idiom; and (3) purging metaphors, a psychological fusion of exorcism as a persuasive iteration of a familiar problem-solution technique and exorcism as a generic form or structuring logic occurs. The significance of exorcism does not lie in its ability to subdue swelling bodies that vomit and utter profanities; rather, the significance of exorcism results from its symbolic practice as a bodily dispossession, as a promise of recovery through the purging of something previously hidden or unnamed from a given body. As a vocal deliverance, exorcism is a psychosomatic purging, the expelling of an unwanted, alien, and contaminating "bad voice" from a good body (Conner 154–158).

The theological discursive form of exorcism also names and organizes public anxieties about the ineffability of evil and violence. Because of the central role of calling or evocation, naming, and expulsion, the genre exemplifies the way in which our capacities to speak and name are used toward mass therapeutic ends (Ellis 32–61). In this section, I argue that the first connection between the purging of political bodies (namely the social body or body politic) and the religious form of exorcism in contemporary political discourse occurs during the Cold War. Then, I describe the recent rhetoric of George W. Bush as a return of this repressed but deeply inscribed logic of religious transformation.

Political Exorcism in the Twentieth Century

Although actual, bodily exorcisms have only recently surfaced as a therapeutic practice at the end of the twentieth century (Cuneo xii–xv), motifs of the genre have thrived in political discourse for quite some time. One prominent appearance of demonology as a rhetorical idiom in the last century occurred during the "Red Scare" after the first World War, culminating in Senator Joseph McCarthy's ruthless hunt for hidden Communists (see Darsey, 128–150; Shrecker). McCarthy characterized the U.S. as a "Christian" body "infested" with "atheistic communism" ("Speech on Communists") and recommended that these demons be identified and "cast-out" of the polity. The secrecy, invisibility, and/or insidious silence of these metaphorical demons suggest that the genre of exorcism adheres to what Richard Hofstadter describes as a "paranoid style in American politics" (3–40), a style that attempts to arouse the fear of hidden or invisible forces conspiring to take over the body politic. Even so, exorcism is much more than being part of a paranoid style because the motifs of the exorcist genre concentrate on a body subject to violent and evil forces. Further, unlike the Catholic stress on the necessity of evidence of demonic invasion (the dialogic character), the exorcism common in U.S. political discourse is more self-sealing, evangelical, and Protestant, stressing the unseen and silent character itself as evidence for mandating a war-like intervention.

Cold War discourse featured two distinct iterations of exorcism and the demonic. The less common *internal* iteration was found in the discourse of those opposed to Cold War policies, particularly those who characterized the American body as possessed by malicious forces in a manner resembling the pathogen metaphors of McCarthy. Robert Ivie observes,

> Contrary to tradition, Cold War "idealists" have attempted to decivilize America's image rather than the enemy's. By relying upon metaphorical concepts such as MAD, PATHOLOGY, SICK, and FORCE, they have portrayed the United States as the irrational, coercive, and aggressive agent of extermination, urging Americans to follow instead the path of love, friendship, trust, and empathy. Thus, they have called for a redeeming act of self-mortification . . . asking in effect that it purge itself of savagery. . . . (119)

Ivie argues that those opposing Cold War policies, such as Henry Wallace, often described the U.S. polity as a body infected with negative forces: "neurotic," "sick," "afflicted," "obsessed," "psychopathic," "fester," "infection," "rot," and "suicide" were among the many metaphors Wallace used to characterize the body politic. The infecting "negative force" was "the force of Satan," and ultimately "Wallace's critique of the Cold War was driven by an ideal image . . . of a spiritually awakened America engaging the Soviet Union in peaceful competition to heal an economically sick world . . ." (107–111).

The second, more typical iteration of exorcism incorporates the monster-making logic of spiritual warfare: the American polity is a healthy body in danger of possession by external demons. This iteration justifies preemptive, militaristic actions as a hunt for hidden evil abroad. President Ronald Reagan's speech to the House of Commons on June 8, 1982, presents one well-known example of externally focused or *exogenous exorcism,* in which the United States is conflated with the totality of human being itself in a spiritual battle between the good and evil. He characterizes evil and good as forces in a supernatural conflict between democracy and "Marxist-Leninism":

> ... we see totalitarian forces in the world who seek subversion and conflict around
> the globe to further their barbarous assault on the human spirit. What then, is our
> course? Must civilization perish in a hail of fiery atoms? Must freedom wither in a
> quiet, deadening accommodation with totalitarian evil?

Reagan's so-called "Evil Empire" speech before the National Association of Evangelicals on March 8, 1984, also presents a spiritual battle between good and evil ("President Reagan's Speech"). Reagan asks audiences to "pray for the salvation of all of
those who live in [Soviet] totalitarian darkness—pray they will discover the joy of
knowing God," ultimately because "they are the focus of evil in the modern world."
Further, there is "sin and evil in the world, and we're enjoined by Scripture and the
Lord to oppose it with all our might." In both speeches, Reagan portrays the American body as synonymous with a global body wrestling with "evil," and he justifies U.S.
action as a "global campaign for democracy" to exorcise and destroy the "tyrannies
which stifle the freedom and *muzzle* the self-expression of the people" (my emphasis).

Reagan's rhetoric extends what Michael Rogin has termed the "countersubversive
tradition" of "political demonology" into a global context with conspicuously corporeal metaphors (Rogin xiii). Reagan conflates a conceptual United States with the global body's striving toward a freedom out of the "darkness."[8] By characterizing this
globalizing rhetoric as a spiritual battle, Reagan and his handlers attempted to avoid
the charge of globalism: "This is not cultural imperialism," he said, "it [the global
campaign] is providing the means for genuine self-determination and protection for
diversity." In other words, Reagan's imperialist objectives were intended to restore the
"good voice" to the world body, purging the bad voices that "muzzle" its self-expression onto the "ash heap of history" ("Speech to the House"). George W. Bush's recent
speeches closely model the Reaganesque purging of an exogenous evil, right down to
the justification of global action, suggesting that speechwriters may have revisited
Reagan's famous remarks. This time, however, the demons are to be cast into "history's unmarked grave of discarded lies" (Bush, "Address to a Joint Session").

George W. Bush's Revival of Exorcism

Public perception of the smoke demon after 9/11 represents an anthropomorphism
of evil confined to a very limited symbolic repertoire. It is not a coincidence that the
image of the smoke demon and its popular dissemination in newspapers, magazines,
and the Internet occurred shortly after President Bush announced that the presidency
would be blamelessly prophetic. After almost a decade of presidential rhetoric virtually
absent of evangelical themes, the events of 9/11 all but guaranteed their return.

Bush's initial addresses to the U.S. citizenry described a spiritual battle between
good and evil. In his third address on 9/11, the president declared that "thousands of
lives were suddenly ended by evil, despicable acts of terror" ("They Cannot Dent"
par. 1). In his address from the Cabinet Room on September 12, Bush remarked that
"[t]his will be a monumental struggle of good versus evil, but good will prevail"
("Bush Address from Cabinet Room" par. 3).

These spiritually themed speeches cast the president as a healing exorcist. First,
he identified a public body and asked his audience to relive trauma: "Thousands of
lives were suddenly ended by evil, despicable acts of terror. The pictures of airplanes
flying into buildings ... have filled us with disbelief, terrible sadness and a quiet,
unyielding anger." The public body brought into being was the American polity,
which was signaled in almost every speech by constitutive language that identified

"unification," first in "grief," and then in "anger." Remarks such as "the resolve of our great nation" ("Freedom Itself" par. 3), "Americans from every walk of life unite in our resolve" ("They Cannot Dent" par 2), "Our unity is a kinship of grief and a steadfast resolve to prevail against our enemies" ("Address at the Episcopal" par. 8), and "They're [the American people] united in their resolve to help heal the nation" ("Remarks By President At Photo" par. 8) worked to forge the public body in the context of crisis. The term "national character" has also appeared frequently as a signifier for the American body since its first appearance in Bush's address to the grieving at the Episcopal National Cathedral on September 14, 2001 (par. 6).

Having identified the social body as "American," the president then located the negative force that divided our body as none other than "evil." Initially, the force was described as a vague "terrorism" ("Remarks by the President after Two Planes" par. 3) and later as "a faceless coward" ("Freedom Itself" par. 1). But in the third and final speech of the day it was clear that "evil" would be its lasting name, signaling the demonic idiom; the speech closed with a reading of Psalm 23: "Even though I walk through the valley of the shadow of death, I fear no evil because you are with me" ("They Cannot Dent" par. 2). From this point onward, an infecting "evil" is repeatedly invoked as a spiritual entity that invades and possesses the bodies of "evil doers" and "evil ones" ("President Holds Prime Time"). Phrases such as, "in the face of all this evil" ("National Day of Prayer" par. 3), "to . . . rid the world of evil" ("Address at the Episcopal National Cathedral" par. 3), "to secure our country and *eradicate* the evil of terrorism" ("Radio Address," 15 September 2001, par. 3), and "[These terrorists] *represent* evil and war" ("Remarks by the President at the Islamic Center" par. 3; my emphasis), are typical of the kind of evil invoked. To protect the body politic from further invasions, "the search is under way for those who are behind these evil acts," revealing an aggressive campaign abroad to find and *name* the demons.

In his address to the nation on September 20, the president became an exorcist claiming righteousness: "Every nation in every region has a decision to make: Either you are with us, or you are with the terrorists," professed Bush. This stance clearly marks the brand of exorcism underway as an evangelical Protestant one more typical of the U.S. prophetic tradition. The prophetic rhetorical tradition is characterized by an "inflexible posture of righteousness," concludes James Darsey, and this righteousness leaves no room for deliberation or evidence (Darsey 1–34). The president adopted a prophetic mode of address in his many speeches after 9/11 by using frequent biblical references and the language of spiritual warfare.[9] Using the idiom of civil religion (Bellah 1–21), the evangelical themes of Bush's speeches place the presidency into the pastoral and preacherly mode, as opposed to what Richard Pierard and Robert Linder term the priestly mode (291–293). Bush's rhetoric is patently Protestant and less dialogic or Catholic than that of more "priestly" presidents, such as Nixon or Harrison (Wilson). "I appreciate diplomatic talk," the president said at a news conference on 24 September 2001, "but I'm more interested in action and results. I am absolutely determined—absolutely determined—to *rout* terrorism out where it exists and bring them to justice" ("President Holds Prime Time" par. 59; my emphasis).

The *American* exorcism only lasted a month. By October, the American body was fortified by a "steel resolve" and attention shifted to the bodies of other countries and, eventually, the global body itself. In his remarks on September 20th, Bush prefigured the turn to the global body when he remarked that this "is not . . . just America's fight. . . . This is the world's fight," and that "we are supported by the collective will of the world." "We defend not only our precious freedoms," argued Bush, "but also the freedom of people everywhere. . . ." Although Bush's later speeches repeat the theme of fortifying the interior against an exterior threat, the initial identification of the U.S. public as a possessed body shifted to a full-blown "global campaign against terror" beginning in October ("Radio Address," 6 October 2001, par. 1). "The best defense against terror is a global offensive against terror," argued the president ("Gov. Ridge Sworn-In"). Although "the attack took place on American soil, . . . it was an attack on the heart and soul of the civilized world" ("President Holds Prime Time" par. 3).

Bush described the external "evildoers" in a manner that parallels the way in which evangelical Protestants describe how demons "hide" in bodies, thus necessitating an exorcism to coax them out. The most common language used to characterize "evil ones" referred to their "hiddenness" in the global body—eventually, in the mountainous caves of Afghanistan. "Hunting down" was a favored metaphor: "[I] have ordered that the full resources of the federal government . . . conduct a full-scale investigation to hunt down and find those folks who committed this act" ("Remarks by the President After Two" par. 2); "the United States will hunt down and punish" ("Freedom Itself" par. 1); "This enemy hides in shadows and has no regard for human life" ("Bush Address From Cabinet Room" par. 1); "we will find those who did it; we will smoke them out of their holes" ("Whatever It Takes" par. 3). In the September 20th address, Bush characterized the Middle East as harboring hidden demons, "parasites" who "burrow deeper into caves and other entrenched hiding places" ("Address to a Joint Session of Congress"). In this way, Bush positioned himself as an exorcist ready to purge the global body of the demons that possess its cavities. He asked the public to expect "a lengthy campaign unlike any other we have ever seen," and concluded "we will starve the terrorists of funding . . . driving them from place to place until there is no refuge or no rest." Four days later, the rhetorical embodiment of these hidden, evil forces was made explicit: "I will say it again—if you *cough him up* [Osama bin-Laden], and his people, today, that [sic] we'll reconsider what we're doing in your country [Afghanistan]" ("President Holds Prime Time" par. 68; my emphasis).

In the previous State of the Union Address delivered by Clinton, the focus was overwhelmingly deliberative. Bush's address on September 20th, which he characterized as an early State of the Union Address, contrasts sharply because it is strangely celebratory and repetitive, repeatedly following an order provided by one line in the introduction: "Our grief has turned to anger and anger to resolution." Similar to a neurotic's compulsion to repeat, Bush's speeches return to the proverbial primal scene, the "point of pain" or source of grief, again and again, reestablishing a mood of "crisis." Throughout what has been dubbed the "Justice Will Be Done" speech, Bush reminds the audience of grief and then attempts to create a sense of resolute anger and blind determination. For example, after the requisite meditation on common values and the construction of a public body in the introduction, Bush then abruptly comments that "On September the 11th, enemies of freedom committed an act of war against our country," which is followed by a maudlin reference to Pearl Harbor (another "point of pain" for many Americans). Bush continues that "Americans have known surprise attacks, but never before on thousands of civilians." These remarks are followed by mention of al Qaeda as a "perversion" of Islam, and then remarks that describe a "hidden" threat, and finally, a stalwart list of demands to the "Taliban." He said, "Deliver to the United States all of the leaders of al Qaeda who hide in your land." Similarly, after reminding us of "atrocity" and the terrorists' attempt to "end lives," Bush prescribes driving the evil out "until there is no refuge or no rest." At the end of the speech, Bush recalls "great loss," and "grief and anger," characterizing our predicament as "the dark threat of violence." He emphasizes, "I will not forget the wound to our country and those who inflicted it," thus recasting the U.S. as a body besieged. Finally, he calls for "patient justice" and "the rightness of our cause" to help vanquish the demons. He returns the audience to neurotic compulsion and trauma in order to amplify an angry "resolution," resembling the physical ambivalence of actual, bodily exorcisms that can last for days. The end result is, of course, physical and psychological exhaustion.

In light of this repetition, the faith-healing tone of both "Justice Will Be Done" and his 2002 State of the Union Address resembles the pattern Barry Brummett terms "contemporary apocalyptic." Both speeches model the "grief-to-anger-to-righteous action" pattern that begins with a recounting of "shock and suffering," "terror," a "sorrow and pain that will never completely go away," and "discoveries" that, unfortunately, "confirmed our worst fears," creating a sense of catastrophe and grief for the audience. Although a resolution is promised in the State of the Union Address, no particular time period is specified for closure. Further, the secret pattern explaining reasons behind the crisis is sketchy at best. Instead of the promise of an imminent ending, the president describes overcoming "evil with greater good" as a lengthy process; the enemy is not so much Osama bin Laden and the al Qaeda network as it is the diffuse and insidious force of "evil" that motivates them. At the end of his speech, Bush proclaims a fated victory for freedom, as its "momentum" is unstoppable, but he also carefully notes that "evil is real and must be opposed." This pattern is not apocalyptic, but a continual, immanent purging of the world body of a demonic force.

As the final statement of U.S. policy during this period, the 2002 State of the Union Address condenses the exorcist themes appearing in the post-9/11 speeches; although the genre is easier to recognize across the body of speeches delivered since the attacks, the State of the Union does exemplify the four steps of calling, naming, battling, and expelling an evil force.

In light of the repetitive calls to return to the original trauma, this speech is not so much a *recognition* or assessment of a chaotic state of affairs as it is an emotion-producing *preparation* for an exorcism of the global body—that is, for U.S. aggression abroad. The State of the Union revisits the primal scene by forcing audiences to relive the trauma of the event and reopen the symbolic wound left by the "terrorists," such as in the emotional appeal of the fourth introductory paragraph:

> For many Americans, these four months have brought sorrow and pain that will never completely go away. Every day a retired firefighter returns to ground zero to feel closer to his two sons who died there. At a memorial in New York, a little boy left his football with a note for his lost father: "Dear Daddy, please take this to Heaven. I don't want to play football until I can play with you again someday."

Further, Bush claims "madness and destruction" is imminent as "thousands of dangerous killers" wait "like ticking time bombs, set to go off without warning." "Time is not on our side," worries the president, but he concludes he "will not wait on events while dangers gather." These remarks disturb audiences and are intended to prepare their collective, global body for submission to the will of the presidential exorcist. Once the tone of fear, sorrow, and imminent danger is set, the official U.S. exorcist can commence with the summons.

Emotionally primed, the audience seeks evocation of the demon housed in the public body. Like the ritual of bodily exorcism, the president describes the demonic threat as hidden and interior in a besieged and wounded body. Phrases such as, "We have seen the depth of our enemies' hatred," "the depth of their hatred is equaled by the madness and destruction they design," and "a terrorist underworld . . . operates in remote jungles and deserts, and hides in the centers of large cities" not only specify the intensity of "evil" by degree, but also bespeak an inside/outside logic. As the many references to "hiding in holes" in earlier speeches locate these demons *inside a body,* so does the "hiding" metaphors here locate them in places *unseen.* The president mimics the evangelical plea that people are often unaware of their harboring demons, that the demonic is "hidden" or secreted away and must be coaxed out against their will. The American body is also called into being again here, signaled by anthropo-morphisms such as "the true character of this country" and "deep in the American character," as an example for the global body to achieve; our exemplary purified body is used to justify the global ritual.

By equating the American body with the "will of the world"—the body free of evil toward which all should aspire—Bush's speech strongly resembles Reagan's address to the House of Commons in 1982, and to some extent, the "Evil Empire" speech. Like Reagan's speeches, Bush's speech masks the globalization of U.S. ideol-ogy as a prophetic, imperial righteousness vouchsafed by God. Toward the end of the speech, we learn the speechwriters are aware of the possible perception of imperialism when they remark that "we have no intention of imposing our culture, but America will always stand firm for the non-negotiable demands of human dignity," a remark that closely resembles Reagan's qualification concerning imperialism in his 1982 address.[10] Elsewhere the president demands that the "values" deep in the American body should be advocated "around the world" to secure peace. Because our "enemies view the entire world as a battlefield," the United States "must pursue them wherever they are," and militaristic action can be understood as an attempt to exorcise the worldly body of the demons hidden deep inside the deserts and jungles of our worldly geography. Finally, purged of our own demons we have realized a new spiritual awak-ening. Now we can turn to the global body completely and blamelessly.

Who are the demons that need to be confronted? What are their names? For Bush, these demons certainly possess individual people—bin Laden and his follow-ers—but the speech implies that even if these hateful individuals have been captured or destroyed, the true source of the demonic will not be spirited away. There is a nam-ing, but this only is a naming of infected hosts since evil is a disembodied spiritual force. There are "terrorist" groups such as "Hamaz, Hezbollah, Islamic Jihad and Jaish-i-Mohammed" that have infected the world body for a long time and that also need to be vanquished. Further, a number of "regimes of terror" comprise foreign state bodies that will continue to harbor "evil." These state bodies, notably Iraq, Iran, and North Korea, compose an "axis of evil" and a "grave and growing danger" that threatens peace and freedom.[11] Even the identification of state bodies, however, fails to identify the true source of the demonic. Just as Reagan repeatedly chose to charac-terize the world body as being plagued by competing *forces,* the best and most frequent name given by Bush to the cause of bodily harm is the plain and deeply ambiguous term "evil."[12]

In the third main section of the State of the Union, Bush again turns from the glo-bal body to the American body to detail its safety, enumerating the fortifications against the demonic. Among the more memorable fortifications are more military spending, the establishment of an office of Homeland Security, economic stimuli leading to the creation of "good jobs," and the creation of USA Freedom Corps. In this way, Bush fulfills the patterned expectations of a State of the Union address. His transition from the meditation and assessment to policy is remarkable, particularly in terms of its navigation of the U.S. body politic and the global body:

> Our war on terror is well begun, but it is only begun. This campaign may not be finished on our watch, yet it must be and it will be waged on our watch. . . . Our first priority must always be the security of our nation, and that will be reflected in the budget I send to Congress. My budget supports three great goals for America: We will win this war, we will protect our homeland, and we will revive our economy.

Because of the role of bodies, that is, the need to fortify an already healthy body internally and the need to exorcise the global body externally, Bush is able to move smoothly from the angry and epideictic to a calm, optimistic, deliberative laundry list of policy recommendations. "We will prevail in the war, and we will defeat this recession," is a transitional phrase that smoothly links the internal and the external with the president as the link. Absent the notion of strengthening an already healthy body threatened by external "forces of evil," the transition ceases to make sense.

Having recovered our good voice, Bush urges the public to recognize that "this time of adversity offers a unique moment of opportunity, a moment we must seize to change our culture." Echoing Bush senior's "1000 points of light," by performing a "million acts of service and decency and kindness," the president assures the audience that "we can overcome evil with greater good." There is clearly the call to conscience typical of religious transformation, the urging to dig deeper, beyond the infecting spirits, to find the True Spirit of Faith, thus letting God (back) in: "Deep in the American character there is honor, and it is stronger than cynicism. And many have discovered again that even in tragedy—especially in tragedy [the hallmark of transformation]—God is near." The call here is characteristic of American pragmatism. It asks for the audience to exorcize itself continually while the presidential exorcist and his helpers go to expel the demons abroad.

Concluding Remarks: Whither Deliverance?

The media portrayal of physical exorcisms in recent years and the post 9/11 oratory of George W. Bush tracks the resurgence of exorcism as a generic form in the popular imagination. I have argued that just as some people found demons in the smoke of the World Trade Center's destruction in their attempts to organize and contain anxiety, so did Bush's speechwriters amplify the "terrorist" attacks on U.S. soil as a violent, spiritual confrontation with hidden, malicious forces. I have also suggested that the generic pattern of exorcism is the counterpart to conversion and part of a larger form of religious transformation. Exorcism can be identified as a formal logic that (1) constructs a rhetorical body; (2) features a spiritual battle between the forces of good and evil; and (3) contains metaphors that speak to the purging of something invisible or silent. Once these signs are identified, the pattern of exorcism will feature (1) the summoning of an evil infecting force; (2) the ritual naming of that force; (3) a symbolic battle with the named force; and (4) the demand for the force to leave.

This essay also underscores the importance of recasting our understanding of genre to take it beyond the mere description or classification of texts into an understanding of invention and reception as a largely unconscious process. Genres are labels for *psychological* forms that are persuasive because they stimulate the pleasures of repetition. The function of the generic critic is to bring social forms into conscious awareness by restoring them to their verbal character—by describing them, in language, as iterations of a recurring social form. Although genres are constrained by what appears in texts, it is important to underscore the field of genre is social. Recognizing the social existence of genre affords the generic critic some degree of creativity in "naming" the genre, however, insofar as genres are names for forms that elude consciousness, *genres can only capture forms incompletely* because form is, essentially, a repetition (or a kind of "work"), not a substance.

Genres are one of many ways to fix or stabilize the movement of discourse (suasion).[13] Exorcism is the key to a particular form of religious transformation that presents the body as a trope, a site of symbolic warfare, naming the presence of forces of evil and purging these forces. It should be underscored, however, that exorcism is a generic form that includes witch hunts, inquisitions, and similar, forceful modes of religious transformation. The forceful purging of bodies from infecting forces is a global iteration of religious transformation that need not model the model of calling, naming, battling, and expelling. Nevertheless, exorcism is a common, psychosomatic form in many cultures around the world.

One very important reason why "exorcism" is a useful description of Bush's recent rhetoric is because it helps us to see better the enthymematic function of "evil," and how the use of evil in demon-making sets a civil pedagogy—a subtle form of discipline—into motion. By using a charged yet vague label, a speaker can demonize entire peoples and justify violence as a necessity. Describing the racial Other as "evil" is a civil lesson in the intolerance of righteousness. For example, President Bush's initial speech inadvertently subjected many American Muslims to abuse, discrimination, and some physical violence. This reaction necessitated a speech by the president stressing that most Muslims were peaceful and Islam is a peaceful religion.

In closing, it should be said that the president's 2002 State of the Union Address is a kind of discursive exorcism lacking *deliverance* because the speech itself does not proclaim the exorcism a success. In the exorcist logic of presidential discourse, "evil" is a force that repetitively takes many guises. Bush demonstrates these guises in the following passage:

> The last time I spoke here, I expressed hope that life would return to normal. In some ways it has. In others it never will. Those of us who have lived through these challenging times have been changed by them. We've come to know truths that we will never question: Evil is real, and must be opposed. Beyond all differences of race or creed, we are one country, mourning together and facing danger together.

Bush's speech ends with a glimpse of optimism: "And in this great conflict, my fellow Americans, we will see freedom's victory." But he precludes optimism with the reminder that the demon still thrives abroad, still threatens the U.S. body. He says that we are discovering, and "especially in tragedy," that these dark forces impose a dreadful but necessary choice. "Our enemies send other people's children on missions of suicide and murder," and our enemies "embrace tyranny and death as a cause and creed." In other words, in the shadow of these many ills, the exorcism must never end.

Notes

[1] Of course, this observation is not new. See Burke, *Religion* vi.

[2] The word "demon" derives from the Greek *daemon,* "a supernatural being of a nature intermediate between that of gods and men"—not necessarily an evil spirit. As a result of the influence of Christian theodicy, however, demons are commonly associated with ill-will.

[3] Monster making is distinct from scapegoating, which works to alleviate guilt via an Oedipal logic of projection; see Burke, *Philosophy* 39–46.

[4] Exposés on exorcism during this period are numerous. For representative examples, see "Business Boom Brings Theological Debate" A65; Greg Burke 74; and Fountain A16.

[5] For example, rhetorical scholars have looked at *The Exorcist* as a popular means of organizing anxiety concerning the problem of evil during profound social changes in institutionalized religion and politics in the 1970s; none have sought to understand exorcism as a genre. See Frentz and Farrell 40–47; Lazenby 50–56; Medhurst 73–92; and Schuetz 92–101.

[6] This phrase is borrowed from a description of Freud's interpretive technique in Ritchie Robertson's forward to *The Interpretation of Dreams* (xix–xx).

[7] Exorcism is celebrated by members of the movement as an extremely common practice in the Bible. In fact, it is mentioned numerous times throughout the New Testament. See Matthew 8:16, 8:30–32, 9:32–33, 10:1, 12:22, 12:43–45, 15:22–28, 17:15–18; Mark 1:23–26, 3:22–26, 5:6–20, 6:7, 7:25–30, 9:18–29, 16:9, 16:17; Luke 4:33–35, 4:41, 8:2–3, 8:28–36, 9:41–42, 11:14–20; and Acts 16:16–18, 19:13–16.

[8] The classic examination of the relationship between the natural and public body is Kantorowicz, esp. 81–114.

[9] It is not surprising that his chief speechwriter, Michael Gerson, is an evangelical Christian who studied theology at one of the most conservative evangelical schools in the country, Wheaton College. See Bumiller A16; and Kiefer 1.

[10] Compare to Reagan's remarks in the "Speech Before the National Association of Evangelicals": "Now, obviously, much of this new political and social consensus I've talked about is based on a positive view of American history, one that takes pride. . . . But we must never forget that no government schemes are going to perfect man. . . . Our nation, too, has a legacy of evil with which it must deal . . . the long struggle of minority citizens for equal rights, once a source of disunity and civil war, is now a point of pride. . . . But whatever sad episodes exist in our past, any objective observer must hold a positive view of American history, a history that has been the story of hopes fulfilled and dreams made into reality."

[11] Notably, the original phrase was "axis of hatred," which the evangelical speechwriter Michael Gerson changed to "axis of evil." See Bumiller A16.

[12] In some sense, the naming of the possessing demon as "evil" mirrors Jesus' famous exorcism of a man in the gospel according to Mark: "For [Jesus] said unto him, Come out of the man, thou unclean spirit. And [Jesus] asked him, What is thy name? And [the demon] answered, saying, My name is Legion, for we are many" (Mark 5: 6–20). Legion is thus not a single possessing demon, but a host of demons (presumably with their own, individual names). On a symbolic register, naming the demon who haunts us as simply "evil" functions much like the name "Legion." Evil is a name for innumerable malignant spirits hosted by any number of "terrorists" in any number of places. Hence Bush's exorcism presented in the State of the Union risks failure, but it is a productive failure insofar as failing to exorcise evil makes it possible to repeat exorcisms everywhere indefinitely.

[13] Campbell and Jamieson note that "using a system of critical categorization that is but one among many, how can [one] claim truth of any sort . . . ? Our answer is that . . . [if] the use of a particular genre or group of genres proves illuminating, provides insights otherwise unavailable, then it is true by definition. But it is never the *only* truth, and it is always a tentative truth in that the critical argument holds only until a better argument is made" (*Deeds* 8).

Works Cited

Bellah, Robert N. "Religion in America." *Daedalus* 96 (1967): 1–21.

Benoit, William L. "Beyond Genre Theory: A Genesis of Rhetorical Action." *Communication Monographs* 67 (2000): 178–192.

Brookey, Robert Alan and Robert Westerfelhaus. "Pistols and Petticoats, Piety and Purity: *To Wong Foo,* the Queering of the American Monomyth, and the Marginalizing Discourse of Deification." *Critical Studies in Media Communication* 18 (June 2001): 141–156.

Brown, Karen McCarthy. *Mama Lola: A Vodou Priestess in Brooklyn.* Berkeley: University of California Press, 1991.

Brummett, Barry. *Contemporary Apocalyptic Rhetoric.* New York: Praeger, 1991.

Bumiller, Elisabeth. "White House Letter; A New Washington Whodunit: The Speechwriter Vanishes." *New York Times* 4 March 2002: A16.

Burke, Greg. "If You Liked the Movie . . . A Horror Classic is Back—and So is Exorcism, an Old Rite Getting New Respect." *Time* 2 Oct. 2000: 74.

Burke, Kenneth. *The Philosophy of Literary Form: Studies in Symbolic Action,* 3rd Ed. Berkeley: University of California Press, 1973.

———. *The Rhetoric of Religion: Studies in Logology.* Berkeley: University of California Press, 1970.

———. *Counter-statement.* Berkeley: University of California Press, 1968.

Bush, George W. "Address at the Episcopal National Cathedral in Washington, D.C. on the Occasion of the National Day of Prayer and Remembrance" 14 Sept. 2001. Americanrhetoric.com. 24 Jan. 2003 (http://americanrhetoric.com/speeches/bushmemorialaddress.htm).

———. "Bush Address from Cabinet Room Meeting" 12 Sept. 2001. Americanrhetoric.com. 24 Jan. 2003 (http://americanrhetoric.com/speeches/ bushcabadd91201.htm).

———. *A Charge to Keep: My Journey to the White House.* New York: HarperCollins, 2001.

———. "Freedom Itself Was Attacked This Morning" 11 Sept. 2001. Americanrhetoric.com. 24 Jan. 2003 (http://americanrhetoric.com/speeches/ bushtxt1.htm).

———. "National Day of Prayer and Remembrance" 13 Sept. 2001. Americanrhetoric.com. 24 Jan. 2003 (http://americanrhetoric.com/speeches/ ntlprayerday.htm).

———. "President Bush's Address to a Joint Session of Congress and the American People" ("Justice Will Be Done") 20 Sept. 2001. Americanrhetoric.com. 24 Jan. 2003 (http://americanrthetoric.com/speeches/gwbushjointsessionspeech9–20–01.htm).

———. "President Delivers State of the Union Address" 29 Jan. 2002. The White House Online. 24 Jan. 2003 (http://www.whitehouse.gov/news/releases/2002/01/ 20020129–11.htm1).

———. "President Holds Prime Time News Conference" 11 Oct. 2001. The White House Online. 24 Jan. 2003 (http://www.whitehouse.gov/news/releases/2001/10/ 20011011–7.html).

———. "Radio Address of the President to the Nation" 15 Sept. 2001. The White House Online. 24 Jan. 2003 (http://www.White House.gove/news/releases/2001/09/ 20010915.html).

———. "Radio Address of the President to the Nation" 6 Oct. 2001. The White House Online. 24 Jan. 2003 (http://www.White House.gov/news/releases/2001/10/ 20011006.html).

———. "Remarks by the President after Two Planes Crash Into World Trade Center" 11 Sept. 2001. The White House Online. 24 Jan. 2003 (http://White House.gov/ news/releases/2001/09/20010911.html).

———. "Remarks by the President at the Islamic Center of Washington, D.C." 17 Sept. 2001. Americanrhetoric.com. 24 Jan. 2003 (http://americanrhetoric.com/speeches/ bushislamicpeace.htm).

———. "They Cannot Dent the Steel of American Resolve" 11 Sept. 2001. Americanrhetoric.com. 24 Jan. 2003 (http://americanrhetoric.com/speeches/ bushspch9–11–01.htm).

———. "'Whatever It Takes, As Long as It Takes' to Defeat Terrorists" 15 Sept. 2003. U.S. Department of State, International Information Programs Online. 24 Jan. 2003 (http://usinfo.state.gov/topical/polterror/01091510.htm).

"Business Boom Brings Theological Debate; Scholars Say Family Problems, Interest in Occult Fuel Interest." *The Washington Post* 7 Dec. 2000, A65.

Callinicos, Alex. *Against Postmodernism: A Marxist Critique.* New York: St. Martin's Press, 1989.

Campbell, Karlyn Kohrs and Kathleen Hall Jamieson. *Deeds Done In Words: Presidential Rhetoric and the Genres of Governance.* Chicago: Chicago University Press, 1990.

———. (Eds.). *Form and Genre: Shaping Rhetorical Action.* Falls Church: Speech Communication Association, 1978.

———. "Introduction." *Southern Speech Communication Journal* 51 (1986): 294.

Carroll, Robert Todd. "Pareidolia." Skeptic.com Webpages (n.d.). 21 Feb. 2002 (http://skeptic.com/pareidol.html).

Cassirer, Ernst. *Language and Myth.* Trans. Susanne K. Langer. New York: Dover Publications, 1946.

Clinton, William J. "Clinton's State of the Union Speech" 27 Jan. 2000. Inside Politics 1 Sept. 2002 (http://www.insidepolitics.org/speeches/clinton00.htm).

Conley, Thomas. "The Linnaean Blues: Thoughts on the Genre Approach." *Form, Genre, and the Study of Popular Discourse.* Ed. Herbert W. Simons and Aram A. Aghazarian. Columbia: University of South Carolina Press, 1986. 59–78.

Connor, Steven. *Dumbstruck: A Cultural History of Ventriloquism.* New York: Oxford University Press, 2000.

Cuneo, Michael W. *American Exorcism: Expelling Demons in the Land of Plenty.* New York: Doubleday, 2001.

Darsey, James. *The Prophetic Tradition and Radical Rhetoric in America.* New York: New York University Press, 1997.

Delbanco, Andrew. *The Death of Satan: How Americans Have Lost the Sense of Evil.* New York: Farrar, Straus, and Giroux, 1995.

Dwyer, Graham. *The Divine and the Demonic: Supernatural Affliction and its Treatment in North India.* New York: Routledge, 2003.

Ellis, Bill. *Raising the Devil: Satanism, New Religions, and the Media.* Lexington: University Press of Kentucky, 2000.

Fountain, John W. "Exorcists and Exorcisms Proliferate Across U.S." *New York Times* 28 Nov. 2000: A16.

Frentz, Thomas S. and Thomas B. Farrell. "Conversion of America's Consciousness: The Rhetoric of *The Exorcist*." *Quarterly Journal of Speech* 61 (1975): 40–47.

Guthrie, Stewart Elliott. *Faces in the Clouds: A New Theory of Religion.* New York: Oxford University Press, 1995.

Gutterman, David S. "Presidential Testimony: Listening to the Heart of George W. Bush." *Theory and Event* 5 (2001): 31 pars. 1 Dec. 2001 (http://muse.jhu.edu/journals/theory_and_event/v005/5.2gutterman.html).

Headley, Stephen Cavana. *From Cosmogony to Exorcism in a Javanese Genesis: The Split Seed.* New York: Oxford University Press, 2001.

Hebdige, Dick. "The Impossible Object: Towards a Sociology of the Sublime." *New Formations* 1 (1987): 47–76.

Hofstadter, Richard. *The Paranoid Style in American Politics: And Other Essays.* Cambridge: Harvard University Press, 1996.

Ingebretsen, Edward J. *At Stake: Monsters and the Rhetoric of Fear in Public Culture.* Chicago: Chicago University Press, 2001.

Ivie, Robert L. "Metaphor and the Rhetorical Invention of Cold War Idealists." *Cold War Rhetoric: Strategy, Metaphor, and Ideology.* Ed. Martin J. Medhurst, Robert L. Ivie, Philip Wander, and Robert L. Scott. New York: Greenwood Press, 1990, 103–127.

Jameson, Fredric. *The Political Unconscious: Narrative as a Socially Symbolic Act.* Ithaca: Cornell University Press, 1981.

Kantorowicz, Ernst H. *The King's Two Bodies.* Princeton: Princeton University Press, 1997.

Kapferer, Bruce. *A Celebration of Demons: Exorcism and the Aesthetics of Healing in Sri Lanka.* Washington: Smithsonian Institution Press, 1991.

Kiefer, Francine. "Where Can a Guy Write a State of the Union Speech?" *The Christian Science Monitor* 28 January 2002: 1.

Larson, Bob. *In the Name of Satan: How the Forces of Evil Work and What You Can Do to Defeat Them.* Nashville: Thomas Nelson Publishers, 1996.

Lazenby, Walter. "Exhortation as Exorcism: Cotton Mather's Sermons to Murderers." *Quarterly Journal of Speech* 57 (1971): 50–56.

McCarthy, Joseph. "Speech on Communists in the State Department (1950)." Cable News Network. 9 June 2008 (http://www.cnn.com/SPECIALS/cold.war/episodes/06/documents/mccarthy/).

Medhurst, Martin J. "Image and Ambiguity: A Rhetorical Approach to *The Exorcist.*" *Southern Speech Communication Journal* 44 (1978): 73–92.

Mikkelson, Barbara and David P. Mikkelson. "Images of World Trade Center Fire Reveal the Face of Satan." Urban Legend Reference Pages (21 Sept. 2001). 21 Feb. 2002 (http://snopes.com/rumors/wtcface.htm).

Miller, Carolyn R. "Genre as Social Action." *Quarterly Journal of Speech* 70 (1984): 151–167.

O'Leary, Stephen D. *Arguing the Apocalypse: A Theory of Millennial Rhetoric.* New York: Oxford University Press, 1994.

Pierard, Richard V. and Robert D. Linder. *Civil Religion and the Presidency.* Grand Rapids: Academie Books, 1988.

Reagan, Ronald. "Address to the British House of Commons (June 8, 1982)." Cable News Network. 9 June 2008 (http://www.cnn.com/SPECIALS/2004/reagan/stories/speech.archive/empire.html).

Rogin, Michael P. *Ronald Reagan, the Movie: And Other Episodes of Political Demonology.* Berkeley: University of California Press, 1988.

Rosemarin, Adena. *The Power of Genre.* Minneapolis: University of Minnesota Press, 1985.

Russell, Jeffrey Burton. *The Devil: Perceptions of Evil from Antiquity to Primitive Christianity.* Ithaca: Cornell University Press, 1977.

———. *Lucifer: The Devil in the Middle Ages.* Ithaca: Cornell University Press, 1986.

———. *Mephistopheles: The Devil in the Modern World.* Ithaca: Cornell University Press, 1990.

———. *The Prince of Darkness: Radical Evil and the Power of Good in History.* Ithaca: Cornell University Press, 1992.

———. *Satan: The Early Christian Tradition.* Ithaca: Cornell University Press, 1987.

Schrecker, Ellen. *Many Are the Crimes: McCarthyism in America.* New York: Little, Brown and Company, 1998.

Schuetz, Janice. "*The Exorcist:* Images of Good and Evil." *Western Speech Communication* 39 (1975): 92–101.

Wagner, Doris M. *How to Cast Out Demons: A Guide to the Basics.* Ventura, CA: Regal Books, 2000.

Wilson, Kirt. "The Problem with Public Memory: President Benjamin Harrison Confronts the 'Southern Question.'" Eighth Annual Presidency Conference. Texas A&M University, College Station. 1 March 2002.

Wise, Terry S. *Fundamentals of Spiritual Warfare.* Needham Heights, MA: Simon and Schuster Custom Publishing, 1996.

Family Photographs
A Generic Description
Sharon M. Varallo

In this essay, I will describe and analyze three photographs to determine if a genre of family photographs exists. I am interested in family communication and want to discover ways in which family members rhetorically construct themselves as a unit. Toward that end, I address the situational requirements necessary for a particular response, a description of the artifacts collected, an analysis of the substantive and stylistic features of the artifacts, and an overall pattern of organization for this genre.

Situational Requirements

The first step in generic description is the observation of similarities in rhetorical responses to particular situations. In other words, in order for an artifact to exist that might be called a *family photograph*, a number of elements must be present. The elements on which I briefly focus include the need for a family, a camera, a photographer, and an audience:

(1) The most obvious element required to be present is a family. The definition of *family* is much broader now than it has been in years past, as evidenced by new descriptors such as *blended families*, which did not exist a short time ago. The situational requirement, therefore, is a broadly defined one: whether the group members consider themselves to be traditional or nontraditional, the subjects being photographed must perceive themselves to be a family.

(2) The presence of a camera is necessary to the situation. Because many cameras are relatively inexpensive, they are accessible to the general population; people from almost every economic class, therefore, are able to present themselves as a family in front of a camera.

(3) A photographer must be present. Unless the photograph is taken with a camera with time-delay capability, family photos are taken with a non-family member as onlooker and producer.

(4) An audience is required. Why else would a family stop, pull together, smooth hair, and smile broadly at no one in particular? The family members know that the photograph will capture them in a particular moment, so they collect themselves enough to present themselves in ways that clearly show they are a family. The family itself could be the audience the photograph most persuades; in collecting family photos, we constantly reassure ourselves that we are members of the culturally valued group called a *family*.

Description of Artifacts

The artifacts I have chosen to analyze are three photographs of family groups. They include the Varallo family photograph, the Chryslee-Miller family photograph, and the Marty-Rhoades family photograph. All of the photographs are of immediate family members, and all of the families are white and middle class.

This essay was written while Sharon M. Varallo was a student in Sonja K. Foss's rhetorical criticism class at Ohio State University in 1994. Used by permission of the author.

The Varallo family photograph was taken in December, 1973, during the Christmas holiday season. The photograph shows a mother, father, son, and daughter standing in front of a Christmas tree. The tree, decorated with plastic confections, is positioned in front of a window covered with white patterned curtains. The children are standing in front of their parents. The father's arm is encircling his wife, who, in turn, is touching her daughter. The son stands independently. The females are wearing primarily red, and the males are dressed primarily in white.

The Chryslee-Miller family photograph was taken in May of 1992 prior to a graduation ceremony for the older son. The photograph includes a mother and father and two sons, one of whom is dressed in a graduation cap and gown. The family members are standing in a line, all in close proximity to one another, obviously convening around the graduating son. The mother has her arms around both her sons, the father has his arm around his older son, and the younger son has his arm around his mother. The photograph was taken in front of a tree in the family's backyard.

The Marty-Rhoades photograph was taken during a vacation trip to visit family in August, 1992. The photograph includes two women who are partners and co-parents and their seven-year-old daughter. This family is shown huddled on a rock that is jutting out into the ocean, and the background is of the water and shoreline reefs. Both women are touching their daughter, and she appears to be leaning against them. They all are wearing casual clothing.

Substantive and Stylistic Elements

A substantive and stylistic analysis of the photographs uncovers the meanings present in the artifacts. In the case of non-discursive artifacts such as photographs,

The Varallo family. (All images also included in color photo gallery.)

The Chryslee-Miller family.

The Marty-Rhoades family.

substantive and stylistic elements cannot be separated; thus, both will be discussed together. This stage of generic description finds the similarities in the artifacts and considers what those similar elements might signify. As similarities in the photographs are uncovered, their importance or unimportance to a genre of family photographs also is addressed.

First, the children tend to be positioned in front of and physically lower than the adults. In the Varallo and Marty-Rhoades photographs, the children are positioned in front of and physically lower than the adults; this positioning is not surprising given that the children are, after all, shorter than the parents. However, in many family photographs where the children are taller than the parents, the children often are positioned so they are shorter than the parents. Julia Hirsch (1981) discusses a possible reason for this feature of family photography:

> The authority of these conventions, like the hold of traditional family roles which still makes us want strong fathers and nurturing mothers, loving children and sheltering homes, is difficult for any of us to resist. Professional as well as amateur photographers still place families in poses that express and cater to these longings. (p. 12)

Hirsch's revelation of the family as a metaphor for all of humankind gives any representation of the family a much greater significance. Families pose for formal photographs to show themselves as a family *should* be. The positioning of the subjects to ensure the distinction between the matriarch/patriarch and the children seems necessary to the genre.

A second similarity is that all the people are sitting or standing in close proximity to one another. Perhaps some of this closeness is required for everyone to fit into the picture, but the picture could be taken from a distance to produce a longer shot, so the physical closeness is not a necessity for the photograph itself. This closeness clearly suggests to an onlooker that the family is one unit. By standing near one another, the family members create a distinct and distinguishable group. To fit into the genre of the ideal family photograph, the members should be standing close to one another.

A third similarity related to the first two is that the mothers touch their children, while the fathers are less likely to do so. The Marty-Rhoades mothers are connecting the most obviously with their daughter; their warmth and intimacy are apparent from their comfortable connection with one another. The other mothers also touch their children in "natural" ways that the fathers do not. The Chryslee-Miller father has his hand on his son's shoulder but otherwise does not appear to be touching him and is standing directly forward in an independent stance. The Varallo father is touching only his wife. The connections of the mothers to the daughters show nurturing and protective women, and the separation of the fathers and the sons shows independence and distance: both are the kinds of behaviors that fit within the traditional family mold addressed by Hirsch and are an element necessary to the ideal genre.

Fourth, women seem to have paid more attention to their appearance than the men and, overall, seem to have been concerned more with presenting a pleasing image. The Varallo woman has on make-up and a wig and has thin, finely plucked eyebrows, as was the fashion at that time. The Chryslee-Miller woman has coordinated accessories—a red belt and red earrings—to add flair to her dress. Albeit more subtly, the Rhoades and Marty women also have on jewelry, and the daughter is wearing small post earrings. In all the photographs, the women's dress closely matches that of the other women in the photograph, as if they coordinated their efforts: the Varallo females are wearing red, and the Rhoades and Marty women are dressed similarly in style—they are wearing comfortable, kick-about clothing. Finally, all the women are smiling broadly. These elements combine to present an image of women as, perhaps, the filler of a more nurturing role. After all, the Chryslee-Miller and Varallo fathers—and the adult Chryslee-Miller sons—did not feel the need to smile: they present themselves as more independent and more of what traditionally might be called *strong*. The women perhaps are showing the traditional roles expected of them as part of a family. Their concern with a pleasing image is both individual and group oriented and influences the showing of the entire family.

Yet another characteristic that distinguishes the photographs is their optimism. The Marty-Rhoades family members have open-mouthed smiles as if laughing in response to a joke. The Varallo photograph is of people smiling for the camera, seemingly on command. The Varallo father is the only unsmiling person, and, as such, he stands out. The Chryslee-Miller photograph evidences optimism in yet another way: it celebrates a family milestone as the members have gathered for a son's graduation. These observations coincide with Hirsch's: "Family photographs, so generous with views of darling babies and loving couples, do not show grades failed, jobs lost, opportunities missed . . . . The family pictures we like best are poignant—and optimistic" (p. 118). We are motivated to fit the image. Optimism, not realism, is important to family photographs.

A sixth characteristic feature of the photographs is that the pictures are posed. These photographs, although seemingly natural, are not candid. Everyone except the Chryslee-Miller graduate is looking directly at the camera, and each person seems acutely aware of being photographed. In this way, photographs present a kind of normalcy that is not normal: my family never stood that way unless we were getting our picture taken, and chances are the Chryslee-Miller and Marty-Rhoades families usually did not stand in that fashion on a normal day. This awareness and posing seem important to the genre as well.

The backgrounds in the photographs clearly were important and consciously chosen, perhaps to help represent the image of the family; this is a seventh characteristic of the photographs. All the photographs were taken during a special event, an event that is clear from an analysis of the background details. The Varallo photograph was snapped at Christmas time, and the family members positioned themselves in front of the Christmas tree. The Chryslee-Miller family stood in front of a tree in their backyard, gathered around a graduate. The Marty-Rhoades family, standing with the ocean as a backdrop, were clearly out of the ordinary settings of their usual lives. Part of the catalyst for taking the photographs seems to have been the event itself. Special events, therefore, also may be integral to the ideal family photograph.

The backgrounds in these particular photographs may offer insights into a critique of the genre of family photographs. The decorations on the Varallo tree, for instance, are sugar-coated, plastic candy ornaments. The Christmas tree was a pretend tree, the decorations were pretend confections, and our presentation of ourselves as the ideal family was pretend. We also stood in front of a window, perhaps symbolizing our desire for public approval, and the window is covered with curtains, perhaps symbolizing our need to hide the "real" family. The star on the Christmas tree is directly above the patriarch's head, crown like, giving the male a kingly air. The Chryslee-Miller photograph was taken in front of a tree in the backyard, and part of the house is visible in the background, serving to reinforce the representation of the traditional family. The most open background of all the photographs is in the photograph of the Marty-Rhoades family. Interestingly, their environment is natural. While the Varallo family seems limited to one way of showing a family, the Marty-Rhoades family is the most open of all, not just in background but in the family structure itself. As lesbian partners and parents, they present a family that likely would garner objection in traditional circles. Their family photograph, however, shows a more open, natural setting and clearly shows the most sincere warmth. Their smiles are genuine, while the others, though not necessarily fake, are obviously primarily for the camera.

That these photographs rarely capture the subjects' feet is an eighth characteristic of the genre of family photographs. Only upper torsos are visible in the Varallo and Chryslee-Miller photographs, and we barely see the feet of the Marty and Rhoades women. Although this photographic choice may have some symbolic significance, it does not appear vital to the genre.

Finally, similarities exist in the physical presentations of the photographs. The Marty-Rhoades photograph is enlarged and framed and usually sat on a table in the family's living room. The framing and public showing of the picture added to the impression that the family is special. The photograph was set apart, given a place of honor on a table, put out to be admired and to remind those who saw it most often— the two women and their daughter—that they were, indeed, a family. Although the framing and presentation of the photograph reinforces the ideal family it presents, that the photograph be framed is not vital to the genre. The other two photographs, for instance, are normal-sized photographs and have been in both private and public places, ranging from the "photo drawer" to a bulletin board; they still seem to qualify as participants in this genre.

Organizing Principles of the Genre

In summary, the substantive and stylistic elements that seem vital to the genre include the presentation of:

(1) higher (status) positioning of the patriarch and/or matriarch

(2) close physical proximity of the family members

(3) mothers touching the children and touching more in general

(4) women more concerned with presenting a pleasing image

(5) optimism, usually evidenced in smiles

(6) a posed group

(7) backgrounds showing a special event

If all of these elements are present and the situational requirements are met, a photograph would seem to fit into a distinct category of family photography. From these observations, I conclude that there is, indeed, a genre of family photographs. The necessary elements noted in the previous section are substantial enough to warrant the inclusion of a new genre in the realm of generic criticism.

Conclusion

These photographs undoubtedly serve to convince and reinforce the "proper" family image to society at large and also to the families themselves. The photographs probably serve as a strong element of self-persuasion; in Hirsch's words, perhaps we are both seller and consumer of the idea of the ideal family. Formal family photography deals with character (Hirsch, p. 82), and few are willing to preserve for eternity a flawed image. None of the families evidenced in these photographs remains intact today—all three dissolved through divorce or separation of the parents. Nowhere, however, is family strife shown in any of these photographs. We all have our central identities at stake, and we therefore present ourselves as a unified family, the rules of which implicitly seem to be known.

Reference

Hirsch, J. (1981). *Family photographs*. New York: Oxford University Press.

Beauty in Conflict
Discussion on Art

Danielle Montoya

Artist Ansel Adams is known throughout the world for his landscape photographs set in the American West and Southwest. I received an Ansel Adams calendar for Christmas and found, among the works included, a photograph that seemed to violate the genre of the landscape photograph for which he is known. It is entitled *Discussion on Art* and was taken about 1936, during the time he was completing one of his most famous natural landscape portfolios, *Images 1920–1974*. Unlike any of his other photographs, this work depicts two men in what appears to be an unnatural or constructed setting, and it challenges the characteristic works of Adams through distinct choices of style, form, and composition.

Discussion on Art, 1936. Photograph by Ansel Adams. Used with permission of the Trustees of The Ansel Adams Publishing Rights Trust. All rights reserved.

This essay was written while Danielle Montoya was a student in Karen A. Foss's rhetorical criticism class at the University of New Mexico in 2002. Used by permission of the author.

The purpose of this analysis is to investigate the photograph *Discussion on Art* to discover if it reflects attributes of Ansel Adams's artistic genre and, if so, how the photograph participates in communicating the rhetor's artistic perspective. To explore the work's participation in the genre, I will apply the method of generic rhetorical criticism and, in particular, of generic participation.

I will analyze *Discussion on Art* and its participation in Ansel Adams's artistic genre according to three specific elements of rhetorical genres: (1) situational requirements—the contextual setting that evokes specific rhetorical responses; (2) substantive and stylistic characteristics—the unique features that constitute the content; and (3) the organizing principle—the dynamic formed by the situational and stylistic elements. In the interest of achieving a solid and representative understanding of the artistic genre of the photographs of Ansel Adams, I first analyze seven photographs from the *Images 1920–1974* collection: *Mount Resplendent*, Mount Roboson National Park, Canada, 1928; *Icicles*, Yosemite National Park, California, 1950; *Bicycle*, Yosemite National Park, California, 1937; *Granite Crags*, Sierra Nevada, California, 1927; *Statue and Oil Derricks*, Signal Hill, Long Beach, California, 1939; *Cape Royal from the South Rim*, Grand Canyon National Park, Arizona, c. 1947; and *Silverton, Colorado*, 1951.

Description of the Adams Genre

In the collection of natural landscape photographs available in the seven photographs I analyzed, five patterns of situational and stylistic elements emerge: (1) contrast in natural settings; (2) contrast between light and dark; (3) contrast between high and low; (4) contrast between humans and nature; and (5) contrast between smooth and rough. Each of the seven works participates in all five patterns on some level. However, each composition is unique and individual in the emphasis of the elements of contrast and opposition and how they function in the work.

Contrast in Natural Settings

The primary defining feature of Ansel Adams's artistic genre is that all of the photographs focus on subjects in their natural settings. By *natural setting*, I do not mean that all of the photographs avoid and omit materials or settings that are humanly made; however, the works reflect physical contexts that have been undisturbed or unprovoked by the artist. The settings are free of affectation or artificiality. They are not altered or disguised and are photographed as the artist found them to exist in the physical world.

Each composition is created through the aesthetic contrast and opposition of elements found in the natural setting. For example, *Bicycle* exhibits a humanly made object, the bicycle, in opposition to the natural snow. The human presence is acknowledged but, at the same time, is contrasted with a statement of absence in the collection of snow. Neither the bicycle nor the snow has been altered, disguised, or manipulated by the artist. The composition and contrast exist in the natural, physical world without the influence of the artist.

Icicles found melting on a rock face provide another example of elements found in natural opposition. In *Icicles*, the color and texture of the icicles in the foreground are found in natural contrast with the color and texture of the rocks in the background. The image of contrast occurs naturally and is not altered or corrupted by the artist. Opposition and contrast are found and represented in the setting in which they were discovered by Adams.

Another setting that articulates a perspective of opposition is exposed by Adams in *Statue and Oil Derricks*. Nearly all elements in the composition are humanly created; however, the setting in which they are discovered and photographed is left unchanged and is represented as it exists without the influence of the artist. The natural medium in which the statue was created contrasts with the medium of the oil derricks and industrial park in the background. These two main elements of the work are in striking contrast as they existed and were found by Adams.

Adams chooses to photograph beauty found in the contrast he sees around him in the world, as it exists, without artistic influence, alteration, or manipulation apart from that involved in the selection of the photographic frame. He observes contrast within and between subjects and their environments, emphasizing those elements through his artistic compositions.

Contrast Between Light and Dark

A signature technique to the aesthetic composition of Adams's work is a focus on elements of light and dark. This stylistic practice creates a generic style that emphasizes the contrast and opposition he finds in natural settings. For example, *Mount Resplendent* depicts stark contrast between the layer of white snow and the huge mountain of black rock. Shadows caused by the terrain cause black striping to occur horizontally in the foreground, opposing the same effect that happens vertically in the background. The crevices, crags, and points in the mountain itself add depth and texture through the use of black and white. In the foreground, a chunky shadow is cast amid the smoothness of the horizontal plane of the snow leading to the sheer cliff at the top of the mountain. At the left side of the composition, the dark mountain is contrasted against the light of the sky, giving *Mount Resplendent* an ominous feel. It evokes an awe of the natural beauty contrasted with the stark danger and darkness of the mountain and its elements.

Adams uses the same stylistic technique in *Cape Royal from the South Rim* to capture the awe the viewer experiences in seeing the space, texture, and "grandness" of the Grand Canyon. In this piece, the light and shadow are caught playing on high plateaus and low valleys. The shadow and darkness emphasize the depth of the canyon and obscure the rocks below so that the observer is impressed with a sense of endlessness and void. The shadow and depth are contrasted with the light striking the inclining sides and flat tops of the plateaus. The light also brings focus to the texture of the higher land, detailing the sheer cliffs, jagged inclines, and the step-like layering of the two. Light and darkness are observed and captured as they articulate the contrast that emphasizes the beauty and complexity of the Grand Canyon. Adams articulates his perspective through the photograph, composing an image of contrast to attempt to enhance and accentuate the experience for the viewer.

Images of light and darkness aid in underscoring the opposition present in *Statue and Oil Derricks*. In this composition, the light color of the medium in which the statue was created is enhanced by direct sun on the largest open surface area, making the statue seem to radiate light. Light also enhances the soft curves of the statue, bringing attention to the gentle and feminine presence of the work. A shadow, in contrast, falls across the left side of the face of the image, accentuating the statue's contemplative, downcast, non-threatening air. The gentle, luminescent presence of the statue is contrasted with the darkness of the background. Strong black lines draw attention to the angular, sharp shape of the oil derricks. The strength of steel and the blackness of industry are in direct opposition to the statue. The dark shapes and the black of oil and industry create looming shadowy silhouettes. The statue at the center of the photograph, however, is highlighted by the sun and is a brighter, stronger, more present and powerful image than the opposing oil derricks. Images contrasted in dark and light create the gentle presence as more central to the composition and assist in creating mood and meaning around the statue and oil derricks.

In all of the seven photographs I analyzed, Adams uses elements of light and dark to emphasize and enhance. In the three works discussed, light and dark contribute significantly to the composition. In other works, tension between light and dark is still present but is not as important to the visual aesthetic or perspective of the compositions.

Contrast Between High and Low

Patterns in high and low contrast in Adams's photographs also work to define his artistic genre. *Statue and Oil Derricks* combines aspects of light and dark with aspects of high and low. The statue, higher in the composition, is in contrast with the oil derricks that are lower in the photograph, although the derricks would dwarf the statue if placed next to it. Adams uses height to create the statue as the dominant image and to subvert the appearance of the oil derricks. Levels of height assist the artist in communicating his perspective.

This skill is also employed in *Silverton, Colorado*. Low one-story houses in the foreground are contrasted with the height and mass of the mountains behind them. The low placement of the houses contributes to creating and enhancing the effect of the towering mountains. Although the houses are in the foreground and want to make their presence known, the height of the mountains behind them seems to overpower and overcome them. Portraying the relative height of the mountains and the houses helps to expound the significance and independence of the land and makes clear the view of the artist. Characteristics of high and low are also present and significant in *Cape Royal from the South Rim* and *Granite Crags*. The stylistic application of contrast between high and low helps to define the genre and to highlight significant aspects of the works. The elements of high and low are present in each of the seven photographs and are a qualifying characteristic of the genre. Like the other qualifying characteristics, this one varies across the photographs in emphasis and significance.

Contrast Between Humans and Nature

A tension or contrast between humans and nature is a recurring image and theme in all seven works. Although Adams often photographs landscapes devoid of human presence and undisturbed by human existence, his own presence is articulated through the existence of the photograph. In that sense, each photograph, specifically the most desolate and intimidating settings, is in conflict with the human presence of the artist. Several of the photographs, however, expressly address the contrast of the human presence with nature. *Silverton, Colorado*, for example, portrays the existence of humans as natural. The human presence, represented by houses in the foreground, is not obtrusive, and it does not deface or harm the power and beauty of the mountain behind it. The houses are simply a part of what is real; they are a part of the landscape and construct a natural contrast. The human presence is not destructive here—it just is.

The same presence is found in *Bicycle*. The bicycle indicates the human presence that is contrasted with the suggestion of human absence through the layer of snow that has collected. The existence of people and artificial objects is not seen as an intrusion on nature. They are not seen as blatant disruptions in the natural environment but actually have membership in it. The beauty is created in the contrast the two create as they exist together.

Contrast Between Smooth and Rough

The pattern of beauty in contrast is perpetuated through the stylistic elements of smooth and rough, soft and hard. *Bicycle*, for example, illustrates the contrast between the hard, smooth metal bicycle and the soft and textured snow cover. The contrast of textures underscores other elements of opposition that occur in the composition, such as those of light and dark and human and natural. The tension between textures is also exemplified in *Icicles*. The clear, white icicles are contrasted with the dark, solid, opaque rock beneath. The aesthetic opposition is enhanced by the competition of the textures. The smoothness of the sharp icicles in the foreground contradicts the rough, dull rock face in the background.

This same technique is evident in *Granite Crags*, where the jagged angular rocks cut into the soft cirrus clouds in the background, accentuating the harsh and stark qualities of the formation. Patterns of texture are clear in all seven works and are enhanced and elaborated with contrasts of light and dark, high and low, and human and nature.

All five recurring stylistic and situational characteristics combine to comprise Adams's photographic genre. Beauty and aesthetic appeal are found in natural contrasts the artist finds in the world, as it exists, without influence, alteration, or manipulation by the artist himself. The organizing principle that governs each composition and comprises the genre is beauty in natural opposition.

Generic Comparison with *Discussion on Art*

To determine the generic participation of *Discussion on Art* in Adams's genre, I applied each of the five stylistic and situational characteristics that typify his photographs to the photograph in question.

Contrast in Natural Settings

All seven works analyzed to investigate the generic qualities of Adams's work existed in a natural setting. Each photograph contained evidence of materials or objects created from the earth that exist with and in spite of the human presence. At first glance, *Discussion on Art* seems to stray from this qualifying characteristic. Upon a more careful investigation, however, the generic pattern of opposition in a natural setting is perpetuated.

The photograph suggests that humans in their natural settings are in conflict. As in the seven works definitive of the genre, the artist has found contrast in the world as it exists, without artistic influence, alteration, or manipulation. Adams has photographed what he wants the audience to believe is spontaneous. The work captures a scene that is unprovoked and undisturbed by the artist. In accordance with the generic quality, Adams observes contrast among subjects and between subjects and their environments, emphasizing those elements through the aesthetic composition.

Contrast Between Light and Dark

Elements of light and dark accentuate the natural opposition found in the photograph. The white flower is contrasted with the dark suit to emphasize the symbols of what is considered genteel and civilized. Just a few inches lower on the darkness of the suit is the contrast of the light hand beginning to grip the suit in an act that violates the social control implied by the suits and the flower. The light areas in the dark background also draw attention to the female figure positioned similarly to the impassioned man in the center. The contrast of light and dark that is carried through both figures opposes the gentle nurturing nature of the female and the aggressive threatening nature of the male. The contrast between man and woman in the work also underscores the contrast and opposition of the central action in the photograph. The light areas in the work are only the hands and faces of the characters in the composition. These areas, in contrast to the overall darkness of the work, highlight the placement of the faces in the photograph.

Contrast Between High and Low

Adams's use of light and dark aligns the faces of *Discussion on Art* on an incline from right to left. While the man on the right is confronted, he does not display intimidation by lowering himself to his aggressor; however, the aggressor is attempting to assert power by raising himself over and leaning into his opponent. The higher and lower positioning of the bodies in the composition highlights the conflict and activity in the center of the photograph. The figure highest in the composition, however, is the woman in the background. Her position asserts her importance, strength, and power as a central figure in the piece despite her placement in the background. The high and low visual aesthetics work in combination with contrasts of light and dark to emphasize the opposition taking place on many different levels in the work.

Contrast Between Humans and Nature

Light and dark and high and low also work to stress the conflict between humans and nature in the photograph. The conflict underscored in this stylistic pattern becomes the conflict between humans and their own nature. The setting implied by the title is an art museum, calling for a level of class, gentility, and civilization. The dark suits and accentuating flower highlight the push and desire for social control, propriety, and decency. These characteristics are contrasted with the nature of the humans embroiled in the conflict and unable to adhere to imposed social control. Although humans are perceived to be of a higher order, their baseness is the animalistic quality they cannot escape.

Contrast Between Smooth and Rough

The textures of civilized and uncivilized, refined and rough around the edges, are polarized facets of the same entity in *Discussion on Art*. Texture is elaborated not with what can be seen as visually tactile but occurs metaphorically between civilized and uncivilized, man and woman. The softness of the gentle and nurturing woman is a stark contrast to the rough and hard aggressive nature of the man. The texture is found in the language we construct around the nature of man, woman, and human nature. The aesthetic visual elements in the work underscore the evidence of natural opposition and contrast found in the setting and communicated through the work.

Concluding Observations

Discussion on Art, seemingly not part of Ansel Adams's artistic genre, exhibits the recurring patterns of situational and stylistic qualities characteristic of that genre.

Characteristics of all five elements of the genre are apparent in *Discussion on Art*, qualifying the work as a participant in Adams's aesthetic genre. Through this genre, the artist's insights and observations are communicated and perpetuated.

Beauty in natural opposition communicates the patriarchal idea that humans' natural setting is conflict. The nature of humans drives them to assert their personal perspective. As human beings, we constantly strive to have our perspectives and presence asserted and validated. We judge our value and worth by the acceptance of our ideas and opinions by others and, as history has shown, we turn to violence and conflict to force acceptance of our presence and perspective by others.

The participation of *Discussion on Art* in the genre of Adams's photography also communicates that we are in conflict with what we perceive to be the nature of humankind. Men are socially expected to be the aggressor, violent, in conflict, hard, and rough, while women are forced to ignore that which we name natural to humanity and remain soft, kind, and nurturing. Woman is asked to ignore the human tendency to assert her perspective and presence aggressively. She must stand in the background and accept her socially defined place and nature, just as man accepts his. Both sexes are in conflict with the culturally created social reality imposed on them. The beauty, then, is the contrast between the human nature and the expectations we place on ourselves that create the conflict and opposition, the natural shadows, the plateaus that we allow to surface, and the valleys we subvert.

As a rhetorical vehicle, Adams obscures and enlightens perspectives, beliefs, views, and opinions that emphasize and communicate beauty in conflict. Each of his masterpieces contributes to this perspective and functions as a medium that expresses the rhetor. The genre allows the artist to reinforce his perspective and presence through repetition in themes and style. The patterns that characterize the genre act as an echo to the social reality constructed and communicated by the artist, and we are able to see and appreciate the beauty in conflict.

An Uncommon Rap Music Video

Lacey N. Stein

For many of today's most popular rap artists, the maintenance of a certain kind of personal image is fundamental to their success. This image is frequently one that portrays the artist as a model of powerful autonomy gained through a variety of negative means. Among the routes used to achieve their elite status and success, their lyrics suggest, are the emotional and physical domination and even violation of others. Such lyrics suggest that the rappers achieve their elite positions through domination of and even the inflicting of harm on others.

Rappers who construct such images have been subjected to criticism from a multitude of sources, including yesterday's top rappers. LL Cool J, for example, laments the connection between power and misogyny in many rap lyrics: "The only power a lot of young males have is power over women. So they dwell on it" (Waldron, 1996). Darryl McDaniel, founding member of the rap group Run-D.M.C., is concerned about how his son will perceive rappers' images, explaining that he does not "want him thinking that . . . slapping bitches is what he has to do" (Croal, Davis, Gates, & Samuels, 2000). In response, many rap artists have defended their lyrics as reflective of their individual everyday realities (Croal, Davis, Gates, & Samuels, 2000).

One artist who has thrived in the rap industry for nearly two decades claims to work against conveying an image of power achieved through the domination of others. Common, formerly known as *Common Sense*, is a rapper who frequently speaks out against the violent and misogynistic lyrics of other rap artists (Wikipedia, 2007) and chooses in his lyrics to deal with subjects such as love, the value of life, and personal growth (Yahoo! Music, 2002). In spite of his alternative views, Common is still generally categorized as a rapper (Wikipedia, 2007). Because he has prospered in the mainstream rap industry but claims to disagree with the image of today's most popular rap artists, I am interested in discovering whether he maintains his convictions within his music videos and, if so, whether his work fits the genre of rap music videos.

In 2005, Common released a video for his single "Go" that, superficially, seems to contradict some of his espoused beliefs. The video begins with Common sitting on the couch in what audiences can presume is his apartment. A woman who appears to be Common's girlfriend enters the room and sits down next to him. They begin talking and laughing while holding hands and kissing. The two then walk hand in hand to the bedroom, where they become more physically intimate and begin to undress one another.

The video changes at this point, and the audience is able to see into Common's thoughts. Titles are given to the couple's actions using superimposed text that labels the artist's sexual fantasies with his girlfriend as they lie in the bed. As the video progresses, Common begins picturing anonymous women, rather than his girlfriend, set against nondescript backgrounds. These women are accompanied by text that describes each one as a "Fantasy" followed by a number. The fantasizing continues until the numbers begin spinning into the thousands, and the fantasy women move from his mind onto the bed that Common was just sharing with his girlfriend. As the women surround him

This essay was written while Lacey N. Stein was a student in Sonja K. Foss's rhetorical criticism class at the University of Colorado Denver in 2007. Used by permission of the author.

and begin touching him, Common shakes his head slightly, and viewers are brought back into reality from his imagination, where he sees his girlfriend—and only his girlfriend. In the final shots of the video, Common's apartment disappears and is replaced by a close-up of his hand holding his girlfriend's hand. The two of them then walk off together into a cityscape that is appearing slowly in front of them.

To determine whether the video for "Go" participates in the genre of rap music videos, I first will analyze rap music videos to establish the components of this genre using the method of generic criticism—in particular, generic participation. This method of criticism involves describing a genre, focusing on the situational requirements, substantive and stylistic elements, and the organizing principle that links the elements together. This description is followed by a second step in which the critic describes the situational elements, substantive and stylistic strategies, and organizing principle of the artifact in question. In the final step, the critic compares the artifact to the genre to discover if it participates in that genre.

Description of the Genre of Rap Music Videos

I chose to analyze three videos from artists who are referred to as *rappers* by authoritative figures in the music business. I chose these specific videos because, according to MTV, these videos were some of the most requested by viewers and most frequently played on the channel in 2005 when Common's video for "Go" was released. The videos I examined are "Just a Lil Bit" by 50 Cent, "Pimpin' All Over the World" by Ludacris, and "Gold Digger" by Kanye West.

In the video for "Just a Lil Bit," 50 Cent is shown rapping with three women standing near him. In one scene, the group is shown sitting on the beach; in another, the four are shown standing next to a pool. These shots are interspersed with the video's plotline, which begins with 50 Cent and the three women stepping off a plane in a tropical location. Each of these women, one by one, meets a local man and leads him off to a separate, private setting. In these private settings, each of the women becomes physically intimate with the man and then murders him, each in a different way. Each of these occurrences is followed by a shot of 50 Cent being physically affectionate with the woman. In the conclusion of the video, police are searching the three locations to which the men were led, and 50 Cent carries a suitcase full of money through airport security to board a plane with the three women.

In Ludacris's video for "Pimpin' All Over the World," a plotline emerges that is significantly less dramatic than the one found in the 50 Cent video. Ludacris visits the beautiful seaside city of Durban, South Africa, where he meets local vendors and plays on the beach. The main plotline shows Ludacris wooing a local young woman: He buys her jewelry, takes her on safari and on a carriage ride, and sees a traditional tribal dance performance with her. These shots are combined with a variety of shots that show Ludacris hanging out with friends and rapping on the beach and in the African wilderness.

Kanye West's music video for "Gold Digger" is not governed by a narrative but is comprised largely of four basic kinds of shots. The audience sees West rapping against a fuchsia backdrop; backup vocalist Jamie Foxx sings against a similar backdrop; a variety of women pose as live-action models on the covers of mock magazines; and a solitary woman dressed in a tight black dominatrix costume dances while making swift, harsh, stabbing movements with a glowing dagger-like weapon.

Situational Elements

Superficially, the three videos for rap songs seem rather different; however, a closer examination reveals similarities in their situational, substantive, and stylistic elements. In terms of the situational elements, the rap videos obviously are designed to sell the music the rappers produce. But they are set up to sell the music in a particular way. I propose that the situational requirements for the rap music video genre revolve around the inclusion of a constellation of visual markers of achievement that audiences expect to see. Rap music videos depict artists as visually successful in terms of money, clothing, power, and lifestyle, modeling a successful life to which fans can aspire. By meeting these situational requirements within their videos, successful rap artists ensure that their fans are appeased and that their musical careers continue to flourish.

Substantive and Stylistic Elements

Commonalities also characterize the videos in terms of substantive and stylistic elements. These elements include power claimed by the artist, accumulation and display of wealth, and the depiction of women as sex objects. Although each of these videos handles these elements in a different manner visually, they are extremely important to the meaning of each video, which would be significantly altered if these elements were not present.

Power Claimed by the Artist.   Within the videos' visual representations, power is crucial in some way to each artist. In 50 Cent's video, he clearly is in charge of the microcosm presented. For example, the video opens with mock credits as though the audience is about to watch a traditional film "starring 50 Cent as 'El Jefe,'" a Spanish term that means "the boss." Although 50 Cent arrives in a place that is foreign to him, he automatically holds power there. Furthermore, 50 Cent has control over the three women with whom he works, and they do his dirty work by luring anonymous, wealthy men to secluded places so that they can steal money from the men and kill them. This violence also gives power to the rapper because he is literally taking the wealth and the lives of other men. The video's conclusion completes the notion that 50 Cent holds authority over all others because he has eluded the local police and is shown headed to another destination where he cannot be discovered.

Similarly, in "Pimpin' All Over the World," Ludacris is treated as a powerful man despite his foreign surroundings. The video begins with Ludacris pulling over to the side of a dirt road in the African desert to ask a native man for directions to Durban. Visually, power is automatically granted to Ludacris because he is sitting in his vehicle looking down on the seated man as they talk. In addition, Ludacris is driving a luxurious sport utility vehicle, in contrast to the local man, a vendor who is selling inexpensive goods in the middle of nowhere. The contrast indicates that Ludacris is obviously privileged in comparison to this individual. In spite of this, the vendor seems thrilled to help Ludacris reach his destination and even thanks the rapper for talking to him.

The attitude of subservience the vendor demonstrates is a consistent theme in the video. Once Ludacris is in Durban, the locals he encounters seem elated by his presence. The vendor from whom Ludacris buys jewelry smiles widely at him while throwing her arms in the air wildly to express her thanks. The man who pulls the carriage in which Ludacris rides jumps in the air occasionally and seems to be laughing out loud as though his joy cannot be contained, even though his job is laborious and even demeaning. Similarly, the men who perform the traditional African dance direct their attention toward Ludacris, although there are many other people in the audience.

Notions of power are visually represented in other ways in Kanye West's video for "Gold Digger." Much like 50 Cent's video, this video begins with mock credits. Here, however, the only people who are mentioned are the video's director and the song's artists, Kanye West and Jamie Foxx. Although this video includes a few other men and many women, the only individuals who are worthy of recognition are the three men. The opening credits also include text that reads, "Beware of the Gold Digger." The term *gold digger* is slang for a woman who attempts to involve herself romantically with a man in order to better herself financially. This text suggests that the men in the video—specifically the song's artists—are threatened with losing their economic power because of women. This concept is reinforced several times when West is shown rapping while a woman dances erotically around him, and he either ignores her by refusing to look at her or by turning his back to her. When he does address the woman, he does so by waving his index finger back and forth at her as if to indicate that she should stop trying to attract his attention.

Accumulation and Display of Wealth.   Closely related to the idea that power is fundamental to the persona of the rappers in the videos is the notion that the accumulation and display of wealth are of great importance. 50 Cent seems to gain his power from his possession of money in that the women who work for him do so for monetary profit. In fact, money is important enough that the main character is willing to murder multiple people for it. Also, in spite of their immoral and criminal actions, 50 Cent and his female companions show no remorse for their behavior. Instead, financial abundance is seen to compensate for criminal behavior because they are shown wearing elegant clothing in lavish settings intended for leisure. The characters presented in this plot appear to be primarily motivated by an interest in acquiring wealth.

In Ludacris's video, the plotline is entirely dependent on the fact that the artist is wealthy. Ludacris would not be able to visit Durban, buy expensive jewelry to impress women, or go on safari if he were not financially well off. Not only does he have enough money to do such fantastic leisurely activities, but he is also shown driving an expensive vehicle; wearing conspicuous, pricey jewelry; and using costly video cameras and cellular phones during his stay in this tourist location. Audience members are led to believe that his trip to Durban is not necessarily a unique experience because many Polaroid pictures are shown throughout the video of Ludacris in tourist spots all over the globe. Essentially, this artist has enough money to go wherever he chooses and to do and see whatever he pleases. Wealth is presented as a major priority for this individual, and he clearly reaps the benefits of being wealthy.

The entire premise behind the song and video "Gold Digger" depends on the importance of wealth. A woman dances around a well-dressed Kanye West in an attempt to involve herself with him and thus gain access to his wealth. This woman is not alone, however; numerous women are shown in the video, and this goal is the common denominator among all of them. Foundational to this video is the importance of protecting wealth once it has been obtained.

Women as Sex Objects.   In all three of the videos, the female characters are reduced visually to being sex objects and/or villains of some kind. In "Just a Lil Bit," the opening credits introduce 50 Cent first, then the women, who are named *Face*, *Tata*, and *Diabla*. With the term *face* as her name, physical appearance becomes the most important characteristic of one of the women. Similarly, the word *tata* can be used as slang to refer to a woman's breasts, making the entire being of the second woman into an erogenous zone. Finally, the word *diabla* is the feminine form of the Spanish term for *devil*, suggesting that the third woman is evil personified. These women are also costumed consistently in skimpy clothing or underwear and are shot in ways that draw attention to their breasts, legs, and buttocks. Furthermore, these women are not only highly sexual beings, but they use their sexual prowess to aid in the committing of brutal crimes.

In a similar vein, the women seen in "Gold Digger" are extremely sexualized in a manner that suggests transgression. Again, all of the women in this video are scantily clad, generally wearing only lingerie. When they appear as live-action models on the covers of mock magazines, they are reduced to one-dimensional creatures whose primary function is to be viewed. Although these women exist to be aesthetically pleasing, they still pose a threat to viewers because the magazines on which they appear have titles such as *Vixen*, *Sinful*, *Pre-Nupt*, and *Smoke*. Such titles send the message that anyone who chooses to interact with these women—rather than just looking at them—will be in danger because these women are wicked. The paradigm for this kind of woman is represented multiple times in the video with the image of the woman in the dominatrix costume who stabs at the air violently with her glowing dagger. Audiences, then, are presented with visuals that reduce women to objects of sex and perpetrators of violence.

In Ludacris's video, women are not vilified, but they are commodified because of their sex appeal. In each of the Polaroid pictures that shows Ludacris in a variety of vacation spots around the world, he is posing with a different woman. This suggests that Ludacris views women simply as part of the local flavor of his present location—they are attractions to be toured or toys that exist merely to provide him with fleeting entertainment. Although he gives most of his attention to one woman in this plotline, he is shown flirting with a variety of other women, sometimes in front of her. Also, he clearly lacks respect for this primary female character when he rips off her skirt in a playful manner while they are on the street together; the woman responds with laughter. These visuals imply that women enjoy being disrespected and serving mainly as figures of sexuality. As in the other two videos, women here are generally wearing little clothing, and their breasts, thighs, and buttocks are fully or partially exposed. In Ludacris's life of leisure and luxury, women can be traded up like baseball cards and are important solely because of their sexuality.

Organizing Principle

The situational, substantive, and stylistic characteristics of the videos suggest that the organizing principle of the genre is conventional patriarchy. Patriarchy is a system in which men and their perspectives are featured and in which they are granted power and prestige. Women, in this system, are seen as subordinate to men and function primarily to address the needs and desires of men and assume the roles men dictate for them. The power the rappers claim in these videos, the wealth they are accorded, and the depiction of women as only sexual beings all reinforce the notion that men are in charge and have the power to create the world as they like. The situational elements reinforce this claim by providing visual evidence that the men are, indeed, powerful and privileged.

Generic Comparison with Common's Video

To determine whether Common's video for the song "Go" should be categorized as participating in the rap video genre, I now will apply the characteristics of the genre to his video, comparing and contrasting them in terms of situational, substantive, and stylistic elements and the organizing principle that links them.

Situational Elements

The other rap videos seek to appeal to fans and sell music—the situational requirements of all rap music videos—through the construction of an image of power through a particular set of visual cues. These cues link the rapper to external indicators of wealth such as money, pricey clothing, gold jewelry, adulation of others, and ability to travel. In contrast, Common constructs his situational requirements differently. The situational exigence his video addresses is the need to model a new kind of power for his fans. This is an innate power available to anyone, and it is not dependent on external markers for its achievement or manifestation. Instead, it is rooted in the demonstration of values in interaction with others such as respect, support, mutuality, and equality—in other words, power *with* rather than power *over*.

Substantive and Stylistic Elements

Power Claimed by the Artist.   In the three videos that I examined previously, the artists derive their power through their interactions with other people: 50 Cent expresses power by controlling the female characters presented and by taking the lives and money of other men, Ludacris's power is established by his manipulation of women and the respect that others show him, and Kanye West's authority is presented as a given and is maintained by preventing women from having access to his money.

In his video, Common does not appear to claim or be awarded power in these ways. The person with whom he interacts most frequently is the woman who plays the character of his girlfriend. The concept of power does not seem to be prominent within the depiction of their relationship in that their laughter, conversation, and physical affection are consistently mutual and reciprocal. They work together and share power equally.

When Common is shown interacting with the numerous women of his fantasies, he has the opportunity to display a masculine sexual prowess similar to that demonstrated by Ludacris in his video. Common, however, does not seize this opportunity. Instead, he physically and mentally returns to his girlfriend—his imagination disappears as he chooses to spend his reality with her. Also, unlike the men in the other rap videos, the girlfriend character begins to undress Common while they are in bed together. This situates him on a more equal plane with the female characters in this video who are not fully clothed.

Moreover, rather than being presented as a sort of demigod, Common seems like a normal, fallible man who nearly succumbs to the temptations of his imagination but then reprimands himself for almost doing so and chooses to ground his life in his healthy relationship with his girlfriend. Not only does Common reject the chance to gain power through the manipulation of women, but the conclusion of this video suggests that Common embraces the notion that the public eye will view his girlfriend as his equal rather than his inferior. Unlike the artists in the rap video genre, Common seems not to see his own power as a priority, and Common is not filmed in a style that grants him superiority over others.

Accumulation and Display of Wealth.   Music videos found in the rap video genre place emphasis on the value of acquiring wealth by showing posh settings and glamorous costumes and by devoting a great deal of screen time to consumption and money. In the video for "Go," wealth and visuals associated with money are not featured prominently. The video takes place almost entirely within Common's apartment, which is decorated tastefully and conservatively. Although it does not look like a lower class home, it is not marked by an exaggerated sense of wealth. In addition, Common does not don expensive suits or accessorize with flashy jewelry but wears business-casual clothing. The woman who portrays Common's girlfriend is shown wearing an elegant, but simple, flattering costume throughout the video. The fantasy women in the video wear skimpier, more ostentatious clothing, but these characters are imaginary and are not presented as realistic. Finally, there is never a time during which money, consumption, and financial gain are represented in the video.

Women as Sex Objects.   In generic rap videos, women tend to be depicted as objects defined exclusively by their sexuality and/or their demonic tendencies. The women in Common's imagination are temptresses who function exclusively to please him physically. These women are further reduced to existing solely as sex objects because they are scantily clad in lingerie and labeled with text as numbered fantasies. However, as soon as this vision of women becomes tangible and Common is given the chance to interact with these kinds of female characters, he invalidates this vision of women by restoring his emotional bond with his girlfriend, who is presented as a well-rounded individual. Essentially, the difference between Common's video and generic rap videos lies in the fact that women are depicted in different ways. The fantasy women are wholly sexual beings, while his girlfriend is shown as an individual for whom sexuality is only one aspect of her persona. Generic rap videos display extremely limited roles for women; Common's video resists that stereotype.

Organizing Principle

In contrast to the organizing principle of conventional patriarchy that I suggested marks rap music videos, the organizing principle of Common's video is a valuing of relationships over wealth and power. Realistic relationships that engage the whole person, his video suggests, are of greater value than wealth and the capacity to dominate others.

Conclusion

The situational, substantive, and stylistic elements that serve as a foundation for generic rap music videos depict rappers as powerful and wealthy men who interact with women only as sex objects. These elements limit the capabilities of women by reducing them to sexual—if not violent—commodities and also present a restricted view of men, showing that they only can earn power and respect by manipulating others and achieving financial success. Common's video for the song "Go" is not founded in the same situational and stylistic elements and thus does not participate in the rap music video genre. Common displays courage by making a video for mainstream audiences to be aired on a mainstream channel that eschews the generic boundaries typically associated with rap music videos. As a result, he provides an alternative perspective to each of the three substantive and stylistic markers of the genre. That his video is aired and apparently well received by audiences suggests the possibility of opening up the genre to allow for the presentation of modes of living and values other than the domination of others through power, money, and sex.

Works Cited

Croal, N., Davis, A., Gates, D., & Samuels, A. (2000, October 9). Battle for the soul of hip-hop. *Newsweek, 136,* 58–66.

Music Television. *2005 MTV Yearbook.* Retrieved October 6, 2007 from http://www.mtv.com/music/yearbook/index.jhtml?contentId=1535988

Waldron, C. (1996, June). Effects of rap music on today's young black men. *Ebony Man, 11,* 50–54.

Wikipedia. *Common (rapper).* Retrieved October 6, 2007 from http://en.wikipedia.org/wiki/Common_%28rapper%29

Yahoo! Music. (2002, December 30). *Interviews.* Retrieved October 6, 2007 from http://music.yahoo.com/read/interview/12028288

The Rhetoric of Huey P. Newton

Davi Johnson

Although scholars across disciplines are paying increasing attention to the Black Panther Party (BPP) and Huey P. Newton (e.g., Cleaver & Katsiaficas, 2001; Hilliard & Weise, 2002; Jeffries, 2002; Jones, 1998), rhetoricians appear hesitant to engage this multidisciplinary inquiry. The groundwork for such studies exists within rhetoric (Campbell, 1972; Courtright, 1974), and the recent focus on Black leaders of the 1960s makes now a fitting time for renewed attention to Newton and the BPP (e.g., Gallagher, 2001; Terrill, 2000, 2001; Yousman, 2001). Despite these patterns, there are no recent analyses of the BPP or Newton from an explicitly rhetorical perspective. This neglect is somewhat surprising given the discipline's history of a strong interest in social movements generally and radical Black movements specifically (see, for instance, Burgess, 1968/2001; Campbell, 1971; Cathcart, 1978/2001; Goldzwig, 1989; Gregg, 1971/ 2001; Scott, 1969; Scott & Brockriede, 1969; Scott & Smith, 1969/ 2001). Analyses of radical activism typically attempt to justify unconventional tactics falling outside of traditional norms of public communication. These justifications are motivated by the observation that standards of rationality and decorum often preserve dominant interests by making common channels of rhetorical influence inaccessible to oppressed classes. Although these approaches offer considerable insight into the discursive operations of radical Black movements, they frequently give short shrift to the more traditional strategies employed by Black rhetors and the interrelationships between diverse rhetorical acts.

Examining Newton's oratory within a critical orientation attentive to rhetorical traditions, I draw attention to the polyphonic qualities of social movement discourse and situate the BPP within a diverse tradition of radical Black rhetoric. Specifically, I examine Newton's mastery of the jeremiad as a major form of his public address. Although the jeremiad has long been recognized as a traditional and even hegemonic form of rhetorical practice within the American tradition, there is an ongoing debate concerning its potential to function as a mechanism for social change (Bercovitch, 1978; Murphy, 1990; Owen, 2002). In short, because the jeremiad rests on appeals to traditional American values, some argue that the form is ill-suited to radical discourses and inevitably reifies conservative values. However, the Afro-American jeremiad has been recognized as a unique modification of the jeremiad, adapted for a Black audience, and more accommodating to activist purposes. Newton's public address combined elements from both the Afro-American jeremiad and the jeremiad in general. His speech indicates that foundational values and their historical traditions are always constructed rhetorically; hence, they are constantly available for redefinition and reappropriation. Newton strategically situated traditional American values within a historical perspective that allowed him to redefine the American dream as a socialist paradise where equality becomes consonant with equitable distribution of economic resources.

By focusing primarily on Newton's 1970 address to the Revolutionary People's Constitutional Convention (RPCC), I hope to simultaneously emphasize the tradi-

Davi Johnson, The Rhetoric of Huey P. Long. *Southern Communication Journal*, 2004, vol. 70:1, pp. 15–30. Permission granted by Taylor & Francis.

tional aspects of Newton's seemingly radical rhetoric and illustrate the amenability of the jeremiad to arguments for substantial social change. In short, Newton's mastery of a conservative rhetorical form casts doubt on typical accounts that treat him and his organization as an aberrant and isolated social movement unconnected to broader rhetorical traditions.[1] Additionally, his subtle articulation of a radical content within this conservative form lends insight into the ways in which the jeremiad can function in the service of social change, further developing existing scholarship on the activist potential of the jeremiadic form (e.g., DeSantis, 1999; Howard-Pitney, 1990). Newton's failure to supplant his image as a radical militant suggests that the success of the jeremiad is not dependent on its activist or conservative content, but is instead a function of the rhetor's relationship to his or her audience. In this essay, I summarize the historical significance of Newton and his relationship to the BPP, examine the jeremiadic rhetorical tradition, and illustrate the complexity of both Newton's rhetoric and jeremiadic discourse.

Huey P. Newton and the Black Panther Party

As the primary leader of the BPP, Newton has come to symbolize and embody not only the Party but also the very concepts of Black power and militancy associated with the late 1960s and early 1970s. Although Breslauer (1995) describes Newton as "the symbol of resistance for a movement which boasted particularly dynamic speakers" (p. F1), Newton was neither an enthusiastic nor a particularly gifted public speaker. In his autobiography, Newton (1973) reflected, "I am not very good at talking to large groups; nor do I enjoy it. Abstract and theoretical arguments interest me most, but they lack the rhetorical fire to hold audiences" (p. 172). Indeed, Newton had little opportunity to speak in public due to confinement. The BPP was founded by Newton and Bobby Seale in October 1966, and Newton was arrested for the murder of John Frey barely one year later on October 28, 1967.[2] Newton's arrest had the paradoxical effect of catalyzing the movement as thousands of mostly young Black people were mobilized to challenge what they had long perceived as an unjust and corrupt legal system. Thousands of supporters ranging from discontented college students to wealthy Hollywood types attended the "Free Huey!" rally organized by the Panthers to draw national attention to the plight of their leader. Newton was not released until August 5, 1970. While he was behind bars, the BPP had grown from its humble Oakland origins into a national organization with considerable membership, aided in no small part by relentless media fascination with the gun-toting, beret-wearing Panthers.

Popular conceptions of the BPP as militant no doubt provided some benefit to the Party in terms of recruitment and national visibility; however, these negative depictions continue to shape the legacy of Newton and his movement. The BPP is viewed as "the image of Black militancy" and "a potent symbol of racial chaos and upheaval," in stark contrast to popular conceptions of the "down-by-the riverside dream of Martin Luther King, Jr." (Del Vecchio, 1999; Hughes, 1998; Weiss, 1999). These accounts of BPP militancy are so frequent that they constitute what Singh (1998) describes as the "Panther effect," where "the figure of the Black Panthers evokes the catastrophic sense of America's permanent racial chasm itself" (p. 62).

The "Panther effect" is not isolated to popular accounts of Newton and the BPP but also shapes scholarly discourse. For instance, Courtright (1974) writes that the BPP crafted a rhetorical strategy around "arming themselves and using their guns to declare their manhood" (p. 249), characterizing members of the movement as militants who viewed rhetoric as an act of force. Doss (1998) similarly focuses on Newton's sexual appeal and aggressive masculinity as the keystone of the BPP's attraction for young people.

My purpose is not to detail the shortcomings or falsehoods of this "Panther mythology" (Jones & Jeffries, 1998, p. 26), as others have succeeded admirably here (e.g., Clemons & Jones, 2001). However, it is important to understand the backdrop against which the rhetoric of Newton and the BPP is confronted. These few examples indicate that in the popular mind as well as in academic scholarship, the Panthers are conceived of as a separatist, militant, and isolated social movement. By examining Newton's discourse in light of its participation in the long-standing jeremiadic tradition, I hope to provide resources for better understanding the complexity of the BPP and its associated mythology.

I have chosen to focus on Newton's September 5, 1970, address to the Revolutionary People's Constitutional Convention (RPCC) in Philadelphia, delivered only a month after his release from prison. The RPCC address is historically significant because it is Newton's first major public speech after his release from prison. The speech is rhetorically significant because it is the first explication of Newton's mature thought, which would come to be dubbed "revolutionary intercommunalism" for its emphasis on the economic interconnectedness of global communities (see Jeffries, 2002, pp. 78–82).

The Jeremiadic Tradition

Recent scholarship emphasizes the importance of attending to rhetorical traditions as a method of situating diverse and polyphonic oratory. Influenced in part by Campbell's (1986) concept of cultural grammar, Murphy (1997) defines rhetorical traditions as methods of organizing the "'social knowledge' of communities" and making available "symbolic resources for the invention of arguments aimed at authoritative public judgments" (p. 72). The flexibility of this approach allows critics to situate rhetorical texts within diverse argumentative traditions and account for the polyphonic and heteroglossic nature of complex discursive arrangements. By encouraging an examination of the "dialogic encounter between immediate problems and ongoing rhetorical forms," the critic may simultaneously evaluate the historical specificity of rhetorical phenomena and draw comparisons with other phenomena to invoke broader theoretical generalizations (Murphy, 1997, p. 74). Like Murphy, Jasinski (1997) employs the theoretical insights of Bakhtin to study the interaction of diverse traditions circulating within "dynamic, heteroglot, and polyphonic" rhetorical forms (p. 24). Similarly, Browne (2002) argues that Jefferson's inaugural is "at once forward looking and indebted to certain rhetorical traditions" (p. 413), and he teases out these traditions to better situate Jefferson's oratory. Finally, such an orientation allows the critic to move beyond ideological criticism and attend to the "sheer rhetoricality" of texts that construct or invoke "cultural fictions" shaped by historical patterns (see Hartnett, 2002, pp. 2–3, 24).

The jeremiad has frequently been described as a rhetorical tradition employed in diverse contexts, from campaign speeches (Ritter, 1980) and environmental policy proposals (Buehler, 1998) to anti-slavery appeals (DeSantis, 1999). The jeremiad is viewed as the secular adaptation of a sermonic form adopted from the European pulpit by the Puritans. For the latter, the jeremiad became less a pessimistic prediction of inevitable social decline and instead a complex doctrine of both lamentation and celebration that called upon a chosen people to turn from their errant ways and commit themselves fully to their sacred mission.³ The "modern jeremiad" (Ritter, 1980) is a secular discourse that has replaced religious authority with the foundational values of the American dream. In this turn to civil religion, as Ritter (1980) describes, "the scriptures have been replaced by a rendering of the national past" and the sacred texts invoked are no longer Biblical, but the words of Jefferson, Lincoln, and the nation's founding documents (p. 158).

Ritter (1980) distinguishes between the past and history to emphasize the way in which jeremiadic discourse constructs a particular vision of the past rather than attempts to document historical fact. As Bercovitch (1978) explains, the jeremiad rests on ideological consensus and cultural myth rather than social reality, and Buehler (1998) notes that rhetors can offer unique constructions of the past to justify their current proposals. Although the jeremiad is often distinguished by common formal features (Carpenter, 1978), the content is at once common and particular: Rhetors traditionally participate in the invocation of American civil religion by calling upon foundational values as the basis of their persuasive appeals, but the ways in which these values and their historical contexts are constructed and interpreted are often widely disparate. The rhetorical power of the jeremiad is, as Buehler (1998) effectively pinpoints, its ability to link even extreme proposals for change to concepts and ideals that already have currency in the audience's worldview.

The Afro-American Jeremiad

Moses (1982) suggests that the jeremiad is a particularly apt resource for Black rhetors for this ability to blend conservative ideals with a radical vision. For Moses (1982), Black Americans' cultural identity or sense of group identification is not intrinsic but is the product of the maintenance of a "social mythology" accounting for the origin and destiny of Black peoples (p. vii). While this social mythology is itself a rich source of rhetorical traditions, it also participates in traditions common to the American people in general, specifically the jeremiadic and messianic rhetoric associated with American civil religion. The myths of "manifest destiny" associated with American civil religion are often appropriated to confirm a special, messianic purpose for Black Americans, and the jeremiadic tradition is invoked to account for the particular sufferings borne by these chosen people. For Moses (1982), this tradition is a fusion of assimilation and separatism and is a response to the amphibious experience of simultaneous immersion and oppression within American society. Howard-Pitney (1990) similarly defines the Afro-American jeremiad as a messianic rhetorical form that signals both a faith in the American promise and a faith in the missionary destiny of the Black race, a position often associated with ideologies of Black nationalism. While Black nationalism is often conceived of as a separatist philosophy because of its frequent emphasis on territorial independence (Moses, 1996), its rhetorical manifestations participate in both assimilationist and separatist visions (Moses, 1990). Black rhetors including W.E.B. du Bois, Frederick Douglass, and Malcolm X have made use of the jeremiad to challenge the nation to reform its errant ways and live up to its promises of freedom and equality (Howard-Pitney, 1990). In short, the jeremiad allows rhetors to criticize American society while simultaneously expressing faith in its ideals, resulting in a discourse that is at once separatist and integrationist. Although the jeremiad is often thought of as a conservative rhetorical form, Howard-Pitney (1990) points out that assenting to mainstream values provides an "ideological shield" for the advancement of more radical criticism, and that this assent often involves a subtle refashioning of the mainstream values or cultural fictions invoked (p. 187).

Newton and the RPCC

Although theorists have recognized that radical and apparently discrete rhetorical acts frequently participate in more conservative or socially accepted traditions (Burgess, 1968/2001; Scott, 1973/2001), there have been limited attempts to situate the BPP or Newton within historical traditions and the impressions of aberrancy and isolationism fostered by mainstream media accounts persist. Katsiaficas (2001) pinpoints practices "emphasizing superficial characteristics and ignoring deeper connections to broader historical currents" (p. viii) as a primary factor in common misconceptions about the aims and ideals of Newton and the BPP. Although Newton's early public discourse contained jeremiadic elements, his later RPCC address appealed to a broad coalition of politically engaged citizens by downplaying racial division and highlighting economic injustice as the nation's original sin in hallmark jeremiadic form. Yet, though Newton fully participated in the traditional jeremiadic form, his originality is in recasting traditional American values in an economic language that makes the American dream consonant with a socialist vision. The strategic use of the jeremiadic tradition in the advocacy of a radical vision attests to the potential for the jeremiad to function in the service of arguments for social change and, conversely, illustrates the extent to which seemingly radical discourse participates in long-standing rhetorical traditions.

The RPCC address is considered Newton's first articulation of his mature philosophy dubbed "revolutionary intercommunalism" (Jeffries, 2002, p. 71). Newton's interest in the international situation was strong since the inauguration of the BPP,[4] as evidenced by the Party's platform including a demand for a UN plebiscite to determine the destiny of the Black community (see Foner, 1995, pp. 2–3). Like King, Newton strongly opposed the Vietnam War, and he articulated his protest by offering to send BPP members as troops in support of North Vietnam. As Newton's thought developed, he came more and more to recognize the inability of nation-states to function autonomously in a global society linked economically where large corporations rather than strong national governments regulated the world's populations. Abolitionist and civil rights rhetors have frequently emphasized the international arena in their articulations of the unique plight of African Americans.

The RPCC itself was crafted with a strong global emphasis and included, among similar activities, a "Workshop on Internationalism and Relations with Liberation Struggles around the World" (see Cleaver & Katsiaficas, 2001, p. 289). Indeed, Newton's success at articulating the global dimensions of the Black struggle for equality led Stuart Hall to credit the Panthers and similar organizations with the transformation of the "third world" from a geographical descriptor to a metaphor encompassing social, economic, and cultural relations (Singh, 1998, p. 67). Newton's development of the international argument is evident in his address delivered at the RPCC, a convention designed with the express purpose of mimicking American colonial subjects by drafting a new Constitution better able to guarantee the promises contained in the original. As such, the context of the RPCC gave Newton ample opportunity to refine his own vision of the American dream and situate his audience historically as vital participants in the pursuit of the nation's original vision.

Specifically, Newton presented a jeremiad premised on three major strategies: (a) a historical narrative that situates the American dream in a material context, (b) an emphasis on the chasm between the rhetorical promise of America's founding and the social reality of its unfolding, and (c) an appeal to the audience to view themselves as special people with unique ability to bring about social change through the pursuit of socialist alternatives to the existing politico-economic structure. Although Newton's address was, for the most part, color-blind, he subtly carved out a particular role for Black Americans, dabbling in the messianic rhetoric that infused his earlier speeches.[5] In general, the jeremiad functions by constructing its audience as a chosen people specifically designated to bring about desired changes. Specifically, the Afro-American jeremiad appeals to Black Americans to recognize themselves as a special people whose disproportionate sufferings confirm their privileged role in bringing about social change. Newton employed these rhetorical techniques to address a racially diverse audience without neglecting the racially specific tenets of the BPP's philosophy. With an emphasis on the materiality and actuality of historical processes in the context of idealist and visionary values, Newton effectively redefined the American dream in a material context, implying that the true fulfillment of the American dream lies not in capitalist progress but revolutionary socialism.

Redefining the American Dream: Newton's Dialectical Materialism

The jeremiad is consistently defined as including appeals to foundational values, secular or spiritual. However, the meanings of these values are not given, rather these values function as "empty signifiers" or "floating signifiers," concepts that possess widespread and even universal appeal despite their fluctuating and contingent connotations. Newton was acutely conscious of the rhetorical nature of values and the extent to which their meanings are determined by their historical situations, particularly by the material factors that provide the context for their interpretation and understanding. In an address given at Boston College shortly after his RPCC address, Newton (1970/2002) described his method:

> If we are using the method of dialectical materialism, we don't expect to find anything the same even one minute later because "one minute later" is history. If things are in a constant state of change, we cannot expect them to be the same. Words used to describe old phenomena may be useless to describe the new. (p. 26)

The twin emphasis on a dynamic material reality and the resulting contingency of language was central to the development of Newton's thought. Although Newton exhibited some suspicion about resurrecting linguistic elements associated with the past, his consistent appeals to American values illustrate his acumen at rhetorically adapting these values to new situations to serve his specific ends.

The RPCC provided an apt staging ground for Newton to develop his particular version of American values. Katsiaficas (2001) writes that the RPCC is the "key to unlocking the mystery of the aspirations of the 1960s movement," an event that, though neglected by most historians, is "the most momentous event in the movement during this critical period in American history" (p. 142). The RPCC, held in Philadelphia and primarily organized by the Panthers, was attended by an extraordinary alliance of persons and organizations, ranging from the Students for a Democratic Society to the Gay Liberation Front. Participants gathered to hear several speakers, most notably Newton, and to attend workshops with the goal of drafting and ratifying a new constitution. Newton's address was carefully crafted to take full advantage of the convention's theme.

Newton (1970/1999) opened his RPCC address with a genealogy of sorts, situating the promises of the Declaration of Independence in a specific material context. He stated:

> Two centuries ago the United States was a new nation conceived in liberty and dedicated to life, liberty, and the pursuit of happiness. . . . The United States of America was born at a time when the nation covered relatively little land, a narrow strip of political divisions on the Eastern seaboard. The United States of America was born at a time when the population was small and fairly homogeneous both racially and culturally. Thus the people called Americans were a different people in a different place. Furthermore, they had a different economic system. The small population and the fertile land available meant that with the agricultural emphasis on the economy, people were able to advance according to their motivation and ability. It was an agricultural economy and with the circumstances surrounding it Democratic Capitalism flourished in the new nation. (p. 156)

It is interesting that Newton (1970/1999) did not initially challenge the common patriotic mythology of America's origination. Instead, Newton (1970/1999) affirmed this myth by describing the nation's founding in positive terms as the initiation of "Democratic Capitalism," a seemingly equitable system where people were "able to advance according to their motivation and ability" (p. 156).

Rather than refute this popular legend of origins, Newton (1970/1999) radically contextualized this beginning by emphasizing the specificity of demographic and economic circumstances. The racial and cultural homogeneity of the populace in combination with an agricultural economy made possible the equitable opportunity for advancement intrinsic to Newton's definition of Democratic Capitalism. Thus, Newton participated in a certain idealization of America's birth, assenting to foundational myths associating the nation's founding with life, liberty, and the pursuit of happiness not merely as ideal principles but as real material possibilities potentiated by unique demographic and economic conditions.

Newton's claim that at the nation's birth "the people called Americans were a different people in a different place" foreshadowed his development of a historical narrative that described the specific changes that fundamentally altered the meaning of these critical values. The nation developed into a "multi-limbed giant," expanding geographically and drawing populations from Africa, Asia, Europe, and South America. As a result of this geographic distribution and population explosion, a nation conceived by a homogeneous population in relative geographical isolation developed into a large, heterogeneous, and geographically expansive population. Newton (1970/1999) stated, "This change in the fundamental characteristics of the nation and its people substantially changed the nature of American society" (p. 157). Accompanying changes in the economic structure of the nation, as "a rural and agricultural economy became an urban and industrialized economy" where farming was replaced by manufacturing, had profound consequences for Democratic Capitalism:

> The Democratic Capitalism of our early days became caught up in a relentless drive to obtain profits until the selfish motivation for profit eclipsed the unselfish principles of democracy. Thus 200 years later we have an overdeveloped economy which is so infused with the need for profit that we have replaced *Democratic Capitalism with Bureaucratic Capitalism.* The free opportunity of all men to pursue their economic ends has been replaced by constraints (confinement) placed upon Americans by the large corporations which control and direct our economy. They have

> sought to increase their profits at the expense of the people, and particularly at the expense of the racial and ethnic minorities. (Newton, 1970/1999, p. 157)

Economic changes favoring profit and the concentration of wealth in industries accompanied by a diversification of the population have resulted in, according to Newton, a present situation where minorities are specifically disadvantaged by a system that no longer allows for the equality of opportunity necessary for Democratic Capitalism. Newton (1970/1999) invented a new term to distinguish the economic realities of the current age from the more equitable social system present at the nation's founding: Bureaucratic Capitalism. Through this historical contextualization, Newton was able to simultaneously affirm the mythology of America's egalitarian foundations while condemning the modern manifestations of profit motive and racial inequality.

Appeals to foundational values, such as equality of opportunity and the individual pursuit of life, liberty, and happiness, are often used as arguments against regulations that would impede the development of industrial strength and global capitalism. Newton (1970/1999) strategically situated these values in a specific historical context to suggest that industrial capitalism mutates these values to such a degree that they are no longer recognizable. Although this historical narrative is no doubt as simplistic as the fables it refutes, the accuracy of Newton's (1970/1999) historiography is less interesting than its rhetorical utility. Through the lens of his dialectical materialism, Newton resituated American history in such a way that modern capitalism appears as a perversion of America's foundational values. As Newton continued his jeremiad, he developed the distinction between Democratic and Bureaucratic Capitalism to emphasize the hypocrisy endemic to modern America.

Ideals versus Reality: Diagnosing America's Hypocrisy

When viewed from the perspective of Howard-Pitney's (1990) definition of the three elements constitutive of the rhetorical structure of the jeremiad, the initial part of Newton's address framing American values in a specific historical/material context fulfilled the first function, outlining the promise or ideal state subsequently abandoned. The second aspect, criticism of present declension or description of the retrogression from that promise, was carried out through Newton's distinction between Democratic and Bureaucratic Capitalism, which comes to be defined as a contradiction between the promise of the idea of the United States and its unfolding material reality. As Darsey (1997) and Scott (1973/2001) have noted, radical rhetors often employ a "conservative voice," claiming to be more true to traditional values than the mainstream society. Newton participated in this conservative voice by highlighting the hypocrisy operative in a society where rhetorical ideals and material reality are fundamentally at odds.[6]

Newton (1970/1999) developed the second section of his speech by describing specific manifestations of the contradictions that lie at the heart of modern society. He stated, "The history of the United States, as distinguished from the promise of the idea of the United States, leads us to the conclusion that our sufferance is basic to the functioning of the government of the United States" (p. 157). This conclusion is evidenced by examining "the basic contradictions found in the history of this nation" (p. 157). Newton continued to document the case for majority freedom and minority oppression by examining two distinct historical examples: the case of the American Indians and the case of slavery.

Newton's (1970/1999) choice of the American Indians as his first instance of evidence for American hypocrisy was a strategic way to modify the almost exclusive focus on the situation of Black Americans found in his early discourse. This example provided a more nuanced perspective with the capability of appealing to a racially diverse audience while lending his rhetoric a more neutral and scientific tone. Newton (1970/1999) continued, "We find evidence for *majority freedom and minority oppression* in the fact that the expansion of the United States Government and the acquisition of lands was at the unjust expense of the American Indians, who are the original possessors of the land and still its legitimate heirs" (p. 158). Newton cited the Trail of Tears and disappearance of other Indian nations as evidence of "the unwillingness and inability of this government and this government's Constitution to incorporate racial minorities" (p. 158).

Newton (1970/1999) introduced his next example in parallel fashion, giving the appearance of a scientific investigator providing a litany of factual data in support of hypotheses: "We find evidence for majority freedom and minority oppression in the fact that even while the early settlers were proclaiming their freedom, they were deliberately and systematically depriving Africans of their freedom" (p. 159). These "basic contradictions" were developed in the resulting three-fifths clause that denied African Americans the status of full human beings in the interests of territorial expansion. These contradictions were, for Newton, not peripheral or accidental aberrations that could be corrected through simple legal remedies. He described:

> These compromises were so basic to the thinking of our forebears that legal attempts to correct the contradictions through Constitutional amendments and civil-rights laws have produced no change in our condition. We are still a people without equal protection and due process of law. We recognize then that the oppressive acts of the United States Government when contrasted with the testaments of freedom, carry forward a basic contradiction found in all legal documents upon which this government is based. (p. 158)

Here, Newton was both providing evidence of the nation's fall from its founding ideals as well as providing the foundation for his later arguments for radical social change.

Although Newton would ultimately conclude his jeremiad by arguing for a fulfillment of America's founding promise, this fulfillment could not be achieved through existing legal mechanisms. In order to argue for a substantial revamping of America's political and economic structure, Newton was required to effectively solder the nation's fall from its originating ideals to its current politico-economic arrangement. Thus, Newton argued that the hypocrisy manifested in the treatment of the American Indians and Black slaves was not peripheral to the design of the nation's political economy, but was in fact basic and central to its functioning.

Newton (1970/1999) walked a fine rhetorical line in order to both assent to founding ideals and argue for a radical undermining of the nation's political, economic, and legal structure. Even in the excerpt above, however, he continued to positively value the ideals associated with America's promise (for instance, equal protection and due process of the law) while thoroughly condemning the material structure that had since unfolded. Newton developed this line of thought by describing the contradiction between a majority who "have seen the fruits of their labors in the life, liberty, and happiness of their children and grandchildren" and a Black minority who "have seen the fruits of their labors in the life, liberty, and happiness of the children and grandchildren of their oppressors" (p. 159). The appeal to foundational values persisted alongside a condemnation of the material structures developed to achieve these values.

Newton's (1970/1999) critique of America's political and economic structure was extended to a criticism of the mainstream civil rights movement as an organization attempting to use the existing structure to achieve its ends. Newton situated himself as one who previously shared the civil rights movement's hope that the government would modify its practices to include minorities. He continued, "We did not recognize, however, that any attempt to complete the promise of an eighteenth-century revolution in the framework of a twentieth-century government was doomed to failure" (p. 159). Just as the specific material circumstances made equal opportunity possible at the nation's birth, its material circumstances at the time of Newton's speech were incompatible with the rhetorical ideals of America's promise. These material circumstances included the concentration of wealth in the hands of a few industries in an increasingly globalized economy. Thus, the "Constitution set up by their ancestors to serve the people no longer does so, for the people have changed" and "the people of today stand waiting for a foundation of their own life, liberty and pursuit of happiness" (Newton, 1970/1999, p. 159).

Newton (1970/1999) paralleled the globalization of the economy with the early shift from Democratic to Bureaucratic Capitalism, outlining a cycle of hypocrisy that can only be broken with a new material order. He says:

> We note that the government continues its pattern of practices which contradict its democratic rhetoric. We recognize now that we see history repeating itself, but on an international as well as national scale. The relentless drive for profit led this nation to colonize, oppress, and exploit its minorities. This profit drive took this nation from democratic capitalism and underdevelopment to bureaucratic capitalism and overdevelopment. Now we see this small ruling class continues its profit drive by oppressing and exploiting the peoples of the world. . . . We gather here today to let it be known at home and abroad that a nation conceived in liberty and dedicated to life, liberty, and the pursuit of happiness has in its maturity become an imperialist power dedicated to death, oppression and the pursuit of profits. (p. 160)

Newton's historical examples of the American Indians and the Black slaves were connected to broader contradictions associated with the concentration of wealth in the hands of a few at a global level, providing a historical narrative that effectively highlighted the hypocrisy central to America's democratic rhetoric. Newton continued to assent to these rhetorical ideals, invoking life, liberty, and the pursuit of happiness as worthwhile and just promises that could not be fulfilled without substantial changes in the economic and political structure of American, and even global, society. By describing this hypocrisy and tightly linking it to America's existing legal and economic system, Newton fulfilled the jeremiadic requirement of delineating America's fall from its foundational promises while laying the groundwork for his later arguments for radical social and economic change.

Defining the American Dream Materially: Newton's Radical Jeremiad

The jeremiad has been distinguished as rhetorical genre not only by its structural components (i.e., construction of promise, explanation of failure to achieve the promise, and resolving prophecy) but also by the particular way in which it defines its audience. Carpenter (1978) explains that the jeremiad "accomplishes its goals rhetorically by a process leading readers to view themselves as a chosen people confronted with a timely if not urgent warning that unless a certain atoning action is taken, dire consequences will ensue" (p. 104). The Afro-American jeremiad in particular has been described as a rhetoric that constructs a unique identity for African Americans as chosen people whose disproportionate suffering is directly related to their special role as agents for social change (Howard-Pitney, 1990; Moses, 1982). Newton's (1970/1999) jeremiad combined racially specific and universal appeals to an ethnically diverse audience, ultimately calling on themes of a universal humanity to ground his claims for socialism.

After his historical narrative outlining America's foundation and fall from its original democratic promise, Newton (1970/1999) initiated a significant break and recited the platform of the BPP. Each of the 10 planks are similarly worded, beginning with "The Black Panther Party calls for . . ." followed by a specific component of the platform. For instance, "The Black Panther Party calls for freedom and the power to determine our destiny" (p. 160). The inclusion of the BPP platform is somewhat curious given the restrained, race-neutral approach of the rest of the speech. Even when Newton cited the case of slavery and Black Americans as examples for American hypocrisy, these instances were cited in an academic, almost scientific tone and were not articulated as emotional appeals to a racially specific audience. The BPP platform as vociferous political advocacy (it is highlighted in capital letters in the print version of his address) seems out of place amid the restrained, abstract discourse that surrounds this section.

There are at least two possible explanations for this break: First, Newton, famous for founding the BPP, could be living up to the expectations of both his Black and mixed audiences that he would address the unique plight of Black Americans and rally members of the BPP to further action. Second, though the BPP platform was racially specific (only Blacks could be members of the Party), its appeals had a universal cast—freedom, full employment, decent housing, etc. are not racially specific goals, nor were they worded as aims exclusive to the BPP or Blacks in general. Thus, Newton could have been subtly highlighting the universality of the BPP's platform by including the platform within this speech. The inclusion of the BPP platform is reminiscent of Newton's earlier rhetoric that was heavily messianic in character—perhaps here he was reminding Blacks that although the project of reconstructing American society is universal, Blacks and the Black Panthers specifically were the vanguard of the revolution and had a particular role to play in a more general social movement.

After this break, Newton (1970/1999) resumed his speech with potent appeals to his audience, encouraging them to see themselves as uniquely situated to bring about substantial change in the national and global order. Here, Newton took full advantage of the context of his address, associating his present audience with the nation's founders and capitalizing on the rhetorical resources provided by the associations between the historical and the modern constitutional convention. Newton again stated that the very structure of current society is contradictory and continued:

> For this reason we assemble a Constitutional Convention to consider rational and
> positive alternatives. Alternatives which will place their emphasis on the common
> man. Alternatives which will bring about a new economic system in which the
> rewards as well as the work will be equally shared by all people—a Socialist

framework in which all groups will be adequately represented in the decision making and administration which affects their lives. Alternatives which will guarantee that all men will attain their full manhood rights, that they will be able to live, be free, and seek out those goals which give them respect and dignity while permitting the same privileges for every other man regardless of his condition or status. (pp. 161–162)

Newton had come full circle from the initial stages of his address where he outlined the promises of America. His concluding advocacy resonated with these American ideals, "to live, be free, and seek out those goals which give them respect and dignity," emphasizing equality of opportunity that is defined in material, specifically economic, terms ("a new economic system in which the rewards as well as the work will be equally shared by all people").

For Newton (1970/1999), the renewal of America's early ideals was only possible through a rewriting of the Constitution, the task for which his immediate audience had assembled. Although Newton did not believe in the realistic efficacy of such an undertaking,[7] he capitalized on the rhetorical situation and used the Convention's ostensible purpose to make his point that the founding ideals could not be realized within the prevailing political, economic, and legal setting.[8]

Newton (1970/1999) concluded his address by appealing to universal human characteristics, transcending race and nationality and implying a truly global audience:

> The sacredness of man and of the human spirit requires that human dignity and integrity ought to be always respected by every other man. We will settle for nothing less, for at this point in history anything else is but a living death. WE WILL BE FREE and we are here to ordain a new Constitution which will ensure our freedom by enshrining (cherishing) the dignity of the human spirit. (p. 162)

Although Newton's jeremiad did not include a specific scenario of catastrophe that would result barring immediate action by his audience, his stark reminder that the status quo is "a living death" provided a compelling rationale for the construction of a new Constitution, which for Newton became consonant with replacing existing social structures with a socialist order. For Newton, nothing less than the universal human spirit and dignity of man were at stake and he encouraged his audience to view themselves as uniquely well situated to achieve noble and consequential ends.

Conclusion

Newton's (1970/1999) RPCC address fulfills the functions of jeremiadic discourse while explicitly refashioning the cultural fictions associated with the American Revolution and the promises of the founding documents. Economic equality emerges as the central component necessary for the realization of the ideals of life, liberty, and the pursuit of happiness declared at the nation's inauguration. Newton's abstract and argumentatively sophisticated address ultimately resulted in ambivalent consequences. Newton (1973) wrote that the crowd seemed displeased when their expectations of militant demagoguery were not fulfilled:

> As I talked, it seemed to me that people were not really listening or even interested in what I had to say. Almost every sentence was greeted with loud applause, but the audience was more concerned with phrasemongering than ideological development. I am not a good public speaker—I tend to lecture and teach in a rather dull fashion—but the people were not responding to my ideas, only to an image, and

though I was very excited by all the energy and enthusiasm I saw there, I was also disturbed by the lack of serious analytical thought. (p. 332)

Yet, Newton's proclivity toward abstract thought and academic discourse resulted in an invitation to speak with Erik Erikson at a series of roundtable discussions hosted by Yale University only a few months after his RPCC address (subsequently published as Newton & Erikson, 1973).

Though Newton was aware of his shortcomings as a public orator, his RPCC address and his other writings evidence the fact that, for Newton, language mattered. In the history of disagreement over the capacity of the jeremiad to operate as an expression of dissent in the service of radical social change, critics suspicious of a progressive function for the jeremiad often fail to account for the profoundly rhetorical nature of traditional values and the capacity for them to be appropriated and rhetorically redefined in the service of arguments for significant change. For instance, Murphy (1990) writes that the jeremiad transforms dissent "into a rededication to the principles of American culture" and hence precludes a critical examination of the system or the Establishment (p. 402). He subsequently states that the jeremiad is severely limited and "cannot serve as a vehicle for social criticism" (p. 404) because it is doomed to rely on the precepts of the past. Although Murphy's presuppositions about the jeremiad are to an extent accurate, what he fails to realize is the fact that the past and the "principles of American culture" are not static entities or predetermined forms, but radically contingent possibilities amenable to diverse rhetorical visions.

Thus, it is true that Newton's jeremiad involves "a rededication to the principles of American culture," but in his rhetorical vision, these principles become consonant with socialism. As Hartnett (2002) points out, these American principles are cultural fictions that have no foundational meaning but are always rhetorical products open to refashioning and rearticulation. Newton radicalized the meaning of traditional values, but his participation in a conservative rhetorical form casts doubt on common portrayals of Newton as a radical demagogue who was wholly in opposition to mainstream society. His strategy of "dissent by assent" indicates Newton's considerable skill at taking part in mainstream rhetorical traditions and his mastery of the discourse of traditional American values.

Ultimately, perhaps more can be learned from Newton's failures than his successes. Although Newton successfully infused a conservative rhetorical form with an undeniably radical content by refashioning traditional values in socialist garb, Newton failed to change his popular image as an aggressive demagogue. Ironically, though Newton's mastery of a rhetoric of traditional values could not supplant his public image as a militant, his immediate audience faulted him precisely for his failure to live up to this militant persona. These twin failures indicate the importance of attending to contextual factors when considering the political possibilities of the rhetorical jeremiad. Scholars who argue that the jeremiad is inherently a conservative discourse take as case studies rhetors who were viewed already as authoritative "insiders" in relation to their target audience when they spoke (Buehler, 1998; Murphy, 1990; Ritter, 1980).

DeSantis (1999) explicitly recognizes that a successful jeremiad is only possible when the speaker is clearly perceived as a member of the community he/she is addressing. Because Newton was already considered an outsider, a militant revolutionary who posed a threat to traditional values, even if he had articulated a more reformist content (for instance a moderate redefinition of the American tradition), he could not have improved his public image. If the jeremiadic form limits radical advocacy, perhaps this is not because the jeremiad's necessary appeals to traditional values amount to a restriction on content (because values can always be redefined to accommodate revolutionary visions). Rather, as DeSantis (1999) suggests, and Newton's example confirms, the success of the jeremiad largely depends on the status of the enunciator in relation to his/her audience. Murphy (1990) argues that the "'jeremiahs' gain in prestige and stature because they are perceived as speaking for fundamental national values" (p. 411), but the Newton study suggests a different formulation—jeremiads can successfully speak for fundamental national values only when they *already* have the requisite prestige and stature. Murphy concludes that the "rhetorical form of the jeremiad clearly limits the range of political choices that are available" to the rhetor (p. 412), however, Newton's address illustrates that these limitations are misunderstood when they are simply viewed as formal restrictions on content. The jeremiad's success (or failure) is not a direct function of its political content, but its success is limited to instances where an insider, one who is already perceived as rightfully sharing or claiming ownership of community values, refashions these values for new purposes. Thus, Newton's example suggests that future work on the jeremiad cannot limit itself to textual analysis but must attend to contextual factors, particularly the relationship between the rhetor and audience.

Newton's socialist vision was in many respects radical, to be sure, but by artfully defining this vision with a traditional vocabulary, Newton showed that his rhetorical orientation was not, or at least not solely, one of opposition and negation, but a skillful blend of assent and redefinition. Newton (1973) wrote of the importance of language in crafting visions for the future and interpreting events of the past:

> The Black Panthers have always emphasized action over rhetoric. But language, the power of the word, in the philosophical sense, is not underestimated in our ideology. We recognize the significance of words in the struggle for liberation, not only in the media and in conversations with people on the block, but in the important area of raising consciousness. Words are another way of defining phenomena, and the definition of any phenomenon is the first step to controlling it or being controlled by it. (p. 181)

Though Newton and the BPP were unique and in many ways more radical than their contemporaries, they participated in a tradition of Black activism spawning centuries. In the face of the persistent "Panther mythology" that still exists today, it is time for rhetorical scholars to revisit the legacy of the Black Panther Party and examine the richness and diversity of their contributions to American public address.

Notes

[1] Jones and Jeffries (1998) provide an excellent review of the general tendency to mythologize Newton and the BPP, specifying the frequent focus on the organization as radical and isolated from other social movements. In specifically rhetorical scholarship, Courtright (1974) and Campbell (1972) focus on the radical nature of the BPP and its leaders. In her insightful examination of Eldridge Cleaver's rhetoric, Campbell (1972) situates the Panthers within a "rhetoric of dissent, confrontation, alienation, and revolution" (p. 142). Courtright (1974) more boldly writes that the BPP crafted a rhetorical strategy around "arming themselves and using their guns to declare their manhood" (p. 249).

[2] Newton was not convicted for the murder of Frey. In a three-month long trial, Newton presented over 4,000 pages of testimony, including the Declaration of Independence. He was convicted of manslaughter and sentenced to 2–15 years before the California Court of Appeals reversed the conviction in a 51-page opinion. Details about the trial are available in Foner's (1995) introduction to *The Black Panthers Speak* as well as Newton's (1973) autobiography and *War Against the Panthers,* Newton's (1996) published dissertation.

[3] For a detailed examination of the genealogy of the jeremiad, see Bercovitch (1978).

[4] See, for instance, Clemons and Jones (2001) as well as Cleaver (1998).

[5] Newton's messianic tendencies surface throughout his career and are implied by the titles of his autobiography, *Revolutionary Suicide* (1973), and his published speeches, *To Die for the People* (1999). His (1967/2002; 1967/2002) early speeches, including "In Defense of Self-Defense I" and "In Defense of Self-Defense II," also exhibit a strong messianic character.

[6] Darsey (1997) states, "It is common for radicals to claim to be the true keepers of the faith; they oppose their society using its own most noble expressions and aspirations" (p. 9). In a much earlier essay dedicated to this issue, Scott (1973/2001) writes, "Dwelling on the hypocrisy of the dominant society, the radical is quite apt to sound the conservative voice. . . . Unable or unwilling to be free of some quite traditional values, the radical is likely to claim in some way or another that he is true to those values whereas conventional people betray them" (p. 85).

[7] See Hilliard, 1993, pp. 302–304, 312–313. Newton viewed the RPCC as a misplaced expenditure of resources trying to attempt a national organization rather than a more practical focus on building local bases of power. Additionally, the RPCC bore the mark of Eldridge Cleaver's planning and Newton and Cleaver were increasingly divided on their visions for the future of the movement.

[8] Although the Black Panther Party was born in the spirit of Black nationalism, by the late 1960s Newton firmly espoused socialism as the best method of political and economic organization. Newton's emphasis on international socialism later developed into "revolutionary intercommunalism," an ideology that included a critique of the nation-state along with its socialist framework. Newton was skeptical of the RPCC's ability to bring about a socialist alternative. For Newton, the RPCC was not radical enough and only a true revolution on a global scale would bring about the structural changes necessary to achieve social and economic justice. Additionally, the RPCC was too much talk and too little action—Newton and the BPP had always emphasized action. For instance, the early Oakland-based programs offering free breakfast for children and free shoes and clothing to needy community members were part of the Panthers' struggle to bring about real change through grassroots activism. For a good discussion of Newton's socialist vision and the Party's ideological development, see Jeffries (2002).

References

Bercovitch, S. (1978). *The American jeremiad*. Madison: University of Wisconsin Press.

Breslauer, J. (1995, January 19). Taking Huey off posters and onto the stage. *Los Angeles Times*, p. F1.

Browne, S. (2002). "The Circle of Our Felicities": Thomas Jefferson's First Inaugural Address and the rhetoric of nationhood. *Rhetoric & Public Affairs, 5,* 409–438.

Buehler, D. O. (1998). Permanence and change in Theodore Roosevelt's conservation jeremiad. *Western Journal of Communication, 62,* 439–458.

Burgess, P. G. (2001). The rhetoric of Black power: A moral demand? In C. E. Morris, III & S. H. Browne (Eds.), *Readings on the rhetoric of social protest* (pp. 180–190). State College, PA: Strata. (Original work published 1968)

Campbell, J. A. (1986). Scientific revolution and the grammar of culture: The case of Darwin's "Origin." *Quarterly Journal of Speech, 72,* 351–376.

Campbell, K. K. (1971). The rhetoric of radical Black nationalism: A case study in self-conscious criticism. *Central States Speech Journal, 22,* 151–160.

Campbell, K. K. (1972). An exercise in the rhetoric of poetic justice. In *Critiques of contemporary rhetoric*. Belmont, CA: Wadsworth.

Carpenter, R. (1978). The historical jeremiad as rhetorical genre. In K. K. Campbell & K. H. Jamieson (Eds.), *Form and genre: Shaping rhetorical action* (pp. 103–117). Falls Church, VA: Speech Communication Association.

Cathcart, R. (2001). Movements: Confrontation as rhetorical form. In C. E. Morris, III & S. H. Browne (Eds.), *Readings on the rhetoric of social protest* (pp. 102–112). State College, PA: Strata. (Original work published 1978)

Cleaver, K. (1998). Back to Africa: The evolution of the international section of the Black Panther Party (1969–1972). In C. E. Jones (Ed.), *The Black Panther Party reconsidered* (pp. 211–251). Baltimore: Black Classic Press.

Cleaver, K., & Katsiaficas, G. (Eds.). (2001). *Liberation, imagination, and the Black Panther Party*. New York: Routledge.

Clemons, M. L., & Jones, C. E. (2001). Global solidarity: The Black Panther Party in the international arena. In K. Cleaver & G. Katsiaficas (Eds.), *Liberation, imagination and the Black Panther Party* (pp. 20–29). New York: Routledge.

Courtright, J. A. (1974). Rhetoric of the gun: An analysis of the rhetorical modifications of the Black Panther Party. *Journal of Black Studies, 4,* 249–267.

Darsey, J. (1997). *The prophetic tradition and radical rhetoric in America.* New York: New York University Press.

Del Vecchio, R. (1999, January 7). A full revolution: Ex-Panthers invoke 1960s passion for 2000 Oakland council race. *The San Francisco Chronicle,* p. A15.

DeSantis, A. D. (1999). An Amostic prophecy: Frederick Douglass; *The Meaning of Fourth of July for the Negro. Journal of Communication and Religion, 22,* 65–92.

Doss, E. (1998). Imaging the Panthers: Representing Black power and masculinity, 1960s–1990s. *Prospects: An Annual of American Cultural Studies, 23,* 484–512.

Foner, P. S. (Ed.). (1995). *The Black Panthers speak.* New York: Da Capo Press.

Gallagher, V. (2001). Black power in Berkeley: Postmodern constructions in the rhetoric of Stokely Carmichael. *Quarterly Journal of Speech, 87,* 144–157.

Goldzwig, S. R. (1989). A social movement perspective on demagoguery: Achieving symbolic realignment. *Communication Studies, 40,* 202–228.

Gregg, R. B. (2001). The ego-function of the rhetoric of protest. In C. E. Morris, III & S. H. Browne (Eds.), *Readings on the rhetoric of social protest* (pp. 45–59). State College, PA: Strata. (Original work published 1971)

Haiman, E. S. (2001). The rhetoric of the streets: Some legal and ethical considerations. In C. E. Morris, III & S. H. Browne (Eds.), *Readings on the rhetoric of social protest* (pp. 10–25). State College, PA: Strata. (Original work published 1967)

Hartnett, S. (2002). *Democratic dissent & the cultural fictions of Antebellum America.* Urbana: University of Illinois Press.

Hilliard, D. (1993). *This side of glory: The autobiography of David Hilliard and the story of the Black Panther Party.* Boston: Little, Brown.

Hilliard, D., & Weise, D. (Eds). (2002). *The Huey P. Newton reader.* New York: Seven Stories.

Howard-Pitney, D. (1990). *The Afro-American jeremiad: Appeals for justice in America.* Philadelphia: Temple University Press.

Hughes, J. (1998, May 3). Former Panther Eldridge Cleaver: A relic with a cause. *The Seattle Times,* p. L5.

Jasinski, J. (1997). Heteroglossia, polyphony, and *The Federalist Papers. Rhetoric Society Quarterly, 27,* 23–46.

Jeffries, J. L. (2002). *Huey P. Newton: The radical theorist.* Jackson: University Press of Mississippi.

Jones, C. E. (Ed.). (1998). *The Black Panther Party reconsidered.* Baltimore: Black Classic Press.

Jones, C. E., & Jeffries, J. L. (1998). "Don't believe the hype": Debunking the Panther mythology. In C. E. Jones (Ed.), *The Black Panther Party reconsidered* (pp. 25–56). Baltimore: Black Classic Press.

Katsiaficas, G. (2001). Organization and movement: The case of the Black Panther Party and the Revolutionary People's Constitutional Convention of 1970. In K. Cleaver & G. Katsiaficas (Eds.), *Liberation, imagination and the Black Panther Party* (pp. 141–155). New York: Routledge.

Moses, W. J. (1982). *Black Messiahs and Uncle Toms.* University Park: Pennsylvania University Press.

Moses, W J. (1990). *The wings of Ethiopia.* Ames: Iowa State University Press.

Moses, W. J. (Ed). (1996). *Classical Black nationalism.* New York: New York University Press.

Murphy, J. M. (1990). "A Time of Shame and Sorrow": Robert F. Kennedy and the American jeremiad. *Quarterly Journal of Speech, 76,* 401–414.

Murphy, J. M. (1997). Inventing authority: Bill Clinton, Martin Luther King, Jr., and the orchestration of rhetorical traditions. *Quarterly Journal of Speech, 83,* 71–89.

Newton, H. P. (1973). *Revolutionary suicide.* New York: Ballantine.

Newton, H. P. (1996). *War against the Panthers: A study of repression in America.* New York: Harlem River Press.

Newton, H. P. (1999). To the Revolutionary People's Constitutional Convention: September 5, 1970. In T. Morrison (Ed.), *To die for the people* (pp. 156–162). New York: Writers and Readers Publishing.

Newton, H. P. (2002). In defense of self-defense: June 20, 1967. In D. Hilliard & D. Weise (Eds.), *The Huey P. Newton reader* (pp. 134–137). New York: Seven Stories Press.

Newton, H. P. (2002). In defense of self-defense II: July 3, 1967. In D. Hilliard & D. Weise (Eds.), *The Huey P. Newton reader* (pp. 138–141). New York: Seven Stories Press.

Newton, H. P. (2002). The correct handling of a revolution: July 20, 1967. In D. Hilliard & D. Weise (Eds.), *The Huey P. Newton reader* (pp. 142–146). New York: Seven Stories Press.

Newton, H. P. (2002). Speech delivered at Boston College: November 18, 1970. In D. Hilliard & D. Weise (Eds.), *The Huey P. Newton reader* (pp. 160–179). New York: Seven Stories Press.

Newton, H. P. (2002). On Pan-Africanism or communism, December 1, 1972. In D. Hilliard & D. Weise (Eds.), *The Huey P. Newton reader* (pp. 248–254). New York: Seven Stories Press.

Newton, H. P., & Erikson, E. H. (1973). *In search of common ground.* New York: Laurel.

Owen, S. A. (2002). Memory, war and American identity: *Saving Private Ryan* as cinematic jeremiad. *Critical Studies in Media Communication, 19,* 249–282.

Ritter, K. W. (1980). American political rhetoric and the jeremiad tradition: Presidential nomination acceptance addresses, 1960–1976. *Central States Speech Journal, 31,* 153–171.

Scott, R. L. (1969). Justifying violence: The rhetoric of militant Black power. In R. L. Scott & W. Brockriede (Eds.), *The rhetoric of Black power* (pp. 132–145). New York: Harper & Row.

Scott, R. L. (2001). The conservative voice in radical rhetoric: A common response to division. In C. E. Morris, III & S. H. Browne (Eds.), *Readings on the rhetoric of social protest* (pp. 74–87). State College, PA: Strata. (Original work published 1973)

Scott, R. L., & Brockriede, W. (Eds.). (1969). *The rhetoric of Black power.* New York: Harper & Row.

Scott, R. L., & Smith, D. K. (2001). The rhetoric of confrontation. In C. E. Morris, III & S. H. Browne (Eds.), *Readings on the rhetoric of social protest* (pp. 26–33). State College, PA: Strata. (Original work published 1969)

Singh, N. P. (1998). The Black Panthers and the "undeveloped country" of the left. In C. E. Jones (Ed.), *The Black Panther Party reconsidered* (pp. 57–107). Baltimore: Black Classic Press.

Terrill, R. E. (2000). Colonizing the borderlands: Shifting circumference in the rhetoric of Malcolm X. *Quarterly Journal of Speech, 86,* 67–85.

Terrill, R. E. (2001). Protest, prophecy, and prudence in the rhetoric of Malcolm X. *Rhetoric & Public Affairs, 4,* 25–53.

Weiss, H. (1999, February 22). "A Huey P. Newton Story" at the Museum of Contemporary Art. *Chicago Sun Times,* p. 23.

Yousman, B. (2001). Who owns identity? Malcolm X, representation, and the struggle over meaning. *Communication Quarterly, 49,* 1–18.

Additional Samples of Generic Criticism

Achter, Paul J. "Narrative, Intertextuality, and Apologia in Contemporary Political Scandals." *Southern Communication Journal*, 65 (Summer 2000), 318–33.

Al-Ali, Mohammed Nahar. "Religious Affiliations and Masculine Power in Jordanian Wedding Invitation Genre." *Discourse & Society*, 17 (November 2006), 691–714.

Aly, Bower. "The Gallows Speech: A Lost Genre." *Southern Speech Journal*, 34 (Spring 1969), 204–13.

Andrews, James R. "They Chose the Sword: Appeals to War in Nineteenth-Century American Public Address." *Today's Speech*, 17 (September 1969), 3–8.

Bass, Jeff D. "The Rhetorical Opposition to Controversial Wars: Rhetorical Timing as a Generic Consideration." *Western Journal of Speech Communication*, 43 (Summer 1979), 180–91.

Bennett, W. Lance. "Assessing Presidential Character: Degradation Rituals in Political Campaigns." *Quarterly Journal of Speech*, 67 (August 1981), 310–21.

Benoit, William L., and Susan L. Brinson. "AT&T: 'Apologies Are not Enough.'" *Communication Quarterly*, 42 (Winter 1994), 75–88.

Benoit, William L., Paul Gulliform, and Daniel A. Panici. "President Reagan's Defensive Discourse on the Iran-Contra Affair." *Communication Studies*, 42 (Fall 1991), 272–94.

Benoit, William L., and Robert S. Hanczor. "The Tanya Harding Controversy: An Analysis of Image Restoration Strategies." *Communication Quarterly*, 42 (Fall 1994), 416–33.

Blair, Carole. "From 'All the President's Men' to Every Man for Himself: The Strategies of Post-Watergate Apologia." *Central States Speech Journal*, 35 (Winter 1984), 250–60.

Bostdorff, Denise. "George W. Bush's Post-September 11 Rhetoric of Covenant Renewal: Upholding the Faith of the Greatest Generation." *Quarterly Journal of Speech*, 89 (November 2003), 293–319.

Brown, Stephen H. "Generic Transformation and Political Action: A Textual Interpretation of Edmund Burke's Letter to William Elliot, Esq." *Communication Quarterly*, 38 (Winter 1990), 54–63.

Brummett, Barry. "Premillennial Apocalyptic as a Rhetorical Genre." *Central States Speech Journal*, 35 (Summer 1984), 84–93.

Brummett, Barry. *Rhetorical Dimensions of Popular Culture*. Tuscaloosa: University of Alabama Press, 1991, pp. 125–46, 147–71.

Bryant, Donald C. "The Speech on the Address in the Late Eighteenth-Century House of Commons." *Southern Speech Communication Journal*, 51 (Summer 1986), 344–53.

Butler, Sherry Devereaux. "The Apologia, 1971 Genre." *Southern Speech Communication Journal*, 37 (Spring 1972), 281–89.

Campbell, Karlyn Kohrs. "The Rhetoric of Women's Liberation: An Oxymoron." *Quarterly Journal of Speech*, 59 (February 1973), 74–86.

Campbell, Karlyn Kohrs, and Kathleen Hall Jamieson, eds. *Form and Genre: Shaping Rhetorical Action*. Falls Church, Virginia: Speech Communication Association [1978], several essays, pp. 75–161.

Carlson, A. Cheree. "John Quincy Adams' 'Amistad Address': Eloquence in a Generic Hybrid." *Western Journal of Speech Communication*, 49 (Winter 1985), 14– 26.

Carlton, Charles. "The Rhetoric of Death: Scaffold Confessions in Early Modern England." *Southern Speech Communication Journal*, 49 (Fall 1983), 66–79.

Carpenter, Ronald H., and Robert V. Seltzer. "Situational Style and the Rotunda Eulogies." *Central States Speech Journal*, 22 (Spring 1971), 11–15.

Clark, Thomas D. "An Exploration of Generic Aspects of Contemporary American Campaign Orations." *Central States Speech Journal*, 30 (Summer 1979), 122–33.

Clark, Thomas D. "An Exploration of Generic Aspects of Contemporary American Christian Sermons." *Quarterly Journal of Speech*, 63 (December 1977), 384–94.

Connell, Ian, and Dariusz Galasiski. "Academic Mission Statements: An Exercise in Negotiation." *Discourse & Society*, 9 (October 1998), 457–79.

DeWitt, Jean Zaun. "The Rhetoric of Induction at the French Academy." *Quarterly Journal of Speech*, 69 (November 1983), 413–22.

Downey, Sharon D. "The Evolution of the Rhetorical Genre of Apologia." *Western Journal of Communication*, 57 (Winter 1993), 42–64.

Farrell, Thomas B. "Political Conventions as Legitimation Ritual." *Communication Monographs*, 45 (November 1978), 293–305.

Foss, Karen A. "Out from Underground: The Discourse of Emerging Fugitives." *Western Journal of Communication*, 56 (Spring 1992), 125–42.

Fulkerson, Richard. "*Newsweek* 'My Turn' Columns and the Concept of Rhetorical Genre: A Preliminary Study." In *Defining the New Rhetorics*. Ed. Theresa Enos and Stuart C. Brown. Newbury Park, CA: Sage, 1993, pp. 227–43.

Gold, Ellen Reid. "Political Apologia: The Ritual of Self-Defense." *Communication Monographs*, 45 (November 1978), 306–16.

Gronbeck, Bruce E. "The Rhetoric of Political Corruption: Sociolinguistic, Dialectical, and Ceremonial Processes." *Quarterly Journal of Speech*, 64 (April 1978), 155–72.

Hammerback, John C., and Richard J. Jensen. "Ethnic Heritage as Rhetorical Legacy: The Plan of Delano." *Quarterly Journal of Speech*, 80 (February 1994), 53–70.

Hatch, John B. "Beyond *Apologia*: Racial Reconciliation and Apologies for Slavery." *Western Journal of Communication*, 70 (July 2006), 186–211.

Hearit, Keith Michael. "From 'We Didn't Do It' to 'It's Not Our Fault': The Use of Apologia in Public Relations Crises." In *Public Relations Inquiry as Rhetorical Criticism: Case Studies of Corporate Discourse and Social Influence*. Ed. William N. Elwood. Westport, CT: Praeger, 1995, pp. 117–31.

Hogben, Susan, and Justine Coupland. "Egg Seeks Sperm. End of Story . . . ? Articulating Gay Parenting in Small Ads for Reproductive Partners." *Discourse & Society*, 11 (October 2000), 459–85.

Hoover, Judith D. "Big Boys Don't Cry: The Values Constraint in Apologia." *Southern Communication Journal*, 54 (Spring 1989), 235–52.

Ivie, Robert L. "Images of Savagery in American Justifications for War." *Communication Monographs*, 47 (November 1980), 279–94.

Jamieson, Kathleen Hall, and Karlyn Kohrs Campbell. "Rhetorical Hybrids: Fusions of Generic Elements." *Quarterly Journal of Speech*, 68 (May 1982), 146–57.

Johannesen, Richard L. "The Jeremiad and Jenkin Lloyd Jones." *Communication Monographs*, 52 (June 1985), 156–72.

Jones, John M., and Robert C. Rowland. "A Covenant-Affirming Jeremiad: The Post-Presidential Ideological Appeals of Ronald Wilson Reagan." *Communication Studies*, 56 (June 2005), 157–74.

Kahl, Mary. "Blind Ambition Culminates in Lost Honor: A Comparative Analysis of John Dean's Apologetic Strategies." *Central States Speech Journal*, 35 (Winter 1984), 239–50.

King, Janis L. "Justificatory Rhetoric for a Female Political Candidate: A Case Study of Wilma Mankiller." *Women's Studies in Communication*, 13 (Fall 1990), 21–38.

Kruse, Noreen Wales. "Apologia in Team Sport." *Quarterly Journal of Speech*, 67 (August 1981), 270–83.

Lucas, Stephen E. "Genre Criticism and Historical Context: The Case of George Washington's First Inaugural Address." *Southern Speech Communication Journal*, 51 (Summer 1986), 354–70.

Martin, Howard H. "A Generic Exploration: Staged Withdrawal, the Rhetoric of Resignation." *Central States Speech Journal*, 27 (Winter 1976), 247–57.

McClure, Kevin R., and Lisa Laidlaw McClure. "Postmodern Parody: *Zelig* and the Rhetorical Subversion of Documentary Form." *Qualitative Research Reports in Communication*, 2 (Fall 2001), 81–88.

McMullen, Wayne J. "Gender and the American Dream in *Kramer vs. Kramer*." *Women's Studies in Communication*, 19 (Spring 1996), 29–54.

Miles, Edwin A. "The Keynote Speech at National Nominating Conventions." *Quarterly Journal of Speech*, 46 (February 1960), 26–31.

Mueller, II, Alfred G. "Affirming Denial through Preemptive Apologia: The Case of The Armenian Genocide Resolution." *Western Journal of Communication*, 68 (Winter 2004), 24–44.

Nelson, Jeffrey. "The Defense of Billie Jean King." *Western Journal of Speech Communication*, 48 (Winter 1984), 92–102.

Olson, Kathryn M. "Completing the Picture: Replacing Generic Embodiments in the Historical Flow." *Communication Quarterly*, 41 (Summer 1993), 299–317.

Orr, C. Jack. "Reporters Confront the President: Sustaining a Counterpoised Situation." *Quarterly Journal of Speech*, 66 (February 1980), 17–32.

Pullum, Stephen J. "Sisters of the Spirit: The Rhetorical Methods of Female Faith Healers Aimee Semple McPherson, Kathryn Kuhlman, and Gloria Copeland." *Journal of Communication and Religion*, 16 (September 1993), 111–25.

Quimby, Rollin W. "Recurrent Themes and Purposes in the Sermons of the Union Army Chaplains." *Speech Monographs*, 31 (November 1964), 425–36.

Ritter, Kurt W. "American Political Rhetoric and the Jeremiad Tradition: Presidential Nomination Acceptance Addresses, 1960–1976." *Central States Speech Journal*, 31 (Fall 1980), 153–71.

Rodgers, Raymond S. "Generic Tendencies in Majority and Non-Majority Supreme Court Opinions: The Case of Justice Douglas." *Communication Quarterly*, 30 (Summer 1982), 232–36.

Schwarze, Steven. "Environmental Melodrama." *Quarterly Journal of Speech*, 92 (August 2006), 239–61.

Sefcovic, E. M. I. "Stuck in the Middle: Representations of Middle-Aged Women in Three Popular Books About Menopause." *Women's Studies in Communication*, 19 (Spring 1996), 1–27.

Shaw, Punch. "Generic Refinement on the Fringe: The Game Show." *Southern Speech Communication Journal*, 52 (Summer 1987), 403–10.

Short, Brant. "Comic Book Apologia: The 'Paranoid' Rhetoric of Congressman George Hansen." *Western Journal of Speech Communication*, 51 (Spring 1987), 189–203.

Simons, Herbert W. "'Going Meta': Definition and Political Applications." *Quarterly Journal of Speech*, 80 (November 1994), 468–81.

Simons, Herbert W., and Aram A. Aghazarian, eds. *Form, Genre, and the Study of Political Discourse*. Columbia: University of South Carolina Press, 1986, numerous essays, pp. 203–77.

Stoda, Mark, and George N. Dionisopoulos. "Jeremiad at Harvard: Solzhenitsyn and 'The World Split Apart.'" *Western Journal of Communication*, 64 (Winter 2000), 28–52.

Valley, David B. "Significant Characteristics of Democratic Presidential Nomination Speeches." *Central States Speech Journal*, 25 (Spring 1974), 56–62.

Vande Berg, Leah R. Ekdom. "Dramedy: *Moonlighting* as an Emergent Generic Hybrid." *Communication Studies,* 40 (Spring 1989), 13–28.

Vartabedian, Robert A. "Nixon's Vietnam Rhetoric: A Case Study of Apologia as Generic Paradox." *Southern Speech Communication Journal,* 50 (Summer 1985), 366–81.

Vivian, Bradford. "Neoliberal Epideictic: Rhetorical Form and Commemorative Politics on September 11, 2002." *Quarterly Journal of Speech,* 92 (February 2006), 1–26.

Ware, B. L., and Wil A. Linkugel. "They Spoke in Defense of Themselves: On the Generic Criticism of Apologia." *Quarterly Journal of Speech,* 59 (October 1973), 273–83.

Weaver, Ruth Ann. "Acknowledgment of Victory and Defeat: The Reciprocal Ritual." *Central States Speech Journal,* 33 (Fall 1982), 480–89.

White, Cindy L., and Catherine A. Dobris. "A Chorus of Discordant Voices: Radical Feminist Confrontations with Patriarchal Religion." *Southern Communication Journal,* 58 (Spring 1993), 239–46.

Wooten, Cecil W. "The Ambassador's Speech: A Particularly Hellenistic Genre of Oratory." *Quarterly Journal of Speech,* 59 (April 1973), 209–12.

For a more complete bibliography of genre studies, see: Fisher, Walter R. "Genre: Concepts and Applications in Rhetorical Criticism." *Western Journal of Speech Communication,* 44 (Fall 1980), 296–99; and Simons, Herbert W., and Aram A. Aghazarian, eds. *Form, Genre and the Study of Political Discourse.* Columbia: University of South Carolina Press, 1986, pp. 355–77.

Ideological Criticism

When rhetorical critics are interested in rhetoric primarily for what it suggests about beliefs and values, their focus is on ideology. In an ideological analysis, the critic looks beyond the surface structure of an artifact to discover the beliefs, values, and assumptions it suggests. An ideology is a pattern of beliefs that determines a group's interpretations of some aspect(s) of the world. These beliefs reflect a group's "fundamental social, economic, political or cultural interests." Another way to think about an ideology is as a mental framework—the language, "concepts, categories, imagery of thought, and the systems of representation" that a group deploys to make sense of and define the world or some aspect of it.[1]

The primary components of an ideology are evaluative beliefs—beliefs about which there are possible alternative judgments.[2] We can see such an ideology in the following set of beliefs about the issue of immigration:

- Too many people come to our country.
- Immigrants only come here to live off welfare.
- Most immigrants are economic refugees.
- Immigrants fill up inexpensive housing and take jobs from people who need them.
- Immigrants face growing resentment in the inner cities.
- The government must send back illegal immigrants.
- Immigration has to be restricted to "real" refugees only.[3]

Beliefs such as these that comprise an ideology around immigration serve as the foundation for the knowledge, attitudes, motives, and predilections of groups that adhere to this ideology. Other examples of ideologies are patriotism, anti-Communism, Christianity, multiculturalism, conservatism, anti-terrorism, and survivalism. Ideologies also can be less formal, as evidenced in the ideologies embedded in 12-step programs, reality-television shows, testing as the means for judging quality in education, and dieting. Each of these ideologies includes a set or pattern of beliefs that evaluates relevant issues and topics for a group, provides an interpretation of some domain of the world, and encourages particular attitudes and actions to it.

Ideological criticism is rooted in basic conceptualizations about ideologies and how they function. Primary is the idea that multiple ideologies—multiple patterns of belief—exist in any culture and have the potential to be manifest in rhetorical artifacts. Some ideologies, however, are privileged over others in a culture, and ideologies that present oppositional or alternative perspectives on the subjects to which they pertain are sometimes repressed. The result is a dominant way of seeing the world or the development of a hegemonic ideology in certain domains. Hegemony is the privileging of the ideology of one group over that of other groups. It thus constitutes a kind of social control, a means of symbolic coercion, or a form of domination by more powerful groups over the ideologies of those with less power.[4] When an ideology becomes hegemonic in a culture, certain interests or groups are served by it more than others. The hegemonic ideology represents experience in ways that support the interests of those with more power.

When an ideology becomes hegemonic, it accumulates "the symbolic power to map or classify the world for others."[5] It invites "us to understand the world in certain ways, but not in others."[6] A dominant ideology controls what participants see as natural or obvious by establishing the norm. Normal discourse, then, maintains the ideology, and challenges to it seem abnormal. A hegemonic ideology provides a sense that things are the way they have to be; it asserts that its meanings are the real, natural ones. In a culture where the ideology of racism is hegemonic, for example, the privilege accorded to whites seems normal, as does the lack of opportunity accorded to individuals of other races. If practices in the culture concerning people of color are questioned, the questions are viewed as abnormal.

The dominance of one group's ideology is visible in the discourse about the Iraq War initiated by the United States in 2003. Although many perspectives and ideologies were involved in the discourse about whether the United States should invade Iraq—those of religious leaders, politicians, President George W. Bush, members of his cabinet, Iraqi citizens, military officers, pacifists, backers of the president, and skeptical citizens—the dominant perspective that emerged and functioned as hegemonic was that of the president and his cabinet members. Because they were the ones with access to classified information about the situation in Iraq and terrorist activity, they had the capacity to hide or to release the information available to them; the ability to converse with world leaders to try to enlist their support; and guaranteed media coverage of their words and actions. Their perspective became privileged over that of other perspectives.

To maintain a position of dominance, a hegemonic ideology must be renewed, reinforced, and defended continually through the use of rhetorical strategies and practices. Resistance to the dominant ideology is muted or contained, and its impact thus is limited by a variety of sophisticated rhetorical strategies. Often, in fact, these strategies incorporate the resistance into the dominant discourse in such a way that the challenge will not contradict and even may support the dominant ideology. In a culture in which an ideology of racism is dominant, for example, questions about why people of color are not given equal opportunities may be muted by representations of these people as lacking in internal motivation. Thus, the argument that they are not given equal opportunities is seen as irrelevant and thus is unable to have much impact on the dominant ideology.

The rise to dominance of particular ideologies is not always as deliberate and conscious a process as the above description makes it seem. We all are subjected to dominant perspectives in the most mundane and ordinary activities of our lives. All of the institutions in which we participate embody particular ideologies. Our educational system, for example, shapes students in particular directions; part of its complex ideology teaches obedience to orders and the necessity to follow rules. Religion, families, the media, the legal system, and popular culture perpetuate various ideologies and convince participants in a culture to accept those ideologies. Although we may adhere, as individuals, to ideologies different from one that is hegemonic, we cannot help but participate in the hegemonic ideology as we participate in our culture through activities such as watching television, browsing through popular magazines, and attending school.

A number of scholars have contributed to the development of ideological criticism in the communication field, including Teun A. van Dijk,[7] Philip C. Wander,[8] Michael Calvin McGee,[9] Raymie E. McKerrow,[10] Janice Hocker Rushing and Thomas S. Frentz,[11] Lawrence Grossberg,[12] Celeste Michelle Condit,[13] and Dana L. Cloud.[14] These scholars have been influenced by a number of different perspectives and philosophies in their development of ideological approaches to criticism.

One perspective that informs ideological criticism is structuralism, a series of projects in which linguistics is used as a model for attempts to develop the "grammars" of systems such as myths, novels, and genres. Claude Lévi-Strauss, for example, analyzed a wide range of myths to discover their structure or grammar.[15] By constructing such grammars—systematic inventories of elements and their relationships, structuralists gain insights into the ideologies of artifacts because the grammars embody and provide clues to those ideologies.

A form of structuralism that many ideological critics have found useful is semiotics or semiology, the science of signs. Developed by Ferdinand de Saussure[16] and Charles Sanders Peirce,[17] semiotics is a systematic attempt to understand what signs are and how they function. Semioticians have a broader definition of signs than the one presented in chapter 1. They define signs as units that can be taken as substitutes for something else, such as words, font styles, camera angles, colors, clothing, and gestures. Semiotics provides a way to study components of an artifact as clues to its meaning and ideology. Among those who have contributed to the development of semiotics and its use in ideological criticism are Roland Barthes,[18] Arthur Asa Berger,[19] and Kaja Silverman.[20]

Marxism also informs the work of many ideological critics.[21] As an intellectual system, Marxism is a way of analyzing cultural products in terms of the social and economic practices and institutions that produce them. Although Marxist critics—such as Theodor Adorno,[22] Louis Althusser,[23] Walter Benjamin,[24] Bertolt Brecht,[25] Terry Eagleton,[26] Jürgen Habermas,[27] Georg Lukács,[28] and Herbert Marcuse[29]—differ in their interpretations and applications of Marxism, they are united by the belief that material conditions interact with and influence the symbols by which groups make sense of their worlds. These scholars believe ideological forms are more than ideas, beliefs, and values. They have a material existence and are embodied in cultural institutions such as schools, churches, and political parties and in artifacts such as paintings, novels, and speeches.

Yet another influence on ideological criticism is deconstructionism, which sometimes is called *poststructuralism* because it developed after and in response to structuralism. The philosophy and critical method of deconstructionism is most closely associated with Jacques Derrida,[30] and its foremost American exponent is Paul de Man.[31] The purpose of deconstructionism is to deconstruct the self-evidence of central concepts—to subject to critical analyses the basic structures and assumptions that govern texts and the development of knowledge. Methodologically, deconstruction is directed to the questioning of texts—taking apart and exposing their underlying meanings, biases, and preconceptions—and then transforming or reconceptualizing the conceptual fields of those texts.

Postmodernism, a theory of cultural, intellectual, and societal discontinuity, also influences much ideological criticism. Postmodern theories are based on the notion that our culture has moved into a new phase—one that follows the period of modernism, which championed reason as the source of progress in society and privileged the foundation of systematic knowledge. The new form of society has been transformed radically by media and technology, which have introduced new forms of communication and representation into contemporary life. This postmodern society requires new concepts and theories to address the features that characterize the new era: fragmentation of individuals and communities; a consumer lifestyle; a sense of alienation; and a destabilization of unifying discourses and principles. The postmodern project is useful to ideological critics in that it provides information about the context for many contemporary artifacts and suggests the exigence to which many of these artifacts and their ideologies respond. Among the primary contributors to theories of postmodernism are Jean-François Lyotard,[32] Jean Baudrillard,[33] and Fredric Jameson.[34]

Another source from which ideological critics draw is cultural studies, an interdisciplinary project focused around the idea that relations of power within a society are embedded in and reproduced through cultural creation. Critics who work from this perspective seek to uncover oppressive relations and the forces available that have the potential to lead to liberation or emancipation. As a loosely unified movement, cultural studies dates to the Birmingham Centre for Contemporary Cultural Studies in Great Britain, founded in 1964 by Richard Hoggart[35] and later headed by Stuart Hall.[36] Although theorists associated with cultural studies adopt diverse approaches, including Marxist, poststructuralist, postmodern, feminist, and Jungian perspectives, they tend to share some basic assumptions about cul-

The Hay-Wain by Hieronymus Bosch (see essay that starts on p. 71).

The Varallo family (see essay that starts on p. 166).

The Chryslee-Miller family (see essay that starts on p. 166).

The Marty-Rhoades family (see essay that starts on p. 166).

Top: Portland Building.
Left: Humana Building.
Both buildings were
designed by architect
Michael Graves.

Images Courtesy of Michael
Graves & Associates.

The Humana Building is discussed in chapter 7
(pp. 215–217, 219, and 220). The Portland Building is
analyzed in a sample essay beginning on p. 300.

TOP: *Buffalo Bill—The Scout* by Gertrude Vanderbilt Whitney. LEFT: A statue of Buffalo Bill welcomes visitors to the Buffalo Bill Museum (see essay that starts on p. 225).

Buffalo Bill photographs by Brian L. Ott.

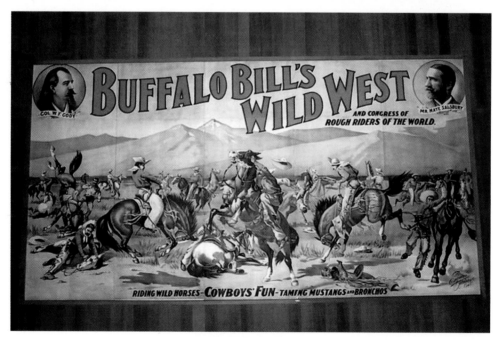

TOP: Stagecoach used in Buffalo Bill's Wild West show.
BOTTOM: Promotional poster for Buffalo Bill's Wild West (see essay that starts on p. 225).

Portland Building, designed by architect Michael Graves (see essay that starts on p. 300).

Photographs by Judy Bowker.

I See What You Mean by Lawrence Argent (see the discussion that starts on p. 359).
Photograph by Sonja K. Foss.

ture. Culture, they believe, consists of everyday discursive practices, with these discursive practices both embodying and constructing a culture's ideology. They see artifacts of popular culture as legitimate data for critical analysis because they are places where struggles take place over which meanings and ideologies will dominate.

Articulation as a theory and critical method also contributes to ideological criticism. An offshoot of cultural studies, articulation theory has been developed primarily by Ernesto Laclau, Chantal Mouffe,[37] and Stuart Hall.[38] The term *articulation* has had a variety of "medical, biological and enunciative meanings. But in every case, the word suggests some kind of joining of parts to make a unity."[39] In the context of ideological criticism, *articulation* means establishment of a relationship among elements (such as beliefs, practices, and values) so that their identity is transformed. The notion of articulation guides the "critic's attention to specific connections between ideological elements" to identify "ideology's systemic and structural levels of operation."[40] A critical focus on articulation also involves analysis of the connection of these elements to "social, political, economic, and technological practices and structures"[41] to discover how they construct certain "ways of thinking, being, and acting in the world as possible or not."[42] The end of an analysis focused on articulation is "to understand how meaning is ideologically constructed within the level of complex social formation."[43]

Feminism and feminist criticism also contribute in key ways to ideological criticism. Many feminist scholars and critics conceptualize feminism as the effort to eliminate relations of domination not just for women but for all individuals. They employ feminist or ideological criticism to discover how the rhetorical construction of identity markers such as gender are used as a justification for domination, how such domination is constructed as natural, and how that naturalness can be challenged. Feminist scholarship and criticism began in the communication discipline with three key texts. In Karlyn Kohrs Campbell's "The Rhetoric of Women's Liberation," published in 1973, she suggested that the rhetoric of the contemporary women's movement consists of substantive and stylist components so distinctive that it constitutes a unique genre.[44] This essay thus constituted the first effort to reconceptualize rhetorical constructs from a feminist perspective. An essay by Cheris Kramer (now *Kramarae*), "Women's Speech: Separate but Unequal?," published the following year, raised the possibility of sex-linked linguistic signals, but Kramarae also urged that women as language users be considered individually rather than as part of a general category. Her essay thus foreshadowed the development of an emphasis on differences among women for purposes of theorizing.[45] In "The Womanization of Rhetoric," published in 1979, Sally Miller Gearhart challenged a fundamental tenet of rhetorical studies—the definition of rhetoric as persuasion—and suggested that feminism necessarily transforms rhetorical constructs and theories.[46]

Regardless of the specific perspectives they embrace, the primary goal of ideological critics is to discover and make visible the ideology embedded in an artifact. As a result of an ideological analysis, a critic seeks to explicate the role of communication in creating and sustaining an ideology and to discover whose interests are represented in that ideology. Such an analysis provides a critical distance on existing relations, clearing a space in which existing arrangements can be evaluated and perhaps altered. By describing relationships that exist within an artifact and between the artifact and its context, it calls them into question, opening the way for change and for the envisioning of new kinds of relationships.

Procedures

Using the ideological method of criticism, a critic analyzes an artifact in a four-step process: (1) selecting an artifact; (2) analyzing the artifact; (3) formulating a research question; and (4) writing the essay.

Selecting an Artifact

Virtually any artifact can serve as an artifact for ideological criticism because ideologies exist everywhere. Every artifact takes an evaluative position on various subjects simply by the rhetorical choices that were made in creating that artifact. Although you may be tempted to select a political text for an ideological analysis, other kinds of artifacts often can produce less obvious insights. Artifacts of popular culture such as advertisements, television shows, basketball games, concerts, coffee houses, computer games, lawn ornaments, films, Web sites, and songs are often sites where ideology is rhetorically packaged and sold and where ideological conflicts are played out. Audiences are often less resistant to ideological messages in such artifacts because they do not expect to see them there, and such artifacts thus are often more productive and interesting to analyze.

Analyzing the Artifact

A critic who explores an artifact for the ideology it manifests does so in four steps: (1) identifying the presented elements of the artifact; (2) identifying the suggested elements linked to the presented elements; (3) formulating an ideology; and (4) identifying the functions served by the ideology.

Identifying Presented Elements

The first step in an ideological analysis is to identify and focus on rhetorical aspects of the artifact that provide clues to its ideology. The critic seeks to identify the assumptions or premises behind the artifact that constitutes its ideology. Your task, then, is to examine individual signs that point to ideological tenets in the artifact, working back to the often implicit ideology through the rhetorical content and form of the artifact.

An easy way to begin the process of identifying the assumptions that construct a particular ideology for an artifact is to code your artifact for presented and suggested elements.[47] Identification of presented elements involves identifying the basic observable features of the artifact. These might be, for example, major arguments, types of evidence, images, particular terms, or metaphors. In visual artifacts, physical features such as shapes and colors constitute presented elements. Whatever form your artifact assumes, you are looking for observable aspects of the artifact that provide clues to its ideology. Note these major elements or features of the artifact and make a list of them.

For example, let's say the artifact you are analyzing is the Humana Building in Louisville, Kentucky. This building is the headquarters of the Humana Corporation, a health-benefits company, and it was designed by architect Michael Graves. In this building, you might identify the major presented elements as follows:[48]

- granite
- massive scale
- L shape
- pyramid shape at the top of the building
- rounded shaft down the south side of the building
- façade columns
- water flowing down each side of the entrance
- glass panels
- crossed lines
- grid-like steel truss
- marble floor of geometric shapes in the lobby
- rotunda formed by six marble columns
- information booth
- works of art throughout the interior
- wood
- 25th floor with a sitting room, reception hall, auditorium, and terrace.

The Humana Building. Image Courtesy of Michael Graves & Associates. (Image also included in color photo gallery.)

Ideological criticism gives you the opportunity to focus your analysis on a particular subject of interest to you. You may choose to do ideological criticism because you are particularly interested in the ideologies related to a particular subject, and you want to analyze only the ideology concerning that subject in your artifact. You might be interested, for example, in the ideology of an artifact in terms of the environment and what it suggests about how to think about environmental issues. Or maybe you are particularly interested in the conception of gender embedded in an artifact or any difference that is often denigrated—race, class, sexual orientation, religion, and ability, for example. In such cases, you want to focus on identifying key presented elements of the artifact related to your topic of interest.

Feminist criticism, for example, is ideological criticism with a particular interest in gender. In this kind of criticism, your identification of presented elements would be selective, focused on those aspects of the artifact that depict women and men, femininity and masculinity. Similarly, ideological critics with a particular interest in race would discover the construction of race implicit in a particular ideology, and when they identify presented elements, they would select ones that have to do with race in the artifact and ignore those that have to do with the environment, for example.

Identifying Suggested Elements

In the second step of ideological criticism, the critic articulates ideas, references, themes, allusions, or concepts that are suggested by the presented elements. This is the step at which you identify the meanings suggested by the elements that will serve as the basis for ideological tenets. Take your list of presented elements and generate at least one idea or concept you believe each one suggests.

In the Humana Building, for example, the presented elements might reference the following suggested elements:

- granite: permanence, durability, wealth
- massive scale: grandeur, awe
- L shape: tombstone, memorial, cash register
- pyramid shape: ziggurat, a terraced tower of Assyria and Babylonia
- rounded shaft: column
- façade columns: order, ceremony, decorum
- water: sustenance, purification, cleanliness
- glass panels: water (a lake or pond), flags hung in a row
- crossed lines: crosses
- steel truss: bridges
- lobby: wealth, grandeur, permanence (marble), Pantheon (patterned floor and vaulted ceiling), cemetery (ordered geometric shapes on the floor)
- rotunda: tomb or mausoleum
- information booth: security guards or caretakers
- works of art: wealth and treasure
- wood: expensive coffin
- 25th floor: elegant mansion (sitting room), outdoor plaza and grand ballroom (reception area), church (auditorium with crosses), outdoor garden (terrace)

The two lists you prepare of the presented and suggested elements will not appear as lists in the essay you write. These lists are tools to help you discover the ideology in the artifact. Your analysis transforms the key presented and suggested elements into an ideology, and that is the next step of ideological criticism.

Formulating an Ideology

In the third step of ideological criticism, the critic groups the suggested elements into categories and organizes them into a coherent framework that constitutes the ideology you suggest is implicit in your artifact. To discover this ideology, you want to figure out what major ideational clusters, themes, or ideas characterize all or most of your suggested elements. Notice that, at this step in the process, you are no longer dealing with the presented elements you identified. Your attention is on the suggested elements alone. (You will bring the presented elements in as support for your ideological tenets when you write your essay, but, for now, your attention is on the ideas suggested by those presented elements.)

The suggested elements of the Humana Building, for example, cluster into two major categories—death and wealth. Death emerges as a key idea from the suggested elements because several of them call attention to memorial structures used to commemorate the lives of those who have died. The granite and marble used on the exterior of the building are materials used on tombstones. The pyramid-like structure at the top of the building has a tomb-like quality in its allusion to the sacred burial place of kings. The rounded shaft that bisects the building is symbolic of a grave marker. The most obvious "memorial," though, is the inner circle of the rotunda, where visitors feel the quiet and sanctity of a mausoleum. The information attendant, in this context, becomes a caretaker or guard of the dead.

The suggested elements also can be grouped into various rituals associated with death. The references to water are symbolic of the purification rituals that many cultures perform in preparation for the burial of a body. The references to bridges and rivers call up the water journeys connected with death in various cultures. The various art works displayed throughout the building might be viewed as the treasures buried with individuals in their tombs. The "flags" hung on the side of the building—the glass panels—can be seen as banners hung in mourning.

Many of the suggested elements also reference the various settings or context used by the living to deal with death. The 25th floor of the building contains several of these contexts. The sitting room is the "living room" of the funeral parlor, which is suggested by the reception hall. This hall also can be viewed as an outdoor plaza where mourners carry the body in ceremonial processional to the cemetery. The auditorium, with its church-like references, is a place where survivors eulogize the dead. Finally, the terrace suggests a cemetery or sanctuary where survivors may visit the dead.

In addition to the funerary references, various elements of the Humana Building suggest the theme of wealth. The materials of granite and marble are expensive and somewhat precious. The art works, because of their age or the reputations of their creators, are valuable. The theme of wealth is referenced by the stately elegance and ballroom style of the 25th floor and the cash-register shape on the top of the building.

Using major themes such as death and wealth, formulate the ideology of your artifact clearly and succinctly. This might take the form of a single sentence, or it may require two or three sentences. If you need more words than that to explain the ideology, you probably have not come up with the core idea of the ideology yet. You also will find that the statement you formulate for the ideology you discover in the artifact usually makes a good thesis or preview for your essay.

The following questions might help you articulate the ideology in the artifact you are analyzing:

- What is the preferred reading of the artifact?
- What does the artifact ask the audience to believe, understand, feel, or think about?
- What claim do the arguments being made in the artifact support?
- What particular characteristics, roles, actions, or ways of seeing does the artifact commend?
- What values or general conceptions of what is and is not good are suggested?
- What doesn't the artifact want the audience to think about?
- What ways of seeing does it ask the audience to avoid?
- What alternative interpretations of the world are possible to the one offered by the ideology in the artifact?
- What does the artifact suggest is unacceptable, negative, undesirable, marginal, or insignificant?

If you are still having trouble developing a clear, coherent, and succinct statement of the ideology of the artifact you are analyzing, you might find it helpful to think about whether the suggested elements have something to say about any of the following elements, which are typical components of an ideology. You might very well discover that your suggested elements offer perspectives on some or all of these categories. Note that you want to answer these questions from within the ideology—not from any external knowledge you have about those who adhere to a particular ideology:

- *Membership.* According to the ideology, who are adherents to the ideology or members of the group that espouses the ideology? Where are they from? What do they look like? Who can become a member of the group?
- *Activities.* What do those who espouse the ideology do? What is expected of them?
- *Goals.* Why do those who are committed to the ideology do what they do? What do they want to realize?
- *Core belief.* What one major idea best characterizes the essence of the ideology?
- *Defining event.* What event, invention, time period, movement, court case, or condition had the most influence on shaping the ideology?
- *Sacred text.* What document, book, or film best captures the commitments embedded in the ideology?

- *Ultimate authority.* Who or what is the sanctioning agent or highest authority, according to the ideology? Is it, for example, a set of documents such as annual reports and stock indexes? A method of rating such as best-seller lists or box-office receipts? A deity such as God, Great Spirit, or Mother Earth?

- *Values/norms.* What are the main values embedded in the ideology? How do adherents to the ideology evaluate themselves and others? What things should they do or not do?

- *Position and group-relations.* Who are the supporters of the group members? Who are the enemies or opponents?

- *Resources.* What are the essential social resources the group has or needs to have?[49]

Ideologies may contain beliefs that are clearly articulated in all of the above categories, but you are likely to find that the ideology implicit in most artifacts focuses on only one or perhaps a few areas. The ideology of feminism, for example, focuses primarily on one goal—to eliminate relations of oppression and domination in our culture. In contrast, a Christian ideology focuses on values, while the ideology of capitalism focuses on the resource dimension—freedom of the market as the means to achieve resources.[50] In the case of the Humana Building, the ideology identified deals with the goals and values of the Humana organization and says very little about the other elements.

Here are some samples of ideologies that critics have articulated as a result of engaging in ideological criticism of various artifacts. They give you an idea of the form you want to use to articulate the ideology that emerges from your analysis:

- Judy Chicago's work of art *The Dinner Party* empowers and legitimizes women's authentic voice through three primary strategies: "(1) The work is independent from male-created reality; (2) it creates new standards for evaluation of its own rhetoric; and (3) women are clearly labeled as agents."[51]

- The children's book *Daddy's Roommate* presents an ideology that acknowledges and challenges homosexual stereotypes by embedding homosexual relationships within the American dream. The book's ideology is one in which an un-American family meets the "criteria for the economic status, characters, and activities that mark fulfillment of a very American dream."[52]

- The ideology that undergirds the film *Pocahontas* constructs Pocahontas as "a prisoner, wrongfully and immorally trapped within a backward and pre-scientific culture." The film "enacts the colonialist narrative and in so doing legitimates a cultural framework rooted in racism, anti-miscegenation, patriarchy, and capitalism."[53]

- The Delta Blues Museum presents to visitors an ideology that promotes "'authentic' images of primitiveness and impoverishment— iconic symbols that reflect larger, more encompassing, blues mythic narratives—that arguably satisfy (White) tourists who share culturally specific memories of the blues. At the same time, these mythic narratives serve to racially reinscribe predictable and stereotypical images of the downtrodden, dispossessed blues subject."[54]

- The Woman's Building at the 1893 World's Columbia Exposition affirms the "dominant rhetoric of 'civilization' as White and male" by co-opting minority voices "to serve the interests of the dominant narrative."[55]

- The Humana Building "is a memorial to those who have suffered or died because of its system of health care—a system that emphasizes profit over charity. . . . The images of death linked to the Humana Corporation serve as monuments to those whom Humana has served not for reasons of charity but for reasons of profit—and the service has been less than it would have been in a hospital dedicated to care rather than profit."[56]

Identifying the Functions Served by the Ideology

In the final step of ideological criticism, your task is to discover how the ideology you constructed from the artifact functions for the audience who encounters it and the consequences it has in the world. Does it encourage the audience to accept a particular position on a social issue? Does it present a view of a condition that is naïve, misguided, or inappropriate for some reason? How does the ideology encourage audience members to construct themselves? Does the ideology present something as natural and normal in the artifact so that audiences do not question a particular perspective? Does it represent a marginalized perspective that it invites the audience to consider?

Formulating a Research Question

Ideological criticism is a kind of criticism in which your research question can be specifically about your artifact, although you might want to explain why knowing the ideology of a particular artifact is important if you formulate such a question. One or more of the following questions are likely to serve as your research question in ideological analysis: "What is the ideology manifest in this artifact?" "Who are the groups or voices whose interests are represented, served, or favored in the ideology?" "What are the implications of the ideology for the world in which it participates?"

Writing the Critical Essay

After completing the analysis, you are ready to write your essay, which includes five major components: (1) an introduction, in which you discuss the research question, its contribution to rhetorical theory, and its significance; (2) a description of the artifact and its context; (3) a description of the method of criticism—in this case, ideological analysis; (4) a report of the findings of the analysis, in which you identify the ideology manifest in the artifact and the rhetorical strategies that promote it over other ideologies; and (5) a discussion of the contribution the analysis makes to rhetorical theory.

Sample Essays

In the essays that follow, critics analyze a variety of artifacts to discover the ideologies they embody. Greg Dickinson, Brian L. Ott, and Eric Aoki analyze the Buffalo Bill Museum to discover what vision of the West it constructs for visitors. In their analysis of the television show *Queer Eye for the Straight Guy*, Celeste Lacroix and Robert Westerfelhaus identify the ideology of the show and suggest that it functions to allow gays and lesbians only temporary and controlled access to the cultural mainstream. In her analysis of the Web sites of three United Nations agencies, Khadidiatou Ndiaye seeks to answer the question: "How inclusive is the ideology of UNICEF, UNFPA, and UNAIDS as portrayed in these organizations' Web sites?"

Notes

[1] Teun A. van Dijk, *Ideology: A Multidisciplinary Approach* (Thousand Oaks, CA: Sage, 1998), p. 69; and Anne Makus, "Stuart Hall's Theory of Ideology: A Frame for Rhetorical Criticism," *Western Journal of Speech Communication*, 54 (Fall 1990), 499.

[2] For a more detailed explanation of beliefs and ideology, see van Dijk, pp. 28–52.

[3] van Dijk, p. 66.

[4] Antonio Gramsci is credited with the initial conceptualization of this notion of hegemony. See Antonio Gramsci, *Selections from the Prison Notebooks*, trans. and ed. Quintin Hoare and Geoffrey N. Smith (1971; rpt. New York: International, 1987).

[5] Stuart Hall, "The Toad in the Garden: Thatcherism Among the Theorists," in *Marxism and the Interpretation of Culture*, ed. Cary Nelson and Lawrence Grossberg (Urbana: University of Illinois Press, 1988), p. 44.

[6] Alan O'Connor, "Culture and Communication," in *Questioning the Media: A Critical Introduction*, ed. John Downing, Ali Mohammadi, and Annabelle Sreberny-Mohammadi (Newbury Park, CA: Sage, 1990), p. 36.

[7] van Dijk; Teun A. van Dijk, *Communicating Racism: Ethnic Prejudice in Thought and Talk* (Newbury Park, CA: Sage, 1987); Teun A. van Dijk, *News Analysis: Case Studies of International and National News in the Press* (Hillsdale, NJ: Erlbaum, 1988); and Teun A. van Dijk, *Elite Discourse and Racism* (Newbury Park, CA: Sage, 1993).

[8] Philip C. Wander, "Salvation Through Separation: The Image of the Negro in the American Colonization Society," *Quarterly Journal of Speech*, 57 (February 1971), 57–67; Philip C. Wander, "The John Birch and Martin Luther King Symbols in the Radical Right," *Western Speech*, 35 (Winter 1971), 4–14; Philip C. Wander, "The Savage Child: The Image of the Negro in the Pro-Slavery Movement," *Southern Speech Communication Journal*, 37 (Summer 1972), 335–60; Philip Wander and Steven Jenkins, "Rhetoric, Society, and the Critical Response," *Quarterly Journal of Speech*, 58 (December 1972), 441–50; Philip Wander, "*The Waltons*: How Sweet It Was," *Journal of Communication*, 26 (Autumn 1976), 148–54; Philip Wander, "On the Meaning of *Roots*," *Journal of Communication*, 27 (Autumn 1977), 64–69; Philip Wander, "The Angst of the Upper Class," *Journal of Communication*, 29 (Autumn 1979), 85–88; Philip Wander, "Cultural Criticism," in *Handbook of Political Communication*, ed. Dan D. Nimmo and Keith R. Sanders (Beverly Hills: Sage, 1981), 497–528; Philip Wander, "The Ideological Turn in Modern Criticism," *Central States Speech Journal*, 34 (Spring 1983), 1–18; Philip Wander, "The Aesthetics of Fascism," *Journal of Communication*, 33 (Spring 1983), 70–78; Philip Wander, "The Rhetoric of American Foreign Policy," *Quarterly Journal of Speech*, 70 (November 1984), 339–61; Philip Wander, "The Third Persona: An Ideological Turn in Rhetorical Theory," *Central States Speech Journal*, 35 (Winter 1984), 197–216; Richard Morris and Philip Wander, "Native American Rhetoric: Dancing in the Shadows of the Ghost Dance," *Quarterly Journal of Speech*, 76 (May 1990), 164–91; and Philip C. Wander, "Introduction: Special Issue on Ideology," *Western Journal of Communication*, 57 (Spring 1993), 105–10.

[9] Michael C. McGee, "In Search of 'The People': A Rhetorical Alternative," *Quarterly Journal of Speech*, 61 (October 1975), 235–49; Michael C. McGee, "'Not Men, but Measures': The Ori-

gins and Import of an Ideological Principle," *Quarterly Journal of Speech*, 64 (April 1978), 141–54; Michael Calvin McGee, "The 'Ideograph': A Link Between Rhetoric and Ideology," *Quarterly Journal of Speech*, 66 (February 1980), 1–16; Michael Calvin McGee, "The Origins of 'Liberty': A Feminization of Power," *Communication Monographs*, 47 (March 1980), 23–45; Michael Calvin McGee and Martha Anne Martin, "Public Knowledge and Ideological Argumentation," *Communication Monographs*, 50 (March 1983), 47–65; Michael Calvin McGee, "Secular Humanism: A Radical Reading of 'Culture Industry' Productions," *Critical Studies in Mass Communication*, 1 (March 1984), 1–33; Michael Calvin McGee, "Another Philippic: Notes on the Ideological Turn in Criticism," *Central States Speech Journal*, 35 (Spring 1984), 43–50; Allen Scult, Michael Calvin McGee, and J. Kenneth Buntz, "Genesis and Power: An Analysis of the Biblical Story of Creation," *Quarterly Journal of Speech*, 72 (May 1986), 113–31; Michael Calvin McGee, "Power to the {People}," *Critical Studies in Mass Communication*, 4 (December 1987), 432–37; and Michael Calvin McGee, "Text, Context, and the Fragmentation of Contemporary Culture," *Western Journal of Speech Communication*, 54 (Summer 1990), 274–89.

[10] Raymie E. McKerrow, "Critical Rhetoric: Theory and Praxis," *Communication Monographs*, 56 (June 1989), 91–111; and Raymie E. McKerrow, "Critical Rhetoric in a Postmodern World," *Quarterly Journal of Speech*, 77 (February 1991), 75–78.

[11] Janice Hocker Rushing, "The Rhetoric of the American Western Myth," *Communication Monographs*, 50 (March 1983), 14–32; Janice Hocker Rushing, "*E.T.* as Rhetorical Transcendence," *Quarterly Journal of Speech*, 71 (May 1985), 188–203; Janice Hocker Rushing, "Mythic Evolution of 'The New Frontier' in Mass Mediated Rhetoric," *Critical Studies in Mass Communication*, 3 (September 1986), 265–96; Janice Hocker Rushing, "Ronald Reagan's 'Star Wars' Address: Mythic Containment of Technical Reasoning," *Quarterly Journal of Speech*, 72 (November 1986), 415–33; Janice Hocker Rushing, "Evolution of 'The New Frontier' in *Alien* and *Aliens*: Patriarchal Co-optation of the Feminine Archetype," *Quarterly Journal of Speech*, 75 (February 1989), 1–24; Janice Hocker Rushing, "Power, Other, and Spirit in Cultural Texts," *Western Journal of Communication*, 57 (Spring 1993), 159–68; Thomas S. Frentz and Thomas B. Farrell, "Conversion of America's Consciousness: The Rhetoric of *The Exorcist*," *Quarterly Journal of Speech*, 61 (February 1975), 40–47; Janice Hocker Rushing and Thomas S. Frentz, "The Frankenstein Myth in Contemporary Cinema," *Critical Studies in Mass Communication*, 6 (March 1989), 61–80; Janice Hocker Rushing and Thomas S. Frentz, "Integrating Ideology and Archetype in Rhetorical Criticism," *Quarterly Journal of Speech*, 77 (November 1991), 385–406; and Thomas S. Frentz and Janice Hocker Rushing, "Integrating Ideology and Archetype in Rhetorical Criticism, Part II: A Case Study of *Jaws*," *Quarterly Journal of Speech*, 79 (February 1993), 61–81.

[12] Lawrence Grossberg, "Marxist Dialectics and Rhetorical Criticism," *Quarterly Journal of Speech*, 65 (October 1979), 235–49; Lawrence Grossberg, "Is There Rock after Punk?" *Critical Studies in Mass Communication*, 3 (March 1986), 50–73; and Lawrence Grossberg, "Cultural Studies and/in New Worlds," *Critical Studies in Mass Communication*, 10 (March 1993), 1–22.

[13] Celeste Michelle Condit, "Hegemony in a Mass-Mediated Society: Concordance about Reproductive Technologies," *Critical Studies in Mass Communication*, 11 (September 1994), 205–30; and Celeste Michelle Condit, "The Rhetorical Limits of Polysemy," *Critical Studies in Mass Communication*, 6 (June 1989), 103–22.

[14] See, for example, Dana L. Cloud, *Control and Consolation in American Politics and Culture Rhetorics of Therapy* (Thousand Oaks, CA: Sage, 1998); Dana L. Cloud, "Hegemony or Concordance? The Rhetoric of Tokenism in Oprah Winfrey's Rags-to-Riches Biography," *Critical Studies in Mass Communication*, 13 (June 1996), 115–37; "'To Veil the Threat of Terror': Afghan Women and the <Clash of Civilizations> in the Imagery of the U.S. War on Terrorism," *Quarterly Journal of Speech*, 90 (August 2004), 285–306; and Dana L. Cloud, "The Rhetoric of <Family Values>: Scapegoating, Utopia, and the Privatization of Social Responsibility," *Western Journal of Communication*, 62 (Fall 1998), 387–419.

[15] See, for example, Claude Lévi-Strauss, *The Savage Mind* (Chicago: Chicago University Press, 1966); and Claude Lévi-Strauss, *Totemism*, trans. Rodney Needham (Boston: Beacon, 1963).

[16] See, for example, Ferdinand de Saussure, *Course in General Linguistics*, ed. Charles Bally, Albert Sechehaye, and Albert Reidlinger, trans. Roy Harris (London: Duckworth, 1983).

[17] See, for example, Charles Sanders Peirce, *Peirce on Signs: Writings on Semiotic*, ed. James Hoopes (Chapel Hill: University of North Carolina Press, 1991).

[18] See, for example, Roland Barthes, *Elements of Semiology*, trans. Annette Lavers and Colin Smith (1964; rpt. New York: Noonday, 1967); and Roland Barthes, *Mythologies*, trans. Annette Lavers (1957; rpt. New York: Noonday, 1972).

[19] See, for example, Arthur Asa Berger, *Signs in Contemporary Culture: An Introduction to Semiotics* (New York: Longman, 1984); and Arthur Asa Berger, *Media Analysis Techniques* (Newbury Park, CA: Sage, 1991).

[20] Kaja Silverman, *The Subject of Semiotics* (New York: Oxford University Press, 1983).

[21] See, for example, Karl Marx and Frederick Engels, *The German Ideology: Parts I and III*, ed. Roy Pascal (New York: International, 1947); and Karl Marx, *The Grundrisse*, ed. and trans. David McLellan (New York: Harper and Row, 1971).

[22] See, for example, Theodor Adorno, *Aesthetic Theory*, ed. Gretal Adorno and Rolf Tiedmann, trans. C. Lenhardt (London: Routledge and Kegan Paul, 1984); and Theodor Adorno, *The Jargon of Authenticity*, trans. Knut Tarnowski and Frederic Will (Evanston, IL: Northwestern University Press, 1973).

[23] See, for example, Louis Althusser, *For Marx*, trans. Ben Brewster (1965; rpt. London: Allen Lane, 1969); and Louis Althusser, *Lenin and Philosophy and Other Essays*, trans. Ben Brewster (New York: Monthly Review, 1971).

[24] See, for example, Walter Benjamin, *Illuminations*, ed. Hannah Arendt, trans. Harry Zohn (New York: Schocken, 1968); and Walter Benjamin, *Understanding Brecht*, trans. Anna Bostock (London: NLB, 1977).

[25] See, for example, Bertolt Brecht, *Brecht on Theatre*, ed. and trans. John Willett (New York: Hill and Wang, 1964).

[26] See, for example, Terry Eagleton, *Marxism and Literary Criticism* (Berkeley: University of California Press, 1976); and Terry Eagleton, *The Function of Criticism: From the Spectator to Post-Structuralism* (London: Verso, 1984).

[27] See, for example, Jürgen Habermas, *Communication and the Evolution of Society*, trans. Thomas McCarthy (Boston: Beacon, 1979); Jürgen Habermas, *The Theory of Communicative Action, Volume I: Reason and the Rationalization of Society*, trans. Thomas McCarthy (Boston: Beacon, 1984); and Jürgen Habermas, *The Theory of Communicative Action, Volume II: Lifeworld and System: A Critique of Functionalist Reason*, trans. Thomas McCarthy (Boston: Beacon, 1987).

[28] See, for example, Georg Lukács, *History and Class Consciousness*, trans. Rodney Livingston (London: Merlin, 1971); and Georg Lukács, *The Historical Novel*, trans. Hannah Mitchell and Stanley Mitchell (London: Merlin, 1962).

[29] See, for example, Herbert Marcuse, *An Essay on Liberation* (Boston: Beacon, 1969); and Herbert Marcuse, *Counterrevolution and Revolt* (Boston: Beacon, 1972).

[30] See, for example, Jacques Derrida, *Writing and Difference*, trans. Alan Bass (Chicago: University of Chicago Press, 1978); Jacques Derrida, *Margins of Philosophy*, trans. Alan Bass (Chicago: University of Chicago Press, 1982); and Jacques Derrida, "Structure, Sign, and Play," in *The Structuralist Controversy*, ed. Richard Macksey and Eugenio Donato (Baltimore: Johns Hopkins Press, 1972), pp. 247–72.

[31] See, for example, Paul de Man, *Blindness and Insight: Essays in the Rhetoric of Contemporary Criticism* (New York: Oxford University Press, 1971); and Paul de Man, *Allegories of Reading: Figural Language in Rousseau, Nietzsche, Rilke, and Proust* (New Haven: Yale University Press, 1979).

[32] See, for example, Jean-François Lyotard, *The Postmodern Condition: A Report on Knowledge*, trans. Geoff Bennington and Brian Massumi (1979; rpt. Minneapolis: University of Minnesota Press, 1984).

[33] See, for example, Jean Baudrillard, *Simulations* (1981; rpt. New York: Semiotext(e), 1983); and Jean Baudrillard, *The Mirror of Production*, trans. Mark Poster (St. Louis: Telos, 1975).

[34] See, for example, Fredric Jameson, *Postmodernism, or the Cultural Logic of Late Capitalism* (Durham, NC: Duke University Press, 1991); and Fredric Jameson, *The Geopolitical Aesthetic: Cinema and Space in the World System* (Bloomington: Indiana University Press, 1992).

[35] See, for example, Richard Hoggart, *The Uses of Literacy: Aspects of Working-Class Life, with Special Reference to Publications and Entertainments* (New York: Oxford University Press, 1970); and Richard Hoggart, *On Culture and Communication* (1971; rpt. New York: Oxford University Press, 1972).

[36] See, for example, Stuart Hall, "The Rediscovery of 'Ideology': Return of the Repressed in Media Studies," in *Culture, Society and the Media*, ed. Michael Gurevitch, Tony Bennett, James

Curran, and Janet Woolacott (London: Methuen, 1982), pp. 56–90; Stuart Hall, "Encoding/ Decoding," in *Culture, Media, Language*, ed. Stuart Hall, Dorothy Hobson, Andrew Lowe, and Paul Willis (London: Hutchinson, 1980), pp. 128–38; and Stuart Hall and Tony Jefferson, eds., *Resistance Through Rituals: Youth Subcultures in Post-War Britain* (London: Hutchinson, 1976).

[37] Ernesto Laclau, *Politics and Ideology in Marxist Theory* (London: New Left, 1977); and Ernesto Laclau and Chantal Mouffe, *Hegemony and Socialist Strategy: Towards a Radical Democratic Politics* (London: Verson, 1985).

[38] Hall, "Rediscovery of 'Ideology'"; and Stuart Hall, "Signification, Representation, Ideology: Althusser and the Post-Structuralist Debates," *Critical Studies in Mass Communication*, 2 (June 1985), 91–114.

[39] Jennifer Daryl Slack, "The Theory and Method of Articulation in Cultural Studies," in *Stuart Hall: Critical Dialogues in Cultural Studies*, ed. David Morley and Kuan-Hsing Chen (New York: Routledge, 1996), p. 115.

[40] Makus, p. 503.

[41] Makus, p. 496.

[42] Jennifer Daryl Slack, "Communication as Articulation," in *Communication as . . . Perspectives on Theory*, ed. Gregory J. Shepherd, Jeffrey St. John, and Ted Striphas (Thousand Oaks, CA: Sage, 2006), p. 225.

[43] Makus, p. 503.

[44] Karlyn Kohrs Campbell, "The Rhetoric of Women's Liberation: An Oxymoron," *Quarterly Journal of Speech*, 59 (February 1973), 74–86.

[45] Cheris Kramer, "Women's Speech: Separate but Unequal?" *Quarterly Journal of Speech*, 60 (February 1974), 14–24.

[46] Sally Miller Gearhart, "The Womanization of Rhetoric," *Women's Studies International Quarterly*, 2 (1979), 195–201.

[47] This vocabulary and method were developed by Marla Kanengieter. See Marla R. Kanengieter, "Message Formation from Architecture: A Rhetorical Analysis," Diss. University of Oregon 1990; and Sonja K. Foss and Marla R. Kanengieter, "Visual Communication in the Basic Course," *Communication Education*, 41 (July 1992), 312–23.

[48] This analysis of the Humana Building is from Foss and Kanengieter.

[49] van Dijk, *Ideology*, pp. 69–70; and Mark Gerzon, *A House Divided* (New York: Putnam, 1996).

[50] van Dijk, *Ideology*, p. 70.

[51] Sonja K. Foss, "Judy Chicago's *The Dinner Party*: Empowering of Women's Voice in Visual Art," in *Women Communicating: Studies of Women's Talk*, ed. Barbara Bate and Anita Taylor (Norwood, NJ: Ablex, 1988), p. 17.

[52] Dara R. Krause, See Vang, and Shonagh L. Brent, "Americanizing Gay Parents: A Feminist Analysis of *Daddy's Roommate*," in Sonja K. Foss, *Rhetorical Criticism: Exploration & Practice*, 3rd ed. (Long Grove, IL: Waveland, 2004), p. 185.

[53] Derek T. Buescher and Kent A. Ono, "Civilized Colonialism: *Pocahontas* as Neocolonial Rhetoric," *Women's Studies in Communication*, 19 (Summer 1996), 147, 151.

[54] Stephen A. King, "Memory, Mythmaking, and Museums: Constructive Authenticity and the Primitive Blues Subject," *Southern Communication Journal*, 71 (September 2006), 247–48.

[55] Andrew F. Wood, "Managing the Lady Managers: The Shaping of Heterotopian Spaces in the 1893 Chicago Exposition's Woman's Building," *Southern Communication Journal*, 69 (Summer 2004), 289, 290.

[56] Foss and Kanengieter, p. 317.

Memory and Myth at the Buffalo Bill Museum

Greg Dickinson, Brian L. Ott, and Eric Aoki

Introduction

The story of the American frontier is a foundational myth. It both reveals how Americans view themselves as "Americans" and informs the actions they take on a local and global stage (Slotkin, 1992, p. 10). Like all national (hi)stories, it is a dynamic myth, adapting to the demands of an age and the psychological needs of those who would tell the story as their own. It is a story that first began to be told in the eighteenth century, and one that took on particular importance in the late nineteenth century when Frederick Jackson Turner (1994) first read his paper, "The Significance of the Frontier in American History," to an audience of nearly 200 historians gathered in Chicago during the World's Columbian Exhibition:

> Up to our own day American history has been in large degree the history of colonization of the Great West. The existence of an area of free land, its continuous recession, and the advance of American settlement westward, explain American development. (p. 31)

But it was another figure of that time, William Frederick "Buffalo Bill" Cody, who popularized the story of the frontier. Born in Iowa territory in 1846, William Cody was many things—a frontiersman, civilian scout, Pony Express rider, and hunting guide. He did not become a well-known public figure, however, until the early 1870s when pulp novelist Ned Buntline transformed Cody into the legendary hero, Buffalo Bill. The dime novel press was a key force in fostering national and international interest in the West (Kasson, 2000, p. 201), and "more dime store novels were written about 'Buffalo Bill' than any other western character" (Sorg, 1998, p. xiii). Had Buffalo Bill remained *merely* a colorful character in dime novel fiction, then the history of the West may have been remembered very differently than it was for much of the twentieth century.

But Cody was an entrepreneur. Recognizing the public's appetite for narratives of western settlement, especially those involving clashes with Indian "savages," he embraced the image of Buffalo Bill and "re-created himself as a walking icon" (White, 1994, p. 11). In 1883, Cody launched a carnivalesque arena show known as Buffalo Bill's Wild West, which blended his life experiences with the exploits of his mythic alter ego, Buffalo Bill, into a master narrative of the frontier. "Fact" and "fiction" became indistinguishable (Slotkin, 1992, pp. 81–82). Although the images of the frontier it presented were highly selective, dramatized, and romanticized, "the Wild West . . . seemed like an invitation into living history" (*Buffalo Bill Museum,* 1995, p. 31). A renowned storyteller and showman, Cody "never referred to his Wild West as a show" (White, 1994, p. 7), and audiences in the United States and Europe saw the Wild West as a serious attempt to tell the history of the West (Slotkin, 1992, pp. 67–68). By the time it ended its run in 1913, "Buffalo Bill was the most famous American of his time" (Tompkins, 1992, p. 179) and he "typified the Wild West to more people in more parts of the world than any other person" (Lamar, 1977, p. 230).

In telling the story of the frontier, Buffalo Bill's Wild West "defined the quintessential American hero" (*Buffalo Bill Museum,* 1995, p. 28) and brought "the essence of the American West to the world" (*Treasures,* 1992, p. 8). With its dramatic images of untamed lands and cowboy heroes, frontier mythology is distinctly Anglo and "American" in character, for as Will Wright (2001) asserts, the White "cowboy represents the American idea, not just American history" (p. 2). Over the past half century, both the stories of the frontier and the key sites in which those stories are told have changed, but the frontier myth has remained a vital part of U.S. national identity (Wright, p. 10). To gain a richer understanding of how the frontier myth is constructed in contemporary U.S. culture, we turn to the Buffalo Bill Historical Center (BBHC) and more particularly the Buffalo Bill Museum (BBM). The BBM is, we believe, especially well suited for examining memory, myth, and their intersection, both because of its significance as a museum of Western history and its particular connection to Buffalo Bill.

It is difficult to contest the importance of the BBHC as a key site in the construction of public memory regarding the "Old West." Composed of five internationally acclaimed museums (The Buffalo Bill Museum, Whitney Gallery of Western Art, The Plains Indian Museum, The Cody Firearms Museum, and The Draper Museum of Natural History), the Center encompasses over 300,000 square feet, making it the largest history and art museum between Minneapolis and the West Coast. Once described by author James Michener as "The Smithsonian of the West" (Buffalo Bill Historical Center, 2001, p. 4), the BBHC "is widely regarded as this country's finest western museum" (*Visitor's guide*). Although the whole complex certainly deserves analysis, the Center's size and complexity constrain what can be adequately addressed in one journal paper. More importantly, Buffalo Bill and the museum dedicated to his life provide the authorial voice for the entire Center and activate the central narrative of the frontier in constructing a national identity. Therefore, our analysis focuses on only the Buffalo Bill Museum, which establishes the narrative form of the Center and addresses many of the rhetorical issues raised by the BBHC as a whole. Based on its rhetorical invitations to collective memory and national identity, we argue that the Buffalo Bill Museum privileges images of Whiteness and masculinity, while using the props, films, and posters of Buffalo Bill's Wild West to carnivalize the violent conflicts between Anglo Americans and Native Americans.

In order to illustrate this claim, we first briefly outline the history of the museum itself. We then chart the material and symbolic ways that history museums function as rhetorical invitations to collective memory and national identity. Third, we move to an analysis of the Buffalo Bill Museum and to the specific ways it privileges Whiteness and masculinity, and carnivalizes the violent colonization of the West. Finally, we reflect upon what an analysis of the BBM suggests, not only about the construction of a particular nationalized myth, but also about the roles that White masculinity and carnivalized violence play in that myth.

The Building of the Buffalo Bill Museum

Although we do not wish to perpetuate an intentional fallacy, briefly tracing the history of the Buffalo Bill Museum and Buffalo Bill Historical Center can help clarify the ideological and economic forces that shaped the construction and function of the museum. The Buffalo Bill Museum started as little more than a local institution. Housed in a small log building designed as a replica of William Cody's TE ranch house (just outside of Cody, Wyoming), the museum was an odd collection of Buffalo Bill and Western memorabilia, taxidermied animals, historic firearms, the putative scalp of Cheyenne Chief Yellow Hair, and a display of locally produced art (Nicholas, 2002, p. 449).

From the very beginning, however, the founders of the museum had national aspirations. By 1924, sculptor Gertrude Vanderbilt Whitney (an heir to significant fortunes) had purchased better land for the museum (adjacent to the original Buffalo Bill Museum and site of the current complex), built a Buffalo Bill memorial sculpture (*The Scout*), and transported it to Cody using her own money (Bartlett, 1992, pp. 46–53). Her initial gift was valued at $50,000. However, this gift was dwarfed by the support of William Robertson Coe, who became the institution's most important Eastern supporter (Bartlett, 1992, pp. 117–118). Born and raised in England, Coe believed that Americans took their traditions for granted (Nicholas, 2002, p. 450). Coe focused his attention and considerable financial resources to educate Americans in these traditions, and he saw the Buffalo Bill Museum as a powerful site for this pedagogy. Located in the heart of Wyoming, a state that Coe believed was still "fresh with the pioneer spirit" (quoted in Nicholas, 2002, p. 452), the Buffalo Bill Museum could "tell the deep cultural stories about the West" (Nicolas, 2002, p. 459). Further funding for building the Buffalo Bill Museum itself came through the sale of Buffalo Bill commemorative rifles built by Winchester, which was owned at the time by John Olin. On the market in the late 1960s, the rifles were priced at $129.95 with $5.00 per rifle going to the BBM. Revenue from the sales of the rifles totaled approximately $825,000, enough to build the BBM wing of the Center.[1]

This short history of the funding and the building of the Buffalo Bill Museum raises three important issues. First, by the late 1950s and 1960s, the BBM was designed as an educational institution, a purpose that is reflected today in the institution's mission statement: "The Buffalo Bill Historical Center is a museum that educates the public by advancing knowledge about the American West through acquiring, preserving, exhibiting and interpreting collections" (J. Hedderman, personal communication, March 8, 2004). Second, supporters' interests in the museum were primarily national, not local, in scope. The museum was designed to attract audiences from across the nation, and the representations in the museum narrate a story of national significance.[2] Finally, the museum's location in Wyoming was and is crucial both to its pedagogical mission and its growth into a nationally recognized institution (Nicholas, 2002, pp. 439, 449). As Bartlett (1992) asserts, "the Historical Center is devoted to the history of the American West, and perhaps no other region in the United States is still so untarnished by modern times, still so genuinely western" (p. 4). The BBHC also interacts with other major sites of memory including Mount Rushmore and the uncompleted Crazy Horse Memorial. Like the BBHC, these memorials draw on and reinforce a discourse of heroism as modes narrating, or, in the case of the Crazy Horse Memorial, resisting the story of the nation (Blair & Michael, 2004). The Buffalo Bill Museum, then, serves as a pedagogical site, working to teach its visitors about the Old West and in so doing inculcating a particular vision not only of "the West" but also of what it means to be American. As a social and educational institution, the museum offers, in Benson and Anderson's (1989) terms, constructed and thus structured invitations to meaning (p. 3). The purpose of this paper is to explore these structured invitations.[3] We turn now to the ways by which museums create these invitations.

History Museums, Public Memory, and National Identity

History museums are a popular way for U.S. Americans to engage the past, and more importantly, they are perceived by the public to be the most trustworthy source of information about the past (Rosenzweig & Thelen, 1998, p. 21). In interviews conducted by Rosenzweig and Thelen (1998), individuals expressed a belief that history museums provide relatively unmediated access to the past—a judgment that does not appear to vary by sex, ethnicity, or class (p. 21). The artifacts, images, and narratives of the museum are understood to be "real" and thus reliable markers of the past. Finally, museum visitors feel particularly connected to the past when visiting museums (Rosenzweig & Thelen, pp. 19–21). As pedagogical institutions, then, history museums are compelling sites.

The perceived truthfulness of history museums, as well as their size, scope, and complexity, pose unique challenges for rhetorical critics (Armada, 1998, p. 235). However, such critics, who have increasingly turned their attention to the material spaces of memory (Blair & Michael, 1999; Blair, Jeppeson, & Pucci, 1991; Dickinson, 1997; Gallagher, 1995, 1999; Hasian, 2004; Katriel, 1994), are well positioned to understand the *suasory* force of history museums. Rhetorical critics bring an understanding of the interaction between texts and audiences to these sites. Historians have the tools to argue about the factual accuracy of museums (Loewen, 1999), art critics and art historians can evaluate artifacts in the appropriate aesthetic contexts (Dubin, 1999; Fryd, 1992), and scholars in American Studies are equipped to trace the political and economic forces in creating museums (Nicholas, 2002). Scholars of rhetoric, by contrast, consistently point to the ways that museums make claims on audiences (Armada, 1998; Gallagher, 1995, 1999). Rhetoric's concern with textual invitations therefore turns our attention to the *ways* material sites engage audiences in compelling historical narratives. Since our focus is on these material expressions, our aim in this section is to identify the three primary rhetorical practices of history museums: collecting, exhibiting, and (re)presenting.

Collecting

First and foremost, museums engage in the practice of collecting. Exhibit curators seek, locate, archive, preserve, and ultimately legitimate certain artifacts (both material and discursive) and not others (Gaither, 1992, p. 61). Since museums "constantly select and discard from the limitless realm of material memory" (Crane, 2000, p. 9), the appeal to memory is always selective, incomplete, and partial. To be collected means to be valued, and, in the case of museums, it means to be valued institutionally (Kavanagh, 1996, p. 6; Zelizer, 1995, p. 224). The BBM's collection of domestic artifacts from Cody's family life as well as its collection of Wild West artifacts selectively values certain elements of Cody's history, namely his status as a born Westerner and as an author of Western history. However, through exclusion, the practice of collecting also erases elements of Cody's life and the history of the West. History museums are, therefore, sites of both remembering and forgetting (Kavanagh, p. 6). In functioning as sites of forgetting, museums have the potential to cleanse, absolve, or relieve visitors of painful, conflictual histories. Traditionally, history museums have collected primarily material artifacts, which, unlike oral discourse, anchor the transient character of memory (Blair, 1999, pp. 30–50; Nora, 1989, p. 13; Zelizer, p. 232). Objects are not simply representations of the past, they are concrete fragments of the past, and thus they solidify memory, asserting that this particular past really happened; objects stand as embodied testaments to a particular memory (Rosenzweig & Thelen, 1998, p. 21). It is vital, therefore, that critics attend to the materiality of museums, and to the precise ways that visitors experience and interact with tangible artifacts.

Exhibiting

In addition to collecting, museums are engaged in the practice of exhibiting—of situating, locating, and (re)contextualizing artifacts in actual spaces. "Space has always helped define the boundaries of memory" (Zelizer, 1995, p. 223), and the spatial location of the museum as well as the placement of objects and testimonials within the museum work to orient visitors toward the past in particular ways (Hutton, 1993, p. 78). First is the matter of *site specificity,* which deals with the relation between the site of the gallery and the space unconfined by the gallery. Museums are fashioned by the contents and materials of their physical locations, be they industrial or "natural" (Suderburg, 2000, p. 4), and thus it matters where memory is activated. Museums are constitutive elements in a larger landscape, a landscape that, as Blair and Michael (1999) argue, offers "rules for reading" the museum and offers specific subject positions for visitors (pp. 58–59). As we have already suggested, the BBM's location in Wyoming is central both to its existence and to its pedagogical force. Upon entering the museum, visitors are already prepared to learn the lessons of the conquering of the West.

A second concern with exhibition is that of *installation,* which refers to the practice of placing an artifact in the "neutral" void of a gallery or museum. In removing an artifact from its original context, the placement of artifacts within a museum necessarily alters their meanings (Armada, 1998, p. 236; Maleuvre, 1999, p. 1). In a museum, an artifact's meaning is shaped by how the visitor arrives at it, by how movement through the museum is organized and directed (Bennett, 1995, pp. 180–186), and by the associations and dissociations fostered by juxtaposition with and proximity to other artifacts (Crane, 2000, p. 4; Suderburg, 2000, p. 5). As our analysis of the BBM suggests, the order of the exhibition creates a certain epistemology of the site, providing visitors with reading strategies to help decode the meanings as they move through the space. Regardless of how the visitors begin their visit in the BBM, they experience artifacts of Buffalo Bill's "real" life first. Visitors necessarily attend to Buffalo Bill's career as a showman *only after* learning that Buffalo Bill was a "real hero," and that this personal history served as the foundation in creating the Wild West. The ordering of the museum, then, asserts that the story Buffalo Bill tells in his Wild West, and, by extension, the story the BBM tells, is but a telling of the way it really was.

(Re)presenting

(Re)presenting constitutes the third key practice of museums. Through their various modes of display, museum curators and designers interpret artifacts and render them meaningful. The (re)presentational strategies of museums vary greatly from curiosity cabinets and life-size, dioramic environments to automated voice-overs and televisual presentations. The placards, curator's notes, brochures, and exhibit catalogues scattered throughout museums further shape the meanings of the artifacts on display. Historically, the display of artifacts in museums has been about separation, spectacle, and surveillance, as visitors have "gazed" at artifacts that are preserved and protected behind rope barriers and glass walls (Bennett, 1995, pp. 59–86). Increasingly, however, museums seeking to foster "lived experience" with artifacts have featured fully immersive, interactive environments. The United States Holocaust Memorial Museum in Washington, DC, for example, seeks to "encourage its visitors to reflect upon the moral and spiritual questions raised by the events of the Holocaust as well as their own responsibilities as citizens of a democracy" (*Mission statement*) by having visitors adopt the personas of Holocaust victims and survivors as they move through the museum. Using simulated environments, modern museums often claim to deliver visitors a more "authentic" experience of history.

Through the intersecting practices of collecting, exhibiting, and (re)presenting, history museums construct a story of the past—a story that is, above all, about "identities of people in the present" (Armada, 1998, p. 235), about "defining who people are and how they should act" (Karp, 1994, p. 4). As key civic and public institutions, argue Appadurai and Breckenridge (1992), "museums . . . represent national identities both at home and abroad [and] . . . serve as ways in which national and international publics learn about themselves and others" (p. 44). Museums of Western history—drawing on the centrality of the West to define America and utilizing the rhetorical power of history museums more generally—are among the most important sites in constructing, disseminating, and maintaining national identity, as well as in reminding us what it means to be "American." Understanding how history museums promote "social unity" (Bodnar, 1992, p. 13) even as they struggle to be sensitive to and reflexive about our cultural differences is the task of the next section.

Whiteness, Masculinity, and the Carnivalization of Violence in the Buffalo Bill Museum

Our analysis of the BBM is based on two weekend-long visits, one in 2002 and one in 2003. The three of us spent well over 20 hours each in the BBHC, devoting much of that time to our exploration of the BBM. During our time in the museums, we took photographs of the exhibits, collected documents provided by the institution, visited the on-site archives, and took extensive notes of our observations about the space and the ways the space was used by visitors. We have drawn on e-mail and phone conversations with Josie Hedderman, an administrator of the BBHC, as well as utilized Richard Bartlett's (1992) book *From Cody to the World* published by the BBHC, the BBHC Web site, and the Center's pamphlets for background information about the institution. In what follows we employ first person narrative of our first visit in portions of our analysis to emphasize the ways traveling to and through the museum influences the rhetorical force of the site.

Cody, Wyoming, and the BBHC are located near the center of the 10,000 square miles that compose the Big Horn Basin. For most visitors, travel to the BBHC takes a significant commitment of time and effort. Indeed, our own initial trip conditioned our experience of the Center. We first traveled to the Buffalo Bill Museum from Fort Collins, Colorado, in April of 2002. After seven hours of travel by car, we found ourselves in the middle of Wyoming and deep in the heart of the West. The further northwest we journeyed along State Route 120, the fewer signs of "civilization" we encountered. By the time we had passed through two consecutive towns with populations of 10, the landscape appeared to us as vast, barren, and uninterrupted (Figure 1). Encompassing nearly 98,000 square miles, Wyoming is geographically the ninth largest state in the country (*Profile of general*) but has the smallest population of any U.S. state. Surrounded on all sides by open range, the partially clouded sky stretched a

Figure 1

Photographs in Figures 1–8 by Brian L. Ott.

seemingly endless distance in every direction. In describing her own response to this landscape Jane Tompkins (1992) writes:

> It is environment inimical to human beings, where a person is exposed, the sun beats down, and there is no place to hide. But the negations of the physical setting—no shelter, no water, no rest, no comfort—are also its siren song. Be brave, be strong enough to endure this, it says, and you will become like this—hard, austere, sublime. (p. 71)

Like Tompkins' response to the Wyoming plains, our understanding of this landscape as "the West" is already culturally informed. For over 100 years, Wyoming has served as a central symbol in thinking about the West. In the late nineteenth century, painters and novelists like Fredric Remington and Owen Wister declared Wyoming the "last stronghold of Anglo-Saxon America" (Nicholas, 2002, p. 439). These images articulate powerfully with the larger "Myth of the Frontier," which asserts:

> the conquest of the wilderness and the subjugation or displacement of the Native Americans who originally inhabited it have been the means to our achievement of a national identity, a democratic polity, an ever-expanding economy, and a phenomenally dynamic and "progressive" civilization. (Slotkin, 1992, p. 10)

In the late nineteenth century, Buffalo Bill, Wyoming's most famous resident, became the ideal embodiment of the frontier hero (Slotkin, pp. 75–76). However, Cody's death did not mark the end of this myth. Indeed, the myth is replayed throughout the twentieth century, and as we will see, serves as a motivating narrative structure of the BBM. The repetition of the myth in movies, novels, and political discourse structures our experience of traveling to Cody and the museum.

On our first visit to the Center during the last weekend of April 2002, it was bit-
terly cold and snow was falling lightly. As we approached the complex, we noticed a
large bronze statue of a horse and rider flanking the Center on an adjoining hill.
Closer inspection revealed that the impressive 12 ft. 5 in. sculpture was of Buffalo Bill
Cody (Figure 2), posed in "his historic role as a scout, bending down to read the trail
while signaling with his rifle" (*Treasures,* 1992, p. 13). The location of Gertrude
Vanderbilt Whitney's *Buffalo Bill—The Scout* allows its heroic figure to survey the adjacent valley and mountain range. The statue captures what, at some level, visitors
already know—that they are in cowboy country, in Buffalo Bill's territory, which he
austerely oversees with his gaze and gun. We wanted to study the statue more closely,
but the cold was unbearable and we proceeded quickly to the Center's entrance.
There, a second, and yet very different, statue of Buffalo Bill greeted us (Figure 3).
With gun draped casually at his side, Cody tips his hat as if welcoming visitors into his
home. Although the BBHC houses five "separate" museums, the statues of Cody outside the Center are the first and most obvious of many signs that the story visitors will
hear is Cody's to tell. He is both its narrator and chief protagonist.

Having been introduced to the institution's narrator, we entered the BBHC. The
space immediately inside the Center, like the landscape that surrounds it, is expansive
and airy. After paying our $15 admission fee, we found ourselves standing in the cen-
ter of the "Orientation Gallery," facing a family of bison grazing on tall range grass
(Figure 4). The taxidermied animals are made to appear "natural," to conceal any
human activity and agency in their preservation. As the sole artifact in the Orientation Gallery, the bison perform an important orienting function. They serve to "natu-
ralize" the story that is just now beginning to unfold, to guarantee that the people and
events visitors will learn about were simply colorful features of the landscape and

Figure 2

(Image also included in color photo gallery.)

Figure 3

(Image also included in
color photo gallery.)

Figure 4

inevitable stages in the natural "development" of the West. Father, mother, and calf affirm a "natural" history of the West, one of life cycles, seasonal change, and uncorrupted states. The bison obscure the fact that art, whether taxidermied or classical, "is not [only] nature but nature existing by and for humans" (Maleuvre, 1999, p. 214). In the accompanying placard, culture is further subordinated to nature, "The West is a land of symbols: the cowboy, the warrior of the plains, the horse and the six shooter. But perhaps no more representative symbol of the West exists than the American bison, commonly known as the buffalo." This installation functions mythically to transform, as Barthes (1972) argues, "history into nature" (p. 129). The bison, already coded as natural, are stripped of their historical importance as sustenance for Plains Indians and, just as tellingly, are stripped of the history of their violent demise. To dispel any remaining doubt left open by the image of the installation, the placard discursively transforms the bison from their place in historical conflicts into nothing more (or less) than a "symbol of the West."

As symbolically important as the buffalo are, even more important is Buffalo Bill and the museum dedicated to his/story. The Buffalo Bill Museum is brightly lit with incandescent and florescent fixtures recessed in the ceiling and the displays. Its space functions rhetorically, like Buffalo Bill's Wild West, "[to] put the epic western experience into an orderly narrative." The museum is divided into four parts, the Cody Family Room, Local History Room, Wild West Room, and Young Buffalo Bill. That these four "independent" exhibits work to tell a coherent, well-ordered story is evident from the outset. Upon entering the museum, visitors are greeted by a large image of Buffalo Bill in full vaquero stage outfit, sharing his story with eight captivated children huddled on his lap and at his feet (Figure 5). This same image introduces the BBM in the *Treasures from Our West* (1992) catalogue (p. 9) sold at the gift shop, and a nearly identi-

Figure 5

cal image graces the cover of the Center's *Visitor's Guide*. The poster of Buffalo Bill suggests visually what the accompanying placard confirms discursively—that the story is Cody's to tell. "Buffalo Bill," the placard reads, "is perhaps best remembered as a storyteller. The story he told—through his life and his show—was heard by millions in America and abroad. To many of the children and grandchildren of those who saw him, Buffalo Bill *is* the Wild West" (italics original). In subtly shifting from his role as narrator ("as a storyteller") to his role as participant, as real life Western figure ("through his life and show"), the placard lends credence and authenticity to Cody's history.[4] Moreover, the closing phrase ("Buffalo Bill *is* the Wild West") functions synecdochically to suggest that Cody's story is not simply *a* history, but *the* history of the West.

The first exhibit, the Cody Family Room, exercises a similar authorizing function. It showcases an array of furniture and personal items from Cody's home in North Platte, Nebraska. The various artifacts from Cody's home materially document his life on the frontier and guarantee that his story of the West is *grounded* in lived experience. The location of this exhibit prior to the Wild West Room is significant as it frames how visitors come to the showman stage of his life. The spatial layout symbolically suggests that Cody is a Westerner *first* and that his life as a Westerner is the basis for the (hi)story told in his Wild West "show."

In addition to grounding history in lived experience, the Family Room is important because of its definition of family. By unreflectively exhibiting Cody's home as an archetypal example of "frontier life," the family room naturalizes Whiteness as the invisible center of that life. As there is an entire museum at the BBHC dedicated to the "cultural backgrounds, traditions, values, and histories" of the Plains Indians (*Visitor's Guide*), it is tempting to dismiss this critique. Locating the culture of the Plains Indians in a separate museum, apart from a generic history of the frontier, however, is precisely the installation practice that decenters the American Indian. The Plains Indian Museum claims to reflect a *particular* set of cultural experiences, while the Buffalo Bill Museum—although utterly silent about its White ethnic bias—claims, according to the membership brochure, to represent the "culture of the Western frontier" (*We're Making History*). This exclusion of Native Americans from the narrative of Anglo American history is typical of Western histories (Lake, 1991, pp. 124–125; Morris & Wander, 1990, pp. 165–166). Indeed, with the frontier myth, Native Americans serve as the "savage" opposite to Anglo Americans' "civilization" and culture (Slotkin, 1992, pp. 14–16).

Situated between the Cody Family Room exhibit and the Wild West exhibit is the Local History Room. On our visit, this room was filled with a collection of contemporary "Western" furniture created by local artisans and furniture makers. The spatial movement through these three exhibits, then, follows a past, present, past temporal structure. The interruption of the past by the present did not seem odd to any of us as we moved through the BBM, and none of us commented on it during our visit. The West of the present seemed to "fit right in line" with the West of the past—its bulky, rustic, natural all-wood furniture indicating the same strength and ruggedness of character suggested by the artifacts in the Cody Family Room. The movement from past to present to past again is virtually seamless and suggests that the qualities embodied in the artifacts of the Local History Room are a product of place, not time. The West, visitors are told, is timeless, and its unchanging landscape promises a certain (stereo)type of hero.[5] Judging by the accompanying surnames, the furniture in the Local History

Room was created exclusively by artisans of European descent and reflects a collecting practice that, once again, treats White ethnic identity as the invisible norm in Western culture. The exhibit's relative location in the Buffalo Bill Museum as well as its unreflective treatment of White culture *as* Western culture extends and confirms the story of Western life introduced by the Cody Family Room—a story that *begins* with and is *centered* on White Western settlement. The Native American is, thus far, altogether absent from the museum's history of the frontier. Beginning the story *when* and *as* it does functions rhetorically to reaffirm "settlement" myths by treating the land as unoccupied and untamed prior to the arrival of (White) frontiersmen. The Plains Indians come onto the scene only after museum visitors are introduced to *typical* (read as White and patriarchal) frontier life, and even then they are represented not as an indigenous people but as one of the "novelties" and "challenges" faced by early settlers.

Since the stated purpose of the Buffalo Bill Museum is "to interpret his [Cody's] story in the context of the history and myth of the American West," and since "Indians were vital" in Cody's own "master narrative of the West," it is worth noting that the first and only images of American Indians that visitors encounter in the BBM are in the third exhibit, the Wild West Room. The relegation of Native Americans to the Wild West exhibit suggests that, for the museum, they are peripheral to the history of the American frontier and constructs them primarily as objects of spectacle and entertainment, as an exoticized ethnic Other. The representation of cowboys and Indians in the Wild West exhibit is intriguing because it perpetuates many of the same stereotypes and images as Buffalo Bill's Wild West, even as it carnivalizes the show's foundational trope—that of Indian/White violence.[6] To better understand this partial homology, it is necessary to examine the exhibit's collection and display of artifacts and contrast them with the images and discourses from Buffalo Bill's Wild West. The Wild West Room is composed of three types of museum artifacts: costumes and props from Buffalo Bill's Wild West, a short video of historical footage from the show, and a collection of promotional posters for it.

The Wild West exhibit features an impressive array of costumes and props from Buffalo Bill's actual Wild West (which itself claimed to be presenting the actual history of the West). Visitors are invited to peruse show-related items such as costumes, saddles, and firearms. Accompanied by short identifying placards and photographs of Cody in costume (Figure 6), the artifacts in this portion of the exhibit are largely decontextualized. The fringed and beaded buckskin shirts and broad Stetson hats reproduce the (stereo)typical image of the cowboy found widely in popular culture. By tapping into popular images of the cowboy—images that were shaped significantly by Cody's *theatrical* attire—the costumes serve to affirm Cody's authenticity as a cowboy (Kasson, 2000, p. 40). Completing the familiar image of the cowboy is a collection of firearms from the show, including William "Doc" Carver's Colt .45 revolver and Annie Oakley's Winchester .32 rifle.[7] Absent from the exhibit and its history of the frontier is any discussion or analysis of the role firearms played in the slaughter of the buffalo or in the violent conflicts between American Indians and Whites. Instead, the firearms gesture to the sharp-shooting skills of individuals like Doc Carver and Annie Oakley, reducing guns to objects of play and aesthetics.

Among the most impressive artifacts from Buffalo Bill's Wild West is the stagecoach (Figure 7) purchased by Cody from the Cheyenne and Black Hills stage line in 1883 to portray Indian stagecoach raids. In Buffalo Bill's Wild West, the "Attack on the Stagecoach" was one of the many popular skits that told of Indian aggression,

Figure 6

Figure 7

(Image also included in color photo gallery.)

White female victimization, and male heroism (White, 1994, p. 27), but the museum does not comment on the political implications of how the stagecoach was used in the show. In failing to contextualize its artifacts or to problematize the Wild West's version of history, the Wild West exhibit perpetuates the show's stereotypical image of the cowboy, while repressing the violence that was a central feature of the show. The Wild West exhibit draws, then, on the narrative of Buffalo Bill's Wild West as its founding story, while the Wild West itself is a founding narrative of the West that continues to haunt U.S. imagination, a narrative simply reinforced by the museum itself (Slotkin, 1992, pp. 81–82).

The only components of the Wild West exhibit in which Indian/White violence is explicitly (re)presented are the Wild West film and promotional posters for the show. In both instances, the images of violence are sparse and heavily coded as "entertainment." The video is a short, black-and-white film of actual footage from Buffalo Bill's Wild West. It plays continuously on a small television monitor situated in front of several rows of cushioned benches inside a mock arena canopy. The canopy bears a striking resemblance to the large image of a Wild West "tent" in a nearby display case and furnishes the space with a carnival atmosphere. The images are grainy and unsteady, giving the film a nostalgic, but clumsy, feel. Thus, the footage of an Indian-led attack on a stagecoach and the passengers' eventual rescue by Buffalo Bill is almost humorous. The image does not, by contemporary standards, seem particularly violent or realistic, and the assemblage of the performers, both "cowboys and Indians," at the end of the film reminds viewers of its fictional nature.

Several of the promotional posters for the show also depict clashes between Native Americans and Whites, but the depictions are cartoonish in style and do not invite serious reflection on the actual violence that characterized westward expansion. Promotional posters for Buffalo Bill's Wild West are the most prevalent artifacts in the Wild West exhibit, and in some cases, fill an entire wall (Figure 8), but there is no explanation in the museum of what relation the images in the posters bear to history and myth. With no discourse to contextualize the images in the posters, visitors learn more about advertising of the time than about Indian/White relations. In fact, the sole placard dedicated to Wild West posters focuses on the role of posters in nineteenth-century advertising and the process of stone lithography used to print them. The placard structures the visual images into a story of progress both of technology and of advertising. The slim possibilities for oppositional readings of the White/ Native American relationships are displaced into the realm of "entertainment" and into a discourse of technological and economic development.

The artifacts, video, and posters in the Wild West exhibit operate as simulacra. They are images that materially testify only to another set of images (that is, Buffalo Bill's Wild West) for which there is no historical referent. But with no reflection on Buffalo Bill's history of the frontier as told through his Wild West, the engulfing presence of genuine, tangible, precious, historical artifacts fosters the appearance of "real" history. The near endless photographs of Buffalo Bill, along with the meticulous preservation and thus celebration of his clothing, riding equipment, and firearms, obscures the fact that "Buffalo Bill" is himself a fictional, popularly manufactured image of the cowboy. So, by the time visitors reach the final exhibit in the Buffalo Bill Museum, Buffalo Bill seems more *real* than William Cody and it matters not that Cody's experiences as a Pony Express Rider and Civil War private in the Seventh Kansas Volunteer Cavalry are detailed in an exhibit titled "Young Buffalo Bill."

Figure 8

(Image also included in color photo gallery.)

Although the experiences and events recounted in this exhibit precede Cody's creation of the Wild West arena show, the Young Buffalo Bill exhibit temporally follows the Wild West exhibit in the museum. As visitors near the exit of the BBM, this historical reversal functions to remind them that Buffalo Bill was not simply a showman, but that he was also a genuine Western hero.[8] It is here, for instance, that visitors learn Cody was awarded the Congressional Medal of Honor for valor.

There is a sense in which the Cody Family Room and Young Buffalo Bill function for the BBM in the same way as "real" artifacts of the West functioned in Buffalo Bill's Wild West. In both cases, the authenticity of the artifacts in these exhibits asserts the authenticity of Buffalo Bill as hero and narrator of the West. Both the Wild West and contemporary history museums, including the BBM, garner their trustworthiness in similar ways. Visitors are positioned as though they are in the presence of the "real" and unmediated elements of the past (Rosenzweig & Thelen, 1998, p. 21). The "authenticity" of the BBM, however, is even more complex than that of the Wild West. For here the artifacts from Cody's youth and from his life as a showman are accorded the same kind of historical authenticity. The stagecoach on exhibit is the "real" stagecoach from the "real" show, a show that claimed reality based in part on the fact the stagecoach had a pre-show life as a "real" stagecoach. Visitors, then, engage in both a history of the West and history of the representation of the West, a representation that relied on the authenticity of its props and its hero as justification. The props—already accorded authenticity by Buffalo Bill at the turn of the twentieth century—are given a double authenticity in the museum: they are, at once, authentic markers of the real West and authentic props of the Wild West.

These multiplying levels of authenticity and simulacra cover profound absences. Much of Cody's life story is not told in this exhibit or the museum, such as his reputation as an "Indian slayer" beginning at the age of 11 (Carter, 2000, pp. 30–32; Croft-Cooke & Meadmore, 1952, p. 120; Lamar, 1977, p. 230; Nash, 1992, p. 80; Russell, 1960, pp. 214–235) or his role as "the greatest killer of buffaloes whom the old West produced" (Neider, 1958, p. 219). This absent history is crucial to the museum's rhetoric and more generally to the myth of the frontier (Slotkin, 1992, pp. 13–14). Cody's exploits as Indian and buffalo killer are displaced onto the violent but neutralized images of the Wild West. The violence is not absent but carnivalized. The posters, the decontextualized attack on the stage coach, the rifles of Annie Oakley and of Doc Carver all represent an acknowledgement of the violent colonization of the West but an acknowledgement that continually defers political engagement of the history of Western colonization. The BBM, in deferring and carnivalizing Cody's part in the violent conquest of the West, invites visitors to defer their own responsibilities for the violent colonization of the West (Morris & Wander, 1990, pp. 165–166).

Dime novels and early biographies about Buffalo Bill were filled with accounts of Indian slaying and buffalo hunting, and Buffalo Bill's Wild West "made the conquest of savages central [to life on the frontier]. . . . His spectacles presented an account of Indian aggression and white defense; of Indian killers and white victims" (White, 1994, pp. 11, 27). For Buffalo Bill, the cowboy was a romantic figure, whose heroism was closely tied to his hunting and fighting skills, to his ability live off the harsh land and to fend off the "savages." For the BBM, the cowboy remains a romantic, celebrated figure, who—as a placard titled "The Cowboy," informs museum visitors—"represents the best in all Americans. . . . We admire him for his independence, his honesty, his modesty and courage." To appeal to contemporary audiences the BBM recodes cowboy heroism into categories other than violence. By mid-twentieth-century, after all, public sentiment was shifting. The blind extermination of buffalo at the close of the nineteenth century had nearly caused their extinction and Buffalo Bill's narrative of the frontier with its badly abused (read: White) conquerors was deemed inverted by historians. Thus, the violence so central to Buffalo Bill's life and to the Wild West are replaced by images of Buffalo Bill and stage Indians as entertainers, co-performers, and "friends." The cowboy is celebrated for his sharp shooting skills, but only as they relate to glass bobbles; he is praised for his riding and wrangling skills, but only as they relate to ranching. The cowboy remains a hero because he overcame an indomitable setting—a setting that the BBM, in confining Native Americans to the Wild West Room, suggests was his for the taking.

Constructing Public Memory and National Identity: Reflections on White Masculinity, Carnivalized Violence, and Manifest Destiny

The BBM is one site in which the story of the American West is told, one place where the myth of U.S. origins is dramatized and replayed; as such, the BBM draws on and helps constitute larger memory structures for national identity. In this final section we point to these memory structures and suggest the ways the BBM is a crucial institution in the creation of a vision of national identity that rests on White masculinity, carnivalized violence, and manifest destiny.

The Western nation-state and its attendant values of individualism, democracy, self-determination, and equality rest on the purposefully forgotten oppressions and rejections of the "Other." As scholars have recently argued, European, Anglo, and U.S. American modernities depended on a consistent expansion of Western ways of being, foisting onto the colonized Other values of savagery, communalism, and domination while reserving for the Western actor the privileged values of civilization, democracy, and freedom (Shome & Hegde, 2002, p. 254). The colonization of American Indians in the U.S. proceeded differently from many other colonizing discourses. This difference can, in part, be attributed to the ways the U.S. colonization of native peoples occurred within its own geopolitical boundaries, allowing the U.S. to represent its "expansionist motives as essential to nation-building, denying the imperial" (Anderson & Domash, 2002, p. 126). This nation building colonial impulse was justified, in part, by the rhetoric of manifest destiny, which claimed that westward expansion was not simply necessary for political or economic reasons but was, instead, a moral or even religious duty of the nation. Yet this form of colonization carried with it difficult contradictions. As Anderson and Domash argue, "the experiences of colonizing internally brings to the fore . . . contradictions inherent in national identities forged from positioning the colonized as both them and us" (p. 126). Creating and maintaining U.S. national identity, then, depends on creating stories that negotiate these contradictions, "stories that deny and assert the presence and significance of internal 'others'" (Anderson & Domash, p. 126).

Implicitly drawing on the language of manifest destiny and suturing itself into the larger myth of the frontier, the BBM enters into these contradictions, representing Buffalo Bill in particular and cowboys more generally as benign heroes who "civilize" the land. This civilizing maneuver allows Buffalo Bill to escape the charges of imperial violence under the guise of offering to both Native Americans and Euro Americans an improved and more productive land and life. The museum, through its practices of collection, exhibition, and (re)presentation, celebrates the White, male, civilizing colonizer—the one who brings the goods of modern society to an otherwise untamed land (Kirsch, 2002, p. 549; Ollund, 2002, p. 133; Slotkin, 1992, pp. 10–16, 75–76). In this setting Buffalo Bill becomes an ideal hero: White and male, a grand weaver of grand narratives, he tells a story of the West and of America that negotiates the contradictions of internal colonization. The museum is doing much more than simply conveying the biography of a particular cowboy and showman; it is, instead, telling and retelling a narrative of colonization and civilization. In promoting this memory, the museum materially and symbolically constitutes and reconstitutes the modernist story of the U.S. nation state. In motivating this particular memory, the museum draws on and creates the cultural resources not just of the frontier and cowboy myth but the larger and abstract values of self-determination, rugged individualism, and heroism.

The continuing desire for the BBM's version of Western history is dramatically illustrated by public response to the West as America exhibit at the National Museum of American Art in 1991. That show, whose purpose was "to critically reexamine received wisdom about American history, intergroup relations, and the American character" (Dubin, 1999, p. 156), became one of the most intensely debated exhibits in museum history. The show's catalog, edited by William H. Truettner, along with the exhibit's placards, consistently highlighted the ideological biases of Western Art (Truettner, 1991; Wolf, 1992, pp. 423–425). Critical responses to the exhibit were swift and vitriolic. After his visit on opening day, historian and Library of Congress librarian emeritus Daniel Boorstein wrote in the show's notebook: "A perverse, historically inaccurate destructive exhibit! No credit to the Smithsonian" (quoted in Dubin, p.

160). Commentator Charles Krauthammer, in his *Washington Post* editorial, called the show "tendentious, dishonest and, finally, puerile" (p. A19). Other commentators argued that the show was the worst of revisionist history and political correctness, undermining fundamental U.S. American values (Dubin, p. 161). Recent academic work interrogating the frontier myth no doubt heavily influenced the history of the West presented in the West as America exhibit. Although the exhibit indicates that alternative visions of the West *are* representable, the resistance to this different vision of the West demonstrates the continuing importance of the traditional Western narrative to U.S. American culture.

The BBM offers no "revisionist" history of the West nor succumbs to "political correctness." Quite the opposite, in fact, for the heroic narrative told by Buffalo Bill at the end of the nineteenth century returns in the BBM as a story about a story—a fully realized simulacrum (Baudrillard, 1983).[9] The BBM (re)tells the heroic narrative that celebrates Euro American colonization of the West while carnivalizing the violence of colonization in a dreamscape of the Wild West. More than simply representing the memory of Cody's entertaining violence, the museum serves as a way for visitors to at once acknowledge and avoid the memory of the violence that constructed the West as the "West." The memory of violence is transformed into an image of an image; the death-*making* acts constitutive of "winning" the West become the death-*defying* tricks of the Wild West. The colonization of the American Indian becomes a hyper-dramatic play—a performance that simultaneously enacts and denies the racialized oppressions inherent to the story of the West. This carnivalization and neutralization of the violence of colonization speaks to us not only about our relations with the land and the peoples of the West in the late nineteenth and early twentieth century but also to our understandings of Whiteness, Western colonization, and racialized violence in the twenty-first century.

Notes

[1] See Bartlett, 1992, pp. 152–154. The museum continues to depend almost exclusively on private financing from entrance fees, donations, and grants. State and federal funds have served a minor role in funding this museum (J. Hedderman, personal communication, March, 8, 2004).

[2] See Bartlett, 1992, p. 119. The Center draws visitors from across the country and around the globe. According to the Center's records, visitors come to the Center from nearly every state in the U.S. while less than 5% of the visitors are from other countries. Most visitors come from the West, in particular California, with Colorado, Texas, Washington, Montana, and Wyoming also "well represented" (J. Hedderman, personal communication, March, 8, 2004).

[3] We will be engaging in a reading of the museum guided primarily by structuralist reading practices. Audiences do not necessarily accept the invitations offered by the text; indeed, some actively resist them. We suggest, however, that history museums may be particularly powerful as structures of meaning. Further, as important as polysemy and resistance are, exploration of preferred meanings and structured invitations remains a crucial component of criticism. The literature on this debate is too large to cover here. For excellent contributions to this debate, see Fiske (1986) and Condit (1989).

[4] Museum visitors are further assured of Cody's authenticity by the placard's second paragraph, titled "Civil Honors," which highlights his relation to other well-known historical figures. "We live in a skeptical age," the placard continues. "Many people doubt that anyone like Buffalo Bill, particularly a *showman,* could measure up to the legends. But at the turn of the century, Buffalo Bill was probably the best-known American in the world. He was consulted on Western matters by every president from Grant to Wilson. He counted among his friends such artists and writers as Frederic Remington and Mark Twain. He was honored by royalty, praised by military leaders, and feted by business tycoons."

[5] The notion of a "timeless" West is evident in a wide variety of discourses throughout the BBHC, such as this quotation from the *Treasures from Our West* (1992) catalogue: "Cody died in 1917, but he, and the West in which he lived, did not vanish" (p. 8).

[6] According to White (1994), "Cody's Wild West told of violent conquest, of wrestling the continent from the American Indian peoples who occupied the land. Although fictional, Buffalo Bill's story claimed to represent a history. . . . The bullet, the Wild West program declared, was 'the pioneer of civilization'" (p. 9).

[7] Annie Oakley, referred to as "*little* sure shot" in promotional literature for the Wild West, did not significantly challenge or disrupt the *masculine* image of the cowboy. She was by far the most famous female performer to participate in "cowboy activities" such as sharp shooting, bronc riding, and steer roping. "Women constituted roughly just ten percent of an exhibition's cast" (Wood-Clark, 1991, p. 16), and they were more commonly cast in stereotypically feminine roles such as "the prairie flower" or "damsels in distress."

[8] Bartlett, writing in 1992, continues to connect William Cody and Buffalo Bill through Cody's real life exploits:

Here was a man of humble origin so respected that millionaires vied for the opportunity of entertaining him—and found him as suave and sophisticated as any gentleman born to the purple. Here was a showman who was heeded as a spokesman for the West, for the Indian, and, overseas, for America. Here was a man with a dime-novel reputation who had really earned fame on the frontier as a scout and guide, who could ride with any horseman and shoot with any marksman, and who followed animal tracks and read Indian sign as surely as the fictional Leatherstocking. William Frederick Cody was his real name, but the world knew him best as—Buffalo Bill. (pp. 3–4)

[9] Near the end of his life and in the years after the Wild West was no longer profitable, Buffalo Bill took several farewell tours across the United States. Slotkin (1992) suggests that the appeal of these tours was not so much a nostalgia for the West before its "closing" but instead a nostalgia for the spectacle of the Wild West (p. 87). This nostalgia for both the West and Wild West is alive and well in the BBM. Indeed, in the museum the difference between the West and the Wild West is slim.

References

Anderson, K., & Domash, M. (2002). North American spaces/postcolonial stories. *Cultural Geographies, 9,* 125–128.

Appadurai, A., & Breckenridge, C. (1992). Museums are good to think: Heritage on view in India. In I. Karp, C. Kreamer, & S. Lavine (Eds.), *Museums and communities: The politics of public culture* (pp. 34–55). Washington, DC: Smithsonian Institution Press.

Armada, B. (1998). Memorial agon: An interpretive tour of the National Civil Rights Museum. *Southern Communication Journal, 63,* 235–243.

Barthes, R. (1972). *Mythologies* (A. Lavers, Trans.). New York: Hill and Wang. (Original work published 1957)

Bartlett, R. (1992). *From Cody to the world: The first seventy-five years of the Buffalo Bill Memorial Association.* Cody, WY: Buffalo Bill Historical Center.

Baudrillard, J. (1983). *Simulations* (P. Foss, P. Patton, & P. Beitchman, Trans.). New York: Semiotext(e).

Bennett, T. (1995). *The birth of the museum: History, theory, politics.* New York: Routledge.

Benson, T., & Anderson, C. (1989). *Reality fictions: The films of Frederick Wiseman.* Carbondale, IL: Southern Illinois University Press.

Blair, C. (1999). Contemporary U.S. memorial sites as exemplars of rhetoric's materiality. In J. Selzer & S. Crowley (Eds.), *Rhetorical bodies* (pp. 16–57). Madison, WI: The University of Wisconsin Press.

Blair, C., Jeppeson, M., & Pucci, E. (1991). Public memorializing in postmodernity: The Vietnam Veterans Memorial as prototype. *Quarterly Journal of Speech, 77,* 263–288.

Blair, C., & Michael, N. (1999). Commemorating in the theme park zone: Reading the astronauts memorial. In T. Rosteck (Ed.), *At the intersection: Cultural studies and rhetorical studies* (pp. 29–83). New York: Guilford Press.

Blair, C., & Michael, N. (2004). The Rushmore effect: *Ethos* and national collective memory. In M. Hyde (Ed.), *The ethos of rhetoric* (pp. 158–196). Columbia, SC: University of South Carolina Press.

Bodnar, J. (1992). *Remaking America: Public memory, commemoration, and patriotism in the twentieth century.* Princeton, NJ: Princeton University Press.

Buffalo Bill Historical Center: Best of the West. (2001). *Cody Country: Gateway to Yellowstone Park* [Brochure]. Cody, WY: Cody Enterprise Publication.

Buffalo Bill Museum. (1995). [Catalogue]. Cody, WY: Buffalo Bill Historical Center.

Carter, R. (2000). *Buffalo Bill Cody: The man behind the legend.* New York: John Wiley and Sons, Inc.

Condit, C. (1989). The rhetorical limits of polysemy. *Critical Studies in Mass Communication, 6,* 103–123.

Crane, S. (2000). Introduction. In S. Crane (Ed.), *Museums and memory* (pp. 1–13). Stanford, CA: Stanford University Press.

Croft-Cooke, R., & Meadmore, W. S. (1952). *Buffalo Bill: The legend, the man of action, the showman.* London: Sidgwick and Jackson Limited.

Dickinson, G. (1997). Memories for sale: Nostalgia and the construction of identity in Old Pasadena. *Quarterly Journal of Speech, 83,* 1–27.

Dubin, S. (1999). *Displays of power: Memory and amnesia in the American museum.* New York: New York University Press.

Fiske, J. (1986). Television: Polysemy and popularity. *Critical Studies in Mass Communication, 3,* 391–408.

Fryd, V. (1992). *Art and empire: The politics of ethnicity in the United States capitol, 1815–1860.* New Haven, CT: Yale University Press.

Gaither, E. (1992). "Hey that's mine": Thoughts on pluralism and American museums. In I. Karp, C. Kreamer, & S. Lavine (Eds.), *Museums and communities: The politics of public culture* (pp. 56–64). Washington, DC: Smithsonian Institution Press.

Gallagher, V. (1995). Remembering together: Rhetorical integration and the case of the Martin Luther King, Jr. Memorial. *Southern Communication Journal, 60,* 109–119.

Gallagher, V. (1999). Memory and reconciliation in the Birmingham Civil Rights Institute. *Rhetoric and Public Affairs, 2,* 303–320.

Hasian, M., Jr. (2004). Remembering and forgetting the "final solution": A rhetorical pilgrimage through the U.S. Holocaust Memorial Museum. *Critical Studies in Media Communication, 21,* 64–92.

Hutton, P. (1993). *History as an art of memory.* Hanover, VT: University of Vermont.

Karp, I. (1994). Introduction: Museums and communities: The politics of public culture. In I. Karp, C. Kreamer, & S. Lavine (Eds.), *Museums and communities: The politics of public culture* (pp. 1–18). Washington, DC: Smithsonian Institution Press.

Kasson, J. (2000). *Buffalo Bill's Wild West: Celebrity, memory, and popular history.* New York: Hill and Wang.

Katriel, T. (1994). Sites of memory: Discourses of the past in Israeli pioneering settlement museums. *Quarterly Journal of Speech, 80,* 1–20.

Kavanagh, G. (1996). Making histories, making memories. In G. Kavanagh (Ed.), *Making histories in museums* (pp. 1–14). New York: Leicester University Press.

Kirsch, S. (2002). John Wesley Powell and the mapping of the Colorado plateau, 1869–1879: Survey science, geographical solutions, and the economy of environmental values. *Annals of the Association of American Geographers, 92,* 548–572.

Krauthammer, C. (1991, May 31). Westward hokum: Political correctness comes to the Smithsonian. *The Washington Post,* p. A19.

Lake, R. (1991). Between myth and history: Enacting time in Native American protest rhetoric. *Quarterly Journal of Speech, 77,* 123–152.

Lamar, H. (Ed.). (1977). *The reader's encyclopedia of the American West.* New York: Thomas Crowell Company.

Loewen, J. W. (1999). *Lies across America: What our historic sites get wrong.* New York: The New Press.

Maleuvre, D. (1999). *Museum memories: History, technology, art.* Stanford, CA: Stanford University Press.

Mission statement. (2004). The United States Holocaust Memorial Museum. Retrieved March 11, 2003, from http://www.ushmm.org/museum/council/index.utp?content= mission.htm

Morris, R., & Wander, P. (1990). Native American rhetoric: Dancing in the shadows of the ghost dance. *Quarterly Journal of Speech, 76,* 154–191.

Nash, J. (1992). *Encyclopedia of Western lawmen and outlaws.* New York: Paragon House.

Neider, C. (Ed.). (1958). *The great West.* New York: Coward-McCann, Inc.

Nicholas, L. (2002). Wyoming as America: Celebrations, a museum, and Yale. *American Quarterly, 54,* 437–465.

Nora, P. (1989). Between memory and history: *Les lieus de mémoire. Representations, 26,* 7–24.

Ollund, E. (2002). From savage space to governable space: The extension of United States' judicial sovereignty over Indian country in the nineteenth century. *Cultural Geographies, 9,* 129–157.

Profile of general demographic characteristics: 2000 (Wyoming). (2002, July 11). U.S. Census Bureau. Retrieved October 31, 2004, from http://factfinder.census.gov/servlet/ QTTable?ds_name=DEC_2000_SF1_U&geo_id=04000US56&qr_name=DEC_ 2000_SF1_U_DP1

Rosenzweig, R., & Thelen, D. (1998). *The presence of the past: Popular uses of history in American life.* New York: Columbia University Press.

Russell, D. (1960). *The lives and legends of Buffalo Bill.* Norman, OK: University of Oklahoma Press.

Shome, R., & Hegde, R. (2002). Postcolonial approaches to communication: Charting the terrain, engaging the intersections. *Communication Theory, 12,* 249–270.

Slotkin, R. (1992). *Gunfighter nation: The myth of the frontier in twentieth-century America.* New York: Atheneum.

Sorg, E. (1998). *Buffalo Bill: Myth and reality.* Santa Fe, NM: Ancient City Press.

Suderburg, E. (2000). Introduction: On installation and site specificity. In E. Suderburg (Ed.), *Space, site, intervention: Situating installation art* (pp. 1–22). Minneapolis, MN: University of Minnesota.

Tompkins, J. (1992). *West of everything: The inner life of westerns.* New York: Oxford University Press.

Treasures from our west. (1992). [Catalogue]. Cody, WY: Buffalo Bill Historical Center.

Truettner, W. (Ed.). (1991). *The West as America: Reinterpreting images of the frontier, 1820– 1920.* Washington, DC: Smithsonian Institution Press.

Turner, F. (1994). The significance of the frontier in American history. In J. Faragher (Ed.), *Rereading Frederick Jackson Turner: "The significance of the frontier in American history" and other essays* (pp. 31–60). New Haven, CT: Yale University Press.

Visitor's guide: Buffalo Bill Historical Center. (2002). [Brochure]. Cody, WY: Buffalo Bill Historical Center.

We're making history "happen!" (2002). [Brochure]. Cody, WY: Buffalo Bill Historical Center.

White, R. (1994). Frederick Jackson Turner and Buffalo Bill. In J. Grossman (Ed.), *The frontier in American culture: An exhibition at the Newberry Library, August 26, 1994–January 7, 1995* (pp. 7–65). Berkeley, CA: University of California Press.

Wolf, B. (1992). How the West was hung, or, when I hear the word "culture" I take out my checkbook. *American Quarterly, 44,* 418–438.

Wood-Clark, S. (1991). *Beautiful daring Western girls: Women of the Wild West shows.* Billings, MT: Artcraft Printers.

Wright, W. (2001). *The Wild West: The mythic cowboy and social theory.* London: Sage Publications.

Zelizer, B. (1995). Reading the past against the grain: The shape of memory studies. *Critical Studies in Mass Communication, 12,* 214–239.

From the Closet to the Loft
Liminal License and Socio-Sexual Separation in *Queer Eye for the Straight Guy*

Celeste Lacroix and Robert Westerfelhaus

Since its 2003 debut, Bravo's *Queer Eye for the Straight Guy* has attracted a large and loyal audience. As Robinson (2004) reports, *"Queer Eye* was an instant hit and became the cable channel's most watched program ever" (p. 4G).[1] Episodes aired during the series' first season generated the "No. 1 cable results among the Adults 25–54 and 18–49 demographics . . . making Bravo cable's No. 1 ad-supported network in prime time in both these key categories" (Rogers, 2003, p. 1). The series' popularity prompted Bravo's parent network, NBC, to recycle episodes during its prime-time programming.[2] Capitalizing upon the show's success, Bravo airs *Queer Eye UK* and has launched a spin-off, *Queer Eye for the Straight Girl*. The series has spawned such spoofs as Comedy Central's *Straight Plan for the Gay Man*. In 2004 it won the Emmy Award for Outstanding Reality Program (Paulsen, 2004).[3]

Queer Eye "was created by David Collins, a gay man, and developed by David Metzler, a straight man" (Rogers, 2004, p. 1). Initially, Bravo "marketed the show to women 18 to 49 with a secondary target of gay men" (Friedman & Linnett, 2003, p. 4).[4] The series celebrates the sophisticated tastes and make-over prowess of a quintet of self-identified gay men, referred to as the Fab Five, who consist of Ted Allen, "food and wine connoisseur"; Kyan Douglas, "grooming guru"; Thom Filicia, "design doctor"; Carson Kressley, "fashion savant"; and Jai Rodriquez, "culture vulture" ("Fab Five," 2004, p. 1). The show's premise is simple: "Each week their mission is to transform a style-deficient and culture-deprived straight man from drab to fab" ("About us," 2004, para. 2). *Queer Eye* is positioned thus at the intersection of two trends in American television programming. Its rigidly formulaic format follows that of other "unscripted" reality remake shows in which a person and/or a home is radically and rapidly transformed. In addition, the series provides yet another venue for the growing presence of openly gay men and women on American television.[5]

From a queer theory perspective, the series offers much to celebrate. The visibility of openly gay men, the positive way they are represented, and their easy fraternization with straight men are welcome additions to the television landscape.[6] Not surprisingly, *Queer Eye* was given a GLAAD Award in 2004. Still, there is cause for critical concern. The show unquestioningly reaffirms the straight/gay dichotomy reflective of, and central to, mainstream culture's heteronormative[7] bias and the homophobia this bias fosters. Additionally, the Fab Five are often depicted in ways that reinforce rather than challenge traditional stereotypical notions regarding gay men. The decorating, fashion, and grooming prowess they flaunt are skills gay men purportedly possess in abundance. These are, of course, the same standard concerns queer media criticism has raised for several decades.

There is an additional cause for concern. *Queer Eye* illustrates the construction by mainstream media of a new kind of Closet, which we call "the Loft"[8] because of the

Lacroix, Celeste and Westerfelhaus, Robert. "From the Closet to the Loft: Liminal License and Socio-Sexual Separation in *Queer Eye for the Straight Guy,*" *Qualitative Research Reports in Communication* 6 (1): 11–19. Permission granted by Taylor & Francis.

term's connection to one of the show's conventions and because of how this new Closet functions to contain queers and queer sexuality.[9] The defining feature of the traditional Closet was an invisibility that was the product of heterosexist hostility toward queers and of the strategic reaction of queers to this hostility. Today, queers have become quite visible and rightly refuse to remain hidden, but just as a literal closet holds as well as hides things, the Loft serves to contain queers, and especially queer sexuality, in order to protect the social mainstream from the supposed danger posed by queer "contamination." In the case of *Queer Eye,* this containment is accomplished through a ritual formula that inverts the traditional sequence characteristic of rites of passage. This inversion grants the show's protagonists permission to enter temporarily the heterosexual mainstream only to be relegated to the Loft's cultural, geographical, and sexual exile by each episode's end.[10]

Queer Eye as an Inverted Rite of Passage

In addition to entertaining and informing us, the media also offer powerful ritualized experiences that draw from and reinforce core social values (Aden, 1999; Couldry, 2003; Vande Berg, 1995). Heterosexist values frequently find ritual expression in mainstream films and television shows (Dow, 2001; Gross, 1998; Westerfelhaus & Brookey, 2004). We suggest that the heteronormative formula followed by *Queer Eye* has much in common with those rites of passage that have traditionally helped negotiate important social transitions and enabled societies to manage the potential threat these transitions pose to the social order. These rites follow a tripartite pattern, consisting of preliminal rites of social separation, liminal rites of transition, and postliminal rites of social (re)integration into the social body (Turner, 1967; van Gennep, 1960). The same three ritual elements are present in *Queer Eye* but are sequentially inverted, beginning with integration and ending with separation. This inverted ritual order allows queers temporary and controlled access to the cultural mainstream while ensuring that they pose no threat of socio-sexual contamination by their continued presence there.

Queer Eye opens each episode with *integration* of the Fab Five into a straight man's life, followed by a *liminal* phase in which the show's gay leads are given license to remake that man and his home in accordance with a defined "mission" that provides them the necessary—and always temporary—transgressive permission to invade the straight world in order to set it right. (A typical show has the Fab Five providing some "fashion-challenged" straight man with grooming and decorating tips intended to make him and his place more attractive to a girlfriend or wife, thus salvaging an endangered heterosexual relationship.) Episodes typically end with the Fab Five ensconced in their well-appointed loft, viewing via video how their most recent makeover project performs during a date, a party, or some social event. In their loft, they are geographically and socio-sexually *separated* from the straight man they had befriended and are reduced to voyeurs who may view and comment upon, but no longer participate in, the heterosexual social order they have helped repair. To illustrate how this inverted rite of passage plays out, we examine two representative episodes—one drawn from *Queer Eye's* first season and one from the second.

Integration

Rapid ritual integration of the Fab Five into a straight man's life and home happens early in each episode. The Fab Five race off in their SUV toward their next "project," the details of which are conveyed in a style campily reminiscent of the old television series *Mission: Impossible*. In an episode entitled "Queer Eye for Our Production Guy" (Collins et al., 2003), featuring Andrew Lane, the Fab Five attempt to "fix" one of their own—a *Queer Eye* crew member. Tired of Andrew's "Drew Carey look-alike" style, the team's mission is to prepare him for a "Big Boy Date" with his girlfriend, Diana. In an episode entitled "Taking on the Twins" (Collins et al., 2004), the Fab Five help twin brothers David and Brandon Bravo organize a "Grand party for Grandpa." In carrying out these missions, they quickly invade their clients' lives and spaces.

Liminal License

Liminality is central to rites of passage sequentially and in terms of ritual focus. Aden (1999) describes liminality as both a transitory state and a transitory process. Those liminally positioned are, according to Turner (1967), betwixt-and-between, paradoxically a part of and yet apart from society. This liminal status provides the ritual logic for the license to violate selected socio-cultural rules sometimes granted ritual participants undergoing a rite of passage (Westerfelhaus & Brookey, 2004). The Fab Five's liminal status renders them "safe," thus defining their otherwise transgressive intrusion into the heterosexual mainstream tame, temporary, and ritually situated to serve the needs of the heteronormative mainstream through fulfillment of their well-defined mission.

Liminal license permits the Fab Five to tease and touch their straight subjects in ways regarded as taboo in other contexts. *Queer Eye* episodes are filled with such transgressions. In the episode featuring Andrew Lane, the Fab Five pull his shirt down and complain about his hairy back. Carson combs that hair and kids, "Let's take this sweater off . . . we can tease it; it'll look like angora! People will think you have cashmere!" Later, while driving to a day spa, the following exchange occurs:

Andrew: This spa . . . this isn't like some kind of bathhouse, is it?

Carson: No, for God's sake. No sexual overtones . . . that's extra.

Ted: Unless you create them.

[Minutes later, Carson leans toward Andrew:]

Carson: Just rub your cheek up against me . . . this is for my work. I just need to tell Kyan . . . just rub up.

[Andrew reluctantly does so.]

Kyan (to Andrew): Ohmigod, you're gay now! You're homosexual!

Andrew: Did you put the gay on me?

Carson: I put the gay on you. For twenty-four hours you're gonna be buying flip-flops at Jeffrey's.

The episode featuring the Bravo Twins is also filled with sexually charged banter and touching. The Twins enjoy wrestling. At the beginning of the episode, they wrestle each other. Later, Brandon wrestles with Carson, throws him on a bed, and puts him in a leg lock. Carson is speechless, with his head locked in close proximity to Brandon's crotch. When released, he fans his face and comments archly, "That was fun. . . ." Such homo*social* bonding stops short of homo*sexual* behavior, in keeping with Sedgwick's (1985) observation that there is a strictly observed limit to male bonding in "straight" contexts. Though *Queer Eye's* formula affords the Fab Five liminal license to flirt with and flaunt homoerotic interest in their "straight" clients, they are not permitted to engage in actual sexual contact with them. Instead, queers and any hint of queer sexuality are ritually removed from the heterosexual world by each episode's end.

The Loft as Socio-Sexual Separation

Rites of passage begin with separation of ritual initiates from the social mainstream and end with their (re)integration. In the case of *Queer Eye*, this pattern is reversed. Since gays are *a part from* rather than *a part of* the mainstream, their inclusion—rather than exclusion—ruptures the mundane and begins the ritual. Ritual logic dictates that separation is thus necessary to bring narrative closure. Typically, episodes of *Queer Eye* conclude with the Fab Five in their loft seated alone before a television viewing how their newest made-over straight man acquits himself during the event for which they prepared him. Their social separation is illustrated at that moment in the Bravo Twins' episode where the Twins read a poem extolling the Fab Five's influence upon their lives and the bonds (albeit temporary) they have formed with them. At the conclusion of this reading, which is mediated via video, the Twins turn to the camera and say, "We love you guys!" The ritually removed Fab Five raise their beers to the Twins' video image and salute them from the remoteness of the Loft. Once the liminal phase is concluded, direct contact between straight men and their gay benefactors is no longer sanctioned.

Queer Eye's formula reinforces the heteronormative order by privileging heterosexual relationships. While the Fab Five are safely contained in the Loft, the show's straight men purge themselves of any homoerotic contamination they might have acquired from cavorting with the Fab Five. This is often accomplished through a dinner date or some other obviously and traditionally heterosexual encounter. In the Andrew Lane episode, the Fab Five's playful flirting with him is replaced at show's end with a rather forced interest in his girlfriend and the success of the date, for which they congratulate themselves. Even those episodes that do not conclude with some overtly heterosexual ritual encounter still end with the heteronormative social order devoid of any ongoing queer contamination. In the episode featuring the Bravo Twins, no one who is openly queer is shown attending the party the Fab Five have helped organize.

Historically, gays have been excluded from open participation in America's mainstream culture. In the end, the Fab Five are excluded from the heterosexual world they had intruded upon and are reduced to acting as voyeurs who may watch but not participate in the heterosexual world they helped heal. In contrast to the classic Closet, which denigrated those it contained, the Loft literally and symbolically elevates queers even as it separates them from the heterosexual mainstream. In this respect, it is an example of the dehumanizing rhetoric of deification identified by Brookey and Westerfelhaus (2001) in their analysis of *To Wong Foo, Thanks for Everything! Julie Newmar.* Like that film's protagonists, the Fab Five are depicted in deified terms in relation to the straight people whose problems they solve.

This dynamic is reminiscent of the filmic and literary construct of the "Noble Savage," whose strength and bravery are superior to those of his "masters," but who serves and sacrifices for them, and in the end supports a social order that serves the interests of his oppressors rather than himself. In much the same way, the Fab Five are seemingly superior to the heterosexuals they serve and whose social order they support, and like *To Wong Foo's* drag queen trio, who at film's end gaze down upon the magic they have wrought from the safe (from a heterosexist perspective) distance of a second story balcony, the Fab Five are removed from the heterosexual order and relegated to viewing the results of their work from the physical and symbolic exile of the Loft. The metaphor of the Loft better reflects the way queers are currently depicted in much of the mainstream media than does the old metaphor of the Closet. Though both are forms of enforced socio-sexual exile, the Closet conjures images of a dark, shameful "hiding place" on the periphery of the mainstream community, while the Loft is a gilded cage in which queers are comfortably confined even as they are celebrated.

Conclusion

Bravo should be applauded for airing a series that celebrates the exploits of openly gay men, but as Hart (2003) warns, while inclusion of queer characters on television is important, what "the producers opt to do with those characters . . . is equally important" (p. 606). Queer criticism needs to be especially attentive to the ways ostensibly positive representations of gay and lesbian characters can serve to tame and contain queer experience (Brookey & Westerfelhaus, 2001). Through the socio-sexual distancing they promote, media rituals of the type analyzed here negotiate the tension between the heterosexist social order and the increased visibility and growing political power of gays. This tension is managed by taming queers—and containing queer experience—while seemingly celebrating them. Continued critical attention should be paid to the way shows such as *Queer Eye* recuperate heteronormative values even while providing gays with increased visibility. We look forward to the day when such critical scrutiny is no longer needed, when queers are no longer excluded from the social mainstream unless their presence is ritually tamed and rendered temporary, when instead of being exiled to the Loft the Fab Five and their partners can join the Bravo Twins's family and party with them.[11] We would like to join that party.

Notes

[1] According to Levin (2003), "*Queer Eye's* premiere set new records for the low-rated cable network [Bravo]" (p. 3D).

[2] These reruns also drew high ratings. Wallenstein (2003b) suggests that the "series undoubtedly gained new viewers from its trial run on NBC in prime time July 24" (p. 3, section 2). Friedman and Linnett (2003) report:

> Audience numbers for the July 29 "Queer Eye" [*sic*] in its fourth airing on Bravo, shot up 62% from the prior week, according to Nielsen Media Research, earning the cable network its highest-ever rating. "This is the break-out show of the summer on any network, cable or network," crowed Jeff Zucker, president-NBC entertainment. (p. 4)

O'Steen (2004) notes that the "show started out on Bravo in February 2003 with 1.6 rating and doubled its audience in its initial 11-week run. It has become so popular that slightly reedited installments have been used to bolster ratings on the parent network, NBC" (p. 22). According to Littleton (2003), during the week ending August 24, 2003, a special NBC airing of *Queer Eye* "wound up beating CBS' 10 p.m. 'Without a Trace' rerun despite 'Trace's' advantage from the 'CSI' lead-in" (p. 6, section 2).

[3] *Queer Eye* is not the only such program aired by the network. *Boy Meets Boy* and *Gay Weddings* are two other examples. These shows, however, are not nearly as popular with mainstream audiences as *Queer Eye*. Indeed, as noted by the *Hollywood Reporter*, the series finale of *Boy Meets Boy* attracted only 1.6 million viewers, while the episode of *Queer Eye* that immediately followed it drew an audience of 3.3 million ("'Queer Eye' ratings," 2003). We note, though, that *Queer Eye* has attracted a smaller audience in its second and third seasons. This pattern is typical of the life-cycle of formulaic reality-based television shows that do not employ significant casting changes to generate continued interest (as opposed to, for example, *The Apprentice, Survivor,* and *The Real World*).

[4] Targeting this demographic (females aged 18–49) makes commercial sense. As Vivi Zigler, senior vice president of marketing and advertising services at the NBC Agency, explains, "Gay men are not measured by Nielsen (Media Research). . . . Women 18–49 is a more salable demo" (quoted in Wallenstein, 2003a, p. 1, section 2).

[5] Regarding the growing visibility of gays on television, see Battles and Hilton-Morrow (2002) and Hart (2003).

[6] We acknowledge that using the term "positive" with respect to representation of queers and queer sexuality is troublesome. In this context, we simply mean that the Fab Five are not depicted as being sexual prey or predators, as sick or as criminal; while funny, they are not mere comedic relief.

[7] As defined by Herman (2003), "Heteronormativity encompasses, at a basic level, the view that heterosexuality is natural and normal for individuals and society . . . heteronormativity does not just construct a norm, it also provides the perspective through which we know and understand gender and sexuality in popular culture" (p. 144; see also Westerfelhaus & Brookey, 2004; Cooper, 2002; Epstein & Steinberg, 1997).

[8] We capitalize "Loft" when using the word in reference to the construct of socio-sexual containment that is the focus of our analysis. We do not do so when referring to the physical loft in which the Fab Five end each episode.

[9] We use the noun "queer" in preference to other terms because we see the term as inclusive of anyone whose sexuality lies, as Erni (1998) puts it, "outside of foundationalist gender and sexual norms" (p. 161).

[10] This inverted rite of passage takes place within the context of, and is a ritual response to, a broader social drama that is still unfolding. A social drama, as defined by Turner (1957, 1980), is a ritual means of addressing those conflicts that threaten the social order. According to Turner, such dramas assume a processural form that unfolds in four parts: breach, crisis, redress, and an integration that restores or changes the status quo. The Stonewall riots of 1969 gave rise to a Gay Rights Movement that has significantly changed the socio-sexual landscape. These changes represent a serious—though partial—breach of the social conventions (customs, laws, rules, etc.) that had once governed mainstream society's attitudes toward and treatment of queers and which thus served to perpetuate their marginalization. Not surprisingly, this breach has brought about a growing sense of crisis. One symptom of this crisis was the failed attempt in 2004 to amend the Constitution so as to prohibit the legalization of gay marriage. Turner argues that crises of this kind require some form of ritualized redressive response if social stability is to be maintained. Unlike the Ndembu cultural context in which Turner began his study of ritual, ours is a media saturated-society in which many people often turn to films and television to satisfy their ritual needs (Aden, 1999; Couldry, 2003; Vande Berg, 1995; Westerfelhaus & Brookey, 2004). *Queer Eye* is illustrative of the ritual response of much of the mainstream media to the crisis posed by the increased visibility of queers and their demands to be accorded the same rights that others take for granted. It is for this reason that we have chosen to examine this series. Before moving on to that examination, we note that at this time it is unclear whether this social drama will end with an integrative return to or a rupture of the socio-sexual status quo. Much of what happens will depend on how *Queer Eye* and other similar and opposing mediated rituals play out in the public sphere.

[11] *Queer Eye* has aired occasional holiday specials in which a group of selected straight "clients" and their families come together to celebrate Christmas or Thanksgiving with the Fab Five. These shows represent brief and temporary departures from the standard ritual formula toward which the series quickly reverts.

References

About us. (2004). Bravo: *Queer Eye for the Straight Guy.* Retrieved August 30, 2004 from http://www.bravotv.com/Queer_Eye_for_the Straight Guy/About_Us/.

Aden, R. C. (1999). *Popular stories and promised lands: Fan cultures and symbolic pilgrimages.* Tuscaloosa, AL: The University of Alabama Press.

Battles, K., & Hilton-Morrow, W. (2002). Gay characters in conventional spaces: *Will and Grace* and the situation comedy genre. *Critical Studies in Media Communication, 19,* pp. 87–105.

Brookey, R. A., & Westerfelhaus, R. (2001). Pistols and petticoats, piety and purity: *To Wong Foo,* the queering of the American monomyth, and the marginalizing discourse of deification. *Critical Studies in Media Communication, 18,* pp. 141–156.

Collins, D., Williams, M., Metzler, D., Berwick, F., Introcaso-Davis, A., & Barcellos, C. (Executive Producers). (2004). Taking on the twins: Episode 127 [Television series episode]. *Queer Eye for the Straight Guy.* New York: Bravo.

Collins, D., Williams, M., Metzler, D., Berwick, F., Introcaso-Davis, A., & Barcellos, C. (Executive Producers). (2003). Queer Eye for our production guy: Episode 105 [Television series episode]. *Queer Eye for the Straight Guy.* New York: Bravo.

Cooper, B. (2002). *Boys Don't Cry* and female masculinity: Reclaiming a life and dismantling the politics of heterosexuality. *Critical Studies in Media Communication, 19,* pp. 44–63.

Couldry, N. (2003). *Media rituals: A critical approach.* London: Routledge.

Dow, B. J. (2001). *Ellen,* television, and the politics of gay and lesbian visibility. *Critical Studies in Media Communication, 18,* pp. 123–140.

Epstein, D., & Steinberg, D. I. (1997). Love's labours: Playing it straight on the *Oprah Winfrey Show*. In D. I. Steinberg, D. Epstein, & R. Johnson (Eds.), *Border patrols: Policing the boundaries of heterosexuality* (pp. 32–65). London: Cassell.

Erni, J. N. (1998). Queer figurations in the media: Critical reflections on the Michael Jackson sex scandal. *Critical Studies in Mass Communication, 15,* pp. 158–180.

Fab Five. (2004). Bravo: *Queer Eye for the Straight Guy*. Retrieved August 30, 2004 from http://www.bravotv.com/Queer_Eye_for_the_Straight_Guy/Fab_Five/.

Friedman, W., & Linnett, R. (2003, August 4). Madison + Vine: Getting piece of the "Eye." *Advertising Age, 74,* p. 4.

Gross, L. (1998). Minorities, majorities and the media. In T. Liebes, & J. Curran (Eds.), *Media, ritual and identity* (pp. 87–102). London: Routledge.

Hart, K. R. (2003). Representing gay men on American television. In G. Dines, & J. M. Humez (Eds.), *Gender, race, and class in media: A text-reader* (2nd ed.) (pp. 597–607). Thousand Oaks, CA: Sage.

Herman, D. (2003). "*Bad Girls* changed my life": Homonormativity in a women's prison drama. *Critical Studies in Media Communication, 20,* pp. 141–159.

Levin, G. (2003, July 30). Repeats still rule in ratings race. *USA Today,* p. 3D.

Littleton, C. (2003 August 27). "CSI" leaves competition in the dust: CBS hit tops in viewers; "Queer Eye" surprises NBC. *Hollywood Reporter, 380,* p. 6(2).

O'Steen, K. (2004). "Queer Eye for the Straight Guy": Vivi Zigler VP, marketing and advertising services, the NBC agency and Bravo. *Television Week, 23,* p. 22.

Paulsen, W. (2004, September 21). *Queer Eye for the Straight Guy* wins 2004 Emmy for Outstanding Reality Program. *Reality TV World.* Retrieved October 29, 2004 from http://www.realitytvworld.com/index/articles/story.php?s=2908.

"Queer Eye" ratings chic for Bravo. (2003, September 8). *Hollywood Reporter, 380,* p. 20(1).

Robinson, G. (2004, May 30). "Queer Eye" designer does heaviest work on show. *The (Charleston, SC) Post and Courier,* p. 4G.

Rogers, S. (2004, January 18). NBC to air "Queer Eye for the Straight Guy" marathon on Superbowl Sunday. *Reality TV World.* Retrieved June 30, 2004 from http://www.realitytvworld.com/index/articles/story.php?s=2172.

Rogers, S. (2003, November 20). New "Queer Eye" episode kicks off new episodes run with strong ratings. *Reality TV World.* Retrieved June 30, 2004 from http://www.realitytvworld.com/ index/articles/story.php?s=2012.

Sedgwick, E. K. (1985). *Between men: English literature and male homosexual desire.* New York: Columbia University Press.

Turner, V. (1957). *Schism and continuity in an African society: A study of Ndembu village life.* Manchester: Manchester University Press.

Turner, V. (1967). *The forest of symbols: Aspects of Ndembu ritual.* Ithaca, NY: Cornell University Press.

Turner, V. (1980). Social dramas and stories about them. *Critical Inquiry, 7*(4), pp. 141–168.

van Gennep, A. (1960). *The rites of passage.* Chicago: The University of Chicago Press. (Original work published 1908.)

Vande Berg, L. R. (1995). Living room pilgrimages: Television's cyclical commemoration of the assassination anniversary of John F. Kennedy. *Communication Monographs, 62,* pp. 47–64.

Wallenstein, A. (2003a, July 28). Bravo targets 2 demos with shows. *Hollywood Reporter, 379,* p. 1(2).

Wallenstein, A. (2003b, July 31). Bravo's gay power couple: "Boy," "Queer" score solid numbers. *Hollywood Reporter, 379,* p. 3(2).

Westerfelhaus, R., & Brookey, R. A. (2004). At the unlikely confluence of conservative religion and popular culture: *Fight Club* as heteronormative ritual. *Text and Performance Quarterly, 24,* pp. 302–326.

Cyber Ideology
An Ideological Criticism of the UNICEF, UNAIDS, and UNFPA Web Sites

Khadidiatou Ndiaye

The possibilities offered by the Internet have given people with the desire to make the world a global village the opportunity to make their dream a reality. The world is getting much closer because people everywhere now have an opportunity to share their beliefs, culture, and views online. Companies, agencies, and associations have seized the opportunity and are using the Internet to improve their accessibility and to allow people all over the world to read their messages.

As a global system representing 189 nations of the world, the United Nations (UN) can be considered the forum of the world, an organization that works to bring the world together to solve global issues. For such an organization, the Internet's potential for reaching populations all over the world is enormous, and UN officials were quick to tap into this potential. The foreword to *The Internet: An Introductory Guide for United Nations Organizations* addresses the importance of the Internet to the United Nations' work:

> The Internet is clearly a phenomenon of global significance. The implications for the United Nations family of organizations are tremendous. United Nations agencies have at their fingertips not only an effective tool for collaborative work, but also a far-reaching and popular mechanism for disseminating information to the entire global community. This works both ways: United Nations agencies become immediately accessible to a worldwide group of Internet users as well. (The U.N. joins the net, 1996, p. 1)

This global significance is due to the Internet's potential for erasing physical and social boundaries. Today, all agencies of the United Nations have structured Web sites.

In this essay, I offer an ideological criticism of the Web sites of the United Nations Children's Fund (UNICEF), the United Nations Populations Fund (UNFPA), and the Joint United Nations Programme on HIV/AIDS (UNAIDS). Using these three Web sites as artifacts for analysis, I will explore how inclusive the ideologies of UNICEF, UNFPA, and UNAIDS are as portrayed in these organizations' Web sites.

The question of inclusiveness is important in looking at the three Web sites because of the agencies' identity and public message. UNAIDS, UNFPA, and UNICEF are agencies of unity; they represent the world's efforts to fight relevant issues together. Because these agencies rely on the world's support to exist, they reinforce daily the principles of unity and talk often about working for all of the world's population. Analyzing the inclusiveness of the Web sites will allow us to see if they "practice what they preach." Looking at their Web sites is even more important if we consider the fact that the Internet is becoming one of the primary ways in which United Nations agencies communicate with the populations represented by the UN. Exploring the question of inclusiveness will make visible who is truly represented.

This essay was written while Khadidiatou Ndiaye was a student in Karen A. Foss's rhetorical criticism class at the University of New Mexico in 2002. Used by permission of the author.

Logging On: The Three Web Sites at a Glance

UNICEF, UNFPA, and UNAIDS are United Nations agencies dealing with social issues, including children's well-being, women, population concerns, and HIV/AIDS. The following descriptions of the Web sites of each of the agencies focus only on the main pages of the Web sites because these pages hold the central message provided by the agencies. That central message is the main vehicle through which the ideology is presented.

The United Nations Children's Fund (UNICEF) Web Site

The UNICEF Web site's main page is divided into four frames, one horizontal frame on top and three vertical frames. The UNICEF logo is placed in a prominent place on the top left of the page. The Web site is the most colorful of the three Web sites analyzed. The page uses two background colors, red as the main and orange for the top frame. Other colors are also used to separate the main points. There are three pictures on the page, with the first taking up considerable space. It features children wearing costumes and make-up, and all the children are carrying little boxes in forms of buses with the UNICEF inscription. The caption for this first picture reads: "It's time to Trick or Treat for UNICEF. This Halloween, children are collecting money to help children in developing countries." The children are all smiling, and most of the children look to be white, although discerning the race of two children is difficult because of the make-up they are wearing.

The second picture, which is much smaller, is of a young girl carrying an infant. The two children are looking directly at the camera; they are definitely not smiling and seem to be sad. We cannot tell how the two are dressed because the only clearly identified items are a scarf covering the young girl's head and a hat for the infant. On the bottom of the picture is the word "Afghanistan," suggesting that the two children are from that country.

The third picture is also small (the same size as the second one), and it captures the profile of a young girl. The young girl is white, is not smiling, and looks sad. There is no reference to her nationality, and at the bottom of the picture are the words "social monitor support."

There are also two images in the same frame with the small pictures. In the first image is a stack of books with the words "our shared future" on the top and "Achebe-Morrison" on the bottom of the page. The last image has a map of Southern Africa and the words "updated" in small letters and "Southern African Crisis" in large capital letters. In the most prominent area of the page, the logo of UNICEF is used as a background with the words "United Nations Special Session on Children . . . Landmark goals for children . . . Click here for complete coverage" prominently placed in the middle of the box.

The Web page is interactive; the user sees additional topics just by placing the cursor on one of the main options. These options are "UNICEF in Action," "Highlights," "Information Resources," "Donations, Greeting Cards, & Gifts," "Press Centre," "Voices of Youth," and "About UNICEF."

The United Nations Population Fund (UNFPA) Web Site

The UNFPA Web site uses primarily three colors—dark blue, light blue, and white. There are three frames: one horizontal at the top of the page and two vertical, with the first vertical a margin frame. The UNFPA logo is located on the top left of the page with the dark blue background. There are two pictures on the page, one of which is very prominent and takes up almost the entire main frame. The picture depicts a woman carrying an infant in her arms. Both are looking directly at the camera with a grave—almost sad—expression. There is a series of phrases to the left of the picture: "UNFPA responds to Afghan Crisis" is written in large letters and "Relief Effort Aims to Save Women's Lives" and "How Can You Help" in smaller letters. The second picture is quite small and is located at the bottom of the page. The image is slightly faded and depicts a young woman staring directly into the camera with a neutral expression on her face. The caption below the picture is "UNFPA Initiative against Fistula."

The vertical margin frame is divided into three parts. The first part is called "Key Issues" and offers the following link topics: "Safe Motherhood," "Adolescent and Youth," "Gender Equity," "HIV/AIDS," "Population and Development Strategies," "Emergencies," and "Reproductive Health Commodities." The second part of the margin frame is titled "Global Reach," and its topics include "Africa, Arab States & Europe," "Asia & the Pacific," "Latin America & the Caribbean," and "Technical Support." The final frame is titled "Executive Board" and offers only one topic: "UNDP/UNFPA Executive Board."

Another important aspect of the UNFPA Web site is the "Latest News" feature, which offered three topics at the time of this analysis: "UNFPA Launches Two-Year Campaign to Fight Obstetric Fistula in Sub-Saharan Africa," "Afghan Health Officials to Learn from Iran's Experience," and "Malawi Food Crisis and Reproductive Health Concerns." In addition, the Web site has link options for journalists and information regarding a campaign titled "34 Million Friends Campaign."

Joint United Nations Programme on HIV/AIDS (UNAIDS) Web Site

The third Web site used in this analysis is the UNAIDS Web site. Compared to the first two Web sites, the UNAIDS Web site is rather plain. No pictures are used, and the only image the Web site contains is the international symbol of AIDS, the red ribbon. The page has three vertical frames of equal size and one bottom frame. The logo of UNAIDS is located in the left in a prominent area. The content of the page is divided into topics, and red headings separate the topics links. The headings are "Latest News," which includes four separate topics. The first heading reads: "New education action plan launched," "Monitoring the declaration of the commitment on HIV/ AIDS," and "AIDS fight under resourced." The second heading, "What's New," has 10 topics ranging from "UNAIDS report on the global HIV/AIDS epidemic" to "Cosponsor news." The "Upcoming Events" heading highlights an upcoming "Microcredit Summit," and the fourth heading, "Elsewhere on the Web," has one topic: "The Future of AIDS." The bottom frame has a library of information on the following topics: "For Journalists," "About UNAIDS," "Publications," "HIV/AIDS Info," and "Special Sections."

From Surface to Real Ideologies

An ideology is a pattern or set of ideas, assumptions, beliefs, values, or interpretations of the world by which a group operates. As a large organization with members all over the world, the United Nations has a very public and obvious ideology centered on globalization—bringing people all over the world together. "It's your world," its slogan states, suggesting that individuals should take ownership of the world and its problems.

The public ideology of bringing the world together to solve problems is the basis for the surface ideology of the three Web sites. Surface ideology, in this context, refers to the central message the Web sites want to convey or the message the Web sites' design teams believe they are presenting. I named this surface ideology "working for the world," and the strategies used to convey it are openness and action.

Openness as a strategy refers to the inviting aspect of the Web sites. The Web sites want the viewers to feel that they are welcome. Openness is a preliminary strategy in that viewers cannot see how the Web site is "working for the world" if they are not inclined to spend time exploring the Web site. By using openness as a strategy, the Web-site designers want to keep their audience interested long enough to see how the agencies are, indeed, working for the world.

The use of colors, clearly organized layouts, and pictures help present this openness. Pleasing colors are used in all three Web sites; the use of red, blue, and orange within the Web sites serves to limit users' potential apprehensions. These colors are almost playful and are designed to make users feel at ease.

The next element used to convey openness is clarity. Providing a simple and organized layout is a way to invite users to return to the Web site. Viewers who can easily find the information they need will be more likely to feel invited and to return to the Web site.

A final strategy for achieving openness is through the use of pictures. The pictures in the UNICEF and UNFPA Web sites reinforce this sense of an easily accessible Web site because the user can click on each of these pictures for further information. The openness strategy is designed to make viewers feel that they are part of these agencies and to invite them to log on to visit their Web sites so they can see how the agencies are working for them.

Once the viewers feel welcome enough to log on and visit the Web sites, then the Web sites work to show how the three agencies are "working for the world" using a strategy of action. All three Web sites use a considerable amount of space to describe the work the agencies are doing and to show the world they are working hard. This strategy allows them to show the viewer the extent to which they are "working for the world." The action strategy is presented primarily through the use of text. There are several headings referring to news on each page, and reports are emphasized in all three Web sites.

The surface ideology of "working for the world" fits well with the public message of unity and globalization. The designers of the Web sites use the strategies of openness and action to convey the ideology that the agencies work for everyone, enacting the United Nations' slogan, "It's your world." Through these Web sites, the agencies seem to add, "It's your Web site." After close analysis, however, this surface ideology turns out to be just that—a message that stops at the surface.

Not-So-Global Ideology: The Real Ideology

I will argue that, in spite of the UN's advocating unity around the world, the Web sites of the agencies analyzed are not inclusive. The ideology presented through these agencies' Web sites is not inclusive because Third World countries are presented as victims needing help, and the Web sites are more concerned with the images of the agencies than with meeting the needs of different groups.

Helper/Helped Ideology: Victims not Equal Partners

The pictures found in the UNICEF and UNFPA Web sites suggest an ideology of helper/helped, where people from developing nations need help, which is provided by people from the West. The strategies used to convey this ideology include pictures, captions, and type of information provided.

The pictures ask the audience to feel sorry for the people represented. The first picture that serves to convey this ideology is found in the UNFPA Web site. The picture of a woman carrying a child is a prominent one; it is large and is the first thing the viewer sees. The woman and child are looking directly at the camera, and they have grave facial expressions; the child looks downright sad. A second picture that uses the same technique is found on the UNICEF Web site. This picture features a young girl carrying a child; it is much smaller and not as prominent, but it still has the same effect. What this second picture lacks in size, it makes up for in emotional impact in that a young child carrying an infant evokes even more pity. The absence of the mother in this picture is another reason to feel sorry for these children—a young girl has to care for an infant who presumably has lost her mother.

The pictures in the UNICEF and UNFPA Web site may differ in size and prominence, but they use the same strategy to make the Web-site viewer feel sorry for these individuals. I call this technique the *pity appeal*. In this strategy, individuals from developing nations are portrayed as people for whom the audience should feel sorry. African author Aidoo (1995) provides a critique of this appeal to pity by describing the commonly used portrayals of African woman in Western media:

> She is breeding too many children, she cannot take care of, and for whom she should expect other people to pick up the tab. She is hungry and so are her children . . . she is half-naked, her drooped and withered breasts are well exposed; there are flies buzzing around the faces of her children; and she has a permanent begging bowl in her hand. (p. 39)

These stereotypes are not exclusively used for African women; they often apply to the representations of all individuals of developing nations. These individuals usually are depicted as people who need help, whose cause needs to be adopted, and whose misery needs to be erased.

The pity appeal is also used by organizations looking for donations such as World Vision, Children International, ChildReach, Save the Children, and Compassion International. The same style of pictures emphasizing a strategy of pity can be found at the Web sites of all five organizations.[1] The point is not to put on trial the strategies used by organizations such as Children International but to question what the UN agencies are suggesting to their audiences by using this technique. Unlike the United Nations, organizations such as Save the Children and Compassion International do not have as primary a mission to bring the world together; they are looking for financial assistance for children.

One can argue that by using pity as the basis for appeal, UNICEF and UNFPA are only suggesting that these countries also need help. They are asking people to participate in helping solve global problems. This argument would work if we did not notice the individuals who are the victims—the ones portrayed as needing help. The two pictures discussed earlier are clear as to the individuals they represent—they both refer to Afghanistan. In the UNICEF Web site, the other pictures presented work to complement this idea. First, in opposition to the picture of the sad young girls is the picture of laughing children dressed in Halloween costumes. Most of these children are white and, since they are celebrating Halloween, we can assume that they are from the West (Halloween is a Western holiday). This assumption is reinforced by the caption of the picture, "It's time to Trick or Treat for UNICEF. This Halloween, children are collecting money to help children in developing countries." Through this caption and the contrast of the pictures, a hierarchy of children is established. The happy smiling children of the West are working to help the poor, sad children in developing countries.

Other elements in the UNFPA Web site contribute to establishing this hierarchy of helped and helper. In addition to the pity appeal that the women and child pictured represent, the headlines also serve to reinforce this idea by providing only negative ideas of developing countries. The headlines talk about the Malawi food crisis, fighting obstetric fistula in Sub-Saharan Africa, and yet another southern Africa crisis.

Also important to note is that the stories that deal with the developing world being helped and the West as a helper are clearly labeled so that the Web-site viewer can access these stories from the main page of the Web site. There are two Web-site elements with no links to a geographical area. The first is a picture showing the profile of a young white girl captioned with the words, "social monitor support." To understand what the picture was about, I clicked on its link and was surprised to see that it deals with the economic crisis in Western Europe. To understand that the picture dealt with this crisis, the viewer had to click on the link. This is not necessary for all the crises related to the developing world because they are clearly labeled. In other words, the one instance in which the West needs help is hidden on the Web site—those aspects that do not fit the helper/helped ideology are not visible. This is also true for a second element with no geographical ties—an image with the words "our shared future" and in smaller letters "Achebe-Morrison." The story deals with acclaimed African author Chinua Achebe working on a fiction series for children. This story of a citizen of the developing world serving as a helper is relegated to the second level of the Web site.

Using contrasting pictures, headlines, and the systematic placing of labels, the Web sites of UNICEF and UNFPA do not suggest an inclusive ideology where equal partners work together. Rather, they use strategies such as an appeal to pity and non-inclusion to present the developing world as the sad victim that requires help from the West.

The Web Site: A Place to Shine?

Another area that prevents the UNAIDS, UNICEF, and UNFPA Web sites from living up to their public ideology of bringing people together is their underlying tone. These Web sites do not invite the audience to think about their role in these global issues but rather to consider all that the agencies are doing. Priority is given to stories about what the agencies have done and all of the work in which they are involved. In other words, the Web sites serve to make the agencies look good by highlighting their participation in many projects. The strategy used to accomplish this is an emphasis on news and action reports.

Information related to news is highlighted in all three sites. It is not only placed in a prominent area of the site to catch the audience's attention, but it also is repeated. For example, two out of the three major headings of the UNAIDS Web site deal with news. The repetition is clear; the first heading is titled "Latest News" and the second "What's New." In the same Web site, there is a heading titled "For Journalists" that once again provides news. The other two Web sites also prioritize news. UNICEF has a press center option and a "What's New" option strategically placed at the top of the page. The third Web site—that of UNFPA—has three options for news: The main part of the page has "the latest news link," another option for "more news options or features," and another news link on the top of the page. I first saw this intensity and repetition of the news option as a positive aspect of the page. My opinion on this changed later as I explored in more depth the Web sites' ideology.

The news in these Web sites is not used to inform the audience and meet its needs; rather, it is a vehicle that serves the interests of the agencies. The news stories are all about what the agencies are doing, not what is important to the audience. For example, the most important news item for UNAIDS is "the education plan launched." UNFPA uses, interestingly enough, the same language and talks about "launching a campaign." UNICEF uses the largest part of the Web site to cover a special session on children, and the audience is asked to "click for complete coverage." These examples show that news is used in the Web sites to spotlight the agencies and not to inform people about relevant issues. The result of this desire to "shine"—to use the Web site as a vehicle for flaunting or boasting about the agency's work—is a suppression of voices. If what is important—what is newsworthy—is related to the agencies, then the voices of the people these agencies serve are not given a chance to be heard. The people from the 189 countries are not given the chance to use or be heard on these Web sites. These Web sites should not be places for the agencies to shine but rather an opportunity for their members to work together to solve problems related to children's lives, population, and AIDS.

Three Web Sites: Three Missed Opportunities

The potential of the Internet for bringing unity and working together will continue to grow as cyber cafes open in even the most remote areas of the world. As agencies of the UN, the world's largest organization, UNICEF, UNFPA, and UNAIDS are vehicles for the ideology of bringing people together. A close examination of these agencies' Web sites, however, reveals a disturbing ideology. The ideology excludes people of developing nations by presenting them as victims—as people whose only role is to accept the help provided by the West. The Web sites lose the potential to provide a forum for people all over the world as they equate newsworthy with self-recognition. They do not allow for mutual help or true information exchange. In the end, what is clear is that the three Web sites analyzed are not inclusive and miss the opportunity to bring people together to make the lives of children better, to address population concerns, and to fight the ravages of AIDS.

Inclusiveness is increasingly common as an objective for communication in our global era. As we become aware of the richness that diverse perspectives provide in trying to solve the world's problems, rhetors are encouraged to use rhetorical strategies that invite diverse perspectives and to consider those perspectives seriously. This analysis suggests that this laudable objective is more difficult to achieve than we might have imagined. Despite apparently careful and creative efforts by the designers of the UN Web sites to communicate their inclusiveness and welcoming of myriad perspectives, many features of the Web sites divide and dismiss as much as they include. This analysis suggests that the construction of some groups as needy and others as agents, the featuring of the problems of one group and the hiding of the problems of another, and a focus on the organizational rhetor's own accomplishments rather than the accomplishments or interests of its members all belie the inclusiveness that the Web sites signal through their openness and their action orientation. Perhaps the contradiction is intentional; the organizations may be seeking to convey an image of one kind while genuinely harboring some ideological beliefs that contradict that. Another possibility is that, with the new technology of the Web, the many ways in which inconsistencies within messages can occur have not yet been explicated. Web sites are exciting new communicative sites with tremendous potential for community building, even at an international level, but whether this potential will be realized in true unity or in separation and division clearly is as yet unknown.

Note

[1] Web sites for the five organizations are (1) World Vision: http://www.worldvision.co.nz (2) Children International: http://www.children.org (3) ChildReach: http://www.childreach.com (4) Save the Children: http://www.savethechildren.net (5) Compassion International: http://www.ci.org

References

Aidoo, Ama A. (1995). The African women today. In O. Nnaemeka (Ed.), *Sisterhood, feminisms and power: From Africa to the Diaspora* (pp. 39–50). Trenton, NJ: Africa World Press.

The U.N. joins the net. *The Futurist*, Washington; Jan./Feb. 1996.

UNAIDS: Joint United Nations Programme on HIV/AIDS (n.d.). Retrieved October 29, 2002, from http://www.unaids.org.

UNFPA: United Nations Population Fund (n.d.). Retrieved October 29, 2002, from http://www.unfpa.org.

UNICEF: United Nations Children's Fund (n.d.). Retrieved October 29, 2002, from http://www.unicef.org.

Additional Samples of Ideological Criticism

Acosta-Alzuru, Carolina. "'I'm Not a Feminist . . . I Only Defend Women as Human Beings': The Production, Representation, and Consumption of Feminism in a *Telenovela*." *Critical Studies in Media Communication*, 20 (September 2003), 269–94.

Altman, Karen E. "Consuming Ideology: The Better Homes in America Campaign." *Critical Studies in Mass Communication*, 7 (September 1990), 286–307.

Behling, Laura L. "Reification and Resistance: The Rhetoric of Black Womanhood at the Columbian Exposition, 1893." *Women's Studies in Communication*, 25 (Fall 2002), 173–96.

Birmingham, Elizabeth. "Reframing the Ruins: Pruitt-Igoe, Structural Racism, and African American Rhetoric as a Space for Cultural Critique." *Western Journal of Communication*, 63 (Summer 1999), 291–309.

Bodroghkozy, Aniko. "'We're the Young Generation and We've Got Something to Say': A Gramscian Analysis of Entertainment Television and the Youth Rebellion of the 1960s." *Critical Studies in Mass Communication*, 8 (June 1991), 217–30.

Brouwer, Daniel C., and Aaron Hess. "Making Sense of 'God Hates Fags' and 'Thank God for 9/11': A Thematic Analysis of Milbloggers' Responses to Reverend Fred Phelps and the Westboro Baptist Church." *Western Journal of Communication*, 71 (January 2007), 69–90.

Cloud, Dana L. "Operation Desert Comfort." In *Seeing Through the Media: The Persian Gulf War*. Ed. Lauren Rabinovitz and Susan Jeffords. New Brunswick, NJ: Rutgers University Press, 1994, pp. 155–70.

Cloud, Dana L. "The Rhetoric of <Family Values>: Scapegoating, Utopia, and the Privatization of Social Responsibility." *Western Journal of Communication*, 62 (Fall 1998), 387–419.

Condit, Celeste Michelle. "Hegemony in a Mass-Mediated Society: Concordance about Reproductive Technologies." *Critical Studies in Mass Communication*, 11 (September 1994), 205–30.

Cooks, Leda M., Mark P. Orbe, and Carol S. Bruess. "The Fairy Tale Theme in Popular Culture: A Semiotic Analysis of *Pretty Woman*." *Women's Studies in Communication*, 16 (Fall 1993), 86–104.

Coupland, Justine, and Angie Williams. "Conflicting Discourses, Shifting Ideologies: Pharmaceutical, 'Alternative' and Feminist Emancipatory Texts on the Menopause." *Discourse & Society*, 13 (July 2002), 419–45.

Delgado, Fernando Pedro. "Chicano Ideology Revisited: Rap Music and the (Re)articulation of Chicanismo." *Western Journal of Communication*, 62 (Spring 1998), 95–113.

Dickinson, Greg. "Joe's Rhetoric: Starbucks and the Spatial Rhetoric of Authenticity." *Rhetoric Society Quarterly*, 32 (Fall 2002), 5–28.

Dickinson, Greg, Brian L. Ott, and Eric Aoki. "Spaces of Remembering and Forgetting: The Reverent Eye/I at the Plains Indian Museum." *Communication and Critical/Cultural Studies*, 3 (March 2006), 27–47.

Dow, Bonnie J. "Femininity and Feminism in *Murphy Brown*." *Southern Communication Journal*, 57 (Winter 1992), 143–55.

Dow, Bonnie J. "Hegemony, Feminist Criticism and *The Mary Tyler Moore Show*." *Critical Studies in Mass Communication*, 7 (September 1990), 261–74.

Downey, Sharon D. "Feminine Empowerment in Disney's *Beauty and the Beast*." *Women's Studies in Communication*, 19 (Summer 1996), 185–212.

Downey, Sharon D., and Karen Rasmussen. "The Irony of *Sophie's Choice*." *Women's Studies in Communication*, 14 (Fall 1991), 1–23.

Dubrofsky, Rachel E. "*The Bachelor*: Whiteness in the Harem." *Critical Studies in Media Communication*, 23 (March 2006), 39–56.

Fabj, Valeria. "Motherhood as Political Voice: The Rhetoric of the Mothers of Plaza de Mayo." *Communication Studies*, 44 (Spring 1993), 1–18.

Fang, Yew-Jin. "'Riots' and Demonstrations in the Chinese Press: A Case Study of Language and Ideology." *Discourse & Society*, 54 (October 1994), 463–81.

Fassett, Deanna L., and John T. Warren. "The Strategic Rhetoric of an 'At-Risk' Educational Identity: Interviewing Jane." *Communication and Critical/Cultural Studies*, 2 (September 2005), 238–56.

Flores, Lisa A., and Dreama G. Moon. "Rethinking Race, Revealing Dilemmas: Imagining a New Racial Subject in *Race Traitor*." *Western Journal of Communication*, 66 (Spring 2002), 181–207.

Franklin, Sarah. "Deconstructing 'Desperateness': The Social Construction of Infertility in Popular Representations of New Reproductive Technologies." In *The New Reproductive Technologies*. Ed. Maureen McNeil, Ian Varcoe, and Steven Yearley. London: MacMillan, 1990, pp. 200–29.

Frentz, Thomas S., and Thomas B. Farrell. "Conversion of America's Consciousness: The Rhetoric of *The Exorcist*." *Quarterly Journal of Speech*, 61 (February 1975), 40–47.

Frentz, Thomas S., and Janice Hocker Rushing. "Integrating Ideology and Archetype in Rhetorical Criticism, Part II: A Case Study of *Jaws*." *Quarterly Journal of Speech*, 79 (February 1993), 61–81.

German, Kathleen M. "Frank Capra's *Why We Fight* Series and the American Audience." *Western Journal of Speech Communication*, 54 (Spring 1990), 237–48.

Goltz, Dustin Bradley. "Laughing at Absence: *Instinct* Magazine and the Hyper-Masculine Gay Future?" *Western Journal of Communication*, 71 (April 2007), 93–113.

Hackett, Robert A., and Zuezhi Zhao. "Challenging a Master Narrative: Peace Protest and Opinion/Editorial Discourse in the U.S. Press During the Gulf War." *Discourse & Society*, 5 (October 1994), 509–41.

Haines, Harry W. "'What Kind of War?': An Analysis of the Vietnam Veterans Memorial." *Critical Studies in Mass Communication*, 3 (March 1986), 1–20.

Halualani, Rona Tamiko. "The Intersecting Hegemonic Discourses of an Asian Mail-Order Bride Catalog: Pilipina 'Oriental Butterfly' Dolls for Sale." *Women's Studies in Communication*, 18 (Spring 1995), 45–64.

Hanke, Robert. "Hegemony Masculinity in *thirtysomething*." *Critical Studies in Mass Communication*, 7 (September 1990), 231–48.

Hanke, Robert. "The 'Mock-Macho' Situation Comedy: Hegemonic Masculinity and its Reiteration." *Western Journal of Communication*, 62 (Winter 1998), 74–93.

Hariman, Robert, and John Louis Lucaites. "Public Identity and Collective Memory in U.S. Iconic Photography: The Image of 'Accidental Napalm.'" *Critical Studies in Media Communication*, 20 (March 2003), 35–66.

Hayashi, Reiko. "Helping!?: Images and Control in Japanese Women's Magazines." *Women's Studies in Communication*, 18 (Fall 1995), 189–98.

Hayden, Sara. "Teenage Bodies, Teenage Selves: Tracing the Implications of Bio-Power in Contemporary Sexuality Education Texts." *Women's Studies in Communication*, 24 (Spring 2001), 30–61.

Henke, Jill Birnie, Diane Zimmerman Umble, and Nancy J. Smith. "Construction of the Female Self: Feminist Readings of the Disney Heroine." *Women's Studies in Communication*, 19 (Summer 1996), 229–49.

Hoerrner, Keisha L. "Gender Roles in Disney Films: Analyzing Behaviors from Snow White to Simba." *Women's Studies in Communication*, 19 (Summer 1996), 211–28.

Illouz, Eva. "Reason Within Passion: Love in Women's Magazines." *Critical Studies in Mass Communication*, 8 (September 1991), 231–48.

Japp, Phyllis M. "Gender and Work in the 1980s: Television's Working Women as Displaced Persons." *Women's Studies in Communication*, 14 (Spring 1991), 49–74.

Jasinski, James. "The Feminization of Liberty, Domesticated Virtue, and the Reconstitution of Power and Authority in Early American Political Discourse." *Quarterly Journal of Speech*, 79 (May 1993), 146–64.

King, Stephen A. "Memory, Mythmaking, and Museums: Constructive Authenticity and the Primitive Blues Subject." *Southern Communication Journal*, 71 (September 2006), 235–50.

Kray, Susan. "Orientalization of an 'Almost White' Woman: The Interlocking Effects of Race, Class, Gender, and Ethnicity in American Mass Media." *Critical Studies in Mass Communication*, 10 (December 1993), 349–66.

Loeb, Jane Connelly. "Rhetorical and Ideological Conservatism in *thirtysomething*." *Critical Studies in Mass Communication*, 7 (September 1990), 249–60.

LaFountain, Marc J. "Foucault and Dr. Ruth." *Critical Studies in Mass Communication*, 6 (June 1989), 123–37.

Lessl, Thomas M. "Science and the Sacred Cosmos: The Ideological Rhetoric of Carl Sagan." *Quarterly Journal of Speech*, 71 (May 1985), 175–87.

Lester, Neal A., and Maureen Daly Goggin. "In Living Color: Politics of Desire in Heterosexual Interracial Black/White Personal Ads." *Communication and Critical/Cultural Studies*, 2 (June 2005), 130–62.

Lewis, Charles. "Hegemony in the Ideal: Wedding Photography, Consumerism, and Patriarchy." *Women's Studies in Communication*, 20 (Fall 1997), 167–87.

Lindenfeld, Laura. "Visiting the Mexican American Family: *Tortilla Soup* as Culinary Tourism." *Communication and Critical/Cultural Studies*, 4 (September 2007), 303–20.

Marvin, Carolyn. "Theorizing the Flagbody: Symbolic Dimensions of the Flag Desecration Debate, or, Why the Bill of Rights Does Not Fly in the Ballpark." *Critical Studies in Mass Communication*, 8 (June 1991), 119–38.

McGee, Michael Calvin. "The Origins of 'Liberty': A Feminization of Power." *Communication Monographs*, 47 (March 1980), 23–45.

Moore, Stephen H. "Disinterring Ideology from a Corpus of Obituaries: A Critical Post Mortem." *Discourse & Society*, 13 (July 2002), 495–536.

Morris, Richard, and Philip Wander. "Native American Rhetoric: Dancing in the Shadows of the Ghost Dance." *Quarterly Journal of Speech*, 76 (May 1990), 164–91.

Murphy, John M. "Domesticating Dissent: The Kennedys and the Freedom Rides." *Communication Monographs*, 59 (March 1992), 61–78.

Myrick, Roger. "Making Women Visible through Health Communication: Representations of Gender in AIDS PSAs." *Women's Studies in Communication*, 22 (Spring 1999), 45–65.

Nakayama, Thomas K. "Show/Down Time: 'Race,' Gender, Sexuality, and Popular Culture." *Critical Studies in Mass Communication*, 11 (June 1994), 162–79.

Nomai, Afsheen J., and George N. Dionisopoulos. "Framing the Cubas Narrative: The American Dream and the Capitalist Reality." *Communication Studies*, 53 (Summer 2002), 97–111.

Oates, Thomas P. "The Erotic Gaze in the NFL Draft." *Communication and Critical/Cultural Studies*, 4 (March 2007), 74–90.

O'Brien, Pamela Colby, "The Happiest Films on Earth: A Textual and Contextual Analysis of Walt Disney's *Cinderella* and *The Little Mermaid*." *Women's Studies in Communication*, 19 (Summer 1996), 155–83.

Olbrys, Stephen Gencarella. "*Seinfeld's* Democratic Vistas." *Critical Studies in Media Communication*, 22 (December 2005), 390–408.

Orbe, Mark P. "Constructions of Reality on MTV's *The Real World*: An Analysis of the Restrictive Coding of Black Masculinity." *Southern Communication Journal*, 64 (Fall 1998), 32–47.

Ott, Brian L., and Eric Aoki. "Popular Imagination and Identity Politics: Reading the Future in *Star Trek: The Next Generation*." *Western Journal of Communication*, 65 (Fall 2001), 392–415.

Parry-Giles, Trevor. "Character, the Constitution, and the Ideological Embodiment of 'Civil Rights' in the 1967 Nomination of Thurgood Marshall to the Supreme Court." *Quarterly Journal of Speech*, 82 (November 1996), 364–82.

Parry-Giles, Trevor. "Ideological Anxiety and the Censored Text: Real Lives at the Edge of the Union." *Critical Studies in Mass Communication*, 11 (March 1994), 54–72.

Palmer, David L. "Virtuosity as Rhetoric: Agency and Transformation in Paganini's Mastery of the Violin." *Quarterly Journal of Speech*, 84 (August 1998), 341–57.

Perkins, Sally J. "The Myth of the Matriarchy: Annulling Patriarchy through the Regeneration of Time." *Communication Studies*, 42 (Winter 1991), 371–82.

Perkins, Sally J. "The Rhetoric of Androgyny as Revealed in *The Feminine Mystique*." *Communication Studies*, 40 (Summer 1989), 69–80.

Perkins, Sally J. "*The Singular Life of Albert Nobbs*: Subversive Rhetoric and Feminist Ideology." *Women's Studies in Communication*, 16 (Spring 1993), 34–54.

Rasmussen, Karen. "*China Beach* and American Mythology of War." *Women's Studies in Communication*, 15 (Fall 1992), 22–50.

Rogers, Richard A. "Deciphering Kokopelli: Masculinity in Commodified Appropriations of Native American Imagery." *Communication and Critical/Cultural Studies*, 4 (September 2007), 233–55.

Rojo, Luisa Martin. "Division and Rejection: From the Personification of the Gulf Conflict to the Demonization of Saddam Hussein." *Discourse & Society*, 6 (January 1995), 49–80.

Roy, Abhik. "The Construction and Scapegoating of Muslims as the 'Other' in Hindu Nationalist Rhetoric." *Southern Communication Journal*, 69 (Summer 2004), 320–32.

Rushing, Janice Hocker. "*E.T.* as Rhetorical Transcendence." *Quarterly Journal of Speech*, 71 (May 1985), 188–203.

Rushing, Janice Hocker. "Evolution of 'The New Frontier' in *Alien* and *Aliens*: Patriarchal Co-optation of the Feminine Archetype." *Quarterly Journal of Speech*, 75 (February 1989), 1–24.

Rushing, Janice Hocker. "Mythic Evolution of 'The New Frontier' in Mass Mediated Rhetoric." *Critical Studies in Mass Communication*, 3 (September 1986), 265–96.

Rushing, Janice Hocker. "Putting Away Childish Things: Looking at Diana's Funeral and Media Criticism." *Women's Studies in Communication*, 21 (Fall 1998), 150–67.

Rushing, Janice Hocker. "The Rhetoric of the American Western Myth." *Communication Monographs*, 50 (March 1983), 14–32.

Rushing, Janice Hocker. "Ronald Reagan's 'Star Wars' Address: Mythic Containment of Technical Reasoning." *Quarterly Journal of Speech*, 72 (November 1986), 415–33.

Rushing, Janice Hocker, and Thomas S. Frentz. "The Frankenstein Myth in Contemporary Cinema." *Critical Studies in Mass Communication*, 6 (March 1989), 61–80.

Salvador, Michael. "The Rhetorical Subversion of Cultural Boundaries: The National Consumers' League." *Southern Communication Journal*, 59 (Summer 1994), 318–32.

Sanchez, Victoria E., and Mary E. Stuckey. "Coming of Age as a Culture: Emancipatory and Hegemonic Readings of *The Indian in the Cupboard*." *Western Journal of Communication*, 64 (Winter 2000), 78–91.

Scult, Allen, Michael Calvin McGee, and J. Kenneth Kuntz. "Genesis and Power: An Analysis of the Biblical Story of Creation." *Quarterly Journal of Speech*, 72 (May 1986), 113–31.

Sellnow, Deanna D. "Music as Persuasion: Refuting Hegemonic Masculinity in 'He Thinks He'll Keep Her.'" *Women's Studies in Communication*, 22 (Spring 1999), 66–84.

Shah, Hemant, and Michael C. Thornton. "Racial Ideology in U.S. Mainstream News Magazine Coverage of Black-Latino Interaction, 1980–1992." *Critical Studies in Mass Communication*, 11 (June 1994), 141–61.

Short, Brant. "'Reconstructed, But Unregenerate': *I'll Take My Stand*'s Rhetorical Vision of Progress." *Southern Communication Journal*, 59 (Winter 1994), 112–24.

Shugart, Helene A. "Crossing Over: Hybridity and Hegemony in the Popular Media." *Communication and Critical/Cultural Studies*, 4 (June 2007), 115–41.

Shugart, Helene A. "On Misfits and Margins: Narrative, Resistance, and the Poster Child Politics of Rosie O'Donnell." *Communication and Critical/Cultural Studies*, 2 (March 2005), 52–76.

Shugart, Helene A. "Reinventing Privilege: The New (Gay) Man in Contemporary Popular Media." *Critical Studies in Media Communication*, 20 (March 2003), 67–91.

Shugart, Helene A. "She Shoots, She Scores: Mediated Constructions of Contemporary Female Athletes in Coverage of the 1999 U.S. Women's Soccer Team." *Western Journal of Communication*, 67 (Winter 2003), 1–31.

Sloop, John M. "'Apology Made to Whoever Pleases': Cultural Discipline and the Grounds of Interpretation." *Communication Quarterly*, 42 (Fall 1994), 345–62.

Sloop, John M. "Riding in Cars Between Men." *Communication and Critical/Cultural Studies*, 2 (September 2005), 191–213.

Smith, Cynthia Duquette. "Discipline—It's a 'Good Thing': Rhetorical Constitution and Martha Stewart Living Omnimedia." *Women's Studies in Communication*, 23 (Fall 2000), 337–66.

Solomon, Martha. "'With Firmness in the Right': The Creation of Moral Hegemony in Lincoln's Second Inaugural." *Communication Reports*, 1 (Winter 1988), 32–37.

Stein, Sarah R. "The *1984* Macintosh Ad: Cinematic Icons and Constitutive Rhetoric in the Launch of a New Machine." *Quarterly Journal of Speech*, 88 (May 2002), 169–92.

Stormer, Nathan. "Embodying Normal Miracles." *Quarterly Journal of Speech*, 83 (May 1997), 172–91.

Taylor, Bryan C. "Fat Man and Little Boy: The Cinematic Representation of Interests in the Nuclear Weapons Organization." *Critical Studies in Mass Communication*, 10 (December 1993), 367–94.

Taylor, Bryan C. "Register of the Repressed: Women's Voice and Body in the Nuclear Weapons Organization." *Quarterly Journal of Speech*, 79 (August 1993), 267–85.

Tierney, Sean M. "Themes of Whiteness in *Bulletproof Monk, Kill Bill*, and *The Last Samurai*." *Journal of Communication*, 56 (September 2006), 607–24.

Trujillo, Nick. "Hegemonic Masculinity on the Mound: Media Representations of Nolan Ryan and American Sports Culture." *Critical Studies in Mass Communication*, 8 (September 1991), 290–308.

Trujillo, Nick. "In Search of Naunny's History: Reproducing Gender Ideology in Family Stories." *Women's Studies in Communication*, 25 (Spring 2002), 88–118.

Trujillo, Nick. "Interpreting (the Work and the Talk of) Baseball: Perspectives on Ballpark Culture." *Western Journal of Communication*, 56 (Fall 1992), 350–71.

Trujillo, Nick, and Leah R. Ekdom. "Sportswriting and American Cultural Values: The 1984 Chicago Cubs." *Critical Studies in Mass Communication*, 2 (September 1985), 262–81.

Vande Berg, Leah R. "*China Beach*, Prime Time War in the Post-feminist Age: An Example of Patriarchy in a Different Voice." *Western Journal of Communication*, 57 (Summer 1993), 349–66.

Wander, Philip C. "The Aesthetics of Fascism." *Journal of Communication*, 33 (Spring 1983), 70–78.

Wander, Philip C. "The Angst of the Upper Class." *Journal of Communication*, 29 (Autumn 1979), 85–88.

Wander, Philip C. "The John Birch and Martin Luther King Symbols in the Radical Right." *Western Speech*, 35 (Winter 1971), 4–14.

Wander, Philip C. "On the Meaning of *Roots*." *Journal of Communication*, 27 (Autumn 1977), 64–69.

Wander, Philip C. "The Rhetoric of American Foreign Policy." *Quarterly Journal of Speech*, 70 (November 1984), 339–61.

Wander, Philip C. "Salvation Through Separation: The Image of the Negro in the American Colonization Society." *Quarterly Journal of Speech*, 57 (February 1971), 57–67.

Wander, Philip C. "The Savage Child: The Image of the Negro in the Pro-Slavery Movement." *Southern Speech Communication Journal*, 37 (Summer 1972), 335–60.

Wander, Philip C. "*The Waltons:* How Sweet It Was." *Journal of Communication*, 26 (Autumn 1976), 148–54.

Watts, Eric K. "An Exploration of Spectacular Consumption: Gangsta Rap as Cultural Commodity." *Communication Studies*, 48 (Spring 1997), 42–58.

Weiss, Julie H. "Mothers as Others: The Construction of Race, Ethnicity, and Gender in Self-Help Literature of the 1940s." *Women's Studies in Communication*, 18 (Fall 1995), 153–63.

Wilson, Kirt H. "Towards a Discursive Theory of Racial Identity: *The Souls of Black Folk* as a Response to Nineteenth-Century Biological Determinism." *Western Journal of Communication*, 63 (Spring 1999), 193–215.

Xiao, Xiaoyu, and D. Ray Heisey. "Liberationist Populism in the Chinese Film *Tian Xian Pei*: A Feminist Critique." *Women's Studies in Communication*, 19 (Fall 1996), 313–33.

Xing, Lu. "An Ideological/Cultural Analysis of Political Slogans in Communist China." *Discourse & Society*, 10 (October 1999), 487–508.

Zagacki, Kenneth S. "The Rhetoric of American Decline: Paul Kennedy, Conservatives, and the Solvency Debate." *Western Journal of Communication*, 56 (Fall 1992), 372–93.

Metaphor Criticism

Metaphors are nonliteral comparisons in which a word or phrase from one domain of experience is applied to another domain. Derived from the Greek words *meta*, meaning "over" and *phereras*, meaning "to carry," metaphor involves the process of transferring or carrying over aspects that apply to one object to a second object. When we describe an economic downturn in the Silicon Valley using metaphors such as "it has been in a tailspin," "Silicon Valley is the Mecca for startups," "the bottom fell out," "something will have to pick up the slack," and "the Web breathed new life into the Valley," we are describing an industry using terms from domains such as aviation, religion, sailing, and medicine.

A metaphor joins two terms normally regarded as belonging to different classes of experience. These two terms or the two parts of a metaphor are called the *tenor* and the *vehicle*. The tenor is the topic or subject that is being explained. The vehicle is the mechanism or lens through which the topic is viewed.[1] Other terms that are used to distinguish the two parts of a metaphor are *target domain* and *source domain*. The conceptual domain we are trying to understand is the target domain, and the conceptual domain we are using as a lens viewing for the target is the source domain. In other words, the "target domain is the domain that we try to understand through the use of the source domain."[2] In the metaphor, "My roommate is a pig," for example, the roommate is the tenor, the target, or the subject being addressed, and the pig is the vehicle, the source, or the lens being applied to the subject we are seeking to understand.

The two terms of a metaphor are seen to be related by a "system of associated commonplaces," entailments, or characteristics. In their interaction to create a metaphor, the characteristics associated with the vehicle or source are used to organize conceptions of the tenor or target.[3] In the metaphor "My roommate is a pig," we use one system of commonplaces (those

267

dealing with pigs) to filter or organize our conception of another system (that of the roommate). In the correspondences between the characteristics of the tenor and the vehicle, some qualities are emphasized and others are suppressed. In addition, we recognize that there are both similarities and differences between the two systems of characteristics.[4]

The first extended treatment of metaphor was provided by Aristotle, who defined metaphor as "the transference of a name from the object to which it has a natural application."[5] Aristotle's definition set the direction for the study of metaphor as decoration or ornamentation. From this perspective, metaphor is seen as a figure of speech or linguistic embroidery that the rhetor uses only occasionally to give extra force to language. As Aristotle explains, metaphor "gives clearness, charm, and distinction to the style."[6] Cicero's view of metaphor is similar: "there is no mode of embellishment . . . that throws a greater lustre upon language."[7] To summarize this perspective on metaphor, metaphors "are not necessary, they are just nice."[8]

When metaphor is seen as decoration, it is regarded as a deviant form of language—as extraordinary rather than ordinary language. As Aristotle suggests, metaphors "create an unusual element in the diction by their not being in ordinary speech."[9] Thomas Hobbes, writing in the sixteenth and seventeenth centuries, echoes this notion, suggesting that metaphor frustrates the process of communicating thoughts and knowledge. He considers metaphor to be one of four abuses of speech because we "deceive others" when we use metaphor.[10] Richard Whately expresses a similar view of metaphor, suggesting that the use of metaphor departs "from the plain and strictly appropriate Style."[11]

When metaphor is seen as linguistic embellishment that makes it different from the typical use of language, rules are needed to limit its use in effective rhetoric. Throughout the history of the treatment of metaphor, strong warnings have been given against the improper use of metaphor. Although Aristotle states that metaphor is not something that can be taught,[12] he provides guidelines for its proper use. A metaphor, for example, should not be "ridiculous," "too grand," "too much in the vein of tragedy," or "far-fetched."[13] Cicero's writings on metaphor provide another illustration of the kinds of rules offered for its proper use. A metaphor must bear some resemblance to what it pictures, and it should give clarity to a point rather than confuse it.[14]

In contrast to the view of metaphor as decoration, metaphor now is seen as a major means for constituting reality. We do not perceive reality and then interpret or give it meaning. Rather, we experience reality through the language by which we describe it; description *is* the reality we experience. Metaphor is a basic way by which the process of using symbols to construct reality occurs. It serves as a structuring principle, focusing on particular aspects of a phenomenon and hiding others; thus, each metaphor produces a different description of the "same" reality. In Max Black's words: "Suppose I look at the night sky through a piece of heavily smoked glass on which certain lines have been left clear. Then I shall see only the stars that can be made to lie on the lines previously prepared upon the screen, and the stars I do see will be seen as organized by the screen's structure. We can think of a metaphor as such a screen."[15]

The metaphors "we select to filter our perceptions and organize our experience" are important because "when you choose a metaphor you are also choosing its rules, along with the roles and scripts that those rules dictate."[16] Metaphors contain implicit assumptions, points of view, and evaluations. They organize attitudes toward whatever they describe and provide motives for acting in certain ways. The metaphor that "time is money" illustrates how the use of a particular metaphor can affect our thought and experience of reality. This metaphor, reflected in common expressions in our culture such as, "This gadget will *save* you hours," "I've *invested* a lot of time in her," and "You need to *budget* your time," leads us to experience the reality of time in a particular way. Because we conceive of time as money, we understand and experience it as something that can be spent, budgeted, wasted, and saved. Long-distance telephone charges, hotel-room rates, yearly budgets, and interest on loans are examples of how time is experienced as money. We expect to be paid according to the amount of time worked, and we decide whether to engage in certain activities according to whether the time spent will be sufficiently valuable.

Another case of how our selection of a particular metaphor affects our perception of reality is the metaphor that "argument is war." That we tend to see an argument through the metaphor of war is evidenced in such expressions as, "He *attacked* my argument," "I *demolished* her argument," "I *won* the argument," and "He *shot down* all of my arguments." As a consequence of the war metaphor, we experience an argument as something we can win or lose. We view the person with whom we engage in the argument as an opponent. We may find a position indefensible and thus abandon it and adopt a new line of attack.[17] In contrast, if we used a different metaphor on argument—"argument is a dance," for example—participants would be seen as partners. Their goals would be to perform in a balanced, harmonious, and aesthetically pleasing way; to collaborate to produce a finely coordinated performance; and to continue working until the dance was perfected.

Let's say we choose a metaphor of knitting or gardening to talk about argument. Instead of "it's easy to *shoot holes* in her arguments," we might say, "it's easy to *find dropped stitches* in her arguments" or "it's easy to *pick out the dead flowers* of her arguments." Rather than making statements such as "you can't *drop your guard* with her around," we might say, "you can't *lay down your needles* with her around" or "you can't *stop watering* with her around."[18] The point is that, with the selection of a different metaphor, we would view and experience arguments differently.[19]

Linguist Suzette Haden Elgin provides an example of how a choice of metaphors affects our interpersonal interactions. In this example, a woman accuses her coworker of lying in a meeting. He is operating on the basis of the metaphor LIFE IS A FOOTBALL GAME, while she is operating on the metaphor LIFE IS A TRADITIONAL SCHOOLROOM. They disagree about what counts as a lie because of these different metaphors:

> On the football field it's perfectly okay to pretend you have the ball
> when you don't have it, or to pretend you're going to run one direction

and then run the other way. That's not lying, it's just "the way the game is played." It's not only okay, it's admired and rewarded. . . . In the traditional schoolroom, on the other hand, if a statement is false it's a lie. Period; end of discussion. You not only don't get rewarded for lying, you get punished.[20]

Because of these different metaphors, then, the coworkers are likely to "have radically different understandings of what happened and why," and "disagreement and hostility [are] almost inevitable."[21]

Likewise, we would adopt different actions as a response to terrorism depending on the metaphor used to describe it. George W. Bush conceptualizes terrorism through the metaphor of hunt and gather, which encourages us "to imagine terrorists as animals and to concede the President unlimited power to 'gather' information and 'hunt' these animals."[22] In contrast, if we described a response to terrorism in computer terms, *danger* would be "defined in terms of a threat to your operating system." The solutions would involve "virus protection and backing up your files." Under this system, responding appropriately to terrorism would mean developing "a system that allowed every American to constantly 'download' updates about new threats." Just as they do with their computers, "Americans could participate in keeping themselves informed. . . . [T]he more active they were at updating and 'backing up' their 'files,'" the greater degree of security they would experience. As a result, Americans would be likely to experience a lessening of anxiety, in contrast to the increase in anxiety they feel in the hunt and gather frame.[23]

An earthquake frame would define *danger* regarding terrorism still differently—this time as "an inevitable natural disaster." The question would be "not if the 'big one' will come, but when it will come." Protection from the quake would lie in the planning and design of buildings: "Security comes from knowing that your house and the buildings in your town are safe from terrorist bombs" because "design innovations have been made to decrease potential damage in case of an attack." Security in this frame also would be enhanced by "knowing as much as possible about 'fault line' activity—about what is happening in the world that might lead to more terrorism."[24] Whatever metaphor is used to label and experience a phenomenon, then, suggests evaluations of it and appropriate behavior in response.

When metaphor is seen as a way of knowing the world, it plays a particular role in argumentation. Metaphor does not simply provide support for an argument; instead, the structure of the metaphor itself argues. The metaphor explicates the appropriateness of the associated characteristics of one term to those of another term and thus invites an audience to adopt the resulting perspective. If the audience finds the associated characteristics acceptable and sees the appropriateness of linking the two systems of characteristics, the audience accepts the argument the metaphor offers.[25]

Steven Perry explains how metaphor constitutes argument in his study of the infestation metaphor in Hitler's rhetoric: "Hitler's critique of the Jew's status as a cultural being . . . is not illustrated by the metaphor of parasitism; it is *constituted* by this metaphor."[26] The figurative language is not supplementary or subordinate to the argument; it is itself Hitler's argument. The listener or reader who does not reject the interaction of the characteristics of *infestation* and *Jews* has accepted a claim about what the facts are and the evaluation expressed in the metaphor. A metaphor, then, argues just as typical argumentative structures do, but it usually does so more efficiently and comprehensively.[27]

The use of metaphor as argument also can be seen more recently in the 2004 presidential election in the United States, when George W. Bush was running against John Kerry. Metaphor scholars such as George Lakoff and Jeffrey Feldman suggest that metaphor had a major impact on the outcome of that election because of the metaphor on which conservatives built their arguments, choosing "words that invoked powerful sets of unspoken ideas that structured the entire debate. These ideas described a worldview of how the country should work that ultimately trumped and undermined every possible statement made by progressive candidates."[28] Lakoff explains the frame as a metaphor of a family with a strict father who protects the family in the dangerous world, supports the family, and teaches his children right from wrong.[29] As a "strict father, you tell the children how to develop, tell them what rules they should follow, and punish them, when they do wrong."[30] When this metaphor was used to frame the major issues of the campaign, the Democrats were unprepared to counter it in any effective way and thus were unable to garner the support of the majority of the American public.

Because of the key role that metaphors play in framing perceptions and thus action and argumentation, change can be generated by changing metaphors. Gloria Anzaldúa is a proponent of the conscious choice of new metaphors to evoke individual and social change. Shifting metaphors means changing perspectives—making new connections and seeing in new ways—for both the creator of and the audience for the metaphor. She provides an example when she shifts the metaphors associated with the term *bearing* in an effort to empower her audience to see and act in new ways: "Haven't we always borne jugs of water, children, poverty? Why not learn to bear baskets of hope, love, self-nourishment and to step lightly?"[31]

Feldman suggests that the process of using metaphors to reframe an issue or a debate in the public realm and thus to create social change involves five steps: (1) "Stop Repeating their Words," which means stop using the language of the previous metaphor to talk about an issue because that simply reinforces the current frame; (2) "Go to Another Frame," which involves deliberately seeking out new perspectives on an issue; (3) "Build a New Frame," selecting and developing some other vehicle that captures the new perspective; (4) "Break it Down," breaking the metaphor that is the new frame into "bite-sized pieces" that can be used in ads, Web sites, and speeches; and (5) "Framing is Action," by which he means that, because "political action is a non-stop conversation unfolding in words and images," framing the debate is as real a form of political action as, for example, registering new voters.[32]

A number of theorists in various fields have helped to develop the perspective that metaphor is a primary means by which phenomena in the world become objects of reality or knowledge for us.[33] George Lakoff and Mark Johnson were instrumental in introducing the notion that metaphor is pervasive in everyday language and thought. [34] Kenneth Burke takes a similar view, suggesting that metaphor plays a critical role "in the discovery and description of 'the truth.'"[35] "If we employ the word 'character' as a general term for whatever can be thought of as distinct (any thing, pattern, situation, structure, nature, person, object, act, role, process, event, etc.)," he explains, "then we could say that metaphor tells us something about one character as considered from the point of view of another character. And to consider A from the point of view of B is, of course, to use B as a *perspective* upon A."[36] In the communication field, Michael Osborn[37] and Robert L. Ivie[38] have been instrumental in theorizing and applying this perspective on metaphor.

Procedures

Using the metaphor method of criticism, a critic analyzes an artifact in a four-step process: (1) selecting an artifact; (2) analyzing the artifact; (3) formulating a research question; and (4) writing the essay.

Selecting an Artifact

Choose an artifact for metaphor criticism that contains some explicit metaphors. At one level, of course, all language is metaphoric, but you will find metaphor criticism easier and more useful if you apply it to artifacts that contain some surface metaphors.

Analyzing the Artifact

In criticism in which metaphors are used as units of analysis, a critic analyzes an artifact in four steps: (1) examining the artifact for a general sense of its dimensions and context; (2) isolating the metaphors in the artifact; (3) sorting the metaphors into groups according to vehicle or tenor; and (4) discovering an explanation for the artifact.[39]

Examining the Artifact as a Whole

The first step for a critic is to become familiar with the text or elements of the artifact and its context to gain a sense of the complete experience of the artifact. Attention to the context is particularly important because, although some metaphors generally are understood in particular ways without attention to the context in which they are used, the meaning of most metaphors must be reconstructed from clues in the setting, occasion, audience, and rhetor. The meaning of calling a person a *pig*, for example, would be different when applied to a police officer by a crowd yelling "racist pig" than if applied to a teenager in her messy room. Information about the context of the artifact can be gathered in a variety of ways, including a review of rhetoric contemporaneous with the artifact, the audience's reactions to the artifact, and historical treatments of the context.

Isolating the Metaphors

The second step in a metaphor analysis is to isolate the metaphors employed by the rhetor. A brief selection from Martin Luther King, Jr.'s speech "I Have a Dream" illustrates the procedure for isolating metaphors in an artifact. The introduction of King's speech includes this passage:

> Five score years ago, a great American, in whose symbolic shadow we stand today, signed the Emancipation Proclamation. This momentous decree came as a great beacon light of hope to millions of Negro slaves, who had been seared in the flames of withering injustice. It came as a joyous daybreak to end the long night of their captivity.

Six metaphors can be found in this passage: *in whose symbolic shadow we stand, great beacon light of hope, seared in the flames of withering injustice, daybreak,* and *long night of their captivity.* Although, in many artifacts, only the vehicle is actually present in metaphors and the tenor is implied, in this passage, King includes both tenor and vehicle in most of his metaphors. The tenor of hope is seen through the vehicle of a beacon light, injustice is flame, the Emancipation Proclamation is daybreak, and captivity is the long night. His metaphor of standing in the symbolic shadow of Lincoln, however, does not explicitly include a tenor. Implied is a tenor of history and past struggles that cast their shadow and lend their spirit to the current situation. In the process of isolating metaphors in your artifact, then, look for metaphors where both tenor and vehicle are present and for those where only the vehicle is stated.

Sorting the Metaphors

You now have reduced your artifact to a list of metaphors. The next step of the process involves sorting the metaphors you have identified into groups, looking for patterns in metaphor use. The metaphors are sorted or grouped according to either vehicle or tenor, depending on your interest and the kinds of insights that are emerging for each in the analysis. If you want to discover how a rhetor conceptualizes a particular subject, group together all of the vehicles used to depict that subject. For example, if you note that a rhetor describes a workplace using terms such as *zoo, asylum, snake pit, jungle,* and *firestorm,* you are sorting the metaphors according to vehicles, and the tenor remains the same.

If you are interested in a rhetor's general worldview, identify all of the metaphors you find in the artifact. You are likely to discover a number of different tenors or topics and a number of different vehicles used to frame those topics. The major tenors and vehicles that appear in a text serve as an index to how the rhetor sees the world. In this case, you are sorting metaphors around the tenors in the artifact. In Martin Luther King, Jr.'s speech, for example, the metaphors used by King can be grouped into tenors that deal with blacks, the Constitution, and the United States.

Discovering an Explanation for the Artifact

In this step, the groups of metaphors—metaphors organized around either tenors or vehicles—are analyzed to develop an explanation for your artifact. You probably chose to analyze your artifact because there is some aspect of the artifact that doesn't fit or that you cannot explain. Perhaps you like the artifact and cannot explain its appeal for you. Perhaps it disturbs you, but you don't know why. Perhaps it seems unusual in some way. Your coding of the metaphors, in which some aspects of tenors, vehicles, or both are revealed as significant, can provide an explanation for your initial reactions.

Use the principles of frequency and intensity to discover what is significant about the metaphors and provide an explanation of your artifact. If vehicles from the same category are used repeatedly to describe many different tenors, for example, the frequency suggests an important pattern and an insight about the artifact. If your analysis identifies a very unusual vehicle to describe a particular tenor, that would be significant based on intensity. Metaphors that stand out because of frequency and intensity in tenors and/or vehicles, then, suggest areas where something is going on that can help explain the artifact.

The significant features that emerge from your metaphor analysis may suggest various kinds of explanations for your artifact. An explanation, for example, may deal with the image the vehicles convey of the topics discussed by the rhetor, the ideas that are highlighted and masked as a result of the metaphors used, the attitudes and values for which the metaphors argue, or the effects the particular metaphors are likely to have on the audience. Your explanation also might lie in how the rhetor's identity or actions are shaped by the metaphors selected.

Formulating a Research Question

Your research question for a metaphor analysis depends on whether your explanation of the artifact features tenor or vehicle. If you are featuring a particular tenor and are interested in the vehicles used to describe the tenor, your question would be about the tenor or topic and the implications of the selection of the particular vehicles for the rhetor's worldview, the audience's perception of the topic, or the way in which debates or controversies about the topic might play out in the world. If your analysis features the vehicles used by a rhetor to discuss many different tenors or topics, your research question would be about the implications of constructing a world as the rhetor has done for the rhetor, the audience, or a public controversy. Your interest also might be in how a particular metaphoric construction can be countered through an alternative metaphoric frame or the types of actions that are likely to be adopted by someone who adopts a particular metaphor for conceptualizing an issue.

Writing the Essay

After completing the analysis, you are ready to write your essay, which includes five major components: (1) an introduction, in which you discuss the research question, its contribution to rhetorical theory, and its significance; (2) a description of the artifact and its context; (3) a description of the method of criticism—in this case, metaphor analysis; (4) a report of the findings of the analysis, in which you reveal the metaphors, their patterns, and their function in the artifact; and (5) a discussion of the contribution the analysis makes to rhetorical theory.

Sample Essays

The following essays provide samples of criticism in which metaphors are used as units of analysis to answer various research questions. In Benjamin R. Bates's essay on the metaphors used by George Bush in his effort to build a military coalition in the Persian Gulf War, he is guided by the research question, "What strategies can be used to build international coalitions of nations to cooperate effectively on a joint venture such as war?" In his analysis of an essay by Allan Gurganus on his experience as a soldier in Vietnam, Ryan H. Blum asks the research question, "How can marginalized groups express resistance to a hegemonic rhetoric?" Marla Kanengieter-Wildeson's essay analyzing a building by architect Michael Graves focuses on visual metaphors, and her analysis is directed toward answering the research question, "How are ideologies subverted through the use of visual metaphors?" She combines ideological and metaphor criticism to answer this question.

Notes

[1] The terms *tenor* and *vehicle* were suggested by I. A. Richards, *The Philosophy of Rhetoric* (London: Oxford University Press, 1936), p. 96. David Douglass discusses confusion over these terms in "Issues in the Use of I. A. Richards' Tenor-Vehicle Model of Metaphor," *Western Journal of Communication*, 64 (Fall 2000), 405–24.

[2] Zoltán Kövecses, *Metaphor: A Practical Introduction* (New York: Oxford University Press, 2002), p. 4.

[3] The term *associated commonplaces* was suggested by Max Black, *Models and Metaphors: Studies in Language and Philosophy* (Ithaca, NY: Cornell University Press, 1962), p. 40. *Entailments* was suggested by George Lakoff and Mark Johnson, *Metaphors We Live By* (Chicago: University of Chicago Press, 1980), p. 9.

[4] For more on the notion of differences in the operation of metaphor, see Richards, *The Philosophy of Rhetoric*, p. 127.

[5] Aristotle, *Poetics*, 21.

[6] Aristotle, *Rhetoric*, 3.2.

[7] Cicero, *On Oratory and Orators*, 3.41.

[8] Andrew Ortony, "Metaphor: A Multidimensional Problem," in *Metaphor and Thought*, ed. Andrew Ortony (Cambridge: Cambridge University Press, 1979), p. 3.

[9] Aristotle, *Poetics*, 22.

[10] Thomas Hobbes, *Leviathan*, ed. C. B. MacPherson (1651; rpt. New York: Penguin, 1951), pt. 1, ch. 4, p. 102.

[11] Richard Whately, *Elements of Rhetoric* (New York: Harper, 1864), pt. 3, ch. 2.3.

[12] Aristotle, *Poetics*, 22.

[13] Aristotle, *Rhetoric*, 3.34.

[14] Cicero, 3.39.

[15] Black, p. 41.

[16] Suzette Haden Elgin, *How to Disagree Without Being Disagreeable: Getting Your Point Across with the Gentle Art of Verbal Self-Defense* (New York: John Wiley, 1997), p. 79.

[17] Lakoff and Johnson, pp. 4, 7–9.

[18] M. J. Hardman, "Metaphorical Alternatives to Violence—Report from a Workshop," *Women and Language*, 21 (Fall 1998), 43–44.

[19] Lakoff and Johnson, pp. 4, 7–9.

[20] Elgin, p. 78.

[21] Elgin, p. 78.

[22] Jeffrey Feldman, "Frameshop: 'Hunt and Gather,'" January 4, 2006, retrieved January 15, 2006, from http://jeffrey-feldman.typepad.com.

[23] Feldman, p. 2.

[24] Feldman, p. 3.

[25] Steven Perry, "Rhetorical Functions of the Infestation Metaphor in Hitler's Rhetoric," *Central States Speech Journal*, 34 (Winter 1983), p. 230; and Carroll C. Arnold, *Criticism of Oral Rhetoric* (Columbus, OH: Charles E. Merrill, 1974), p. 203.

[26] Perry, p. 230.

[27] Michael Leff, "I. Topical Invention and Metaphoric Interaction," *Southern Speech Communication Journal*, 48 (Spring 1983), 226.

[28] Jeffrey Feldman, *Framing the Debate: Famous Presidential Speeches and How Progressives Can Use Them to Change the Conversation (and Win Elections)*. (Brooklyn, NY: Ig Publishing, 2007), p. 5.

[29] George Lakoff, *Don't Think of an Elephant! Know Your Values and Frame the Debate*. White River Junction, VT: Chelsea Green, 2004), p. 7.

[30] Lakoff, p. 11.

[31] Gloria Anzaldúa, "Foreword to the Second Edition," *This Bridge Called My Back: Writings by Radical Women of Color*, ed. Cherre Moraga and Gloria Anzaldúa, 2nd ed. (New York: Kitchen Table: Women of Color, 1983).

[32] Feldman, *Framing the Debate*, pp. 9–12.

[33] For summaries of the history of the treatment of metaphor, see: Michael M. Osborn, "The Evolution of the Theory of Metaphor in Rhetoric," *Western Speech*, 31 (Spring 1967), 121–32; and Mark Johnson, "Introduction: Metaphor in the Philosophical Tradition," in *Philosophical Perspectives on Metaphor*, ed. Mark Johnson (Minneapolis: University of Minnesota Press, 1981), pp. 3–47.

[34] Lakoff and Johnson.

[35] Kenneth Burke, *A Grammar of Motives* (1945; rpt. Berkeley: University of California Press, 1969), p. 503.

[36] Burke, pp. 503–04.

[37] Michael M. Osborn and Douglas Ehninger, "The Metaphor in Public Address," *Communication Monographs*, 29 (August 1962), 223–34; John Waite Bowers and Michael M. Osborn, "Attitudinal Effects of Selected Types of Concluding Metaphors in Persuasive Speeches," *Communication Monographs*, 33 (June 1966), 147–55; Michael Osborn, "Archetypal Metaphor in Rhetoric: The Light-Dark Family," *Quarterly Journal of Speech*, 53 (April 1967), 115–26; Osborn, "The Evolution of the Theory of Metaphor in Rhetoric"; and Michael Osborn, "The Evolution of the Archetypal Sea in Rhetoric and Poetic," *Quarterly Journal of Speech*, 63 (December 1977), 347–63.

[38] Robert L. Ivie, "The Metaphor of Force in Prowar Discourse: The Case of 1812," *Quarterly Journal of Speech*, 68 (August 1982), 240–53; Robert L. Ivie, "Speaking 'Common Sense' About the Soviet Threat: Reagan's Rhetorical Stance," *Western Journal of Communication*, 48 (Winter 1984), 39–50; Robert L. Ivie, "Literalizing the Metaphor of Soviet Savagery: President Truman's Plain Style," *Southern Communication Journal*, 51 (Winter 1986), 91–105; and Robert L. Ivie, "Metaphor and the Rhetorical Invention of Cold War 'Idealists,'" *Communication Monographs*, 54 (June 1987), 165–82.

[39] These steps in the process of metaphor criticism came largely from Ivie, "Metaphor and the Rhetorical Invention of Cold War 'Idealists,'" pp. 167–68.

Audiences, Metaphors, and the Persian Gulf War

Benjamin R. Bates

For nearly fifty years, the world was simple. In the bipolar system, one was aligned with the United States or with the Soviet Union. With the end of the Cold War, this world was gone. The post-Cold War era became more complex as the world entered a transition stage between a bipolar world and an allegedly unipolar one. Nitze correctly noted that "a time of transition is bound to be a time of uncertainty. Old guideposts are gone or quickly fading and new landmarks need to be sorted out and established" (1990, p. 11).

In this post-Cold War world, the stumbling for a coherent international policy, and some would say the justification for such a policy, made for an unclear course. Then, as if to test the new international waters, Saddam Hussein directed Iraqi troops to invade Kuwait. Although there had been minor skirmishes involving the United States, Iraq's 1990 invasion was the first substantial challenge to America's post-Cold War preponderance (Hippler, 2000). The American response was also seen as the moment of *krisis* in which the United States would functionally declare whether it had unipolar pretensions or would become an active participant in multipolar collective security, a moment with broad implications for American foreign policy (Maynes, 2000; Nitze, 1990). The American response was not a unilateral eviction of Iraqi forces from Kuwait. Instead, an international coalition was assembled, several U.N. resolutions were passed, and then, after attaining U.N. authorization, American-led forces from 28 nations waged air- and land-based war.

The invasion of Kuwait was *not* enough to cause mass international outcry for the "globocop" to return to her beat. The U.S.-led coalition did not represent the deployment of the American behemoth against Saddam Hussein, whilst being cheered by the international crowd (Mermin, 1996). Instead, the American-led coalition was a feat of engineered international elite opinion. The conclusion given by *Foreign Affairs* in the midst of Operation Desert Shield/Desert Storm is apt:

> George Bush did not blunder into war. At each juncture over a six-month period he weighed his options and made his choices. The president had to maintain an unprecedented and fragile coalition, retain domestic support for what might end in war, and bring increasing pressure to bear against an opponent whose very rationality was open to question. ("The road to war," 1990, p. 4)

If Bush did not blunder into the war, then how did he build and maintain the coalition that was necessary to the successful prosecution of the war? Instead of seeing it as blundering or inevitable, analysts should see that the American leadership was constructed as necessary.

To explore the construction of American leadership, I will examine George Bush's diplomatic efforts as rhetorical efforts. I will first outline the importance of Bush's international audience, one composed of opinion leaders from other countries that could enable the military coalition. After indicating some of the constraints that an international audience places on foreign policy rhetoric, I will note the importance of Bush's mass-mediated public speeches as a representative anecdote for the persua-

Benjamin Bates, Audiences, Metaphors, and the Persian Gulf War. *Communication Studies*, 2004, vol. 55(3), pp. 447–463. Permission granted by Taylor & Francis.

sion of this international audience. Using metaphoric cluster analysis, I then will read these speeches. After discussing the use of metaphoric clusters of SAVAGERY and CIVILIZATION in these speeches, I will indicate how the international audience adopted these metaphors in their own language after meeting with the president. Finally, I offer some conclusions about Bush's use of metaphor and its implications for our readings of war rhetoric.

The Importance of Multiple Audiences

To successfully prosecute the Persian Gulf War, the United States needed to build a coalition. Yet, when exploring how this coalition was built, the foreign policy literature has assigned the success to the genius of George Bush's diplomacy and left it there (see Nacos, 1994 for a review). This genius, though, needs to be made palatable to those who would follow the policies proposed. Moreover, there are two audiences that must be considered in the decision to use American force: "the domestic audience on which the authority rests, and the international system that influences the effectiveness of major White House policies" (Rose, 1988, p. 18). Without the support of the American people, the U.S. could not have sustained involvement. Without the support of the international community, the coalition may have never been built, or, having been built, have shattered.

The American public was essential to the Persian Gulf War. Throughout Operation Desert Shield, Bush received about 60 percent approval for his policies and attained over 80 percent approval when Desert Storm began (Bennett & Lepgold, 1994, p. 52). Many communication scholars saw Bush's actions as essential to gaining and maintaining this domestic public approval. Communication scholars have identified a number of strategies that Bush used to persuade the domestic public, including rally-around-the-flag effects (Norrander & Wilcox, 1993), analogic reasoning (Stuckey, 1992), agenda-setting (Iyengar & Simon, 1993), *a fortiori* reasoning (Olson, 1991), military information control (Bennett & Manheim, 1993), media cleansing (Griffin & Lee, 1995), and polarization themes (Hallin & Gitlin, 1993). Although they disagree on how he did it, the communication literature agrees that Bush built a domestic consensus. This consensus, however, does not take into account international constraints. The commitment of nearly thirty nations' soldiers shows that the decision-makers in the Persian Gulf War were not only Americans but also a fragmented and diverse group of international actors.

Taking this international audience seriously does not mean that the arguments that persuade the international audience are hermetically sealed from the arguments that persuade the domestic audience. Indeed, in many cases, there is not a strict line dividing the domestic from the international. Some appeals that might work well with a domestic audience, however, are unlikely to be persuasive to an international audience. For example, appeals to American nationalism, American civil religion, or American exceptionalism may work well for an American audience but are unlikely to persuade British, Omani, or Senegalese audiences. Other appeals, though, may persuade both domestic and international constituencies. Appeals that cross audiences are particularly important in war rhetoric. As Keen (1986) puts it, "the hostile imagination has a certain standard repertoire of images it uses to dehumanize the enemy" that crosses spaces, times, and cultures (p. 13; see also Osborn, 1967). In creating appeals, then, if the president wants to offer an interpretive frame that can persuade domestic *and* international constituencies, he or she should select images that come from this standard repertoire.

These cross- and intercultural appeals, though, have been little studied as rhetoric in the traditional sense of public address. Rhetoric and public address scholars have largely left the question of international persuasion to students of political science or diplomatic history. Because rhetoricians approach these questions with a different set of tools and perspectives than do political scientists or diplomatic historians, rhetoricians may be able to contribute uniquely to the understanding of acts that require the persuasion of auditors outside of U.S. borders or acts that take place on a global stage. In an increasingly interconnected and globalized world, rhetoricians should be more than willing to assist in bearing this burden.

The international audience is not composed of all the people who live outside the borders of a given state. Rather than being the persuasion of the whole *cosmopolis,* international persuasion can be considered the persuasion of opinion leaders that hold power in other states. By opinion leaders, I mean those who have the power to set national agendas: heads of government; policy ministers; economic, media, and military leaders; and the like. A measure of how well opinion leaders are persuaded can be constructed based on whether or not they begin to speak in the same terms as the president. Chilton and Ilyin (1993) and Grundmann, Smith, and Wright (2000) have found that as opinion leaders begin to use similar justifications, there is evidence that they have begun to share national interests and agendas with one another.

In constructing persuasive appeals to international opinion leaders, the president cannot simply speak however he or she wishes. There are four things the president must do to successfully persuade international opinion leaders (see Nye, 2002 for a review). First, the president should identify appropriate international opinion leaders for persuasion. For different issues, different opinion leaders should be contacted. For example, in advocating human rights policies, the president may find that religious and charitable opinion leaders are the most appropriate audience, while for military issues, heads of government and military leaders may need to be consulted. Second, the president should create the appearance of dialogue. That is, while the president may employ public speeches, opportunities for direct response, as in personal diplomacy, should also be available so that the international opinion leader feels that he or she is being consulted about policy, not merely directed. Third, the president must realize that the greatest resource he possesses is *ethos* and, therefore, should strive for transparency and consistency in all messages. Finally, the president should emphasize common values and collective interests in his messages.

George Bush did all four of these things. The Persian Gulf War was framed as a military issue. Bush, therefore, sought to persuade the heads of other states to join the American military coalition. Bush also created the appearance of consultation and dialogue through telephone diplomacy and personal consultations. Telephone calls, personal visits, and shuttle trips by aides were channels of persuasion that advocated the same message: joining the military coalition was in the best interests of whatever head of state to whom Bush was speaking. Finally, as I will indicate below, Bush used these channels to express a consistent motive force that emphasized common values and collective interests. Bush framed the act of joining the coalition and opposing Saddam Hussein through metaphoric clusters; he advocated the coalition as the embodiment of CIVILIZATION standing against Saddam Hussein's SAVAGERY.

Accessing International Persuasion:
Bush's Speeches as Representative Anecdote

Despite the large number of international actors involved and the heterogeneity of their abilities and interests, there were grounds for believing that swift international action would be taken against Iraq. Several nations issued statements condemning the invasion, and the U.N. Security Council approved Resolution 660 overnight. Although Operation Desert Shield began less than a week after the invasion of Kuwait and was conducted under the U.N.'s authority, the initial deployment was largely made up of American troops. Rosegrant (1994) clarifies that, "except for the ever-enthusiastic British and a couple of Arab nations," the U.S. appeared to be acting alone (p. 236). Rosegrant (1994) states that, through "telephone diplomacy" and intense lobbying, other countries eventually provided support. What is missing from Rosegrant's case study, however, is *how* the United States persuaded these states into joining.

Although the best resources for understanding Bush's rhetorical tactics would be to obtain transcripts of his private telephone calls and minutes of his high-level meetings, these resources are unavailable. Given the consistency between the mass-mediated addresses given by Bush and other discourses surrounding the Gulf War, the Bush administration's grand rhetorical strategy becomes clear. Because Bush's public statements are internally consistent, I treat Bush's public speeches as a representative anecdote. Burke (1969) argues that the representative anecdote allows the rhetorician to engage an extensive body of discourse even as she or he reduces that discourse to a smaller set for closer analysis. Burke states that the analyst can use this smaller set to derive a "motivational calculus" that drives the larger discourse. In selecting a set of texts as the representative anecdote, the motivational calculus derived from the smaller set "must be representative of the subject matter" and "must be supple and complex enough to be representative of the subject matter it is designed to calculate. It must have scope. Yet it also must possess simplicity" (Burke, 1969, p. 60).

I choose Bush's mass-mediated addresses for several reasons. As mass-mediated and public statements, these addresses were accessible to both a domestic and an international audience, increasing the scope of the speeches' coverage as a representative anecdote. This selection necessarily leaves out some of his total discourse. Nevertheless, these speeches also gain scope in terms of the time frame they cover. Bush's first speech in this set (Bush, 1990a) was delivered on August 8, 1990, immediately after the Iraqi invasion. The last speech (1991c) was delivered on January 16, 1991, just as Operation Desert Storm began. The eleven speeches chosen here provide an outline of Bush's primary rhetorical tactics. This range also provides the necessary suppleness and complexity. As speeches given at different times, it was possible for Bush to adapt his arguments to the needs of the moment. Additionally, as the actions advocated moved from a defensive military posture to an offensive one, the strategies deployed in each speech could have changed to support changed goals. Despite the opportunity for strategic change, however, the metaphoric cluster analysis performed below indicates that, throughout, Bush retained the same basic rhetorical strategies.

There are also good reasons for assuming a correspondence between Bush's mass-mediated addresses and the more private discourses. The most basic reason to assume a correspondence is that there historically has been such a correspondence (Bose, 1998; Boyle, 1990; Fensch, 2002). Holsti (1989) indicates that this correspondence should be a common trend, as, for effective international relations, individual policy makers must have transparency and consistency in foreign policy. Moderating or reversing one private statement in a public setting can opacify foreign policy making by creating actual or apparent inconsistencies in policy and thus damage international influence. Indeed, the need for consistency between public and private statements is so important that McEvoy-Levy (2001) asserts that the president makes speeches about foreign policy to show that he or she is committed to the "operational code" expressed in the private statements.

The general trend of correspondence is probably also true of Bush's rhetoric and his private meetings. Bush and Brent Scowcroft (1998) and James Baker (1995) have stated that their administration was aware that consistency was necessary to avoid misunderstandings with allies. Bush also asserts that the president uses private meetings with foreign leaders to extend public presidential statements (Bush & Scowcroft, 1998). Given Bush's recognition of the need for a consistent body of statements, his public rhetoric can be read as a self-chosen representative anecdote as well as a representative anecdote chosen by the analyst.

Metaphor as an Analytic Paradigm

Bush's speeches, as a representative anecdote, clearly fall into the category of war rhetoric. In the analysis of war speeches and other discourses that draw on war as an organizing principle (Johnson's war on poverty, Bush's war on drugs, etc.), one of the central concepts for rhetorical analysis has been metaphor. Although metaphor is often thought of as just a figure of speech, it can be central to rhetorical invention. Ivie (1987) puts it well: "elaborating a primary image into a well formed argument produces a motive, or interpretation of reality . . . the form of the argument actualizes and literalizes the potential of the incipient figure" (p. 166). By using the metaphor's comparison of two unlike things, the image of one is replaced with the image of another in the listener's mind. Although words do not change reality through material transmogrification, the way the world *becomes real* to auditors can change when a metaphor is used effectively (Lakoff & Johnson, 1980). When one thing is substituted for another, it can cause the auditor to "view the entailments of the metaphors as being true" even when there is no literal basis for doing so (Lakoff & Johnson, 1980, p. 157). Metaphor is not a simple substitution of one term for another but a way of creating a powerful perceptual link between the two things.

This creation of similarity by substitution becomes particularly powerful in war rhetoric. In war rhetoric, metaphors are often used to reshape public perceptions of the enemy so that there is no alternative to war. Rather than seeing metaphors as illustrative, they become constitutive of reality. The advocacy of war presents, embellishes, and, ultimately, literalizes the metaphor (Ivie, 1982). That is, once the label has been applied, speeches cement the application of the metaphor as an *accurate,* not merely *decorative,* description because the constant deployment of the metaphor's imagery becomes the accepted way of viewing the subject (Ivie, 1985).

Ivie (1987) outlines a five-step model for doing metaphoric analysis. First, the critic should familiarize him or herself with the speaker's text and context. The critic should then select a set of texts as a representative anecdote. After this selection, the critic should closely read the representative anecdote and mark the central vehicles employed by the rhetor. The entailments of the metaphor should then be outlined by looking at the context in which the vehicles occur. Finally, the critic should analyze the vehicles and their entailments for patterns of usage that reveal the speaker's system of metaphoric concepts. Ivie concludes that revealing this system will also determine the possible courses of action that auditors can take after hearing the metaphor and its entailments.

Although Ivie only looks at American perceptions and American metaphoric use, metaphoric analysis can also be used to understand international audiences' reactions. Metaphors, if properly universalized, enact a conceptual model that allows "all sides to find ideological justification for political action" because metaphors provide meaning on a scale beyond personal interpretation (Burrows & Wallace, 1972, p. 250). Core motives, such as SAVAGERY, ORDER, or CHAOS, are likely to transcend ideological interpretation and be accepted as valid by multiple audiences. Such metaphors also activate connotations about the subject of the metaphor across cultures. As such, archetypal metaphors can be inserted into multiple cultural and ideological frameworks while retaining their rhetorical force because they allow individual cultures to translate the denotative vehicle of the metaphor literally while still retaining the idiomatic expression of the original (Chilton & Ilyin, 1993).

Some metaphors clearly meet this test, as Keen's (1986) study of war metaphors in propaganda shows. The terms of war propaganda metaphors (e.g. SAVAGE, RAPIST, or FACELESS HORDE) can be found in almost all cultures' propaganda, and the connotations of literally translated terms remain the same across them. Not all metaphors, though, have this archetypal appeal. For example, Mario Cuomo's "wagon train" metaphor at the 1984 Democratic Convention makes sense in American culture but if translated into Russian, Peruvian, or Congolese cultures, the connotations of a literally translated "wagon train" are unlikely to match up with the original. Therefore, if a rhetorician wants "to speak to audiences beyond his own people," the speaker will use archetypal metaphors for their "persuasive power, their potential for cross-cultural communication, and their time-proofing" (Osborn, 1967, p. 117). In Bush's Persian Gulf addresses, the archetypal metaphoric clusters he activates have the potential to become effective transcultural war rhetoric.

Analysis and Interpretation: The Savage and Civilization Clusters

Two metaphoric clusters dominate Bush's address: the SAVAGE metaphor and the CIVILIZATION metaphor. Ivie (1980) appropriately argues that the analyst should examine war rhetoric for symbolic oppositions; a negative motive force should be assigned to the other and a positive motive force should be assigned to one's self. Although Ivie has discussed SAVAGERY extensively (Ivie, 1980, 1982, 1984, 1985), its counterpart, CIVILIZATION, has been relatively underdiscussed, even in Ivie's own work. The positive motive force is portrayed as the supplement to the negative motive force rather than being seen as an equally important term in the dialectic. In the Persian Gulf War, SAVAGERY is the core motivation to do *something* about Iraq's invasion of Kuwait. The CIVILIZATION metaphor explains how the *particular* action was justified. Although Ivie (and others) provide excellent analyses of the SAVAGE metaphor, they have often neglected the other half of the symbolic opposition. Both sides of the motivational dialectic should be investigated, as they are mutually supportive and provide a more complex understanding of rhetorical action and the advocacy of war. Examining the CIVILIZATION metaphor explains why the U.S.-led action became acceptable in the Gulf War. In addition, the CIVILIZATION cluster may play a role in justifying military action in general.

To create the appearance of Iraq as a threat to all, Bush consistently employed a cluster of terms centered on the SAVAGE metaphor. Ivie (1982) indicates that the SAVAGE creates the perception that an uncontrolled and uncivilized Other is preparing for war. Bush claims that the world, excepting Iraq, has advanced from the primal state, as Saddam's actions are a "dark relic from a dark time" (1990f, p. 1332). Saddam and his troops are portrayed as savages, indeed as sub-humans, throughout Bush's speeches. He calls Saddam's government a "barbaric" (1990d, p. 1239) user of "inhuman aggression" (1990c, p. 1218) that is based in "the rule of the jungle" (1990c, p. 1219) and that aims for "the law of the jungle to supplant the law of nations" (1990f, p. 1333). Iraqis perform the acts of savages. Bush's audiences are told that the Iraqis are not soldiering in Kuwait but that they have engaged in "outrageous and brutal acts of aggression" (1990a, p. 1107): they have "maimed and murdered innocent children" (1991c, p. 43), performed "mass hangings" (1990h, p. 1673), and allowed "babies [to be] pulled from incubators" (1990h, p. 1673). Moreover, they have "raped, pillaged, and plundered" (1991c, p. 43); "ransacked and pillaged" (1990e, p. 1317); and engaged in the "rape of Kuwait" (1991b, p. 12). These are *not* the acts of soldiers but of barbarians. What is more, even if the Iraqi troops are seen as soldiers, they are "genocidal" (1990f, p. 1332) and fight in "blitzkrieg fashion" (1990a, p. 1107), sounding once more "the guns of August" (1990f, p. 1331) for the world. These parallels to the Nazis are further developed so that the leader of the amoral troops becomes central. Saddam is "a tyrant bent on aggression" (1990b, p. 1175), an "aggressive dictator" (1990a, p. 1108), and a "classic bully" (1990h, p. 1673). A failure to oppose him would allow "terrible weapons and terrible despots" (1990f, p. 1332) to fulfill their "power-hungry" (1990g, p. 1669) desires for the "tyranny of dictatorial conquest" (1990h, p. 1673). On top of his tyrannical pursuits, Saddam refuses to see himself as subject to law, another characteristic of the savage. His "aggression and international lawlessness" (1990b, p. 1174) motivate him to "unlawful occupation" (1990e, p. 1318); a "campaign of terror" (1991b, p. 12); and "aggression, terror, and blackmail" (1991a, p. 11). Driven by his "hands of injustice" (1990b, p. 1174) Saddam's "enormous war machine" (1990a, p. 1108) has facilitated his "treachery and aggression" (1990e, p. 1318). The refusal to oppose Saddam's savagery will lead to the "grim nightmare of anarchy" (1990f, p. 1333) where "unprovoked aggression" (1990h, p. 1673; 1990g, p. 1669; 1990f, p. 1331) enables the "invading, bullying, and swallowing whole of a peaceful neighbor" (1990g, p. 1669).

The SAVAGE metaphor, which Ivie claims has been employed throughout American military history, also works well in the Persian Gulf War. If Saddam Hussein could be successfully compared to a savage, then the metaphor can begin to serve a constitutive function. Bush uses a series of what Ivie (1984) calls "decivilizing vehicles," terms that "provide starting points for constructing political realities which soon become self-contained interpretations in the guise of independently verified truths" (p. 42–43). The SAVAGE cluster can be broken down to several decivilizing vehicles; the comparisons to jungle animals, Nazis, machines, and criminals serve to reinforce the idea of SAVAGERY. Stuckey (1992) and Ivie (1996) indicate that the domestic audience accepted these decivilizing vehicles. Because Saddam was cast into the savage mold, his behavior became a threatening force. Further acts of aggression became further proof that the Iraqis were savages, as the metaphor had been transformed from a figure of speech into a (quasi-)accurate description of reality.

If Osborn's (1967) discussion of metaphor is taken seriously, good reasons for why the metaphor succeeded internationally can also be found. If a people views itself as civilized (which nearly all do), then the savage should be seen as a threatening force in a universal sense. Rather than seeing Bush's labeling of the Iraqis as savages as hyperbole, the labeling constructs the Iraqis transculturally. In order for a person not to see Saddam Hussein as a savage, s/he must argue that violations of international law, aggression against a sovereign state, and the murder of children are not the acts of a savage. This interpretation is unlikely. Rather, it becomes easier to substitute the *reality* of Saddam as a savage for the *comparison* of Saddam to a savage. Instead of seeing the invasion of Kuwait as a response to Kuwait's theft from Iraqi oil fields (or any of the other assertions made by Iraq), the action becomes much simpler: a band of savages has invaded Kuwait. If the relatively messy field of international resource scarcity or state-based competition can be avoided by simplified explanations, the international perception that something must be done can be increased. Bush's comparison of the Iraqis to savages was meant to do just this, to provide a reason for the CIVILIZED international community to oppose the Iraqi invasion.

The comparison of the Iraqis to SAVAGES may have required action, but the requirement for action does not necessarily entail *how* the auditor should respond. Given the suspicions surrounding American motivations, an American-led force might not be seen as the best option for retaliation. Moreover, responding militarily to aggression would allow critics to claim that the coalition was as savage as the initial invasion. To respond to both concerns, Bush employed a cluster of terms centered on the CIVILIZATION metaphor. Unlike Saddam Hussein's illegal actions, Bush assures the auditor that the coalition follows "the rule of law" (1990b, p. 1174; 1990c, p. 1219; 1990f, p. 1332; 1991c, p. 44); that as "enshrined in international law" (1990a, p. 1108) a "jury of [Iraq's] peers" (1990f, p. 1332) has applied "standards of justice and fairness" (1990e, p. 1318) and judged Iraq guilty. In order to be "stronger in the pursuit of justice" (1990c, p. 1219), someone must carry out the "will of the world community" (1990e, p. 1318; 1991b, p. 12). It is here that the auditor can see it is *not* an American action but a world action. The coalition would represent a "new partnership of nations united by principle" (1990g, p. 1668): a set of "cooperative measures" (1990a, p. 1108) where "the rest of the civilized world" (1990e, p. 1318) stood "side-by-side" (1990c, p. 1218; 1990h, p. 1673; 1991b, p. 12) in "unity and cooperation" (1990h, p. 1330). This "categorical rejection of aggression" (1990e, p. 1318) was adopted by "an unprecedented coalition" (1991b, p. 12) after "unparalleled international consultation" (1990a, p. 1107). This "consultation, cooperation, and collective action" (1990f, p. 1332) expressed the "international commitment to peace" (1990b, p. 1174) and wanted to make Iraq a "peaceful and cooperative member of the family of nations" (1991c, p. 43). To further distinguish the coalition's CIVILIZATION from Iraq's SAVAGERY, the military action was actually peaceful and just. The action was "wholly defensive" (1990a, p. 1109) and would employ "peaceful means" (1990d, p. 1240; 1991b, p. 13). Coalition troops "will not initiate hostilities, but they will defend themselves" (1990a, p. 1109). As "the world prayed for peace" (1991c, p. 43), any resulting actions would provide a "safer and better world" (1990g, p. 1669) that is "freer from the threat of terror" (1990c, p. 1219) and usher in "a time of peace for all peoples" (1990a, p. 1108). The "security and stability of the Persian Gulf" (1990a, p. 1108; 1990b, p. 1174; 1990c, p. 1219) and "the world's best hope for peace" (1990b, 1174) would come from a "peaceful international order" (1990c, p. 1219; 1990d, p. 1239) that would make the world "more secure in the quest for peace" (1990c, p. 1219). The "atmosphere of peace, rapprochement, cooperation, and optimism"

(1990e, p. 1318) would provide "civilized standards of international conduct" (1990f, p. 1333) and support "civilized values around the world" (1990c, p. 1219). Moreover, the regime of "peace and justice" (1991c, p. 43) would allow a "world wide explosion of freedom" (1990h, p. 1672). This "age of freedom" (1990a, p. 1108) would fulfill the "defense of principle and the dream of a new world order" (1990c, p. 1222).

The CIVILIZATION cluster provides insight into Bush's justification for the American-led coalition and to other states' support for it. Although Ivie (1984) emphasizes decivilizing vehicles, Bush's rhetoric evidences a parallel set of "civilizing vehicles." These civilizing vehicles provide a powerful motive force that gives international opinion leaders a cause to fight for—a positive motive force—to balance the negative motive force of SAVAGERY, the motive force that gives the international opinion leaders something to fight against. These civilizing vehicles provide good reasons for the U.S. to ask other states to join the coalition. Rather than casting the U.S. as a crusading paladin, Bush emphasized collective action. Not only is it collective action, but it is communal, as the comparisons to partnership and family show. Critics of war must answer the claim that the American-led coalition was in response to the will of the world community. Clearly, Bush's claims can be refuted. Any refutation, however, faces formidable obstacles such as the U.N. Security Council vote, the 28-member military coalition, and the international economic sanctions imposed on Iraq.

The presence of a transnational structure guiding the American-led coalition's actions is not enough to guarantee the CIVILIZATION metaphor. Had Bush stopped at stating that the coalition was international and, thus, rightly guided, it would be a metaphor of CONTROL. The U.S. also had to deal with the appealing claim that "two wrongs don't make a right"; that, if it was wrong for Iraq to use military force against Kuwait, it may also be wrong to use force against Iraq. In order to reinforce the claim of CIVILIZATION, the coalition had to be placed squarely into the maintenance of stability and security rather than destructiveness. This may be why Bush framed the action as defensive up to, and including, the deployment of troops into Iraq's territory. Moreover, the U.S. claim incorporates long-term ramifications of joining the coalition as well as short-term ones. The immediate use of force would provide the best chance for a peaceful world order, even if the short-term cost was disruptive. Even in the short term, the actions were needed to avoid the destruction of world civilization. As with the SAVAGE metaphor, these claims appear hyperbolic at first glance. Nonetheless, there is method to these metaphors: if the SAVAGE metaphor shows the extremity of the threat posed by Iraq, then an equally strong force must be raised to oppose it. Thus, it requires CIVILIZATION to erect a defense against Saddam's SAVAGERY.

Speaking the President's Language

Through these antithetical metaphors, a choice is given to members of the international community. Should they side with Saddam, they are not only siding with a savage, but they are also casting themselves out of the community of civilized nations. Should they side with the coalition, these same states are welcomed into the family of nations as civilized peoples and not partners of depraved states like Iraq. By crafting the choice as he did, Bush's rhetoric gives the auditor little room for resistance. Instead, the choice is made for the auditor; the auditor must join the coalition against Iraq in order to maintain his or her position in the civilized world. Because the SAVAGE metaphor alone does not explain acquiescence to American leadership, the CIVILIZATION metaphor is necessary to Bush's rhetoric.

Bush's success in persuading a domestic audience to support intervention in the Persian Gulf is well documented. When it comes to his persuasion of international leaders, however, the proof of Bush's success has been that 28 states contributed to the military coalition. An interpretation that each of these 28 states acted out of its own national interest in a classical realist sense could be constructed. Given that there were varying degrees of national interest (Nitze, 1990); a fear expressed by some coalition members that their participation would support U.S. hegemony (Hippler, 2000; Maynes, 2000); and, in some states with large Muslim populations, attempts by Saddam to disrupt the coalition (Heilman, 1991), these national interests, even if true, may have required presidential persuasion to encourage these states to participate *with* the United States in a military coalition.

Bush and his high-ranking aides have indicated that their private and public statements were largely concordant (Bush & Scowcroft, 1998; Baker, 1995). Other evidence of concordance exists. Kenneth Burke (1969) may be correct that rhetoric should not be thought of "in terms of some one particular address" but rather "as a more general *body of identifications* that owe their convincingness much more to trivial repetition and dull daily reënforcement" (p. 26). If Burke is correct, then the evidence of whether Bush's SAVAGE and CIVILIZATION metaphoric clusters were persuasive should not come from the addresses he makes alone. Instead, examining the statements made by foreign leaders after their meetings with Bush may indicate whether they adopted Bush's tropes to talk about the situation in Iraq. If these leaders also deploy the SAVAGE and CIVILIZATION clusters, then their repetition and reinforcement of the metaphors are proof of the rhetoric's success.

A review of the *Public Papers of the President* indicates that Bush and several foreign leaders met privately to discuss the Persian Gulf situation. Selecting the remarks, question-and-answer sessions, joint statements, and press meetings following these discussions with foreign leaders—the international targets of Bush's persuasion—gives a snapshot of the leaders' reactions. These items indicate that the foreign leaders began to discuss the Persian Gulf situation by using Bush's tropes. That is, they discussed the Iraqi invasion in terms of SAVAGERY and the coalition response in terms of CIVILIZATION.

Bush first met with traditional allies from England and Canada. At a joint press conference, Prime Minister Margaret Thatcher asserted that the U.N. decision to impose sanctions and evict Iraq has "become law in all the countries of the world," indicating that "the world is condemning the [Iraqi] action" ("Remarks," 1990a, p. 1106). Thatcher indicates that "sanctions will be properly and effectively enforced . . . against what we all totally and utterly condemn," the actions that place Iraq outside of the communal "all" and brand it as the intolerable other ("Remarks," 1990a, p. 1106). At the same conference, NATO Secretary General Manfred Woerner agreed that the West needed to "show cohesion, determination, and to make it clear [Saddam's actions] cannot be accepted in this world" ("Remarks," 1990a, p. 1106). Thatcher rearticulated her support at a meeting in France. She stated that she and Bush "see so similarly on most things," particularly the need "to stay firm in defense, because you never know what uncertainties may arise" when dealing with a person like Saddam (Remarks, 1990g, p. 1636). What is certain, however, is that Saddam's actions are "evil. The things that are going on in Kuwait are terrifying. They are brutal. And most people understand that evil has to be stopped" (Remarks, 1990g, p. 1637). Canadian Prime Minister Brian Mulroney agreed with these assessments. Mulroney claimed that Saddam is "a rogue leader who sought to annex another nation and believed he could conduct himself with impunity" (Remarks, 1990b, p. 1167). As such, Mulroney states that Iraq's actions were "an abuse" of the "fundamental privileges of democratic and civilized nations," and Canada's participation in a coalition would be "to make sure that the fundamental rule of international law is respected" (Remarks, 1990b, p. 1168).

Other European actors articulated the metaphoric clusters. Italian Prime Minister and European Community President Giulio Andreotti argued that the United States was acting in accord with all of Europe. Andreotti stated, "the close relationship of the United States of America and the European Community constitutes a point, and has constituted a point, of great strength for the maintenance of stability and peace in the world" (Remarks, 1990e, p. 1592). Andreotti indicated that, if Iraq "were allowed to occupy and to annex a country without any opposition, then this would mean the end of the juridical order system which exists in the world" (Remarks, 1990e, p. 1592). That is, the order of civilization itself, one based on common international law, is threatened by Iraq's actions. Moreover, Andreotti states that the international community's reaction to Iraqi aggression must be forceful and immediate, as "we must have this policy of cooperation and security guide always our steps in the future in our decisions" (Remarks, 1990e, p. 1593).

Similarly, Czech President Vaclav Havel and German Chancellor Helmut Kohl each announced support for the coalition. Havel stated, "Czechoslovakia has made it very clear on a number of occasions that it is necessary to resist evil, that it is necessary to resist aggression" (Question, 1990, p. 1628). Additionally, Havel indicates that he does not support resisting "evil" based on Czech advantage alone but states that "it is my opinion that all the resources that are expended on resisting aggression anywhere in the world finally turned to the good of all humankind," whereas simple aggression only benefits the aggressor (Question, 1990, p. 1628). Likewise, Kohl stated that he and Bush "were in agreement that it is very important, indeed, that the international community stand together here, stand fast in the coalition. And this on the basis of the U.N. resolutions, in the sense that we want to see respect for international law restored" (Remarks, 1990f, p. 1635). By opposing the international community and international law against Saddam's aggression, Kohl supported Bush's descriptions of the Iraqi regime.

The United States also requested the assistance of its former arch-nemesis, the Soviet Union. Instead of asserting that the United States could act alone, Bush met with Soviet President Mikhail Gorbachev. At the end of their meeting, they issued a joint statement. Bush and Gorbachev adopted the SAVAGE/CIVILIZATION dichotomy, stating that we "are united in the belief that Iraq's aggression must not be tolerated. No peaceful international order is possible if larger states can devour their smaller neighbors" (Soviet Union, 1990, p. 1203). The joint statement argued that the desire for peace did not bar civilized nations from countering Iraq's savage aggression. The presidents claimed, "our preference is to resolve this crisis peacefully, and we will be united against Iraq's aggression. . . . [W]e are determined to see this aggression end. . . . We must demonstrate beyond all doubt that aggression cannot and will not pay" (Soviet Union, 1990, p. 1204). When asked to clarify his position on the coalition, Gorbachev indicated that all of the nations in the coalition were also "involved in the participation of the world community in one form or another," declaring that his support was not coerced by the U.S. (Joint, 1990, p. 1212). Gorbachev stated that the members of the coalition believed "it's unacceptable to the United States, it's unacceptable to the Soviet Union, and it would be unacceptable to any other state" to allow Saddam to practice aggressive behaviors and to go unpunished (Joint, 1990, p. 1212). Rather than allowing Iraqi aggression, Gorbachev, like Bush, argues that "the international community working together" can come to "a peaceful solution" that will oust Saddam from Kuwait (Joint, 1990, p. 1212).

Bush also engaged in personal diplomacy with Middle Eastern leaders. They also adopted the SAVAGE and CIVILIZATION metaphors. Turkish President Turgut Ozal stated that "Bush has shown exceptional leadership . . . for the whole community of nations since the outbreak of this crisis," as Bush was "instrumental in the mobilization of a united front against the aggression" (Remarks, 1990c, p. 1286). After further lauding Bush's leadership, Ozal stated that for his "sagacious and determined stand" against Iraqi aggression, Bush "deserve[d] the appreciation of the civilized world all over" (Remarks, 1990c, p. 1286). The Amir of Kuwait, Sheikh Jamir Sabah, also praised Bush's actions as they "are based on the solid foundation of common values and principles" (Remarks, 1990d, p. 1318). The Amir claimed that "the unity of the international community in support of our position against aggression and occupation" reflected a common "determination of all nations and peoples of the world to put an end to armed aggression as any country's foreign policy tool" and to support the values of "peace, rapprochement, cooperation, and optimism" (Remarks, 1990d, p. 1318). Later, the Amir praised "the honorable stance taken by the world community" against Iraq, as it placed the world "on the side of justice and righteousness in an unprecedented manner as to make it a turning point in international relations" (Remarks, 1990h, p. 1661). In particular, the Amir lauds the United States for helping "again to dissipate the dark shadow cast by another dictator on the land of the free" and thus clearing "the darkness" that has befallen Kuwait and responding to "unprecedented inhuman treatment" sponsored by Iraq (Remarks, 1990h, p. 1661).

Hosni Mubarak, the president of Egypt, articulated similar sentiments. He claimed that Iraq's invasion "is a threat to peace and security everywhere and a grave violation of the rule of law. It undermines the very foundation of our modern civilization" (Remarks, 1990i, p. 1676). In response to the threat against civilization, Mubarak states that the coalition will help "to advance the cause of peace and fraternity and all nations, to stand for eradication of injustice and the elimination of war and violence, and to contribute to the construction of a new world order" (Remarks, 1990i, p. 1676).

Following these rounds of diplomacy, Bush outlined the coalition's position. After lining up the ambassadors from the coalition countries outside the White House, Bush remarked:

> What you see here is living proof that the international coalition arrayed against Saddam's aggression remains deep and wide. We're talking now about some 28 countries that have committed their forces of one kind or another to this extraordinary historic effort. Every country represented here agrees that the 12 Security Council resolutions that are now on the books make clear what is required. . . . [I]t is not simply the United States against Iraq; it is really Iraq against the world. (Remarks, 1990j, p. 1801)

By allowing Bush to speak for them and by appearing in solidarity, the ambassadors represent their countries as fully aligned with Bush. The visual display and the concordance expressed by the national leaders indicate that there was a common vocabulary articulated for the Persian Gulf situation. On the one side were Iraq and its savagery. On the other were the coalition and its commitment to the ideals of civilization. The metaphors of SAVAGERY and CIVILIZATION had created a motive force that could be, and apparently was, accepted by an audience of international leaders. Through this agreement and, perhaps, the rhetorical efforts of George Bush, a coalition that could strike against Iraq had been formed.

Implications and Conclusions

The investigation of how an international audience would evaluate the decision to go to war, rather than the traditional focus on the domestic audience, may seem odd. Usually, the only audience that concerns an American president is the domestic one, as far as communication researchers are concerned. This makes sense for many research questions, as polls, elections, and other mechanisms that are used to evaluate political leaders are used on a domestic audience. In the Gulf War, however, the international audience was an additional enabling audience for Bush's plan. If Gurevitch is right that "the Gulf War was 'acted out' on a global stage," then any paradigm that treats the domestic audience as the only concern is sure to miss important constraints and opportunities (1995, p. 447). As Bush's rhetoric evidences, the need to shape opinion on a global scale has already arrived. Bush was able to shape successfully global public opinion, at least as far as international leaders were concerned. The domestic *polis* is only part of the audience. As Bush needed to persuade elite opinion on a global scale, his rhetoric is designed for the global *cosmopolis*.

In arguing that Bush was able to persuade other states to join the coalition, I do not claim that it was solely Bush's rhetoric that made this possible. Material conditions allowed Bush to take advantage of certain exigencies (namely, the invasion of Iraq) for particular audiences (one domestic, the other international). The existence of a material concern, though, does not guarantee action will take place. Instead, the deployment of rhetoric allows a leader to shape the international *perception* of events. In the Persian Gulf War, Bush was able to use metaphors to translate Iraq's actions through decivilizing vehicles so that Saddam Hussein came to be seen as a SAVAGE and to translate the American-led response through a dialectical metaphor that portrayed the coalition as the defender of CIVILIZATION. As archetypal metaphors, SAVAGERY and CIVILIZATION called on motive forces within the audiences to support a particular action. Although the invasion of Kuwait by Iraq was seen as a crisis, the action required to respond to it was unclear. By labeling the Iraqis SAVAGES and encouraging support for international CIVILIZATION, Bush was able to make the coalition appear more feasible to international actors and gain their support.

A related implication is that, having used an international coalition once in the face of the SAVAGE to maintain CIVILIZATION, the U.S. may be expected to do so in the future. Bennett and Lepgold argue that "few countries other than the United States can lead international coalitions successfully, and even for the United States demanding conditions must be met," including soliciting support from allies *while* taking the lead (1994, p. 74). This need to gain international consent explains why Bush needed to (re)create the exigency as the world against Saddam Hussein instead of allowing the situation to be seen as two states opposed to each other (Gurevitch, 1995). The need for international support and "proof" that it was *not* an American program required the U.S. to make the invasion of Kuwait seem more than a border dispute. Instead, by using the SAVAGE metaphor to describe the Iraqis, these troops were transformed from being the world's fourth largest military into the world's largest band of savages. Also, Bush's use of the CIVILIZATION metaphor took pluralism, multipolarity, and integration seriously, as he indicated that the repulsion of Iraq was the will of the international community, not just the U.S. Although he did offer a choice that would enable recalcitrant states to oppose the decision, Bush's rhetoric allowed many divergent views to be captured under the trope of CIVILIZATION. The moment a state's leaders accepted that they were being addressed as responsible members of the world community and as civilized peoples, their decision was made for them. In order to maintain their position in the family of civilized nations, they had to oppose the savagery of the Iraqis.

The acceptance of the SAVAGE and CIVILIZATION metaphors by multiple opinion leaders overseas is not without cost. Having chosen the metaphor of CIVILIZATION and the material enactment of that metaphor through a coalition once, the U.S. may be expected to do so in future international actions. As Rosegrant (1994) indicated, this was one of the most significant concerns that the U.S. faced. The reliance on the coalition may have this effect during the Clinton presidency, as American military actions in Somalia, Rwanda, East Timor, and the Balkans all took place under U.N. approval. Having argued once that civilized states act together to meet the will of the world community, while savage states act alone and outside of it, future actions taken by the U.S. may also be judged by this standard. George W. Bush's most recent war against Iraq did not have the approval of the United Nations. The earlier literalization of unapproved military action as the act of a savage may easily transform him into a savage in the eyes of the international community. Indeed, in a U.N. debate over the second Persian Gulf War, George W. Bush was cast into the role of the savage by several ambassadors. In these debates (Security Council, 2003), the Iraqi ambassador claimed that the war was "a blatant violation of international law and the Charter of the United Nations" (p. 4), the Indonesian representative argued that the war was "the willful action of the powerful" against the weak (p. 8), and the observer for the Arab League stated that Bush was concerned only with "the imposition of absolute power, plans, and schemes" (p. 5). The representatives of several other states argued that the American actions were in violation of international law and that George W. Bush's failure to abide by this law made him little better than Saddam Hussein. This resistance indicates that metaphors in foreign policy do not simply vanish after they have been employed. They become, instead, part of a common understanding in the world community. As such, the deployment of metaphor by the elder Bush is likely to influence readings of international events for some time to come.

The final implication that this study of Bush's rhetoric has is that there are some limits to metaphor. If metaphors are as compelling as some portray them to be, then why did Bush have to use military force when he did? Having constructed an international coalition in support of CIVILIZATION against SAVAGERY, it would seem that he could bide his time. Bush had to act decisively when he did because he could not be sure that the coalition could be sustained long enough for sanctions to work and was aware that a prolonged conflict would have strained the unity of the collation as well (Freedman & Karsh, 1991). The materiality of force, however, does not challenge the understanding of metaphor. Instead, the need to act on the metaphoric construct ensures that the metaphor will hold as a persuasive trope. Although metaphors do carry connotations for redefining reality, the use of a metaphor does not guarantee that it will hold in the long term. Instead, the central rule of metaphor use is simple: "for the metaphor to be maintained, it must be satisfying to the user" (Hastings, 1970, p. 183). The metaphor of SAVAGERY and CIVILIZATION does seem clear enough, but one can only call one's opponent a savage for a certain time. After a while, others will become convinced that s/he cannot be a savage because action to correct their barbarism has not been taken.

The failure to act out the implications of a metaphor is severe—it leads to the collapse of the metaphor. This is why Ford's "war on inflation" failed to serve him well. Although he declared it a "war," his program collapsed because he could not "act politically or guarantee the authenticity of the metaphor which, once invoked, demanded more of him than he was willing or able to give" (Stelzner, 1977, p. 297). The risk of metaphoric collapse may explain why Bush acted when he did. The strain placed on the coalition may have broken it if action was not taken, thus making it impossible for Bush to deliver on the CIVILIZATION metaphor. He would not have been able to present a united world community with an enforceable will had the splits in that community grown too deep. Acting too soon, oddly enough, would have the same effect, as it would disrupt the SAVAGE metaphor. Had the diplomatic option not been given enough time to work out, it would have been easy to see the coalition as just as savage as the Iraqis, thus making it difficult to carry out the political implications of the metaphor. As the two metaphors worked in an antithetical relationship, the failure of either the SAVAGE or CIVILIZATION metaphors would have made international action more constrained. In short, the war occurred when it did not only because it was militarily and politically the most opportune time but also because it allowed a rhetorical coherence to the international actions. The study of other military events, such as revisiting Ivie's case studies, may indicate whether metaphors have similarly shaped military timing in the past.

The use of the SAVAGE and CIVILIZATION metaphors was necessary for the American-led coalition to succeed in Iraq. Yet, their employment also constrained action at the time and may do so in the future. To overcome international constraints and ensure that the action against Iraq would not be seen as an American vendetta, the U.S. could not act alone. By employing the metaphor of SAVAGERY, the U.S. gave the international community a good reason to oppose Iraq. Through the CIVILIZATION metaphor, Bush gave the international community a reasonable means to oppose Iraq. The two worked together in a dialectical relationship to ensure international support for American-led military action. Having made American interests appear subservient to international will, the U.S. may find itself trapped into asking for international support in future actions. The objections made at the U.N. at the onset of the 2003 Persian Gulf War may only be the first rumbles of discontent against a U.S. that does not seek the approval of the international community. Although the support of the international community can add important justifications for action, it does pose a fundamental risk—the world may *not* agree with American actions. The assumption that everyone will always agree with American actions is laughable. Despite the success of Bush's rhetoric in the short term, his metaphoric choices may influence how international opinion leaders view American action in the future. What the long-term impacts of Bush's rhetorical choices will be can only be seen in the coming years.

References

Baker, J.A., III. (1995). *The politics of diplomacy.* New York: G.P. Putnam's Sons.

Bennett, A. & Lepgold, J. (1994). Burden-sharing in the Persian Gulf war. *International Organization, 48,* 39–75.

Bennett, W.L. & Manheim, J.B. (1993). Taking the public by storm: Information, cueing, and the democratic process in the gulf conflict. *Political Communication, 10,* 331–352.

Bose, M. (1998). Words as signals: Drafting Cold War rhetoric in the Eisenhower and Kennedy administrations. *Congress & the Presidency, 25,* 23–41.

Boyle, P.G., ed. (1990). *The Churchill-Eisenhower correspondence, 1953–1955.* Chapel Hill: University of North Carolina Press.

Burke, K. (1969). *Rhetoric of motives.* Berkeley: University of California Press.

Burrows, E.G. & Wallace, M. (1972). The American revolution: The ideology and psychology of national liberation. *Perspectives in American History, 6,* 167–306.

Bush, G.H.W. (1990a, August 8). Address to the nation announcing the deployment of United States armed forces to Saudi Arabia. *Public papers of the Presidents of the United States: George Bush* [hereafter abbreviated as *Public papers].* Washington: USGPO. 1107–1109.

Bush, G.H.W. (1990b, August 29). Radio address to the United States armed forces stationed in the Persian Gulf region. *Public papers.* Washington: USGPO. 1174–1175.

Bush, G.H.W. (1990c, September 11). Address before a joint session of the Congress on the Persian Gulf crisis and the federal budget deficit. *Public papers.* Washington: USGPO. 1218–1222.

Bush, G.H.W. (1990d, September 16). Address to the people of Iraq on the Persian Gulf crisis. *Public papers.* Washington: USGPO. 1239–1240.

Bush, G.H.W. (1990e, September 28). Remarks following discussions with Amir Jabir al-Ahmad al-Jamir al-Sabah of Kuwait. *Public papers.* Washington: USGPO. 1317–1319.

Bush, G.H.W. (1990f, October 1). Address before the 45th session of the United Nations General Assembly in New York, New York. *Public papers.* Washington: USGPO. 1330–1334.

Bush, G.H.W. (1990g, November 22). Remarks to the United States army troops near Dhahran, Saudi Arabia. *Public papers.* Washington: USGPO. 1668–1670.

Bush, G.H.W. (1990h, November 22). Remarks to allied armed forces near Dhahran, Saudi Arabia. *Public papers.* Washington: USGPO. 1671–1674.

Bush, G.H.W. (1991a, January 5). Radio address to the nation on the Persian Gulf crisis. *Public papers.* Washington: USGPO. 10–11.

Bush, G.H.W. (1991b, January 8). Message to allied nations on the Persian Gulf crisis. *Public papers.* Washington: USGPO. 12–13.

Bush, G.H.W. (1991c, January 16). Address to the nation announcing allied military action in the Persian Gulf. *Public papers.* Washington: USGPO. 42–45.

Bush, G.H.W. & Scowcroft, B. (1998). *A world transformed.* New York: Alfred A. Knopf.

Chilton, P. & Ilyin, M. (1993). Metaphor in political discourse: The case of the "common European house." *Discourse & Society, 4,* 7–31.

Fensch, T., ed. (2002). *The Kennedy-Khrushchev letters: Top secret.* New York: New Century.

Freedman, L. & Karsh, E. (1991). How Kuwait was won: Strategy in the Gulf War. *International Security, 16(2),* 5–41.

Griffin, M. & Lee, J. (1995). Picturing the Gulf War: Constructing an image of war in *Time, Newsweek,* and *U.S. News & World Report. Journalism and Mass Communication Quarterly, 72,* 813–825.

Grundmann, R., Smith, D., & Wright, S. (2000). National elites and transnational discourses in the Balkan war. *European Journal of Communication, 15,* 299–320.

Gurevitch, M. (1995). Taken by storm: The media, public opinion, and U.S. foreign policy in the gulf war. *Public Opinion Quarterly, 5.9,* 445–447.

Hallin, D.C. & Gitlin, T. (1993). Agon and ritual: The Gulf War as popular culture and as television drama. *Political Communication, 10,* 411–424.

Hastings, A. (1970). Metaphor in rhetoric. *Western Speech, 34,* 181–194.

Heilman, R.K. (1991). The Middle East and the New World Order: Rethinking U.S. political strategy after the Gulf War. *International Security, 16(2),* 42–75.

Hippler, J. (2000). Foreign policy, the media, and the Western perception of the Middle East. In K. Hafez (Ed.). *Islam and the West in the mass media.* Cresskill: Hampton Press. 67–88.

Holsti, O.R. (1989). Models of international relations and foreign policy. *Diplomatic History, 13,* 15–43.

Ivie, R.L. (1980). Images of savagery in American justifications for war. *Communication Monographs, 47,* 279–294.

Ivie, R.L. (1982). The metaphor of force in prowar discourse: The case of 1812. *Quarterly Journal of Speech, 68,* 240–253.

Ivie, R.L. (1984). Speaking "common sense" about the Soviet threat: Reagan's rhetorical stance. *Western Journal of Speech Communication, 48,* 39–50.

Ivie, R.L. (1985). Literalizing the metaphor of Soviet savagery: President Truman's plain style. *Southern Speech Communication Journal, 51,* 91–105.

Ivie, R.L. (1987). Metaphor and the rhetorical invention of Cold War "idealists." *Communication Monographs, 54,* 165–182.

Ivie, R.L. (1996). Tragic fear and the rhetorical presidency: Combating evil in the Persian Gulf. In M.J. Medhurst (Ed.). *Beyond the rhetorical presidency.* College Station: Texas A & M UP. 153–178.

Iyengar, S. & Simon, A. (1993). News coverage of the Gulf crisis and public opinion: A study of agenda-setting, priming, and framing. *Communication Research, 20,* 365–383.

Joint conference of President Bush and Soviet President Mikhail Gorbachev in Helsinki, Finland. (1990, September 9). *Public papers.* Washington: USGPO. 1204–1213.

Keen, S. (1986). *Faces of the enemy.* San Francisco: Harper & Row.

Lakoff, G. & Johnson, M. (1980). *Metaphors we live by.* Chicago: University of Chicago Press.

Maynes, C.W. (2000). America's fading commitment to the world. In M. Honey & T. Barry (Eds.). *Global focus: U.S. foreign policy at the turn of the millennium.* New York: St. Martin's. pp. 85–106.

McEvoy-Levy, S. (2001). *American exceptionalism and U.S. foreign polity: Public diplomacy at the end of the Cold War.* New York: Palgrave.

Mermin, J. (1996). Conflict in the sphere of consensus? Critical reporting on the Panama invasion and the Gulf War. *Political Communication, 13,* 181–194.

Nacos, B.L. (1994). Presidential leadership during the Persian Gulf conflict. *Presidential Studies Quarterly, 24,* 543–561.

Nitze, P.H. (1990). America: An honest broker. *Foreign Affairs, 69(4),* 1–14.

Norrander, B. & Wilcox, C. (1993). Rallying around the flag and partisan change: The case of the Persian Gulf war. *Political Research Quarterly, 46,* 759–770.

Nye, J.S. (2002). *The paradox of American power: Why the world's only superpower can't go it alone.* New York: Oxford UP.

Olson, K.M. (1991). Constraining open deliberations in times of war: Presidential war justification for Grenada and the Persian Gulf. *Argumentation and Advocacy, 27,* 64–79.

Osborn, M. (1967). Archetypal metaphor in rhetoric: The light-dark family. *Quarterly Journal of Speech, 53,* 115–126.

Question-and-answer section with reporters following discussions with President Vaclav Havel in Prague, Czechoslovakia. (1990, November 17). *Public papers.* Washington: USGPO. 1626–1628.

Remarks and an exchange with reporters following a meeting with Prime Minister Margaret Thatcher of the United Kingdom and Secretary General Manfred Woerner of the North Atlantic Treaty Organization. (1990a, August 6). *Public papers.* Washington: USGPO: 1105–1106.

Remarks and a question-and-answer session with reporters in Kennebunkport, Maine, following a meeting with Prime Minister Brian Mulroney of Canada. (1990b, August 27). *Public papers.* Washington: USGPO. 1166–1172.

Remarks following discussion with President Turgut Ozal of Turkey. (1990c, September 25). *Public papers.* Washington: USGPO. 1285–1287.

Remarks following discussion with Amir Jabir al-Ahmad al-Jabir al-Sabah of Kuwait. (1990d, September 28). *Public papers.* Washington: USGPO. 1317–1319.

Remarks following discussion with Giulio Andreotti, Prime Minister of Italy and President of the European Council. (1990e, November 13). *Public papers.* Washington: USGPO. 1592–1593.

Remarks and a question-and-answer session with reporters following a luncheon with Chancellor Helmut Kohl in Ludwigshafen, Germany. (1990f, November 18). *Public papers.* Washington: USGPO. 1635–1636.

Remarks and an exchange with reporters following a meeting with Prime Minister Margaret Thatcher of the United Kingdom in Paris, France. (1990g, November 19). *Public papers.* Washington: USGPO. 1636–1640.

Remarks and a question-and-answer session with reporters in Jeddah, Saudi Arabia, following a meeting with Amir Jabir al-Ahmad al-Jabir al-Sabah of Kuwait. (1990h, November 21). *Public papers.* Washington: USGPO. 1661–1664.

Remarks and a question-and-answer session with reporters following discussions with President Mohammed Hosni Mubarak in Cairo, Egypt. (1990i, November 23). *Public papers.* Washington: USGPO. 1676–1683.

Remarks and a question-and-answer session with reporters following discussions with Allies on the Persian Gulf crisis. (1990j, December 17). *Public papers.* Washington: USGPO. 1801–1803.

Rose, R. (1988). *The postmodern president.* Chatham: Chatham House.

Rosegrant, S. (1994). *The gulf crisis: Building a coalition for war.* Cambridge: Harvard University, Kennedy School of Government Case Program.

Security Council holds first debate on Iraq since start of military action; Speakers call for halt to aggression, immediate withdrawal. (2003, March 26). United Nations Document Accession Number SC/7705.

Soviet Union-United States joint statement on the Persian Gulf crisis. (1990, September 9). *Public papers.* Washington: USGPO. 1203–1204.

Stelzner, H.G. (1977). Ford's war on inflation: A metaphor that did not cross. *Communication Monographs, 44,* 284–297.

Stuckey, M.E. (1992). Remembering the future: Rhetorical echoes of World War II and Vietnam in George Bush's public speech on the gulf war. *Communication Studies, 43,* 246–256.

The road to war. (1990). *Foreign Affairs, 70*(1), 1–5.

Making the Familiar Foreign
Dissent and Metaphor Surrounding the Iraq War

Ryan H. Blum

In his article "Captive Audience," which appeared in the April 6, 2003, issue of *The New York Times Magazine*, Allan Gurganus links his experiences as a Vietnam veteran with his concern over the conflict in Iraq. In so doing, he makes the case that the portrayal of war is far removed from the brutal reality of active combat and that the role of the wartime soldier irreparably alters the life of a young person. The author's concern for the conflict in Iraq stems from his lost youth, which is attributed to a reluctant participation in the Vietnam conflict.

Gurganus's is a cautionary tale, one that on its face seeks to undermine the communication that has emerged from the popular media and the Bush administration. The success of this piece is found neither in its motives nor intentions. Rather, clues to the strength of the article are found in its stylistic details—those metaphors that move the piece beyond the polemic into the artistic and provide the reader with a corrective to the comforting rhetoric surrounding the U.S. conflict in Iraq. His essay thus offers one strategy to counteract the rhetorical influence of a dominant group. In particular, I explore the question of how marginalized groups express resistance to a hegemonic rhetoric—in this case, a rhetoric that has been strengthened and personalized by the close relationship between the media and a presidential administration.

Metaphoric criticism is a method of rhetorical criticism rooted in the assumption that stylistic details like metaphors are not superfluous. Instead, they are seen as crucial elements in forwarding the rhetorical vision of a rhetor. Although short in length, "Captive Audience" contains a number of effective metaphors that further an introspective sentiment eschewed by the dominant ideology.

Undertaking an exploration of metaphors in a given work can take two forms—an analysis of tenor (the primary subject) or an analysis of vehicle (frame). In the case of Gurganus's essay, readers are offered a wide variety of vehicles, and the relationships between them are not immediately evident. I begin my exploration of Gurganus's metaphors with a sampling of the metaphors based on their tenor.

The first group of metaphors relates to a soldier's inability to articulate an involvement in Vietnam. For instance, readers are offered the colloquial expression for being gay—"coming out"—as a metaphor for admitting that one is a Vietnam veteran. Then there is the pairing of a "lead-lined meat locker" with the unshared memories of combatants. At another point, Gurganus captures the idea of a soldier's inability to make sense of the politics behind the conflict in the metaphorical phrase, "don't speak the local language."

Other metaphors are assigned to the experience of being a soldier and the duties that must be performed in that role: "Heavy lifting" is defined as the work of military personnel, as is the term "killing chores." The metaphor "trapped boys" stands in for the soldiers themselves, while the Vietnam experience is a "Children's Crusade." Similarly, "Dante's 11th circle" is equated with the experience of armed conflict.

This essay was written while Ryan H. Blum was a student in Sonja K. Foss's rhetorical criticism class at the University of Colorado Denver in 2003. Used by permission of the author.

Another tenor is related to the identities of the individuals involved in the war experience, both at home and abroad. For instance, "the old guys" are politicians and generals. In addition, the name "Larry" is used as a metaphor for the average soldier, and "Al" is a metaphor for the father of the average soldier. Linking "Uncle Sam" with the draft board continues this sort of familial metaphor.

As compelling as these metaphorical tenors are, a more insightful glimpse into Gurganus's rhetorical strategy is available through a focus on the associations entailed by the vehicles themselves. I now turn my attention to the vehicles used to explain how Gurganus's article opposes the rhetoric of the Bush administration and mainstream media. In doing so, I focus on the attributes surrounding three primary groupings of metaphorical vehicles: unappealing locations, uncomfortable actions, and seemingly familiar but unknown others.

The first category of vehicles—unappealing locations—contains items like the "lead-lined meat locker," "Dante's 11th circle," and "booths without doors." Even on their faces, each of these imaginary places offers no comfort. There is a palpable sense of pain or vulnerability associated with these phrases that unsettles the placidity of the reader. Moreover, the horror that we are to imagine is undefined; we lack further description or experience to envision the scene. This is the first in a series of depersonalizations that characterize the process by which Gurganus begins to overturn the rhetorical devices of those in power—the familiar, the personal, the comforting—with the frightening unfamiliarity of chaos that constitutes military activity.

The second associative frame consists of actions that are uncomfortable. The vehicles that develop this sentiment are "heavy lifting," "killing chores," negotiating "a learning curve," admitting difference/"coming out," "thawing," muteness/"an inability to speak the local language," and a "crusade of children." Acting in any one of these ways, much less all of them, would be distressing. Such distress acts as a foil to the rhetoric of those in favor of military activity in Iraq. When the United States began its invasion, both the secretary of state and the vice president made comments regarding the effortlessness with which American success would be achieved. The metaphorical associations created by the author dissipate the illusion of comfort provided by the popular media and the Bush administration.

The final vehicular association—seemingly familiar but unknown people—is a grouping of names that employs the guise of familiarity to achieve its ends. The characters provided to the readers, "Al," "Larry," "Uncle Sam," "the old guys," and the "Burger King," seem to profess a degree of acquaintance. Upon reflection, however, these are individuals with whom we never will become intimate. Even though we know their names, Al and Larry are as much of a mystery as those old guys and the Burger King. Unlike the dominant political communication emerging from our leaders and the media, where reporters are "embedded" with units so that we learn the names of grunts, platoon leaders, and generals, the world created by Gurganus sounds familiar while making us feel foreign. Here, a name may be printed upon a uniform, but the person behind it is camouflaged. This disorientation serves to make the reader feel alienated and out of place, creating an opportunity for introspection.

Considering the sentiment generated through these three categories, a more cohesive understanding of the metaphorical terrain is possible. Readers are provided with an unappealing montage of locations, places distant from the comforts assured by the administration. There is also a list of actions that individuals are not likely to enjoy, which moves readers farther from a desired sense of security. Finally, readers are presented with characters who appear familiar but are mysterious and possibly threatening (old, avuncular, and hierarchical). Taken together, readers are placed in the position of being strangers in a strange land.

The disassociation rendered by these metaphors explains how a marginalized rhetor—a war protestor—may overturn the reassuring vision created by a presidential administration and a sympathetic or cooperative media. The communication coming from those in power is decidedly positive, familiar, and comforting. Through his efforts, Gurganus takes readers' assumptions of place, activity, and person and throws them into chaos. Once an audience becomes unsure of these rhetorical elements, doubts about the claims of the dominant group may surface. This promise of resistance can explain how a marginalized group may overcome the close relationship between the media and those in control of political activity.

Captive Audience

Allan Gurganus
The New York Times Magazine
April 6, 2003

From 1966 to 1970, I disappeared from snapshots. I hid, even from my parents' camera. See, I was ashamed, of the uniform. I'd tried for "conscientious objector" in my Carolina county and was laughed out of the office. So, avoiding six years in a federal pen, I spent four in bell-bottoms, floating just off Southeast Asia. Buddies wore their caps cocked, making this assigned life feel more personal. I wore my uniform as a prisoner wears his. Why am I finally "coming out" about all this? I never ever speak of it. The new war drives me. My "service" years I freeze-dried. Till last week, I kept them stashed in the dark rear corner of a lead-lined meat locker. Now they're thawing—fact is, "My name is Allan and I am secretly . . . B-32-37-38." Name, hometown and serial number, that's what Iraqi captors ask of our latest P.O.W.'s. These kids' faces are banged up, squinty. Eyes shocked and awed at gunpoint, they recall me to myself. Such dulled innocence drives me to confess.

If you live long enough, you can become your own parent. I am now that to me, even a granddad. Against the Defense Department, I so long to defend my former grandson self and all these other kids. A graying 55-year-old homeowner can see just how young 18 really is! I served in another such Children's Crusade. I'm qualified to call it a disaster. Even the generals who were in charge back then admit that now. The same guys are helping plan this new one. I was a kid enlisted, against his will, to do the heavy lifting for a nation launched on a mission botched from the start. The entrance imperative: all macho force. The exit strategy? None whatever. Only very young kids would be fool enough to go that far and do as told. Some claim they didn't even mind. I myself remember. And, for me, and for this new crop, I mind. I'm watching.

I know these trapped boys from the inside. Perfect physical specimens, they are cocksure about absolutely everything because they know next to nothing. From a commander's perspective, of course, that's very good. These kids signed up mostly to get some education. Their parents couldn't swing the loans. No college otherwise. All they know of war is from Dolby-deafening action movies. Mainly these kids rage in the fist of the hormonal, the impulsive, the puppy-playful. Girl-crazy, full of stock-car lore and vague dreams of executive glory—great soldier material.

It's spring here, and my jonquils have never been more plentiful and lush, but I walk around as if hooked by black extension cord to CNN, memories de-icing. It comes from my feelings for them. For those idiotic gung-ho kids who really believe they are making up the rules, who consider they are rugged individualists (and therefore take orders beautifully). Many probably never had a plane ride before (it sure was long!), only to sleep all night under a tarp in a sandstorm sitting up against some truck (nobody my age could walk for a week after doing that). And already they write home: "Don't worry about me, Mom. We'll straighten out this mess fast. Just keep my Camaro washed good." I also sent such letters. It is reassuring to reassure. Love becomes a kind of sedative for whatever killing chores you're forced to do tomorrow.

I want to tell you, I have never known a loneliness like it. It's Dante's 11th circle, to be dressed in ugly clothes exactly like 4,000 others, to be called by a number, to be stuck among men who will brag and scrap and fight but never admit to any terror, any need. To sleep in bunks stacked five high, to defecate in booths without doors, you sitting with knees almost meeting the knees of a hunched stranger. To know that you are so much smarter than the jobs assigned, to guess that you are serving in a struggle you can neither approve nor ever understand because the old guys in charge—guys whose sons are safe, golfing at home—they don't speak the local language, either.

During the soldiers' first week, except for blowing sand, it might all seem a lark. Decisions are made by others who give you enough trigger-finger wiggle room so that you can feel a bit expressive, as baby-faced as terrifying. Such volunteers are as intentionally cut off from the effects of their killing as any placated 8-year-old glazed over the lethal thumb work of his Gameboy. These G.I.'s imagine glory, girlfriends waiting at home. The geopolitical picture is as far beyond their reach as the notion that learning a Kurdish dialect just might save their lives.

After my own tour of duty ended, I slouched home and simply sat there for six days, scared to leave my parents' house, too tired to drive a car. "So . . . what are your plans?"—my father saw my state yet chose to treat me with all the tender care of a corporate job interviewer. But Mom must have noticed that the family album featured no photos of me since the draft. So she gathered up my medals, awards for nothing more than my offering my body as another vote against the Cong. Mom assembled these little trophies I was meant to care about. A pretty red-and-yellow ribbon and its bronze coin called the Vietnam Expeditionary. Mom bought a craft-shop shadow box, a nice one too, real wood, and lined with red velvet-like plush for displaying family heirlooms. She arranged my citations under glass, protecting them. But I'd won too few to make a really pleasing pattern. So Mom dipped into my old Boy Scout badges, fleshing out my history with the brass of "God and Country." Then she added my childhood Sunday School pin for perfect attendance. "You see? Impressive." She handed it over. I thanked her and sat staring down at it. Whenever my folks visited, I would get it out and prop it up somewhere until they left. It usually stayed in the attic, where it dwells, I guess, today. In some cardboard box stacked with letters I've really been meaning to answer since '79 or so. But thanks anyway, Mom. Not your fault. Not mine. But whose then?

The latest captured Americans from a downed helicopter squat here on camera, and you see their inexperience in how they're big-eyed scared as kids at their first horror flick. Boys hang their heads with a shame almost sexual. They're blaming themselves for crashing, guilty at how sand can spoil the rotor blades of our most costly chopper. These kids mainly "volunteered," to get ahead. And now, this learning curve. They are prisoners because to start at Burger King, even for a go-getter like Larry here, would get him to only assistant manager in, say, three or four years, and you can't do too darn much on 12 grand a year, can you? These are the ambitious kids, the "good kids," the ones who wanted to make something useful and shapely of their lives.

Now they know that Mom will see them, captured, on "Alive at Five." They know she'll cover her mouth while screaming: "Al, come quick. It's Larry! They got our Larry!"

My parents believed in honor, duty and rendering up firstborns to Uncle Sam. For them Sam was at least as real as Santa. Avuncular, if somewhat overdressed in stripes and gambler's goatee, he tended to look stern and to point right out at you. So when he knocked at our door and said he wanted me, my folks grinned: "He's hiding in the back bedroom, writing essays for the draft board all about peace and Quaker stuff. Though, fact is, he grew up Presbyterian. We'll go get him. Won't take a sec. You comfortable there?"

This week's young captives might just be released. Some will come home, back to their folks' ghetto stoops or trailers or tract houses strung with computer-generated welcomes, personalized, too. Their college years are still ahead of them. So look on the bright side. Bones that young knit fast. And, after a while, even after all the pain and not knowing why they did it, they will get to call this "their" war. And, of course, the medals will be splendid.

Architectural Metaphor as Subversion
The Portland Building

Marla Kanengieter-Wildeson

Susanne Langer described the role and function of architecture as shaping a culture's image by creating a human environment that expresses "characteristic rhythmic patterns within that culture."[1] She explains:

> Such patterns are the alternations of sleep and waking, venture and safety, emotion and calm, austerity and abandon, the tempo and the smoothness or abruptness of life; the simple forms of childhood and the complexities of full moral stature, the sacramental and the capricious moods that mark a social order.[2]

As these rhythmic patterns transform and shift within a specific culture, so do the symbols, icons, and monuments built by its members. Whether its language is the ideal symmetry of Greek *arete* expressed by the builders of the Parthenon or the sterility of Orwell's *1984* raised by the technocrats of steel and glass boxes, architecture relies on a poetic process—a process characterized by the use of metaphor.

In this essay, I will argue that, through the use of metaphor, architectural forms can subvert or reaffirm existing ideologies, and I will demonstrate this process in architect Michael Graves' Portland Building. In 1980, the city of Portland, Oregon, chose Michael Graves' design for its new public service building. Completed in 1982, the building sits on a 200-foot-square block between the City Hall on the east, the County Courthouse on the west, a public transit mall on the north, and a park on the south. Since its construction, the Portland Building remains an enigma in American architecture. Some have called the building's design "offensive rather than open and inviting,"[3] "a joke,"[4] and "dangerous,"[5] while others have proclaimed that it "would be a landmark from inception"[6] and "brings some not-so-old but almost forgotten American traditions to life."[7] That the Portland Building has influenced the landscape of architectural design and caused people to think and talk about their environment is clear.

I suggest that Graves, through his use of metaphor, has molded a carefully articulated statement that reshapes traditional notions about government institutions. His non-discursive message reaffirms the belief that humans play an intrinsic role in civic affairs and concurrently subverts the conventional assumption that efficient governmental bureaucracies are imperious, inelegant, and immutable rather than hospitable and humane.

The first metaphor Graves incorporates in the Portland Building is the metaphor of the building as toy. He associates various dimensions of the building with children's toys and activities, thus extending toy-like images to a building that is supposed to be the epitome of efficiency. For example, many geometric shapes—trapezoidal figures, squares, and rectangles—flippantly decorate the facade, with the shapes fitting together much like a three-dimensional puzzle. The toy metaphor also is characterized by the shape of the building—a truncated jack-in-the-box—flanked on four sides by small, square, blackened windows, evoking images of small building blocks used by children in their play. Approaching the Fifth Avenue entrance, the building reveals

This essay was written while Marla Kanengieter-Wildeson was a student in Sonja K. Foss's rhetorical criticism class at the University of Oregon in 1989. Used by permission of the author.

The Portland Building, Portland, Oregon, 1989. Photograph by Mary Rose Williams.
(Images of the Portland Building also included in the color photo gallery.)

the features of a robotic face, complete with two eyes (two inverted, three-dimensional triangles) staring out in wide-eyed wonder. Across the top of the columns on the sides of the building are bas-relief "ribbons," reminiscent of colorful streamers on May poles. The two-dimensional quality of these ribbons is cartoonish, and, as one reviewer notes, the building "looks as though it just won first prize at the county fair."[8] Thus, these playful accoutrements serve as facetious caricatures of the red tape usually associated with government.

The building's anthropomorphic quality is the second metaphor Graves uses to engage viewers. Richard Sennett underscores the prevalence of the human form in the history of architecture when he argues that in "the course of urban development master images of 'the body' have frequently been used, in transfigured form, to define what a building or an entire city should look like."[9] The building as human is seen in the Portland Building's three-part structure—a structure like that of a human body—legs (the base of the building is weighted in green), torso (the middle section is painted a parchment color), and head (coiffed in a receding tier). The context in which these images occur invites the metaphor of the body politic. By endowing the building with human form, Graves takes the bite out of Portland's political machine. Instead of an austere, looming edifice housing cynical politicians, nameless workers, or, in the words of T. S. Eliot, "hollow men," the Portland Building is shaped into a humane structure—one that reflects the kind of citizens visitors hope work inside. The building's humanlike characteristics celebrate the role of humans, not machines, in civic affairs.

The third metaphor Graves employs is a metaphor of building as romance. The Portland Building embraces a feeling of sensuality rather than utility. Citizens generally assume that a public service building first and foremost is functional. They have been conditioned to think that, in such buildings, walls are gray, furniture is brown, and lighting is fluorescent. Instead of the colorless neutrality of black, gray, and shiny steel dominant in virtually every streamlined slab of the modernist style, however, the Portland Building is dipped in a soft color scheme of pastels—maroon, blue, and green. The colors and the way in which they interact with light suggest the ambience of a Maxwell Parrish painting. By integrating color, form, light, and shadow, Graves erases the mundane and replaces it with a careful mixture of the sublime and the sensuous—with romance.

Although viewers and users of the Portland Building may appreciate it from an aesthetic perspective, my concern as a rhetorical critic is to understand how Graves' metaphors work in generating particular rhetorical responses to the building. The metaphors Graves selected work to encourage a transformation of viewers' usual attitudes toward government because they are rooted in and strongly linked to various positive patterns of experience. Graves references and articulates specific images and experiences that tend to generate positive emotions and to be associated with desirable and valued dimensions of human life (childhood memories, the joy of human contact, and romance). By juxtaposing these with equally strong but negative referents connected with government (bureaucracy, political machinery, sterility, and red tape), Graves gives visitors an opportunity to reconstruct their frame of reference for the offices and processes the building houses. The Portland Building's metaphors create a dialogue with visitors, encouraging them to readjust their perceived order—giving them an opportunity to reconstruct that order in a more positive way. The Portland Building, then, subverts the existing ideology of bureaucracy and invites citizens to revise their perspectives when approaching their city governmental structures—adopting a perspective of optimism, humor, and perhaps even delight.

I suggest that non-discursive metaphors often play a major role in the environment created by architecture; thus, such metaphors deserve the attention of rhetorical critics. Such non-discursive metaphors suggest that buildings are more than aesthetic sites upon which verbal discourse takes place; rather, through the metaphors they suggest, they can become, literally, a ground of ideology and argument, reaffirming conventional perspectives or, as in the case of the Portland Building, inviting viewers to apprehend, experience, and interpret their worlds in new ways.

Notes

[1] Susanne Langer, *Feeling and Form* (New York: Charles Scribner's, 1953) 96.

[2] Langer 96.

[3] Gary Clark, letter, *Oregonian* 4 Mar. 1980: B6.

[4] Robert K. Schroeder, letter, *Oregonian* 16 Mar. 1980: D2.

[5] Wolf von Eckhardt, "A Pied Piper of Hobbit Land," *Time* 23 Aug. 1983: 62.

[6] Steve Jenning, "Architects Favor Temple Design for City Office Building," *Oregonian* 18 Feb. 1980: B1.

[7] Vincent Scully, "Michael Graves' Allusive Architecture," *Michael Graves Building and Projects 1966–1981*, ed. Karen Vogel Wheeler, Peter Arnell, and Ted Bickford (New York: Rizzoli, 1982) 297.

[8] John Pastier, "First Monument of a Loosely Defined Style," *AIA Journal* 72 (May 1983): 236.

[9] Richard Sennett, *Flesh and Stone, the Body and the City in Western Civilization* (New York: W. W. Norton, 1994) 24.

Additional Samples of Metaphoric Criticism

Adams, John Charles. "Linguistic Values and Religious Experience: An Analysis of the Clothing Metaphors in Alexander Richardson's Ramist-Puritan Lectures on Speech." *Quarterly Journal of Speech*, 9 (February 1990), 58–68.

Aden, Roger C. "Back to the Garden: Therapeutic Place Metaphor in *Field of Dreams*." *Southern Communication Journal*, 59 (Summer 1994), 307–17.

Aden, Roger C. "Entrapment and Escape: Inventional Metaphors in Ronald Reagan's Economic Rhetoric." *Southern Communication Journal*, 54 (Summer 1989), 384–400.

Aden, Roger C., and Christina L. Reynolds. "Lost and Found in America: The Function of Place Metaphor in *Sports Illustrated*." *Southern Communication Journal*, 59 (Fall 1993), 1–14.

Akioye, Akin A. "The Rhetorical Construction of Radical Africanism at the United Nations: Metaphoric Cluster as Strategy." *Discourse & Society*, 5 (January 1995), 7–31.

Benoit, William L. "Framing Through Temporal Metaphor: The 'Bridges' of Bob Dole and Bill Clinton in Their 1996 Acceptance Addresses." *Communication Studies*, 52 (Spring 2001), 70–84.

Billig, Michael, and Katie MacMillan. "Metaphor, Idiom and Ideology: The Search for 'No Smoking Guns' Across Time." *Discourse & Society*, 16 (July 2005), 459–80.

Blankenship, Jane. "The Search for the 1972 Democratic Nomination: A Metaphorical Perspective." In *Methods of Rhetorical Criticism: A Twentieth-Century Perspective*, ed. Bernard L. Brock and Robert L. Scott (Detroit: Wayne State University Press, 1980), pp. 321–45.

Brown, Richard Harvey. "Rhetoric and the Science of History: The Debate Between Evolutionism and Empiricism as a Conflict in Metaphors." *Quarterly Journal of Speech*, 72 (May 1986), 148–61.

Brummett, Barry. "The Representative Anecdote as a Burkean Method, Applied to Evangelical Rhetoric." *Southern Speech Communication Journal*, 50 (Fall 1984), 1–23.

Carpenter, Ronald H. "America's Tragic Metaphor: Our Twentieth-Century Combatants as Frontiersmen." *Quarterly Journal of Speech*, 76 (February 1990), 1–22.

Charteris-Black, Jonathan. "Britain as a Container: Immigration Metaphors in the 2005 Election Campaign." *Discourse & Society*, 17 (September 2006), 563–81.

Chiang, Wen-Yu, and Ren-Feng Duann. "Conceptual Metaphors for SARS: 'War' Between Whom?" *Discourse & Society*, 18 (September 2005), 579–602.

Cooper, Brenda, and David Descutner. "Strategic Silences and Transgressive Metaphors in *Out of Africa*: Isak Dinesen's Double-Voiced Rhetoric of Complicity and Subversion." *Southern Communication Journal*, 62 (Summer 1997), 333–43.

Daughton, Suzanne M. "Metaphorical Transcendence: Images of the Holy War in Franklin Roosevelt's First Inaugural." *Quarterly Journal of Speech*, 79 (November 1993), 427–46.

Farrell, Thomas B., and G. Thomas Goodnight. "Accidental Rhetoric: The Root Metaphors of Three Mile Island." *Communication Monographs*, 48 (December 1981), 271–300.

Feldman, Jeffrey. *Framing the Debate: Famous Presidential Speeches and How Progressives Can Use Them to Change the Conversation (and Win Elections)*. Brooklyn, NY: Ig Publishing, 2007.

Ferrari, Federica. "Metaphor at Work in the Analysis of Political Discourse: Investigating a 'Preventive War' Persuasion Strategy." *Discourse & Society*, 18 (September 2007), 603–25.

Fitzgibbon, Jane E., and Matthew W. Seeger. "Audiences and Metaphors of Globalization in the DaimlerChryslerAG Merger." *Communication Studies*, 53 (Spring 2002), 40–55.

Flowerdew, John, and Solomon Leong. "Metaphors in the Discursive Construction of Patriotism: The Case of Hong Kong's Constitutional Reform Debate." *Discourse & Society*, 18 (May 2007), 273–94.

Foss, Sonja K., and Anthony J. Radich. "Metaphors in 'Treasures of Tutankhamen': Implications for Aesthetic Education." *Art Education*, 37 (January 1984), 6–11.

Graves, Michael P. "Functions of Key Metaphors in Early Quaker Sermons, 1671–1700." *Quarterly Journal of Speech*, 69 (November 1983), 364–78.

Gribbin, William. "The Juggernaut Metaphor in American Rhetoric." *Quarterly Journal of Speech*, 59 (October 1973), 297–303.

Ivie, Robert L. "Literalizing the Metaphor of Soviet Savagery: President Truman's Plain Style." *Southern Speech Communication Journal*, 51 (Winter 1986), 91–105.

Ivie, Robert L. "Metaphor and the Rhetorical Invention of Cold War 'Idealists.'" *Communication Monographs*, 54 (June 1987), 165–82.

Ivie, Robert L. "The Metaphor of Force in Prowar Discourse: The Case of 1912." *Quarterly Journal of Speech*, 68 (August 1982), 240–53.

Jamieson, Kathleen Hall. "The Metaphoric Cluster in the Rhetoric of Pope Paul VI and Edmund G. Brown, Jr." *Quarterly Journal of Speech*, 66 (February 1980), 51–72.

Jensen, J. Vernon. "British Voices on the Eve of the American Revolution: Trapped by the Family Metaphor." *Quarterly Journal of Speech*, 63 (February 1977), 43–50.

Kaplan, Stuart Jay. "Visual Metaphors in the Representation of Communication Technology." *Critical Studies in Mass Communication*, 7 (March 1990), 37–47.

Koch, Susan, and Stanley Deetz. "Metaphor Analysis of Social Reality in Organizations." *Journal of Applied Communication Research*, 9 (Spring 1981), 1–15.

Koller, Veronika. "'A Shotgun Wedding': Co-occurrence of War and Marriage Metaphors in Mergers and Acquisitions Discourse." *Metaphor and Symbol*, 17 (2002), 179–203.

Kuusisto, Riikka. "Heroic Tale, Game, and Business Deal? Western Metaphors in Action in Kosovo." *Quarterly Journal of Speech*, 88 (February 2002), 50–68.

Lawrence, Windy Y. "Debilitating Public Deliberation: Ronald Reagan's Use of the Conversation Metaphor." *Southern Communication Journal*, 72 (January–March 2007), 37–54.

Mechling, Elizabeth Walker, and Jay Mechling. "The Jung and the Restless: The Mythopoetic Men's Movement." *Southern Communication Journal*, 59 (Winter 1994), 97–111.

O'Brien, Gerald V. "Indigestible Food, Conquering Hordes, and Waste Materials: Metaphors of Immigrants and the Early Immigration Restriction Debate in the United States." *Metaphor and Symbol*, 18 (2003), 33–47.

Osborn, Michael. "Archetypal Metaphor in Rhetoric: The Light-Dark Family." *Quarterly Journal of Speech*, 53 (April 1967), 115–26.

Osborn, Michael, and John Bakke. "The Melodramas of Memphis: Contending Narratives During the Sanitation Strike of 1968." *Southern Communication Journal*, 63 (Spring 1998), 220–34.

Owen, William Foster. "Thematic Metaphors in Relational Communication: A Conceptual Framework." *Western Journal of Speech Communication*, 49 (Winter 1985), 1–13.

Patthey-Chavez, G. Genevieve, Lindsay Clare, and Madeleine Youmans. "Watery Passion: The Struggle Between Hegemony and Sexual Liberation in Erotic Fiction for Women." *Discourse & Society*, 7 (January 1996), 77–106.

Perry, Stephen. "Rhetorical Functions of the Infestation Metaphor in Hitler's Rhetoric." *Central States Speech Journal*, 34 (Winter 1983), 229–35.

Ritchie, David. "Monastery or Economic Enterprise: Opposing or Complementary Metaphors of Higher Education?" *Metaphor and Symbol*, 17 (2002), 45–55.

Santa Ana, Otto. "'Like an Animal I was Treated': Anti-Immigrant Metaphor in U.S. Public Discourse." *Discourse & Society*, 10 (April 1999), pp. 191–224.

Semino, Elena, and Michela Masci. "Politics is Football: Metaphor in the Discourse of Silvio Berlusconi in Italy." *Discourse & Society*, 7 (April 1996), 243–69.

Smith, Ruth C., and Eric M. Eisenberg. "Conflict at Disneyland: A Root-Metaphor Analysis." *Communication Monographs*, 54 (December 1987), 367–80.

Solomon, Martha. "Covenanted Rights: The Metaphoric Matrix of 'I Have a Dream.'" In *Martin Luther King., Jr., and the Sermonic Power of Public Discourse*, ed. Carolyn Calloway-Thomas and John Louis Lucaites. Tuscaloosa: University of Alabama Press, 1993, pp. 66–84.

Stelzner, Hermann G. "Analysis by Metaphor." *Quarterly Journal of Speech*, 51 (February 1965), 52–61.

Stelzner, Hermann G. "Ford's War on Inflation: A Metaphor that Did Not Cross." *Communication Monographs*, 44 (November 1977), 284–97.

Straehle, Carolyn, Gilbert Weiss, Ruth Wodak, Peter Muntigl, and Maria Sedlak. "Struggle as Metaphor in European Union Discourses on Unemployment." *Discourse & Society*, 10 (January 1999), 67–99.

van Teefelen, Toine. "Racism and Metaphor: The Palestinian-Israeli Conflict in Popular Literature." *Discourse & Society*, 5 (July 1994), 381–405.

Wood, Jennifer K. "Balancing Innocence and Guilt: A Metaphorical Analysis of the US Supreme Court's Rulings on Victim Impact Statements." *Western Journal of Communication*, 69 (April 2005), 129–46.

Narrative Criticism

Alasdair MacIntyre has described the human being as "essentially a story-telling animal."[1] Narratives organize the stimuli of our experience so that we can make sense of the people, places, events, and actions of our lives. They allow us to interpret reality because they help us decide what a particular experience is about and how the various elements of our experience are connected.[2] "By creating stories out of the raw material of our experience," we not only "establish coherence for ourselves" but "create meaningful discursive structures that may be communicated and shared."[3] Narrative, then, constitutes "both a way of knowing about and a way of participating in the social world."[4]

Narratives are found in many different kinds of artifacts. They constitute the basic form of most short stories, novels, graphic novels, comic strips, films, plays, and songs. They also can occur in rhetoric that is less obviously narrative—our dreams, conversations with friends, interviews, speeches, and even visual artifacts such as paintings and quilts.[5] There is also the life story each of us constructs that defines who we are and allows us to see meaning in our lives, which makes even our identity a story.[6]

Although we certainly can identify stories when we hear them, a good starting place for practicing narrative criticism is to clarify what a narrative or a story is. Narratives can be distinguished from other rhetorical forms by four characteristics. A primary defining feature of narrative discourse is that it is comprised of at least two events. These events may be either active (expressing action) or stative (expressing a state or condition). "The mice ran after the farmer's wife" expresses action and thus is an active event, while "the mice were blind" expresses a state or condition and thus is a stative event. "The blind mice ran after the farmer's wife" is not a narrative because it includes only one event—the mice running after the farmer's wife. "The blind mice ran after the farmer's wife, who cut off their tails with a carving knife" is a narrative because it involves two events (in this case, two active events).

A second characteristic of a narrative is that the events in it are organized by time order. A narrative is not simply a series of events arranged randomly—it is at least a sequence of events. The order does not have to be chronological and may involve devices like flashbacks and flashforwards, but at least the narrative tells in some way how the events relate temporally to one another. "The girl swam, the girl ate breakfast, the girl did homework, and the girl went to a movie" lacks a clear temporal order because the order in which these events occurred is not clear. This sentence thus is not a narrative. In contrast, "the girl swam before breakfast, spent the day doing homework, and went to a movie in the evening" is a narrative because the order of events the statement recounts is clear.

A third requirement for a narrative is that it must include some kind of causal or contributing relationship among events in a story. Narratives depict change of some sort, and this third requirement defines the nature of that change by stipulating the relationship between earlier and later events in the story. Sometimes an earlier event in a narrative causes a later event, as when a woman burns a letter that sets off a forest fire. In other narratives, an earlier event cannot be said to have caused a later event, but the earlier event is necessary for the later event to occur. For example, in a story in which a student is trying to gain admission to law school, the student's application is a necessary condition for the later event of rejection, although the application cannot be said to have caused the rejection. Some kind of causal or contributing relationship between early and late events in a story, then, defines a narrative.

A fourth requirement for a narrative is that it must be about a unified subject. "Elvis recorded his first hit record, Benazir Bhutto was assassinated in Pakistan, the soldiers fought the Iraqis near Baghdad, and Jane Austin wrote novels" is not a narrative because it is about disconnected subjects. At a minimum, there must be one unified subject for a narrative—it must be primarily about Elvis or Bhutto, for example.[7]

Symbols other than narratives, of course, help us structure the world in very much the same way that stories do. But stories or narratives do so in a unique way. A narrative is substantially different from a set of instructions, an argument with a claim and evidence, a definition, or a contract, for example. What makes it different is that the narrative creates for both the storyteller and the audience a personal involvement in the narrated world and the act of narrative. We all can remember the experience of being totally engrossed in a story we were reading or that someone was telling us. This involvement is "an internal, even emotional connection individuals feel which binds them to other people as well as to places, things, activities, ideas, memories, and words,"[8] and such a felt connection is more likely to result from narratives than from most other kinds of discourse. Even the choice to tell a story in a communicative situation suggests intimacy, informality, and friendliness,[9] all conditions that facilitate involvement. Three major features of narratives account for the involvement that narratives are likely to generate. The narrated world that is created in a story involves participants because that world is particular, sharable, and personal.[10]

The fact that the narrated world created in a story is *particular* is a key way in which stories are involving. Specific and detailed descriptions and images activate listeners' personal imaginations and remind them of their own past experiences, inviting them to connect their experiences to those of the storyteller: "The storyteller takes what he tells from experience—his own or that reported by others. And he in turn makes it the experience of those who are listening to his tale."[11]

Narratives involve audiences in ways that other forms of discourse do not because they are intersubjectively *sharable*. The narrated world is a shared world because it is a joint achievement by the storyteller and the audience. To experience the narrated world, both the narrator and the audience must recognize the discursive form of the story and understand the story's meaning. The storyteller and the audience, in other words, are sharing moments of experience around both the form and content of the story. This connection "sends a metamessage of rapport between the communicators, who thereby experience that they share communicative conventions and inhabit the same world of discourse."[12]

The *personal* subjective evaluation that occurs when a listener or reader participates in a story is another way in which narrative form generates involvement. Narrative "is always involved in the question of whether an action" is "proper or incorrect,"[13] so the narrator invites the audience members to share the moral evaluation being offered of the narrated world. When audience members enter this world, they have to respond in some way to the evaluation of the world as it is presented by the narrator. As they consider the evaluative judgments of the narrator, they engage their own ethical and moral inclinations, thus providing another means of involvement in the story.[14]

The study of narrative discourse has a long history that dates back to classical Greece and Rome, where both Aristotle and Quintilian wrote about narration.[15] In the communication discipline, the work of Walter R. Fisher has been most influential in developing our understanding of the narrative paradigm.[16] Arthur Bochner and Carolyn Ellis have theorized the use of narrative for studying interpersonal relationships,[17] suggesting that to "have or be in a relationship is to have or be in a story."[18] The performance perspective on communication, in which human beings and cultures are seen as constituting themselves through performances of various kinds, including stories, is another component of the study of narrative. This approach is represented by the work of Victor Turner,[19] Clifford Geertz,[20] Richard Bauman,[21] and Dwight Conquergood.[22] Other contributions to the development of narrative theory and inquiry come from the discipline of folklore, which began with the collection of "narratives, songs, and quaint beliefs" of peoples of other cultures in an effort "to find not only meaning, but art, in everyday activities."[23]

Contributions to the study of narrative have come as well from many disciplines in the social sciences, including anthropology, psychology, and psychiatry. Mary Catherine Bateson's *Peripheral Visions* (1994), Norman K. Denzin's *Interpretive Ethnography* (1997), Donald E. Polkinghorne's *Narrative Knowing and the Human Sciences* (1988), Roy Schafer's *Retelling a Life* (1992), Robert Coles's *The Call of Stories* (1989), and Barbara Czarniawska's *Narrat-*

ing the Organization (1997) are examples of such contributions. Disciplines in the humanities that have contributed to the study of stories include Donald P. Spence and Robert S. Wallerstein's *Narrative Truth and Historical Truth* (1982); David Carr's *Time, Narrative, and History* (1982); and Carolyn Heilbrun's *Writing a Woman's Life* (1988).[24]

Procedures

Using the narrative method of criticism, a critic analyzes an artifact in a four-step process: (1) selecting an artifact; (2) analyzing the artifact; (3) formulating a research question; and (4) writing the essay.

Selecting an Artifact

Any artifact that is a narrative or includes a narrative within it is appropriate for the application of a narrative analysis as long as the artifact meets the four criteria for a narrative. It should contain at least two events and/or states of affairs that are temporally ordered, and the earlier events in the sequence should be necessary conditions for later events. The artifact also should be one where at least one unified subject is present. Possible artifacts include children's books, short stories, novels, films, monologues by comedians, letters, interviews in which individuals tell stories, or speeches. You can use nondiscursive artifacts for narrative analysis, but be aware that they may require more creativity in your application of the narrative method than discursive texts do.

Analyzing the Artifact

The basic procedure for conducting narrative criticism involves two primary steps: (1) identifying the objective of the narrative; and (2) identifying the features of the narrative to discover how they accomplish the objective. The first step involves identifying the work the narrative appears designed to perform in the world, and the second involves analyzing the strategies selected to accomplish the objective. Some critics may choose to do a third step as well: (3) assessing or evaluating the narrative according to the particular objective.

Identifying the Objective of the Narrative

Your first step in a narrative analysis is to identify the objective of the narrative or the action the story appears designed to perform in the world. This is your best guess of what situation or condition the story is addressing. As a story goes out into the world, it performs an action of some kind, it produces outcomes or consequences, or it does a certain kind of rhetorical work: "People tell stories in order to *do* certain things," to attain "interactional aims."[25] Your aim in this step is to identify what you believe this aim or objective is.

You can determine the objective of a narrative by a number of things. If you can trust that the storyteller isn't trying to deceive you and, in fact, does know her purpose for telling a particular story, you can choose to rely on the storyteller's statement of what the objective is. Because such reports are often nonexistent or unreliable, however, you probably want to focus on the objective from the audience's perspective. You are likely to be able to gain some idea of what the objective of a story is by the context in which the narrative is told. A funeral, for example, is a context that suggests that a particular kind of story will be told, in contrast to a political campaign, which requires different kinds of stories because of the particular situation. Who the storyteller is and who the audience is also will provide you with clues to the objective. If the storyteller is a minister or a comedian, for example, those roles could give you very specific and accurate information about the aims of many of the stories they tell. If the audience is made up of children, professors, or medical professionals, you also might be able to narrow the objectives of the stories that are likely to be told to each type of audience respectively. The story itself also will give you clues as to the action or intervention it seems designed to accomplish in the world. The nature of the narrated world that is developed, including the settings, the characters, and other features, will provide you with clues as to the action the narrative is supposed to be performing. If the story contains a lot of humor, swear words, and raunchy characters, for example, those are clues that this story has a different objective from one characterized by biblical characters, respectful and serious language, and inspirational themes.

Use all of the resources available to you, then, to identify an objective, function, or action you believe the story aims to perform in the world. When you use the resources available to you to name the objective of a narrative, you are not naming *the* objective the story is performing but *an* objective. The objective is your best guess of how the narrative is functioning in the world. Multiple interpretations are possible of what the objective is, but you are attempting to name one that you can support from your investigation of the story and its context.

While certainly not complete, the following list includes some objectives that commonly characterize stories:

- To help the storyteller or the audience function more effectively in the present
- To encourage action
- To defend or justify an act
- To legitimize an act
- To adjust to an event or condition
- To repair or restore order
- To heal from loss or disappointment
- To comfort or bring relief
- To teach, instruct, or offer lessons
- To convey truths and values about a culture
- To socialize into a community
- To inculcate obedience
- To challenge perceptions of a situation
- To clarify thinking or to make sense of something

- To gain self-knowledge
- To redeem or renew
- To construct identity
- To entertain
- To maintain or create community
- To counter received or conventional knowledge
- To honor, memorialize, or commemorate
- To manage or resolve conflict

Identifying the Features of the Narrative

After you have identified a major objective of the narrative you are analyzing, your next task is to determine the features of the story that contribute to the achievement of that objective. Identify the strategies being used in the narrative that support that objective. A storyteller makes choices about how to shape a story, so here your focus is on the key choices made by the storyteller that contribute to the story's objective. The following questions allow you to explore the primary features of the narrative to see how the objective is supported and implemented. For each of these elements, see if there is a link between how the element is developed and the objective you identified for the narrative.

Setting.   What is the setting or scene in the narrative? Is there a change in setting over the course of the narrative? How does the setting relate to the plot and characters? How is the particular setting created? Is the setting textually prominent—highly developed and detailed—or negligible?[26]

Characters.   Who are the main characters in the narrative? Are some of the characters nonhuman or inanimate phenomena, described as thinking and speaking beings? What are the physical and mental traits of the characters? In what actions do the characters engage? Do the traits or actions of the characters change over the course of the narrative?

How are the characters presented? Are they flat or round? A flat character has one or just a few dominating traits, making the behavior of the character highly predictable. Round characters, in contrast, possess a variety of traits, some of them conflicting or even contradictory. Their behavior is less predictable than that of flat characters because they are likely to change and to continue to reveal previously unknown traits.[27]

Narrator.   Is the narrative presented directly to the audience, or is it mediated by a narrator? In direct presentation of the narrative, the audience directly witnesses the action, and the voice speaking of events, characters, and setting is hidden from the audience. In a narrative mediated by a narrator, the audience is told about events and characters by a narrator whose presence is more or less audible. If a narrator is audible, what in the narrative creates a sense of the narrator's presence? What makes the narrator intrusive or not?

What kind of person is the narrator? A narrator who apologizes, defends, and pleads is different from one who evaluates, criticizes, and preaches. What kind of vocabulary does the narrator use? Does the narrator favor certain types of words, sentence structures, metaphors, or types of arguments? Is the narrator wordy and verbose or straightforward and direct? Does the narrator adequately connect the various elements of the narrative to one another to create a cogent and meaningful narrative? What is the narrator's attitude toward the story being told, the subject matter of the story, the audience, and him- or herself?

If the narrative is being presented orally, what characterizes the narrator's pitch, pauses, tone of voice, gestures, emphasis, pronunciation, and other features of speech? Style also may be visual in narratives that are predominantly or exclusively visual, accomplished through such elements as types of shots in video or film, motions in dance, or styles of painting.

What kinds of powers are available to the narrator? What kind of authority does the narrator claim?[28] What is the point of view adopted by the narrator? Point of view is the perceptual and psychological point of view in the presentation of the narrative. Is the narrator omniscient, knowing the outcome of every event and the nature of every character and setting? Does the narrator tell the story from a god-like vantage point? Is the narrator omnipresent—able to skip from one locale to another in the narrative? Is the narrator allowed to range into the past or future or restricted to the contemporary story moment? Does the narrator engage in time and space summarizing, a process in which vast panoramas and large groups of people are seen from the narrator's exalted position? Does the narrator go beyond describing to engage in commentary such as interpretation and evaluation? Does the narrator engage in metanarrative discourse—discourse in which the narrative itself is discussed and elements in the narrative are commented on explicitly—such as definitions of terms or translations of foreign words? How does the narrator report characters' discourse? Does the narrator use direct forms of representation, in which the exact words of the characters are reported? Does the narrator use indirect forms, in which the characters' speech and thought are paraphrased, suggesting more intervention by the narrator?

How reliable is the narrator? In unreliable narration, the narrator's account is at odds with the audience's inferences and judgments about the story. The audience concludes that the events and characters depicted by the narrator could not have been as the narrator describes them. If the story is unreliable, what seems to be the cause of the narrator's unreliability—gullibility, innocence, or a desire to mislead?[29]

Events.   What are the major and minor events—plotlines, happenings, or changes of state—in the narrative? Major events in a story are called *kernels*. These are events that suggest critical points in the narrative and that force movement in particular directions. They cannot be left out of a narrative without destroying its coherence and meaning. Minor plot events, called *satellites*, are the development or working out of the choices made at the kernels. Their function is to fill out, elaborate, and complete the kernels. Satellites are not crucial to the narrative and can be deleted without disturbing the basic story line of the narrative, although their omission would affect the form of the narrative and the form's rhetorical effects.[30]

How are the events presented? Are they characterized by particular qualities? How fully are the kernels developed by satellites? How do the satellites affect the nature of the kernels? Are the events active (expressing action) or stative (expressing a state or condition)?[31]

Temporal Relations.   What are the temporal relationships among the events recounted in the narrative? Do events occur in a brief period of time or over many years? What is the relationship between the natural order of the events as they occurred and the order of their presentation in the telling of the narrative? Does the narrator use flashbacks and flashforwards, common devices to reorder events as they are narrated?[32] How is the story that is told located in time with respect to the act of narrating it? Is the telling of the story subsequent to what it tells—a predictive or prophetic form? Is the telling in present tense, simultaneous or interspersed with the action depicted? Is the narration in the past tense, coming after the events recounted?[33]

What is the speed of the narrative? Speed is the relationship between the length of time the events in the narrative go on and the length of the narrative. Are particular events and characters narrated with higher speed than others? Does use of speed emphasize some events and characters over others?[34]

Causal Relations.   What cause-and-effect relationships are established in the narrative? How are connections made between causes and effects? Is cause presented prior to effect or after it? How clearly and strongly are the connections between cause and effect made? Which receives the most emphasis—the cause or the effect? What kinds of causes are dominant in the narration? Are events caused largely by human action, accident, or forces of nature? In how much detail are the causes and effects described?

Audience.   Who is the person or people to whom the narrative is addressed? Is it addressed to an individual, a group, or the narrator him- or herself? Is the audience a participant in the events recounted? What are the signs of the audience in the narrative? What can be inferred about the audience's attitudes, knowledge, or situation from the narrative? Is the audience represented in a detailed or sketchy manner? What seems to be the narrator's evaluation of the audience's knowledge, personality, and abilities?[35]

Theme.   What is the major theme of the narrative? A theme is a general idea illustrated by the narrative. It is what a narrative means or is about and points to the significance and meaning of the action. Themes are ideas such as "good triumphs over evil," "everyone can succeed with hard work," "kindness is a virtue," and "violence is sometimes justified." How is the theme articulated in the narrative? How obvious and clear is the theme?[36]

Type of Narrative.   What type of story is the narrative? There are many forms stories can assume, but four conventional forms identified by Northrop Frye in *Anatomy of Criticism* are comedy, romance, tragedy, and irony.[37] In a comedy (which is not always humorous, by the way), the protagonist challenges an established authority and wins happiness and stability in the end. In a romance (which does not always involve love), the protagonist completes a quest against an enemy and emerges victorious and enlightened. A tragedy is a narrative form in which a protagonist tries to achieve a goal but falls short because of an inability to overcome flaws or faults. In a narrative of irony, the protagonist is trapped and lacks agency and control over the situation, which is one of chaos, confusion, and sadness. Comedy and romance are optimistic in tone, while tragedy and irony are pessimistic.

Let's assume that you are analyzing a narrative where you have established that its primary objective is to challenge an audience's support for a war. You would want to go through all of the dimensions of a narrative to check to see which ones seem to be the most influential in accomplishing that objective. You might discover, for example, that a graphic, bloody setting and characters who are ordinary citizens who endure the brunt of the consequences of war are the major dimensions that accomplish this objective. You would focus on these dimensions and downplay those elements that appear to have little link to the objective when you write up the analysis.

Assessing the Narrative

You may stop your narrative analysis with the first two steps—identifying the objective and discovering how the strategies enable the objective to be accomplished. You also may choose to complete a third step, which is evaluation. Evaluation of the narrative you have analyzed can be done in one of two ways: (1) Scrutiny of the objective itself to determine whether it is an appropriate one; and/or (2) Assessment of the strategies used in the narrative to see whether they accomplish the objective and allow the narrative to work in the world in the way in which the objective suggests.

In the first kind of evaluation, you reflect on the legitimacy or soundness of the objective given what you know about the rhetorical situation in which it took place—the context, the storyteller, the audience, and the like. Perhaps you argue that the particular objective a narrative performed was not appropriate for the occasion and thus did not effectively address what was going on. A narrative that has as its objective providing comfort to the friends and family of someone who has been murdered may not be an appropriate objective if the audience is focused on revenge. You also could argue, of course, that the objective of providing comfort is a legitimate one if the objective of the narrative the audience members want to tell—securing revenge—seems like it would damage them or the community.

In the second option for evaluation, you compare the features of the story to the objective the story is designed to perform to see how well the features and the objective align. You want to evaluate whether the narrative actually performs the objective you believe it is designed to accomplish—whether the particular choices made by the rhetor in creating the story accomplish the objective for telling it. The criteria to use in assessing this alignment derive from the objective of the story, so the criteria will be different for each narrative analysis. A few examples will clarify the kinds of criteria you might use in assessing alignment between an objective and narrative strategies. Notice how the criteria differ substantially according to the objective identified for the narrative.

Let's assume that a narrative is aimed at conveying truths or values about a culture. Using this objective as your criterion for judgment, your focus would be on the elements of the narrative that serve as an index to the values embedded in the narrative. You would be interested in discovering whether the narrative captures truths or values that are representative of the culture and whether it presents those truths and values as appealing so that audiences will want to support and maintain them.

Perhaps you have a narrative designed to encourage an audience to adopt a particular view of a situation. Your criterion for assessment in this situation might be the persuasibility of the story. In this kind of analysis, your attention would focus on the aspects of the narrative that make it compelling. You also might find that the coherence of the narrative is relevant to a story's capacity to persuade—whether the narrative hangs together, has internal consistency, or has adequate connections within it.[38]

If you are analyzing a story that is working to allow a rhetor to defend or justify action, you might be interested in whether the narrative demonstrates fidelity. Fidelity is the truth quality of the narrative—whether it represents accurate assertions about reality or rings true with what you know to be true. Fidelity as a standard for the evaluation of narrative can be problematic because frequent disagreement occurs among audience members in determining what corresponds to actual reality and is "true."[39] A view of fidelity as correspondence to the facts of the real world might better be replaced, then, with correspondence to facts within the community or the context in which the narrative is told.[40] Thus, your interest could be in whether the objective of defense is developed believably in the story—whether its narrated world corresponds to facts in the community in which the story is being told.

If the narrative is supposed to help an audience adjust to an event or condition, you would be interested in whether the narrative provides useful ideas for adjusting—whether it provides strategies that might work in the lives of the audience members. Using this criterion, the focus in your analysis would be on whether those aspects of the narrative that constitute ways of adjusting to a situation—such as the death of a loved one, loss of a job, or the theft of a prized possession—actually would provide "equipment for living"[41] for adjusting to loss.

Formulating a Research Question

As a result of identifying the objective of the story, the features of the narrative selected to achieve that objective, and perhaps assessing whether or not the objective and the narrative features align, you can develop the research question for your essay. You might choose to focus on just one of these three steps in your question if one of them stands out for you as the most significant and compelling aspect of the narrative. Your research question might be about the objective of the narrative, the nature of strategies that accomplish particular objectives, or the appropriateness of a narrative objective.

Writing the Essay

After completing the analysis, you are ready to write your essay, which includes five major components: (1) an introduction, in which you discuss the research question, its contribution to rhetorical theory, and its significance; (2) a description of the artifact and its context; (3) a description of the method of criticism—in this case, narrative criticism; (4) a report of the findings of the analysis, in which you reveal one or more items of interest— the objective of the narrative, the key features used to accomplish the objective, and/or alignment between the objective and the features; and (5) a discussion of the contribution the analysis makes to rhetorical theory.

Sample Essays

In the following samples of narrative criticism, narratives are used to answer a variety of research questions. In his essay, Aaron Hess answers the questions, "What functions do narrative histories as presented in video games perform for players?" and "How are those functions accomplished?" In their essay, Thomas A. Hollihan and Patricia Riley focus on the themes of the narratives they analyze as they ask the research questions, "How do therapeutic narratives accomplish their objectives?" and "What are the impacts of these narratives on their audiences?" Laura S. More, Randi Boyd, Julie Bradley, and Erin Harris analyze an essay by Leslie Marmon Silko to answer the question, "What narrative elements encourage an audience to perceive a culture different from their own in a positive light?"

Notes

[1] Alasdair MacIntyre, *After Virtue: A Study in Moral Theory* (1981; rpt. Notre Dame, IN: Notre Dame University Press, 1984), p. 216.

[2] W. Lance Bennett, "Storytelling in Criminal Trials: A Model of Social Judgment," *Quarterly Journal of Speech*, 64 (February 1978), 1–22; and Catherine Kohler Riessman, *Narrative Analysis* (Newbury Park, CA: Sage, 1993), pp. 1–4.

[3] Danièle M. Klapproth, *Narrative as Social Practice: Anglo-Western and Australian Aboriginal Oral Traditions* (New York: Mouton de Gruyter, 2004), p. 3.

[4] Arthur P. Bochner, Carolyn Ellis, and Lisa M. Tillmann-Healy, "Relationships as Stories," in *Handbook of Personal Relationships: Theory, Research and Interventions*, 2nd ed., ed. Steve Duck (New York: John Wiley, 1997), p. 308.

[5] Some theorists distinguish among various kinds of communication and see narrative as functioning differently in each, but I am not making such distinctions. See, for example, John Louis Lucaites and Celeste Michelle Condit, "Re-constructing Narrative Theory: A Functional Perspective," *Journal of Communication*, 35 (Autumn 1985), 90–108; and Thomas B. Farrell, "Narrative in Natural Discourse: On Conversation and Rhetoric," *Journal of Communication*, 35 (Autumn 1985), 109–27.

[6] Dan P. McAdams, *The Stories We Live By: Personal Myths and the Making of the Self* (New York: Guilford, 1993), pp. 6–7. Also see Dan P. McAdams, *The Redemptive Self: Stories Americans Live By* (New York: Oxford University Press, 2006).

[7] This is the definition of narrative proposed by Noël Carroll, "On the Narrative Connection," in *New Perspectives on Narrative Perspective*, ed. Willie van Peer and Seymour Chatman (Albany: State University of New York Press, 2001), pp. 22–34. For other definitions on narrative, see Klapproth, *Narrative as Social Practice*, pp. 89–105.

[8] Deborah Tannen, *Talking Voices: Repetition, Dialogue, and Imagery in Conversational Discourse* (New York: Cambridge University Press, 1989), p. 12.

[9] Klapproth, *Narrative as Social Practice*, p. 119.

[10] Klapproth, *Narrative as Social Practice*, pp. 116–27; Tannen, *Talking Voices*, pp. 9–35.

[11] Walter Benjamin, *Illuminations*, ed. Hannah Arendt, trans. Harry Zohn (New York: Shocken, 1968), p. 87.

[12] Tannen, *Talking Voices*, p. 13.

13 Charlotte Linde, *Life Stories: The Creation of Coherence* (New York: Oxford University Press, 1993), p. 121.

14 Klapproth, *Narrative as Social Practice*, p. 127.

15 For a good summary of Aristotle's and Quintilian's discussions of narrative, see Lucaites and Condit, "Re-constructing Narrative Theory."

16 Walter R. Fisher, *Human Communication as Narration: Toward a Philosophy of Reason, Value, and Action* (Columbia: University of South Carolina Press, 1987). For responses to Fisher, see: Barbara Warnick, "The Narrative Paradigm: Another Story," *Quarterly Journal of Speech*, 73 (May 1987), 172–82; Robert C. Rowland, "Narrative: Mode of Discourse or Paradigm?" *Communication Monographs*, 54 (September 1987), 264–75; and Michael Calvin McGee and John S. Nelson, "Narrative Reason in Public Argument," *Journal of Communication*, 35 (Autumn 1985), 139–55.

17 See, for example, Arthur P. Bochner and Carolyn Ellis, "Personal Narrative as a Social Approach to Interpersonal Communication," *Communication Theory*, 2 (May 1992), 165–72; and Bochner and Ellis, "Relationships."

18 Bochner and Ellis, "Relationships," p. 310.

19 See, for example, Victor W. Turner and Edward M. Bruner, eds., *The Anthropology of Performance* (Urbana: University of Illinois Press, 1986).

20 See, for example, Clifford Geertz, *The Interpretation of Cultures* (New York: Basic, 1973).

21 See, for example, Richard Bauman, *Verbal Art as Performance* (Long Grove, IL: Waveland, 1977).

22 See, for example, Dwight Conquergood, "Between Experience and Meaning: Performance as a Paradigm for Meaningful Action," in *Renewal and Revision: The Future of Interpretation*, ed. Ted Colson (Denton, TX: Omega, 1986), pp. 26–59.

23 Kathleen Glenister Roberts, "Texturing the Narrative Paradigm: Folklore and Communication," *Communication Quarterly*, 52 (Spring 2004), 132, 134.

24 D. Jean Clandinin and F. Michael Connelly, *Narrative Inquiry: Experience and Story in Qualitative Research* (San Francisco: Jossey-Bass, 2000), pp. 4–17.

25 Klapproth, *Narrative as Social Practice*, p. 102.

26 For more on setting, see Seymour Chatman, *Story and Discourse: Narrative Structure in Fiction and Film* (Ithaca, NY: Cornell University Press, 1978), pp. 101–07, 138–45; Robert Liddell, *A Treatise on the Novel* (London: Jonathan Cape, 1947), pp. 110–28; and Gerald Prince, *Narratology: The Form and Functioning of Narrative* (New York: Mouton, 1982), pp. 73–74.

27 For more on characters, see Chatman, *Story and Discourse*, pp. 119–38, 198–209; Prince, *Narratology*, pp. 13–16, 47–48, 71–73; and Gérard Genette, *Narrative Discourse: An Essay in Method*, trans. Jane E. Lewin (Ithaca, NY: Cornell University Press, 1980), pp. 169–85.

28 Susan Sniader Lanser suggests that a narrator's authority arises from three features: status, a function of the narrator's credibility, sincerity, and storytelling skill; contact, the pattern of the narrator's relationship with the audience; and stance, the narrator's relationship to the story being told. Susan Sniader Lanser, *The Narrative Act: Point of View in Prose Fiction* (Princeton, NJ: Princeton University Press, 1981), pp. 85–94.

29 For more on the narrator, see Chatman, *Story and Discourse*, pp. 146–262; Prince, *Narratology*, pp. 7–16, 33–47, 50–54, 115–28; Genette, *Narrative Discourse*, pp. 185–211; and Bauman, *Verbal Art*, pp. 61–79.

30 For more on kernel and satellite events, see Chatman, *Story and Discourse*, pp. 53, 54; and Prince, *Narratology*, pp. 83–92.

31 Active and stative events are discussed by Prince, *Narratology*, pp. 62–63.

32 For more on temporal relations, see Prince, *Narratology*, pp. 48–50, 64–65; and Seymour Chatman, "What Novels Can Do That Films Can't (and Vice Versa)," in *On Narrative*, ed. W. J. T. Mitchell (Chicago: University of Chicago Press, 1980), p. 118.

33 For more on the relationship between story time and narrating time, see Paul Ricoeur, "Narrative Time," in *On Narrative*, ed. W. J. T. Mitchell (Chicago: University of Chicago Press, 1980), pp. 165–86; Chatman, *Story and Discourse*, pp. 63–84; and Genette, *Narrative Discourse*, pp. 33–160, 215–27. Genette distinguishes among three categories of relations: order (the order in which the events of the story are presented), duration (the relation of the time it takes to read out the narrative to the time the story-events themselves lasted), and frequency (number of representations of story moments).

34 For more on speed of the narrative, see Prince, *Narratology*, pp. 54–59.

[35] For more on the audience, see Prince, *Narratology*, pp. 16–26; and Genette, *Narrative Discourse*, pp. 259–60.

[36] For more on theme, see Prince, *Narratology*, p. 74.

[37] Northrop Frye, *Anatomy of Criticism* (Princeton, NJ: Princeton University Press, 1957).

[38] Fisher, *Human Communication*, p. 88.

[39] Herbert Halpert, "Definition and Variation in Folk Legend," in *American Folk Legend: A Symposium*, ed. Wayland D. Hand (Berkeley: University of California Press, 1971), p. 51.

[40] This view of fidelity was suggested by: Richard Bauman, *Story, Performance, and Event: Contextual Studies of Oral Narrative* (New York: Cambridge University Press, 1986), p. 12; William F. Lewis, "Telling America's Story: Narrative Form and the Reagan Presidency," *Quarterly Journal of Speech*, 73 (August 1987), 288–89; and Farrell, "Narrative in Natural Discourse," pp. 122, 123.

[41] Kenneth Burke, *The Philosophy of Literary Form: Studies in Symbolic Action* (1941; rpt. Berkeley: University of California Press, 1973), pp. 293–304.

"You Don't Play, You Volunteer"
Narrative Public Memory Construction in
Medal of Honor: Rising Sun

Aaron Hess

In 2003, video gamers across the country relived World War II, this time in their living rooms. Through the simulated environment of *Medal of Honor: Rising Sun*, gamers were treated to a historical tale produced by Electronic Arts (EA). Noted for its popularity and realism (Kobrin, 2004), *Medal of Honor: Rising Sun* offers the tale of Joseph Griffin, the player character through whom gamers fight in the jungles of Guadalcanal, on the streets of Singapore, and upon Japanese aircraft carriers. The memory of World War II, however, is tainted with a selective retelling of the events that not only glamorizes the war but constructs an Orientalist image of the Japanese Empire, as narrative and ludologic analyses of the game will show. While other war video games arguably glamorize war, such as *Aces of the Pacific* or *Axis & Allies*, *Medal of Honor: Rising Sun* combines violence with history, providing gamers with a seemingly educational and realist portrayal of the era. Its first-person perspective provides gamers with direct contact with its narrative and immerses players into its historical narrative.

Medal of Honor: Rising Sun ends with this message: "[O]ur deepest appreciation to the Veterans of World War II. Only due to your relentless courage and sacrifice does our freedom stand strong today. Thank you."

While such memorializing language might be expected to be inscribed in granite blocks at Pearl Harbor or in Washington, DC, unsuspecting gamers may be surprised by this patriotic dedication, unusually placed at the end. Biesecker (2002) argues that commemorative history about World War II circulates through both popular film and official memorials. Specifically, she argues that "popular cultural representations of the 'Good War' . . . constitute one of the primary means through which a renewed sense of national belonging is persuasively being packaged and delivered to U.S. audiences" (p. 394). War films such as *Saving Private Ryan* have created a public culture organized around the notion of the "good citizen." The artifacts "promote social cohesion by rhetorically inducing differently positioned audiences . . . to disregard rather than actively seek to dismantle the inequitable power relations that continue to structure collective life in the United States" (p. 394).

Another prominent place for the reception of meanings and memory regarding World War II is in digital gaming. Computer-mediated environments, such as multiple user dungeons, chat rooms, and especially gaming, have reached increasing complexity and realism. Through digital gaming, historical events become interactive simulations that constitute a participatory public memorial. *Medal of Honor: Rising Sun* players participate in a pseudo-fictive epic of the bombing of Pearl Harbor, raids on Guadalcanal, and the destruction of the Japanese Empire. Through multiple spliced narratives, including footage from the era, personal letters from home, and interviews with veterans, the video game offers a complex and interactive representation of the events in the Pacific theater.

Aaron Hess, "You Don't Play, You Volunteer": Narrative Public Memory Construction in *Medal of Honor: Rising Sun*. Permission granted by Taylor & Francis.

Public Memory

Public memory operates as a means of remembering the past and politicking the future. As a society, "our collectivity is deeply intertwined with our capacity for and enactment of remembrance" (Phillips, 2004, p. 1). Cultural knowledge of history has a public sense, where official and vernacular recountings collide (Hauser, 1999). Policy directions are derived from popular expression concerning recent or historical events, and the use of public memory assists in this process. While control over historical events may seem distant from policy making, determination of a historical past profoundly affects the grand histories and narratives of present culture (Bodnar, 1992). These cultural foundations guide experiences into present and future deliberations. Indeed, collective and legal "slivers of memory are constantly recirculating in our legal and public spheres, inviting us to engage in ritualized practices that bring either celebration or condemnation of particular historical decisions" (Hasian & Carlson, 2000, p. 42). Many kinds of public memory monuments have been analyzed, both official (Foss, 1986) and vernacular (Carlson & Hocking, 1988; Jorgensen-Earp & Lanzilotti, 1998). The changing environments, locations, and experiences of memory through digital outlets have yet to be studied in depth. I argue that the use of narrative memorializing in interactive space creates an experience of public memory, giving video game players an active but private (in the home) role in memory making.

As Cohen and Willis's (2004) analysis of National Public Radio's Sonic Memorial shows, digital media environments provide empowering spaces and "broad possibilities for listeners, as audience members, to participate in the construction and dissemination of aural histories" (p. 593). Foot, Warnick, and Schneider (2005) compared the construction of digital and offline memorials of 9/11 to understand the differences in form between individually and officially produced memorials. New issues of interactive potentiality call forth questions of vernacular production in cyberspace, intertextuality, and the personalization of public tragedy. Web memorials blur distinctions between vernacular and institutional commemoration practices; personal grief emulates public memorial, and official memory enacts vernacular speech. Similarly, Hoskins (2003) recognizes that technological advancements and the "electronification" of collective memory have created an environment that "involves a 'presentist' lens being used to view, interpret and record (and rerecord) events of the moment in the round-the-clock (and round-the-globe) watch of the news networks" (p. 8). Memory has become instantaneously accessible as it is created on new media, including television and the World Wide Web. Crogan (2003) argues that Microsoft's *Combat Flight Simulator 2: WW II Pacific Theater* and other war games embody "the classic task given to historical discourse—the prevention of history repeating itself" (p. 296). In a similar vein, Atkins (2003) argues that the game *Close Combat* is located "in this 'space between' what is fact and what is fiction, and brings the question of what 'realism' might mean within historical game-fictions to the fore" (p. 88).

The use of digital interactive media, then, highlights an exceptional location of public memory, whereby the creation of memory via a public artifact is experienced in private spaces. Users are invited to take part in history from their living rooms, replicating the museum, from a video game console. New questions of digital memory should be asked: What happens to *public* memory when it is experienced away from public spaces and in *private* homes? How do uses of digital memory draw from traditional uses of memory? What medium-specific strategies do users of digital technologies employ?

Constructions of public memory, whether digital or traditional, narrate history through commemoration. In constructing these narratives, both individually and officially produced memorials selectively draw upon interpretations of past events. "This value attached to narrativity in the representation of real events arises out of a desire to have real events display the coherence, integrity, fullness, and closure of an image of life that is and can only be imaginary" (White, 1987, p. 24). Consequently, scholars who investigate historical narration pay attention to the ideological function of historicizing and memorializing; they question claims of "truth" in official stories. Indeed, White (1987) asks: "Could we ever narrativize without moralizing?" (p. 25). Given historical narration's impossible task of accurately recreating past events, historical narratives are investigated for their strategic details and omissions—which may influence future policy making. Bodnar (1992) discusses the differences between vernacular memory and official memory: "[T]he shaping of the past worthy of public commemoration in the present is contested and involves a struggle for supremacy between advocates of various political ideas and sentiments" (p. 13). In either case, recollections of the past serve the interests of various opposing groups as history is written and rewritten.

White (1999) regards new genres of postmodern parahistorical representation as blurring the distinction between real and the imaginary. Examining pseudo-historical texts that resemble fact, such as Oliver Stone's *JFK,* White notes that these texts are authored as fiction, yet the public may receive them as historical fact. "What is at issue here is not the facts of the matter regarding such events but the different possible meanings that such facts can be construed as bearing" (p. 70). Such pseudo-historical documents challenge scholars to address how the construction of public memory in fictional historicized forms affects the vernacular sense-making of grand historical events.

Discussing World War II films, Biesecker (2002) argues that *Saving Private Ryan* articulates a sense of nostalgia and patriotism:

> In exposing us to countless trembling, perspiring, gagging, punctured, drowning and bleeding bodies, bodies with missing arms, legs, eyes, and faces before informing us of their individual histories, Spielberg's Omaha Beach scene effectively promotes our patriotic identification with *all* of them while blocking our subjective identification with any *one* of them. (p. 396)

The graphic detail creates viewers' affective response to the film in the way White (1999) articulates by providing an emotionally charged yet seemingly factual tale of World War II. "Through its narrative frame, *Saving Private Ryan* rhetorically expresses, justifies, and induces nostalgia for a national *future* in which each individual's debt to the republic may be paid in minor acts of 'privatize[d] patriotism'" (Biesecker, 2002, p. 398). Extending Biesecker's (2002) argument into war video games, through which players not only see the images of history but also play them out, I highlight how interactive memory in the private sphere entices players to begin their "privatized patriotism."

Medal of Honor: Rising Sun (hereafter *Rising Sun*) is situated within the genres of adventure/war and first-person shooter games. The war gaming genre includes a vast array of games, many of which utilize historical details such as *Brothers in Arms* or the *Call of Duty* series. Many are based on fiction, such as *Gears of War* or *Resistance: Fall of Man. Rising Sun,* released in 2003, was listed second in the top fifteen best-selling games for that year ("Best-Selling Video Games," 2003). Electronic Arts' (EA) wide success with its *Medal of Honor* series, including *Medal of Honor: Allied Assault, Medal of*

Honor: Frontline, Medal of Honor: Pacific Assault, and others, has been specifically attributed to the realism of its gameplay (Dy, 2002). In 2003, the game earned $60 million in sales, "more than many movies take in at the box office" (Snider, 2004, p. 1D).[1]

The game follows U.S. marine Joseph Griffin, the player-character, as he completes eight missions, in part motivated by his brother's missing-in-action (MIA) status. The first mission follows the bombing of Pearl Harbor: the player must escape from a ship while shooting down Japanese fighter pilots and bombers. Subsequent missions take Griffin through jungles, riverboats, and enemy aircraft carriers as he searches for his MIA brother and fights the Japanese Empire. Outside of gameplay are the "unlockable" special features, rewards for successful completion of missions, and bonus objectives. These include newsreel footage from the era covering the progression of the war, interviews with Allied veterans and weapons experts, and (fictional) sentimental letters from Griffin's sister back home that track what was going on in the United States during the war.

Modern war games, especially the *Medal of Honor* series, have won critical acclaim for their historical accuracy and realism. At its release, *Rising Sun* was "making a name for itself with its realistic storylines, intense battles and unique History Channel-style atmosphere" (Kobrin, 2004). Noted for its realism and historical accuracy, the series marks a movement in game development toward historically based games with educational overtones. "Medal of Honor took a more cerebral approach, with a cinema-quality musical score, attention to historic detail and a 'Saving Private Ryan' vibe that made the game feel like a movie" (Hartlaub, 2003, p. D2). *PC Magazine* commended its "realistic environments on land and sea" (Harsany & Sarrel, 2003, p. 190). Even *Military History* stated that reviewing the game's historical information with one's children enables parents "to teach them that Pearl Harbor is more than a Ben Affleck movie" (Dy, 2004, p. 90). This treatment of the game as an educational tool gives credence to its acceptance by the public as a documentary of public history and memory regarding the events of World War II, especially Pearl Harbor. In an unusual move, "to ensure that the game is as authentic as possible," EA hired Captain Dale Dye, who assisted the development team as a military technical adviser (Polak, 2003, p. T26). Dye, describing his involvement with EA, called the *Medal of Honor* series "a long-overdue salute to the men and women who freed the world from tyranny and oppression" (Snider, 2002, p. 4D). This use of military advisers underscores the development of the game as a historically accurate memorial rather than a pastime activity.

Ludology

Game studies, or ludology,[2] offers "an analysis of computer games and game cultures as critical locations for understanding the role of digital technologies in mediating and constituting the social interaction and organization of subjects in late modern information societies" (Simon, 2006, p. 66). Scholars have approached games with an array of theories, including critical and literary theories (Bogost, 2006), social interactionism (Ondrejka, 2006), and ethnography (Boellstorff, 2006; Taylor, 2006). Communication scholars often focus on violent aspects of video games and their effects on users (Jansz, 2005; Lachlan, Smith, & Tamborini, 2004). Stahl (2006) argues that the war game genre has created "virtual citizen soldiers" (p. 125) who have become increasingly detached from critical deliberation about the causes of war.

Drawing from prominent theorists in the growing field of ludology, I take an interdisciplinary approach to *Medal of Honor.* Ludology has complicated the scholarship on video games, especially in terms of narratology. Aarseth (2004) argues that simply applying literary notions of narratology to video game research is to commit "theoretical colonialism" (p. 54). In other words, video games must be recognized as more than just narratives and are deserving of a nuanced theory of ludology. Other ludologists emphasize the difference between video games and previous media. Juul (2001) warns video game scholars not to ignore the effect of interactivity: "The non-determined state of the story/game world and the active state of the player when playing a game has huge implications for how we perceive games." Acknowledging Aarseth's and Juul's concerns, I combine narrative and ludologic rhetorical criticism, examining the construction of meaning and gameplay in *Rising Sun.*

Narrative and Ludologic Criticism

I will provide a standard narrative analysis of the game, including its structure, themes, and characters. Narrative criticism has been a valuable tool for scholars seeking to make arguments about "the users of the stories and the state of culture that is revealed in their understanding of symbols" (Sillars & Gronbeck, 2001, p. 212). However, to recognize distinct features of this particular narrative, I consider specific elements that are unique to video games, including immersion in the game and the first-person perspective within its interactive space. Specifically, I examine the spaces where the character-player becomes involved with the narrative and historical plotline of the game. The development of the character of Joe Griffin through the first-person perspective and as a figure of history sets up a space where gamers experience history through the enactment of events filtered through an ideological lens. Finally, following Brookey and Westerfelhaus's (2002) arguments regarding the blurred distinction between primary and secondary texts in new media works, I consider gameplay as the primary text, including the historical newsreels and first-person (Griffin's) narrative. The secondary features are the aforementioned interviews and "Letters from Home." To grasp the full narrative experience, I analyze the intratextual negotiation between primary and secondary narrative structures.

To augment my narrative analysis, I have selected two concepts from ludology, immersion and the first-person shooter perspective, which are fitting given the interactivity of the game in a historical environment. Immersion refers to the "experience of being transported to an elaborately simulated place" or "digital swimming" (Murray, 1997, pp. 98–99). While immersed in the text, the player interacts with its limits, borders, and environment. Advances in technology have created digital destinations with detailed surroundings with movable objects and interactive lighting. "The more persuasive the sensory representation of the digital space, the more we feel that we are present in the virtual world and the wider range of actions we will seek to perform there" (Murray, 1997, p. 125). Of particular importance to the examination of immersion in *Rising Sun* is the ability of the game not only to create an environment of war but to recreate an "authentic" historically driven space to support its parahistorical and "History Channel-style atmosphere" (Kobrin, 2004). The use of the first-person shooter perspective and control create the sense of immersion into a war environment.

Structure and Theme

Rising Sun has two large stories: a meta-narrative and a personal narrative. First, the meta-narrative sets up the larger scope of the personal narrative and its interaction with history. By incorporating newsreels with World War II footage and interviews from veterans who give their account of the events of World War II, the gameplay gains a sense of authenticity and historical accuracy (Dy, 2004). Each story frames the experience of the gameplay at a particular historical location for players. However, as I will show below, the stories are selectively narrated and only offer a perspective of nationalistic pride, omitting details of American war aggression and atrocity.

Different newsreel footage that is played for gamers after they successfully complete each of the eight levels in the game provides a documentary-style backdrop for the gameplay. At the end of each level, gamers view a closing narrative scene that breaks from the first-person shooter gameplay to a third-person perspective of the character. Immediately after this brief sequence, gamers are taken from the personal narrative to a global newsreel narrative that includes clips of the Japanese bombing of Pearl Harbor, Allied prisoners of war being held in camps, or American bombing missions against Japanese aircraft carriers. These black-and-white news clips, replete with historical figures including President Roosevelt and General Douglas MacArthur, construct a surrounding narrative for players as they complete parallel missions from history.

The intersection between the gameplay narrative and the historical narrative is underscored through mission objectives. For example, one meta-narrative for the "In Search of Yamashita's Gold" level details Japan's use of rail to transport "plunder" from Southeast Asia. Railways, built by slave labor from prisoners of war and local populations, transported gold from the defeated nations back to Japan. As the Allies gained control of many of the rail systems, the Japanese, and specifically General Yamashita, hid the gold in various locations across the South Pacific. After watching the documentary, players go on a mission to rescue both the gold and the slave laborers. Thus gamers enact a type of personal historical retribution. Gamers can help end slave-labor working conditions and capture the fortune stolen by a tyrannical government.

After successfully completing levels, gamers watch extra footage in the form of interviews with U.S. war veterans, specifically recorded for *Rising Sun*. The veterans discuss the labor camps, bombing missions, and weaponry. As they speak, newsreel images of the war play in the background, seemingly coupled with the interview. For example, for the "Pearl Harbor" level, United States Marine Don Jensen recalls witnessing the first few planes as they arrived on the horizon. He says when he recognized the "red meatball" on the side of the planes, he knew that the attack was serious. His story depicts scenes of carnage, destruction, and horror. Images in the background abound with bodies burned from the spilled oil, planes being shot down in mid-air, and the wreckages of carriers, thus supporting his speech. While the newsreel footage effectively conjures images of the time from official history, the use of Allied veterans also conjures the vernacular memory of "ordinary people (Bodnar, 1992). These "ordinary soldiers," utilizing a vernacular perspective on the war, narrate the official version of American involvement; the game's images and newsreel footage support their stories. As veterans recall their fellow soldier "buddies," gamers are offered the same set of friends who assist throughout the game. When veterans describe scenes of POW camps being liberated, gamers also experience the "saving" of captured troops.

In this way, the game becomes a type of digital museum allowing visiting gamers to select the items they wish to learn about. Katriel (1994) argues that museums "serve as cultural sites for the articulation of this very basic tension of history and memory jostling for cultural position" (p. 16). She adds that docents perform narratives about tangible museum artifacts to instill biased perspectives in visitors. Similarly, *Rising Sun* uses individual memories to augment newsreel and documentary accounts of World War II. While tangible artifacts are not available through the game, the replication of World War II weaponry is a parallel tactic. For example, the use of the Browning automatic rifle (BAR) becomes a tangible experience narrated by the veteran "docent" Roy Roush. Roush describes the importance of the rifle for U.S. soldiers in the Pacific while holding the weapon on his lap: "The Japanese feared this weapon more than anything else. Even more so than the machine gun. . . . A BAR man could be anywhere. I'm awfully glad I had it . . . I might not have survived if I had not had this." While he speaks, spliced newsreel images of Marines appear and gamers see the rifle in action. Switching from the narrative to the ludological perspective of these artifacts, players use the weapon in battles against the Japanese forces, feeling its weight and vibration through the controller. The combination of docent-like "object narratives" (Katriel, 1994, p. 12) and personal use of artifacts transplants museum visitors into the digitally constructed field.

While newsreel footage and veteran stories construct the meta-narrative, gamers are provided with the personal narrative of the lead character, Griffin, who is taken through a series of missions in the Pacific region. While the overarching plotline is the fight against the Japanese, Griffin's personal story is also told. After the strike on Pearl Harbor, Griffin's brother Donnie is missing in action; later he is believed to have been caught by Japanese forces. Through bits of computer-animated cinema, offered as introductions or conclusions to levels, gamers track the progress of the overall war and the search for Griffin's brother.[3] Griffin's story is also highlighted through bonus material, in the form of "Letters from Home," awarded to the player for certain kinds of success. These letters, written and spoken in the voice of Griffin's sister Mary, highlight not only the loss of Donnie but also citizens' wartime activities. Mary discusses "current" events on the domestic front, coupled with a combination of computer-animated newspaper clippings and photographs. These events, ranging from Roosevelt's "Day of Infamy" speech to women working in factories to the rationing of rubber and other supplies, geographically situate gamers on the front lines, far away from the events of the homeland. The personal letters reinforce a vernacular reading of history (Hauser, 1999). Their vision of the average citizen's life is selectively constructed to omit details of the war that may damage the image of the United States (Japanese internment camps, the effects of rationing on the poor, discrimination against African-American women in the workplace, etc.). Instead, Mary's stories reinforce the Greatest Generation's commitment to national pride, patriotism, national security, and national sacrifice.

The two intertwined stories construct themes of family pride and nationalistic courage. The historical narrative situates America as a victim of a deadly surprise attack. The personal narrative of Griffin's brother serves as an allegory of national victimhood and retribution. By the story's close, Donnie has not been found, leaving a scar on the central character forever, analogous to the mark left at Pearl Harbor. These themes, drawn from both stories within the game, create a sense of national duty and commitment.

Looking beyond the primary storylines to the secondary "Letters from Home," the thematic landscape expands. As Mary describes the scenes from home, another sense of duty to the country appears. Tales of women working in factories coupled with images of Rosie the Riveter, war bond rallies, and limits on personal gasoline use portray civilian dedication to the war effort. That is, in times of war, collective duty equals collective sacrifice; whether on the front lines or at home, national pride should dictate the actions of the individual.

An analysis of structure and theme shows that the narrative in *Rising Sun* valorizes individual action in the name of nationalism. Kammen (1991) argues that "public memory, which contains a slowly shifting configuration of traditions, is ideologically important because it shapes a nation's ethos and sense of identity" (p. 13). The selective use of memory in *Rising Sun* underscores the ideological construction of its narrative details. Stories of death by American hands and the use of nuclear weapons are omitted, giving gamers a sense of pride without problems. Biesecker (2002) claims that Tom Brokaw's book *The Greatest Generation* "engineers a singular version of the 'then' in order to induce its readers to disavow their own primary and political passionate attachments 'now'" (p. 400). Similarly, *Rising Sun* utilizes an interpretation of the past with clear-cut duties and a call for action, which gamers enact through the central character, Griffin.[4] After the console or computer is turned off, gamers may carry the sentiment of appropriate national response into subsequent thinking about international conflicts. Options are limited in the game; the lone response for gamers is violent aggression and the killing of Japanese soldiers. Thus, while the game's version of the war underscores a sense of American victimization, the deadly response to Pearl Harbor is left in the hands of gamers, who seek to destroy each enemy character in the game. Gamers become the embodiment of a nationalistic response that deflects responsibility for the violence away from the game programmers and toward a larger sense of historical obligation.

Character

Rising Sun sets up a clear dichotomy between self and other. Video games, in classic form, often distinguish between the good and bad, usually for the sake of clarity for the player. In *Rising Sun,* the implication of this split is the ideological burden of Orientalism. The construction of the "other," including location within the story and settings of the gameplay, paints the Japanese enemy as a ruthless despot willing to torture. Conversely, the American soldier embodies fraternity, salvation, and technological might.

Construction of the self in the game comes in three primary forms: self as player-character, self as soldier, and self as nation. Each of the three forms is constructed through various scenes in the gameplay, which include cinematic clips, interviews with veterans, and historical footage. From the combination of visuals, the self becomes a heroic soldier willing to sacrifice anything for the sake of the war effort.

First, in the opening dramatic Pearl Harbor scene, gamers are introduced to the self as player-character. Little is known about the character in the first few scenes, except that the self is a victim of a surprise attack. The opening scene features Griffin slowly waking up in his bunk. Around him, discussions of fellow soldiers' romantic interests back home can be heard. Suddenly, an explosion rocks the walls of the carrier, and Griffin bursts into action, giving gamers a first-person perspective. The first level tracks Griffin through the aircraft carrier to the surface, where the Japanese are in full assault on Pearl Harbor. From a ludological standpoint, the initial scenes limit action by prescribing pathways for gamers from which they cannot deviate. However, there are two "bonus objectives" for the player to enact in the tumultuous surroundings. In both cases, gamers must save dying or trapped soldiers. Their pleas for help are easily answered, establishing Griffin's initial identity as heroic. In the next level, the personal story is established with the disappearance of Griffin's brother, Donnie. This player-character is constructed in direct opposition to the Japanese forces. The war becomes deeply personal and political for the player-character. For the remainder of the game, gamers are constantly reminded of their personal obligation to find the brother. In her letters, Griffin's sister expresses hope that Donnie will be found. In the final level, Griffin is captured by enemy forces. In the game's only confrontation with Japanese leadership, an interrogating officer recognizes Griffin's facial features as being similar to that of his brother and inquires about him. However, as a good soldier, Griffin does not respond.

The next form of self is as soldier. This construction expands the personal self into a Marine, including the corresponding duties and responsibilities. At times, the personal responsibility of the soldier outweighs personal commitment to the war effort. In the example above of the Japanese officer's interrogation, the code of silence for a POW is stronger than Griffin's desire to ask the Japanese officer to release potential information about Donnie's whereabouts. Similarly, when the brother is first thought to be lost or dead, the player's commanding officer eulogizes Donnie as a soldier: "He was a good Marine. . . . You can't ask for more than that." Put simply, duty is more important than family. Moreover, the duty of the soldier serves as a constant reminder of appropriate behavior. During the Pearl Harbor level, gamers help protect the remaining ships in the harbor, specifically the *Nevada*. After this is successfully completed, the scene cuts from the first-person shooter perspective to a third-person cinematic view of Griffin and another soldier celebrating. Interrupting the celebration, the commanding officer exclaims: "Now you listen up, Marines! Take a look out there! . . . I hope none of you ever see a day like this again. . . . Nobody will ever know what it was like, maybe only the ones who lived through it." This commanding officer directs the character toward appropriate behavior (fighting back) and duty as a Marine.

Finally, the self is constructed as nation. Intricately tied to the notion of self as soldier, this identity draws upon other soldiers and civilians to create a sense of national identity. Game scenes, including newsreels and veteran interviews, first represent the nation as a victim. As argued earlier, the sense that America was attacked without provocation implies a national identity of initial neutrality forced into action in World War II. Various American actions before the bombing of Pearl Harbor, such as the naval blockade of oil trade routes into Japan, are left out, reinforcing America's supposed neutrality. Second, the nation is constructed as a savior of Pacific Rim countries. Martin Clemens, an Allied veteran of the war, discusses the interaction between Allied forces and the Solomon Islanders. He recounts a Solomon Islander who approached him with news, saying, "Master, me sorry too much, Japan fleety come." The use of "master" indicates a sense of superiority as the Allied forces intervened in the Pacific conflicts. In other instances, the American and Allied forces are seen liberating Pacific natives and POWs caught during earlier battles. Finally, the self as nation is identified through its technological and military prowess. Both newsreel footage and interviews with veterans often discuss weaponry. The national self is represented as having not only superior moral justification for its presence but also the means to conquer the enemy. Discussions range from the aforementioned BAR to the use of Black Cat fighter jets to attack Japanese carrier fleets. As expected in discussions of war, the combination of moral and mechanical feats poses a contradictory dynamic, especially as the player proceeds to enact the moral responsibility of saving lives by killing thousands.

While the use of superior weaponry and moral justification underscore the self in the game, the "other" is constructed in two primary and often contradictory ways: as crafty enemy and as Oriental. From the initial strike on Pearl Harbor, the enemy is realized as stealthy and powerful. The skies are littered with hundreds of planes, relentless in their attack, destroying the American fleet in Hawaii. In an interview, veteran Don Jensen discusses one of the more memorable experiences of the attack, the "mass confusion" of the hour-long bombing. In one historical sketch, the attack on Pearl Harbor is called "devastating," destroying the "once invincible American fleet." These statements construct the enemy as powerful and capable. The Japanese are a "war machine" with a "superior naval fleet" that "forces" the Americans to surrender. As an enemy, the Japanese are strategic in their military tactics and exert considerable pressure upon Allied forces.

The Japanese forces are also constructed as despotic and barbaric. As in most first-person shooter games, the enemy characters are limited to three or four different personas, through facial constructions and attire. The attacking soldiers use not only their firearms as weapons but also bayonets and samurai swords. During combat, Japanese language is heard but not translated, creating the enemy as even more foreign to (presumably) American gamers. Early in the game, Griffin helps stop some Japanese solders from torturing a captured prisoner of war. The newsreel scenes depict the horrors of POW camps and the treatment of native populations in the Pacific theater by Japanese forces. Images of emaciated POW bodies,[5] similar to those of Holocaust victims, serve to vilify the enemy and compare Japanese to Nazis. When the player is captured in the final level, the Japanese commanding officer threatens Griffin: "You have caused me a great deal of pain, but this is nothing compared to the torture you are about to encounter." In both the interviews with veterans and in the commands from Griffin's superior officer, the Japanese soldiers are referred to as "Japs." This racial slur, while accurate in its historical usage, reifies the superiority of Western gamers over the Japanese people. Said (1979) describes Orientalism as a "Western style [of] dominating, restructuring, and having authority over the Orient" (p. 3). While contradicting the image of the powerful "other," the depictions of the enemy using primitive weapons (swords) rather than modern weaponry (gamers single handedly take out a Japanese aircraft carrier) construct an inferior enemy dominated by Western interests.

One interesting character is Ichiro "Harry" Tanaka, Griffin's Japanese-American soldier "buddy," who assists in many of the solo missions in the game. Tanaka meets up with Griffin halfway through the game in Singapore and supports him in the remaining missions. In the final level, Tanaka uses his Japanese language skills and racially constructed body to help infiltrate a Japanese aircraft carrier. Later, he saves Griffin from imminent torture and death at the hands of a Japanese officer. In this final moment, Tanaka sacrifices his body by tackling the commanding Japanese officer; he is caught in the shuffle, and the officer slices his throat.[6] This final surrender of the only Japanese-American character has significant symbolic value in the overall construction of public memory.[7] If one were to locate the plight of Japanese-Americans during the war, given that *Rising Sun* omits the story of American internment camps, its account of Japanese-Americans, then, is in terms of bodily sacrifice. The story of Tanaka suggests that Japanese-Americans were willing to sacrifice their bodies for the American war effort. Moreover, their suffering and deaths come at the hands of the Japanese Empire. *Rising Sun's* ideological reconstruction of the Japanese-

American experience denies recognition of the American citizens imprisoned by the U.S. government. If, as Bogost (2006) argues, "the interpretation of a game relies as much or more on what the simulation excludes or leaves ambiguous than on what it includes" (p. 105), these narrative reconstructions of World War II have a profound impact on the nature of memory about the Pacific Rim. Griffin, a white soldier ordered to seek revenge upon a racially marked enemy, is privileged in the remembrance of suffering. The omission of American atrocities during the same era reifies the notion of American moral supremacy.

The Interactive Domain

The video game medium has unique features, and the gameplay provided in *Rising Sun* differentiates the game from film or television representations of war. The immersion of players into the environment of the historical narrative has considerable consequences for its reception as an authentic memory of World War II. Of particular focus is the first level of the game, which sets the stage for players' subsequent experiences. One remarkable and unusual aspect of this game is its rapid immersion into the world of Pearl Harbor. When the game is initially loaded, the usual menu and game options are skipped. Instead, the game's logo appears. The logo morphs into a postcard on the wall of Griffin's bunk and then the view pans out to show the dormitory on the USS *California*. Suddenly, the carrier and surrounding bunks shake; a vibration is felt in the controller. A commanding officer bursts into the dormitory and orders everyone to action. Seconds later, gamers are thrown into combat against the Japanese. This immediate immersion into the game reinforces the historical event as a surprise attack upon unknowing and innocent American soldiers. Gamers, also victims of surprise, follow the course of history through a spectacular visual narrative of the events of December 7, 1941.

After Griffin escapes from the doomed USS *California*, he is thrown into the ocean; other soldiers nearby are shot and killed through the water. Swimming to the surface, Griffin is taken aboard a smaller gunship and is directed to attack any Japanese bombers and escort the USS *Nevada* away from vulnerable areas. During this level/scene, immersion into the game is at its most intense. While the gunship is repaired, gamers witness the USS *Arizona* being bombed and destroyed. After the destruction, the gunship navigates through the wreckage; someone exclaims, "Oh my God, we've lost the *Arizona*!" With fire, ash, and smoke in the air and bodies littered across the ocean, the scene documents the carnage in vivid graphics and interactive camera angles. Notably, at this moment, the otherwise relentless attack on the harbor has gone quiet, allowing gamers to act as voyeurs of the devastation, taking in detail without distraction from the Japanese aircraft. In this immersive environment, the game becomes a museum displaying artifacts of the attack. This museum, however, creates a perspective unknown to the collective memory of Pearl Harbor. While these scenes are similar to those in films such as *Tora! Tora! Tora!* and *Pearl Harbor,* this interactive environment allows gamers to tour the scene in the first person. Moreover, immediately after experiencing the destruction, gamers are prepared to respond by exacting revenge on the Japanese. Thus, immersion into the game creates a sense of historical immediacy.

This immersive text functions similarly to the railway cars and authentic scenes constructed at Holocaust museums. Young (1993) argues that created experiences, used frequently by museums, encourage a "critical blindness" (p. 344) in visitors: The visitor's position as a victim from the past deflects attention to the potential victims of future holocausts. Similarly, the placement of gamers inside a victim's perspective on Pearl Harbor distracts from the politics of war and instead focuses on the need for counterattack and vengeance. Remembrance of the event feeds the cycle of war and violence.

The game continues, providing other environments unique to World War II, such as the jungles of Guadalcanal and the streets of Singapore. The use of era-specific weaponry and attire contributes to the sense of historical accuracy. Coupled with the "docent" veterans throughout the game, immersion into the world of *Rising Sun* entails a trip through an ideologically structured museum of the Pacific theater.

In addition to their immersion into the historical environment, gamers also have the means of control. *Medal of Honor* utilizes the popular first-person shooter perspective, which provides gamers with primary control of the story's characters. The environment is constrained by impassable borders; the limits of the game force the player to continue on a predetermined narrative path. Levels are divided by short cinematic clips that provide details of the next mission. Interestingly, however, the game does not set time limits on the play in any particular section; this allows for thorough exploration of the digital environment, as does the physical control given to gamers, which allows them a 360-degree view. Weapons can be fired while moving or from a stationary zoom. This allows for quick-reflex dodging and striking or stealthy attacks upon unsuspecting enemies. The flexibility of control enables a personalization of the war gaming experience. Highlighting the "feel" of the game (on the X-Box version) are vibrating controls that signal to the player the use of weapons, proximal explosions, and being struck by a bullet. These sensations assist in recreating a wartime environment.

In tandem with the immersive environment, the style of control for gamers attempts to capture the atmosphere and experience of World War II. However, as with all simulations, the representation falls dangerously short of the real. For example, during scenes of urgency, gamers are encouraged to act quickly; in others, gamers are allowed to run through a level at their leisure. Once the enemies are killed in any given location, the environment can be fully explored without penalty. This may increase appreciation for the immersive environment, with its intricate detail; however, it also pulls the experience away from the constant perils of war. Similarly, while gamers "feel" the vibrations of the controller when using weapons or when in proximity to explosions, the experience of war obviously cannot be fully replicated. Other games in the war genre have attempted to capture this realism, such as *Call of Duty,* in which gamers experience "shell-shock" through a combination of vibrating controls and blurred vision on the screen. This attempted replication of war sensations has profound implications for the construction of public memory of war. While some research into the nature of violent video games (see Bryce & Rutter, 2006) has argued that violence in video games is damaging for gamers, in the case of historical war video games such as *Rising Sun*, games may not be violent *enough* to realize fully the horror of war. Again, since fully representing war is impossible, the limited participation of *Rising Sun* gamers leads to a critical blindness regarding modern warfare.

Implications

I found that *Rising Sun's* use of intertwined narratives constructs a story of historical and personal vengeance. Gamers are directed to seek revenge for both the destruction of Pearl Harbor and the disappearance of the central character's brother. In analyzing character, I found first that the self is constructed as morally and technologically superior, heroic, and nationalistic. Through multiple self-identities, gamers become involved with the narrative on a personal, role-specific (soldier), and nationalistic level. In contrast, the enemy is constructed as simultaneously powerful, crafty, barbaric, and despotic. Through scenes of tortured fellow soldiers and the greed of a plundering Japanese empire, the "other" is constructed as an evil, morally inferior race set on world domination. Tanaka, who sacrifices his body for the sake of the national war effort against the Japanese, is the only Japanese-American, and there is no mention of any other Japanese-American internment. Finally, my analysis of the interactive domain highlights the museum-like quality of the game. Through the use of authentic World War II weaponry, recreated participatory scenes of the bombing of Pearl Harbor, and the docent-like explanations from veterans, gamers are immersed into the representation of World War II. Gamers are led to believe that the game, in its drive for authenticity, accurately portrays the era. The game becomes a type of interactive public memory, where gamers not only see history but partake in its selective (re)making.

While this interactive environment exists in the privacy of the home, it continues the nationalistic project of films such as *Saving Private Ryan* and *Pearl Harbor.* As the bombs strike Griffin's bunk in the USS *California*, World War II begins again in living rooms. The participatory function of the game personalizes and privatizes the public memory of World War II. First, while the story being told is static (there is only one way to win the game), the experience is dynamic. The personalization of the game through styles of play, whether stealthy sniping or active assault, reinforces the narrative at both individual and collective levels. Second, the location of the game within the private sphere of play (in the home) creates a distinctly violent memory of the era. The shooting down of "Jap" fighters after the initial strike on Pearl Harbor within the immersive museum-like environment instructs gamers to respond violently to national tragedy. While public memorials may instruct visitors to commemorate the dead and their sacrifice, *Rising Sun* only offers violence in its dedication. Third and finally, the reconstruction of war through ludological spaces is an attempt to capture the sensations associated with war. *Medal of Honor,* as noted by popular sources, is believed to capture an authentic experience of war. However, these simulations induce a critical blindness to the reality of war. Historical war games encourage gamers to be unreflective on the experience of war and discourage the possibility of peace (see also Stahl, 2006). Indeed, as the U.S. military reaches out to the war gaming genre as a recruitment tool (Schiesel, 2005), new games will branch into other modern conflicts. As this occurs, gamers should realize that not only are these stories ideologically driven, but they are also a far cry from the true destruction of modern warfare.

Biesecker (2002) calls for researchers to "critically engage these extraordinary popular and rapidly multiplying commemorative rhetorics in whose renovated narratives of national belonging our future may (not) lie" (p. 406). I have approached a new genre of collective memory that carries similar popular memorial intentions. As this analysis demonstrates, historical war games attempt to create an experiential history, placing gamers inside the war rather than witnessing it from the camera's purview. The proliferation of war games for popular consumption, including *Medal of Honor, Call of Duty, Red Orchestra,* and *America's Army*, brings the politics of remembrance to a new audience of consumers. *Rising Sun,* by overlaying interviews from veterans and historical newsreels upon gameplay, creates an experience that moves beyond pleasure and play. Instead, gamers are provided with "narrative histories" that "are presumed to inhere either to the events themselves . . . or in the facts derived from the critical study of evidence bearing upon those events" (White, 1999, p. 24). The danger of this teaching lies in its subtle form: gamers come for entertainment and walk away with selective memories of past conflicts.

Notes

[1] In international business news publications, *Medal of Honor: Rising Sun* was consistently ranked among the top ten best-selling games (see "Weekly Top Ten," 2004). Notably, the game was popular in Japan, although this means, effectively, that players kill Japanese soldiers to defeat their own country (see Thompson, 2004).

[2] The word *ludology* comes from the Latin word *ludus,* or game. Ludology takes an interdisciplinary perspective, combining computer sciences, social sciences, and humanities.

[3] The notion of rescuing a single person in the midst of war highlights a similarity between the game and *Saving Private Ryan;* this may be intended to engage audiences familiar with the film. This act also seems to reinforce the nature of *personal* responsibility for a *world* war, which accentuates the sense of both film and game as pushing for a contemporary return to nationalistic pride, as Biesecker (2002) argues.

[4] Gamers may also recall war scenes from *Saving Private Ryan, Band of Brothers,* or *Pearl Harbor* and their narratives of lost comrades, fraternal bonding, and romance within tragedy. Viewers familiar with *Pearl Harbor* or *Tora! Tora! Tora!* may recall scenes of floating bodies in the water or skies with hundreds of Japanese bombers approaching Hawaii. Other cultural artifacts may assist in connecting *Medal of Honor* into a larger public dialogue of World War II popular culture.

[5] The use of emaciated bodies also seems to call forth other images from World War II familiar to gamers. Specifically, images of rescued Holocaust prisoners in concentration camps, also with emaciated bodies, come to mind as a part of the moral obligation to fight in the war.

[6] Similarly, the construction of Tanaka indirectly references the politics of suspicion at the time. In one scene, Tanaka reappears after a brief absence. As he approaches, he makes his presence known, shouting, "Don't shoot! It's me, Tanaka!" This alerting of the player to his English language presence shifts the focus from his racially constructed body.

[7] Ehrenhaus (2001) goes beyond analysis of text in *Saving Private Ryan* to consider the nature of national remembrance.

References

Aarseth, E. (2004). Genre trouble: Narrativism and the art of simulation. In N. Wardip-Fruin & P. Harrigan (Eds.), *First person: New media as story, performance, and game* (pp. 45–55). Cambridge, MA: MIT Press.

Atkins, B. (2003). *More than a game: The computer game as fictional form.* Manchester, UK: Manchester University Press.

Best-selling video games. (2003, December 26). *USA Today,* p. 15D.

Biesecker, B. (2002). Remember World War II: The rhetoric and politics of national commemoration at the turn of the 21st century. *Quarterly Journal of Speech, 88,* 393–409.

Bodnar, J. (1992). *Remaking America: Public memory, commemoration, and patriotism in the twentieth century.* New Jersey: Princeton University Press.

Boellstorff, T. (2006). A ludicrous discipline?: Ethnography and game studies. *Games and Culture, 1,* 29–35.

Bogost, I. (2006). *Unit operations: An approach to video game criticism.* Cambridge, MA: MIT Press.

Brookey, R. A., & Westerfelhaus, R. (2002). Hiding homoeroticism in plain view: The *Fight Club* DVD as digital closet. *Critical Studies in Media Communication, 19,* 21–43.

Bryce, J., & Rutter, J. (2006). Digital games and the violence debate. In J. Bryce & J. Rutter (Eds.), *Understanding digital games* (pp. 205–222). Thousand Oaks, CA: Sage Publications.

Carlson, A. C., & Hocking, J. E. (1988). Strategies of redemption at the Vietnam Veterans' Memorial. *Western Journal of Communication, 52,* 203–215.

Cohen, E. L., & Willis, C. (2004). One nation under radio: Digital and public memory after September 11. *New Media and Society, 6,* 591–610.

Crogan, P. (2003). Gametime: History, narrative, and, temporality in *Combat Flight Simulator 2.* In M. J. P. Wolf & B. Perron (Eds.), *The video game theory reader* (pp. 275–301). New York: Routledge.

Dy, B. (2002, December). The software bookshelf. *Military History, 19*(5), 96.

Dy, B. (2004, August). Two new WWII titles. *Military History, 21*(3), 90.

Ehrenhaus, P. (2001). Why we fought: Holocaust memory in Spielberg's *Saving Private Ryan. Critical Studies in Media Communication, 18,* 321–337.

Foot, K., Warnick, B., & Schneider, S. M. (2005). Web-based memorializing after September 11: Toward a conceptual framework. *Journal of Computer-Mediated Communication, 11*(1), article 4. Retrieved March 19, 2006, from http://jcmc.indiana.edu/vol11/issue1/foot.html

Foss, S. A. (1986). Ambiguity as persuasion: The Vietnam Veterans Memorial. *Communication Quarterly, 34,* 326–340.

Harsany, J., & Sarrel, M. D. (2003, December 9). Console. *PC Magazine, 22*(22), 190.

Hartlaub, P. (2003, December 2). A game your gramps would love: Nice historic detail in "Over Normandy." *The San Francisco Chronicle,* p. D2.

Hasian, M., Jr., & Carlson, A. C. (2000). Revisionism and collective memory: The struggle for meaning in the *Amistad affair. Communication Monographs, 67,* 42–62.

Hauser, G. A. (1999). *Vernacular voices: The rhetoric of publics and public spheres.* Columbia, SC: University of South Carolina Press.

Hoskins, A. (2003). Signs of the Holocaust: Exhibiting memory in a mediated age. *Media, Culture and Society, 25,* 7–22.

Jansz, J. (2005). The emotional appeal of violent video games for adolescent males. *Communication Theory, 15,* 219–241.

Jorgensen-Earp, C. R., & Lanzilotti, L. A. (1998). Public memory and private grief: The construction of shrines at the sites of public tragedy. *Quarterly Journal of Speech, 84,* 150–170.

Juul, J. (2001). Games telling stories? A brief note on games and narratives. *Game Studies, 1.* Retrieved March 19, 2006, from http://www.gamestudies.org/0101/juul-gts/

Kammen, M. (1991). *Mystic chords of memory: The transformation of tradition in American culture.* New York: Alfred A. Knopf.

Katriel, T. (1994). Sites of memory: Discourses of the past in Israeli and pioneering settlement museums. *Quarterly Journal of Speech, 80,* 1–20.

Kobrin, C. (2004, April 15). "Medal of Honor: Rising Sun" a lowdown, dirty game. *The Oracle.* Retrieved October 27, 2006, from LexisNexis database.

Lachlan, K. A., Smith, S., & Tamborini, R. (2004). Models for aggressive behavior: The attributes of violent characters in popular video games. *Communication Studies, 56,* 313–329.

Murray, J. H. (1997). *Hamlet on the holodeck: The future of narrative in cyberspace.* New York: Free Press.

Ondrejka, C. (2006). Finding common ground in new worlds. *Games and Culture, 1,* 111–115.

Phillips, K. R. (2004). *Framing public memory.* Tuscaloosa, AL: University of Alabama Press.

Polak, S. (2003, August 19). Day the Rising Sun rained death: Play IT. *The Australian,* p. T26.

Said, E. W. (1979). *Orientalism.* New York: Vintage Books.

Schiesel, S. (2005, February 17). On maneuvers with the Army's game squad. *The New York Times,* p. G1.

Sillars, M. O., & Gronbeck, B. E. (2001). *Communication criticism: Rhetoric, social codes, cultural studies.* Long Grove, IL: Waveland.

Simon, B. (2006). Beyond cyberspatial flaneurie: On the analytic potential of living with digital games. *Games and Culture, 1,* 62–67.

Snider, M. (2002, February 4). New appreciation for combat soldiers and WWII veterans. *USA Today,* p. 4D.

Snider, M. (2004, June 10). War games launch all-out sales assault. *USA Today,* p. 1D.

Stahl, R. (2006). Have you played the War on Terror? *Critical Studies in Media Communication, 23,* 112-130.

Taylor, T. L. (2006). *Play between worlds: Exploring online game culture.* Cambridge, MA: MIT Press.

Thompson, C. (2004, February 25). Player, attack thyself. *Slate Magazine.* Retrieved March 9, 2007, from LexisNexis database.

Weekly top ten. (2004, August 16). *Townsville Bulletin/Townsville Sun,* p. 30. Retrieved March 9, 2007, from LexisNexis database.

White, H. (1987). *The content of the form.* Baltimore: Johns Hopkins University Press.

White, H. (1999). *Figural realism: Studies in the mimesis effect.* Baltimore: Johns Hopkins University Press.

Young, J. E. (1993). *The texture of memory: Holocaust memorials and meaning.* New Haven, CT: Yale University Press.

The Rhetorical Power of a Compelling Story
A Critique of a "Toughlove" Parental Support Group

Thomas A. Hollihan and Patricia Riley

> It has recently been said that almost the bitterest and most hopeless tragedies of all
> are the tragedies of parents with bad children. The tragedy of children with bad
> parents is no less acute. . . .
>
> R. Cowell, *Cicero and the Roman Republic*, 1967, p. 298.

Families through the ages have been troubled by misbehaving and, at times, delinquent children. In 49 B.C., Cicero blamed his brother for his nephew Quintus' treacheries saying: "His father has always spoilt him but his indulgence is not responsible for his being untruthful or grasping or wanting in affection for his family, though it perhaps does make him headstrong and self-willed as well as aggressive" (Cicero, cited in Cowell, 1967, p. 299). Twenty centuries later, contemporary researchers, practitioners, and theorists continue to investigate the exceedingly complex interaction of parental actions, societal and cultural pressures, genetic predispositions, and children's behavioral choices that too often culminate in disaster or despair. Such studies still reflect Cicero's penchant for locating blame for juvenile delinquency in parental actions: e.g., parents who drink too much (Morehouse & Richards, 1982); parental relationships characterized by a great deal of conflict (Emery, 1982); parents who are lax in discipline (Fischer, 1983); abusive parents (Paperny & Deisher, 1983); or parents who fail to provide good nutritious food for their children (Stasiak, 1982).

Rather than suffer the disparagement of neighbors and relatives, or the accusations of teachers and counseling professionals, many parents try to cope with their problem children alone (Nemy, 1982). Recently, a program called "Toughlove" has begun to provide parents of delinquent children with emotional support and hope for solutions to their common problems. "Toughlove" proselytizes that it is not the parents who are failing, it is their children. Founded by Phyllis and David York, the Toughlove groups promote highly disciplined child-rearing practices in an attempt to stop unruly teenagers from controlling households, to rid parents of guilt feelings, and to enable parents and non-problem children to lead a normal family life (Nemy, 1982).

The Toughlove approach has attracted a great deal of national attention. It was endorsed by Ann Landers (1981), reported in *Time* ("Getting Tough," 1981), *People* ("David and Phyllis," 1981), *Ms.* (Wohl, 1985), and the *New York Times* (Nemy, 1982), and was featured on the *Phil Donohue Show* and ABC's *20/20*. Partially as a result of this publicity, there are currently more than four-hundred Toughlove groups in the United States and Canada (Nemy, 1982).

A recent Gallup Poll reported that 37 percent of the respondents felt that the main problem with parents today was that they did not give their children sufficient discipline (cited in Wohl, 1985). The increased popularity of the Toughlove program has undoubtedly been a response to these sentiments. Toughlove has been credited with having sparked a series of books advising parents on how to discipline their children (Wohl, 1985; Bodenhamer, 1984; Sanderson, 1983; and Bartocci, 1984).

From *Communication Quarterly*, 35 (Winter 1987), 13–25. Used by permission of the Eastern Communication Association and the authors.

Toughlove, like Alcoholics Anonymous, operates primarily through a system of self-help groups that attempt to better people's lives, help them cope with crises, and teach them their own limitations (Alibrandi, 1982; Pattison, 1982; Pomerleau, 1982). A rhetorical study of Toughlove should give insight into the appeal of this group and into the process that similar self-help groups use to become support systems. More importantly, the study of Toughlove will permit researchers to focus on how members are acculturated into the Toughlove philosophy, and how this philosophy guides their lives.

This study involved the observation of a series of Toughlove group meetings and an analysis of the flow of messages during these meetings. The form of these messages can best be described as the telling of individual stories, and ultimately the development of a shared group story. The study is grounded in the notion that these shared stories give insight into the group members' beliefs, actions, and worldviews, and into the process through which they attempt to change their lives. This perspective is best explicated in Walter R. Fisher's (1984) notion of the "narrative paradigm."

In developing the "narrative paradigm," Fisher (1984) asserted that human beings were essentially storytelling creatures and that the dominant mode of human decision making involved the sharing of these stories. Such stories contained "good reasons" which provided insight into the proper courses of human action. According to this perspective, the world consists of a set of stories from which people must choose. People are thus constantly engaged in storytelling and in evaluating the stories they are told (Fisher, 1984, pp. 7–8).

Where the rational world paradigm would expect individuals (advocates) to possess knowledge of subject matter and of the requirements of argumentative form—thereby creating experts with a capability for argument beyond that possessed by naïve advocates—the narrative paradigm presumes that all persons have the capacity to be rational. Rationality is thus a function of the "narrative probability" and "narrative fidelity" of a given story—the degree to which stories hang together, their ability to make sense of encountered experience, and whether they corroborate previously accepted stories (Fisher, 1984).

Shared stories play an important role in the lives of those who tell them, for they are a way for people to capture and relate their experiences in the world. These stories respond to people's sense of reason and emotion, to their intellects and imagination, to the facts as they perceive them, and to their values. People search for stories which justify their efforts and resolve the tensions and problems in their lives, and desire stories that resolve their dissonance and are psychologically satisfying.

Those who do not share in the storytelling—those whose life experiences demand different types of stories—might view particular stories as mere rationalization, but this is to miss the very nature of the storytelling process. In this framework, one person's life story is another's rationalization, but if a story serves a useful purpose to those who tell it or listen to it, that story likely will be retold in the generative process of narrative understanding.

This study has three major goals: (1) to operationalize Fisher's narrative paradigm through actual observations; (2) to identify the Toughlove story; and (3) to critique the appeal of that story and discuss its possible consequences.

Method

A Toughlove group in a Los Angeles suburb was observed during four consecutive, three-hour meetings. Two researchers attended the meetings and took extensive notes, each attempting to copy down as many of the participants' comments as possible in order to capture the essence of the discussion. We were not allowed to tape record the sessions because the group leaders feared that the presence of taping equipment might "chill" the participants and prevent them from talking in detail about their problems.

The group leaders (two women who founded the group after experiencing difficulties with their own children) were briefed about the nature of the study prior to the first observation. One of the leaders introduced us before our first meeting with the group and asked if anyone objected to our presence. No one objected. We explained to the group that we were interested in watching real-life groups as a part of a small group research project underway at a local university. After each meeting, the Toughlove group leaders were asked if the group's participants had behaved differently due to our presence. On each occasion, the leaders indicated that there appeared to be no differences in the group members' interactions. After the last observation we conducted interviews with several randomly selected group members. Each interviewee was asked if they felt the observation affected the group in any way. Again, no differences were reported.

Following the final observation, each observer's notes were prepared for analysis. While it would have been preferable to have access to complete transcripts of the group meetings, we discovered that our written notes were quite detailed and provided us with a great deal of rhetoric for analysis. We proceeded by first comparing our notes and eliminating issues of disagreement, and second, subdividing the information into actual remarks made by group members and our own comments about the group's process. We next subdivided the group members' statements into three categories that emerged from the notes: (1) story-lines ("Story-lines have beginnings, middles, and ends which give individual actions meanings, provide unity and self-definition to individual lives . . ." (Frentz, 1985, p. 5); (2) questions or comments to other parents; and (3) procedural issues (mainly leader comments).

Our approach is similar to a "mini-ethnography" where the observers are also the message analysts (Knapp, 1979). This perspective ensures that the highly emotional tone of the meeting, together with the dramatic nature of narrative fiction, are captured in the analysis. After the study was completed, the group as a whole was debriefed.

The Group

The group had been in existence for just over one year when the observations took place. While the group had a nucleus of eight parents who always attended the meetings, the group's size increased significantly during the observation period. Twelve persons attended the first observed meeting, but by the fourth meeting there were more than thirty parents. The growing attendance may have resulted from a story on the group which appeared in a local newspaper. Following the last observed meeting the group split into two smaller groups in order to maintain the close personal atmosphere necessary for the highly emotional, self-disclosive discussions. All of the participating parents had experienced, or were in the midst of experiencing, a family crisis precipitated by their child's (or children's) behavior.

Parents came from a variety of occupational and sociocultural backgrounds, but they were predominantly from middle-class, blue-collar families. They were also primarily Caucasian (one Hispanic couple attended, but no Blacks or Asians). Several couples attended, but most of the members were women. Many were single parents— mothers and fathers—and the vast majority of the women worked outside of the home.

The problems faced by these parents were generally quite serious, including simple acts of rebellion, physical assaults, and threats of murder. The most common problems were drug and alcohol abuse. To illustrate the kinds of behavioral problems discussed by the group, a description of some of the children follows (all names are fictitious):

Ellen—A 13-year-old female who skips school, steals from her parents, and during the time of the observation had run away from home.

Bill—A 15-year-old male who struck his father's head against the headboard of his bed while he was asleep.

Mark—An 18-year-old male who had been arrested for theft, breaking and entering, assault, and selling drugs. At the time of the observations, he was serving a one-year sentence in a juvenile correction facility.

Angie—A 15-year-old female who carried a knife, had physical altercations with her mother, threatened her father by describing a dream in which she murders him, and was involved in a youth gang.

John—A 16-year-old male who had beaten his mother with a baseball bat, assaulted her with a knife, and painted "fuck the fat ugly bitch" on their living room wall.

Maria—A 12-year-old female who had run away from home and who was, during the time of observation, a prostitute.

Keith—A 24-year-old male who had no job, refused to leave home, and who threatened to beat his mother because she refused to allow him to smoke marijuana in their living room.

Analysis of the parents' stories showed drug or alcohol abuse to be present in slightly more than two-thirds of the cases. The remainder of the cases seemed to reflect either problems of general disobedience or psychological/emotional disturbances. It was not uncommon for parents to come to group meetings with blackened eyes or other visible bruises from violent confrontations with their children. Many parents reported that they were terrified of their own children and, in several cases, parents claimed that their children had threatened them with violence merely because they planned to attend the Toughlove meeting.

The Sharing of the Toughlove Story

In each meeting, individual tales of fear and helplessness were transformed into hope and perseverance as these stories were woven into shared narrative fiction. If parents truly loved their children, they could not let them destroy themselves or their families; they had to be tough—this was the Toughlove story.

The meetings can best be described as extended storytelling sessions where the members, together, created a powerful, compelling, and cohesive story. Numerous sagas of their children's triumphs over drugs or alcohol were often repeated as part of the "ritual" acculturation of the new members. This was far more than imparting information to the newcomers; the retelling was always a highly emotional experience for the parents, often tearful at the start, ending in the quiet determination that they had regained control over their lives. Through the storytelling, the parents transformed their lives into a moral drama, suffused with righteousness, that absolved them of their guilt and restored orderliness and discipline to their lives. The retelling of these stories provided examples that Toughlove parents could survive and even con-quer crises, kept members involved in the day-to-day life of the group, and preserved a sense of community among the members.

The Toughlove story promised a new beginning. The group's regular members described their desperation before they discovered Toughlove, and contrasted these feelings with the solace they felt once they embraced the Toughlove way of life. Although new members initially may have been reticent to tell their tales in the pres-ence of strangers, their need to talk to someone was apparent as they blurted out their stories in a torrent of emotions.

In this drama, the parents left forever their roles as weak victimized players whose offspring tyrannized them and wreaked havoc on society. The Toughlove narrative empowered them to take charge of their families and demand the respect due them as elders. They would never again be failures, for only their children could lose in the Toughlove story. As one parent declared: "You have not failed—it is your children who are failing. Kids have to learn the consequences of their own actions." Still another added: "We made it easy for them, we covered the sharp edges so they would not bump into things when they learned to walk. We made it too easy—they never had to fight—we went to battle for them. Now they know how to push buttons and use us." Thus if their children were delinquent, they *chose* to be that way, and there are times when there is nothing that parents can do to modify their children's behavior. One group member asserted: "Sometimes you have to realize that your kid is a loser and that there isn't a damn thing that you can do about it." Group members nodded their assent.

Thematic Analysis

The narrative fiction created by this Toughlove group contained several key themes. First, individual tales were interwoven to explain the "good reasons" for abandoning the predominant rival story—the modern approach to child-rearing. In their drama, the old-fashioned values, characterized by strict discipline, were pur-ported to be superior to today's methods of raising children. The group members often blamed "TLC" (tender loving care) for the problems they had with their chil-dren. One father observed: "While TLC works for some kids it is a bust with others." Another father chimed in, "The best way to raise kids is with discipline—strict disci-pline—that's how our parents did it and we sure didn't cause them these kinds of problems." Several group members claimed that they had tried to use the modern approach in raising their own children but that it had failed. These same parents expressed pride that they now had the courage to condemn these modern approaches. As one mother adamantly claimed: "Everything we are learning here in Toughlove is contrary to Dr. Spock." The other members readily agreed.

This call for a return to traditional values had fidelity because it resonated with stories from the parents' youth, and because the loss of the old ways accounted for the traumas they had experienced. In this sense, the Toughlove narrative was one of his-torical renewal, a promise that the past could be recreated and the security and com-fort of a bygone era recaptured (Bass, 1983). Parents frequently told stories from their own childhood—about how it felt to "go to the woodshed." They commented that they had feared their own parents at times, but they also respected them. Their own children, they sadly agreed, neither feared nor respected them. As one mother noted: "We raised our kids like they did on TV and not the way we were raised. It always worked on TV. It sure didn't work in my house."

These parents believed they were good people who had been misled. The Toughlove narrative was appealing because it confirmed their self-perceptions and absolved them of their failures. They may have been too kind, too lenient, not tough enough, but it was their children who had really failed because they took advantage of their parents' kindness.

A second major theme of the Toughlove narrative was the parents' disdain for the child service professionals. The professionals became villains in the story for two primary reasons. First, the parents claimed these professionals were too quick to blame them for the failures of their offspring. Virtually all of the parents attending the meetings complained that they had been told by counselors, teachers, principals, and others that they were responsible for their children's behavioral problems. Second, these professionals were condemned as highly vocal proponents of the "modern" approaches to child-rearing. Thus they were spokespersons for the dominant rival story—a story which, for the parents, lacked narrative coherence and fidelity, and a story which reflected an unrealistic approach to raising children. Accounts of visits to counselors were always a central part of an evening's storytelling. These "experts" were portrayed as naïve—"book smart" but "experience dumb"—and many group members related tales of their children "snowing" or "hoodwinking" the experts and bragging about it on their way home. Thus the professionals were depicted as part of the problem rather than as part of the solution.

Toughlove parents viewed the child-care professionals' rival story as detrimental because it suggested that parents and children shared the responsibility for the problems in the home. The parents believed that this story gave their children an excuse to continue misbehaving. As adherents to the Toughlove narrative, the parents discounted the possibility that they were partially to blame for the problems in their homes. Several parents recalled that counselors had mentioned their drinking problems or marital difficulties as potential causes for their children's misdeeds, but they claimed that it was "just a cop out" for kids to blame their parents for these problems. The Toughlove story, however, allowed parents to blame their children for their own problems, and doing so did not seem to make this story any less probable. On several occasions parents asserted: "This problem with my son is destroying my marriage." Or, "My daughter's behavior is causing me to drink too much."

In their role as experts on juvenile problems, supplanting the professionals, Toughlove parents placed most of the blame on their children and external factors. The enemies in the drama became the professionals, the media, the permissiveness of society, their children's friends, the lack of discipline in the schools, or modern approaches to child-rearing. If they as parents could be faulted at all, it was only that they had relied on the rival story and in so doing had become estranged from the "old-fashioned" values with which they had been raised.

The third central theme of the Toughlove narrative was that the system is pro-child, and that they could best cope with their problem children by depending on, and supporting, each other. The Toughlove group meeting was exalted as the one place where parents knew there would be people willing to listen to their problems without judging them. Group members consistently reported that the social service agencies, the schools, the police, and the juvenile courts were of little help. The consensus of the group members was that "the laws protect kids, but it is parents who need protection."

The parents agreed that neither teachers nor police were helpful. The consistent story-line was that the schools did not teach, teachers could not control their students, and students were permitted to use drugs right on the school grounds. The police refused to come when they were called, and if they did come, they generally took the teenager's side in the dispute. One woman recalled that after her daughter was arrested for selling drugs the police picked her up to take her to a juvenile facility. On the way the officer was kind enough to stop by a friend's house so the girl could pick up her hairdryer.

The tales which recounted the utter helplessness these parents felt in coping with their past crises played an important part in the development of the group's shared story. If parents could not trust "the system" to resolve their problems, then they were all the more dependent on their fellow group members.

In this narrative fiction, the police and the juvenile system were both materially and symbolically anti-parent. The group members discussed how important it was to learn to protect themselves from the law. Several parents explained that their children had filed complaints against them, alleging child neglect or abuse, while their offspring were in fact destroying all harmony in the home and terrorizing their families. The group also discussed in great detail their responsibilities in providing for minor children. One woman insisted: "All parents are required by law to provide is a roof over their head and minimally sufficient clothing." Another mother told the group how she left home to escape from her son, leaving him only a loaf of bread and a jar of peanut butter to eat. The common thread running through most of these stories was the declaration that the police and the courts did not take these complaints seriously and failed to realize that these children represented a genuine threat to their parents and siblings. One angry mother related how the police told her that they could do nothing even though her son, whom she had thrown out, had returned to steal her possessions and destroy her furniture. The police refused to act because her house was still considered the boy's home, and, according to the officer, "A kid can't steal from himself, and can destroy his own house if he wants to."

Consistent with this theme, group members jointly developed language strategies to convince the police to arrest their children the next time they were called to the house. Several parents explained that the police would not take a teenager away the first, second, or even the third time they were summoned, but after that, if you labeled your child "incorrigible" you will have "hit upon the right legal mumbo-jumbo" to get him/her arrested. Other valuable information was given via stories—one mother explained that parents can report their kid missing after he leaves the house, "then after the police find him and bring him to the station you can refuse to pick him up, not accept custody. Then they have no choice, they have to put him somewhere else. That's what I did." She was upset because her son had been selling drugs in her house.

In contrast to the lack of help available from more conventional sources, the Toughlove narrative dramatized that if parents needed assistance they could always call upon another group member. As one of the group leaders recalled: "Crises don't happen between 8 A.M. and 5 P.M. when the social workers are willing to help. But if you are having trouble with your kid, even if it is midnight, you can call another Toughlove mom or dad. We will come by. These folks have come to my house when I needed help. And I've gone to theirs." Another member declared: "Kids have always had gangs. Now we have one too." Thus the Toughlove narrative encouraged parents to take heart—they had formed their own social services system, a support group that could circumvent or beat the system if necessary.

The fourth, and last, prominent theme in the narrative called for parents to put Toughlove into action by setting "bottom lines" for their children. These were the rules their children had to obey if they wanted to live with their family. The key to this strategy was that parents had to enforce their bottom lines, no matter what. The bottom lines set by individual parents were frequently discussed during the meetings. They included: you will not drink, you will not use drugs, you will attend school, you will meet this curfew, you will clean up after yourself, you will not entertain someone of the opposite sex in your bedroom, etc. By spelling out the behaviors appropriate for each of their children, and enforcing them, the Toughlove parents reinforced the shared group story that strict discipline was the answer to their troubles. Youths who did not meet their bottom lines were told they could no longer live at home. Although ejecting a son/daughter from the house was to occur only as a last resort, several parents in this group had forced their children to leave home even though they had nowhere else to go. Two other parents managed to have their children detained in Juvenile Hall, a county detention facility, and one had committed her son to a private detoxification center. The group's leader said the message contained in these stories was a simple one: "Set rules for your kids. If they don't follow them, tell them, 'don't let the door hit you on your way out.'" The Toughlove story thus characterized even these very unhappy outcomes as positive developments. It was presumed better to be rid of these problem children than it was to have to endure the profound disruptions that they caused in the home.

Newcomers were warned that instituting the bottom lines was no easy task, as the group leaders and regulars related anecdotes regarding their children's initial difficulties when the new rules were set. One woman recalled that her daughter kept breaking the rules, so she refused to prepare her meals. Since her daughter could not even find the can opener in the kitchen, the mother found that she gained the girl's cooperation fairly quickly. One father told the group that his daughter's bottom line was to do well in school. To make up for lost time, she had to attend classes regularly, go straight home after school and not have visitors, do her homework, and also help keep the house clean. He discovered that all she did was talk on the phone all afternoon, so he removed the phones from his home every morning and locked them in the trunk of his car so that she could not contact her friends during the day. New Toughlove members quickly understood that they were being prepared for a different type of battle than they were accustomed to, but one that they could hope to win.

During each meeting the group went through the reinforcing ritual of calling upon individual parents and asking them to describe what happened in their homes during the past week. Parents were asked to list the bottom lines they had set, and report whether or not their children had lived up to these rules. If a parent reported that one or more of the rules had been violated, the other group members cross-examined him/her to determine if the offending child had been suitably punished. Parents who showed signs of weakness were criticized, and parents who claimed they had been tough in enforcing the rules were praised by the other group members. This "grilling" of the parents allowed the Toughlove old-timers to give encouragement to parents who were not used to standing firm. The Toughlove narrative left little room for "extenuating circumstances."

During this segment of storytelling, numerous parents exclaimed that their children were now behaving very differently as a result of the Toughlove program. Several expressed the conviction that they had finally managed to "win the respect" of their children—now that they could no longer be pushed around. These parents, furthermore, noted that while their children initially rebelled against the rules, they ultimately accepted them, because "children want and need discipline." The narrative was additionally strengthened when several parents commented that their children were happy that they had found Toughlove.

Most parents would leave the meeting after the story-telling/testimonial session appearing more relaxed than when they arrived, imbued with the Toughlove spirit, and vowing to spread the word. Others, battered by recent crises, would remain to exchange sorrows, advice, hugs, and telephone numbers before braving the trip home.

Implications of the Toughlove Story

The Toughlove narrative proved to be comforting, engaging, predictable, and persuasive. Parents joined the group during times of crisis, many feeling as if they had failed because they had been unable to instill socially appropriate values and attitudes in their children. Shamed by the reactions of friends, relatives, and child-care experts, and resentful of a system that could not help and only blamed them for allowing such a disgraceful state of affairs to exist, they readily embraced the Toughlove narrative as an alternative for their problems.

Human communication works by identification, and these parents discovered that no one else understood life with delinquent children except other parents in similar circumstances. The rational world, with its scientific notions of child psychology and "Dr. Spock type experts," could not "speak" to them. The experts' story, which blamed them for their children's conduct, denied their own experiences and did not contain the formal or substantive features necessary for adherence. The Toughlove narrative met their needs and fulfilled the requirements for a good story, narrative probability—what constitutes a coherent story—and narrative fidelity—that a story rings true with a hearer's experience (Fisher, 1984). The story was probable because it was based on old fashioned values, it restored the social order, and it placed blame where it belonged, on the shoulders of their disobedient and abusive offspring. The rival story which placed at least partial blame on the parents for their children's conduct was viewed as less probable. The story met the test of narrative fidelity because it resonated with their own feelings that they were essentially good people whose only failing had been that they were too permissive and not as tough as their own parents had been.

The Toughlove story was compelling because it so completely absolved parents of their guilt and relieved their sense of failure. The story also provided parents with a course of action that, at best, showed their children who was in charge and established rules they had to follow to remain part of the family, and at worst, allowed the remainder of the household to lead normal lives after the delinquent youth was "shown the door."

Despite the obvious appeal of these new "tough" approaches to child-rearing, however, they are not without risk. The dimension of the Toughlove story which holds that children who do not adhere to their bottom lines should be ejected from the house is especially controversial. There is, of course, great danger that the ejected child may be unprepared to face life on his/her own and may in fact become a real threat to him/herself and to society. For instance, John Hinckley's parents were following the Toughlove philosophy when they insisted that their son become financially independent by March 20, 1982, precisely the day that he shot President Reagan and three other men ("Hinckleys," 1984).

Hinckley's father has since embarked on a national speaking tour to warn parents of the dangers in the Toughlove approach, declaring: "For heaven's sake don't kick somebody out of the house when they can't cope. But I'd never heard that before, and it (kicking John out of the house) seemed to me to make a lot of sense at the time" ("Hinckleys," 1984, p. 12). Hinckley's parents now urge other parents who are told to eject their children from home to be sure to seek the advice of those experts they had been told could not be trusted ("Hinckleys," 1984). This warning seems reasonable enough: parents should not take drastic steps when a more conservative means for disciplining children might work equally well—they should always proceed with caution.

Before this or any other rival story is likely to capture the trust and attention of the Toughlove parents, however, it needs to accommodate them as the hopeful, newly self-confident, bearers of old-fashioned values which they have become. If a rival story cannot capture people's self-conceptions, it does not matter whether or not it is "fact." Fisher noted that, "Any story, any form of rhetorical communication, not only says something about the world, it also implies an audience, persons who conceive of themselves in very specific ways" (Fisher, 1984, p. 14). Parents who do not have "problem children" may find the Toughlove story objectionable, but to those parents in the midst of a crisis the story has obvious appeal. The advocates of any rival story can win adherents only by "telling stories that do not negate the self-conceptions people hold of themselves" (Fisher, 1984, p. 14).

The other great danger in the Toughlove story is that it can be readily adapted to fit all children and all situations. For example, during our observation we noted that if parents told the group that they did not believe drugs or alcohol were responsible for their children's bizarre behavior, they were given a lecture on how to substantiate these abuses. Other potential reasons for their children's erratic or destructive behavior, including emotional or psychological disturbances, were dismissed without consideration. The Toughlove story thus proved quite elastic and was easily stretched to permit the conclusion that "bad drugs" or a "bad crowd" caused all behavior problems and, therefore, all required the same remedy.

The pressure to enact the Toughlove story was great; all parents had to play the "enforcer" role that ritualistically proved their faith and imbued them with the credibility and unquestioned support granted only to other Toughlove moms and dads. While the group leaders seemed to be aware of the danger that parents might seek to get a quick-fix to their problems by ejecting their children from the house when far less drastic actions would be more appropriate, the potential danger from such decisions (as characterized by the Hinckley example) never appeared as imminent to the Toughlove parents as was the impending end to the chaos in their lives.

The truth or falsity of the Toughlove story is not really at issue in this study. What is important is that through an analysis we can come to understand the appeal of stories and perhaps even learn how to avoid the creation of stories which might precipitate harmful consequences. Perhaps the most useful outcome of such study is that child-care professionals and social service agencies can learn how to create *better* stories—stories which affirm parents' self-worth, but also help them to deal with the crises in their homes without the risk of worsening those crises by reacting without careful deliberation.

References

Alibrandi, L. A. (1982). The Fellowship of Alcoholics Anonymous. In E. M. Pattison & E. Kaufman (Eds.), *Encyclopedic handbook of alcoholism* (pp. 979–986). New York: Gardner Press.

Bartocci, B. (1984). *My angry son: Sometimes love is not enough*. New York: Donald I. Fine.

Bass, J. D. (1983). Becoming the past: The rationale of renewal and the annulment of history. In D. Zarefsky, M. Sillars, & J. Rhodes (Eds.), *Argument in transition: Proceedings of the Third Summer Conference on Argumentation* (pp. 305–318). Annandale, VA: Speech Communication Association.

Bodenhamer, G. (1984). *Back in control: How to get your children to behave*. Englewood Cliffs: Prentice-Hall.

Cowell, F. R. (1967). *Cicero and the Roman Republic* (4th ed.). Baltimore: Penguin Books.

David and Phyllis York treat problem teenagers with a stiff dose of "Toughlove." (1981, November 16). *People*, p. 101.

Emery, R. E. (1982). Intraparental conflict and the children of discord and divorce. *Psychological Bulletin, 92*, 310–330.

Fischer, D. G. (1983). Parental supervision and delinquency. *Perceptual and Motor Skills, 56*, 635–640.

Fisher, W. R. (1984). Narration as a human communication paradigm: The case of public moral argument. *Communication Monographs, 51*, 1–22.

Frentz, T. S. (1985). Rhetorical conversation, time, and moral action. *Quarterly Journal of Speech, 71*, 1–18.

Getting tough with teens. (1981, June 8). *Time*, p. 47.

Hinckley, J. & Hinckley, J. A. (1985). *Breaking points*. Grand Rapids, MI: Zondervan.

Hinckleys: Family on a crusade. (1984, February 23). *Los Angeles Times*, p. 12.

Knapp, M. S. (1979). Ethnographic contributions to evaluation research: The experimental schools program evaluation and some alternatives. In T. D. Cook & C. S. Reichardt (Eds.), *Qualitative and quantitative methods in evaluation research* (pp. 118–139). Beverly Hills: Sage.

Landers, A. (1981, November). Giving kids "Tough" love. *Family Circle*, p. 34.

Loeber, R. & Dishion, T. (1983). Early predictors of male delinquency: A review. *Psychological Bulletin, 94*, 68–99.

Morehouse, E. & Richards, T. (1982). An examination of dysfunctional latency age children of alcoholic parents and problems in intervention. *Journal of Children in Contemporary Society, 15*, 21–33.

Nemy, E. (1982, April 26). For problem teen-agers: Love, toughness. *New York Times*, p. B12.

Paperny, D. M. & Deisher, R. W. (1983). Maltreatment of adolescents: The relationship to a predisposition toward violent behavior and delinquency. *Adolescence, 18*, 499–506.

Pattison, E. M. (1982). A systems approach to alcoholism treatment. In E. M. Pattison & E. Kaufman (Eds.), *Encyclopedic handbook of alcoholism* (pp. 1080–1108). New York: Gardner Press.

Pomerleau, O. F. (1982). Current behavioral theories in the treatment of alcoholism. In E. M. Pattison & E. Kaufman (Eds.), *Encyclopedic handbook of alcoholism* (pp. 1054–1067). New York: Gardner Press.

Sanderson, J. (1983). *How to raise your kids to stand on their own two feet*. New York: Congdon & Weed.

Stasiak, E. A. (1982). Nutritional approaches to altering criminal behavior. *Corrective and Social Psychiatry and the Journal of Behavioral Technology, Methods and Therapy, 28*, 110–115.

Wohl, L. C. (1985, May). The parent-training game—from "Toughlove" to perfect manners. *Ms.*, p. 40.

York, P. & York, D. (1980). *Toughlove*. Sellersville, PA: Community Service Foundation.

Facilitating Openness to Difference
A Narrative Analysis of Leslie Marmon Silko's
Yellow Woman and a Beauty of the Spirit

Laura S. More, Randi Boyd, Julie Bradley, and Erin Harris

In an increasingly global world, we often encounter people with different belief systems, cultural backgrounds, and lifestyles. We have choices about how to respond to difference—we can ignore it, reject it, seek to understand it, or actively engage it. If we are to live together effectively, understanding and engagement of other cultures seem like the most productive responses to difference. To develop messages that facilitate such understanding and engagement, however, is difficult. Many audience members hold negative stereotypes of those who are different from them, lack interest in engaging different perspectives, or believe that their own culture is superior to other cultures.

In her book *Yellow Woman and a Beauty of the Spirit* (1996), Leslie Marmon Silko provides an example of effective strategies for encouraging audiences to engage and understand difference. The book is a collection of her essays about Native Americans and the injustices they face when confronting the Anglo-American legal system. Silko is Native American, Mexican, and Anglo, and although she spent many years in the Laguna Pueblo in New Mexico, she also attended Catholic schools in Albuquerque and later a public university. Much of her writing is about Pueblo life, but Silko always has felt a tension among her various worlds. Perhaps because she lives in different cultures, she is able to bridge them effectively and to present one to another in ways that encourage an attitude of openness rather than dismissal or rejection.

Using narrative criticism, we will examine one essay, "Yellow Woman and a Beauty of the Spirit," in Silko's book of the same name in an attempt to discover how narrative is used to make a culture appealing to outsiders in ways that encourage engagement with and understanding of that culture. Our focus is on those dimensions of the narrative—events and characters—that allow Silko to achieve this objective in the essay.

Events

The three major events in this narrative have similar kernels and satellites, although each addresses a different issue of Native American culture. The kernel in each event is a description of a cultural practice given directly by the narrator that educates readers about the culture. Each kernel begins with a story from Silko's past that functions as a satellite, providing entertainment and drawing the reader in. When Silko moves from satellite to kernel, the tone of the narrative changes from light-hearted memories to straightforward descriptions. We believe the narrator uses entertaining and involving satellites to support the kernels for a variety of reasons, which we detail below.

The narrative begins with the satellite of Silko's memory of women re-plastering her house. From her description, the reader can easily picture this "crew of Laguna women, in their forties and fifties," who carry ladders and load mud with ease. This description is provided by the narrator to support her claim (and the kernel) that, in her Pueblo, "there is no stigma on being female; gender is not used to control behav-

This essay was written while Laura S. More, Randi Boyd, Julie Bradley, and Erin Harris were students in Sonja K. Foss's rhetorical criticism class at the University of Colorado Denver in 2005. Used by permission of the authors.

ior" (Silko, 1996, p. 66). In this event, Silko moves quickly from the satellite to the kernel; they are both in one paragraph. The satellite lightens the subject on which Silko is trying to educate the reader. Her message in the kernel is strong; it implies Americans do use gender to control behavior. For the reader to hear her claim without becoming too offended, the narrator includes a light-hearted story about admirable women.

The second event deals with age in the Laguna Pueblo. As in the first event, the satellite comes before the kernel and is another of Silko's memories. This memory is about her Grandma Lily, who worked as a Ford Model A mechanic as a teenager and fixed washing machines and other appliances up until the age of seventy-five. This satellite leads into the kernel: "When a person was ready to do something, she did it. When she no longer was able, she stopped" (Silko, 1996, p. 66). The satellite about Grandma Lily's work serves three purposes in the narrative. First, it ties the previous topic of gender into a new topic of age. Second, it provides the reader from a different culture with a real example to support the kernel. It is easy for a person to say age and gender do not matter; however, with an example, an outsider is more likely to trust that this is true. Third, by incorporating familiar items from American culture—Ford's Model A and washing machines—the reader is given a sense of commonality with the Pueblo culture. Providing readers with a means to connect with the stories gives Silko a better chance of educating them about her own culture.

The third event in this narrative addresses sexuality in the Pueblo. The kernel of this event is this: "In the old Pueblo worldview, we are all a mixture of male and female, and this sexual identity is changing constantly" (Silko, 1996, p. 67). Silko spends quite a bit of time trying to support the Pueblo's beliefs on sexuality. The two events discussed earlier were both short and took up one page together; in contrast, this event has a page devoted to it. The length of the event may be due to the strong contrary beliefs her audience members are likely to hold on this subject.

Three satellites help develop the event of fluid sexuality. One is about a man in another village "who wore nail polish and women's blouses and permed his hair" (Silko, 1996, p. 67). Silko says that no one made fun of him because the Pueblo's community depends on every member for its survival. This satellite mimics the tone and feelings of the previous satellites. The narrator uses this story from her own memory to add validity to her claim that sexuality is arbitrary in Pueblo culture.

Silko then moves to describe a famous medicine man named the *Crawler* because of his hunchback. This satellite is not a direct memory of Silko's like the past ones have been but is a story known throughout her culture. This satellite suggests how far back the cultural attitudes about sexuality go. Here the narrator is trying to prove to her audience that diversity is not new in her culture, and differences have been dealt with in a consistent fashion throughout time—with respect and even indifference.

The third satellite of this event also differs from previous events by directly telling about how Native American cultures were changed by Christian missionaries, who introduced the idea of sexual inhibition. According to Silko, before their arrival, a man could act like a woman and marry a man, and the same was true for women. In addition, before the arrival of the missionaries, "marriage did not mean an end to sex with people other than your spouse" (Silko, 1996, p. 67). This final event is Silko's weakest attempt at educating readers from outside her culture. Silko simply lists differences between her culture and American culture and, while examples are provided in the satellites, those examples lack the descriptive and stylistic details of the preceding examples.

In her narrative, Silko uses specific examples from her past to emphasize the cultural beliefs about which she is attempting to educate the audience. The most effective examples are constructed of specific events that have a light-hearted dimension to them. The details help the reader understand how the beliefs described look in action, and the element of fun softens the impact of foreign concepts for readers. The events in the story include pieces of information to which the audience can relate to bring the audience into the story and perhaps into a new cultural belief system. Satellites with these elements break up the monotony of the educational kernels and keep the reader interested and involved in the narrative.

Characters

Not only the events of the narrative but the characters help Silko achieve the objective of facilitating openness to another culture. Characters are important to the audience because they provide a personification of the beliefs being described. Although there are several characters in this narrative, our focus is on the dominant characters and whether they contribute to providing outsiders with an appealing view of the culture.

The "crew of Laguna women" are lively and strong as characters. They are effective because they are highly regarded by the narrator, and readers cannot help but like these women. These characters vividly point to differences in gender roles between the Pueblo and the American cultures. By giving the women attributes that even people from a different culture may wish to emulate, the narrator makes the culture itself appealing to outsiders.

Silko's choice to include her Grandma Lily in the narrative is a good one because the relationship is close. If the narrator had used a person who seemed distant from her (for example, "I once heard of this townswoman who worked on Fords"), the reader might decide that this was a rare event. Grandma Lily, however, encourages readers to reflect on their own grandmothers and their unique talents. In direct contrast to this character is the "young man from a nearby village who wore nail polish" (Silko, 1996, p. 67). Silko's description of the event that involves this man is her weakest, and he also is one of her weakest characters. Whereas sexual and physical differences may not be as common as gender or growing old, the only examples Silko provides for explaining the Pueblo's attitudes on this subject are a young man she has not met and the Crawler, a medicine man from before her time. These two characters are not well developed and are distant from Silko and her readers. Because she does not know them, she cannot provide the detail that would encourage readers to want to try to understand them and to empathize with them.

We also found the characters of the Creator and the missionaries to be significant. The first time the Creator is brought up is to support open roles for women because the Creator is female. The second time she is referenced is to say that all differences are celebrated because the Creator made them. The Creator is not a major character, but these brief references to her give the audience the sense that she is ever present among the Pueblo culture. Because the femaleness of this character may be a foreign idea to many readers, however, Silko might have wanted to spend more time developing the character and legitimizing it as female.

Silko's portrayal of the Christian missionaries is problematic as well for achieving her objective of generating an attitude of openness to the culture. Silko only talks about the missionaries at the end of the narrative on the subject of sexuality in the

Pueblo, and their influence is portrayed in a negative way because they forced the Pueblo culture to change. Silko does nothing in her development of the missionaries' characters to mitigate negative responses readers may have to the contrast between the sexual practices of the two cultures. Audiences are allowed to picture the missionaries as they choose, and many readers may see them as people with superior beliefs and practices and thus to respond negatively to the very different beliefs and practices of the Pueblo culture.

Through characters directly involved in the action of the stories, Silko gives her readers people to whom they can relate. Readers can look up to characters with admirable qualities and can compare the attributes of characters in the story to themselves or to others they know. Such characters draw readers in and encourage them to engage with the culture. Those characters who are radically different from those that readers might experience in their own cultures and who are not well developed, however, may counter the positive view of the culture that is generated by the well-rounded, familiar characters.

Conclusion

Through a narrative criticism of an essay by Leslie Marmon Silko, we have identified some narrative strategies in terms of events and characters that rhetors can use to encourage outsiders to try to understand and engage difference. Kernels that are used to provide key contrasts with the audience's culture can be made more appealing with satellites that provide specific details that draw in audiences, connect to audience's experiences, and lighten the tone of the kernels. Characters who are presented as laudable and admirable, who are like individuals audience members probably have in their own lives, and who are well developed encourage audience members to consider another culture with openness. As a result, they are likely to make the effort to understand and perhaps even to engage that different culture in positive ways.

Works Cited

Silko, L. M. (1996). *Yellow woman and a beauty of the spirit: Essays on Native American life today.* New York: Simon & Schuster.

Additional Samples of Narrative Criticism

Bass, Jeff. "The Appeal to Efficiency as Narrative Closure: Lyndon Johnson and the Dominican Crisis, 1965." *Southern Speech Communication Journal*, 50 (Winter 1985), 103–20.

Brown, William J. "The Persuasive Appeal of Mediated Terrorism: The Case of the TWA Flight 847 Hijacking." *Western Journal of Speech Communication*, 54 (Spring 1990), 219–36.

Burgchardt, Carl R. "Discovering Rhetorical Imprints: La Follette, 'Iago,' and the Melodramatic Scenario." *Quarterly Journal of Speech*, 71 (November 1985), 441–56.

Carlson, A. Cheree. "The Role of Character in Public Moral Argument: Henry Ward Beecher and the Brooklyn Scandal." *Quarterly Journal of Speech*, 77 (February 1991), 38–52.

Carpenter, Ronald H. "Admiral Mahan, 'Narrative Fidelity,' and the Japanese Attack on Pearl Harbor." *Quarterly Journal of Speech*, 72 (August 1986), 290–305.

Christian, Allison. "Contesting the Myth of the 'Wicked Stepmother': Narrative Analysis of an Online Stepfamily Support Group." *Western Journal of Communication*, 69 (January 2005), 27–47.

Collins, Catherine A., and Jeanne E. Clark. "A Structural Narrative Analysis of *Nightline*'s 'This Week in the Holy Land.'" *Critical Studies in Mass Communication*, 9 (March 1992), 25–43.

Deming, Caren J. "*Hill Street Blues* as Narrative." *Critical Studies in Mass Communication*, 2 (March 1985), 1–22.

Dobkin, Bethami A. "Paper Tigers and Video Postcards: The Rhetorical Dimensions of Narrative Form in ABC News Coverage of Terrorism." *Western Journal of Communication*, 56 (Spring 1992), 143–60.

Fisher, Walter R. *Human Communication as Narration: Toward a Philosophy of Reason, Value, and Action*. Columbia: University of South Carolina Press, 1987, several essays, pp. 143–91.

Foust, Christina R., and Charles Soulkup. "Do I Exist?: Transcendent Subjects and Secrets in *The Sixth Sense*." *Western Journal of Communication*, 70 (April 2006), 115–33.

Gerland, Oliver. "Brecht and the Courtroom: Alienating Evidence in the 'Rodney King' Trials." *Text and Performance Quarterly*, 14 (October 1994), 305–18.

Griffin, Charles J. G. "The Rhetoric of Form in Conversion Narratives." *Quarterly Journal of Speech*, 76 (May 1990), 152–63.

Griffin, Charles J. G. "The 'Washingtonian Revival': Narrative and the Moral Transformation of Temperance Reform in Antebellum America." *Southern Communication Journal*, 66 (Fall 2000), 67–78.

Gross, Daniel G. "A Teachers' Strike, Rival Stories and Narrative Agreement." *Nebraska Speech Communication Association Journal*, 31 (Spring/Summer 1992), 47–56.

Hollihan, Thomas A. "The Public Controversy Over the Panama Canal Treaties: An Analysis of American Foreign Policy Rhetoric." *Western Journal of Speech Communication*, 50 (Fall 1986), 368–87.

Jasinski, James. "(Re)constituting Community through Narrative Argument: *Eros* and *Philia* in *The Big Chill*." *Quarterly Journal of Speech*, 79 (November 1993), 467–86.

Katriel, Tamar, and Aliza Shenhar. "Tower and Stockade: Dialogic Narration in Israeli Settlement Ethos." *Quarterly Journal of Speech*, 76 (November 1990), 359–80.

Kelley-Romano, Stephanie. "Mythmaking in Alien Abduction Narratives." *Communication Quarterly*, 54 (August 2006), 383–406.

Kirby, Erika L., M. Chad McBride, Sherianne Shuler, Marty J. Birkholt, Mary Ann Danielson, and Donna R. Pawlowski. "The Jesuit Difference (?): Narratives of

Negotiating Spiritual Values and Secular Practices." *Communication Studies,* 57 (March 2006), 87–105.

Kirkwood, William G. "Storytelling and Self-Confrontation: Parables as Communication Strategies." *Quarterly Journal of Speech,* 69 (February 1983), 58–74.

Kramer, Michael W., and Julie E. Berman. "Making Sense of a University's Culture: An Examination of Undergraduate Students' Stories." *Southern Communication Journal,* 66 (Summer 2001), 297–311.

Lewis, William F. "Telling America's Story: Narrative Form and the Reagan Presidency." *Quarterly Journal of Speech,* 73 (August 1987), 280–302.

Mandelbaum, Jennifer. "Couples Sharing Stories." *Communication Quarterly,* 35 (Spring 1987), 144–70.

Mumby, Dennis K. "The Political Function of Narrative in Organizations." *Communication Monographs,* 54 (June 1987), 113–27.

Olson, Scott R. "Meta-television: Popular Postmodernism." *Critical Studies in Mass Communication,* 4 (September 1987), 284–300.

Ott, Brian L., and Beth Bonnstetter. "'We're at Now, Now': *Spaceballs* as Parodic Tourism." *Southern Communication Journal,* 72 (October–December 2007), 309–27.

Owen, A. Susan. "Oppositional Voices in *China Beach*: Narrative Configurations of Gender and War." In *Narrative and Social Control,* ed. Dennis K. Mumby. Newbury Park, CA: Sage, 1993, pp. 207–31.

Peterson, Tarla Rai. "Telling the Farmers' Story: Competing Responses to Soil Conservation Rhetoric." *Quarterly Journal of Speech,* 77 (August 1991), 289–308.

Poulakos, Takis. "Isocrates' Use of Narrative in the *Evagoras*: Epideictic Rhetoric and Moral Action." *Quarterly Journal of Speech,* 73 (August 1987), 317–28.

Ritter, Kurt. "Drama and Legal Rhetoric: The Perjury Trials of Alger Hiss." *Western Journal of Speech Communication,* 49 (Spring 1985), 83–102.

Rosteck, Thomas. "Narrative in Martin Luther King's *I've Been to the Mountaintop*." *Southern Communication Journal,* 58 (Fall 1992), 22–32.

Rothenbuhler, Eric W. "Myth and Collective Memory in the Case of Robert Johnson." *Critical Studies in Media Communication,* 24 (August 2007), 189–205.

Rowland, Robert C., and John M. Jones. "Recasting the American Dream and American Politics: Barack Obama's Keynote Address to the 2004 Democratic National Convention." *Quarterly Journal of Speech,* 93 (November 2007), 425–48.

Rowland, Robert C., and Robert Strain. "Social Function, Polysemy and Narrative-Dramatic Form: A Case Study of *Do the Right Thing*." *Communication Quarterly,* 42 (Summer 1994), 213–28.

Rushing, Janice Hocker. "Mythic Evolution of 'The New Frontier' in Mass Mediated Rhetoric." *Critical Studies in Mass Communication,* 3 (September 1986), 265–96.

Rushing, Janice Hocker. "Ronald Reagan's 'Star Wars' Address: Mythic Containment of Technical Reasoning." *Quarterly Journal of Speech,* 72 (November 1986), 415–33.

Salvador, Michael. "The Rhetorical Genesis of Ralph Nader: A Functional Exploration of Narrative and Argument in Public Discourse." *Southern Communication Journal,* 59 (Spring 1994), 227–39.

Schely-Newman, Esther. "Finding One's Place: Locale Narratives in an Israeli *Moshav*." *Quarterly Journal of Speech,* 83 (November 1997), 401–15.

Sefcovic, Enid M. I., and Celeste M. Condit. "Narrative and Social Change: A Case Study of the Wagner Act of 1935." *Communication Studies,* 52 (Winter 2001), 284–301.

Smith, Larry David. "Convention Oratory as Institutional Discourse: A Narrative Synthesis of the Democrats and Republicans of 1988." *Communication Studies,* 41 (Spring 1990), 19–34.

Smith, Larry David. "A Narrative Analysis of the Party Platforms: The Democrats and Republicans of 1984." *Communication Quarterly,* 37 (Spring 1989), 91–99.

Smith, Larry David. "Narrative Styles in Network Coverage of the 1984 Nominating Conventions." *Western Journal of Speech Communication,* 52 (Winter 1988), 63–74.

Solomon, Martha. "Autobiographies as Rhetorical Narratives: Elizabeth Cady Stanton and Anna Howard Shaw as 'New Women.'" *Communication Studies,* 42 (Winter 1991), 354–70.

Stuckey, Mary E. "Anecdotes and Conversations: The Narrational and Dialogic Styles of Modern Presidential Communication." *Communication Quarterly,* 40 (Winter 1992), 45–55.

Zelizer, Barbie. "Achieving Journalistic Authority through Narrative." *Critical Studies in Mass Communication,* 7 (December 1990), 366–76.

Pentadic Criticism

Pentadic criticism is rooted in the work of Kenneth Burke, who made significant contributions to our understanding of how and why human beings use rhetoric and to what effect. Many of his ideas have been used as critical methods (see, for example, cluster criticism in chapter 4). In this chapter, the focus is pentadic criticism, derived from Burke's concept of the pentad. It is a method that seeks to answer the question, "What is involved, when we say what people are doing and why they are doing it?"[1] Although Burke does not claim that the pentad is original with him, noting its origins in sources such as Aristotle's *Nicomachean Ethics* and Talcott Parsons's *The Structure of Social Action*, the method as it is used in rhetorical criticism is certainly associated with Burke.

Pentadic criticism is rooted in Burke's notion of *dramatism*, the label Burke gives to the analysis of human motivation through terms derived from the study of drama.[2] Two basic assumptions underlie dramatism. One is that language use constitutes action, not motion. Motion corresponds to the biological or animal aspect of the human being, which is concerned with bodily processes such as growth, digestion, respiration, and the requirements for the maintenance of those processes—food, shelter, and rest, for example. The biological level does not involve the use of symbols and thus is nonsymbolic.

In contrast, action corresponds to the neurological aspect of the human being, which Burke defines as the ability of an organism to acquire language or a symbol system. This is the realm of action or the symbolic. Some of our motives are derived from our animality—as when we seek food to sustain our bodies. Others, however, originate in our symbolicity, as when we strive to reach goals in arenas such as education, politics, religion, and finance. Even our desires in such arenas arise from our symbol system.[3]

355

Burke elaborates on his notion of action at the heart of dramatism by establishing three conditions for action. One is that action must involve freedom or choice. If we cannot make a choice, we are not acting but are behaving mechanically, like a ball hit with a racket. Of course, we never can be completely free, but implicit in the idea of action is some choice. A second condition necessary for action is purpose. Either consciously or unconsciously, we must select or will a choice—we must choose one option over others. Motion is a third requirement for action. While motion can exist without action (as when an object falls, through the force of gravity, to the ground), action cannot exist without motion. Symbolic activity or action is grounded in the realm of the nonsymbolic.[4]

The distinction Burke proposes between motion and action is largely a theoretical one because once organisms acquire a symbol system, we are virtually unable to do anything purely in the realm of motion. Once we have a symbol system, everything we do is interpreted through the lens of that symbol system. To cook a meal, for example, may be considered motion because it satisfies the biological need for food. Yet, creating a meal is impossible without the involvement of our symbolic conceptions of eating. As we choose foods our family members or friends like and set the table and arrange the food on plates in aesthetically pleasing ways, the simple act of eating to sustain ourselves is transformed into symbolically laden messages about ourselves, our friends, and food. Preparing a meal, which has a biological basis, becomes an action.

A second assumption of dramatism is that humans develop and present messages in much the same way that a play is presented. We use rhetoric to constitute and present a particular view of our situation, just as a play creates and presents a certain world or situation inhabited by characters in the play. Through rhetoric, we size up a situation and name its structure and outstanding ingredients. How we describe a situation indicates how we are perceiving it, the choices we see available to us, and the action we are likely to take in that situation. Our language, then, provides clues to our motives or why we do what we do. A rhetor who perceives that one person is the cause of a particular problem, for example, will use rhetoric that names that perception. She will describe the situation in such a way as to feature that person's characteristics and to downplay other elements that may be contributing to the problem. Once you know how rhetors have described situations, you are able to discover their motives for action in the situations and how they justify, explain, and account for that action.[5]

As rhetors describe their situations, they do so using the five basic elements of a drama—*act, agent, agency, scene,* and *purpose*. These five terms constitute what Burke calls the *pentad*, and they are used as principles or a "grammar" for describing any symbolic act fully:

> You must have some word that names the *act* (names what took place, in thought or deed), and another that names the *scene* (the background of the act, the situation in which it occurred); also you must indicate what person or kind of person (*agent*) performed the act, what means or instruments he used (*agency*), and the *purpose*.[6]

If you are acquainted with journalistic writing, you will recognize these terms as the five questions a journalist must answer to write an adequate story about an act or event: who? (agent), what? (act), why? (purpose), when? and where? (scene). Agency is an additional concern—how the act was done.

In addition to terms for act, scene, agent, agency, and purpose, Burke sometimes includes attitude as an element to be considered in an analysis of motivation. Attitude designates the manner in which particular means are employed. The act of cultivating a garden is done through specific agencies such as seeds, plants, and water. To cultivate with extraordinary diligence and care, however, involves an attitude or a "how." Burke states that "on later occasions I have regretted that I had not turned the pentad into a hexad, with attitude as the sixth term."[7] Because he did not, he includes attitude as a part of agent: "in its character as a state of mind that may or may not lead to an act, it is quite clearly to be classed under the head of agent."[8]

Burke uses ratios that link the five terms in pairs as the mechanism for discovering the rhetor's motive in an artifact. The ratios help the critic trace how each term in the pentad is tied to the other terms. A ratio is a pairing of two of the key terms that allows a critic to discover the relationship between them by analyzing how the first term in the pair shapes understanding of the second term. Key terms affect one another in this way because when "we *perceive* a scene, agent, act, agency, purpose, or attitude as having a given nature or quality, or we *characterize* one of those pentadic elements (or accept another's characterization), we 'grammatically' limit potential interpretations of all the other terms." The grammatical limitations, when "taken as a whole, constitute the *motive* for the action in question."[9] Explication of the ratios suggests which term controls the other terms, and in this term, Burke suggests, motive is located.

Procedures

Using the pentadic method of criticism, a critic analyzes an artifact through a four-step process: (1) selecting an artifact; (2) analyzing the artifact; (3) formulating a research question; and (4) writing the essay.

Selecting an Artifact

Virtually any artifact is appropriate for a pentadic analysis. Discursive and nondiscursive artifacts work equally well, and the length and complexity of the artifacts generally do not matter in an application of the pentadic method.

Analyzing the Artifact

In criticism in which the terms of the pentad are used as units of analysis, two operations are performed by a critic: (1) labeling the five terms of *agent, act, scene, purpose,* and *agency* in the artifact; and (2) applying the ratios to identify the dominant term.

Labeling Terms

The first step in a pentadic analysis is to identify the five terms in the artifact from the perspective of the rhetor. Identification of the *agent* involves naming the group or individual who is the protagonist or main character of the situation described in the artifact as it is presented by the rhetor.[10] The agent could be the rhetor himself or another person or group. In a presentation to the jury at a murder trial, for example, a lawyer—the rhetor—could choose as the agent the murderer, the murder victim, or the victim's family. The agent in a speech by the president of the United States is the person, group, or institution that is the primary subject of the speech—perhaps Congress, the CIA, or the president's mother.

The *act* is the rhetor's presentation of the major action taken by the protagonist or agent.[11] A critic who is studying the speeches of the U.S. president, for example, may find that the act is the effort to accomplish health-care reform, with the president serving as the agent. In a speech honoring someone for her community service, the act might be the creation of a literacy program by the person being honored. If the artifact you are studying is the work of an artist, you may find that, in a particular painting, the act is bathing a child, with the agent the woman who is shown doing the bathing.

The means the rhetor says are used to perform the act or the instruments used to accomplish it are labeled the *agency*.[12] In a speech about health-care reform, for example, a president might depict the agency as hard work, careful compromise, or futile attempts to gain the cooperation of the opposing party. In a song about love gone wrong, the agency for the lover's departure might be explained as callous disregard for the protagonist's feelings and needs.

Scene is the ground, location, or situation in which the rhetor says the act takes place—the kind of stage the rhetor sets when describing physical conditions, social and cultural influences, or historical causes.[13] In an inaugural address, for example, a president might describe a scene of division and hatred among Americans. In an environmentalist's testimony before a city council on the impact of a proposed policy on the local environment, the advocate might describe a scene of abundant nature in harmony and balance.

The *purpose* of the act is what the rhetor suggests the agent intends to accomplish by performing the act.[14] It is the rhetor's account of the protagonist's intentions or reason for an action. The purpose for a Native American's protest speech at a Columbus Day celebration, for example, might be to gain recognition for Native Americans' primary role in the creation of American civilization and culture. The purpose attributed to a community volunteer's actions might be to repay the support she received from others early in her life. Purpose is not synonymous with motive. Purpose is the reason for action by the agent that is specified by the rhetor for the agent. Motive is the larger explanation for the rhetor's action, manifest in the rhetorical artifact as a whole.

As you name the five terms in the artifact you are analyzing, be careful not to look for terms that appear to be one type of term but actually are functioning as another type. You want to look for the terms that are functioning in the artifact as act, agent, scene, purpose, or agency. For example, an agent actually may be functioning as a scene and not as an agent in an artifact. Likewise, a scene may be functioning as an agent. In Al Gore's film *An Inconvenient Truth*, for example, the earth, which usually would function as and be labeled as the *scene* in most pentads, is functioning as a character.

Identification of the five pentadic terms results in an overview of the perspective that is being taken by a rhetor of a particular situation. A critic may discover, for example, that a prisoner in Guantanamo who engages in a hunger strike might write a letter to friends and family in which he characterizes his situation in this way:

- Act: Denial of basic rights to an American citizen
- Agent: United States
- Agency: Imprisonment
- Purpose: To fight terrorism
- Scene: Guantanamo prison

This same prisoner, of course, has an unlimited number of options he can use to describe his situation, and each description constitutes a different vocabulary of motives. He could name, for example, the following key terms:

- Act: Hunger strike
- Agent: Himself
- Agency: Courage and self-sacrifice
- Purpose: To publicize injustices at Guantanamo
- Scene: Guantanamo prison

A piece of public art provides a visual example of naming pentadic terms. The city of Denver has installed an outdoor sculpture at its convention center called *I See What You Mean*, created by the artist Lawrence Argent. It is a 40-foot-tall blue bear made of metal that stands on its hind legs and peers into the windows of the convention center (see color photo gallery; black and white image on p. 360). If you were to take the blue bear as your artifact, you might name the key terms in this way:

- Agent: Blue bear
- Act: Looking into the convention center
- Purpose: To see what is going on
- Agency: Curiosity and playfulness
- Scene: Convention center in downtown Denver

Don't be surprised if you discover more than one pentadic set operating in your artifact. You might discover that a rhetor sets up one set of terms at one place in the artifact and offers a second set at a different place in the artifact. You might choose to focus on just one if you are interested primarily in it for some reason or if it is the primary pentadic set developed. But paying attention to all of the pentadic sets within an artifact can yield useful critical insights. You might discover connections or contradictions among pentadic sets that provide insights into the constructed worldview that would not be available to you if you focused on only one of the pentads.[15]

Applying the Ratios to Identify the Dominant Term

The naming of the five terms of the pentad is the first step in the application of the pentadic method of criticism. The next step is to discover which of the five elements identified dominates, is featured in the rhetoric, or is the controlling term. Discovery of the dominant term—the most important term among the five and the term through which everything else happens—provides insight into what dimension of the situation the rhetor privileges or sees as most important. Identifying this term thus enables you to name the motive for the rhetor's construction of the situation.

I See What You Mean by Lawrence Argent. Photograph by Sonja K. Foss. (Image also included in color photo gallery.)

Ratios are used to discover the dominant pentadic element. Application of the ratios involves the systematic pairing of the elements in the pentad to discover the relationship between them and the nature of the influence each has on the other. Each of the five elements, then, may be put together with each of the others to form these 20 ratios: scene-act, scene-agent, scene-agency, scene-purpose, act-scene, act-agent, act-agency, act-purpose, agent-scene, agent-act, agent-agency, agent-purpose, agency-scene, agency-act, agency-agent, agency-purpose, purpose-scene, purpose-act, purpose-agent, and purpose-agency. Application of the ratios involves pairing two terms from those identified in the pentad for your artifact. There is no right ratio with which to begin this process; simply select two of the terms to pair. With each ratio, look for the relationship between these two terms in the rhetor's description of the situation, trying to discover if the first term influences or directs the nature of the second term.

You may begin, for example, by putting together scene and act in a scene-act ratio. This ratio involves asking whether the nature of the scene, as described by the rhetor, affects the nature of the act the rhetor describes. To determine the answer to the question implied by the ratio, you might ask questions such as, "Does the first term in the ratio require that the second term be a certain way?" or "Is there something in the first term that determines the nature of the second term in this ratio?" An act-scene ratio, in contrast, would explore whether the nature of the act dominates—whether the act, as it is described, directs, determines, or shapes the nature of the scene. You may discover that there is a significant relationship between the two terms in a ratio, or you may find that the first term in the ratio has little impact or effect on the second. Let's say the rhetor describes the scene as a country in which oppressive and dangerous conditions exist, freedom is being repressed, and citizens are being denied the opportunity for self-determination. The act is described as the heroic invasion of that country. In a scene-act ratio, the scene is portrayed by the rhetor as the precipitating event that generates the act of heroism; there would be no need to perform acts of heroism without the dangerous scene. Thus, the scene dominates over act in this ratio; it affects the nature of the act.

If a critic discovers, on the other hand, that the rhetor describes a scene in which people are content and benefit from a country's political structure and names as the act the invasion of the country by another, the outcome of an exploration of the scene-act ratio would be different. In this case, the scene seems to have little influence on the act, but neither does the act have much effect on the scene. A critic probably would find, after investigating other ratios, that the dominant term of the artifact is something other than scene or act—perhaps agent (the nature of the invading country as a domineering, imperialist power) or purpose (the invading country's goal is to impose its will on other countries to bolster its influence in the world).

As you apply the ratios to discover the relationships among the terms, you will find that you are balancing between your general knowledge of the kinds of relationships that exist among the terms and the relationship that is being set up within the artifact. Let's return to an analysis of the sculpture of the blue bear in downtown Denver, where you have named the agency as curiosity and playfulness and the agent as the blue bear. As you are trying to discover the nature of the relationship between the agency and the agent, you might answer the question, "Is there something about this agency that determines this agent or requires that it be a blue bear?" from a general, broad perspective: "No. You don't have to have a cute blue bear to embody curiosity and playfulness—a kitten, for example, could embody those qualities, too." But if you took a more specific perspective and focused on the image Denver actively constructs of itself as a playful city with access to natural resources, then you might answer "yes" to that question because the nature of the character of Denver indeed might require something like the blue bear as an agent to employ the tools of curiosity and playfulness—or at least the bear is not contradictory to that agency. Your first answer draws on general knowledge of how things work in the culture of which the artifact is a part, but the second relies on more normative knowledge—"shared beliefs" in a community "about 'what goes with what' at a given point in time, underlying expectations that one will or should find certain types of agents engaging in certain types of actions, using certain agencies, within certain scenes, for certain purposes."[16]

A burglar trying to steal from a house provides another example of how a critic can use generally shared beliefs about what goes with what in determining which terms affect the nature of others. If you identify a burglar as the agent in a particular pentad, "consider how quickly you can list your own expectations about where you might find him, what he might be doing, when he might be doing it, how he might be doing it, why he might be doing it."[17] At the same time, you would want to consider the characteristics of this particular burglar in this particular setting that might create unique expectations for the relationship of the pentadic terms to one another.

Continue to pair terms in ratios to discover if one term seems to affect or require the nature and character of another. For each of the 20 ratios, note "yes," "no," or "unclear" as the answer to the question of whether the first term in the ratio determines the second. You might have, for example, at the end of this process, a list that looks like this:

scene-act: no
scene-agent: no
scene-agency: no
scene-purpose: yes

act-scene: no
act-agent: no
act-agency: no
act-purpose: no

agent-scene: yes
agent-act: yes
agent-agency: yes
agent-purpose: no

agency-scene: no
agency-act: unclear
agency-agent: no
agency-purpose: unclear

purpose-scene: yes
purpose-act: no
purpose-agent: no
purpose-agency: no

A review of the ratios in this manner produces a pattern that points to the dominant term—the term that receives the most "yes" answers to the question of whether the first term directs or requires the second. In this case, agent is the dominant term because it controls the second term of the ratio more than any of the other terms do.

The process of applying the ratios to discover which term controls or dominates the others is not included in the essay of criticism you write. This is work you do behind the scenes prior to writing the essay. In your essay, you identify the featured or dominant term and provide support for it. This support usually takes the form of a discussion of how the term you propose as the dominant one influences or requires the other terms of the rhetor's description of the situation.

Burke provides a suggestion for gaining a more in-depth view of a rhetor's definition of a situation once you have discovered the dominant term of the pentad. The dominant term can be used to identify the philosophical system to which it corresponds, with that system generating ideas about the definition of a situation, its meaning for rhetors and audiences, and its possible consequences. If *act* is featured in the pentad, Burke suggests, the corresponding philosophy is realism, the doctrine that universal principles are more real than objects as they are physically sensed. This philosophical position is opposite that of nominalism, the doctrine that abstract concepts, general terms, or universals have no objective reference but exist only as names. If *scene* is featured, the philosophy that corresponds is materialism—the system that regards all facts and reality as explainable in terms of matter and motion or physical laws. If *agent* is featured, the corresponding philosophy is idealism, the system that views the mind or spirit as each person experiences it as fundamentally real, with the universe seen as mind or spirit in its essence.

The remaining terms are equated with other philosophical systems. If *agency* is featured, the pragmatic philosophy is the applicable philosophical school. Pragmatism is the means necessary for the attainment of a goal—instrumentalism or concern with consequences, function, and what something is "good for." In this doctrine, the meaning of a proposition or course of action lies in its observable consequences, and the sum of these consequences constitutes its meaning. If *purpose* is featured, the corresponding philosophy is mysticism. In mysticism, the element of unity is emphasized to the point that individuality disappears. Identification often becomes so strong that the individual is unified with some cosmic or universal purpose.[18]

In a speech by an antiabortion advocate on the appropriateness of killing doctors who perform abortions, for example, the rhetor may describe the agent—himself—as a heroic savior, the act as stopping murder, the agency as any means necessary to stop murder, the purpose as saving innocent lives, and the scene as one of desperation in which legal tactics to stop murder have been unsuccessful. You may discover, as a result of application of the ratios, that the dominant term is purpose—to save innocent lives. With purpose featured, those who are persuaded by his argument accept a definition of the situation centered on purpose. The corresponding philosophy is mysticism, which features identification with a cosmic or universal purpose. You then could speculate that the motivating force for the rhetor and those who share his definition of the situation is a belief that they are representatives of divine will, doing God's work of honoring human life. The sacredness of this mission allows whatever acts are necessary to fulfill it.

A pentadic analysis reveals a rhetor's perspective or worldview, but be aware that a worldview can be constructed for various rhetorical purposes. Be careful that you do not confuse the construction of the situation your analysis reveals with the rhetor's actual worldview. When you analyze a text produced by a rhetor to express that person's view of a situation, you may be tapping into that rhetor's worldview—at least according to that rhetor's ability to express it. But you also may be analyzing the rhetor's representation of a situation for rhetorical purposes. In such cases, a rhetor may be constructing a situation and presenting it rhetorically through particular key terms, but that presentation does not represent the rhetor's personal worldview. Lawyers, for example, often develop the terms of a pentad to construct a worldview as they advocate for a client, but that worldview and the motive it reveals are not representative of their personal perspective on that situation. Advertisers and politicians are others who often construct pentadic scenarios to describe situations that differ from their own personal views.

Formulating a Research Question

Knowing a rhetor's worldview—whether it is constructed to express that rhetor's genuine perspective or to function rhetorically in some way—can be the basis for understanding many different rhetorical processes, so the research questions asked by critics using the pentadic method of criticism vary widely. You can ask questions about, for example, the significance of a particular term as controlling, the nature of a message in which a particular term is controlling, or the implications of particular constructions of the world and motives for rhetorical processes or public controversies.

Writing the Essay

After completing the analysis, you are ready to write your essay, which includes five major components: (1) an introduction, in which you discuss the research question, its contribution to rhetorical theory, and its significance; (2) a description of the artifact and its context; (3) a description of the method of criticism—in this case, pentadic analysis; (4) a report of the findings of the analysis, in which you identify the five pentadic terms in your artifact and suggest which one is dominant; and (5) a discussion of the contribution the analysis makes to rhetorical theory.

Sample Essays

Following are three sample essays in which pentadic analysis is used to discover the ways in which rhetors have chosen to describe their situations. David A. Ling uses the terms of the pentad to explore and evaluate Edward Kennedy's efforts to persuade an audience to see him as the victim of an accident rather than as responsible for it. The implicit research question that guides Ling's analysis is, "What types of definitions of situations are effective in enabling rhetors to regain credibility?" In her pentadic analysis of Project Prevention, Kimberly C. Elliott seeks to answer the question, "What strategies can be used to appeal to multiple and diverse audiences?" In the third sample, Danielle C. Cornell uses pentadic elements as units of analysis to explore a proanorexia text to understand a possible motive for self-inflicted dangerous acts.

Notes

[1] Kenneth Burke, *A Grammar of Motives* (1945; rpt. Berkeley: University of California Press, 1969), p. xv.

[2] For a discussion of dramatism, see: Kenneth Burke, *Language as Symbolic Action: Essays on Life, Literature, and Method* (Berkeley: University of California Press, 1966), p. 54; Kenneth Burke, *The Philosophy of Literary Form* (1941; rpt. Berkeley: University of California Press, 1973), p. 103; Burke, *A Grammar of Motives*, pp. xxii, 60; Kenneth Burke, "The Five Master Terms: Their Place in a 'Dramatistic' Grammar of Motives," *View*, 2 (June 1943), 50–52; Kenneth Burke, "Dramatism," in *International Encyclopedia of the Social Sciences*, ed. David L. Sills (New York: Macmillan/Free, 1968), VII, 445–52; and Kenneth Burke, "Rhetoric, Poetics, and Philosophy," in *Rhetoric, Philosophy, and Literature: An Exploration*, ed. Don M. Burks (West Lafayette: Purdue University Press, 1978), pp. 32–33.

[3] The distinction between action and motion is discussed in: Burke, "Dramatism," p. 445; Kenneth Burke, *Permanence and Change: An Anatomy of Purpose* (1954; rpt. Indianapolis: Bobbs-Merrill, 1965), pp. 162, 215; Burke, *Language as Symbolic Action*, pp. 28, 53, 63, 67, 482; and Kenneth Burke, *The Rhetoric of Religion: Studies in Logology* (Berkeley: University of California Press, 1970), pp. 16, 274.

[4] Burke discusses conditions required for action in: *The Rhetoric of Religion*, pp. 39, 188, 281; *A Grammar of Motives*, pp. 14, 276; *The Philosophy of Literary Form*, p. xvi; and "Dramatism," p. 447.

[5] For more on the process of sizing up a situation through rhetoric, see Burke, *The Philosophy of Literary Form*, pp. 1, 6, 109, 298, 304.

[6] Burke, *A Grammar of Motives*, p. xv.

[7] Kenneth Burke, *Dramatism and Development* (Barre, MA: Clark University Press, 1972), p. 23.

[8] Burke, *A Grammar of Motives*, p. 20.

[9] Clarke Rountree, "Instantiating 'The Law' and its Dissents in *Korematsu v. United States*: A Dramatistic Analysis of Judicial Discourse," *Quarterly Journal of Speech*, 87 (February 2001), 4.

[10] For a discussion of agent, see Burke, *A Grammar of Motives*, pp. 20, 171–226.

[11] For a discussion of act, see Burke, *A Grammar of Motives*, pp. 227–74.

[12] Agency is discussed in Burke, *A Grammar of Motives*, pp. 275–320.

[13] Scene is discussed in Burke, *A Grammar of Motives*, pp. xvi, 12, 77, 84, 85, 90; Burke, *The Rhetoric of Religion*, p. 26; and Burke, *Language as Symbolic Action*, p. 360.

[14] For a discussion of purpose, see Burke, *A Grammar of Motives*, pp. 275–320.

[15] J. Clarke Rountree, III, "Coming to Terms with Kenneth Burke's Pentad," *American Communication Journal*, 1 (May 1998), 4–5.

[16] Rountree, "Coming to Terms," p. 3.

[17] Clarke Rountree, *Judging the Supreme Court: Constructions of Motives in* Bush v. Gore (East Lansing: Michigan State University Press, 2007), p. 14.

[18] Burke, *A Grammar of Motives*, pp. 128–30.

A Pentadic Analysis of Senator Edward Kennedy's Address to the People of Massachusetts July 25, 1969

David A. Ling

On July 25, 1969 Senator Edward Kennedy addressed the people of the state of Massachusetts for the purpose of describing the events surrounding the death of Miss Mary Jo Kopechne. The broadcasting networks provided prime time coverage of Senator Kennedy's address, and a national audience listened as Kennedy recounted the events of the previous week. The impact of that incident and Kennedy's subsequent explanation have been a subject of continuing comment ever since.

This paper will examine some of the rhetorical choices Kennedy made either consciously or unconsciously in his address of July 25th. It will then speculate on the possible impact that those choices may have on audience response to the speech. The principal tool used for this investigation will be the "Dramatistic Pentad" found in the writings of Kenneth Burke.

The Pentad and Human Motivation

The pentad evolved out of Burke's attempts to understand the bases of human conduct and motivation. Burke argues that "human conduct being in the realm of action and end . . . is most directly discussible in dramatistic terms."[1] He maintains that, in a broad sense, history can be viewed as a play, and, just as there are a limited number of basic plots available to the author, so also there are a limited number of situations that occur to man. It, therefore, seems appropriate to talk about situations that occur to man in the language of the stage. As man sees these similar situations (or dramas) occurring, he develops strategies to explain what is happening. When man uses language, according to Burke, he indicates his strategies for dealing with these situations. That is, as man speaks he indicates how he perceives the world around him.

Burke argues that whenever a man describes a situation he provides answers to five questions: "What was done (act), when or where it was done (scene), who did it (agent), how he did it (agency), and why (purpose)."[2] Act, scene, agent, agency, and purpose are the five terms that constitute the "Dramatistic Pentad." As man describes the situation around him, he orders these five elements to reflect his view of that situation.

Perhaps the clearest way to explain how the pentad functions is to examine Burke's own use of the concept in *The Grammar of Motives*.[3] In that work, Burke argues that various philosophical schools feature different elements of the human situation. For example, the materialist school adopts a vocabulary that focuses on the scene as the central element in any situation. The agent, act, agency, and purpose are viewed as functions of the scene. On the other hand, the idealist school views the agent (or individual) as central and subordinates the other elements to the agent. Thus, both the materialist and the idealist, looking at the same situation, would describe the same five elements as existing in that situation. However, each views a different element as central and controlling. In Burke's own analysis he further suggests philosophical

From *Central States Speech Journal*, 21 (Summer 1970), 81–86. Used by permission of the Central States Speech Association and the author.

schools that relate to the other three elements of the pentad: the act, agency, and purpose. What is important in this analysis is not which philosophical schools are related to the featuring of each element. What is important is that as one describes a situation his ordering of the five elements will suggest which of the several different views of that situation he has, depending on which element he describes as controlling.

This use of the pentad suggests two conclusions. First, the pentad functions as a tool for content analysis. The five terms provide a method of determining how a speaker views the world. Indeed, this is what Burke means when he says that the pentad provides "a synoptic way to talk about their [man's] talk-about [his world]."[4]

A second conclusion that results from this analysis is that man's description of a situation reveals what he regards as the appropriate response to various human situations. For example, the speaker who views the agent as the cause of a problem will reflect by his language not only what Burke would call an idealist philosophy, but he will be limited to proposing solutions that attempt to limit the actions of the agent or to remove the agent completely. The speaker who finds the agent to be the victim of the scene not only reflects a materialist philosophy but will propose solutions that would change the scene. Thus, an individual who describes the problem of slums as largely a matter of man's unwillingness to change his environment will propose self-help as the answer to the problem. The person who, looking at the same situation, describes man as a victim of his environment will propose that the slums be razed and its inhabitants be relocated into a more conducive environment. The way in which a speaker describes a situation reflects his perception of reality and indicates what choices of action are available to him.

The Pentad and Rhetorical Criticism

But what has all this to do with rhetoric? If persuasion is viewed as the attempt of one man to get another to accept his view of reality as the correct one, then the pentad can be used as a means of examining how the persuader has attempted to achieve the restructuring of the audience's view of reality. Burke suggests how such an analysis might take place when he says in *The Grammar of Motives*: "Indeed, though our concern here is with the Grammar of Motives, we may note a related resource of Rhetoric: one may deflect attention from scenic matters by situating the motives of an act in the agent (as were one to account for wars purely on the basis of a "warlike instinct" in people): or conversely, one may deflect attention from criticism of personal motives by deriving an act or attitude not from traits of the agent but from the nature of the situation."[5]

Thus beginning with the language of the stage, the Pentad, it is possible to examine a speaker's discourse to determine what view of the world he would have an audience accept. One may then make a judgment as to both the appropriateness and adequacy of the description the speaker has presented.

Edward Kennedy's July 25th Address

Having suggested the methodology we now turn to a consideration of Senator Edward Kennedy's address of July 25th to the people of Massachusetts. The analysis will attempt to establish two conclusions. First, the speech functioned to minimize Kennedy's responsibility for his actions after the death of Miss Kopechne. Second, the speech was also intended to place responsibility for Kennedy's future on the shoulders of the people of Massachusetts. These conclusions are the direct antithesis of statements made by Kennedy during the speech. Halfway through the presentation,

Kennedy commented: "I do not seek to escape responsibility for my actions by placing blame either on the physical, emotional trauma brought on by the accident or on anyone else. I regard as indefensible the fact that I did not report the accident to the police immediately."[6] Late in the speech, in discussing the decision on whether or not to remain in the Senate, Kennedy stated that "this is a decision that I will have finally to make on my own." These statements indicated that Kennedy accepted both the blame for the events of that evening and the responsibility for the decision regarding his future. However, the description of reality presented by Kennedy in this speech forced the audience to reject these two conclusions.

Edward Kennedy—Victim of the Scene

The speech can best be examined in two parts. The first is the narrative in which Kennedy explained what occurred on the evening of July 18th. The second part of the speech involved Kennedy's concern over remaining in the U.S. Senate.

In Kennedy's statement concerning the events of July 18th we can identify these elements:

The scene (the events surrounding the death of Miss Kopechne)
The agent (Kennedy)
The act (Kennedy's failure to report immediately the accident)
The agency (whatever methods were available to make such a report)
The purpose (to fulfill his legal and moral responsibilities)

In describing this situation, Kennedy ordered the elements of the situation in such a way that the scene became controlling. In Kennedy's description of the events of that evening, he began with statements that were, in essence, simple denials of any illicit relationship between Miss Kopechne and himself. "There is no truth, no truth whatever to the widely circulated suspicions of immoral conduct that have been leveled at my behavior and hers regarding that night. There has never been a private relationship between us of any kind." Kennedy further denied that he was "driving under the influence of liquor." These statements function rhetorically to minimize his role as agent in this situation. That is, the statements suggest an agent whose actions were both moral and rational prior to the accident. Kennedy then turned to a description of the accident itself: "Little over a mile away the car that I was driving on an *unlit* road went off a *narrow bridge* which had *no guard rails* and was built on a *left angle* to the road. The car overturned into a *deep pond* and immediately filled with water." (Emphasis mine) Such a statement placed Kennedy in the position of an agent caught in a situation not of his own making. It suggests the scene as the controlling element.

Even in Kennedy's description of his escape from the car, there is the implicit assumption that his survival was more a result of chance or fate than of his own actions. He commented: "I remember thinking as the cold water rushed in around my head that I was for certain drowning. Then water entered my lungs and I actually felt the sensation of drowning. But somehow I struggled to the surface alive." The suggestion in Kennedy's statement was that he was in fact at the mercy of the situation and that his survival was not the result of his own calculated actions. As an agent he was not in control of the scene, but rather its helpless victim.

After reaching the surface of the pond, Kennedy said that he "made repeated efforts to save Mary Jo." However, the "strong" and "murky" tide not only prevented him from accomplishing the rescue, but only succeeded in "increasing [his] state of utter exhaustion and alarm." The situation described is, then, one of an agent totally at the mercy of a scene that he cannot control. Added to this was Kennedy's statement that his physicians verified a cerebral concussion. If the audience accepted this entire description, it cannot conclude that Kennedy's actions during the next few hours were "indefensible." The audience rather must conclude that Kennedy was the victim of a tragic set of circumstances.

At this point in the speech Senator Kennedy commented on the confused and irrational nature of his thoughts, thoughts which he "would not have seriously entertained under normal circumstances." But, as Kennedy described them, these were not normal circumstances, and this was *not* a situation over which he had control.

Kennedy provided an even broader context for viewing him as the victim when he expressed the concern that "some awful curse did actually hang over the Kennedys." What greater justification could be provided for concluding that an agent is not responsible for his acts than to suggest that the agent is, in fact, the victim of some tragic fate.

Thus, in spite of his conclusion that his actions were "indefensible," the description of reality presented by Kennedy suggested that he, as agent, was the victim of a situation (the scene) over which he had no control.

Kennedy's Senate Seat: In the Hands of the People

In the second part and much shorter development of the speech, the situation changes. Here we can identify the following elements:

The scene (current reaction to the events of July 18th)
The agent (the people of Massachusetts)
The act (Kennedy's decision on whether to resign)
The agency (statement of resignation)
The purpose (to remove Kennedy from office)

Here, again, Kennedy described himself as having little control over the situation. However, it was not the scene that was controlling, but rather it was agents other than Kennedy. That is, Kennedy's decision on whether or not he will continue in the Senate was not to be based on the "whispers" and "innuendo" that constitute the scene. Rather, his decision would be based on whether or not the people of Massachusetts believed those whispers.

Kennedy commented: "If at any time the citizens of Massachusetts should lack confidence in their senator's character or his ability, with or without justification, he could not, in my opinion, adequately perform his duties and should not continue in office." Thus, were Kennedy to decide not to remain in the Senate it would be because the people of Massachusetts had lost confidence in him; responsibility in the situation rests with agents other than Kennedy.

This analysis suggests that Kennedy presented descriptions of reality which, if accepted, would lead the audience to two conclusions:

1. Kennedy was a tragic victim of a scene he could not control.

2. His future depended, not on his own decision, but on whether or not the people of Massachusetts accepted the whispers and innuendo that constituted the immediate scene.

Acceptance of the first conclusion would, in essence, constitute a rejection of any real guilt on the part of Kennedy. Acceptance of the second conclusion meant that responsibility for Kennedy's future was dependent on whether or not the people of Massachusetts believed Kennedy's description of what happened on the evening of July 18th, or if they would believe "whispers and innuendo."

Rhetorical Choice and Audience Response

If this analysis is correct, then it suggests some tentative implications concerning the effect of the speech. First, the positive response of the people of Massachusetts was virtually assured. During the next few days thousands of letters of support poured into Kennedy's office. The overwhelming endorsement was as much an act of purification for the people of that state as it was of Kennedy. That is, the citizenry was saying, "We choose not to believe whispers and innuendo. Therefore, there is no reason for Ted Kennedy to resign." Support also indicated that the audience accepted his description of reality rather than his conclusion that he was responsible for his actions. Guilt has, therefore, shifted from Kennedy to the people of Massachusetts. Having presented a description of the events of July 18th which restricts his responsibility for those events, Kennedy suggested that the real "sin" would be for the people to believe that the "whispers and innuendoes" were true. As James Reston has commented, "What he [Kennedy] has really asked the people of Massachusetts is whether they want to kick a man when he is down, and clearly they are not going to do that to this doom-ridden and battered family."[7] The act of writing a letter of support becomes the means by which the people "absolve" themselves of guilt. The speech functioned to place responsibility for Kennedy's future as a Senator in the hands of the people and then provided a description that limited them to only one realistic alternative.

While the speech seemed to secure, at least temporarily, Kennedy's Senate seat, its effect on his national future appeared negligible, if not detrimental. There are three reasons for this conclusion. First, Kennedy's description of the events of July 18th presented him as a normal agent who was overcome by an extraordinary scene. However, the myth that has always surrounded the office of the President is that it must be held by an agent who can make clear, rational decisions in an extraordinary scene. Kennedy, in this speech was, at least in part, conceding that he may not be able to handle such situations. This may explain why 57 percent of those who responded to a CBS poll were still favorably impressed by Kennedy after his speech, but 87 percent thought his chances of becoming President had been hurt by the incident.[8]

A second reason why the speech may not have had a positive influence on Kennedy's national future was the way in which the speech was prepared. Prior to the presentation of Kennedy's speech, important Kennedy advisers were summoned to Hyannis Port, among them Robert McNamara and Theodore Sorensen. It was common knowledge that these advisers played an important role in the preparation of that presentation. Such an approach to the formulation was rhetorically inconsistent with the description of reality Kennedy presented. If Kennedy was the simple victim of the scene he could not control, then, in the minds of the audience that should be a simple matter to convey. However, the vision of professionals "manipulating" the speech suggested in the minds of his audience that Kennedy may have been hiding his true role as agent. Here was an instance of an agent trying to control the scene. But given Kennedy's description of what occurred on July 18th such "manipulation" appeared unnecessary and inappropriate. The result was a credibility gap between Kennedy and his audience.

A third factor that may have mitigated against the success of this speech was the lack of detail in Kennedy's description. A number of questions relating to the incident were left unanswered: Why the wrong turn? What was the purpose of the trip, etc.? These were questions that had been voiced in the media and by the general public during the week preceding Senator Kennedy's address. Kennedy's failure to mention these details raised the speculation in the minds of some columnists and citizens that Kennedy may, in fact, have been responsible for the situation having occurred: the agent may have determined the scene. If this was not the case, then Kennedy's lack of important detail may have been a mistake rhetorically. Thus, while Kennedy's speech resulted in the kind of immediate and overt response necessary to secure his seat in the Senate, the speech and the conditions under which it was prepared appear to have done little to enhance Kennedy's chances for the Presidency.

Conclusion

Much of the analysis of the effect of this speech has been speculative. Judging the response of an audience to a speech is a difficult matter; judging the reasons for that response is even more precarious. The methodology employed here has suggested two conclusions. First, in spite of his statements to the contrary, Kennedy's presentation portrayed him, in the first instance, as a victim of the scene and in the second, the possible victim of other agents. Second, the pentad, in suggesting that only five elements exist in the description of a situation, indicated what alternative descriptions were available to Kennedy. Given those choices, an attempt was made to suggest some of the possible implications of the choices Kennedy made.

Notes

[1] Kenneth Burke, *Permanence and Change* (Los Altos, CA: Hermes Publications, 1954), p. 274.

[2] Kenneth Burke, *A Grammar of Motives and A Rhetoric of Motives* (Cleveland: The World Publishing Company, 1962), p. xvii.

[3] *Ibid.*, pp. 127–320.

[4] *Ibid.*, p. 56.

[5] *Ibid.*, p. 17.

[6] This and all subsequent references to the text of Senator Edward Kennedy's speech of July 25, 1969 are taken from *The New York Times*, CXVII (July 26, 1969), p. 10.

[7] James Reston, "Senator Kennedy's Impossible Question," *The New York Times*, CXVII (July 27, 1969), section 4, p. 24.

[8] *CBS Evening News*, CBS Telecast, July 31, 1969.

Chappaquiddick Speech

Edward M. Kennedy
July 25, 1969

My fellow citizens:

I have requested this opportunity to talk to the people of Massachusetts about the tragedy which happened last Friday evening. This morning I entered a plea of guilty to the charge of leaving the scene of an accident. Prior to my appearance in court it would have been improper for me to comment on these matters. But tonight I am free to tell you what happened and to say what it means to me.

On the weekend of July 18, I was on Martha's Vineyard Island participating with my nephew, Joe Kennedy—as for thirty years my family has participated—in the annual Edgartown Sailing Regatta. Only reasons of health prevented my wife from accompanying me.

On Chappaquiddick Island, off Martha's Vineyard, I attended, on Friday evening, July 18, a cook-out I had encouraged and helped sponsor for a devoted group of Kennedy campaign secretaries. When I left the party, around 11:15 P.M., I was accompanied by one of these girls, Miss Mary Jo Kopechne. Mary Jo was one of the most devoted members of the staff of Senator Robert Kennedy. She worked for him for four years and was broken up over his death. For this reason, and because she was such a gentle, kind, and idealistic person, all of us tried to help her feel that she still had a home with the Kennedy family.

There is no truth, no truth whatever, to the widely circulated suspicions of immoral conduct that have been leveled at my behavior and hers regarding that evening. There has never been a private relationship between us of any kind. I know of nothing in Mary Jo's conduct on that or any other occasion—the same is true of the other girls at that party—that would lend any substance to such ugly speculation about their character.

Nor was I driving under the influence of liquor.

Little over one mile away, the car that I was driving on the unlit road went off a narrow bridge which had no guard rails and was built on a left angle to the road. The car overturned in a deep pond and immediately filled with water. I remember thinking as the cold water rushed in around my head that I was for certain drowning. Then water entered my lungs and I actually felt the sensation of drowning. But somehow I struggled to the surface alive.

I made immediate and repeated efforts to save Mary Jo by diving into strong and murky current, but succeeded only in increasing my state of utter exhaustion and alarm. My conduct and conversations during the next several hours, to the extent that I can remember them, make no sense to me at all.

Although my doctors informed me that I suffered a cerebral concussion, as well as shock, I do not seek to escape responsibility for my actions by placing the blame either in the physical, emotional trauma brought on by the accident, or on anyone else. I regard as indefensible the fact that I did not report the accident to the police immediately.

Instead of looking directly for a telephone after lying exhausted in the grass for an undetermined time, I walked back to the cottage where the party was being held and requested the help of two friends, my cousin, Joseph Gargan and Phil Markham, and directed them to return immediately to the scene with me—this was sometime after midnight—in order to undertake a new effort to dive down and locate Miss Kopechne. Their strenuous efforts, undertaken at some risk to their own lives, also proved futile.

All kinds of scrambled thoughts—all of them confused, some of them irrational, many of them which I cannot recall, and some of which I would not have seriously entertained under normal circumstances—went through my mind during this period. They were reflected in the various inexplicable, inconsistent, and inconclusive things I said and did, including such questions as whether the girl might still be alive somewhere out of that immediate area, whether some awful curse did actually hang over all the Kennedys, whether there was some justifiable reason for me to doubt what had happened and to delay my report, whether somehow the awful weight of this incredible incident might, in some way, pass from my shoulders. I was overcome, I'm frank to say, by a jumble of emotions, grief, fear, doubt, exhaustion, panic, confusion and shock.

Instructing Gargan and Markham not to alarm Mary Jo's friends that night, I had them take me to the ferry crossing. The ferry having shut down for the night, I suddenly jumped into the water and impulsively swam across, nearly drowning once again in the effort, and returned to my hotel about 2 A.M. and collapsed in my room.

I remember going out at one point and saying something to the room clerk.

In the morning, with my mind somewhat more lucid, I made an effort to call a family legal advisor, Burke Marshall, from a public telephone on the Chappaquiddick side of the ferry and belatedly reported the accident to the Martha's Vineyard police.

Today, as I mentioned, I felt morally obligated to plead guilty to the charge of leaving the scene of an accident. No words on my part can possibly express the terrible pain and suffering I feel over this tragic incident. This last week has been an agonizing one for me and for the members of my family, and the grief we feel over the loss of a wonderful friend will remain with us the rest of our lives.

These events, the publicity, innuendo, and whispers which have surrounded them and my admission of guilt this morning raises the question in my mind of whether my standing among the people of my state has been so impaired that I should resign my seat in the United States Senate. If at any time the citizens of Massachusetts should lack confidence in their Senator's character or his ability, with or without justification, he could not in my opinion adequately perform his duty and should not continue in office.

The people of this State—the State which sent John Quincy Adams and Daniel Webster and Charles Sumner and Henry Cabot Lodge and John Kennedy to the United States Senate—are entitled to representation in that body by men who inspire their utmost confidence. For this reason, I would understand full well why some might think it right for me to resign. For me this will be a difficult decision to make.

It has been seven years since my first election to the Senate. You and I share many memories—some of them have been glorious, some have been very sad. The opportunity to work with you and serve Massachusetts has made my life worthwhile.

And so I ask you tonight, the people of Massachusetts, to think this through with me. In facing this decision, I seek your advice and opinion. In making it, I seek your prayers—for this is a decision that I will have finally to make on my own.

It has been written a man does what he must in spite of personal consequences, in spite of obstacles, and dangers, and pressures, and that is the basis of human morality. Whatever may be the sacrifices he faces, if he follows his conscience—the loss of his friends, his fortune, his contentment, even the esteem of his fellow man—each man must decide for himself the course he will follow. The stories of the past courage cannot supply courage itself. For this, each man must look into his own soul.

I pray that I can have the courage to make the right decision. Whatever is decided and whatever the future holds for me, I hope that I shall have been able to put this most recent tragedy behind me and make some further contribution to our state and mankind, whether it be in public or private life.

Thank you and good night.

A Pentadic Analysis of the CRACK Web Site

Kimberly C. Elliott

CRACK is the acronym for "Children Requiring a Caring Kommunity," the original name of a nonprofit organization that now is called *Project Prevention*. It is a five-year-old, growing grassroots effort to prevent pregnancies among drug- and alcohol-addicted women by paying them to be sterilized or to use long-term birth control. Although CRACK also will pay addicted men to get vasectomies, fewer than 4% of its participants, to date, have been men.

In its first five years, the organization has raised $2 million, grown from a California home office to a staffed office and 28 other offices across the country, and paid almost 1,000 women to be sterilized or to use long-term birth control. Its founder is Barbara Harris, a woman who, with her husband, adopted the fifth, sixth, seventh, and eighth babies born to a drug-addicted mother. Her experience as an adoptive parent of drug-addicted infants inspired her to try to get a bill passed in California to define the birth of an addicted baby as a crime committed by its mother. The legislation also would have mandated long-term birth control for those mothers. After that legislative effort failed, Harris started CRACK.

Supporters and critics of the project abound. Supporters agree with Harris that her efforts are appropriate and effective. Critics deride a solution that fails to address the addiction that underlies the problem. Some view the organization as coercive, in part because it pays participants $200 to become sterilized or to use long-term birth control. Judging by Harris's original effort to help by making criminals of and imposing birth control upon mothers who give birth to addicted babies, one might surmise that Harris believes those mothers are responsible for exposing fetuses to drugs and alcohol and that an appropriate punishment for that behavior is state-imposed sterilization or birth control. Her current effort, however, seeks to appeal to participants by paying them to do as she wishes, rather than physically forcing them into compliance. Project Prevention also seeks to appeal to potential donors for financial support.

In this paper, I will analyze the discourse presented on the organization's Web site to identify the dramas it creates to both facilitate and mask its motivation while appealing to its two major audiences: drug and alcohol addicts and potential cash donors. I will use this example to consider how a rhetor might construct and concurrently present multiple dramas that function to influence multiple audiences that otherwise might reject its message.

The Artifact

Project Prevention's Web site, at cashforbirthcontrol.com, includes on every page photographs of happy, healthy looking children and documents filed under five headings: *The Cause, The Program, The Reasons, How to Help,* and *About Us. The Cause* includes a statement of organizational objectives, news, and testimonials. *The Program* includes a document titled *How We Help the Children,* a modest list of health-care providers, and frequently asked questions (with answers). *The Reasons* section includes a document titled *The Sad Reality,* statistics, and photos of leaders in the organization.

This essay was written while Kimberly C. Elliott was a student in Sonja K. Foss's rhetorical criticism class at the University of Colorado Denver in 2003. Used by permission of the author.

How to Help and *About Us* offer information about project leaders and ways to participate in the project or provide financial support.

Two documents within the Web site describe what Project Prevention does and its stated rationale. One is titled *Objectives* and the other *How We Help the Children.* Other documents, including *The Sad Reality,* which presents two case studies of drug-addicted infants, and *Statistics* offer support for the arguments in *How We Help the Children* and *Objectives.*

Project Prevention's "main objective is to offer effective preventive measures to reduce the tragedy of numerous drug-affected pregnancies." The *Objectives* document describes the problem of "drug-addicted pregnancies" as one that often causes children to suffer and taxpayers to spend "over a million dollars per child." Children may suffer from developmental and health problems and/or from being "bounced around the foster care system."

Within its objectives, the organization says that it will "support" the decision to use birth control while using drugs but that Project Prevention is not concerned with addressing "all problems for addicts," including drug-use prevention and rehabilitation. It adds, "our mission is to reduce the number of drug- and alcohol-related pregnancies to zero. Unlike incarceration, Project Prevention is extremely cost effective and does not punish the participants."

The *How We Help the Children* document explains that participation in the program is voluntary. It asserts, "most participants who choose permanent birth control are those who have already had far more children than most people have in a lifetime." This is the sole mention of children in the text of *How We Help the Children.*

The process for signing up and getting paid $200 is described. This document lists the brands of long-term birth-control products and the sterilization procedures for which participants may be paid. For example, tubal ligations and vasectomies warrant one-time $200 payments, while using Depo Provera for a full year pays $200 each year for participants who can prove they are and remain drug or alcohol addicted.

One paragraph in *How We Help the Children* contemplates how participants spend their $200. It asks, "what does she do with the money she has earned from us?" Although this wording suggests that participants work for and earn their $200, another suggests it is a gift or charity: "we do not monitor where our money is spent." Still another description used for the cash is "a $200 incentive," suggesting the cash is neither compensation earned nor a gift received but a tool used to persuade drug addicts to participate in the program.

Pentadic Analysis

I will analyze this artifact using the dramatist pentad, as conceived by Kenneth Burke, for the purpose of understanding a rhetor's motivation by analyzing the drama(s) a rhetor creates when telling a story. The elements of the pentad—act, agent, agency, scene, and purpose—are the units of analysis I will use.

The Key and Dominant Elements

My analysis of Project Prevention's Web site yielded several pentads partially or fully developed within the rhetoric. Some pentads are internally inconsistent and/or poorly developed. For example, the key elements in one pentad are:

Agent: the organization (Project Prevention)
Act: paying $200 to drug- and alcohol-addicted people to become sterilized
          or to use long-term methods of birth control
Scene: the presence of drug- and alcohol-addicted pregnancies
Purpose: to help children
Agency: preventing drug- and alcohol-addicted pregnancies

An internal inconsistency in this pentad is in the claim of helping children by preventing them from being born. Clearly, helping children cannot be CRACK's real purpose in this drama; it only can be its stated purpose, for the children it purports to help do not/will not exist, and those who never exist cannot be helped. One wonders who the happy and healthy looking children pictured on the Web site are. Are they the children who will never live?

An example of a poorly developed pentad within the Project Prevention rhetoric is one in which pregnancy is personified to serve as an agent. The key elements in that pentad are:

Agent: drug- and alcohol-addicted pregnancies/substance-exposed pregnancies
Act: cause children to suffer, cost taxpayers, and strain the foster care system
Scene: where people use drugs
Purpose: (none offered)
Agency: expose children to substances

This incomplete pentad lacks a purpose. Because the agent (drug-addicted pregnancy) is both fictitious and inanimate, it is on at least two counts incapable of having a purpose for doing anything. In statements like "drug-addicted pregnancies are a two-tiered problem" and "awareness and concern are also growing about the hundreds of thousands of substance-exposed pregnancies that occur each year," the rhetor describes pregnancies that are addicted or exposed rather than addicted women who are pregnant and fetuses that are exposed to substances. Pregnancy, obviously, cannot be addicted to drugs or alcohol, and it does not exist independent of women, but this linguistic construct suggests otherwise. Also, the Project does not seek to stop drug-addicted women from becoming pregnant; rather, it wants to "reduce the tragedy of numerous drug-affected pregnancies."

There are no people in these linguistic constructs. Instead, the agent causing children to suffer, costing taxpayers, and straining the foster care system is pregnancy. Pregnancy clearly cannot act with intent, so this pentad lacks a key term for purpose. This pentad also reveals the implausibility and inconsistency of the drama by asserting that pregnancies expose children to drugs and alcohol, rather than identifying the real agents who might do so.

In my analysis, three complete, consistent, and interacting pentads emerged. Their common thread is prostitution as a metaphor. I have named the three pentads for the roles their agents play in the dramas created rhetorically by Project Prevention:

1. The Pimp
Agent: Project Prevention
Act: solicits financial support and expands the organization
Scene: capitalist, free-market economy
Purpose: to enrich itself, increase its power and influence
Agency: offers a product to donors (the johns), recruits addicts (the prostitutes),
          and pays them a portion of what it collects for the product (control of
          their bodies)

2. The Johns
Agent: financial donors
Act: anonymously buy control of someone else's body
Scene: capitalist, free-market economy
Purpose: gratification through influencing/controlling others
Agency: pay Project Prevention (the pimp)

3. The Prostitutes
Agent: addicts
Act: modify their bodies in exchange for a fee
Scene: capitalist, free-market economy
Purpose: compensation, survival
Agency: according to instructions specified by Project Prevention (the pimp)

In the first pentad, act—soliciting funds and expanding the organization—is the dominant term. The act dominates the dependent agent, makes the agency possible and relevant, and facilitates the purpose. The scene and the act interact symbiotically because the act both benefits from and becomes a part of the scene. Neither term in the act-scene ratio dominates the other.

Agency fully dominates all other terms in the second pentad. Paying Project Prevention is what renders one a financial donor (agent) in this drama, so agency dominates the agency-act ratio by defining the agent. The agency dominates and transcends the scene because it both makes use of the scene and lacks reliance upon it. This agency can be used in any economic system, but it is particularly effective in a capitalist economy in which participants readily enter into agreed-upon (and arguably exploitative) exchanges. In the rhetor's construction of this drama, the specified agency uniquely accommodates the agent's purpose, so agency dominates purpose, too. Similarly, agency dominates act because the act relies upon the agency of paying Project Prevention.

Agency is the dominant term in the third pentad. In the rhetor's drama, addicts are able to collect a fee for being sterilized or using long-term birth control only if they do so according to the instructions specified by Project Prevention, so agency dominates in the agency-act ratio. Because the act can facilitate the purpose only if the agent employs the prescribed agency, the purpose also is dominated by the agency. Neither term is dominant in the agency-agent ratio because, while the agent is influenced by the agency, the agency is not possible for any agent other than addicts. Completion of the act relies upon the agency, so agency dominates the agency-act ratio. Agency dominates the scene by making use of the features of a free-market economy that encourages such agreed-upon exchanges and makes them legal.

The least influential term in the third pentad is purpose. The purpose of receiving compensation to survive is common to a variety of agents, not just addicts, so the agent dominates the purpose-agent ratio. Compensation and survival do not require an agent to modify her or his body in exchange for a fee, so purpose does not dominate the purpose-act ratio. The scene dominates the purpose because a capitalist economy mandates that people seek compensation to facilitate their own survival. Finally, agency dominates purpose because the agency is a determinant in whether the purpose is served in this drama.

Conclusion

The prostitution metaphor in the three pentads in which the agents are cast in the roles of pimps, johns, or prostitutes serves as a multifaceted link among the dramas. Some constants exist. For example, each of the three dramas is set in the same scene. The metaphor also identifies a hierarchy of agents and illuminates an emergent hierarchy of pentads.

The rhetor/pimp/agent is the most powerful of the three agents, acting as a determinant in several elements of the other agents' dramas. For example, even the dominant term in the prostitutes' drama, agency, is as prescribed by the rhetor/pimp/agent from another drama. In the pentad in which the johns are the agent, the dominant term, agency, directly facilitates the dominant term (act) in the pimp's pentad. In other words, when the johns pay the pimp, the pimp's act of soliciting financial support and expanding is accomplished.

All of the dramas identified in the three pentads ultimately serve the rhetor/pimp/agent. It appears that no elements would be allowed in the johns' or the prostitutes' pentads if they in any way undermined the elements of the pimp's drama, in which the rhetor's purpose is served. As revealed in the pentadic analysis, the least powerful element in what I have identified as the least powerful pentad is the prostitutes'/agents' purpose. Although Project Prevention makes some effort to appeal to addicts by offering them compensation, the addict's purpose clearly is of little importance to Project Prevention.

Because these three pentads tell much of the rhetor's story, it is notable that no children appear in any of these dramas. Despite Project Prevention's repetitious claims that its purpose is to "help the children," its entire drama can be performed without the appearance of any children. This is possible because Project Prevention's mission is to prevent the children it "helps" from existing and therefore from appearing anywhere. Indeed, the Web page titled *How We Help The Children* offers no explanation for how Project Prevention helps children. Instead, the page summarizes the agency (the dominant term) in the prostitutes' pentad—the procedures with which an addict must comply to be paid for becoming sterilized or using long-term birth control. The claim that children are central characters in Project Prevention's drama is a deception revealed by this pentadic analysis.

Finally, the prostitution metaphor underscores an exploitation of and the assumed desperation of some drug- and alcohol-addicted women. While some of Project Prevention's rhetoric suggests that it seeks to compensate both women and men for being sterilized, most of its rhetoric is directed at addicted women. Participating women have been paid by an organization to alter their bodies in prescribed ways. If women are influenced to do so by the promised payment of compensation to them and their interest in that compensation is motivated by their need to survive, then they are being exploited. Pimps don't sell exploitation, and neither does Project Prevention. They both sell fantasy and endeavor to hide the desperation motivating women to sell any brand of control over their bodies.

Because Project Prevention plays the role of a pimp in its own drama, it is engaged in promoting that which attracts and hiding that which does not. The three pentads presented within a prostitution metaphor are masked in the organization's Web-site rhetoric by the fictional and incomplete pentad in which "helping children" is the purpose. This universally appealing purpose is one of three prominent constructs the rhetor uses to appeal to and avoid offending members of its two major audiences: potential or current donors and drug- and alcohol-addicted women.

Another effort to avoid offending potential addict/participants, although inconsistently applied, is the use of language suggesting that Project Prevention is not targeting women. In a third major construct that functions to avoid offending potential addicts/participants, the rhetor avoids any suggestion that drug-using women and men who conceive a child are responsible for causing their children to suffer while maintaining that such children do suffer. By separating parents, particularly mothers, from pregnancies with language such as "drug-addicted pregnancies," the organization suggests that pregnancies victimize children. A logical extension of this construct is that pregnancies should be prevented (or ended), but Project Prevention makes no suggestion that terminating a pregnancy is advisable or even possible. Abortion is not even mentioned and therefore does not exist in Project Prevention's drama.

Because pregnancy is described as the problem, rather than parents, drugs, alcohol, substance abuse, or addiction, any effort to help parents for the benefit of children is irrelevant and dismissed. As Project Prevention states on the *Objectives* page of its Web site, "we do not have the resources to solve all problems for addicts including housing, nutrition, education and rehabilitation." Thus, redirecting responsibility for exposing a fetus to alcohol or drugs from parents to pregnancy, whether drug-addicted, substance-exposed, drug-affected, or drug- and alcohol-related, serves both to relieve potential participants of responsibility for their actions and legitimate the organization's dismissal of all the needs of addicts.

Project Prevention's literature employs a varied methodology in attempting both to mask and facilitate its motivation while appealing to at least two very different audiences. It demonstrates how a rhetor might mask its function, character, and motive by creating and presenting fictional dramas, as the rhetor does with its claimed purpose of helping children by preventing them from living. Some such fictional dramas are incomplete, such as the rhetor's construction of pregnancies as agents that victimize children without a purpose.

The rhetoric in Project Prevention's Web site demonstrates how a rhetor might present a creative collection of pentads that alternately clash and coordinate with one another for the purpose of appealing to multiple audiences with multiple motivations. The rhetor may further demonstrate, with this method, reliance upon the notion that audiences will absorb the messages they find most relevant to themselves and overlook or dismiss the others.

Justification of Self-Destructive Behaviors
Pentadic Analysis of "A Letter from Ana"
Danielle C. Cornell

Each day, we participate in activities that are not necessarily good for us. Examples include smoking, driving when we've been drinking, and sky diving, to name just a few. How do we justify such potentially dangerous activities—even ones that may cause death—to ourselves and perhaps to others? This is the question I will explore in this essay. To continue to engage in such activities, we must be able to accomplish this rhetorical act of justification successfully.

The artifact I have chosen to analyze is a letter ostensibly written by Anorexia Nervosa (Ana) to a girl who has the disease of anorexia nervosa. The letter is dated July 31, 2002, and it can be found on many proanorexia Web sites. The letter details the perspective of Ana, who attempts to keep an unknown girl tied to her (the disease) so that both can achieve their shared vision of perfection. The letter clearly was written by someone who has the disease to explain the hold the disease has on her and her reluctance to give it up. Thus, I seek here to discover the motive for the letter's real writer (a girl with anorexia nervosa) as she attempts to justify her reluctance to let go of the disease.

Kenneth Burke created pentadic criticism as a means to understand how and why human beings use rhetoric and to what effect. By analyzing an artifact using this method, a critic can figure out a rhetor's motive for creating an artifact. *Agent*, *act*, *purpose*, *scene*, and *agency* are key terms the critic identifies as constructed in the artifact. *Agent* refers to the person doing the act, *act* is what the agent is doing, *purpose* is why the rhetor does the act, *scene* is where the act is taking place, and *agency* is the means used to accomplish the act. The critic then pairs these terms in ratios to determine the dominant term in which the motive lies.

Analysis of "A Letter from Ana"

There are a number of ways in which the key terms in this letter can be identified. I chose to focus in my naming of the five terms on the friendship that is implied in the letter:

- Scene: World populated by people who are unsuitable as friends
- Act: Inducing compliance
- Purpose: To create identification
- Agency: Honesty and understanding
- Agent: Ana (a special, ideal friend)

Application of the ratios of the key terms suggests that the dominant term in this pentad is agent. When I paired agent with the other terms, it appeared to determine the nature of the other terms or to strongly influence them. With the agent-scene ratio, Ana, the unique, special friend, requires a setting of potential friends who are unsuitable and unworthy. Without such a scene, the agent cannot be special, and the target of affection could be friends with many others. To stand out as the one special friend,

This essay was written while Danielle C. Cornell was a student in Sonja K. Foss's rhetorical criticism class at the University of Colorado Denver in 2005. Used by permission of the author.

Ana must be located in a scene in which no one else is worthy of assuming that role. The agent-act ratio suggests that, because Ana is so special, she has the right and the responsibility to induce the compliance of the girl so that she, too, can participate in the specialness that marks Ana. In the agent-purpose ratio, agent is dominant because when someone is as perfect as Ana is, the target would want to identify with her to share in her perfection and the perfect friendship she offers. Finally, the agent-agency ratio highlights the relationship between the perfect friend of Ana and the means she uses to accomplish the act of inducing compliance—honesty and understanding. These are two of the most valued qualities in a friendship and are what people typically expect they will receive from an ideal friendship. Because she is a model friend, Ana will demonstrate these qualities in her interactions with her friend.

The motive of the letter, centered in agent, is to sustain the friendship or the special connection the rhetor has with Ana. Because Ana is a model and ideal friend, certain things are required to be worthy of her friendship. Someone with anorexia nervosa willingly acquiesces to Ana's demands for compliance (act) in order to create identification (purpose) with such a special person, who clearly is unique in a world of potential friends of lesser quality (scene). If agent is the controlling term, Burke suggests, the corresponding philosophy is idealism, the system that views the mind or spirit as each person experiences it as fundamentally real. Because Ana is an ideal friend whose special qualities make friendship with her highly desirable, she offers in reality something the girl with the disease never believed she could have: a special connection with a superior, perfect ideal.

My analysis of "A Letter from Ana" suggests that individuals may justify self-inflicted, harmful behaviors to themselves to maintain a connection or a relationship with someone or something they see as superior to them or an ideal they want to emulate. They are highly motivated to maintain the connection because its loss would be harmful to themselves and disrespectful to an honored other. The desire to live up to the responsibilities required to maintain that connection and to be careful not to break it may serve as a powerful rationale for engaging in self-destructive behaviors.

A Letter from Ana

Anonymous (Ana)
July 31, 2002

Allow me to introduce myself. My name, or as I am called by so called "doctors," is Anorexia. Anorexia Nervosa is my full name, but you may call me Ana. Hopefully we can become great partners. In the coming time, I will invest a lot of time in you, and I expect the same from you.

In the past you have heard all of your teachers and parents talk about you. You are "so mature," "intelligent," "14 going on 45," and you possess "so much potential." Where has that gotten you, may I ask? Absolutely nowhere! You are not perfect, you do not try hard enough, furthermore, you waste your time on thinking and talking with friends and drawing! Such acts of indulgence shall not be allowed in the future.

Your friends do not understand you. They are not truthful. In the past, when the insecurity has quietly gnawed away at your mind, and you asked them, "Do I look . . . fat?" and they answered "Oh no, of course not," you knew that they were lying! Only I tell the truth. Your parents, let's not even go there! You know that they love you, and care for you, but part of that is just that they are your parents and are obligated to do so. I shall tell you a secret now: Deep down inside themselves, they are disappointed with you. Their daughter, the one with so much potential, has turned into a fat, lazy, and undeserving girl.

But I am about to change all that. I will expect you to drop your calorie intake and up your exercise. I will push you to the limit. You must take it because you cannot defy me! I am beginning to embed myself into you. Pretty soon, I am with you always. I am there when you wake up in the morning and run to the scale. The numbers become both friend and enemy, and the frenzied thoughts pray for them to be lower than yesterday, last night, etc. You look into the mirror with dismay. You prod and poke at the fat that is there, and smile when you come across bone. I am there when you figure out the plan for the day: 400 calories, two hours exercise. I am the one figuring this out, because by now my thoughts and your thoughts are blurred together as one. I follow you throughout the day. In school, when your mind wanders, I give you something to think about. Recount the calories for the day. It's too much. I fill your mind with thoughts of food, weight, calories, and things that are safe to think about. Because now, I am already inside of you. I am in your head, your heart, and your soul. The hunger pains you pretend not to feel is me, inside of you.

Pretty soon I am telling you not only what to do with food, but what to do ALL of the time. Smile and nod. Present yourself well. Suck in that fat stomach, dammit! God, you are such a fat cow!!!! When mealtimes come around I tell you what to do. I make a plate of lettuce seem like a feast fit for a king. Push the food around. Make it look like you've eaten something. No piece of anything . . . if you eat, all the control will be broken . . . do you WANT that?? To revert back to the fat COW you once were?? I force you to stare at magazine models. Those perfect-skinned, white-teethed, waifish models of perfection staring out at you from those glossy pages. I make you realize that you could never be them. You will always be fat and never will you be as beautiful as they are. When you look in the mirror, I will distort the image. I will show you obesity and hideousness. I will show you a sumo wrestler where in reality there is a starving child. But you must not know this, because if you knew the truth, you might start to eat again and our relationship would come crashing down.

Sometimes you will rebel. Hopefully not often though. You will recognize the small rebellious fiber left in your body and will venture down to the dark kitchen. The cupboard door will slowly open, creaking softly. Your eyes will move over the food that I have kept at a safe distance from you. You will find your hands reaching out, lethargically, like in a nightmare, through the darkness to the box of crackers. You shove them in, mechanically, not really tasting but simply relishing in the fact that you are going against me. You reach for another box, then another, then another. Your stomach will become bloated and grotesque, but you will not stop yet. And all the time I am screaming at you to stop, you fat cow, you really have no self-control, you are going to get fat.

When it is over you will cling to me again, ask me for advice because you really do not want to get fat. You broke a cardinal rule and ate, and now you want me back. I'll force you into the bathroom, onto your knees, staring into the void of the toilet bowl. Your fingers will be inserted into your throat, and, not without a great deal of pain, your food binge will come up. Over and over this is to be repeated, until you spit up blood and water and you know it is all gone. When you stand up, you will feel dizzy. Don't pass out. Stand up right now. You fat cow, you deserve to be in pain! Maybe the choice of getting rid of the guilt is different. Maybe I chose to make you take laxatives, where you sit on the toilet until the wee hours of the morning, feeling your insides cringe. Or perhaps I just make you hurt yourself, bang your head into the wall until you receive a throbbing headache. Cutting is also effective. I want you to see your blood, to see it fall down your arm, and in that split second you will realize you deserve whatever pain I give you. You are depressed, obsessed, in pain, hurting, reaching out, but no one will listen. Who cares?!?! You are deserving; you brought this upon yourself.

Oh, is this harsh? Do you not want this to happen to you? Am I unfair? I do things that will help you. I make it possible for you to stop thinking of emotions that cause you stress. Thoughts of anger, sadness, desperation, and loneliness can cease because I take them away and fill your head with the methodic calorie counting. I take away your struggle to fit in with kids your age, the struggle of trying to please everyone as well. Because now, I am your only friend, and I am the only one you need to please.

I have a weak spot. But we must not tell anyone. If you decide to fight back, to reach out to someone and tell them about how I make you live, all hell will break loose. No one must find out, no one can crack this shell that I have covered you with. I have created you, this thin, perfect, achieving child. You are mine and mine alone. Without me, you are nothing. So do not fight back. When others comment, ignore them. Take it into stride, forget about them, forget about everyone who tries to take me away. I am your greatest asset, and I intend to keep it that way.

Sincerely,
Ana

Additional Samples of Pentadic Criticism

Appel, Edward C. "The Perfected Drama of Reverend Jerry Falwell." *Communication Quarterly*, 35 (Winter 1987), 26–38.

Birdsell, David S. "Ronald Reagan on Lebanon and Grenada: Flexibility and Interpretation in the Application of Kenneth Burke's Pentad." *Quarterly Journal of Speech*, 73 (August 1987), 267–79.

Blankenship, Jane, Marlene G. Fine, and Leslie K. Davis. "The 1980 Republican Primary Debates: The Transformation of Actor to Scene." *Quarterly Journal of Speech*, 69 (February 1983), 25–36.

Brown, Janet. "Kenneth Burke and *The Mod Donna*: The Dramatistic Method Applied to Feminist Criticism." *Central States Speech Journal*, 29 (Summer 1978), 138–46.

Brummett, Barry. "A Pentadic Analysis of Ideologies in Two Gay Rights Controversies." *Central States Speech Journal*, 30 (Fall 1979), 250–61.

Cali, Dennis D. "Chiara Lubich's 1977 Templeton Prize Acceptance Speech: Case Study in the Mystical Narrative." *Communication Studies*, 44 (Summer 1993), 132–43.

Carlson, A. Cheree. "Narrative as the Philosopher's Stone: How Russell H. Conwell Changed Lead into Diamonds." *Western Journal of Speech Communication*, 53 (Fall 1989), 342–55.

Cooks, Leda, and David Descutner. "Different Paths from Powerlessness to Empowerment: A Dramatistic Analysis of Two Eating Disorder Therapies." *Western Journal of Communication*, 57 (Fall 1993), 494–514.

Fisher, Jeanne Y. "A Burkean Analysis of the Rhetorical Dimensions of a Multiple Murder and Suicide." *Quarterly Journal of Speech*, 60 (April 1974), 175–89.

Hahn, Dan F., and Anne Morlando. "A Burkean Analysis of Lincoln's Second Inaugural Address." *Presidential Studies Quarterly*, 9 (Fall 1979), 376–89.

Hayden, Sara. "Reversing the Discourse of Sexology: Margaret Higgins Sanger's *What Every Girl Should Know*." *Southern Communication Journal*, 64 (Summer 1999), 288–306.

Ingram, Jason. "Conflicted Possession: A Pentadic Assessment of T. E. Lawrence's Desert Narrative." *KB Journal*, 4 (Fall 2007), 1–23.

Ivie, Robert L. "Presidential Motives for War." *Quarterly Journal of Speech*, 60 (October 1974), 337–45.

Kelley, Colleen E. "The 1984 Campaign Rhetoric of Representative George Hansen: A Pentadic Analysis." *Western Journal of Speech Communication*, 51 (Spring 1987), 204–17.

MacLennan, Jennifer. "A Rhetorical Journey into Darkness: Crime-Scene Profiling as Burkean Analysis." *KB Journal*, 1 (Spring 2005), 1–24.

Nelson, Jeffrey, and Mary Ann Flannery. "The Sanctuary Movement: A Study in Religious Confrontation." *Southern Communication Journal*, 55 (Summer 1990), 372–87.

Peterson, Tarla Rai. "The Meek Shall Inherit the Mountains: Dramatistic Criticism of Grand Teton National Park's Interpretive Program." *Central States Speech Journal*, 39 (Summer 1988), 121–33.

Peterson, Tarla Rai. "The Will to Conservation: A Burkeian Analysis of Dust Bowl Rhetoric and American Farming Motives." *Southern Speech Communication Journal*, 52 (Fall 1986), 1–21.

Procter, David E. "The Rescue Mission: Assigning Guilt to a Chaotic Scene." *Western Journal of Speech Communication*, 51 (Summer 1987), 245–55.

Rountree, Clarke. "Instantiating 'The Law' and its Dissents in *Korematsu v. United States*: A Dramatistic Analysis of Judicial Discourse." *Quarterly Journal of Speech*, 87 (February 2001), 1–24.

Rountree, J. Clarke, III. "Charles Haddon Spurgeon's Calvinist Rhetoric of Election: Constituting an Elect." *Journal of Communication and Religion*, 17 (September 1994), 33–48.

Rountree, J. Clarke, III. "The Speech of Quintus Fabius Maximus Before the Roman Senate, 205 A.D.: Actus, and the Representation of Motives." *Florida Communication Journal*, 20 (Spring 1992), 32–38.

Rushing, Janice Hocker. "Ronald Reagan's 'Star Wars' Address: Mythic Containment of Technical Reasoning." *Quarterly Journal of Speech*, 72 (November 1986), 415–33.

Stewart, Charles J. "The Internal Rhetoric of the Knights of Labor." *Communication Studies*, 42 (Spring 1991), 67–82.

Tonn, Mari Boor, Valerie A. Endress, and John N. Diamond. "Hunting and Heritage on Trial: A Dramatistic Debate Over Tragedy, Tradition, and Territory." *Quarterly Journal of Speech*, 79 (May 1993), 165–81.

Yingling, Julie. "Women's Advocacy: Pragmatic Feminism in the YWCA." *Women's Studies in Communication*, 6 (Spring 1983), 1–11.

Zulick, Margaret D. "The Agon of Jeremiah: On the Dialogic Invention of Prophetic Ethos." *Quarterly Journal of Speech*, 78 (May 1992), 125–48.

Generative Criticism

The previous chapters in this book have provided you with an approach to doing criticism when your starting point is a particular method of criticism. Starting with a method produces some good insights and is a comfortable way to begin doing criticism if you are an inexperienced critic. Most seasoned rhetorical critics, however, engage in rhetorical criticism using a different process, and that process is the subject of this chapter. As useful as the formal methods of criticism are for discovering insights into rhetoric, they do not always allow what is most interesting and significant in an artifact to be captured and explained. In most cases, then, you will want to analyze artifacts without following any formal method of criticism. This kind of criticism is generative in that you generate units of analysis or an explanation from your artifact rather than from previously developed, formal methods of criticism.

A critic who engages in generative criticism analyzes an artifact in a nine-step process: (1) encountering a curious artifact; (2) coding the artifact in general; (3) searching for an explanation; (4) creating an explanatory schema; (5) formulating a research question; (6) coding the artifact in detail; (7) searching the literature; (8) framing the study; and (9) writing the essay.[1]

Encountering a Curious Artifact

Critics sometimes begin the process of criticism with a question they want to answer. If you are interested in finding out about a particular aspect of a rhetorical process and have in mind a specific question that inquires into that process, you could choose an artifact to analyze that allows you to investigate the question. You may be interested, for example, in how rhetors design messages for audiences they know will be hostile. You might choose to study, for example, a speech by the Pope to a group of U.S. nuns who want to be priests or a pro-union essay speech by a union organizer to an anti-union audience.

But most rhetorical critics do not begin with a research question that interests them. The act of criticism usually begins when you encounter an artifact that raises questions for you. You discover a rhetorical artifact that is appealing to you; generates a sense of uneasiness, intrigue, or amazement; or seems unusual in some way. You discover that, for some reason, an object is prompting you to think about some ideas, and you want to try "to understand both the object and [your] interest in it."[2]

Most professional rhetorical critics report that they begin the process of criticism with an artifact they want to study. Thomas S. Frentz and Janice Hocker Rushing, for example, explain such an impetus for criticism in this way: "For us, criticism typically starts as this kind of gut-level, unexamined intuitive feeling about a text(s). If we don't feel intensely about it one way or another—it can be hate, love, disgust, surprise, fear, awe, perplexity—we don't write."[3] Roderick P. Hart uses the term *curious text* to describe his initial interest in a particular artifact and suggests that many "critical projects begin because the critic is baffled." A curious text also can result when you encounter an incomplete argument. You read someone's book or essay and think there is more to the book or essay than has been told.[4]

Critics Elizabeth Walker Mechling and Jay Mechling also explain that "the puzzling texts present themselves first. We do not begin with a theory or method or hypotheses and then search for a case study to demonstrate or illuminate the theory."[5] Their description of how they decided to analyze the civil defense campaigns of the 1950s illustrates particularly well the process of encountering a text as the impetus for criticism. They both remember their parents' absurd efforts to protect their families from nuclear attack, including their development of a plan to evacuate the children from school and the creation of a bomb shelter out of a closet, complete with mattress shoved against the door. As they explain, this

> is the madness we sought to understand. How could our parents, perfectly reasonable people, act in this way? How could we, cynical preadolescents then, also take this world as "natural"? How were we so easily socialized into . . . "nuclear culture"? How did some people in the 1950s resist the socialization, even to the point of creating social movements engaging in civil disobedience meant to thwart civil defense planning? The questions were real and troubling. . . . The stakes of self-understanding were high, both in retrospect for understanding our nuclear socialization, and in prospect for understanding what possibly pathological worldviews have become normal, "naturalized," for us [now]. These questions led us to settle upon the civil defense campaigns and resistances as the texts we would analyze.[6]

As the critics' descriptions suggest, the defining characteristic of an artifact that intrigues and interests you is likely to be something that doesn't fit or that breaks a pattern. Perhaps you like an artifact and can't explain its appeal for you. Perhaps you can't figure out why an artifact had the impact on an audience that it did. Perhaps you encounter an artifact that seems to violate much of what you know about communication, but it seems to be effective anyway. Perhaps an artifact disturbs or angers you, but you don't know why.

I confronted just this kind of curious text with two friends when we went to see the German film *Run Lola Run*. The film is about Lola, who receives a phone call from her boyfriend, Manni, telling her he needs a huge sum of money within 20 minutes or he will be killed by his mobster boss. Lola takes off running to try to get the money and makes three such runs, encountering the same people in different ways and with dramatically different outcomes for each run. We went to *Run Lola Run* to be entertained and had no intention of writing an essay of criticism about the film. When it was over, however, we knew we really liked the film, but we couldn't say why it resonated with us as it did. We knew that the three runs represented three different perspectives on something, but we couldn't figure out what. We also couldn't get the film out of our heads—it continued to nag at us until we finally gave in to its demands and began the process of generative criticism.[7]

Coding the Artifact

After encountering an artifact that you cannot adequately explain, your next step in generative criticism is to do an initial broad-brush coding of the artifact to discover its central features. *Coding* here means that you notice and interpret the major features of the artifact. The features you notice should include some of the major dimensions or components of the artifact that would have to fit into whatever explanation you develop to understand the artifact. As part of this process, think about what you immediately remember about the artifact after encountering it only once. As you examine the artifact, look for what topics are treated and the order in which they appear, the lengths of various segments, and the significant words and images that mark the artifact. If you are analyzing a film, television ad, or music video, you might want to watch it without sound to focus your attention on the visual aspects of the artifact. Listen to it again without the pictures to focus attention on the sound.

In this process of identifying major features of the artifact, use *intensity* and *frequency* as your selection criteria. Intensity guides you to look for aspects of the artifact that seem important or significant—those aspects that stand out in the artifact. Also pay attention to frequency and look for patterns in the artifact—things that are repeated and show up with some regularity. Because these recur, you might guess that they are somehow important in the artifact. Code the artifact according to intensity and frequency several times. Each examination will produce more information about the artifact's major elements, how they change over the course of the artifact, and the relationships and contradictions among the elements.

In our initial coding of *Run Lola Run*, my fellow critics and I watched the film several times and, as we watched, we wrote down images, dialogue, and events that seemed to stand out—features that met the criterion of intensity. We guessed, for example, that the fact that Lola makes three runs is important (and of course, in this case, the three runs also constitute a pattern that we would notice as we paid attention to frequency). We noticed that Lola encounters several people along her runs and thought these various characters might be important, so we noted who they were and what they did in each run. Time seemed to be very important because Manni only has 20 minutes to produce the required money, so we noted that. At the beginning of the film is a scene involving a soccer game, so we also included the game in our coding, thinking it might be significant, especially since a game of roulette appears in the third run. We noted that Lola and Manni seem to be on the outside of mainstream society because they do not have regular jobs, have little money, and dress in Eurotrash clothing.

We also noticed patterns in the film where the same objects, events, or qualities appear repeatedly, and we wrote these down, coding for frequency. The color red initially seemed important in the film: Lola's hair is red, the telephone she answers at the beginning of the film is red, and the liminal bedroom scenes between the runs are filmed through a red filter. The color red, then, appeared to constitute a pattern. Guns used in various ways also seemed to be a pattern. A gun shows up in Manni and Lola's robbery of a grocery story in the first run, in Lola's effort to get money from her father in the second run, and in Manni's effort to retrieve his lost money from a tramp in the third run. We noted these and other patterns in the film.

After identifying the major features of the artifact, the next part of the coding process is to interpret them. You also could think of the two aspects of this process as presented and suggested elements—the presented elements are the data or what you observe, and the suggested elements are what they evoke or reference. Write a paraphrase, phrase, or label that describes what you are seeing in a passage, quotation, or image or what it might mean. You can write your codes in the margin of a discursive text or on another piece of paper if you are analyzing a film, TV program, Web site, or visual image. The exact label you use as you code does not have to be very precise at this time. These labels are just general indicators of what you are seeing and probably will not be used in your actual essay. Our coding of the first run of *Run Lola Run*, for example, produced the following features and interpretations:

1. *Feature:* Menacing-looking clock. *Interpretation:* Time as a monster.
2. *Feature:* Tick-tock sound on the sound track. *Interpretation:* Urgency, time passing.
3. *Feature:* Cartoon Lola runs through a clock surrounded by teeth. *Interpretation:* Time as a monster.
4. *Feature:* Manni taunts Lola and claims she can't help him. *Interpretation:* Asking help of those who can't help.
5. *Feature:* Lola's father shakes his head "no" as she mentally reviews people she can ask for money. *Interpretation:* Asking help of those who can't help.
6. *Feature:* Manni turns down an offer of 500 marks from a friend. *Interpretation:* Refuses resources.

7. *Feature:* Lola stops for men carrying a pane of glass. *Interpretation:* Glass ceiling, obstacle.

8. *Feature:* Lola kneels before her father to ask him for the money. *Interpretation:* Adoption of low-status position.

9. *Feature:* Lola rejects invitation to buy a bike. *Interpretation:* Refuses resources.

10. *Feature:* Lola passes the tramp who has Manni's money and doesn't see him. *Interpretation:* Blind to resources.

11. *Feature:* Lola screams in fear at a dog on the stairs. *Interpretation:* Fearful for no reason.

12. *Feature:* Guard at bank says, "Little Miss wants to see Big Daddy." *Interpretation:* Construction of Lola as subordinate.

13. *Feature:* Lola and Manni rob a grocery store. *Interpretation:* Illegal means, employment of a strategy likely to fail.

14. *Feature:* Lola is shot by a police officer. *Interpretation:* Death of something, punishment.

As you develop your interpretations of the features, try not to bring in other people's theories—stay focused on the data of your artifact. Obviously, you cannot clear your mind of everything you know about communication as you code. But as much as possible, let the data reveal insights to you independent of any preconceived theories. This will insure the originality of the explanation you develop. Be careful about coding according to what you want to find or what you are certain you will find. If you know what you are going to find, you already have your explanation for the artifact.

Remember that you will have to explain how you came to your interpretation of the data of the artifact. Your interpretive claims will have to make sense to someone else, so frequently ask yourself the question, "Could I explain this to someone else so they would be able to see how I moved from my observations of a feature to the interpretation I've given it?" For example, we see Lola's kneeling before her father to ask him for money as evidence for her adoption of a stance of inferiority and low power. If someone were to ask us how we came to this interpretation from this gesture in the film, we could explain that low-status people tend to engage in nonverbal behavior that suggests their low power, and kneeling is a classic sign of that stance. We also could argue that the person who is physically located above another tends to be the one with higher status. You do not need to go through this process with every interpretation of every feature of your artifact because much of this happens intuitively and almost automatically, but this is the process you should be able to do for a skeptical reader.

Many critics find writing or typing notes in a list helpful during the interpretation process. Leave some space between each observation/interpretation that you make. Physically cut the observations you have made apart so that each idea or observation is on a separate strip of paper. Then group the strips that are about the same thing and put them in one pile; group those that are about another topic and put them in another pile. Give labels to your piles—name them with a word or phrase that captures what you are seeing in the codes that made you want to group them together. In our case, after we cut our codings apart and began putting them together in piles that seemed to reflect the same principle or idea, we had a number of categories:

1. *Material conditions as threats and obstacles*
   Menacing-looking clock.
   Tick-tock sound on the sound track.
   Cartoon Lola runs through a clock surrounded by teeth.
   Lola stops for men carrying a pane of glass.
   Lola screams in fear at a dog on the stairs.

2. *Refusing help*
   Manni taunts Lola and claims she can't help him.
   Manni turns down an offer of 500 marks from a friend.
   Lola rejects invitation to buy a bike.
   Lola passes the tramp who has Manni's money and doesn't see him.

3. *Rhetorical strategies doomed to fail*
   Lola's father shakes his head "no" as she mentally reviews people she can ask for money.
   Lola and Manni rob a grocery store.
   Lola is shot by a police officer.

4. *Assumption of inferior position*
   Lola kneels before her father to ask him for money.
   Guard at the bank says, "Little Miss wants to see Big Daddy."

The categories will enable you to begin to see the general themes that characterize the artifact. At the end of this initial coding process, you have a set of broad features, ideas, or topics that you believe might serve as clues to an explanation of the artifact. Something seems to be going on in the artifact in terms of these features that you believe will help explain the artifact. At this point, however, you do not yet see a pattern that puts the features together. We ended our initial coding process thinking that *Run Lola Run* might have something to do with feminism, gender, relationships between marginalized and dominant groups, rhetorical strategies used by subordinate groups, agency, time, and games because our initial coding produced piles of observations/interpretations in these categories.

At this point, you might want to mark in some way which slips of papers are in which piles so you could re-create them if you want to after trying another grouping. Sort the slips again to force yourself to come up with another way of organizing your interpretations. You might want to feature different ideas, downplay others, interpret features differently, and try to capture different kinds of possible relationships among the codes. What this process does is encourage you to stretch beyond an initial, obvious way of categorizing the observations/interpretations and to open up other possibilities for seeing your data. There are many other categories in which we could have grouped our observations/interpretations of the first run in *Run Lola Run*. A different category, for example, from the data noted above, might have been a label such as *lack of support for others*, which could include the codes of Lola's father shaking his head "no," Manni taunting Lola, and Manni turning down a friend's offer of money.

Searching for an Explanation

Your next task is to search for an already existing or conventional way to explain the artifact. An explanation is likely to come in the form of a theory about an aspect of rhetoric or a construct from a theory. If you have been a student of communication for a while, you will bring to an artifact a repertoire of ideas and tools that can serve as possible explanations. If you are not yet very familiar with the communication discipline and its theories, you might want to do a miniature literature review at this time to discover if theories or concepts exist that can explain to your satisfaction your curiosity about your artifact. In addition, theories and concepts from outside the communication discipline may be relevant in your search for an explanation. Investigate journal articles and books related to the categories of themes your coding of the artifact revealed. Research that has been done on the artifact or on similar artifacts by others also might offer useful explanations. You may discover in an artifact, for example, elements that suggest to you Karlyn Kohrs Campbell's theory of a feminine rhetorical style. You then would look in the artifact for features of a feminine rhetorical style and construct your explanation from this application.

When you analyze an artifact using already existing concepts or theories, the temptation is often to engage in what is sometimes called *cookie-cutter criticism*, where all artifacts studied through the lens of the same method or theory come out looking exactly the same. For example, if you decide that what is going on in a speech by Barack Obama that is most significant has something to do with his use of the characteristics of a feminine style, you will focus your analysis on the components of Campbell's notion of a feminine style—a personal tone; use of personal experience, anecdote, and examples as evidence; an inductive structure; audience participation; and identification between speaker and audience. Likewise, if you are analyzing a poem by Maya Angelou and something in the poem suggests that a feminine style may be part of your explanation for what intrigues you about it, again you would analyze the poem for those five components. You may not find the same things are going on in terms of the precise enactment of a feminine style in the two artifacts, but you would have molded your artifact into one where what is significant about it must fit into those five components. When you do this, you risk missing more significant and interesting things in your artifact. In addition, when the data are made to fit the theory, your essay of criticism sometimes illustrates the theory more than it illuminates your artifact. With such an approach, you usually are not encouraged to go beyond the confines of those concepts or theories for an explanation for your artifact.

But what usually happens is that your search for a conventional explanation does not produce one that satisfactorily explains the artifact. Gilbert B. Rodman provides an excellent example of a search for—and rejection of—conventional explanations for a curious artifact. He noticed that, for "a dead man, Elvis Presley is awfully noisy. His body may have failed him in 1977, but today his spirit, his image, and his myths do more than live on: they flourish, they thrive, they multiply."[8] He asks the questions: "Why is Elvis

Presley so ubiquitous a presence in U.S. culture? Why does he continue to enjoy a cultural prominence that would be the envy of the most heavily publicized living celebrities?" He tries out a number of explanations—capitalism, fandom, and postmodernism—and suggests that none of them

> manages to provide a compelling or convincing account of why Elvis enjoys the current cultural ubiquity he does. . . . What the approaches . . . ultimately do is explain how Elvis is just like any (and every) other star and how his story can be stitched back into the larger fabric of media, culture, and society. The problem here, however, is not that there are no similarities between Elvis and other stars, but that the phenomenon at hand is only interesting because it *exceeds* the normal expectations of capitalism, fandom, and postmodernism. In the end, then, these potential solutions to the puzzle of Elvis's contemporary ubiquity don't explain the phenomenon so much as they explain it away; transforming a unique and unusual range of texts and practices into just another example of a supposedly already understood cultural phenomenon.[9]

We thought for a while that *Run Lola Run* could be explained by the three views of love/rhetoric in Plato's *Phaedrus*. But we not only discovered that these three views of rhetoric did not begin to explain what was going on in the film but also that an analysis built on this theory largely would have illustrated Plato's theory, would not have added anything new to it, and would have restricted our insights about the artifact. As an explanation, the theory, in other words, felt laminated onto the film instead of derived from its unique features.

What is most likely to happen after searching for an explanation of your artifact is that you will find a theory or construct that explains some pieces of your artifact but not all of them. It might explain one aspect or dimension of the artifact, but it does not account for all of the major dimensions you noticed in your initial coding. In this case, you do not yet have an adequate and satisfactory explanation of the artifact.

Creating an Explanatory Schema

If a conventional explanation for your artifact does not exist, you must develop your own explanatory schema for it—an explanation that comes from your thinking about the data of your artifact. Your objective in generating an explanatory schema is to discover a better explanation for your artifact than what was offered by the theories and constructs you tried out on your artifact in your search for a conventional explanation.[10] An explanatory schema is a framework for organizing your insights about the artifact in a coherent and insightful way. It is an explanation of what is going on in the artifact derived from an analysis of the artifact itself. It connects all or most of the features that emerged from your broad-brush coding of the artifact. An explanatory schema also can be thought of as a theory—the components of the schema are concepts in the theory, and the patterns among the concepts in the schema are statements of relationship in the theory. An explanatory schema, then, will be about some things—some constructs or concepts—and it will explain how those constructs or concepts relate to one another.

The explanation we developed for *Run Lola Run* is an example of an explanatory schema. Our explanation for the film is that it presents three different agentic orientations—patterns of interaction that predispose individuals to a particular enactment of agency. An agentic orientation is composed of three components—a particular interpretation of structure (persons, places, and events); the selection of a response to that interpretation of structure; and the experience of an outcome in line with those choices. Each agentic orientation, then, has different conceptions of structural conditions, takes a different response to the perception of those conditions, and generates a different outcome.

An explanatory schema does more than provide an explanation for what is intriguing to you about an artifact. It also serves as the structure of the essay you will write to present your analysis. Its component parts are the headings and subheadings of the findings or analysis section of your essay. In the case of our analysis of *Run Lola Run*, for example, we organized our analysis section around the headings of *victim, supplicant,* and *director* when we wrote up our analysis and divided each of those into subsections of *structural conditions, response,* and *outcome*.

Although you can formulate an explanatory schema just by sitting alone at your desk and thinking, three techniques can be useful in your efforts to develop this schema. They speed up the process of developing a schema by providing sparks or prompts that can move you in new directions so that you are able to think in creative and insightful ways about your artifact. The three techniques are: (1) cutting and sorting codes; (2) engaging in a conceptual conversation; and (3) brainstorming.

Cutting and Sorting Codes

One technique that can help in the development of an explanatory schema makes use of the notes you made about the artifact in the initial coding step. If you used the process of cutting and sorting codes, you can make use of your piles again to help you create an explanatory schema. List the labels you have given the piles and cut them apart so that each label is on a separate strip of paper. You then can move the labels (which represent features/interpretations) around to see how you can put them in relation to one another in a way that provides an explanation for your artifact. Some of our piles for *Run Lola Run*, for example, were *material conditions as threats and obstacles, refusing help, rhetorical strategies doomed to fail,* and *assumption of inferior position.* When we listed our labels on a piece of paper, cut them apart, and began to play around with how they could be connected to provide an explanatory schema for *Run Lola Run*, we asked questions such as: "Is there something that all these have in common?" "What picture do these present of Lola in this run?" "Are there inconsistencies among the themes/labels?" "To what ideas do all of these point?"

Engaging in a Conceptual Conversation

A second technique that facilitates the process of formulating an explanatory schema is to have a conversation with someone else or even a small group of people about your artifact. Your task in this conversation is to talk about the initial coding you did, explain what you are seeing in the artifact, clarify terms, and explain what in the artifact you find intriguing or baffling. Also describe what was unexplained by the previous theories you tried out as explanations for the artifact. Encourage your conversational partner to ask exploratory, open-ended, defining, doubting, connecting, and probing questions. The only requirements for good conversational partners are that they are patient, genuinely willing to listen, ask questions when they do not understand what you are saying, are curious, have little investment in being right or wrong themselves, and are individuals whose ideas you respect.

Even someone who knows nothing about communication or your topic can be a useful conversational partner and, in fact, these people often make better partners in this effort than people who are trained in communication. Those who know a lot about communication are most likely to help you find explanations for your artifact from conventions, drawing on theories they know about and particularly on theories that resonate with them. They may be less likely to allow an explanation to be generated from the artifact itself. Often, people without a knowledge of the communication discipline ask excellent questions and generate good ideas simply because they don't share your assumptions about communication and are less confined by a specific body of knowledge.

Set aside a significant amount of time for a conceptualizing conversation—it often takes several hours—and hold the conversation someplace where you won't be interrupted. If you can, take notes during the conversation, but this can be difficult to do as you are talking and exploring ideas. Thus, you might want to record the conversation so that you can recapture easily the insights you have along the way.

Brainstorming

A third technique that is useful for developing an explanatory schema is to use formal techniques designed to facilitate creative and original thinking.[11] You might try techniques like those described below to prompt your thinking about your artifact and to help you come to a possible explanation for it. You can use these techniques either alone or in conversation with someone else.

Introducing Random Stimulation

Using this technique, you deliberately introduce apparently irrelevant and unconnected information into your thinking about the artifact. This can be done in a variety of ways. You can open a dictionary, point to a word, and then relate that word to your artifact and the categories that emerged from your coding in as many ways as you can. Another way is to look around the room and select an object. Create as many connections as you can between that object and your topic.

I used this technique to discover an explanation for a group of artworks that intrigued me—works of art known as *body art* that were popular in the 1970s and involved artists using their physical bodies as their medium of expression. These artists, for example, might bite themselves all over their bodies and then apply paint to the bites. I looked up from the desk where I was trying to create an explanatory schema and saw a picture of a clown on the wall, so I began connecting the clown to body art in as many ways as I could. After just a few minutes, I had my explanatory schema: The clown was not the explanation I was seeking, but the insane person was. I constructed an explanation around the notion of insanity, in which the viewer adopts the role of a therapist to make sense of the works. I never would have developed that schema without the image of the clown as a prompt.[12]

Shifting Focus

We are able to pay only limited attention to the things in our world, and we have a choice about where to focus our attention. Because our attention usually settles over the most obvious areas, a slight shift in attention by itself may suggest an explanation for an artifact. In shifting focus, you deliberately turn away from your natural attention areas to see what happens if you pay attention to something else in the artifact. If you are interested in the appeals of a politician to Latino/a voters, your likely attention is to the kinds of appeals the campaign made to these voters. The deliberate selection of a different, less obvious point of attention—the real intended audience for the appeals—might suggest an explanation you had not thought about before. Perhaps the appeals really are directed at white moderate and undecided voters and not at Latinos/as at all.

Three perspectives can be particularly useful for exploring an artifact to discover possible options for a shift in focus. The terms are borrowed from physics—viewing the artifact as a particle, a wave, or a field. A view of the artifact as a particle assumes the artifact is an isolated, static entity or an irreducible constituent of matter. From this perspective, try to name the unique identifying features that differentiate your artifact from similar things. Taking a perspective on the artifact as a wave—a disturbance or an oscillation—you can see the artifact as a dynamic object or event and ask how the artifact is changing, noting movement in time, space, or conceptually. When you explore the artifact as a field, you see it not existing in isolation but as occupying a place in a larger system or network of some kind. You might ask how the components of the artifact are organized in relation to one another and what its position is in a larger system.

For an analysis of the Portland Building, located in Portland, Oregon, and designed by architect Michael Graves, you might generate ideas using this approach in the following ways:

1. Portland Building as a *particle*. What are its constituent units—materials, colors, structure, height, arrangement of rooms, placement on the lot?

2. Portland Building as a *wave*. How does the effect of the Portland Building on its users change as the building ages, the landscape around it changes, and it is used in ways other than those for which

it was designed? How does the building evoke different responses according to the time of day and season in which it is viewed? How have judgments about the building changed over time and according to changing architectural styles? How does the building direct the movement of users within it?

3. Portland Building as part of a *field*. How does the building function as part of the larger field of architecture, the field of Graves's buildings or the items he designs for Target, or the field of the city of Portland? How does the building constitute a system itself, composed of interrelated subsystems? What relationships order the parts of the building and connect them to other units within larger systems?

Obviously, some of these ideas would be able to be developed into an explanation of the Portland Building, and others would not, but the technique of shifting focus provides a way to generate possible explanations. (You can see what the Portland Building looks like in chapter 8 and in the color photo gallery.)

Applying the Topics

If you have studied classical rhetoric, you are likely to be familiar with an ancient system that can be used to generate ideas for an explanatory schema for an artifact—Aristotle's *topoi* or topics. In his book the *Rhetoric*, Aristotle suggested various topics or places to go to discover ideas for arguments, including definition, comparison, contrast, cause and effect, opposites, relation of parts to whole, and conflicting facts. Three of the topics are used below to illustrate how they might generate ideas for explaining the rhetoric of Hillary Clinton as she campaigned for president of the United States in 2008:

1. Definition: How can Clinton's rhetoric be defined? Can it be defined as an effort to remove the gender issue from politics? Can it be defined as an effort to redeem her husband's presidency? Can it be defined as a triumph of feminism?

2. Comparison and contrast: How was Clinton's rhetoric like or unlike that of Geraldine Ferraro, who was Fritz Mondale's vice presidential running mate? How was her rhetoric like or unlike that of Shirley Chisholm and Sonia Johnson, two women who ran for president before her? How was her rhetoric like or unlike that of her male opponents?

3. Cause and effect: What effects might Clinton's rhetoric have on the perceptions of politics by Americans and others? Did Geraldine Ferraro's rhetoric help create an environment in which Clinton's candidacy was taken more seriously? What might be the effects of Clinton's rhetoric on the Democratic Party? What was the effect of Bill Clinton's presidency on his wife's campaign rhetoric?

Reversing

Using the reversal technique, you deliberately move away from what you know about the artifact (or believe you have figured out) and pursue an opposite direction or opposite qualities. Take things as they are in the artifact and turn them around, inside out, upside down, and back to front to see if the reversal generates ideas for an explanation. Reversal would generate thinking about *Run Lola Run* by encouraging us to ask questions such as: Lola is running to save Manni's life; is there a way in which Manni is saving Lola's life? The security guard stands at the entrance to the bank where Lola goes to ask her banker father for the money. Is there something that Lola guards? What does her father guard? Manni's boss demands money by noon. What does the money demand that the boss do? In one of the runs, Manni is killed by an ambulance. If the ambulance doesn't save Manni, who or what does it save?

Questioning

Questioning, or the why technique, provides an opportunity to challenge assumptions you might be holding about an artifact and to pursue various aspects of it in depth. This technique is similar to the child's habit of asking "why?" all the time. The difference is that, in this process, you are likely to know the answer to the questions you are asking. The asking simply encourages you to explore the possibilities and dimensions of the artifact in more detail. At one point in *Run Lola Run*, Lola's father agrees to marry his mistress, even though she is pregnant with another man's baby. Using the questioning technique, you might ask why he would do that. You might answer that he loves her and can ignore the fact that she apparently cheated on him. You would ask "why?" again. Your answer this time might be that he is able to separate his feelings from the material conditions around him. You would ask "why?" again, this time speculating that he has more control over events if he doesn't tie his agency to material conditions. And so on. At some point, an answer may suggest an explanation or part of an explanation for your artifact.

Whatever the means you use to arrive at it, at this time, you have an explanatory schema—an idea for an explanation of your artifact. The next step is to evaluate whether this schema will work as an explanation for your artifact. When you have a schema that explains the artifact well, you will know it in two ways. One is that the schema explains all of the key pieces of the artifact—nothing major about the artifact is left hanging or unexplained. Everything fits. The features you coded earlier as a result of frequency and intensity in the artifact should fit into or be able to be explained by the proposed schema.

A second criterion for judging your schema is whether it feels right. This undoubtedly seems like a strange way to judge an explanatory schema, but a schema that really explains your artifact produces a "got it!" or "ah ha!" feeling. When you come up with an explanation that addresses what intrigued or baffled you about the artifact, you will know this explanation is the one. Admittedly, at the beginning of your career as a rhetorical critic, almost any schema you devise is probably going to feel pretty good. To counter this possibility, try out two different possible explanatory schemas for your artifact. If they both have about the same amount of explanatory value and neither one seems particularly better than the other, you know you probably do not have the best schema you could develop for explaining your artifact.

When you are trying to create an explanatory schema from an artifact, the process often is difficult, frustrating, and takes time. You know something of rhetorical significance is occurring in the artifact but are not yet able to articulate and explain it. Be patient. My coauthor, Karen A. Foss, and I went through three dramatically different schemas for our analysis of Garrison Keillor's monologues on the radio program *A Prairie Home Companion* over the course of several years before we found the one we knew explained the appeal of the monologues for us.[13] Sufficient time and energy spent exploring the artifact eventually will yield an explanation that will enable you to understand the particular artifact better and also to contribute to rhetorical theory.

Formulating a Research Question

When you have constructed an explanatory schema that you believe provides an insightful explanation of your artifact and answers the questions that led you initially into an exploration of the artifact, you are ready to construct your research question. You want to be able to state clearly what your research question is, although you probably will turn the question into a purpose statement in the essay you write. Use the principle behind the TV show *Jeopardy* to create a question for which the explanatory schema you have developed is the answer. For example, the explanatory schema my coauthors and I developed for *Run Lola Run* is that the three runs in the film represent different agentic orientations. As a result of this schema, our research question became, "What is the nature and function of agentic orientation?"

Coding the Artifact in Detail

Following the formulation of your research question, code your artifact again, using the component elements of your explanatory schema. You are doing more in-depth coding here than what you did originally because you are testing your proposed schema against the data of your artifact and developing your schema further. Your research question now guides your coding, so as you analyze the artifact, you are looking for dimensions and qualities pertinent to answering it. As in the initial coding process, you are identifying features of the artifact and interpreting them.

When you have finished the detailed coding of your artifact, make another copy of your observations or codings. Save one copy of the coded artifact for future reference, and physically cut apart the notes or codes on the other copy. In a process much like the one you might have used in your initial coding of the artifact, sort the coded data into piles according to topics, putting all the strips of paper that have to do with the same topic together. Label the piles with a word or phrase that describes what is common to all the observations in that pile. If you can, create a space where you can lay the piles out and keep them out while you write your essay. If you do not have this kind of space, put the piles into separate envelopes and label the envelopes with the labels you put on the piles.

As you did with your initial coding, make a list of the labels of the piles. Cut the labels on this list apart. Play around with the labels, which represent your piles and major ideas, to see how they relate to one another and provide the explanation that is the answer to your research question. You are working to discover what is subordinate to what, what are the overarching categories, and so on. As you engage in this process, you are developing the explanatory schema you have seen until now only in general terms, working out kinks, conceptualizing aspects of it you did not think through before, refining it, and extending it.

When you have your explanatory schema fully developed and you know how the concepts captured by the piles of strips of paper are going to work together in your schema, create the actual labels you will use to name the various components of your schema. Choose these conceptual labels carefully because the components of your schema become the concepts of your theory and the subheadings in the body of your essay. If possible, name the components with labels that are original and not conventional—labels that do not come from existing literature. Clearly, if some part of your schema is a well-known rhetorical process with a known label, you want to use that label, but not everything in your schema should repeat what is already known. If you have new observations and insights, they should produce new labels.

Make your labels parallel with one another and at the same level of abstraction to contribute to your theory's coherence. The labels we gave to the three agentic orientations Lola adopts in *Run Lola Run*—*victim*, *supplicant*, and *director*—although common words, have not been used before to describe options in terms of agency. Thus, they are new in that no theory we know about puts them together in this way.

Searching the Literature

When you have an explanatory schema that explains your artifact in comprehensive and insightful ways, do a miniature literature review of the key concepts in the schema. The purpose for the literature review at this stage is to relate the literature to your explanatory schema so that you can enter conversations in the communication field about the ideas covered by the schema. See if literature exists that can help you elaborate on ideas in your schema, that points you to ways in which you can elaborate on an existing theory, or that makes visible a point of contention where you take issue with a way in which a construct is conceptualized. You are checking concepts and relationships from the literature against your actual data, looking for evidence of whether or not those concepts and relationships apply to the artifact you are analyzing and, if so, the form they take in your artifact. In the case of our analysis of *Run Lola Run*, we reviewed literature on various options by which agency is constituted in rhetorical performances, including the origin of agency, various forms that agency can assume, and the strategies employed by specific agents in response to particular exigencies.

Searching the literature in this way is probably a different way to use literature from the way to which you are accustomed, where you do a literature review at the start of your study to help you design the study. In rhetorical criticism, new ideas should emerge that neither you nor anyone else has thought about previously. If you review all relevant literature before you analyze your artifact, you will be so steeped in the literature that your creative ideas will be constrained and stifled. Because discovery of new ideas is your purpose, you do not want to have knowledge of all the categories relevant to your theory at the beginning of your analysis. Only after a topic has emerged as pertinent to a possible explanation for your artifact do you want to go back to the literature to see if this topic has been studied and, if so, what others have said about it.

You may find yourself facing two common problems when you survey the literature. One is that the literature seems overwhelming because there is so much of it to cover that you have no idea how to begin. A second problem is keeping track of everything you read so you can make use of it effectively. You may find that you have highlighted passages or have stuck Post-it notes on virtually every page of every book and article you have relevant to your subject. The following system of "coding" the literature addresses these problems and enables you to engage the literature in an efficient and manageable fashion.

Coding the literature means gleaning the ideas that are relevant and useful for your project from the literature. Do this coding the first time you read a book or an article instead of reading it first and then going back through it to code. When your literature is gathered and is stacked before you, sit at your computer and take each book or article in turn. Review it for ideas that have a direct bearing on your explanatory schema. When you find such an idea, take notes about it on the computer. Type in single space either a direct quote or a summary of the idea you find useful, and include the source and page number for each note you take. Double or triple space between notes.

Using this system, you are likely to be able to read and code a book in an hour. This is possible because you do not read every word of the book. Use all the clues the book provides to discover what is relevant for your explanatory schema—the table of contents, chapter titles, headings, and the index. For each chapter that seems relevant to your explanatory schema, ask: "Is this chapter relevant for my study?" If it isn't, don't read it, and don't code it. When you come upon a relevant chapter, review it heading by heading and subheading by subheading. Ask at each heading, "Is this section relevant for my explanatory schema?" If it isn't, skip it. When you find something relevant, type a note about it.

If you are not a fast keyboarder, there is another way to code literature that may work better for you. As you read a book or an article, mark in the margin each excerpt or passage that is relevant to your explanatory schema. When you have finished reading a book or an article, take it to a copy machine and make a copy of each page where you marked a passage or passages. On the copied pages, write the source and page in the margin by each passage you have marked.

After you have coded all of the literature, print out two copies of the notes you took during your coding. Keep one as it is for future reference and cut the notes on the other copy apart. If you copied actual pages from books and journals, cut out the passages from each copied page that you have marked. At the end of this process, then, each note or marked passage is on a separate strip of paper, along with a shorthand reference to the source and page number from which the note came.

The next step of the process is to sort the strips into piles according to subject, putting everything that is about the same topic in the same pile. For example, all the strips of paper in one pile might have to do with power, those in another pile with gender, those in another pile with agency, and those in another pile with a disagreement in the communication field about the role that material conditions play in rhetoric. These piles should correspond to the major areas of your explanatory schema because you are only reading literature that is relevant to your explanatory schema.

If you cut apart your codings of your artifact, you now have two types of piles—piles of concepts that came from coding your artifact and piles of notes from your literature review that should be about the same topics as those in your data piles. Compare the ideas about the topics that emerged from the literature review with the insights that you have created in your explanatory schema. Use ideas from the literature as you write up your findings to elaborate on and extend your ideas in the schema. In our presentation of our analysis of *Run Lola Run*, for example, we explain how mortification (self-inflicted punishment) is a rhetorical strategy the characters choose in the first run; we reference Kenneth Burke's ideas about mortification. He provides elaboration for our notion because he suggests that mortification is designed to slay characteristics, impulses, or aspects of the self. This idea fits perfectly with and supports our analysis because we are suggesting that what is being slayed in the first run is the capacity to act apart from the demands of structural conditions.

Framing the Study

The last step of analysis before you begin to write your essay is to decide how to frame your explanatory schema so that it can contribute to a significant conversation in the communication discipline. Your research question may explicitly suggest what this frame is, but in many cases, you can contribute to numerous theoretical conversations with the same research question. If your research question asks a question about how political leaders justify unpopular wars, for example, you can frame your essay as a contribution to an understanding of political discourse, an understanding of war rhetoric, or an understanding of justificatory rhetoric. In the case of our analysis of *Run Lola Run*, we framed our explanatory schema in terms of the relationship between rhetoric and agency and suggested that one piece of that relationship is undertheorized and not adequately explained—what various options are for enacting agency and how different options affect outcomes. But we also could have framed our essay, for example, in terms of communication between marginalized and dominant groups and means for gaining access to the resources of the dominant culture.

Writing the Essay

After completing your analysis, you are ready to write your essay of criticism. The components of this essay are the same as those for an essay when you begin criticism with a method: (1) an introduction, in which you discuss the research question, its contribution to rhetorical theory, and its significance; (2) a description of the artifact and its context; (3) a brief description of the generative method used to analyze your artifact; (4) a report of the findings of the analysis—in this case, your explanatory schema or theory; and (5) a discussion of the contribution the analysis makes to rhetorical theory.

Sample Essays

Three sample essays that were developed using the generative method of criticism follow. The first is the essay I wrote with William Waters and Bernard J. Armada on *Run Lola Run* that came out of the process described in this chapter. As you'll recall, our research question is, "What is the nature and function of agentic orientation?" The second essay, "The Gender of Napoleon and the Power of Dynamite" by M. Rosie Russo, focuses on the question, "How does a nontraditional portrayal of masculinity encourage audiences to question conventional definitions of masculinity?" In her essay on a children's book *Star of Fear, Star of Hope*, Marcia S. Van't Hof analyzes her artifact to answer the question, "What are rhetorical strategies that are effective in introducing children to frightening historical realities?"

A list of additional samples that model generative criticism is not provided following the sample essays, as it was in the previous chapters. Most criticism published in communication journals today uses the generative method, so samples of it are readily available and accessible.

Notes

[1] My thanks to William Waters, who cocreated these steps of the process.

[2] Philip Wander and Steven Jenkins, "Rhetoric, Society, and the Critical Response," *Quarterly Journal of Speech*, 58 (December 1972), 441.

[3] Janice Hocker Rushing and Thomas S. Frentz, "The Frankenstein Myth in Contemporary Cinema: Commentary," in *Critical Questions: Invention, Creativity, and the Criticism of Discourse and Media*, ed. William L. Nothstine, Carole Blair, and Gary A. Copeland (New York: St. Martin's, 1994), p. 155.

[4] Roderick P. Hart, "Wandering with Rhetorical Criticism," in *Critical Questions: Invention, Creativity, and the Criticism of Discourse and Media*, ed. William L. Nothstine, Carole Blair, and Gary A. Copeland (New York: St. Martin's, 1994), pp. 78, 80.

[5] Elizabeth Walker Mechling and Jay Mechling, "The Campaign for Civil Defense: Commentary," in *Critical Questions: Invention, Creativity, and the Criticism of Discourse and Media*, ed. William L. Nothstine, Carole Blair, and Gary A. Copeland (New York: St. Martin's, 1994), p. 120.

[6] Mechling and Mechling, "The Campaign for Civil Defense," p. 119.

[7] Sonja K. Foss, William J. C. Waters, and Bernard J. Armada, "Toward a Theory of Agentic Orientation: Rhetoric and Agency in *Run Lola Run*," *Communication Theory*, 17 (August 2007), 205–30.

[8] Gilbert B. Rodman, *Elvis after Elvis: The Posthumous Career of a Living Legend* (New York: Routledge, 1996), p. 1.

[9] Rodman, *Elvis after Elvis*, pp. 18–19.

[10] This process is much like the grounded-theory approach to analyzing data. See Barney G. Glaser and Anselm L. Strauss, *The Discovery of Grounded Theory: Strategies of Qualitative Research* (Chicago: Aldine, 1967); Anselm Strauss and Juliet Corbin, *Basics of Qualitative Research: Grounded Theory Procedures and Techniques* (Newbury Park, CA: Sage, 1990); and Barney G. Glaser, *Doing Grounded Theory: Issues and Discussions* (Mill Valley, CA: Sociology, 1998).

[11] See, for example, Edward de Bono, *Lateral Thinking: Creativity Step by Step* (New York: Harper Colophon, 1970).

[12] Sonja K. Foss, "Body Art: Insanity as Communication," *Central States Speech Journal*, 38 (Summer 1987), 122–31.

[13] Sonja K. Foss and Karen A. Foss, "The Construction of Feminine Spectatorship in Garrison Keillor's Radio Monologues," *Quarterly Journal of Speech*, 80 (November 1994), 410–26.

Toward a Theory of Agentic Orientation
Rhetoric and Agency in *Run Lola Run*

Sonja K. Foss, William J. C. Waters, and Bernard J. Armada

Lucaites (2003) has called for identification of the wide range of options by which agency—the "capacity to make a difference" (Castor & Cooren, 2006, p. 573)—is constituted in particular rhetorical performances. He notes that "every rhetorical performance enacts and contains a theory of its own agency—of its own possibilities—as it structures and enacts the relationships between speaker and audience, self and other, action and structure" (p. 1). Such a mapping of various options for agency is important in that it can lead to "analytical leverage for charting varying degrees of maneuverability, inventiveness, and reflective choice" (Emirbayer & Mische, 1998, p. 964) in the rhetorical process.

Lucaites' (2003) call has been answered in various ways by those concerned with the relationship between agency and rhetoric. Some seek to locate the origin of agency in various relationships between self and structure, as do, for example, Spivak (1988b), Gaonkar (1993), Conrad and Macom (1995), Lucaites and Condit (1999), Cooren (1999), Gunn (2003, 2006), Gunn and Treat (2005), and Cloud (2005). Some explicate various forms of agency, including the technological, human, and textual, a project undertaken by, among others, Hardy (2004), Cooren (2004), McPhee (2004), and Fairhurst (2004). The various dimensions of the agentic process constitute another focus, exemplified by the work of Emirbayer and Mische (1998) and of Bandura (1989). Others turn their attention to the nature of rhetoric as it constructs or enables agency, represented by the work of Grossberg (1997) and of Campbell (2005). Yet another project concerning agency is to explicate the strategies of agency employed by specific agents in response to a unique exigence, as do Wendell (1990) and Waggoner and O'Brien Hallstein (2001).

We want to take the conversation about rhetoric and agency in a somewhat different direction, which is to theorize a rhetorical mechanism—agentic orientation—that provides various options for the enactment of agency. Agentic orientation is a pattern of interaction that predisposes an individual to a particular enactment of agency. Thus, it is not unlike Bourdieu's (1990) "*habitus*, systems of durable, transposable dispositions, structured structures predisposed to function as structuring structures" (p. 10). Although a construct that others have referenced (Emirbayer & Mische, 1998, p. 964), agentic orientation has not been sufficiently developed to constitute a theoretical and practical option for understanding agency. Our aim in this essay is to explicate the nature and function of agentic orientation and the options available to agents through its application.

We chose to develop the construct of agentic orientation and to map out its various enactments after seeing the film *Run Lola Run,* a German film directed by Tom Tykwer that stars Franka Potente and Moritz Bleibtreu (Arndt, 1998). Watching the film was the most fun we had had at the movies in a while, a response confirmed by the film's positive reception at festivals such as Sundance and Toronto. What pushed us to meet the film's insistent challenge to analyze it was our realization that the film

Foss et al., Toward a Theory of Agentic Orientation: Rhetoric and Agency in *Run Lola Run. Communication Theory,* 2007, Vol. 5(3), pp. 205–230. Permission granted by Blackwell Publishing, Ltd.

has something to say about agency—in particular about the nature and function of agentic orientation.

Run Lola Run features the young lovers Lola and Manni who live on the fringes of the establishment in contemporary Germany. At the start of the film, Lola receives a frantic phone call from Manni, who has lost a small fortune (100,000 Deutschemarks) belonging to his mobster boss, Ronnie, by accidentally leaving it in a subway car, where it is picked up by a tramp. Manni claims that if he cannot produce the money by noon (within 20 minutes), Ronnie will kill him, and he begs Lola for help. Lola takes off running to try to secure the money and to reach Manni by the deadline. She makes three runs in the film, each time encountering the same people, vehicles, and objects but in different ways: a boy and a dog on the stairs of her apartment, a woman with a baby carriage, a group of nuns, a man riding a bike, a security guard at her father's bank, Lola's father, his mistress, Lola's father's friend Mr. Meier, a secretary in the bank, a blind woman, an ambulance, and men crossing the street with a large pane of glass. She attempts to acquire the money in different ways in each run, and the outcomes of the runs are dramatically different.

Scholars and film critics who have analyzed *Run Lola Run* have read it in strikingly different ways. Wood (2006) suggests that the film's message is about the importance of a balance among "the human activities of willing, feeling, and thinking" (p. 110). O'Sickey (2002) asserts that the film is about Lola's effort to become synchronized with Manni in sexual terms. Lauer (2003) suggests that the film imitates the new technology of the Internet, in which "everything is possible upon returning to a previous icon that enables one to access other potentially available albeit previously uninvoked routes" (p. 6). He suggests that the film admonishes viewers not "to accept anything less than . . . a multiplicity of options constantly and joyfully different (and deferred) in a continuously evolving universe" (p. 8). The most common way to read the film is through the metaphor of a game, as Bianco (2004) does, suggesting that the "end/s of the game lost become the possibility of the game continuing . . . a game that is the same and new with each round" (p. 379).

We find all these interpretations credible but are most intrigued by those that focus on agency. Scholars who address agency in the film stop at identifying the message of agency they believe the film offers without describing the processes by which the message is developed and communicated. Tobias (2004), for example, argues that the film develops the theme of "desire that plays out in the context of a female insistence on agency in the face of senior figures whose power is undesirable, and of peers whose impotence is unacceptable" (p. 31). Whalen (2000) reads the film as a coming-of-age fairy tale that disrupts determinism and suggests that "like Lola, we, too, if we work at it, can become the player rather than the played" (p. 40). Evans (2004) also interprets the film's message as one about agency: "The film is about *not* passively accepting one's fate; it is all about changing it" (p. 112). The "film advocates, and portrays," he continues, "a spirit of never-say-die" (p. 114). The construct of agentic orientation, we believe, describes the process by which the agency these critics reference is enacted.

Agentic Orientation

We turn now to an explication of the construct of agentic orientation that we believe *Run Lola Run* offers to an understanding of agency. We begin with the fundamental contribution the film makes to mapping out the construct, which is to point to the components that comprise an agentic orientation. The film suggests that there are three components: a particular interpretation of structure, the selection of a response to that interpretation of structure, and the experience of an outcome in line with those choices. An agentic orientation first takes into account structural or material conditions because every act is an interpretation of a set of conditions. Agency is "always agency *toward* something," and that something is the perceived structure, whether it consists of the "surrounding persons, places, meanings, and events" an agent encounters or "routines, dispositions, preconceptions, competencies, schemas, patterns, typifications, and traditions" (Emirbayer & Mische, 1998, pp. 973, 975). *Run Lola Run,* of course, has the requisite confrontational structure as exigence—Lola and Manni face the classic structural constraints of a lack of money and restrictions of time.

A second component of agentic orientation is a response to structure rooted in processes such as categorization, invention, and symbolization as employed by the agent. The artistry that Campbell (2005) finds so essential to agency finds its place in this second component of agentic orientation. The element of response maps out different responses to structure—different acts that involve certain arrangements with or types of adaptation to structure. In *Run Lola Run,* Lola engages in different kinds of acts in response to her interpretations of structure across the three runs.

Finally, an agentic orientation generates an outcome tied to the choices made concerning structure and act. If agency is action that influences or exerts some degree of control, an agentic orientation must attend to the outcomes generated by particular enactments of agency. Different rhetorical choices should result in different outcomes if those choices make a difference and, of course, they make a dramatic difference in *Run Lola Run.* A third component of agentic orientation, then, is outcome.

Run Lola Run not only identifies structure, act, and outcome—the elements that we posit comprise an agentic orientation—but it also conducts an experiment with different relationships among these elements. It displays on screen three different agentic orientations—three different combinations of structure–act–outcome. The film holds structure constant—both the structural exigence (the need for money and a lack of time) and the material resources of the agents (Lola and Manni have the same amount of education; the same abilities; and the same class, race, and gender across the runs). But it varies agentic orientations—interpretations of structure, acts in response to those interpretations, and the outcomes the agents experience—thereby providing an elegant model for exploring different enactments of agency.

Our process of explicating the three enactments of agency in the film began when we sought an explanation for the varied outcomes of the three runs. We began our search by coding the runs for images, objects, dialogue, qualities, and events that stood out either because of intensity or frequency. When we noticed that the features we had identified within each run formed consistent patterns of interpretation and action, we developed those patterns into the three different agentic orientations that we came to label *victim, supplicant,* and *director.*

Because of constraints of space, we are unable to report all the aspects of *Run Lola Run* that led us to the theory of agentic orientation we develop here. Dimensions of the film we are unable to discuss include, for example, the musical score of the film, the flash-forwards for minor characters, and the bedroom scenes that serve as transitions from one run to the next. Our analysis is also circumscribed by a focus on the character of Lola. Although the characters in each run tend to share a particular agentic orientation so that Lola, Manni, Lola's father, his mistress, and the security guard at the bank all show evidence of the same agentic orientation within each run, we have chosen to focus our analysis on the agency enacted by the title character of Lola, where variations in agentic orientation are most clear. Although we have had to focus on those elements of the film that constitute the most relevant evidence for our claims concerning agentic orientation, the elements we are unable to discuss here are consistent in their development of particular agentic orientations.

We now turn to an explanation of the agentic orientations presented in the three runs of *Run Lola Run*—victim, supplicant, and director. We begin by explaining, for each run, the first two elements of agentic orientation—an understanding of structural conditions and the acts selected to respond to those conditions. We then explicate the third element of agentic orientation—outcomes that align with agentic orientations. We conclude with a discussion of how the mechanism of agentic orientation might be applied.

Run 1: Victim

In the first run, Lola chooses an agentic orientation of victim in which she sees her agency as dependent on structural conditions or external others. She interprets her structural conditions as limited and engages in acts of mortification that declare and reinforce her victimage. In this run, Lola runs to the bank where her father works to ask him for the money. She interrupts a conversation her father is having with his mistress, who has just revealed her pregnancy to him. Lola's father not only refuses to give his daughter the money, but he has her thrown off the premises by the bank's security guard. Lola reaches Manni empty-handed just as he begins to rob a grocery store, and she assists him with the robbery. As they run from the store with the money, they are surrounded by the police, one of whom accidentally shoots and kills Lola.

In the agentic orientation of victim evident in the first run, Lola sees herself as helpless and disempowered, dependent on conditions and individuals external to herself. This agentic option is one in which she "seeks power through an identity of powerlessness" (Wolf, 1993, p. 147) so that everything "is organized around the deprived, frustrated, handicapped subject, and the victim strategy is that of [her] acknowledgement as such" (Baudrillard, 1996, p. 137). Lola interprets her choices for action to be embedded in external sources, making her actions dependent on and determined by other people and things.

Adoption of an agentic orientation of victimage encourages an agent to see expected punishment as an indicator of the correctness of the chosen agentic orientation. Although the punishment is typically seen as an undesirable outcome, the fact that the outcome matches a victim's expectations is soothing to the victim in that it suggests a world that makes sense, a world she can count on, and a world in which she knows how to exist. Lola's father, for example, belittles her and lies to her, agreeing to help her, but he then throws her out of the bank. His actions toward her serve as forms of punishment that constitute proof for Lola that she is a victim. Similarly, when Lola helps Manni rob the grocery store, she reinforces her victim orientation because, against her own judgment, she is helping him do something criminal for which she knows she will be punished. The ultimate punishment for Lola in this run, of course, is death. That she dies is primary evidence of the appropriateness of her adoption of an agentic orientation of victim. Heroic and fiercely loyal, she does everything she can think of to help Manni, but she still loses. The ultimate victim, Lola loses her father, she loses Manni, and she loses her life.

Structural Conditions: Limitations

When Lola adopts a victimage orientation, she interprets her structural conditions in ways that are consistent with an oppressed powerlessness. Because she has chosen a dependent form of agency, she grants ultimate power to structural conditions and sees herself as powerless over her circumstances. Lola's perception that structural conditions limit her agency is most obvious in Lola's view that the time deadline set by Ronnie constitutes a real constraint within which she must operate. The menacing nature of time for Lola is clear in an animated sequence at the beginning of the film when Lola crashes through clock after clock adorned with ugly gargoyles and surrounded by sharp, menacing teeth.

Lola also cedes power to structural conditions by refusing to take responsibility for what happens to Manni and her. She places the blame for events in their lives on conditions, people, or events external to them. The perception that structural conditions are powerful controllers is evident even when Lola explains the sources of the pair's trouble to Manni at the beginning of the film. Lola tells Manni that, because her scooter was stolen, she could not pick him up after he took delivery of the money. Lola took a cab to try to meet Manni, but the cab driver got lost, which meant she could not arrive on time for the scheduled rendezvous with Manni. He thus was forced to take the subway, where he accidentally left the money when the arrival of police flustered him and compelled him to exit the subway car. The stolen scooter, the lost cab driver, the arrival of the police, and the money left on the subway are seen as conditions over which Lola and Manni have no control and that irrevocably determine the course of their lives. "It wasn't my fault, Manni," cries Lola in response to Manni's scapegoating of her for the lost money. "There was nothing I could do."

Lola's view of structural conditions as controlling is also seen when she runs alongside an ambulance after leaving her father at the bank. When the ambulance screeches to a halt to allow several men carrying a large pane of glass to cross an intersection, Lola, too, stops and waits as if she is governed by the rules of traffic that govern the vehicle. Although she is a pedestrian and easily could walk around the glass, she allows the glass to function as an obstacle that must be moved before she can continue rather than something that she can circumvent.

Lola chooses to interpret another structural condition as immutable as well. As Lola's father shoves her through the security door of the bank, he announces, "Now you know. The guy who fathered you never lived to see your birth." He then turns to the security guard and says, "Throw her out, please. Come on! Get her out of here!" His acts reference structural conditions often seen as governing and controlling—paternity, heredity, and institutional power. Lola sees these structural conditions as compelling forces that allow no response other than a tearful acquiescence.

Because Lola views structural conditions as controlling, she sees them as limiting. Instead of attending to the enabling dimensions of and the opportunities presented by the surrounding environment, she sees structural conditions as obstacles. As she runs through the streets of Berlin on her way to her father's office, Lola rejects a young man's offer to sell her the bike he is riding for 50 marks. Lola's sense of victimhood blinds her from seeing resources such as the bike that could help her reach Manni faster. A lack of money is not the issue here; she has enough money on her to buy the bike, evidenced by the 99 marks she produces at the casino entrance in the third run.

Accepting help means she could change her condition, but because an acceptance of assistance would require a change of agentic orientation, she refuses the offer.

Lola's negative attributions to structural conditions sometimes extend beyond limitation to danger. Even when there is no reason to fear a particular condition, she constructs it as dangerous and again reinforces the victim orientation that the presence of such danger appears to dictate. All three runs begin with a short animated vignette in which a cartoon version of Lola runs down the stairs of the apartment and confronts a nasty looking boy and his dog on the stairwell. In the first run, Lola screams in fear when she sees the dog, more fearful of the idea that the dog might harm her than is warranted by the actual dog.

The image of tragic death that frames the first run underscores most dramatically the controlling power of structural conditions for Lola. At the end of the run, death appears as an inescapable force when Lola is accidentally shot by a police officer. Lola's death is a visceral reminder of the power of structural conditions from the standpoint of a victim. As Burke (1970) advises, "death in the natural order becomes conceived as the fulfillment or completion" of a victim orientation (p. 207), and Lola's death in the service of saving Manni epitomizes that stance.

Response: Mortification

The options Lola employs to respond to the strictures of structure also manifest an agentic orientation of victim. She chooses strategies that declare her victimage, maintain it, and repair it when she encounters evidence that she has other options. Her primary response is the strategy that Burke (1970) labels *mortification,* self-inflicted punishment, self-sacrifice, or self-imposed denials and restrictions designed to slay characteristics, impulses, or aspects of the self. He suggests that mortification is the "deliberate, disciplinary 'slaying' of any motive that, for 'doctrinal' reasons, one thinks of as unruly . . . it is a systematic way of saying no to Disorder, or obediently saying yes to Order" (p. 190). In Lola's case, Lola says yes to the order of the structural conditions and slays the possibility for action apart from their demands.

Lola employs a variety of strategies that function to ensure that she does not achieve her goals because accomplishment of those goals would require that she abandon her victim stance. One such strategy is to ask for help from people who are not able to provide it. In the beginning of the film, when Lola mentally and visually reviews the people she could ask for money, her father's face appears among the options, but he shakes his head "no." Although she already knows he will not give her the money, she still makes her request of him. Lola's piercing scream in the first run is also an option designed not to accomplish her presumed objective. In a scene in her father's office, where Lola has interrupted the conversation he is having with his mistress, Lola screams out in frustration at her father's refusal to give her money, shattering a glass clock on the wall. Her scream, which has a distinctly different rhetorical quality and function in the third run, here symbolizes Lola's frustration with time limitations and immutable demands. It is an unfocused act of frustration, however, that does nothing to liberate her from those demands.

Another strategy Lola uses to maintain the agentic orientation of the victim is to announce her victim status publicly, suggesting to herself and others that there are no other viable agentic orientations for her to assume. Lola makes such an announcement when she is placed in circumstances in which she is given the opportunity to assume a position of power yet abdicates it for the position of victim. When Lola enters her father's office, he and his mistress have just kissed, clearly compromising him in his daughter's eyes. He sits down, placing himself in a subordinate position to Lola, who is standing—towering, in fact—over her father. Instead of choosing either to capitalize on this power disparity or to equalize it, Lola kneels in front of her father with her hands in his lap and begs him for the money: "Listen, if I tell you I need your help more than ever in my whole life, and you're the only one who can help me, would you help me?" Although her father is at a disadvantage and the opportunity is presented for her to occupy a position other than victim, Lola chooses verbally and nonverbally to adopt a classic stance of powerlessness.

Individuals who choose victimage as an agentic orientation in response to structural conditions "explore the multiple signs of misfortune to prove" their victim status and use as raw material "misfortune, wretchedness, and suffering" (Baudrillard, 1996, p. 135). As a result, Lola sees structural conditions as controlling and limiting. The rhetoric she employs has the predictable outcome of reinscribing the agentic orientation of victim and of abdicating control in favor of helplessness.

Run 2: Supplicant

In the second run, Lola adopts an agentic orientation of supplicant, enacting emotional, physical, and moral appeals to those who appear to control the structures that impose demands on her. She interprets structural conditions as bequests and engages in the strategy of petitioning to secure any grants her structural environment may be prepared to dispense. In this run, Lola runs to the bank where her father works and, again, her father refuses to assist her, this time forcefully ushering her out of the bank himself. As she exits the bank, Lola grabs the security guard's gun, slips back into the bank, and demands the money from her father, who acquiesces to her demand under gunpoint. Lola leaves the bank with the money and encounters a perimeter the police have installed to catch the bank robber they have been alerted is inside. Mistaken for a bystander, Lola is whisked past the police lines and allowed to continue on her way. She arrives at the designated meeting place with Manni on time with money in hand, but when Manni turns to answer Lola, who is calling his name, he is struck and killed by an ambulance.

In the second run, Lola selects a version of agency under the control of the structural conditions in which she positions herself as a supplicant. This kind of agency appears to accomplish Lola's goals, but it is a hollow and insubstantial form of agency because it is rooted in the structural system's ultimate power to discipline or govern that agency. Because Lola sees her agency as granted and disciplined by others and thus constructs herself as a supplicant, she cedes to others the power to validate her requests. Lola looks momentarily powerful when she is able to subvert the authority of the guard, encoded in his gun, for her own ends. The fact that Lola is ushered to safety by a police officer after she robs the bank is also an apparent accomplishment of her goals. Her ostensible agency is evident again when she shows up just before the fatal deadline with the required amount of money and thereby saves Manni from the feared retribution of Ronnie. Where there is acceptance of a petition, there appears to be agency on the part of the individual.

At the point at which a hegemonic structure is threatened by a supplicant's use of power and no longer tolerates it, however, everything the supplicant has gained loses value because the petition is no longer supported and validated by the sanctioning agent. Empowerment of the supplicant exists only within the limits determined by the structural hegemony, and where there is rejection of a supplicant's petition, the individual remains disempowered and unrewarded. Lola's desire for money is tolerated only until support is withdrawn by structural forces for her petition, at which point her gains lose all value. For example, when Lola holds her father at gunpoint, she is his equal and now apparently has the power to petition to save Manni's life. Lola is, in the absence of resistance, allowed to handle the gun, allowed to rob the bank, and allowed to escape with what she desires most: the lifesaving money. Ultimately, though, if her success is not continually validated by the structure that confronts her, that success is rendered meaningless.

The ultimate function of the granting of bequests by structural conditions is not to facilitate individuals' access to resources but to reify the structure itself. This principle is evident in the fact that although Lola attains the money and reaches Manni by the deadline, Manni is struck and killed by an ambulance. Lola thus gains the resources for which she petitions but is not granted the capacity to save Manni's life—her only purpose for securing the money. Her petition for his life remains invalidated by the structure, a lack of validation underscored when the ambulance, a mechanism of life-rescuing potential, strikes him dead. The ambulance here is both literally and figuratively a hegemonic rescue vehicle that instantly removes Lola's accomplishment and thus preserves the structural power. When the supplicant is granted power, that power still remains the power of structure to preserve itself, always adjusting and returning the granted power to itself in the end.

Structural Conditions: Bequests

In the second run, because Lola is apparently successful in gaining access to the bounty embedded in structure, she appears to have greater control over structural conditions than she does in the first run. Although she is not pinned under the absolute control of structural conditions, she still is limited by the requirement implicit in her supplicant orientation that others recognize or validate her requests for resources. She may or may not receive the grants, dispensed in the form of resources, that others offer. Thus, in this run, Lola does not actually have control over structural conditions because the resources they provide are given and so can be revoked.

The second run contains a number of examples of the kinds of methods used to rein in and control individuals who seek to gain access to structural resources and power. These methods involve subjecting the lives of individuals to controls and regulations in various ways (Foucault, 1979). The use of physical discipline for the purpose of such control is demonstrated when Lola's father strikes her following her request for money. He supplements physical punishment with a normalizing label that is commonly used as a control mechanism: "Have you gone crazy? Think you can do anything you like?" Similarly, as Lola begins her run, the boy on the stairs deliberately trips her, reminding her that the control belongs to some external structure, which can mete out constraints and cripple individuals arbitrarily. At other times, etiquette rules are referenced to remind Lola of the system's control over her actions and the structural resources she desires. "Courtesy and composure are the queen's jewels," the security guard advises her as she enters the bank. He reminds her of this principle again when she first leaves the bank: "It just isn't your day. You can't have everything." The constraining mechanism can also be a simple denial of a request, as when Lola asks the ambulance driver for a lift, and he refuses. But the most obvious example of society's capacity to control behavior comes when Lola's father reminds her that she is being watched in the bank: "There are cameras. You'll never get out of here."

The mechanisms of control used to rein in agency become so ingrained and naturalized for those who enact an agentic orientation of supplicant that they themselves adopt these mechanisms and apply them to themselves. Imprisoning herself by subjecting herself to a power that is ever watchful and arbitrary, Lola in the second run "becomes the principle of [her] own subjection" (Foucault, 1979, p. 203). When the man on the bike offers to sell it to Lola for 50 marks, for example, she refuses with the retort, "It's stolen." Although she has no way of knowing whether the bike has been stolen, she monitors and constrains herself unnecessarily.

Adoption of a supplicant orientation, then, results in the interpretation of structural conditions as bequests that may or may not be conferred. Although the structural conditions appear to be less controlling and the agency of the individual seems to have more impact on those conditions, supplicants still are bound to structural conditions under the control of others. Structural representatives parcel out grants in response to requests, and they are aided in this effort as individuals themselves step up to assume the same disciplinary functions that the constraining mechanisms administer.

Response: Petitioning

In the second run, Lola engages in the act of petitioning, the effectiveness of which depends on her perceived ability to receive a hearing and to appeal successfully to those who appear to control resources that she desires. Lola is the showcase example of petitioning in the second run. She petitions the security guard to be allowed to enter the bank: "Let me in, please," followed by a petition to her father: "I need money." When he refuses her request, she forcefully petitions her father for the 100,000 marks by holding a gun to his head.

Although the claim might be made that the use of a gun constitutes an act of coercion, we assert that Lola's use of the gun in this run constitutes supplication. If she wants to kill her father, the gun can do that. Lola's only goal, though, is to save Manni, and using the gun to kill her father would only make it more difficult for her to achieve that goal. Therefore, Lola's threat is empty. Her father could challenge the gun—call her on her empty threat—but he chooses not to because she is functioning as a supplicant. Rather than demanding what the gun promises—control over her father's life—Lola is petitioning her father to give her the money. Even as he capitulates, he reminds Lola that her control of the money is tenuous and temporary because cameras are recording her actions in the bank.

In the second run, then, Lola is a supplicant whose enactment of agency depends on the discretion of structural power relations. In this orientation, structural resources are seen as bequests, and individuals petition structural forces that may or may not validate their petitions.

Run 3: Director

Lola's choice of agentic orientation in the third run is one of director, a form of agency in which she directs structural conditions and herself in such a way that her desires are affirmed and supported. Consistent with this orientation, Lola sees structural conditions as resources and employs innovating as her primary response. In this run, Lola's father agrees to marry his mistress in a conversation that takes place as Lola runs to the bank. She misses her father, who has left the bank prior to her arrival to have lunch with his friend Mr. Meier, both of whom are killed in a car accident later in the run. Leaving the bank, Lola spies a casino, talks her way in, and wins 100,000 marks by playing roulette, using her piercing scream to will the wheel to stop on the number 20. On her way to meet Manni, Lola hops into the back of a passing ambulance, where she saves the life of the security guard from the bank, who apparently has suffered a heart attack. Manni also secures the required money by retrieving it from the tramp who had picked it up when he left it on the subway car. The run ends with Manni delivering the money to his boss and Lola joining Manni at their designated meeting place, carrying a bag that contains the money she has won.

What is striking about the third run, in contrast to the previous ones, is the individual responsibility and independence both Lola and Manni exhibit. They achieve their goals not by appealing to or controlling others but by using rhetoric to act on and direct themselves. Although Lola began the run acting on behalf of Manni, the fact that the outcome of her efforts is irrelevant to Manni's needs—because he secures the money on his own—converts her run into one of agency on her own behalf.

Even when the conditions around her seem bleakest, in this run, Lola trusts that she will be inspired to find a way to secure the money. She whispers to herself as she runs, "What can I do? What can I do? Come on. Help me. Please. Just this once. I'll just keep on running, okay? I'm waiting. I'm waiting. I'm waiting. I'm waiting." No longer waiting for her father or a robbery to produce the money, she knows that she herself will be the one who will produce it, even though she is as yet unaware of the specific mechanisms she will use. Although her words might be interpreted as a prayer, we suggest that they are a plea to herself to be self-directing and to find her own answer, consistent with her other actions in this run. When she notices the casino, she recognizes it as her answer, even though she appears to know virtually nothing about gambling, evidenced by her question, "How does this work?" asked of the woman at the entrance.

Because the nature of the agentic orientation assumed in the third run is rooted in self-responsibility, Manni's actions become relevant to an exploration of Lola's version of agency in this run. He, too, assumes responsibility for himself and secures the money on his own, belying the frantic phone call in which he tells Lola that her assistance is the only means by which he can succeed. He encounters the tramp who earlier had picked up his money, stops him, and asks him to give the money back with a simple "that's mine." "I know," the tramp replies.

Most indicative of Manni's agency in the third run and a puzzling line of dialogue outside of the context of the director orientation is Manni's greeting to Lola when they meet at the end of the run. Manni is surprised that Lola is out of breath and questions her: "Hey, what happened to you? Did you run here?" Despite the earlier phone call, his questions are rooted in the assumption that she has not been acting on his behalf. Manni's question to Lola that ends the film, "What's in the bag?" is asked in a casual, almost phatic style and, in the context of the previous runs, would be seen as total inattention to or betrayal of Lola. After all, Manni has begged her for help and then acts surprised when she gives it to him. In the context of this run, however, Manni's question is a normal and natural result of two agents acting on their own behalf; there is no expectation that others are responsible for meeting their needs or desires. Manni does not know what is in the bag because he had no expectation that Lola would work to secure the money for him.

Structural Conditions: Resources

Because of her enactment of an agentic orientation of director, Lola interprets structural conditions in this run as resources and not as the obstacles they were for her in the previous runs. Rather than viewing her circumstances as lacking or problematic, she interprets them as strategic opportunities, toolkits, or inventory available for her use—or at least irrelevant or trivial in terms of their impact.

Lola grants structure little power over her, privileging its nature as a construction that can be de- and re-constructed. As Lola runs down the stairs at the start of the third run, she sails over the boy and dog that tripped her earlier and growls at them. She avoids running into people and obstacles she hit in earlier runs, such as a woman pushing a baby carriage. She bounces off the hood of Mr. Meier's car when he stops suddenly to keep from hitting her, running on without injury. When the woman at the casino door tells Lola, "You can't go in like that," Lola acts as if the prohibition has no meaning and enters the casino anyway. She does not even have sufficient money for the 100-mark chit but buys it with only 99 marks 20.

Further evidence of Lola's interpretations of circumstances as resources rather than obstacles in the third run is that she ignores the structural condition of time that is so critical to the plot of the film—Manni must have the money by noon. While each of the first two runs is exactly 20 minutes long in real time, putting Lola at the meeting place with Manni at precisely 12:00, the third run takes over 20 minutes. As Lola leaves the casino, a clock shows the time as 3 minutes before 12:00, after which she catches a ride in the ambulance, where she restores the heartbeat of the security guard, while Manni catches up with the tramp and retrieves his money—sequences that in real time take another 6 minutes. Lola thus arrives at the meeting place at what should be about 3 minutes after noon.

That time does not function as a controlling structural condition for Lola is also evident when she wins at the roulette table in the casino. She always places her bets on the number 20, and, contrary to the experience of most gamblers, she wins each time she plays. She no longer fears the number 20 and has transformed the original 20-minute deadline into a resource. Because Lola does not interpret conditions as the obstacles they were for her in the earlier runs, they lack the capacity to confine her.

Response: Innovating

Adoption of an agentic orientation of director in the third run enables Lola to employ innovative actions. Innovating means creating one's own options and not choosing from among options created by others. Lola's actions are marked by a lack of acceptance of the "masters' descriptions of the real" and an eschewal of the boundaries of the universe as defined by others (Rorty, 1998, p. 216). In this run, Lola writes her own script, and her acts are highly individualistic and idiosyncratic, with "no method or procedure to be followed except courageous and imaginative experimentation" (Rorty, 1998, p. 217).

Lola's actions are not strategies in the sense of planned efforts designed to accomplish certain goals—the types of scripted strategies that in the earlier runs were unsuccessful. A number of images in the third run reinforce the need to be blind to the strategies that are assumed to be effective in addressing the exigencies of structural conditions. Those who appear most at the mercy of their environments in the film play critical roles in envisioning and pointing to ways to address perceived problems independent of apparent structural limitations. In one scene, for example, Manni is waiting to enter a phone booth being used by a blind woman. As she leaves the booth, she looks toward the tramp who has Manni's money, thus directing Manni to look in that direction and discover where his money can be found. An individual who is marked by what usually is considered to be a major structural limitation—blindness—is the one who points Manni to his money. Similarly, Lola runs around rather than through a group of nuns, choosing not to run the gauntlet subjecting her to their approval and system of rules but to operate instead within a system of her own construction. In addition, as Lola runs, waiting for inspiration, her eyes are closed, in contrast to the previous runs, suggesting that her attention is directed inward, and she is blind to the conditions and conventional strategies of the structural world.

Other evidence of Lola's shift from a reliance on external sources to her own creative capacity is suggested in the casino's emergence as a mechanism by which she can exercise agency. Lack of attention to external conditions allows Lola to see the casino in which she wins the money. She spots the casino only when her view is blocked by a truck that screeches to a halt as she crosses in front of it. Because it temporarily stops her physically and blocks her vision—preventing her from continuing on a planned or prescribed path—Lola notices the casino.

Those who develop and limit choices for Lola in previous runs no longer have the power to define and restrict choices for her in the third run. The security guard at the bank, who guards access to the funds, is outside of the bank on a cigarette break when Lola arrives in the third run. Outside of the structural system, no longer the representative of authority, he has stepped outside of his role, opening up new possibilities. The deaths of Lola's father and his friend, Mr. Meier, in a car accident remove the confines of parenthood, enabling Lola to function as her own parent. Similarly, the medical technician in the ambulance, once a director of Lola's fate when he refused to give her a ride, steps aside so she can take over the efforts to save the life of the security guard. In all these instances, structural representatives have become irrelevant. Those who were the authors of Lola's life and created the range of options for her in the earlier runs step aside or disappear.

Individuals move through the world with confidence, the third run suggests, when they are open to innovation. Such agents see the conditions around them as conspiring on their behalf and available for their use. Thus, the money comes easily in this run. Lola places a bet on the black 20 on the roulette wheel, wins, and then places her winnings on the black 20 again. As the ball bounces on the wheel, she lets out an ear-piercing scream that shatters glasses and the clock on the wall, willing the ball to land on the black 20, which it does. Even when the casino manager approaches Lola after the first win and says, "Come with me, please," she replies, "Just one more game." Her self-assured tone suggests that his request is irrelevant—that she will place a second bet, which, in fact, she does. Lola's confidence in her own actions continues when she catches a ride in the back of an ambulance following her successful wins in the casino. She does not ask for permission this time but simply climbs into the back of the ambulance when it stops to allow men carrying a pane of glass to pass in front of it (the men for whom she stopped in the first run).

The power that results when individuals engage their worlds as directors is demonstrated in the third run. It is suggested when the security guard at the bank greets Lola's arrival in the third run with the words, "You've come at last, dear." Lola has come at last to awareness and adoption of the powerful agency of the director. Lola's apparent ability to control the roulette wheel in the casino through the unusual act of a scream also suggests such power. As she leaves the casino, the bystanders who gather to watch her go are awestruck by her power and recognize it as different from theirs. They are still gambling, playing the game using conventional strategies, but they recognize that Lola has freed herself from the game of chance.

Lola's healing of the security guard in the ambulance is another example of her almost magical power. He is dying when she enters the ambulance, and the medical technician's efforts to save him appear to be having little effect. Lola heals him, apparently by holding his hand and focusing her attention on him. Because the source of her power is her own interpretation, which is free from the influence, control, or determination of structure, she has unlimited access to innovative rhetorical options.

As a result of the choice to adopt an agentic orientation of director, both Lola and Manni are in control of the conditions and events they experience, and their efficacy flowers as they see structural conditions as irrelevant to or even supportive of the agency they claim. Because their actions do not follow traditional scripts, they are able to innovate in their structural reality to create outcomes in line with their desires.

Outcomes of Agentic Orientations

We thus far have identified the components of interpretation of structure and response that characterize the three agentic orientations of victim, supplicant, and director presented in *Run Lola Run*. The third component of agentic orientation is outcome, and we now turn our attention to the concomitant outcomes of the agentic orientations. We argue here that choice of agentic orientation dictates the outcomes that agents experience in their lives rather than the strength, power, or persistence of material structures. Choice about what version of agentic orientation to adopt, then, appears to be the critical decision that individuals make in terms of agency.

Clearly, very different outcomes result from Lola's enactment of the three kinds of agentic orientations. In the first run, Lola adopts an agentic orientation of victim, in which she interprets her structural conditions as obstacles and engages in the act of mortification. She and Manni obtain the money they need, but Lola is killed. In the second run, Lola assumes an agentic orientation of supplicant, viewing her structural conditions as bequests bestowed on her by structural power and using petitioning as a primary option for securing those bequests. Lola acquires the money, but Manni dies. In the third run, both Lola and Manni choose agentic orientations of director, assuming that they can direct structural conditions, themselves, and their fate. Structural conditions become resources as they employ innovative responses to secure money and life for both of them.

Run Lola Run supports in a number of ways the claim that an agentic orientation of director is superior to those of victim and supplicant. The structural building of the three runs to a preferred position conforms to the conventions of tripartite narratives (such as those of Goldilocks or the three speeches on love [rhetoric] in Plato's *Phaedrus),* in which inferior alternatives are rejected along the way until the preferred option is reached at the sequence's end. Its ending also suggests that the third run offers the preferred agentic orientation. That Lola and Manni are both alive at the end meets viewers' conventional preferences for happy filmic endings, in contrast to the endings of the two previous runs, where the deaths of the main characters, particularly so early in the film, are shocking to viewers.

The director orientation that *Run Lola Run* advocates contrasts with a normative interpretation of the relationship between agentic orientation and outcome. Such a view would dismiss the feasibility much less the superiority of the director orientation and would suggest that a director orientation can have no direct effect on structural conditions. The outcomes Lola experiences, this interpretation says, are the result of causes such as the flow of time, coincidences of arriving at particular places at particular times, and the accidental encountering of individuals who are either helpful or not.

In contrast, *Run Lola Run's* connection between agentic orientation and outcome suggests a perspective that, while contrary to the normative one, is in tune with a tenet acknowledged by a number of diverse perspectives, ranging from social constructionism to quantum physics. Simply put, it is that symbols create reality (Berger & Luckmann, 1966; Goswami, Reed, & Goswami, 1993; Marshall & Zohar, 1997; Potter, 1996; Sapolsky, 2005; Seligman, 2002; Whorf, 1956; Wolf, 1981). Symbolic choices, *Run Lola Run* argues, can and do affect the structural world. We acknowledge that a belief in this tenet is disputable in the presence of certain kinds of conditions, but we ask our readers to consider seriously for a moment what *Run Lola Run* suggests—the possibility that it might be true under all conditions. Although the reality of everyday life appears prearranged, ordered, and objective, and therefore outside of agents' sphere of influence through processes such as habitualization and materialization (Berger & Luckmann, 1966, pp. 53–67; Butler, 1993, pp. 9, 10), the structural world not only "bears cultural constructions" but is itself a construction (Butler, 1993, p. 28). Choice is the basic mechanism by which the world is manifest, then, and as agents choose (as they do when they adopt an agentic orientation), real, material outcomes are created in line with their choices.

We are not suggesting that agents dictate precisely the outcomes they will experience in their worlds through the symbolic activity of an agentic orientation. We concur with McDaniel (2003) when he suggests that agency "signifies a capacity to invent, but not to control, possible worlds" (p. 1). Agents cannot, simply through choice of agentic orientation, lay out precisely the routes through which their desires will be fulfilled. What we do suggest, however, is that those desires are realized in outcomes that align with agents' choices, although their manifestations may occur in ways not imagined by agents. With a director orientation, the agent trusts that the orientation will open up possibilities, as is the case with Lola in the third run. When Lola takes off running with no idea of how she will obtain the money, her conception of structural conditions as resources and a willingness to innovate allow assistance to come to her in ways she could not have predicted at the outset of her run.

Scholars have offered a number of explanations to account for the kinds of outcomes that result from the agentic orientation of director that *Run Lola Run* "votes" to be the superior one. Among the reasons cited are phenomena such as activation, a complex of beliefs about the agent's own nature (Harré, 1984, p. 95); an internal locus of control, which "makes a considerable difference in the ways that many life experiences will be confronted" (Lefcourt, 1982, p. 183); the representations individuals construct of the world (Danto, 1973); and individuals' perceptions of self-efficacy (Rodin, 1990). Our analysis of *Run Lola Run* suggests three additional explanations for the effectiveness of the agentic orientation of director in terms of its outcomes—reconceptualization of exigence, availability of multiple options, and dissolution of enmity.

One explanation for why the agentic orientation of director produces outcomes in line with agents' desires is that it posits an exigence different from that to which agents often believe they must respond. In traditional conceptions of the agentic process, structural conditions function as the compelling exigence. Individuals are confronted with particular structures that lead to the development of responses based on an understanding of those conditions as controlling and determining. Our analysis of *Run Lola Run* suggests a different exigence for agents. Exigence is the choice of agentic orientation adopted by an agent—whether victim, supplicant, director, or another— and that choice dictates the particular view of structural conditions the agent adopts. From such a perspective, structural conditions are dependent variables that vary according to the nature of the agentic orientation selected.

The consequences entailed by an exigence of agency are dramatically different from those that follow from an exigence rooted in structural conditions. An exigence of structural conditions requires that individuals, working alone or collectively, change all the conditions they see as blocking or diminishing their influence in the world. The task is an enormous and impossible one. If the effectiveness of agency is dependent on making all the structural conditions in agents' worlds or lives align with their own desires or preferences, they cannot ever hope to enact agency effectively.

An exigence of agentic orientation, in contrast, is something that can be chosen and is under the control of the individual. No one can interfere with that choice because its location is internal, and it can be maintained and reinforced with every decision the individual makes. Exigence thus becomes not a constraining force within which agents must work but an opening that enables them to transcend what they previously conceptualized as constraints and limitations. With Anzaldúa (2002), individuals who assume an agentic orientation of director realize that "reactions to events" are the obstacles confronting them and "not something 'real' or unchangeable out there in the outer world" (p. 553).

A second explanation for the positive outcome produced by the agentic orientation of director is that the director orientation makes available the greatest number of options for action for the individual. The agentic orientation of director enables agents themselves to create their own options rather than allowing them to be dictated by predetermined scripts or external others. Even when agents recognize that some of the options before them have been created by others, the very recognition that those choices were created by someone else points to their constructedness and the fact that they thus can be constructed differently. As a result, agents then can choose whether to stay within the array of choices being presented by others or to create options outside of them.

The agentic orientation of director, then, has the capacity to produce a virtually infinite array of options that are constrained only by the desires and imaginations of agents themselves. Arendt (1977) explains the critical role that the capacity to innovate beyond conventional choices plays in agency. She describes the capacity to choose among set alternatives as "a freedom of choice that arbitrates and decides between two given things, one good and one evil" and contrasts it with "the freedom to call something into being which did not exist before, which was not given, not even as an object of cognition or imagination, and which therefore, strictly speaking, could not be known" (p. 151). In *Run Lola Run*, Lola innovates in this latter fashion, evidenced by her choosing to gamble when she knows nothing about it and by her scream in the casino, certainly not a conventional rhetorical strategy. Anzaldúa (2002) explains the results of this kind of choice in this way: "Instead of walking your habitual routes you forge new ones. The changes affect your biology. The cells in your brain shift and, in turn, create new pathways, rewiring your brain" (p. 556).

Agents who adopt a director orientation are able to exploit the "literally fabulous nature of symbol using," as Condit (2003) suggests, taking advantage of the "vast storehouse of variability" available to symbol users "to generate creatively new choices and possibilities" (p. 2). As Davies (2000) explains, when they are acting from such an orientation, agents "can go beyond the given meaning in any one discourse and forge something new, through a combination of previously unrelated discourses, through the invention of words and concepts that capture a shift in consciousness that is beginning to occur, or through imagining not what *is*, but what *might be*" (p. 67). Agency, from the orientation of director, becomes "the actor's capacity to reinterpret and mobilize an array of resources in terms of cultural schemas other than those that initially constituted the array" (Sewell, 1992, p. 19).

An agentic orientation of director also produces the outcomes it does because it dissolves the traditional enmity that exists between agent and structure. The source of the antagonism that characterizes typical agentic efforts is a feeling of limitation and thus anger and hatred toward structures that individuals feel are thwarting them. Such hostility can make the structural "power appear absolute" and the agent's "power insignificant" (Wendell, 1990, p. 28). Griffin (1982) explains the consequences for outcomes of such animosity:

> But the moment I have defined another being as my enemy, I lose part of myself, the complexity and subtlety of my vision. . . . Slowly all the power in my life begins to be located outside, and my whole being is defined in relation to this outside force, which daily becomes more monstrous, more evil, . . . The quality of my thought then is diminished. My imagination grows small. (p. 657)

In the third run, Lola no longer sees structural others as her enemies. This new perspective is particularly evident in Lola's interaction with the security guard at the bank. When Lola discovers him in the back of the ambulance, suffering from an apparent heart attack, she tells the medical technician, "I'll stay with him." She holds his hand, stabilizing his heartbeat, and looks with empathy and concern at the man who, in earlier runs, represents a coercive, domineering structure. From the agentic orientation of director, others are not seen as enemies because they do not control anything that agents do not already have; thus, the source of antagonism and hostility vanishes. An agentic orientation of director, then, insures that the agent's imagination remains large and capable of complexity in interaction with the world.

The perspective on outcomes presented by *Run Lola Run* speaks to and, in fact, transforms a conventional understanding about the kind of agency required to produce outcomes in line with one's desires. We frequently encounter the claim in academic conversations that some individuals or groups lack agency, a view that is prevalent as well in the literature on marginalized groups and agency. Spivak's (1988a) argument that there "is no space from which the sexed subaltern subject can speak" is one example (p. 307); Shome and Hegde (2002) similarly suggest that a condition of nonagency is possible when they reference the existence of an "interstitial space between agency and the lack thereof" (p. 266). Such a perspective suggests that particular individuals or groups cannot control outcomes—cannot exert agency—because they lack a requisite set of life circumstances.

Agentic orientations, however, are achieved within, rather than simply given by, the conditions of individuals' lives. Thus, individuals may be in a dominant position as defined by economic and other structural conditions or in a subordinate position as defined by a lack of access to such resources, but they may choose any agentic orientation and produce any outcome they desire. We acknowledge that such a view may be difficult to accept in extreme cases such as imprisonment or genocide; even in these situations, however, agents have choices about how to perceive their conditions and their agency. Even in these situations, adoption of the agentic orientation of director opens up opportunities for innovating in ways unavailable to those who construct themselves as victims.[1] As Walker (1997) suggests, "Although I assume that very many things human beings have to or want to do are made harder, even excruciatingly costly, by deprivation or oppression," the notion that agency "is out of reach for people under conditions of social disadvantage represents a confusion, a mistake, or a temptation. . . . If lives are distinctively our own because of the distinctive mix of circumstances thrown our way and commitments and attachments we make under those circumstances," the issue "is how well one responds to that lot" (p. 76).

The capacity to generate desired outcomes is available in *Run Lola Run* not only to those with money, high status, or education—those with privilege as it is conventionally conceptualized. Lola's banker father, who clearly is privileged according to conventional definitions of the term, chooses various agentic orientations over the course of the film, including those of victimage (in the first run) and director (in the third). The apparently least privileged exhibit the greatest freedom from the control of structural conditions of all the characters in the film in the third run. Manni, who desperately cries "I'm fucked!" at the start of the film—the cry of a person in a decidedly unprivileged position as traditionally defined—achieves privilege in the third run when the agentic orientation of director becomes so natural for him that he takes it for granted, allowing him to ask casually of Lola at the end of the third run, "You ran here?" Lola herself, of course, exemplifies the capacity of the least privileged to adopt an orientation of director. Traditionally marginalized in that she is a woman, is trying to enact a savior role usually assigned to men, is unemployed, and is relatively poor, Lola still successfully enacts the director orientation.

We acknowledge that a view that anyone has access to an agentic orientation of director and thus to desired outcomes challenges traditional notions of the nature and function of privilege. We believe that the attribution of privilege as it is traditionally conceptualized derives from a particular orientation to agency. A view that someone else is privileged suggests that the privileged person has control over outcomes in a way that the accuser does not. Individuals who lack structural resources and who choose to view someone with those resources as privileged have chosen to reify what is missing from their experience and to interpret it as lack, an emphasis that functions as a filter to prevent them from seeing options available to them. We are not blaming the victim here; in fact, we believe that the view we are articulating empowers rather than blames individuals. We simply are suggesting that a definition of a situation as lacking keeps individuals from being able to see options and to allow agency to work in the world in ways that would not continue to restrict the resources they desire.

That everyone has the same capacity for agency, regardless of access to resources, is not to be confused with the notion that everyone chooses well. With their agency, all individuals may choose situations that make them suffer and reduce their control over structural conditions. Those who make agentic choices that appear less desirable gain at least some rewards from such choices—possibly a greater capacity to attract others to a cause, the generation of positive responses in the form of sympathy, or avoidance of responsibility. Cindy Sheehan provides an example of someone whose adoption of a victim orientation has attracted others to a cause. She is able to generate a following for her antiwar and anti-Bush stance with an emotional appeal centered around her unjust suffering as a result of the Iraq War and Bush's refusal to speak with her. If the unjust suffering were removed or reinterpreted, the emotional appeal that supports her movement would disappear. Our intent is not to impugn Sheehan motives or her cause but to suggest that adoption of a victim orientation can be a rhetorically functional choice for various reasons. *Run Lola Run,* of course, notes that it is not the only available choice.

The view of agency presented in *Run Lola Run,* then, rejects a conventional normative progressive assumption that "human agency primarily consists of acts that challenge social norms and not those that uphold them" (Mahmood, 2005, p. 5). Agency is not consubstantial with resistance to relations of domination; agential capacity is entailed in the multiple ways in which individuals inhabit norms. From such a perspective, "what may appear to be a case of deplorable passivity and docility . . . may actually be a form of agency" (Mahmood, 2005, p. 15). Lola enacts agency in the first and second runs, then, just as much as she does in the third—her agentic choices are simply different.

Applications of Agentic Orientation

The mechanism of agentic orientation answers Lucaites' (2003) call for identification of the range of options by which agency is constituted in particular rhetorical performances. The mechanism readily allows for its application by those who are interested in understanding their agentic options as well as the link between orientation and outcome. Thus, although the characters in *Run Lola Run* do not make decisions or act—their agency, of course, is under the control of the film's director—the mechanism of agentic orientation the film suggests can be used as a didactic tool for individuals outside of the film who are interested in enacting the greatest degree of control over their lives.

Key to application of the mechanism of agentic orientation is the act of interpretation. We agree with those who posit that agency is "shared between agents and the structures they animate" (Anderson, 2004, p. 271). What agentic orientation offers that departs from this perspective on the origin of agency is an insistence that all agentic positions are produced in the same way—through an interpretation of structural conditions. Interpretation of structural conditions creates an agentic orientation, which then creates outcomes in line with that particular orientation. The pragmatic application of agentic orientation thus is this: All individuals have the capacity to move to different agentic positions and to produce new outcomes in their lives because such changes occur through the act of interpretation. The fact that individuals are able to create one agentic orientation is evidence that they can create another. One kind of interpretation results in a particular agentic orientation; reinterpretation changes that orientation.

An example familiar to many of our readers will illustrate how choices of interpretation are played out so that they develop agentic orientations and generate outcomes in alignment with them. The situation is one in which a professor assigns a grade of F to a student's paper. Upon receiving the grade, a student might say, "My professor gave me an F on the paper." With this statement, the student interprets structural conditions as bequests and thus chooses a supplicant orientation. Consequently, she limits her options for response to a set of rhetorical options that involve petitioning—options such as asking for extra credit, pleading with the professor to change the grade, complaining to the department chair or the dean, holding a press conference to proclaim the injustice of the grade, or petitioning the legal system by suing the university. Even if she is given a new grade at the end of her pleas, the student is still relatively powerless in that her agency and efficacy are dependent on someone else's granting of her request.

A change of interpretation substantially changes the student's orientation, options, and outcomes. When the student states instead "I earned a grade of F on the paper," she interprets structural conditions as resources that are available to her and adopts the agentic orientation of director. As a result, she now has available to her a variety of different options that enable her to learn from the paper and to develop her writing skills further. For example, she can secure a tutor, study what was unclear to her when she wrote the paper, make use of the writing center to improve her writing skills, talk with the professor about what went wrong with the paper, ask the professor for good models of papers to help her in the future, continue to work to develop the ideas in the paper more effectively, or even be happy with the grade because she knows it accurately represents the quality of her work. A change in interpretation positions her in a different agentic orientation, makes available different options, and generates different outcomes.

Application of the mechanism of agentic orientation also has implications for the teaching of rhetoric. Geisler (2004) suggests that a primary concern for teachers of rhetoric is to answer the question: "What shall we, as teachers, say to our students about their potential and obligations with respect to becoming rhetorical agents?" (p. 16). Traditionally, the answer to this question has been to teach students to formulate rhetoric in an effort to change structural conditions to create particular outcomes in their lives. We suggest a modification of the traditional approach that would involve teaching students how to use the mechanism of agentic orientation to make rhetorical choices to create their intended outcomes.[2]

Teaching from the perspective of agentic orientation primarily would involve illustrating the chain of connections among: (a) a particular set of interpretations of a set of structural conditions, (b) the agentic orientation that coincides with those interpretations, and (c) the outcomes that manifest in alignment with that agentic position. When they understand the linkages among these three elements, students would be able to adjust their rhetoric to achieve the outcomes they desire. If the students' present outcomes are undesirable and are produced by adopting a particular agentic orientation, then students would understand how to use the mechanism of agentic orientation to rearrange those outcomes. The instructional focus thus would be on isolating and illuminating the chain of structure–act–outcome, allowing students to practice revision or reinterpretation of structural conditions in their rhetorical choices to generate different outcomes. The primary mission of teachers of rhetoric would be to redirect students' focus from trying to change structural conditions to changing their interpretations of those conditions and inventing multiple and innovative options for response to those revised interpretations.[3]

We believe that the possibilities offered by the mechanism of agentic orientation—pedagogical, pragmatic, and heuristic—are exciting in their potential to extend current understandings of agency. At the same time, we recognize a number of questions that remain unanswered concerning agentic orientation and that must be addressed to complete the picture of agency explored in our analysis of *Run Lola Run*. Among them are the factors that affect the selection of agentic orientation by agents, how individuals come to understand the choices that are available to them in agentic orientations, how descriptions of structural conditions are produced so that they appear solid and factual, and how such descriptions can be rhetorically undermined to facilitate different interpretations and thus different agentic orientations. We hope that our efforts here encourage others to contribute to the development of the nascent model of agentic orientation we have offered here and to join us in theorizing an agency ever open to the possibilities of choosing again and choosing something different.

Acknowledgments

The authors would like to thank Karen A. Foss, Christa J. Downer, Joshua Gunn, and François Cooren for their insightful comments on earlier versions of this essay.

Notes

[1] Examples of the agentic orientation of director even in dire circumstances can be seen in the actions of the main characters in two contemporary films: *The Hurricane* (2000), about the unjust imprisonment of boxer Rubin Carter, and *Life is Beautiful* (1997), in which a father helps his son survive a concentration camp.

[2] Some rhetorical scholars suggest that the traditional answer to Geisler's question must change as a result of postmodernism or posthumanism. As is certainly clear by now, our view of agency privileges self over structure; we thus leave to others the concern about how postmodernism or posthumanism affects the teaching of rhetoric.

[3] The idea that change is accomplished by changing oneself and not external conditions is not a new idea with us. It has been explicated by, among others, Anzaldúa (1987), Gearhart (1995), and Johnson (1989, 1991).

References

Anderson, D. (2004). Questioning the motives of habituated action: Burke and Bourdieu on practice. *Philosophy and Rhetoric, 37*, 255–274.

Anzaldúa, G. E. (1987). *Borderlands/La frontera: The new mestiza.* San Francisco: Aunt Lute.

Anzaldúa, G. E. (2002). Now let us shift . . . the path of conocimiento . . . inner work, public acts. In G. E. Anzaldúa & A. Keating (Eds.), *This bridge we call home: Radical visions for transformation* (pp. 540–578). New York: Routledge.

Arndt, S. (Producer), & Tykwer, T. (Director). (1998). *Run Lola Run* [Film]. (Available from Sony Pictures Classics, 550 Madison Avenue, 8th Floor, New York, NY 10022)

Arendt, H. (1977). *Between past and future: Eight exercises in political thought.* New York: Penguin.

Bandura, A. (1989). Human agency in social cognitive theory. *American Psychologist, 44*, 1175–1180.

Baudrillard, J. (1996). *The perfect crime* (C. Turner, Trans.). New York: Verso. (Original work published 1995)

Berger, P. L., & Luckmann, T. (1966). *The social construction of reality: A treatise in the sociology of knowledge.* Garden City, NY: Anchor/Doubleday.

Bianco, J. S. (2004). Techno-cinema. *Comparative Literature Studies, 41*, 377–403.

Bourdieu, P. (1990). *The logic of practice* (R. Nice, Trans.). Stanford, CA: Stanford University Press. (Original work published 1980)

Burke, K. (1970). *The rhetoric of religion: Studies in logology.* Berkeley: University of California Press.

Butler, J. (1993). *Bodies that matter: On the discursive limits of sex.* New York: Routledge.

Campbell, K. K. (2005). Agency: Promiscuous and protean. *Communication and Critical Cultural Studies, 2*(1), 1–19.

Castor, T., & Cooren, F. (2006). Organizations as hybrid forms of life: The implications of the selection of agency in problem formulation. *Management Communication Quarterly, 19*, 570–600.

Cloud, D. L. (2005). Fighting words: Labor and the limits of communication at Staley, 1993 to 1996. *Management Communication Quarterly, 18*, 509–542.

Condit, C. M. (2003, September). *Why rhetorical training can expand agency.* Paper presented at the meeting of the Alliance of Rhetoric Societies, Evanston, IL.

Conrad, C., & Macom, E. A. (1995). Re-visiting Kenneth Burke: Dramatism/logology and the problem of agency. *Southern Communication Journal, 61*(1), 11–28.

Cooren, F. (1999). Applying socio-semiotics to organizational communication: A new approach. *Management Communication Quarterly, 13*, 294–304.

Cooren, F. (2004). Textual agency: How texts do things in organizational settings. *Organization, 11*, 373–393.

Danto, A. C. (1973). *Analytical philosophy of action.* New York: Cambridge University Press.

Davies, B. (2000). The concept of agency. In B. Davies (Ed.), *A body of writing: 1990–1999* (pp. 55–68). Walnut Creek, CA: Altamira/Rowman & Littlefield.

Emirbayer, M., & Mische, A. (1998). What is agency? *American Journal of Sociology, 103*, 962–1023.

Evans, O. (2004). Tom Twyker's *Run Lola Run:* Postmodern, posthuman or "post-theory"? *Studies in European Cinema, 1*(2), 105–115.

Fairhurst, G. T. (2004). Textuality and agency in interaction analysis. *Organization, 11*, 335–353.

Foucault, M. (1979). *Discipline and punish: The birth of the prison* (A. Sheridan, Trans.). New York: Vintage/Random House. (Original work published 1975)

Gaonkar, D. P. (1993). The idea of rhetoric in the rhetoric of science. *Southern Communication Journal, 58*, 258–295.

Gearhart, S. M. (1995). Notes from a recovering activist. *Sojourner: The Women's Forum, 21*(1), 8–11.

Geisler, C. (2004). How ought we to understand the concept of rhetorical agency?: Report from the ARS. *Rhetoric Society Quarterly, 34*(3), 9–17.

Goswami, A., Reed, R. E., & Goswami, M. (1993). *The self-aware universe: How consciousness creates the material world.* New York: Jeremy P. Tarcher/Penguin Putnam.

Griffin, S. (1982). The way of all ideology. *Signs: Journal* of *Women in Culture and Society, 7*, 641–660.

Grossberg, L. (1997). *Bringing it all back home: Essays on cultural studies.* Durham, NC: Duke University Press.

Gunn, J. (2003, September). *The fantastic rhetorical agency debate.* Paper presented at the meeting of the Alliance of Rhetoric Societies, Evanston, IL.

Gunn, J. (2006). Review essay: Mourning humanism, or, the idiom of haunting. *Quarterly Journal of Speech, 92*(1), 77–102.

Gunn, J., & Treat, S. (2005). Zombie trouble: A propaedeutic on ideological subjectification and the unconscious. *Quarterly Journal of Speech, 91*(2), 144–174.

Hardy, C. (2004). Scaling up and bearing down in discourse analysis: Questions regarding textual agencies and their context. *Organization, 11*, 415–425.

Harré, R. (1984). *Personal being: A theory for individual psychology.* Cambridge, MA: Harvard University Press.

Johnson, S. (1989). *Wildfire: Igniting the she/volution.* Albuquerque, NM: Wildfire.

Johnson, S. (1991). *The ship that sailed into the living room: Sex and intimacy reconsidered.* Estancia, NM: Wildfire.

Lauer, A. R. (2003). *Run Lola Run* at the dawn of postmodernity. *Studies in Media & Information Literacy Education, 3*(1). Retrieved November 28, 2006, from http://www.utpress.utoronto.ca/journal/ejournals/simile

Lefcourt, H. M. (1982). *Locus of control: Current trends in theory and research* (2nd ed.). Hillsdale, NJ: Lawrence Erlbaum.

Lucaites, J. L. (2003, September). *Understanding "rhetorical agency."* Paper presented at the meeting of the Alliance of Rhetoric Societies, Evanston, IL.

Lucaites, J. L., & Condit, C. M. (1999). Epilogue: Contributions from rhetorical theory. In J. L Lucaites, C. M. Condit, & S. Caudill (Eds.), *Contemporary rhetorical theory: A reader* (pp. 609–613). New York: Guilford.

Mahmood, S. (2005). *Politics of piety: The Islamic revival and the feminist subject.* Princeton, NJ: Princeton University Press.

Marshall, I., & Zohar, D. (1997). *Who's afraid of Schrödinger's cat?: An A-to-Z guide to all the new science ideas you need to keep up with the new thinking.* New York: Quill/William Morrow.

McDaniel, J. P. (2003, September). *Figuring agency . . . without finality.* Paper presented at the meeting of the Alliance of Rhetoric Societies, Evanston, IL.

McPhee, R. D. (2004). Text, agency, and organization in the light of structuration theory. *Organization, 11,* 355–371.

O'Sickey, I. M. (2002). Whatever Lola wants, Lola gets (or does she?): Time and desire in Tom Tykwer's *Run Lola Run. Quarterly Review of Film & Video, 19*(2), 123–131.

Potter, J. (1996). *Representing reality: Discourse, rhetoric and social construction.* Thousand Oaks, CA: Sage.

Rodin, J. (1990). Control by any other name: Definitions, concepts, and processes. In J. Rodin, C. Schooler, & K. Schaie (Eds.), *Self-directedness: Cause and effects throughout the life course* (pp. 1–18). Hillsdale, NJ: Lawrence Erlbaum.

Rorty, R. (1998). *Truth and progress: Volume 3: Philosophical papers.* New York: Cambridge University Press.

Sapolsky, R. (2005, December). Sick of poverty. *Scientific American, 293*(6), 92–99.

Seligman, M. E. P. (2002). *Authentic happiness.* New York: Free.

Sewell, W. H., Jr. (1992). A theory of structure: Duality, agency, and transformation. *American Journal of Sociology, 98*(1), 1–29.

Shome, R., & Hegde, R. S. (2002). Postcolonial approaches to communication: Charting the terrain, engaging the intersections. *Communication Theory, 12,* 249–270.

Spivak, G. C. (1988a). Can the subaltern speak? In C. Nelson & L. Grossberg (Eds.), *Marxism and the interpretation of culture* (pp. 271–315). Urbana: University of Illinois Press.

Spivak, G. C. (1988b). Subaltern studies: Deconstructing historiography. In R. Guha & G. C. Spivak (Eds.), *Selected subaltern studies* (pp. 3–36). New York: Oxford University Press.

Tobias, J. (2004). Cinema, scored: Toward a comparative methodology for music in media. *Film Quarterly, 57*(2), 26–36.

Waggoner, C. E., & O'Brien Hallstein, D. L. (2001). Feminist ideologies meet fashionable bodies: Managing the agency/constraint conundrum. *Text and Performance Quarterly, 21*(1), 26–46.

Walker, M. U. (1997). Picking up pieces: Lives, stories, and integrity. In D. T. Meyers (Ed.), *Feminists rethink the self* (pp. 62–84). Boulder, CO: Westview.

Wendell, S. (1990). Oppression and victimization: Choice and responsibility. *Hypatia, 5*(3), 15–46.

Whalen, T. (2000). The rules of the game: Tom Tykwer's *Lola Rennt. Film Quarterly, 53*(3), 33–40.

Whorf, B. L. (1956). *Language, thought, & reality: Selected writings of Benjamin Lee Whorf* (J. B. Carroll, Ed.). Cambridge, MA: M.I.T. Press.

Wolf, F. A. (1981). *Taking the quantum leap: The new physics for nonscientists.* New York: Harper & Row.

Wolf, N. (1993). *Fire with fire: The new female power and how it will change the 21st century.* London: Chatto & Windus.

Wood, C. (2006). Sometimes you need the help of the universe: *Run Lola Run. Australian Screen Education, 42,* 107–110.

The Gender of Napoleon and the Power of Dynamite

M. Rosie Russo

In 2004, a quirky feature film popped up in movie theatres across the country and has since sparked a pop-culture phenomenon marked by an almost cult-like adolescent following. That film was *Napoleon Dynamite*. A runaway hit at the Sundance Film festival and winner of "Best Feature Film" at the U.S. Comedy Arts Festival, director Jared Hess' quasi-auteur, quasi-autobiographical film is a reinvention of "the tired structures of the typical teen comedy" (Film Production Notes, p. 3). The film stars previously unknown Jon Heder as the central character, Napoleon, who tramps moon-booted through "life's weirder side, in a nearly alien, small-town world of time machines, martial arts mastery, unselfconscious dance numbers, exasperated sighs, and encyclopedic knowledge of cows" (p. 3), breathing heavily all the while.

The enduring popularity of *Napoleon Dynamite* itself gives credence to the relevance of engaging the film rhetorically. Made on a budget of only $400,000, it has grossed over $10 million since its release (*USA Today*). The town in which *Napoleon Dynamite* was set, Preston, Idaho, has blossomed into a huge tourist attraction since the movie's release. The punk store Hot Topic has developed into the hub for Napoleon paraphernalia, selling everything from t-shirts to lip balm (Weafer, 2005).

The tremendous stir that *Napoleon Dynamite* has caused on the adolescent pop-culture scene is surprising given the unconventional, geeky, eccentric persona Napoleon embodies. Director Jared Hess (2004) describes his creation as "that nerdy kid who sat next to you in math drawing mythical animals, the [person] who you never talked to, or got to know" (p. 3). Napoleon and other such quirky characters are championed in the movie and can be seen foiling the cool, popular kids.

I was immediately intrigued by the film's presentation of such unusual masculinity. In an effort to follow Brod and Kaufman's (1994) template for theorizing masculinities, I want "to emphasize the plurality and diversity of men's experiences, attitudes, beliefs, situations, practices, and institutions" (p. 4) through an analysis of *Napoleon Dynamite*. The film's presentation of such a non-traditional portrayal of masculinity raises the question of how a rhetor encourages an audience to question conventional definitions of masculinity. In this contemporary age of flux gender, *Napoleon Dynamite* serves as an appropriate text for examining the idealization of dynamic conceptions of masculinity. I am interested in highlighting geekiness as a more and more acceptable vein of masculinity and in discovering how this construction is beginning to enjoy credence in popular culture. I explore this question in my analysis of the film and seek to illuminate the ways in which such constructions of masculinity are encouraged and can be accepted in spite of their seeming oddity or unpopularity.

A study of this nature is significant because of its focus on adolescent masculinity. This relevance can be observed more clearly in the comment of Consalvo (2003), who notes, "Past studies of mediated masculinities focus on adult men and fail to interrogate constructions of young or adolescent boys" (p. 28). She continues that these rep-

"The Gender of Napoleon and the Power of Dynamite," by M. Rosie Russo. *Kaleidoscope: A Graduate Journal of Qualitative Communication Research*, Fall, 2006, Vol. 5, pp. 1–16. Permission granted by Department of Speech Communication, Southern Illinois University.

resentations are particularly important because they may show gender as a "process being worked out—rehearsed, refined, and modified" (p. 28). Such a display of gender processes is important because, as Coltrane (1994) writes, "gender is one of the most important organizing principles of societies throughout the world, and because we have too often ignored its influence on men, an explicit focus on masculinities is clearly warranted" (p. 44).

Napoleon is an unapologetic geek who is picked on in school. The "jock" slams him into lockers and practices half-nelsons on him. Other popular kids laugh and smirk at him or simply ignore him altogether. He represents a subordinated aspect of masculinity that is not generally celebrated in contemporary society, and, as Consalvo (2003) notes, includes "outcast" groups of boys in high school, who are harassed by more popular groups. She writes, "subordinate masculinity as a category can serve as a place for alternate representations of masculinity to exist, but this category can be dangerous for those within it" (p. 30). This "subordinate masculinity" is apparent in Napoleon's character and, at times, is "dangerous" for him. Such masculinity can be viewed as also theoretically dangerous in its destabilization of personhood as that which Butler (1990) addresses. She argues that the very notion of "the person" is called into question by the emergence of incoherent and disjointed gendered beings "who appear to be persons but who fail to conform to the gendered norms of cultural intelligibility by which persons are defined" (p. 17). I argue, however, that Napoleon ultimately transforms his oddball, outcast persona into a subversive tool that champions the adolescent geek archetype. This is evidenced in part by the massive impact the film has had on popular culture and countless youth across the country.

I acknowledge that masculinity does not always and is not required to refer to males. I resist the essentialist viewpoint that equates men with masculinity and women with femininity. I realize that men and women are always displaying a hybrid of masculine and feminine traits and that masculinity is a concept that cannot be reduced to residing exclusively in the male body. Nevertheless, as Vavrus (2002) notes, "masculinity is typically associated with males" (p. 357) and as Butler (1990) contends, in such cases, "not biology, but culture, becomes destiny" (p. 8). Therefore, my focus in this essay is on uncovering the masculinity associated with Napoleon's character to demonstrate a range of characteristics available to men (and masculine individuals). As Segal (1990) notes, "A minority of men have always hated the 'masculinity' they felt they were not born with, could never acquire, but which fate remorselessly tried to thrust upon them" (p. 280). The celebrated redefinition of masculinity revealed in this film is significant because it continues to chip away at traditional, hegemonic masculinity.

In this section, I review pertinent literature on traditional hegemonic masculinity and ways it is constructed, as well as the recent changing notions of masculinity. Hegemonic masculinity has been defined in various ways (Boni, 2002; Vavrus, 2002; Mandziuk, 2000; Hanke, 1998; Tripp, 2005; Consalvo, 2003; Kimbrell, 1995; Bell, 1982; Faludi, 1999), but it typically includes characteristics which are focused on insecurity, fear, and self-discipline (Boni, 2002, p. 472). Embodied in traits such as success, status, toughness, heroism, and dominance, masculinity is understood as a homogeneous and monolithic force and a performance of virility (Mandziuk, 2000, pp. 105, 107).

Hegemonic masculinity resists both femininity and homosexuality (Boni, 2002, p. 472). It serves to keep in place one dominant version, comprised ideally of white, middle-class, heterosexual, professional-managerial men. It is ultimately concerned with maintaining the status quo in gender relations (Consalvo, 2003, pp. 29, 30). Clearly, hegemonic masculinity places strict confines on men (and women, consequently). Mandziuk (2000) discusses masculinity as "marked, time and again, as delicate, fragile, provisional; it is under threat, in danger of collapse, it is an impossible ideal" (p. 106). Kimmel (1998) argues that, due to these restrictions, "manhood is only possible for a distinct minority, and the definition has been constructed to prevent others from achieving it" (p. 238).

The constructed, dynamic nature of masculinity, as opposed to the stringent, hegemonic definitions, is increasingly the stance adopted toward masculinity. The term is used to denote characteristics linkable to variant levels of testosterone, which has been socially and culturally associated with men as a result of a broad generalization based on observed characteristics. Ultimately, masculinity is a social rather than a biological notion. Echoing de Beauvoir's (1952) often quoted "One is not born, but rather becomes, a woman" (p. 249), Kimmel and Messner (1998) aptly summarize the issue: "Men are not born; they are made. And men make themselves, actively constructing their masculinities within a social and historical context" (p. xx). And as Tripp (2005) writes, "What we call masculinity is the aggregate of a complex web of characteristics, behaviors, and traits that we have agreed to read as masculine" (p. 186).

Theories of intersectionality prompt me to recognize that the representation of masculinity and the means by which it is constructed, of course, vary by race and class (C. Crenshaw, 1997; K. Crenshaw, 1991; Dace, 1998; Orbe, 1998). Intersectionality has been defined by Collins (2000) as an analysis which claims that such things as race, social class, gender, and sexuality "form mutually constructing features of social organization, which shape [individuals'] experiences and, in turn, are shaped by [individuals]" (p. 299). As a result, Butler (1990) writes, "it becomes impossible to separate out 'gender' from the political and cultural intersections in which it is invariably produced and maintained" (p. 3). Crenshaw (1997) contends that whiteness is rhetorically silenced because there is no need to reference it as it serves as the standard for all that is acceptable. Therefore, I reference black masculinity as an example of a construction of masculinity that challenges (or reinforces) the monolithic white conception of masculinity.

Davis (1983) notes that black masculinity has been associated with a hyperphysicality that involves physical strength, hyper(hetero)sexuality, and physical violence. Henry (2002) identifies these traits as well but chooses to hone in on a particular type of black masculinity that has made its way into contemporary culture within the past two decades—"one defined mainly by an urban aesthetic, a nihilistic attitude, and an aggressive posturing" (p. 114). He contends that this image of black masculinity has developed largely as a result of the commoditization of hip-hop culture and rap music. Diawara (1993) addresses the black masculinity presented in film, arguing that "positive images of racial 'otherness' in mainstream cinema tend to be merely token ones rather than representations that truly address the specificity of black experience" (p. 12). Gates (2004) concurs and extends the point to include sexuality, noting that poor and working class black masculinity is constructed as hypersexual and as a threat to white mainstream culture: "In Hollywood film, the black male body is offered as heroic only when it is contained by a lack of sexuality or action, isolation from a black community, or class" (p. 21). Further, Collins (2005) writes, "assimilated, middle-class Black men are somehow seen as being less manly, as subordinates . . . [and have] been emasculated by the White world" (p. 176). These depictions and representations comprise some of the more popular definitions of black masculinity in contemporary society and continue to flourish because they keep white mainstream culture comfortable.

Organizational literature adds to discourses on intersections of class and masculinity and generally falls into a primitive/civilized dichotomy (Collinson, 1988; Gibson & Papa, 2000; Willis, 1977). Blue-collar labor produces a primitive masculinity of raw physicality, hands-on work, and dirty, sweaty bodies. Conversely, white-collar labor is susceptible to feminization, given its lack of physicality and suppression of the body. It is also thought to be civilized, a notion which makes blue-collar labor prone to charges of being uncivilized, depicting working-class men as "dumb, juvenile, or overgrown brutes" (Ashcraft & Flores, 2003).

Napoleon Dynamite, viewed through an intersectional lens, is set in rural Idaho where most men appear to be white, blue-collar, and working class. Napoleon himself is a white, working class, rural-residing young man. As the preceding discussion implies, Napoleon's gender construction intersects with his class and race. These factors together influence interpretations of his performance of masculinity. A different combination of any of these factors would yield its own unique performance and interpretation of masculinity.

The mainstream media are a primary location for particular constructions of masculinity, and such outlets play an integral part in extending, constraining, and promoting particular ideals as appropriately masculine (Boni, 2002; Tripp, 2005; Consalvo, 2003; Vavrus, 2002; Mandziuk, 2000). In the news media, masculinity is often presented in the form of crime and violence, particularly in terms of black males. In such media, violent masculinity is often equated with heroic masculinity (Consalvo, 2003). The media tell men how they must present themselves, how they must take care of themselves, how they must live, what they must smell like, and how their bodies should look.

The mediation of masculinity through the school system is also important to acknowledge. Schools are incredibly integral to the molding of modern masculinities. Peer culture is extremely important in affecting the ways that masculinities are expressed and developed. Connell (2003) suggests that adolescents learn these constructions and then re-learn them at school: "Mass culture generates images and interpretations of masculinity that flow chaotically into school life and are reworked by pupils . . ." (p. 161).

Just as gender is enacted in the media, it is also enacted and constructed by individuals and comes into existence as people act (Bell, 1982; Butler, 1990; Connell, 2003). The accomplishment of masculinity is social and does not exist as a given essence of individuals' being, apart from their physical and social reality. Seidler (1991) writes, "As boys, we learn constantly to prove our masculinity. We can never take it for granted. This builds enormous tension into contemporary conceptions of masculinity" (p. 33).

In all cases, the constructions of masculinity through the various means are fluid and inconstant, changing over time in response to changing societal mores (Consalvo, 2003). Masculinity and male bodies are discursively and interactionally constructed within the contemporary systems of power and are a product of different relations of power/knowledge, which historically and socially have shaped and disciplined the male body (Boni, 2002). Masculinity, according to social constructionism, is sustained by a continuously negotiated performance and hence is something that has to be achieved, produced, and reproduced (Boni, 2002).

Another key area of literature on masculinity concerns how traditional conceptions of masculinity are being challenged. The United States is experiencing a dramatic shift in thinking about masculinity; it is changing, reflecting men's changing gender relations and self-identities (Boni, 2002; Segal, 1990; Tripp, 2005; Consalvo, 2003; Vavrus, 2002; Connell, 2003; Boon, 2005; Seidler, 1991; Hanke, 1998). If masculinity is accepted as a process of negotiation, Tripp (2005) asserts, "the more we are bombarded by gendered images in our media saturated culture, the more we have to rethink, revise, and/or reorganize the sets of gendered generalizations that we perceive as masculine" (p. 186).

Rigid definitions of (white) masculinity are now being challenged. Tripp (2005) notes, "What once seemed naturally masculine, now no longer reads immediately as such" (p. 186). The traditional role of breadwinner, for example, is being challenged, a role once seen as a core of male identity. There has been a higher level of awareness for raising boys using more loving and expressive methods. There has been a greater prevalence of stay-at-home fathers, which are a marked departure from traditional narratives about family life. We are finding that men can be capable as stay-at-home parents and homemakers. This move modifies a hegemonic masculine ideal by infusing it with nurturance, a traditionally feminized attribute associated with subordinated masculinity (Vavrus, 2002).

The new man is also portrayed as "a young, somehow 'feminine' man" (Boni, 2002, p. 472). Men pay more attention to their physical and emotional health as the male body becomes subject to continuous scrutiny—"it is objectified, exploited, and monitored" (Boni, 2002, p. 467). This feminization of men is evident in men's advertisements, where many of the promises made to women are now being made to men. They are now encouraged to use beauty and body care products, and the advertisers simultaneously legitimize these products for masculine use.

Male consumer culture has also given rise to the "metrosexual," a heterosexual man who grooms himself like a stereotypically gay man. This phenomenon finds straight men liberating themselves from homophobia, leaving themselves open to gay influence and thus to a more expansive idea of what it means to be a man. As Nutter (2004) notes, "No longer adverse to 'gay' traits in the way that straight men of Ronald Reagan's and John Wayne's generation were, the new American man has made his way out of this narrow, homophobic ideal of manhood and embraced a larger world" (p. 19). The metrosexual has allowed "gay" qualities back into the construction of masculinity and has made many straight men realize that they too have been on the losing end of homophobia.

Conversely, hypermasculinity is again being presented in an effort to reinforce masculine dominance. Hypermasculinity is marked by misogyny, homophobia, chauvinism, and excess (Tripp, 2005). Such qualities show the negative side of redefining masculinity. Probably the most familiar example of this hypermasculinity is Robert Bly's mythopoetic men's movement, in which men head into the wild in an attempt to reclaim their inner man. The redefinition of masculinity seeks again to define masculinity in hegemonic terms—it offers, in a sense, a recycled definition. As Kimmel and Kaufman (1994) write, "The mythopoetic men's movement agrees that something is dramatically wrong with American manhood" and "assumes a deep, essential manhood, and its retrieval is the solution" (p. 265). Bly contends that the male of the past 20 years has become a more thoughtful, gentle, easy to please, wimpy Mama's boy. The mythopoetic movement draws on essentialist assumptions about gender distinctions and seeks to retrieve heroic archetypes as models for men. This example of hypermasculinity and other various notions of it represent a backlash in terms of modifying hegemonic conceptions of masculinity.

Analysis: Strategies of Unconventional Masculinity

The dramatically changing standard of masculinity is evidenced in the film *Napoleon Dynamite,* which extends (white) masculinity in a different direction from the notions evident in the literature. I now turn to an analysis of the film to explicate the geeky-masculine persona of Napoleon and explore how the unconventional definition he embodies adds up to cool, socially acceptable masculinity. The method employed for this essay is generative criticism, which offers the greatest freedom in capturing what is most significant about the masculinity in *Napoleon Dynamite* (Foss, 2004). While my focus in the essay is primarily on the central character of Napoleon, he is certainly not the only representation of championed non-traditional masculinity in the film, and I note some instances where other characters reinforce this particular conception of masculinity.

My analysis of *Napoleon Dynamite* proposes four strategies that suggest the means by which the unconventional adds up to cool in a construction of masculinity: (1) Eschewal of "the system"; (2) Flaunting of the individual's unique world; (3) Exhibition of high self-confidence, marked by certainty and passion; and (4) Narrative ambiguity.

Eschewal of the System

Napoleon's character never seems to do what the typical high schooler should or would do. He rides to school everyday on the elementary children's school bus. When the other kids are engaging in group sports or activities at recess or P.E., Napoleon plays tetherball alone. He befriends the new, Mexican exchange student, Pedro, to whom no one else will talk. Instead of a designer salon, Napoleon gets his hair trimmed at "The Cuttin' Corral." Rather than the traditional dog or cat, Napoleon has a pet llama named Tina, which he is responsible for feeding every day after school. Instead of living with his parents (we are never told where they are), he resides with his grandmother and 32-year-old brother, Kip. Kip also represents geeky masculinity, embodying the stereotypical "computer geek" image—engaging in online chat forums for hours, lacking athletic ability, and still residing at home.

In opposition to high-school tradition, Napoleon appears genuinely to enjoy the cafeteria food—in fact, he even stores the leftovers in his pants pocket to eat later in class. Instead of getting a part-time job at McDonald's or at a store in the mall, Napoleon works at a chicken farm, where he receives one dollar an hour—in change. When preparing for the school dance, he buys his suit from a thrift store and asks his Uncle Rico to drive him and his date. Napoleon, sporting this suit rather stylishly in spite of its outdatedness, conjecturably presents an unconsciously metrosexual persona. In contrast, most high schoolers would prefer to buy a nice, new suit and perhaps rent a limo, but not Napoleon. Napoleon is also an extremely proud member of the Future Farmers of America, something that most high schoolers would reject as dorky or uncool. Napoleon, in contrast, embraces it wholeheartedly; in fact, he wins awards for his extensive knowledge of cows. These activities and traits portray a side of masculinity that does not buy into the system of traditional high school life or hegemonic masculinity, which involves the constant struggle to maintain fashion ideals and be accepted by the popular kids.

Flaunting of the Individual World

Because Napoleon does not buy into the system, he is totally ensconced in his own world, and he is not ashamed to flaunt this world. As one reporter framed it, "lanky, leading man Napoleon doesn't seem to be aware of his glaring shortcomings" (Ochieng, 2004). Napoleon reflects this impervious self-presentation in several ways.

While the film appears to be set in contemporary America (we see evidence of the Internet), Napoleon seems stuck in the Eighties—a time period often noted for its awkward, unusual clothing and hair styles. He is always attired in an unvarying assortment of t-shirts from the Eighties (which are always tucked in); he wears black moon boots all the time; and his oversized, thick-lensed glasses look as if they were taken straight out of a family photograph from the Eighties. He also sports a Trapper Keeper as his school gear, a specifically Eighties' piece of paraphernalia. Napoleon's uncle, Rico, also seems "stuck" in the Eighties, dreaming of going back in time and winning the state championship football game. Like Napoleon, Rico also appears socially inept—his girlfriend left him because of his inability to live in the present. He is also clumsy—he throws a football right into his video camera as he attempts to capture his "athleticism" on film. Uncle Rico, then, also contributes to *Napoleon Dynamite*'s conception of geeky masculinity.

Often, Napoleon's world is a fabricated one, a thing of his mind, but one he staunchly flaunts nonetheless. For example, when asked what he did over his summer vacation, he responds with blatantly exaggerated, if not completely untrue, stories about hunting wolverines with a 12-gauge shotgun. He lies about having a hot model girlfriend who lives in Oklahoma, even though the "photograph" he produces as evidence of her existence is clearly from a magazine. His brother, Kip, also lies about the appearance of his online girlfriend, claiming she has "sandy blonde hair," when in actuality, the woman who shows up is African American. Napoleon claims to own nun-chuks and be experienced with a bo-staff and brags about all the gangs at the school that "wanted him," creating some sort of clearly fictional ninja alter-ego. Napoleon also speaks unabashedly about his time in Scout camp, making "an infinity" of multi-colored key chains, an activity at which hegemonic masculinity would shudder.

Truly, Napoleon operates on a separate plane from the rest of the males at his high school and is seemingly unashamed and unaware of this fact. Director Jared Hess (2004) attests to this as well, calling his character "optimistic and oblivious to the world's response" (Production Notes, p. 3). Conventional masculinity would require him to act in a way that would hide his shortcomings, but he lives outside these conventions by staunchly flaunting his own world.

Exhibition of High Self-Confidence

For someone to flaunt so unapologetically such a marginalized and, at times, manufactured masculinity requires possession of a high level of self-confidence. Indeed, Napoleon possesses such self-assurance. In spite of the fact that he gets "beat up" by the jocks at school for being different, he never changes the way he acts. He is very certain of himself and is passionate about the activities in which he engages. For example, he is the only male member of the "Happy Hands Club," which is apparently the school's sign language club; its members are shown performing a hand routine to Bette Midler's "The Rose." The cool kids in the audience are visibly mocking the group, particularly Napoleon. Generally, males want little to do with activities that are viewed as exclusively female. Napoleon, however, is shown very ardently gesticulating, even though he is behind by a beat or two.

Another example of his passion is when he discovers a beat-up VHS tape called *D-quon's Dance Grooves*. Every day after school, he practices in his room and, at the end of the film, he performs a dance routine in front of the whole school to support Pedro's election as school president. The fact that he is willing to do something this flamboyant and impromptu in front of the entire school body displays a high level of self-confidence. Usually, individuals embodying these types of marginalized or subordinate masculinities are not so brazen and self-assured. Napoleon's high self-confidence is further reflected at recess, when he is playing solo tetherball. Napoleon is not discouraged when people do not want to play with him—he continues to play very aggressively against himself. Even the way Napoleon talks throughout the film is certain and passionate. When he buys his suit for the dance at the thrift store, he acknowledges his appreciation for his purchase with an "It's awesome!," expressed so zealously that he seems to struggle to get the words out. When asked by a boy on the school bus, "What are you going to do today Napoleon?" he vehemently responds, "Whatever the heck I feel like I wanna do! GOSH!" His main catch phrase is a fervent "Sweet!"

A high-school student has to be a pretty self-confident person to wear moon boots everyday, claim to own nun-chuks, have a pet llama, and be the only male member of the "Happy Hands Club." The unconventional masculinity Napoleon represents is characterized by a high level of self-confidence and contributes to the overall presentation of the geeky-masculine persona. Conversely, conventional masculinity would expect him to exhibit self-confidence in only those things established as acceptable.

Narrative Ambiguity

The ambiguous nature of the script also contributes to the film's theme of negotiable masculinity. There is no plot to speak of, the characters wind their way through a seemingly arbitrary maze of sub-stories, and there is little closure at the end of the film. In this fragmented narrative style, "stories simply end, with the plot of the narrative unresolved" (Foss & Foss, 1994, p. 421). For example, Napoleon and Deb, the ambiguous love interest of the film, do not explicitly end up together at the end, in stark contrast to typical Hollywood fodder. The audience is given no indication of "happily ever after," there is no passionate kiss, and the friendly game of tetherball on which the final credits close merely supposes that life continues on.

Several reviewers have commented on the lack of plot and closure of the film: "You shouldn't expect a well-developed plot, a moral to the story, or even a common theme" (*Reel Reviews,* 2004). Furthermore Betts (2004) writes, "The plot of the film is pretty non-existent. Everything is basically a five-minute skit with no connection to the rest of the movie. This leaves *Napoleon Dynamite* nothing to accomplish and not much has changed between the beginning of the movie and the end." Ochieng (2004) concurs, "The uniqueness about *Napoleon Dynamite* is the uneventful way it sits there and lets the audience soak in its unassuming charm."

Foss and Foss (1994) identify narrative ambiguity as a feminine discursive style, characterized by continuous processes that "do not provide the relief of an ending . . . or the pleasures that come from resolution" (p. 421). Feminist scholar Trinh (1991) also advocates this prevention of closure and violation of expectations, which disrupts the "commercial and ideological habits of our society" that "favor narrative with as definite a closure as possible" (p. 147). *Napoleon Dynamite*'s ambiguous narrative can be interpreted as just such a disruption. Contemporary audiences are likely to expect a classic Hollywood cinema narrative style, as well as male characters displaying traditionally masculine traits. The film violates these expectations of conventional masculinity and presents a different conception of geeky masculinity.

Conclusion

The four strategies I have detailed—eschewal of the system, flaunting of the individual's unique world, self-confidence, and narrative ambiguity—serve as the means by which the filmmakers of *Napoleon Dynamite* effectively equate geekiness with masculinity. Not only do they successfully equate the two, but they succeed in making this subordinate masculinity something to be desired and achieved. I suggest that Napoleon's hip, geeky expression of masculinity has been so well received—to the point where it is no longer un-hip but rather cool—because it constitutes an ironic vehicle of conventional masculinity and constructs an alternative hegemonic peer group.

Geeky Masculinity from Conventional Masculinity

While the strategies of not buying into the system, flaunting the individual world, and high self-confidence are the means through which geeky masculinity is presented in *Napoleon Dynamite,* they also are representative, to some degree, of conventional definitions of masculinity. These traits are assertive and forceful, qualities that generally are viewed as traditionally masculine. Likewise, the narrative ambiguity of the script affords the filmmakers power over the audience in their lack of resolution of sub-plots and lack of overall closure. The filmmakers know what is going on, but the audience does not. Alternative notions of masculinity are encouraged, then, through an ironic vehicle of conventional conceptions of masculinity.

I propose that this ironic representation is one reason the geeky masculinity of *Napoleon Dynamite* has been championed. Although the presentation of masculinity in the film challenges traditional conceptions, the way it is *conveyed* is remarkable. Hegemonic masculinity is already viewed as the popular ideal. For the geeky-masculine persona, then, the means become the end. Because the strategies used to present it already enjoy established acceptance, they can dictate what other conceptions of masculinity are permitted to join them on the hegemonic pedestal. Hegemonic masculinity is extended beyond its typical borders to further its interests in the domination of gendered lives. The film encourages audiences to consider marginalized definitions of masculinity and ultimately transform those definitions into an acceptable construction through a framework with which audiences are already comfortable—conventional (white) masculinity.

The fact that Napoleon does not become demonized or stigmatized as gay is further evidence of the film's grounding in conventional masculinity. That the film maintains a consistent heteronormative foundation is evident, for example, when Napoleon, Kip, and Uncle Rico are sitting on the couch watching a video. Napoleon gets up to leave the room, leaving Kip and Rico sitting very close together. Rico glances at Kip, who promptly moves over. Although it breaks masculine convention in some respects, *Napoleon Dynamite* brandishes heteronormative power and perpetuates typical homophobia. While *Napoleon Dynamite* presents a seemingly innovative expansion of masculinity, that extension draws its power from the original hegemonic well of masculinity.

Construction of Alternative Hegemonic Group

A second reason for the overwhelming acceptance of the geeky masculinity in the film is the alternative social group that it creates. Because Napoleon is not accepted in the popular peer groups and because he does not allow himself to be completely left by the wayside, he creates for himself and his friends an alternative social space that allows greater freedom of gendered self-expression than do traditional high-school cliques. Napoleon's eschewal of the system, flaunting of his world, high level of self-confidence, and the film's narrative ambiguity all work to create this alternative social space. They portray him as the unwitting leader who forges into un-chartered masculine territory. Although he is not on the cutting edge, he cuts his own edge on the masculine market by refusing to recant his nerdity. He is the supreme, reigning king of geekdom.

The creation of this alternative peer group converts the geeky-masculine conception to cool because it serves as a standard by which other fringe adolescents can proudly be measured. Napoleon allows the audience to compete a bit better with the popular kids. In so doing, however, the group he creates is really no different from popular circles except that it allows for inclusion of a different breed of students—geeky ones. Therefore, this alternate peer group is merely a parallel universe to that of hegemonic cliques, repeating the pattern of a cool place to belong—one that is as hegemonic as the cool groups. While the group allows geeks and nerds to join, it certainly does not want the cool kids to join and thereby adopts exclusionary tactics of its own.

The significance of the fourth strategy, narrative ambiguity, is of particular relevance to the creation of an alternative hegemonic group. While the alternative group seems to follow the same template as that of hegemonic popularity, the results are not the same. Pedro is never flagrantly awarded the presidency (there is a brief shot of a congratulatory cake), Napoleon and Deb never kiss, and the cool kids never afford them any respect. If the filmmakers were to fill in these details or give the story any closure, audiences might begin to recognize it as the same tired script of hegemonic masculinity. As it stands, however, the narrative ambiguity violates those expectations, and audiences are asked to focus their attention not on how the group replicates the very conception of masculinity against which they are rebelling but on this geeky masculinity.

I acknowledge that *Napoleon Dynamite* could be argued merely to be constructing coolness instead of, or in addition to, masculinity—I agree that it does do this. As reporter Martha Irvine wrote concerning the popularity of the film, "Suddenly it's hip to be square." Whatever the reason, "being a nerd, a geek, a dork—whatever you want to call the tragically unhip—is becoming a source of pride" (2005). But as I have explicated in the preceding discussion, I believe the film, in addition to coolness, also constructs masculinity, ultimately conflating the two. The geekiness prevalent in *Napoleon Dynamite* is a masculine geekiness in that the means by which coolness is constructed in the film are hegemonically masculine means. Because femininity is supposed to resist masculinity (and vice versa), coolness would not be constructed for girls through the same means. As Butler (1990) contends, "The presumption of a binary gender system implicitly retains the belief in a mimetic relation of gender to sex whereby gender mirrors sex or is otherwise restricted by it" (p. 6). Were girls to be constructed through these masculine processes, the result would most likely not be coolness, as is the case in *Napoleon Dynamite*. For example, in the film *Welcome to the Dollhouse* (1996), the main character is an adolescent girl who, just like Napoleon, is a geeky outcast and involved in similar school scenarios. But in contrast to Napoleon, her character did not spark a pop culture explosion. The difference, I propose, is that the geekiness of *Napoleon Dynamite* is masculine.

A well-received challenge to hegemonic masculinity such as that presented by *Napoleon Dynamite* is encouraging for males, masculine individuals, and anyone devoted to expanding traditional gender boundaries. As I have suggested in this essay, however, individuals must be consistently alert to the wiles of such conventional definitions, which are forever attempting to creep back into position as the dominant template for masculinity. While I am heartened by *Napoleon Dynamite's* efforts, I charge myself and others to continue to train the critical lens on the gendered slide that is our culture.

References

Ashcraft, K. L. & Flores, L. A. (2003). "Slaves with white collars": Persistent performances of masculinity in crisis. *Text and Performance Quarterly, 23,* 1–29.

Bell, D. H. (1982). *Being a man: The paradox of masculinity.* Lexington, MA: Lewis.

Betts, J. (2004). *Movie review—Napoleon Dynamite.* Retrieved June 28, 2006, from *The Movie Mark* Web site: http://www.themoviemark.com/moviereviews/napoleondynamite.asp

Boni, F. (2002). Framing media masculinities: Men's lifestyle magazines and the biopolitics of the male body. *European Journal of Communication, 17,* 465–478.

Boon, K. A. (2005). Heroes, metanarratives, and the paradox of masculinity in contemporary Western culture. *Journal of Men's Studies, 13,* 301–313.

Brod, H. & Kaufman, M. (1994). *Theorizing masculinities.* Thousand Oaks, CA: Sage.

Butler, J. (1990). *Gender trouble: Feminism and the subversion of identity.* New York: Routledge.

Collins, P. H. (2000). *Black feminist thought: Knowledge, consciousness, and the politics of empowerment.* New York: Routledge.

Collins, P. H. (2005). *Black sexual politics: African-Americans, gender, and the new racism.* New York: Routledge.

Collinson, D. L. (1988). "Engineering humor": Masculinity, joking, and conflict in shopfloor relations. *Organization Studies, 9,* 181–199.

Coltrane, S. (1994). "Theorizing masculinities in contemporary social science." In Brod & Kaufman's (Eds.), *Theorizing masculinities* (pp. 39–61). Thousand Oaks, CA: Sage.

Connell, R. W. (2003). Masculinities, change, and conflict in global society: Thinking about the future of men's studies. *Journal of Men's Studies, 11,* 249–267.

Consalvo, M. (2003). The monsters next door: Media constructions of boys and masculinity. *Feminist Media Studies, 3,* 27–46.

Coon, J., Covel, S., Wyatt, C. (Producers), & Hess, J. (Director). (2004). *Napoleon Dynamite* [Motion picture]. United States: Fox Searchlight Pictures.

Crenshaw, C. (1997). Women in the Gulf War: Toward an intersectional feminist rhetorical criticism. *Howard Journal of Communications, 8,* 219–235.

Crenshaw, C. (1997). Resisting whiteness' rhetorical silence. *Western Journal of Communication, 61,* 253–278.

Crenshaw, K. (1991). Mapping the margins: Intersectionality, identity politics, and violence against women of color. *Stanford Law Review, 43,* 1241–1299.

Dace, K. L. (1998). "Had Judas been a black man . . .": Politics, race, and gender in African America. In J. P. McDaniel and J. M. Sloop's (Eds.), *Judgment calls: Rhetoric, politics, and indeterminacy* (pp. 163–181). Boulder: Westview.

Davis, A. (1983). *Women, race and class.* New York: Vintage.

De Beauvoir, S. (1952). *The second sex.* New York: Bantam/Alfred A. Knopf.

Diawara, M. (1993). *Black American Cinema.* New York: Routledge.

Endearing nerds are dynamite. (2004, August 8). Retrieved November 28, 2005, from Web site: http://usatoday.com

Faludi, S. (1999). *Stiffed: The betrayal of the American man.* New York: William Morrow.

Foss, S. K. (2004). *Rhetorical criticism: Exploration and practice.* Long Grove, IL: Waveland.

Foss, S. K. & Foss, K. A. (1994). The construction of feminine spectatorship in Garrison Keillor's radio monologues. *Quarterly Journal of Speech, 80,* 410–426.

Gates, P. (2004). Always a partner in crime. *Journal of Popular Film and Television, 32,* 20–29.

Gibson, M. K. & Papa, M. J. (2000). The mud, the blood, and the beer guys: Organizational osmosis in blue-collar work groups. *Journal of Applied Communication Research, 28,* 66–86.

Hanke, R. (1998). The "mock-macho" situation comedy: Hegemonic masculinity and its reiteration. *Western Journal of Communication, 62,* 74–93.

Henry, M. (2002). He is a "bad mother *$%@!#": Shaft and contemporary black masculinity. *Journal of Popular Film and Television, 30,* 114–120.

Hess, J. (2004). *Napoleon Dynamite film production notes.* Retrieved November 28, 2005, from Web site http://www2.foxsearchlight.com/napoleondynamite/epk/downloads/aboutFilm/prodNotes.pdf

Irvine, M. (July 7, 2005). *Suddenly it's hip to be square.* Retrieved October 17, 2005, from Web site: http://AssociatedPress.com

J, J. (2004). Movie review. Retrieved June 28, 2006, from Reel Reviews Web site: http://www.franksreelreviews.com/reviews/2004/ napoleondynamite.htm

Kimbrell, A. (1995). *The masculine mystique: The politics of masculinity.* New York: Ballantine.

Kimmel, M. S. & Kaufman, M. (1994). Weekend warriors: The new men's movement. In H. Brod & M. Kaufman's (Eds.), *Theorizing masculinities* (pp. 259–289).Thousand Oaks, CA: Sage.

Kimmel, M. S. & Messner, M. A. (1998). *Men's lives.* Boston: Allyn & Bacon.

Mandziuk, R. M. (2000). Necessary vigilance: Feminist critiques of masculinity. *Review and Criticism, 17,* 105–109.

Nutter, C. (2004). Circling the square. *The Gay and Lesbian Review Worldwide, 11,* 19–21.

Ochieng, F. (2004). Napoleon Dynamite. Retrieved October 17, 2005, from Web site: http://TheWorldJournal.com

Orbe, M. P. (1998). Constructions of reality on MTV's "The Real World": An analysis of the restrictive coding of black masculinity. *Southern Communication Journal, 64,* 32–47.

Segal, L. (1990). *Slow motion: Changing masculinities, changing men.* New Brunswick: Rutgers University Press.

Seidler, V. (1991). Redefining masculinity. *Canadian Dimension, 25,* 33.

Trinh, T. Minh-ha. (1991). *When the moon waxes red: Representation, gender, and cultural politics.* New York: Routledge.

Tripp, D. (2005). "Wake up!": Narratives of masculine epiphany in millennial cinema. *Quarterly Review of Film and Video, 22,* 181–188.

Vavrus, M. (2002). Domesticating patriarchy: Hegemonic masculinity and television's "Mr. Mom." *Critical Studies in Media Communication, 19,* 352–376.

Weafer, M. (2005, March 25). Movie having "Dynamite" impact: Independent film has sparked big merchandise sales. *Messenger-Inquirer.* Retrieved from http://www.messenger-inquirer.com/ frontpage.htm

Willis, P. (1977). *Learning to labor: How working class kids get working class jobs.* New York: Columbia UP.

Star of Fear, Star of Hope
North Star to Reach Reality
Marcia S. Van't Hof

An article in the November 27, 2000, edition of *The Denver Post* included the headline "Holocaust program helps teach tolerance." The feature that followed outlined the dilemma faced by high school teachers: How to teach the teenagers of today about one of the most terrifying historical events of history—the Holocaust. Much pedagogy simply does not connect with teens. Thus, the brutality becomes yet another set of statistics to memorize, or the genocide is presented so graphically that high-school students turn away in simple revulsion. The pedagogy discussed in the *Post* feature involved Teaching Tolerance Trunks "filled with $1,200 worth of books, CD-ROMs, posters, videos, maps, novels and teaching guides" that circulated among Colorado high schools. The trunks were intended to equip teachers "with the materials needed to explain the critical lessons of prejudice, greed, genocide, conformity and injustice" (p. 1A). The need indicated by the Teaching Tolerance Trunks is a need faced by teachers and parents everywhere—how to present the harsh reality of history to young people so that they may begin to process its contemporary lessons.

My analysis in this essay takes up this issue as it applies to an artifact designed for young children. The artifact is a children's picture book, *Star of Fear, Star of Hope*, that has won at least five international awards for children's literature. Written by Jo Hoestlandt and illustrated by Johanna Kang, the book was published in France in 1993, translated by Mark Polizzotti, and published in the United States in 1995. In this essay, I explore how this text employs rhetorical strategies—both visual and verbal—to introduce children to a frightening historical reality.

Star of Fear, Star of Hope is 28 pages long: A first-person narrative illustrated with simple drawings in sepia tones. The narrator is an old woman, Helen, who says that she does not want the world to forget her friend Lydia, so she tells the story that happened years earlier when her friend disappeared. Helen was looking forward to her ninth birthday in July of 1942, and she asked her Jewish friend Lydia to sleep over as part of the celebration. The two friends were telling scary stories before they went to sleep, wanting "to see if our hair would stand on end, like in the comic books" (p. 3). Their stories were interrupted by actual, rather than imagined, frights—the signs and sounds of two frantic, sanctuary-seeking Jewish strangers in the hallway. The two children listened breathlessly as the two called out their code names—"Madame Eleven O'clock" and the "Midnight Ghost"—and scratched and pounded at the apartment doors. After the danger passed, Lydia told Helen's parents that she wanted to go home. Helen's parents complied, and Helen was furious. How could her good friend desert her on the eve of her birthday? But Lydia left her present and went. Helen never saw her again.

The next morning, the streets resounded with shouts, footsteps, and whistles. Out her window, Helen could see a line of marchers guarded by soldiers. The marchers were wearing yellow stars, and they included families like her own. Helen was mystified. " 'They didn't look like robbers,' she thought" (p. 19). When Helen opened the

This essay was written while Marcia S. Van't Hof was a student in Sonja K. Foss's rhetorical criticism class at the University of Colorado Denver in 2000. Used by permission of the author.

present that Lydia had left, she found a handmade paper doll that had a cut-out of Lydia's face pasted on the doll's head. Lydia had made several outfits for the doll, including "a little coat on which she had even drawn a star" (p. 25). Helen wrote Lydia's name on the back of the doll. As the days, weeks, and years passed without Lydia, Helen still held onto the hope that Lydia had lived to become a grandmother like herself, a grandmother who might read *Star of Fear, Star of Hope* to her grandchildren, recognize herself, and call her friend Helen. The elliptical last sentence of the text reads, "I'll always have hope . . ." (p. 27).

Analysis

The unit for analysis for my exploration of *Star of Fear, Star of Hope* is generated by the research question itself. I will scrutinize the traces within the book that provide elements of realism, elements of comfort, and elements of discomfort. An artifact that seeks to introduce children to harsh reality in an effective manner must establish the *reality* of the narrative, allow for the *comfort* of the reading child, and yet introduce the *discomfort* of the harsh reality.

Reality

The story establishes itself as reality rather than fantasy. If children are to begin comprehending the Holocaust, they must understand that these events really happened; they are not the stuff of fantasies or dreams. Hoestlandt accomplishes this effect by her sensory details that signal believable experiences in real life. Lydia's mother breaks with her teeth the thread she is using for the Jewish star (p. 2); Madam Eleven O'clock scratches like a cat on the apartment door (p. 5); the Midnight Ghost has a red face and low voice (p. 7); the two girls, hearts pounding, stand frightened with bare feet on the cold tile floor (p. 7); Helen feels her heart squeeze when she realizes Lydia is gone (p. 23); and she falls asleep cuddled next to her parents (p. 17). With strong sensory details such as these, *Star of Fear, Star of Hope* signals that its narrative takes place in the common reality of children and their families rather than in an imaginary world such as those populated by beasts and fairies. As a real-world story, it invites readers to feel along with the characters as they see, hear, and touch one of the harshest realities two friends will ever face.

In addition, the narrative establishes its place in reality using details of childhood experience to which children easily can relate. For example, Helen says that when her parents came home for the evening, the two girls pretended to be asleep, fearing punishment if they were found up so late (p. 9). The emotions Helen feels when Lydia seemingly deserts her are ones that child readers probably find believable. Helen is so angry with her friend for leaving during her birthday celebration that she does not kiss her goodbye, even when her mother does (p. 13). Helen does not understand her friend's fear, so when Lydia hands her the homemade present and says, "I hope you like it," Helen responds with spiteful words: "I don't care! You're not my friend anymore!" (pp. 13–14). Any child can relate to hasty words spoken in the angry fit of a selfish tantrum. A child also may relate to the cozy security of a parent's bed, a place where Helen is allowed to spend the rest of the night. That such a privilege is unusual for Helen is evident when she says, "Some pretty strange things were happening that night" (p. 17). Because the narrative gives believable details about a child's experience, child readers may be able to accept that "some pretty strange things"—some harsh reality, in this case—really are possible within the circumference of their world.

The illustrations of *Star of Fear, Star of Hope* also signal the reality of the narrative. The characters are realistically and simply drawn; no one is in caricature or larger-than-life form. The sepia tones suggest old photographs, the kind that perhaps child readers have seen of their ancestors. Children may know by the time they read *Star of Fear, Star of Hope* that these photos portray real people who lived in the past. And yet the sepia tones are interrupted, as if to say that the people in this story are not peacefully departed and thus relegated to dusty memory. The interrupting element to the golden brown color scheme is the color red (appearing in the curtain, p. 4; on Lydia's doll, pp. 8, 28; on Lydia's dress, pp. 14–15; and on the paper-doll dress, p. 26). The color red, which is not found in the standard sepia palette, is strongly associated with Lydia and alerts readers to the importance and reality of Lydia as a person.

Child readers are invited to participate in the reality of *Star of Fear, Star of Hope* through yet another visual element. When the text pauses and pictures fill both pages (pp. 15–16 and 21–22), readers need to play out the words of the story in their own imaginations. They "fill in the blanks" at critical moments in the story: Lydia's departure and the marching Jewish families. When children thus accept an invitation to participate in the reality of the story, they will be more likely to incorporate it successfully into their own experience.

Comfort

In addition to the elements of reality employed by *Star of Fear, Star of Hope*, elements of comfort or security are replete in the narrative. For children to accept harsh reality, such elements are necessary to buffer the blow.

The narrative structure itself provides a secure framework upon which other elements of comfort may be built. The narrator, with whom the child reader will relate most readily, is not Lydia herself (a much more frightening perspective) but Helen, a girl-become-woman who happily survived the fearful events of the Holocaust. The plot structure, too, is comfortably familiar. Child readers are introduced to characters, the characters face a problem, the problem is resolved, and order is restored. The "I'll always have hope" ending (with its accompanying cheerful illustration of the two girls) is as close as any Holocaust story can get to the "happily ever after" that children expect.

In addition to the narrative structure itself, smaller scale verbal elements serve as elements of comfort. The story is written simply, with many sentences of three to five words. Nothing is threatening or complex within the vocabulary or syntax. The recurring thematic saying about stars ("Stars at morning, better take warning. Stars at night, hope is in sight") provides a cheerful, familiar element for a children's story—rhyme—whether or not the child knows the rhyme's original context.

Furthermore, *Star of Fear, Star of Hope* makes effective use of the principle of particularization as an element of comfort. Particularization in this narrative allows the story of the Holocaust to be introduced without a child's sensibilities needing to grapple with the whole horror: six million Jews systematically murdered in a national act of racially motivated brutality. *Star of Fear, Star of Hope* focuses its lens not on six million people but on one friendship involving two girls and two families on one day of their lives. The parents featured—Helen's—are close to each other, kind to their daughter, and sympathetic to the plight of the Jews. The other parents—Lydia's—are so dear to Lydia that she retreats into their care when the night at Helen's house becomes scary. A child reading this story does not need to make the emotional and intellectual leap into the entire horror of the Holocaust; the story's particularization simply invites identification with two children and their loving families.

Another element of comfort in *Star of Fear, Star of Hope* is the agency of the narrator. At the beginning of the story, Helen says that neither "the war nor the Germans could keep Lydia and me from going to school, or playing together, or getting into fights and making up, the way friends do all over the world" (p. 2). Even when she loses her friend, Helen is able to write Lydia's name on the doll her friend has left behind (p. 25), and eventually she is able to write the story that tells about her friend so that people still will remember Lydia. Ultimately, the narrator chooses to retain hope. She therefore retains agency and, by logical transfer, readers may retain agency as well. The comfort of some element of control over one's destiny remains.

Finally, the element of comfort that is crucial to any child is clearly present in *Star of Fear, Star of Hope*—a logical explanation for evil. True, children are used to reading stories in which evil is explained by the ugliness of the monsters or the meanness of a bully. This time, the explanation is more complex, but it is a clear and plausible one for child readers. A respected character, Helen's mother, offers it. When Helen offers the explanation for evil that assumes bad luck, Helen's mother sternly replies, "Bad luck almost never comes from the stars above, Helen. And this bad luck certainly doesn't. Unfortunately, it comes from people, from the wickedness of some and the weakness of others. Sometimes it can be so hard to live together" (p. 23). This clear, forceful declaration about the source of evil serves as a foundation upon which a child's more sophisticated understanding may be built. It is a starting place suitable for a child's emotional and intellectual capacities. It is an element of comfort.

The verbal elements of comfort are reinforced by the visual ones. The soft outlines of the human forms are emphasized by the open space, the sharp angles drawn in the background, and the glowingly golden sepia tones. The simple illustrations bring forward the actions and emotions of the human characters. The atmosphere is uncluttered and warm—a strong element of comfort in the face of discomfiting truth.

Discomfort

Sadly, the discomfiting truth must be told, and here we see *Star of Fear, Star of Hope* bringing forward clear elements of discomfort designed to introduce harsh reality to children. These elements do not predominate numerically; just a small dose of frightfulness will suffice. The narrative structure, though basically traditional and therefore comforting, inserts elements of painful mystery. At the very beginning of the story, Lydia's mother denied that the star she is sewing onto Lydia's coat is merely "pretty" but instead says: "The place for stars is in the sky. . . . When people take them down from the sky and sew them on their clothes, it only brings trouble" (p. 2). Helen does not understand what Lydia's mother is saying, but she decides to stop thinking about the stars (p. 3). But disquieting thoughts persist when the girls' playful scary stories turn to scary reality. They hear two fearful strangers in the hallway, strangers with fearful names. Mysterious, frightening events happen in quick succession: Lydia's departure, Madame Eleven O'clock's arrival to stay overnight, the march of Jews watched by armed police, and Lydia's family's empty apartment. Through the lens of a child's consciousness, these events are all difficult to understand. The dawning of comprehension comes gradually to both the narrator and to the child reader. Unreality becomes reality as these frightful, mysterious plot elements unfold. By the end of the story, the falling action is only happy in a limited sense. Even though the narrator has hope, the child reader may realize that Lydia and all those people who were marched down the street probably met a terrible fate.

Additional elements also contribute to discomfort. Several sentences end in ellipses, creating an insecurity about finality, completeness of thought, or satisfying answers. The mostly emotionless faces and dark black lines in the illustrations create a mysterious, foreboding effect. In all, the evil of the Holocaust is not buffered entirely by the narrative's elements of comfort. The disquieting, painful mystery of genocide gradually takes hold through a variety of elements of discomfort employed by the author and illustrator.

Conclusion

Perhaps the Colorado teachers using the Teaching Tolerance Trunks could take a lesson from *Star of Fear, Star of Hope*. The children's text employs a potent triad of elements involving realism, comfort, and discomfort. Whether young learners are seven or seventeen, they need to recognize that harsh reality is indeed real, that it is truly harsh, and yet that some sort of security is possible. Children need to grow into adults who face the full brunt of harsh reality and yet cling to hope. A better world requires the hard work of people who have grappled with evil guided by the assistance of such works as *Star of Fear, Star of Hope*.